Anonymus

Manchester of today - 1888

Anonymus

Manchester of today - 1888

ISBN/EAN: 9783743334953

Manufactured in Europe, USA, Canada, Australia, Japa

Cover: Foto ©ninafisch / pixelio.de

Manufactured and distributed by brebook publishing software (www.brebook.com)

Anonymus

Manchester of today - 1888

MANCHESTER OF TO-DAY

AN EPITOME OF RESULTS

BUSINESS MEN AND COMMERCIAL INTERESTS

WEALTH AND GROWTH

Historical, Statistical, Biographical

PRICE TWO SHILLINGS AND SIXPENCE

THIS BOOK COMPLETE IN ITSELF

HISTORICAL PUBLISHING COMPANY

No. 90, CHANCERY LANE, LONDON; AND AT MANCHESTER AND GLASGOW

Entered at Stationers' Hall

1888

PREFACE.

In presenting MANCHESTER OF TO-DAY to the notice of the reader, the publishers feel that they have no apology to offer for its appearance in the field of literature to which it more particularly appertains. The scope of such a work is, obviously, of an extended character, its fulfilment representing a lengthened period of faithful labour and involving the outlay of considerable capital; and, in view of the object with which the following pages have been prepared—that of portraying with all possible clearness the prominent phases of Manchester's commercial greatness—it is confidently believed that any discrepancy of data which may exist will be overlooked after proper consideration has been given to the nature and requirements of the undertaking. Both the historical and editorial portions of the work will be found authentic and interesting, and, though of necessity brief, present, as they are designed to do, a review of the salient features of this great industrial centre and of the growth and development of leading Manchester industries, in a manner and form that, it is believed, cannot fail to meet with the approval of all. The sketches of mercantile houses, firms and companies which are submitted to the attention of the reader, depict facts connected with those establishments calculated to better acquaint the business man with his fellows in commerce, and more fully familiarise the buyer with the seller. The facts embodied in these articles have been secured after no inconsiderable labour on the part of the publishers, editors, and reporters; and, while justly laudatory, have been compiled with due regard to accuracy and the correct interpretation of the information received. As a carefully prepared review of the wealth and status of notable business men and of the growth of a wide variety of commercial interests—an historical, statistical and biographical epitome of mercantile and municipal results achieved in a great manufacturing city—MANCHESTER OF TO-DAY is, therefore, issued in the confident expectation that it may worthily accomplish the object of its designation, and at the same time, through the medium of its extensive circulation, prove a source of permanent profit to those represented in its pages.

INDEX.

G.

H.

I.

J.

K.

L.

M.

N.

ITS HISTORY, GROWTH, AND IMPORTANCE.

INDUSTRIES, FACTS, FIGURES, AND ILLUSTRATIONS.

A BIRD'S-EYE VIEW.

MANCHESTER is a name which has penetrated to the most distant regions of the habitable globe, and its merchants and manufacturers are known throughout the whole civilized world. To write all that could legitimately be written of Manchester would fill many large volumes, and therefore our readers must be content with a very modest description both of the place itself and of its people. Manchester is a very ancient as well as a very interesting place, though but comparatively little of its early history can be given with absolute certainty. It is a well-known fact that it is mentioned along with Salford, Rochdale, and Radcliffe in Doomsday Book; and these are the *only places* which are named in that famous book in the district now known as South-East Lancashire, the greater portions of which were then either forest or waste lands.

Mr. W. E. A. Axon, M.R.S.L., a most competent and reliable authority, in an article contributed by him some time ago to the "Encyclopædia Britannica," observes in reference to Manchester: "Nearly the only point of certainty in its history before the Conquest is that it suffered greatly from devastations of the Danes, and that in 923 Edward, who was then at Thelwall, near Warrington, sent a number of his Mercian troops to garrison it." The same writer remarks: "It was probably one of the scenes of the missionary preaching of Paulinus; and it is said (although by a chronicler of comparatively late date) to have been the residence of Ina, King of Wessex, and his Queen Ethelberga, after he had defeated Ivor, somewhere about the year 689." It is not necessary to dive deeper into the ancient history of the city, but, though briefly, some facts regarding the Manchester of more recent times may be chronicled. It may be stated that Manchester is distant from London 188 miles by the London and North Western Railway, 189 by the Midland route, and 188¾ by the Great Northern. The distance from Liverpool is 31½ miles. According to the last census (1881), the population of the municipal borough of Manchester was 341,414, and of the parliamentary borough (which includes the townships of Harpurhey, Newton, Bradford, and Beswick), 393,585. In 1885 the city boundary was extended to include Rusholme, Bradford (a local township), and Harpurhey, and the population of the municipal borough was thus raised to 373,583, and of the parliamentary borough to 404,823. Although the town of Salford is, both for municipal and parliamentary purposes, separate and distinct from Manchester, it is quite impossible in a work of this kind to treat them separately except for statistical purposes, inasmuch as they do, in reality, form one immense homogoneous community, and what is applicable to one equally applies to both. It is not therefore out of place to state that the population of Salford, (whose municipal and parliamentary limits are identical), according to the last census, was 176,235. This gives to the combined parlimentary area of Manchester and Salford a total population of 581,058. Of course, as these figures only apply to the year 1881, it can be safely assumed that the population now is over 600,000. A charter of incorporation was granted to Manchester so recently as the year 1838, previous to which the government was vested in a borough reeve, two constables, and other officers, elected or appointed at the Court Leet of the Lord of the Manor.

The municipal government is now composed of nineteen aldermen and fifty-seven councillors, and the city is divided into eighteen wards, or electoral divisions. Manchester became a city by Royal Charter on the 29th of March, 1853. It will scarcely be credited by the present generation, that prior to the passing of the Reform Bill of 1832, neither Manchester nor Salford enjoyed direct Parliamentary representation, whilst places of the utmost insignificance and with a mere handful of electors returned one or more members to the House of Commons. In fact, in some districts single individuals had the power to return members for their pocket boroughs. All such scandals and anomalies as these, however, have happily disappeared, and if the recollection of them be revived by the few amongst the present residents who are old enough to remember those days, it is rather for the purpose of provoking mirth than anger, and doubtless with the desire, too, of impressing upon the young men of this age how much their fathers and grandfathers have accomplished, both in the shape of parliamentary and other reforms, within the last sixty or seventy years. Salford received a Charter of Incorporation on the 16th of

April, 1844, and the Borough is now governed by sixteen aldermen and forty-eight councillors, the borough being divided into twelve wards. It may prove interesting to note that Salford received a charter, constituting it a free borough, from Randle de Blundeville, Earl of Chester, in the reign of Henry III., and that its near neighbour, Manchester, obtained a similar charter about a century afterwards (1301), in the reign of Edward I., from its baron, Thomas Gresley, a descendant of one to whom the manor had been given by Roger of Poictou, who was created by William the Conqueror lord of all the land between the rivers Mersey and Ribble. Both charters are still in existence. The present area of the city of Manchester is 5,927 statute acres, and that of the borough of Salford 5,171, the united areas being 11,098 statute acres. Manchester now returns six representatives to the House of Commons and Salford three, so that the combined representation constitutes a somewhat potent power within the walls of Parliament. In speaking of Manchester (which in this instance may be understood to include Salford), it is impossible to exclude from consideration the fact that it forms the very centre of a number of towns of great magnitude and importance, each returning one or two members to Parliament, amongst which may be mentioned Stockport, Stalybridge, Oldham, Ashton-under-Lyne, Bury, Bolton, and Rochdale. Besides these there are many other populous manufacturing villages, all within a radius of some dozen miles of the city. Nearly every cotton spinner and manufacturer in these places makes Manchester his business headquarters. This circumstance adds enormously to the parliamentary and commercial influence and prestige of the city, and fully entitles it to be styled the great centre of cotton manufacture, and the second city of the Empire. Perhaps no city in the provinces so nearly resembles the metropolis for bustle and excitement, and, certainly, in no provincial centre is there such inexhaustible manufacturing facilities, such an amount of business transacted, or such influential commercial connections maintained as in Manchester.

As in the case of most large cities, the approaches to Manchester, from whichever way the traveller comes, are hardly likely to convey to him a just impression of the Capital of the North. Should he arrive from London, four routes are open to him, all of which unite at Stockport or near it, and convey him over four miles or so of one of the busiest parts of England. On either side is a long, low expanse of fields, traversed by "cinder-paths,"—paths paved, that is to say, with the clinkers from factory furnaces—and dotted with mills, weaving sheds, and cottages for the "hands." As the traveller approaches the end of his journey the houses grow thicker, the chimneys more numerous, and the atmosphere denser. Much the same impression is received by the traveller who approaches Manchester from the north, west, or south. In each case similar features present themselves—industrial activity, mills and factories, ironworks and coal pits innumerable, comfortable-looking cottages, and a smoky and somewhat curiously oppressive atmosphere. However, when the heart of the city is reached the sense of monotony wears off. Even those who arrive by road have to pass through much the same experience. On one side, indeed, there is little change until the voyager has passed the fuliginous town of Oldham. The other roads out of Manchester take one into pleasant suburbs, but he who would reach the rural villages of Northenden, Cheadle, Didsbury, or Stretford must first pass through the regions of Old Garrett and the lower end of the Oxford Road, whilst Eccles and its neighbourhood are approached through the fashionable thoroughfare of Deansgate. Higher Broughton with its pleasant villas, Kersal Moor with its pure air, and pleasant, sociable Cheetham Hill and Prestwich—most attractive and select suburbs—are separated from the city by the less inviting locality of Strangeways.

Every black spot and unsavoury district within the municipal boundaries is being rapidly purified and beautified. No people in England are more ready to display a really generous liberality in all matters which concern their town than those of Manchester. Of this we shall have something to say in its proper place. At present we are concerned only with externals. Manchester is a city of anomalies. It is at once the newest and the oldest of English towns; it is the centre of a vast manufacturing district, and yet is not strictly speaking a manufacturing town; it is one of the plainest, and at the same time one of the handsomest, cities of the kingdom; one of the richest, and yet one of the poorest; it is a Cathedral city, yet a stronghold of Dissent; it has an enormous Roman Catholic population, and is one of the most Protestant towns in the kingdom; and finally, it has in proportion to its population probably more teetotalers than any other town, and yet much strong liquor is consumed within its limits.

The late Mr. W. Harrison Ainsworth says in his preface to "The Manchester Rebels of the Fatal '45," "Little of the old town is now left. The lover of antiquity—if any such should visit Manchester—will search in vain for those picturesque black-and-white timber habitations, with pointed gables and latticed windows, that were common enough seventy years ago. Entire streets embellished by such houses have been swept away by the course of modern improvement, but I recollect them well." At the same time within the town of Manchester the number of factories is yearly decreasing. There is still a forest of chimneys, and the atmosphere is, perhaps, as thick with smoke as ever, but the chimneys which give it forth are those of warehouse steam engines and occasional ironworks. Under the municipal government of Manchester—which, be it said by the way, is administered on the whole in a most admirable fashion—very large sums have been expended on beautifying the city, whilst private enterprise and the public spirit of the inhabitants have done almost, if not quite, as much for the improvement of the place. The change within the last thirty years has been something magical. In the "sixties" the well known street called Deansgate was a narrow, dirty lane, not at all prepossessing, imposing, or attractive. To-day Deansgate is one of the handsomest thoroughfares in England. The old Town Hall has been replaced by a magnificent new building in Albert Square, which is amongst the finest, if not absolutely the finest, in Europe. Manchester, too, boasts Assize and Police Courts such as are to be found nowhere else; while the new Royal Exchange is, except for one or two matters of detail, the most imposing and grandiose edifice of the kind in England.

THE HISTORY OF MANCHESTER

possesses a degree of interest even for those who are not fortunate enough to be natives of the place. It was a town of some consequence in the reign of Henry VIII. During the sixteenth century it largely increased its trade, and became celebrated as the headquarters of the woollen industry. Fustians, baizes, and druggets were largely manufactured, and there were some other minor products. It was not, however, until the cotton trade fairly took root in England that Manchester attained its position of importance. Now the Capital of Cotton is the centre of the most thickly-populated district in the country. A circle of twenty miles radius drawn round the town includes a population of several millions. In point of fact the population and extent of the city are daily increasing. Day by day and week by week the neighbouring towns are approaching more and more nearly to the capital. Comparatively few years ago such places as Bury, Oldham, and Middleton were small isolated villages. To-day they seem almost like parts of Manchester. And with this great material extension there has been an equally great alteration in the habits and manners of the people. The manufacturer of to-day, the merchant, the warehouseman, is a man of very different type from the same class of man three or four generations ago. In the seventeenth and eighteenth centuries the cotton magnates seem to have been of about much the same class as the small shopkeepers of to-day. They were apprenticed in regular form, and for seven years. An indenture dated 1695 is yet extant, from which it would seem that the premium paid was £60. in consideration of which, and of doing an enormous amount of menial work, the future manufacturer was to be instructed in his craft. A writer of the last century tells us that one "eminent manufacturer" of his time "used to be in his warehouse by six in the morning, accompanied by his children and apprentices.

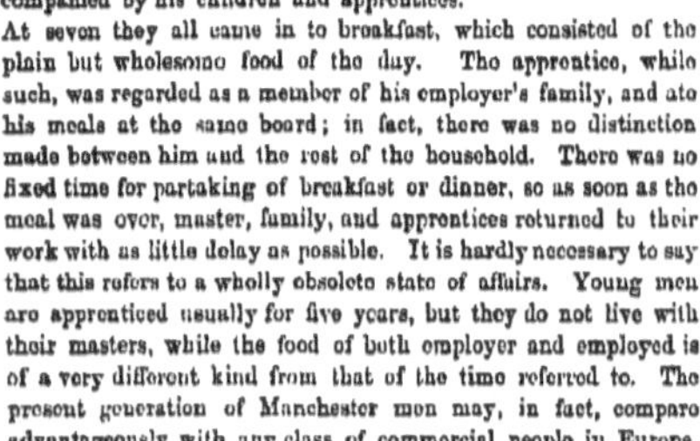

At seven they all came in to breakfast, which consisted of the plain but wholesome food of the day. The apprentice, while such, was regarded as a member of his employer's family, and ate his meals at the same board; in fact, there was no distinction made between him and the rest of the household. There was no fixed time for partaking of breakfast or dinner, so as soon as the meal was over, master, family, and apprentices returned to their work with as little delay as possible. It is hardly necessary to say that this refers to a wholly obsolete state of affairs. Young men are apprenticed usually for five years, but they do not live with their masters, while the food of both employer and employed is of a very different kind from that of the time referred to. The present generation of Manchester men may, in fact, compare advantageously with any class of commercial people in Europe.

Royal Exchange Site, formerly occupied by the above Buildings.

With the progress of education much that formerly distinguished the place is dying out. The letter *h*, for instance, was formerly regarded by many wealthy and conspicuous men as a superfluity—unless, indeed, they displayed a superabundant fondness for it by

View of Manchester, Last Century.

introducing it where it was not wanted. The failing is so comparatively uncommon now as to be a matter for remark. Many influences, of course, have co-operated to bring about this social revolution. For one thing, there has been for many years past a constant and steady influx of new blood from without. As early as the reign of George I. many country gentlemen sent their sons into Manchester, but it is remarked that in those days the treatment of the apprentices was so harsh that they very commonly ran away, and went into the army or to sea. "Other times, other manners." The sons of country gentlemen, of clergymen, and even of men of rank, position, and title, go into Manchester and stay there, thus leavening a society which might otherwise become narrow and provincial in no ordinary degree. It might be invidious to mention names; but it is no secret that amongst the "Young Manchester" of recent years might be seen the sons of one of Scotland's proudest dukes, and of the head of one of the greatest colleges of the greatest university of the world. For a time, however, Manchester life was more than sufficiently provincial in its character. The manufacturers and merchants were seldom rich, and they indulged in very few and very simple pleasures. In the last century, indeed, matters could scarcely be otherwise. The journey to London occupied in 1710 as much as eight or ten days. As late as the year 1742 there was no public conveyance, and a story is told by Dr. Aikin of a lady who having occasion to visit London, postponed her journey until she could find a man who "know the road." Twenty years before there were not more than three or four carriages in the whole of Manchester and Salford. One of them, we are told, belonged to a certain "Madam D.," presumably a well-known personage named Drake, who, having made a fortune in trade, retired from business about the year 1720. It is noted with reference to this old lady that she could never be brought to indulge in tea or coffee, and that when she paid her afternoon visits her friends provided her "with a tankard of ale and a pipe of tobacco"—a taste which was shared by the mother of a deceased M.P. for a Northern borough. One or two other details of social life in the last century are somewhat curious as compared with that of the present day. The daughters of the wealthiest manufacturers, for example, received a regular training in domestic economy. They were all taught to make home-made wines, which were the habitual drink of the wealthiest men in the place. A young manufacturer who incautiously sent for a pint of foreign wine to treat a customer was solemnly rebuked by his seniors for his extravagance. Besides "made wines" the accomplishments of the last century extended to cookery generally, and there is still extant an advertisement of a "pastry school" for young ladies, which was opened in King Street a little after 1760. While the wives and daughters were thus occupied the fathers and brothers attended to their business, and took their pleasure in the evening in a very frugal fashion. About the same time a club of the wealthiest manufacturers in the place was formed. It held its meetings at a tavern, and the expenses were fixed at 4½d.—fourpence for ale and a halfpenny for tobacco. Several years afterwards the tariff was altered, and the members were allowed if they chose to spend sixpence, but no more, in punch. A traditional club of this period is still in existence, but it has, of course, changed its character with the changing years, and is now simply an association of merchants, manufacturers, and so forth, who meet at stated times for social purposes. The original "John Shaw's Club" was held at a public-house in the Market Place. There the merchants and manufacturers met after dinner, and as a contemporary writer remarks, "at six o'clock it was high change." Sixpence only was expected to be spent in punch, though it seems probable that a good deal more was occasionally expended. At eight o'clock John Shaw made his appearance in the club-room with a horsewhip, with which he drove out his

VIEW OF THE CITY OF MANCHESTER IN 1820. TAKEN FROM A PAINTING.

guests. The writer who mentions this club adds that the ladies of Manchester held Shaw in so much esteem that there was no man so often toasted.

THE CATHEDRAL

of Manchester stands on somewhat high ground overlooking the Irwell, near its confluence with the Irk. In the days when the rivers abounded with fish—when the Irk was something better than a turbid stream and the Medlock and the Tib were purling rivulets—the situation of the "Old Church" must have been exceedingly picturesque. It is impossible to say so much for it now. The very commonplace buildings on the opposite side of the river, and the sluggish stream itself, considerably mar the beauty of the site, and leave the attractions of the church to depend upon its architecture and its associations. The present building dates only from a comparatively recent period, but the foundation is a very ancient one, so ancient, indeed, that it is almost impossible to say when there was not a church upon the site. In 1422, however, it was made a collegiate church by Thomas West, Lord de la Warr, who presented himself as the first Warden, and who, although in priest's orders, was allowed to marry, by special dispensation from the Pope, in order that so honourable a family might not become extinct. This foundation was on a really magnificent scale. There were first a Warden with eight Fellows, then for the services of the church two parish priests, two canons, four deacons, six clerks, and six boys of the choir. The fabric itself must have been one of much beauty, for it appears to have cost £3,000. To modern ears the sum may sound absurd, but in the fifteenth century money was so dear that it probably represented about £50,000 of our money. One of the older writers on Manchester antiquities mentions that at the time this church was built the daily wages of a workman were 3d., that ale was 2d. a gallon, that an ox could be bought for £1 15s. 8d., and that wheat was 11s. 3d. per quarter, figures which afford a tolerable standard for comparison. The church was first dedicated to St. Dionis, the Blessed Virgin Mary, and St. George, the name of the first being preserved in that of the street nearly opposite to the front of the building, which is still called Deansgate (Dionis' Gate). Its dedication was, however, changed a century and a half later by Queen Elizabeth, who ordered that the foundation should in future be known as Christ's College. The change of name is typical of the religious life of Manchester "Old Church," which has always held a conspicuous position in the history of the town and county. The original foundation had lasted but little more than a century when it was seized upon by Edward VI., who dissolved the corporation, appointed small pensions to the Warden and Fellows, and confiscated the surplus revenues. From that time forward Manchester became conspicuous for its Protestantism, and although the College was restored in the reign of Mary, it became Catholic again for only a very brief period. Under Mary's restored foundation, one Laurence Vaux, B.D., who is described as a "learned, pious, and conscientious divine," was appointed Warden. Early in the reign of Elizabeth he was expelled from his living, and died in prison in the Gate House of Westminster, "from destitution of the common necessaries of life." His successor was one Herle, whose purity of faith was more remarkable than his honesty of life. He is said to have been a very ardent Protestant, but he managed to waste the Collegiate revenues in the most scandalous way. Killegrew obtained long leases of the College lands at absurdly small rents, Herle pocketing the fines. Nor was this the worst. To prove the ardour of his hatred for Popery, Herle allowed the mob to pillage the church almost as they pleased; "to break down the carved work thereof with axes and hammers," and to carry off the copes and vestments. At last even the patience of Elizabeth's advisers was worn out. Walsingham superseded Herle, and after a time Elizabeth granted a renewed charter of incorporation, changing the dedication, as we have mentioned, to Christ's College. Under this new foundation, which bears date 1578, it was appointed that there should be one Warden, who was required to be in priest's orders, and to have taken a not lower degree than that of Bachelor of Divinity. Associated with him were to be four Fellows, who were to be in priest's orders, and to be of at least the degree of B.A., two chaplains or vicars, four laymen, and four children of the choir. In 1595 Dr. Dee, the celebrated astrologer, alchemist, magician, and what not—a man who seems to have been singularly misrepresented and misappreciated—was appointed Warden under this charter.

It might almost be thought that the ecclesiastical foundation of Manchester had undergone sufficient change, but fresh vicissitudes were in store for it. Charles I. gave a new charter to the Collegiate Church, making some fresh distributions of the College lands and property, and a very few years later came the troubles of the great Civil War, when everything was, to use a homely phrase, turned upside down. The Cathedral—or as it was called then and even now by the old residents, the "Old Church"—was sacked by the Puritans. The few remaining sacred vestments and the small remnant of altar plate were pillaged, and from 1646 to 1660 the whole country was divided into Presbyterian classes. With the Restoration things were slightly improved. The ancient charter was renewed, and the disfigured, dismantled, and mutilated church once more became a "house of prayer." Unhappily, it never seemed to flourish. The prevailing irreligion of the eighteenth century displayed itself in Manchester as elsewhere, and there are many old Manchester men who can tell somewhat striking stories of the lax lives and irreverent habits of the "Fellows" of the last two generations. Even within living memory there have been some curious illustrations of the prevailing tone of irreverence. For example, a story is told of one of the Canons who, whilst reading the Burial Service at the graveside, was annoyed by the grimacing of a Grammar School boy, and broke off at the solemn moment of committing the body to the earth to desire the sexton to "knock that little d——, off the wall." The tradition of celibacy was kept up, and the scandals to which it gave rise may best be left undescribed. The office of Fellow being one of emolument, and having attached to it comparatively few duties, attracted a certain class of idle clerics, whose perfunctory discharge of their few obligations and utter want of a sense of responsibility produced no small amount of harm. The great Oxford movement of 1830 struck, however, upon Manchester with remarkable effect. The policy of the day was to place Bishops in some of the manufacturing centres, and while Ripon was chosen as one of the new sees, Manchester, with infinitely better judgement, was selected for the other. The last Warden under the old charter, the Hon. and Very Rev. W. Herbert, became the first Dean of the new foundation, but died almost immediately afterwards. In July, 1847, the year in which the bishopric was created, Dr. Bowers succeeded to the Deanery, and upon his resignation in 1871 his place was filled by the energetic and active Dr. Cowie, previously rector of St. Lawrence, Jewry, in which capacity he did so much to disprove the alleged necessity for destroying the ancient churches of the City of London. Dr. Cowie was translated from Manchester to the Deanery of Exeter in 1883, and was succeeded by the Very Rev. John Oakley, Dean of Carlisle, who still holds the office. The first Bishop of Manchester was Dr. Prince-Lee. His successor, the late Dr. Fraser, was a man of very considerable scholarship and greatly beloved. The present bishop of Manchester is the Right Rev. Dr. Moorhouse.

THE "SEVEN STARS," SAID TO BE THE OLDEST LICENSED TAVERN IN GREAT BRITAIN.

At the Reformation the cathedral, as we have seen, was wrecked, as parish and collegiate churches generally were, and the soldiers of Cromwell, finished, in part at all events, what the Protestantism of the preceding century had begun. At the beginning of the present century it was exceedingly dilapidated and much disfigured by the churchwardenisms of a past generation, and a partial restoration was accordingly attempted, which was carried on during the fourteen years between 1814 and 1828. As the beauty of Pointed architecture began to be more fully appreciated, the imperfections and shortcomings of the earlier restoration came to be understood, and in 1845 a fresh restoration was commenced. From that time to the present the work has gone on almost without interruption, the result being an almost total reconstruction of the building. Except the mere walls, there is very little left of the church as it stood in the days of Henry VII. The beautiful tower, which is an almost exact reproduction of the old one, but in a better material, is new from foundation to flagstaff. New mullions have been put into the windows, and many of them have been refilled with stained glass, though regarding one or two of the specimens, had more care been bestowed upon the work, they might have been made more worthy of the fane they are intended to ornament. New choir stalls have been erected, a new reredos put up, and ornamental work has been executed. Altogether, a sum of something like £60,000 has been expended on the restoration and beautification of the "Old Church," including the new tower, which was completed in 1868. Of this large sum, at least £23,000 has been expended within the last few years. The results have been satisfactory, and the edifice is now a cathedral more worthy of so great and wealthy a diocese. As a building it has several points of interest. The double aisles and the many chapels will always attract those who are interested in architectural and archæological matters, whilst the very beautiful carved tabernacle work in the choir cannot fail to attract the amateur of ecclesiastical architecture. The old-fashioned galleries have been removed, the inconvenience of some of the internal arrangements, the lowness of the roof, the absence of triforium, and the former sombre appearance of the interior have been remedied, and help to reconcile the casual visitor to the rejection of the project for building a new cathedral on the site of the Infirmary. The scheme was certainly a daring one, but considering the magnificent liberality of Manchester, there was nothing in it to excite surprise amongst those who know the place and the people. The only surprise, in fact, which was felt in many quarters, was that so splendid a notion was dropped so precipitately. The project was carried so far that the drawings for the proposed building were publicly exhibited, and were published in a professional journal some years ago. However, financial and other considerations, combined with the complete and elaborate improvement and restoration of the old cathedral, rendered it inexpedient to proceed with the erection of the new edifice. Unfortunately local feeling is very strong, and

THE SITE OF THE TOWN HALL MAIN BUILDING, FORMERLY OCCUPIED BY DR. WHITE.

RELIGION IN MANCHESTER

has unhappily always been tinged with a certain amount of party spirit. To this fact we may probably attribute a good deal of the hostility with which Dr. Cowie, the predecessor of the present Dean, was received by the people, before they learned to appreciate his unflinching honesty and real capacity for work. On the other hand, the Orangemen muster very strongly, and are conspicuous for their zeal—a zeal, by the way, which might sometimes be advantageously tempered with a little more discretion than is the usual rule. When on one side partisans descend to profane swearing at the clergy in vestry assembled, it is perhaps time for decent people to refuse to identify themselves with the party of the objurgators. So, also, when the supporters of extreme views on the other side announce their intention of defying the law, quiet and peaceable people may be forgiven if they assume the position of Gallio, and "care for none of these things." The fact of the matter is, however, that religious intolerance is a local tradition. One of the greatest heroes of the place is that John Bradford, the so-called martyr, of whom Fox gives so remarkable an account, and whose case reads so very differently in the writings of other chroniclers. When the Revolution came about, Manchester was, as we have seen, a stronghold of the Puritans, who seized upon the church livings and the churches, to appropriate them to their own purposes.

When the Restoration was accomplished, and that protest of the laity against the assumptions of the Presbyterian clergy—the Act of Uniformity—was passed, the majority of the Presbyterians found little difficulty in conforming. Only three ministers in Manchester and one in Salford were ejected, but to commemorate their martyrdom, some of the Dissenters of the town erected, in 1864, a Memorial Hall in Albert Square, in which building the Unitarians frequently hold meetings. The Act of Uniformity was strict as regarded Nonconformists in cities and boroughs, but it allowed them to settle in places which were neither the one nor the other. Manchester answering to this character, speedily became the headquarters of Dissent in the county, and there, under the indulgences of 1672, one of the largest Puritan congregations of the provinces was gathered, under the ministrations of the Rev. Henry Newcome. The people built for themselves a chapel—"a neat but plain edifice"—in Cross Street. In the riots of 1714 the original chapel was pulled down, but a grant having been made by the Treasury, it was restored with primitive simplicity of architecture, and it is now one of the best-known Unitarian chapels in the city, and boasts one of the most wealthy and intellectual congregations in Lancashire. The late Rev. William Gaskell was the minister of this church, and his wife painted in "North and South" the intellectual and metaphysical struggles of her husband's mind in very striking colours. The same body have, besides the chapel in Cross Street, numerous other places of meeting in and about Manchester, one of which, in Upper Brook Street, was erected in 1837, from the designs of the late Sir Charles Barry, and is one of the ornaments of the town.

The Church of England is well represented. Every shade of High, Low, and Broad Churchmanship is to be found. The lover of ritual, altar lights, and high-class ecclesiastical music may go to St. John the Baptist in Renshaw Street, Hulme, where he may hear also a very admirable sermon from the rector, Dr. Marshall. Or should the visitor's taste incline him to the more severe Gregorian modes, St. Alban's, Strangeways, and St. Gabriel's, Hulme, will supply his wants. If, on the other hand, his tastes lead him to prefer the more marked form of Evangelical teaching, St. Ann's, in St. Ann's Square, which is served by a clergyman of considerable local celebrity, the Rev. Canon Tonge, M.A., St. Silas, Higher Ardwick, and St. Paul's, Brunswick Street, will be pointed out as the most desirable places for him to attend. If again his views are, as the little girl in *Punch* once said, "Broad, inclining to High," the Rev. David Ellison, of All Saints', will supply his needs, while if he be of the type known as "Broad, inclining to Low," the church of St. John the Evangelist, Waterloo Road, which is in a sense the private chapel of the Bishop, may be pointed out to his notice. Moderate High Churchmen will find a congenial refuge in the Churches of St. James, Birch-in-Rusholme, and St. Mary, Moss Side, the former of which is served by the Venerable (in every sense of the term) Archdeacon Anson, whilst the latter had until recently the Rev. F. C. Woodhouse, who was one of the most eloquent and forcible preachers amongst the Manchester clergy. Manchester churchmanship is generally, however, of a very sober and rational type, chiefly because of the influence which is exerted upon it by the cathedral. The canons are all parochial clergymen as well as cathedral dignitaries, and the relations between the mother church and the suffragan parishes are unusually close and intimate. As one of the body observed to the present writer some five or six years ago, there is probably no diocese in England in which the views enunciated in Mr. Beresford Hope's work on "The English Cathedral" are so fully carried out as in Manchester. The result to *via media* men is eminently satisfactory. Except at St. Paul's in London, and at the special services at some few of the provincial cathedrals, there is hardly a cathedral in England which has so large, so devout, so intelligent, and so liberal a congregation as that of Manchester, whilst the churches of the city and suburbs bear witness to the rare munificence of the people. A few details of this liberality may be worth giving. We take the churches in their alphabetical order. St. Alban's, Waterloo Road, was built mainly by the anonymous gifts of a gentleman who has taken more pains to conceal his name than less generous givers take to blazon their good deeds. The late Lord Derby presented the site. For St. George's, Pendleton, the site was the free gift of Mr. J. P. Fitzgerald. St. James's, Collyhurst, cost £21,000, the greater part of which sum was raised by private subscription. St. James's, Faulkner Street, cost £30,000, the whole of which was provided by Mr. Stewart, of the Atlas Works. St. John the Evangelist, Oldham Road, was mainly erected by an anonymous benefactor. St. John the Evangelist, Waterloo Road, cost £20,000, and was the sole gift of Mr. Lewis Lloyd. St. Mary's, Moss Side, one of the most splendid churches in or near Manchester, was erected and endowed at the sole cost of the late Mr. Wilbraham Egerton. St. Paul's, Kersal Moor, was erected at great cost by private subscription. SS. Simon and Jude was wholly paid for by a member of the Birley family, and St. Philip's, Chester Street, Hulme, by another member of the same liberal house. Our list cannot pretend to be either full or specially accurate. These good men "have done good by stealth," and without an elaborate search it would be impossible to arrive at all the details of their liberality. One thing, however, is certain, and that is that there are many churches in Manchester in which it is only necessary for the preacher to say on a given Sunday that certain moneys are wanted for special purposes before the following Sunday, to have all that he needs, and something over.

View on the "Irwell." From an old Painting.

Nor are

THE DISSENTERS

by any means behindhand with their contributions for religious and charitable purposes. There are Dissenting ministers in the place who enjoy incomes which sound almost fabulous to those who believe the tradition of the Dissenting clergyman's dependence upon the hardly-extracted contributions of the tradesman and the artisan. When it is mentioned that on one chapel alone the Independent body expended £26,000, and that the income of one popular Dissenting preacher is stated to be some £1,500 a year, it will readily be understood that "the dissidence of Dissent" in

Manchester does not imply sitting still and waiting upon Providence. The following list will, however, show better than any

SALFORD CROSS, WHERE WERE LOCATED THE STOCKS.

general statement the religious activity of the Cotton Capital. Besides the cathedral, with its daily services, and the eighty-two churches belonging to the Church of England, there are in Manchester and Salford—

- 41 Independent Chapels.
- 10 Presbyterian Chapels.
- 45 Methodist Chapels (Wesleyan).
- 3 Methodist New Connection Chapels.
- 19 United Methodist Chapels.
- 18 Primitive Methodist Chapels.
- 3 Primitive Methodist Chapels of other names.
- 11 Unitarian Chapels.
- 11 Baptist Chapels.
- 1 Quakers' Meeting.
- 1 Swedenborgian Chapel.
- 3 Welsh Calvinistic Methodist Chapels.
- 1 "Bible Christian" Chapel (endowed for the support of a sect somewhat akin to that of the Peculiar People, and holding special views on teetotalism, vegetarianism, monogamy, celibacy, and similar subjects).
- 4 Jews' Synagogues.
- 31 Roman Catholic Churches and Chapels.
- 1 Christian Brethren's Chapel.
- 1 German Evangelical Chapel.
- 1 Church of the Greek Catholics.
- 1 Moravian.
- 1 Catholic Apostolic (Irvingite) Church.
- 1 Established Church of Scotland.

In all 291 edifices, large and small, devoted to various religious uses, besides school and mission rooms, the number of which it is impossible accurately to estimate. Notwithstanding these multitudinous divisions, and the somewhat heated party spirit which distinguishes religious matters in Manchester, there are plenty of occasions on which controversial considerations are set aside, and all classes unite for charitable purposes. The principal of these occasions occurs on

WHIT MONDAY,

when the Sunday Schools turn out for a procession through the

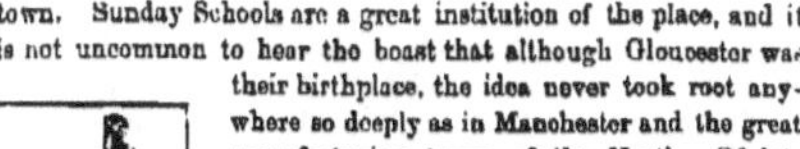

town. Sunday Schools are a great institution of the place, and it is not uncommon to hear the boast that although Gloucester was their birthplace, the idea never took root anywhere so deeply as in Manchester and the great manufacturing towns of the North. Of late years there has been a slightly reactionary feeling against them in certain quarters. One class of critics has urged that it is unnecessary to make Sunday a mere continuation of the rest of the week for those children who are receiving a definite religious education at the day schools. Another has complained that these schools are used for purposes of proselytism; while a third objects to the educational as distinguished from the religious part of them on the ground that the Education Act has done away with the necessity for these irregular and unattached agencies. However, the people who cavil at, or endeavour to depreciate, Sunday schools, are, for the most part, the very parties who deprecate any very particular observance of the Sunday itself, except as a holiday, or a day of bodily rest merely; and therefore, we do not consider their objections entitled to very great weight. Of one thing we feel pretty certain, which is, that no one who has really had any long practical experience of Sunday schools will agree with their detractors, and it would be absurd to accept the opinions of theorists rather than those of indivduals who have laboured in them and have studied their inner workings and effects. That there are occasional abuses in connection with their management may readily be admitted, and that, as an institution, they are not perfect, may also be granted; but what the public have to consider, is this: do they upon the whole, operate beneficially upon society, or otherwise, and are children attending them made better or worse by the instruction received thereat? If it can be shown,

OLD MANCHESTER: THE MARKET PLACE.

as no doubt it can, that in spite of all drawbacks and shortcomings, and even in the face of some admitted abuses, the Sunday school system has been, and still is, a powerful lever for elevating and improving the morals of the rising generation, and has been the means of inculcating social as well as religious obligations in the minds of the young, then Sunday schools ought to be not simply tolerated, but encouraged; and beyond this, they have a right to be liberally supported. The great bulk of the inhabitants of Manchester and neighbourhood are, fortunately, believers in Sunday schools, and duly appreciate their influence for good; and consequently they send their children to them, and, as a result, the numbers attending the various Sunday schools is exceedingly large. It is somewhat difficult to give the aggregate number of Sunday-school children, of all denominations, who walked in procession last Whit Monday (1887), but it is understood that the Church of England schools alone mustered no less than 21,728.

The children of the Sunday schools are taken out in waggons or "lurries" to fields lent by friendly farmers in suburban districts, and are regaled with buns and milk, and entertained with hymn-singing and affectionate addresses from their teachers and other friends. Occasionally, the elder scholars and their teachers are taken in excursion trains to various spots of interest or of natural beauty at a distance. In spite of all attacks, the Sunday schools of Manchester maintain their position and numbers, and the procession of Whit Monday, in which such an immense number of children take part, affords a very striking proof of their continued vitality.

The remainder of Whitsun week is devoted to holiday-making and excursions. Very little business is done during the whole time. Most of the wealthier inhabitants go away altogether, whilst those who are less well endowed with this world's goods content themselves with day excursions to Blackpool, Southport, Lytham, Buxton, Matlock, and the Peak, sometimes extending their peregrinations as far as Windermere or Morecambe Bay, to all of which places the railway companies run special trains.

Market Street, from Market Place. From a Drawing some years ago.

Turning now from social matters we may glance at the

GENERAL ASPECT OF THE PLACE.

Manchester and Salford are usually spoken of as one town, and they are connected by ties of the most intimate kind. Each has its Mayor and Corporation, its separate local administration, its own local rating, and its own way of managing its affairs. Yet the leading men in the two places are identical. The manufacturer who has his mills or his ironworks in Salford has his offices in Manchester, and transacts his business on the Manchester Exchange. Salford is in fact mainly the working-class suburb of Cottonopolis, and fulfils towards it much the same function as that of Southwark to London. It is also the seat of a Roman Catholic bishopric. Between the two towns flows that turbid stream

THE IRWELL,

on the high ground above which the Cathedral is placed. There was a time when the Irwell, with its confluent streams the Irk, the Medlock, and the Tib, must have been a really beautiful river, as will readily be believed by those who have come across it in the neighbourhood of Radcliffe or Bury, winding placidly through a very varied country, and bearing a tribute of fair water to the Mersey. But the hand of man has marred the fair work of Nature, and the Irwell is now, with the exception of the Aire and the Calder, the least attractive stream in the United Kingdom. All over the district through which it passes manufactories have been established, the greater number of which send a large part, if not the whole, of their refuse, solid as well as liquid, into the stream. There are cotton and woollen mills, bleaching, dyeing, calico, and silk printing works, alkali and chemical works, paper mills, tanneries, and hat manufactories. These are scattered over the whole district, and the refuse from all of them—or at all events so much as is not deposited by the way—passes into the Irwell above Manchester, and so gives an impression to the stranger that the city is much dirtier and much more careless of its river than is really the case. Thus Bolton with its multitudinous mills discharges considerable refuse into the Croal, about three miles above its junction with the Irwell. The greater number of the mills and bleachworks of Bury and Tottington stand almost on the brink of the Irwell itself. Rochdale sends its quota of pollution into the Roch before it joins the Irwell, and the Irk leaves Middleton a malodorous brook instead of what it once was, a sparkling trout stream.

In the same way the Medlock, widely known in connection with the author of the "Confessions of an Opium Eater," his brothers, and their juvenile escapades, is studded during the latter part of its course with factories, tanneries, paper mills, and chemical works, each of which contributes its quota of contamination to the Irwell. The effect of all this tremendous influx of refuse into the small and sluggish stream is unpleasantly known in Manchester, and has suggested to local public men the pressing necessity of applying a remedy. In one place, on the Irwell, according to the report of the Rivers Pollution Commissioners, the normal bed of the river was twelve feet nine inches below the present ordinary level of the stream. In 1867 the depth of the stream was only from 3 ft. 6 in. to 4 ft. 6 in., the bed having been raised by the deposit of solid matter during the preceding years at the rate of somewhere about two inches per annum. This solid refuse is not, as would probably be most commonly supposed, mainly composed of sewage, but chiefly consists of the waste from manufactories and other works, and, though quite sufficiently undesirable and more than sufficiently offensive, is not productive of the evil effects which might be expected from such a stream running through the middle of the town. The silting up of the river has at various times produced very severe floods, the low-lying parts of the town—Lower Broughton, for example—having been several times during the last few years flooded by the storm-overflow of the river, greatly to the inconvenience and annoyance of the inhabitants. Beyond such discomfort, however, the evils arising out of this state of the river do not extend very far. Manchester and Salford have a somewhat high death-rate, but it must not be thought that this is attributable in any considerable degree to the waters of the Irwell. In a great and crowded manufacturing centre such as Manchester, many things contribute to produce disease, especially amongst the poorer classes. The mode of life of these people, their over-crowded dwellings and the lack of sanitary conditions under which they live, the early age at which children are put to work, and the unwholesomeness of factory life, all in turn contribute to considerably increase the rate of mortality, and no cleansing or purifying of the Irwell or its tributaries will affect these evils. Radical changes and improvements of a totally different character are needed to grapple with them, and it need not be doubted that the spread of temperance, the diffusion of education, and the many other agencies now at work for ameliorating the condition of the working classes, coupled with scientific discovery and increased sanitary knowledge, will, ere long, produce great transformations in the habits and health of the people generally; and if the evils complained of cannot be entirely removed, their effects will doubtless be reduced to the lowest possible minimum. The Health Committees of Manchester and Salford are composed of men of energy and sound practical knowledge, and they are animated by a desire and determination to do all which the powers invested in them enable them to do, to improve the sanitary condition of the two boroughs, and thus promote the health of the inhabitants. There is little doubt that in the course of a few years hence a very marked change for the better will have taken place, resulting in a greatly reduced death-rate and a healthier community.

MARKET STREET, FROM PICCADILLY, IN 1840.

THE PUBLIC BUILDINGS

which have sprung into existence of late years are rapidly turning what was once one of the ugliest into one of the handsomest cities in the kingdom. That to which the visitor's attention is usually first directed is the exceedingly handsome pile of buildings in Strangeways, which is used for the purposes of

ASSIZE COURTS

It is said, and we believe with perfect truth, that these courts are the most comfortable, commodious, and well-arranged in the kingdom. Certainly in no other courts is there so ample a provision for the public as well as for all persons having business to transact. The building consists of a centre with two wings, and is externally about 250 feet long by 150 feet deep, the architectural effect being enormously enhanced by the wise liberality of the Corporation, who have left an open space in front of the building of more than a hundred feet in depth. The principal feature of the interior is the great hall, the proportions of which are remarkably harmonious but which suffers from the unavoidable want of light. This deficiency is, however, imperceptible on the rare occasions when the coronæ are lighted up, and the spectator can appreciate the size and height of the room. The two principal courts are at the back of this hall. Each of them is 60 feet by 40 feet on the floor, and 40 feet high. Other courts are provided upstairs, and there are large Grand Jury rooms, retiring rooms, offices for the Prothonotary, the Clerk of the Crown, and the other officials of the Courts. The comfort of members of the Bar has been carefully studied. Their library is an exceedingly handsome, commodious, and well-furnished room, divided only from the courts by a corridor—an arrangement the convenience of which will be appreciated by those who have the misfortune to practice in the stuffy and inconvenient dens which are dignified by the name of courts in some parts of the kingdom. On the first floor the Bar mess have a large, lofty, and well-lighted room, communicating by means of a lift with the kitchens in the basement, and on this floor are also the rooms used by the Grand Jury, as well as a smaller court used by the Commissioner when it is found that the two judges cannot get through the work of the Assizes in time. Close to the Courts, and communicating with them by a covered way, are the Judge's lodgings—an exceedingly handsome, commodious, and well-furnished house, admirably adapted for the use to which it is devoted. Immediately behind the courts stands the new

COUNTY GAOL,

which was opened in 1868. This is a very large and imposing building, and embodies all modern improvements in prison architecture and arrangement. It was erected to supersede the "New Bailey," which formerly stood just within the borough of Salford, on the bank of the Irwell—a prison the name of which will be familiar to those who remember the Fenian outbreak and the "Manchester martyrs" of 1867. The new building covers nine acres of ground, and cost £170,000. There are cells for 800 men and 300 women, and the system of management and discipline is so admirable as to be constantly held up as an example for imitation in other prisons. The prisoners are kept constantly employed at various trades, and their work is so far valuable that they practically defray the greatest part of the expense of their maintenance. At the other side of the town, in the Hyde Road, is the City Gaol—a very much smaller establishment, which has just been thoroughly overhauled and repaired. The building and yards cover seven acres of ground, and afford accommodation for about 500 prisoners. The police-courts are in Minshull Street, near to the London Road Station. They are accommodated in a remarkably handsome and convenient building of brick, with stone dressings and in the Venetian Gothic style of architecture. There are four court rooms, each 53 feet by 33 feet, and 36 feet high—light, airy, and convenient. The total cost of the building and furniture was £55,000, and there are few residents of London who have been called by business to any of the metropolitan courts who will not regret that London cannot boast of anything half so commodious or well arranged.

THE RAILWAY STATIONS.

No city in the world possesses finer railway accomodation than Manchester. The chief stations are four in number, namely, the Victoria, the Exchange, the London Road, and the Central Stations. The Victoria Station, which belongs to the Lancashire and Yorkshire Railway Company, is situated at Hunt's Bank, and has the largest area. It has been considerably enlarged during recent years, and its present dimensions are: length, 725 feet; breadth, 656 feet; and area, 52,844 yards. It has thirteen platforms, and four carriage and two foot approaches, of which the principal are those leading from Corporation Street and Strangeways. The platforms are connected by subways. The alterations and additions were designed by the chief engineer of the company, Mr. William Hunt, and are estimated to have cost, exclusive of land, some £170,000. The "Lancashire and Yorkshire" do an

View on the Irwell by Moonlight.

enormous traffic, both in passengers and goods, and their immense station at Hunt's Bank is not at all too great for their passenger requirements. Next in point of size is the new Exchange Station, belonging to the "London and North Western." It stands directly opposite the tower end of the cathedral, on the Salford side of the Irwell, and is approached from Victoria Street by a broad sloping carriage-way which crosses that river. Its elevated position and noble appearance adds greatly to the beauty of the city at that point. The station was erected in lieu of the quarters previously occupied by the company at Hunt's Bank, and it was opened in June, 1884. The building was designed by their engineer-in-chief, Mr. Francis Stevenson, and it has a length of 800 feet, and a breadth of 250 feet, the total area being 200,000 feet. The style of architecture is what is known as the "modern classical." In addition to the entrance from Victoria Street, there is one from Chapel Street, Salford. There is direct communication betwixt the Victoria and Exchange Stations for foot passengers. The London Road Station, also belonging to the London and North

Western Railway Company, is likewise very extensive, although we cannot give its actual dimensions. Some seven or eight years ago it was greatly enlarged at immense cost, the outlay being £300,000. The other is the Central Station, situated in Windmill Street, and belonging jointly to the Cheshire Lines and Midland Railway Companies. This is an entirely new station, and was opened for general traffic in July, 1877. It is not so large as any of the other three, but is, nevertheless, of considerable extent, and is admirably arranged and fitted up. In addition to the foregoing, there is also a station in Oxford Road, which is the headquarters of the Manchester, South Junction, and Altrincham Railway. The Great Northern, and Manchester, Sheffield, and Lincolnshire Railway Company have their headquarters at the London Road Station, with which their system is connected. By the aid of these various railway lines, Manchester is brought into immediate communication with all parts of England, Scotland, and Wales; and whilst passengers can now accomplish a journey to or from Liverpool (31½ miles) in 45 minutes, they can perform a journey to or from the metropolis (188 miles) in 4¼ or 4½ hours.

WATTS' WAREHOUSE AND BUILDINGS.

CHETHAM HOSPITAL AND LIBRARY.

The founder of this establishment was a Manchester worthy, of a type which is happily by no means extinct. He flourished in the middle of the seventeenth century, and having amassed a fortune left it in the hands of trustees, who bought from the Earl of Derby the ruined "Baron's Hall," which up to the time of the Reformation had been used as a residence by the collegiate clergy. The trust under Chetham's will was incorporated by Royal Charter in 1665, and under its provisions a free school was established. The number for whom provision was originally made was forty, but at the present time a hundred boys receive a sound, plain education. They must not be under six years of age and must come from the townships of Manchester, Salford, Crumpsall, Droylesden, Bolton, or Turton. They wear a dress very similar to that of the boys of Christ Hospital in London, and at the age of fourteen they are apprenticed with a premium of £4 and two suits of clothes. That an excellent work is done by the income of this charity is not open to question. But the £4 apprenticeship fee, some people think, might perhaps, be exchanged with advantage for scholarships to enable boys who manifest special ability to prolong their studies, while nothing would be lost if the obsolete and inconvenient dress were replaced by garments of more modern fashion. No change in the *locale* of the school or in its distinctive religious teaching would, however, be likely to meet with much approbation in Manchester. The hundred boys with their Governor sitting on Sunday in a conspicuous place in the Cathedral, are a sacred institution in the eyes of Manchester churchmen.

The Library, which occupies a part of the same building, is one of the oldest free libraries in England, and one of the best and most interesting. It contains 43,000 volumes, and is absolutely and entirely free to every reader. By the will of Humphrey Chetham, £1,000 were left for books and £100 for the building, and, in addition, the residue of his personal estate, which amounted to about £2,000 more, a sum equal in the seventeenth century to about £20,000 to-day. Gradually and slowly additions have been made to the collection of books, until it now numbers amongst its items some of the most interesting relics to be found in the North of England. The gem of the collection is a finely illuminated MS. of Matthew Paris's "Flowers of History," a portion of which is stated to be in the autograph of the author. There are also some splendid Oriental MSS., large collections of books and manuscripts relating to local and general history and antiquities, early English MSS., many magnificently illustrated works on art and natural history, the library of the celebrated Dr. John Bryom, and the collections of that accomplished local antiquarian, the late Mr. John Harland.

At the back of Chetham's Hospital towers that splendid new building the

GRAMMAR SCHOOL.

This building is a standing monument of Manchester liberality, and of the strong local attachment by which Manchester men are as a rule characterised. The school was originally founded as long ago as 1515 by a Lancashire worthy—one Hugh Oldham—whose descendants still inhabit the town, and in whom there is a great amount of local pride. Later on scholarships were founded at both Universities by Sarah, Duchess of Somerset. At various times other munificent gifts have been made to the school; the result being that at the present time there are few grammar schools in the kingdom with so many valuable prizes to boast of. Every year two scholarships tenable for five years at Brazenose College, Oxford, fall vacant, and one exhibition tenable for three years at St. John's College, Cambridge, while every third year there are two such exhibitions vacant. In 1870 a scholarship (the Rickards) of £50 a year was founded, and the late Miss Brackenbury founded six scholarships at Oxford to be held for three years by the best scholar in classics, mathematics, and physical science. There are also four Shakespeare scholarships, and three exhibitions at Owens College. Recently an endowment was bequeathed by the late Mr. E. R. Langworthy, who after providing munificently for his relations bequeathed the sum of £10,000 for the foundation of scholarships. It is to be observed, by the way, that the greater part of this liberality has been displayed of late years. The original foundation has been entirely remodelled, and immense additions have been made to the school property. By the original plan it was provided that the income of the school should be derived from certain mills in the street known as Long Millgate, which Oldham calculated would be sufficient for a grammar school which would educate the boys of Manchester "freely for ever." It was found, however, some years ago that circumstances alter cases, and a pestilent heresy, moreover, had sprung up as to the value of that which is obtained for nothing. The mill rents were falling off; scholarships had to be withheld, and a good deal of uneasiness was felt as to the future of the school. For the time temporary expedients were devised. A scheme was submitted to the Court of Chancery, and, an effort having been made by those who took a public-spirited interest in the school, things went on somewhat better for a while. However, some time afterwards it became evident that something more than had ever before been attempted was necessary. The reputation of the school for scholarship was not likely to suffer for the time, but the stipends of the masters were too inconsiderable to admit of the hope that the best men could in future be induced to come forward. Accordingly a great meeting was held, and one after another the merchants and manufacturers who had been educated at the Grammar School rose to promise their £500, £1,000, or £2,000. The result of that meeting was the erection of the present splendid building, the admission of a large number of students who pay £12 12s. a year, and the extension of "free pupils" to 250. With the income at the disposal of the trustees it has been found possible to obtain the services of some of the most accomplished members of both Universities as masters, and under the able management of the present "High Master"—the Rev. S. Dill, M.A.—the school maintains a standard of scholarship which is probably higher than that attained in any other school of its class in England. The school is not merely a classical and mathematical one—it is also a modern school of the first grade. In addition to all the English subjects usually taught, the boys have the opportunity of acquiring a competent knowledge of the classics, modern languages, mathematics, drawing, and physical science. The institution is on the whole one of which Manchester may well be proud, and although there is a certain amount of feeling in some quarters as to the loss of the "free" character of the school by the introduction of paying pupils, it cannot be denied that the change has been greatly for the better.

View in Mosley Street, Manchester.

At the opposite side of the town, in the Oxford Road, stands another great educational institution, with a history which, though shorter, is not altogether unlike that of the Grammar School.

THE OWENS COLLEGE,

(see Illustration, page 55), though a modern foundation, has made rapid progress in the comparatively few (thirty-seven) years of its existence, and now constitutes the oldest and largest college of the newly created Victoria University. The present buildings are exceedingly handsome, and reflect infinite credit on the architect, Mr. Alfred Waterhouse, to whom Manchester is also indebted for its Assize Courts and New Town Hall. The college originated in the year 1846, when a certain Mr. John Owens, a merchant of Manchester, died, leaving the residue of his property, after paying legacies and charitable bequests, to trustees for educational purposes. The trustees under the will appointed a sub-committee of their number to draw up and report on a plan, which they adopted. They leased the house till then occupied by Mr. Richard Cobden, at the lower end of Quay Street. This house was the property of one of the trustees, who at a later period presented it to the college. In this building the college was opened in March, 1851. The founder's will declared it to be his object to found "an institution for providing the means of instruction in such branches of learning and science as are now and may be hereafter usually taught in the English universities." In accordance with this provision the college was established on what may be called *university lines*, although the novelty of such an enterprise and the exceeding youthfulness of the students (fourteen years having been named by the founder as the *minimum* age of admission), placed great difficulties in the way of realising that ideal. The first principal was the late Professor A. J. Scott, an eloquent lecturer and profound thinker, who by the originality of his teaching, and the strength and dignity of his character, from the first impressed a high type of studentship on the young institution. Professor Scott relinquished the principalship in 1857, retaining his chair of Philosophy and English Literature until his death in 1866. He was succeeded by the present principal, J. G. Greenwood, LL.D., the professor of Greek and Latin, under whom, supported by a long series of energetic and distinguished colleagues, the progress of the college has been steady and uninterrupted. In 1867 it became evident that the college was outgrowing its endowments and the space at the command of the managers. An appeal was therefore made to the public, and the response was speedily visible in the shape of a subscription list such as even in Manchester is not often to be seen. Many thousands of pounds were raised in a few days, and before long a site was secured for the new college, which, availing itself of the Degree Examinations of the London University, to which it has from the first been affiliated, fulfilled the functions of a university for the Capital of Cotton. In the autumn of 1870 the foundation stone of the buildings was laid, and three years later the first portion of them was also opened for the use of the students by the Duke of Devonshire. Great additions have since been made to the establishment, and the college buildings, though not completed, are very extensive; and it is no exaggeration to say that the new buildings are amongst the best in the kingdom, in many respects, for the purposes for which they are designed. Their merit consists less in their ornamental architecture—though in this respect they are not to be despised—than the wise attention to all matters of utility which has been exhibited in planning the interior. As might naturally

WEST VIEW OF ASSIZE COURTS, MANCHESTER.

be anticipated, physical science is a strong point in the curriculum of Owens College. For its study the pupils have the use of laboratories which are justly considered amongst the finest in the kingdom. In 1882 the Manchester Medical School, first and most successful of the medical schools of the provinces, was also amalgamated with the Owens College, and its Museums of Anatomy and *Materia Medica* find a congenial home within its walls. About the same time a department of law, which had for some time existed in germ, was greatly developed, so that, as the historian of Owens College, Mr. Joseph Thompson (a former student of the college and now its treasurer and chairman of the council), says in his recently published work, "It was a university to all intents and purposes except in its machinery and power of granting degrees."

These words had reference to the character of the college before the creation by royal charter of the Victoria University in 1880. Of this university Owens College was declared in the charter to be the first (and at that time the only) constituent college, so that its students obtain their degrees from the university in which it is incorporated, and to which it and the other more recently incorporated colleges in Liverpool and Leeds bear the same relation as the colleges of Oxford and Cambridge bear to those universities.

Sir J. Lyon Playfair M.P., F.R.S., in his address delivered at Aberdeen in 1885, as president of the British Association for the Advancement of Science, says: "Owens College has worthily developed into the Victoria University. Formerly she depended for degrees upon the University of London. No longer will she be like a moon reflecting cold and sickly rays from a distant luminary, for in future she will be a sun, a centre of intelligence, warming and illuminating the regions around her." This graceful tribute to the college from such a quarter cannot fail to be exceedingly gratifying to all its friends and benefactors, no less than to the pupils and governing staff. The actual amount of "residue" received by the trustees from Owens estate for college purposes amounted to £96,654 4s. 6d.; but this sum, great as it undoubtedly is when looked upon as the gift of one individual, is small when compared with the aggregate amount of money which has since been contributed to the various funds of the college, and to found its scholarships, &c., up to the present time. The sum total amounts to some hundreds of thousands of pounds, and includes one bequest from the late Mr. C. F. Beyer, the eminent engineer, of upwards of £100,000. The records of Owens College will reveal an extent of munificence scarcely paralleled in our history for such a purpose. The college library now contains 14,006 volumes, of which number 3,793 have been added during the past year. The late Dr. J. Prince Lee, first Bishop of Manchester, bequeathed his large and valuable library to the college, and many other benefactors have enriched the library by gifts of collections of books or of money for the purchase of books. The library of the Medical Society, the richest outside London, is also deposited within the walls of the college. The residuary legatees of the late Sir Joseph Whitworth, Bart. (who died about a year ago), have paid the whole expense of building and equipping the newly erected laboratory, and have made other large donations to the aggregate value of £13,000. Sir Joseph by his will left to the college shares of the value of £5,000 in "Sir J. Whitworth & Co., Limited."

MANCHESTER CATHEDRAL.

The college, it may be stated, possesses a department for women, and some twelve months ago the late Mrs. Abel Heywood left £10,000 free of legacy duty to form an endowment, "the income arising from such endowment to be applied for the purpose of making proper provisions for the instruction of women in the said college, in such manner as the governors of the said college think fit." The total number of students in the several departments of the college for the year 1886-7 was 1,235, while the six professors and two lecturers of 1851 have grown into twenty-five professors and thirty-five lecturers in 1887. These numbers will give an idea of the magnitude and importance of this famous educational institution.

As showing the wonderful strides which the college has made within the past thirteen or fourteen years, it is noteworthy that when Owens College took over the Medical School in 1872, there were in that school one hundred students. There are now over three hundred in the medical department of the college, and at the present time the numbers attending the lectures on physiology are so large that the lecture theatre in the newly built medical school is too small to conveniently hold them. Owens College, when complete according to Mr. Waterhouse's plan, will form an immense quadrangle and will be a truly splendid and imposing structure.

The portion of the building already completed contains the chemical lecture theatre, museum and laboratories, rooms for experimental physics, engineering and geological museums, lecture rooms and apparatus rooms for natural philosophy, large and small art class-rooms, engineering rooms, and drawing office, mathematical lecture room, and biological lecture rooms and laboratories. Behind the main building there is the chemical laboratory block, said to be the most complete of its kind in the kingdom. Fronting Coupland Street, the medical school has been erected; and facing Oxford Road that portion of the college has been completed which contains the Manchester Museum, consisting of the important collections formerly the property of the Manchester Natural History and Geological Societies.

We have already alluded to the engineering laboratory erected by the residuary legatees of Sir Joseph Whitworth, Bart. Of course the college likewise contains accommodation for the Court of Governors and the general staff, such as a board-room, rooms for the principal and professors, secretary, and other officials, and there is a students' reading-room, the library, freehand drawing room, professors' common room, &c., &c.

There are several temporary erections within the college precincts, which include a gymnasium, and dining-rooms, &c., but these will come down when the quadrangle is completed. Before closing our notice we must explain that Owens College is an entirely distinct institution from the Victoria University. Manchester is by charter the seat of the university, and Owen's College is an incorporated college of the university, as also are University College, Liverpool, and the Yorkshire College, Leeds. The college hospitably provides the university free lodgment within its walls; but the constitution, objects, and management are quite different, and to all intents and purposes they are separate institutions. In conclusion, in reference to this magnificent educational foundation it may be remarked that whilst its rise and progress, hitherto, have been rapid and brilliant, there is no reason to doubt that in its future career it is destined to achieve still greater successes. The founders and benefactors of this noble institution—a fit monument of Manchester's progress and princely liberality—have well merited the lasting gratitude of all future generations of the city's denizens and of those of the entire north of England.

The president of the college is the Duke of Devonshire, K.G., F.R.S.; the chairman of the council and treasurer, Mr. Alderman Joseph Thompson; and the principal and chairman of the senate, Professor J. G. Greenwood, LL.D.

In thus crossing the city, however, we have omitted all mention of the two most remarkable buildings in Manchester, the Exchange and the Town Hall (see illustrations on pages 50

INTERIOR VIEW OF THE CATHEDRAL, MANCHESTER.

and 60), both of which are of modern construction and add materially to the architectural beauty of the neighbourhood in which they are so conveniently and appropriately located.

THE TOWN HALL,

from an elevated point of which, our bird's eye view of Manchester is taken, has been built to replace the somewhat confined and inconvenient buildings in King Street. It should be explained, by the way, that Manchester differs from many other towns, and especially from London, in that the comfort and health of its citizens are made matters of public business, and that consequently the municipal offices are on an unusually extensive scale. The waterworks are the property of the Corporation, and so likewise are the gasworks, the result being that the inhabitants are not merely supplied with gas of the best quality and water of remarkable purity at a very low rate of payment, but that the profits of both undertakings go to provide for public improvements of the grandest kind. Of such public improvements the Town Hall in Albert Square is one of the most remarkable. In the year 1865 it was resolved by the members of the Town Council that the existing accommodation for municipal business was altogether insufficient, and steps were taken to remedy the evil. An Act of Parliament was obtained in 1866, and negotiations with the owners of property in the neighbourhood followed. The result was that a plot of land was secured with a frontage on the largest open space within the city—Albert Square. This piece of ground consists of about 8,648 square yards, and the Corporation in obtaining it made an excellent bargain. Since the New Town Hall rose above the ground, plots of land in the neighbourhood have been sold for seven or eight times the price paid by the town for this site. One plot in particular was pointed out to the present writer a few years ago as having been sold "upon chief"—that is to say, with a ground rent for 999 years—for £30,000, the said piece of ground being about large enough for the erection of a moderate-sized house. The Town Hall itself is probably one of the grandest buildings of the kind in the world. Mr. Waterhouse was once more the architect, and although in externals he has as usual contrived to repeat the idea of his Assize Courts, there can be no question as to the skill with which he has utilised the material at his command. The building has four façades; it is not exactly square, which is unfortunate, but is not the fault of the architect.

Internally the Town Hall is admirably adapted to the purpose for which it has been erected. In the centre is a large courtyard, and around it a series of corridors, 750 feet in length, and 10 feet or 12 feet in width, are arranged. Opening from these corridors are the various public offices connected with the administration of the town, such, for example, as those of the Town Clerk (who is not unfrequently called "King of Manchester,") the Borough Treasurer, the City Surveyor, the Police, Water, Gas, Health, Hackney Coach, Scavenging, Nuisances, Paving, Lamps, Highways, and Market Departments; also for the Local Court of Record, for the Mayor, the Town Council, Committees, and for general public purposes. Altogether there are about 350 rooms in the building, many of which are of very large size. The reception rooms are perhaps the most magnificent in the kingdom. The whole of the first floor of the building, on the front towards Albert Square, a popular promenade, is given up to them, and as that frontage is 387 feet in length it will be easy to form an idea of the grandeur of the suite. In the centre of the building is a hall more than 100 feet long and 50 feet wide, designed for use on public occasions, and communicating with it are the Mayor's state apartments. The "Mayor's Parlour" is, of course, provided for, and also that "snug little chamber behind the Mayor's chair," in which successive incumbents of the Mayoralty of Manchester delight to take counsel with that ablest of municipal advisers, Sir Joseph Heron.

THE ALBERT MEMORIAL

is a truly magnificent tribute to the memory of the lamented Prince Consort, and stands directly opposite the main entrance to the Town Hall, under the tower in Albert Square. It is something after the style of the Albert Memorial in London, but, of course, on a smaller scale. On the 6th of January, 1862, a meeting was held in the Town Hall, and a subscription commenced for raising a monument in Manchester to the late Prince, and the above memorial is the result. The cost of the structure, independent of the statue, amounted to £6,249 15s. 4d., which was defrayed by public subscription, but the statue itself was the gift of the late Alderman Thomas Goadsby, and was presented to the citizens of Manchester by Mrs. Goadsby, his widow, on the 23rd of January, 1867, on which day the inaugural ceremony took place. The statue of the Prince stands upon a neatly carved pedestal, underneath a highly ornamented spiral canopy, and at a considerable elevation above the Square. It is pronounced to be a most faithful and striking effigy. It is the work of the celebrated Matthew Noble. The architect of the canopy, &c., was Mr. Thomas Worthington, of Manchester. Taken as a whole, the Memorial is one of the finest works of art of the kind to be seen anywhere, and it does honour to Manchester, and the spirit of loyalty and affection which prompted its erection.

MANCHESTER WATERWORKS.

The City of Manchester was formerly supplied with water by the Manchester and Salford Waterworks Company, the water being obtained from the River Medlock, which flows through the city, and by means of pumping from a well at Gorton. These works were purchased by the Corporation in or about 1851, but being totally inadequate to meet the immediate and especially the future wants of the city and district, the present works at Longendale were designed and carried out by Mr. J. F. La Trobe Bateman, F.R.S., principally under the powers of Acts of Parliament passed in 1847 and 1848. The situation of the works, which lie near Woodhead, in the valley between the counties of Chester and Derby, about eighteen miles from Manchester, is admirable for collecting a large supply of water, and, as constructed, they form the largest artificial gravitation works in the kingdom. The area of the drainage ground is about 19,300 statute acres, and they yield twenty-five million gallons per day, in addition to the compensation water of about fourteen millions gallons daily sent down the river. The present consumption of water (beyond the compensation) is upwards of twenty million gallons per day. The cost of the old and new works to the 31st March, 1887, was £3,134,424. The following table shows the storage and service reservoirs, with their capacities, &c.:—

Name of Reservoir.	Area of Reservoir.	Capacity of Reservoir.	Depth of Reservoir.	Height of Top Water Level above Ordnance Datum	
	Acres.	Gallons.	Feet.	Feet.	Ins.
Woodhead	135	1,181,000,000	71	782	0
Torside	160	1,474,000,000	84	651	3
Rhodes Wood . . .	54	500,000,000	68	574	6
Vale House. . . .	63	343,000,000	40	503	0
Bottoms	50	407,000,000	48	486	9
Arnfield	39	209,000,000	52	640	4
Hollingworth . . .	13	73,000,000	52	551	9
Godley	15	61,000,000	21	478	0
Denton, No. 1. . .	7	30,000,000	20	321	6
Denton, No. 2. . .	6	23,000,000	20	321	6
Audenshaw, No. 1. .	80	528,000,000	27½	340	0
Audenshaw, No. 2. .	69	371,000,000	22½	328	0
Audenshaw, No. 3. .	102	542,000,000	22¼	323	0
Gorton, Upper . .	34	123,000,000	26	259	0
Gorton, Lower . .	23	100,000,000	29	214	0
Prestwich	4½	20,000,000	22	317	0
Total	854½	6,985,000,000			

The Town Hall, Manchester. (The Finest Municipal Building in the World.)

The area of supply covers eighty-four square miles with a population of about one million persons. In addition to the present works the Corporation have found it necessary, with a prospect of increased trade and population, to secure a further supply of water from Lake Thirlmere, in Cumberland. They have purchased the entire watershed of that lake, which contain 11,000 statute acres, and this will enable them to protect the water from pollution by the prevention of the erection of buildings, working of lead mines, or anything else which would cause contamination. The surface of the lake will be raised, and its present area doubled, by the construction of a small embankment at the outlet, and this arrangement will in itself have the effect of making the lake, lying as it does at the foot of Helvellyn, more consistent with the present surrounding scenery. When the works are completed they will be capable of supplying fifty million gallons per day, and the water will be brought to Manchester by means of tunnels, covered aqueducts, and cast-iron pipes, extending over a distance of about a hundred miles. A portion of the works, comprising the principal tunnels, are now in course of construction, and their execution will be continued from time to time until they are completed, probably in four or five years hence. The water will be dealt with in instalments of ten million gallons per day, five instalments being brought at various intervals of time as may be required. The estimated cost of the works when completed is over £3,000,000.

THE CORPORATION GASWORKS.

The Manchester Corporation are the actual proprietors of the gasworks. It is no flattery to the people of Manchester to speak of them as a thoroughly practical and somewhat shrewd race of men, because it is neither more nor less than the actual truth. Not that there are not practical and shrewd people in other towns and cities in England, but, somehow or other, the public men of Manchester seem to act as well as to think; in other words, when they have once satisfied themselves as to the feasibility of a thing, and that its adoption would be for the benefit of the community, they at once set to work to accomplish it. There is no better illustration of this than the acquiring of the gasworks by the corporation.

In Liverpool and many other large cities, the manufacture and supply of gas is in the hands of public companies, who have parliamentary authority to earn a certain dividend for the shareholders, and only after that dividend has been secured have the gas consumers any claim upon them for a reduction in the price of gas. The result is that the gas consumers in those places have to pay a very much higher price for gas than they would otherwise do, if the gas were manufactured and supplied by the ratepayers, or, in other words, by the corporate authorities. It stands to reason, that if a public company enjoys the monopoly of supplying a town with gas at no fixed price, but at a price which will enable them to pay a dividend of six, eight, or ten per cent., that there is no inducement for them to exercise economy in the management of their works, beyond what may be absolutely necessary in order to secure that dividend.

In the case of a corporation, however, it is very different. When they are the owners of the gasworks, in trust for the ratepayers, it is their interest to keep down the price of gas, just as they would keep down the rates, and to effect this there must be economy and efficient management combined. But, beyond this, every member of the corporation being himself a ratepayer, and having no interest in the gasworks except as such, must naturally be desirous of producing gas at the lowest cost and supplying consumers, who are likewise ratepayers, at a fair and reasonable price. The Manchester Corporation had not been many years in existence when they sought and obtained powers from Parliament to acquire the gasworks which then supplied Manchester, and from that period to the present the gasworks have formed part of the corporate estate. Never did a corporation perform a wiser or a more beneficial service to a community, and every year the citizens of Manchester are reaping the advantages thereof.

Instead of the profits arising from the sale of gas going to make a handsome dividend for speculating shareholders, it goes into the municipal exchequer, and thus helps to lessen the burden of taxation which is borne by the ratepayers. Further than this, the consumers of gas are benefitted to a large extent, for not only is the illuminating power remarkably high in Manchester, but the price per thousand cubic feet is exceedingly low, so that they derive advantages in both ways. The illuminating power of Manchester gas for the year ending 31st March, 1887, averaged 19·44 candles, the standard of comparison being the light of a London standard sperm candle burning at the rate of 120 grains per hour, and this splendid quality has been and is now supplied, at the rate of two shillings and eightpence per thousand cubic feet. Yet, notwithstanding this fact, the Manchester Corporation gas accounts for the year ending 31st March, 1887, showed a gross profit of £92,200, which, after deducting £8,516, the cost of street lighting, exclusive of gas not charged for, and the standing charges of £30,778 for interest, and £27,454 for sinking fund, and crediting £3,463 to suspense account, left the handsome sum of £21,989 to be handed over to the city improvement committee. Altogether, from the year 1862 to the end of March 1887, there has been paid over for improvement purposes, from gas profits, no less than £913,311 19s. 4d. Surely these facts and figures ought to encourage other corporations to follow the example of Manchester, and become the proprietors of their local gasworks. The following figures are worthy of being perused, as showing the extent and capacity of the works. The area of supply is, within the city 5,748 acres; beyond the city, 19,422 acres; beyond the Mersey 4,640 acres; total 29,810 acres.

The extreme limit of supply is ten miles. The length of main pipes laid is 657¼ miles; the length of service pipes 254 miles; total length of pipes, 911¼ miles. The number of street lamps within the city is 9,834; beyond the city, 3,565. Total, 13,399.

There are four separate works, namely, Gaythorn, Rochdale Road, Bradford Road, and Droylsden. The Gaythorn works occupy an area of 8 acres 4,456 yards; Rochdale Road, 9 acres 339 yards; Bradford Road, 39 acres 4,265 yards; Droylsden, 1 acre 519 yards; giving a total area of fifty-nine acres.

The aggregate capacities of the gasholders at each works are as follows: Gaythorn (six gasholders), capacity 3,070,000 cubic feet; Rochdale Road (six gasholders), capacity 4,140,000 cubic feet; Bradford Road (four gasholders), capacity 7,000,000 cubic feet; Droylsden (one gasholder), capacity 82,000 cubic feet. Total, 14,292,000 cubic feet.

In the year ending 31st March, 1887, the total make of gas was, *three thousand and twenty millions of cubic feet*, and the total income was £371,197 14s. Although the gasworks have yielded such handsome profits to the corporation, there has been no undue parsimony or niggardliness either in respect to salaries or general working expenses. The gas department has, indeed, been thoroughly organised throughout, efficiently superintended, and worked with consummate skill and ability.

SALFORD GASWORKS.

The borough of Salford embraces three districts, namely, Salford proper, Pendleton, and Broughton, and these districts are supplied with gas from the Salford Gasworks, which are the property of the Salford Corporation. Of course these works are of far less magnitude than the Manchester works; nevertheless, they are very extensive, as may be deduced from the following facts. For the year ending 25th March, 1887, the gross income of the works amounted to £143,081 4s. 11d., and the expenditure to £87,015 12s. 8d., leaving a balance to be carried to credit of profit and loss account of £56,065 12s. 3d. From this sum, after deducting certain fixed charges, there remained a net balance of £20,092 to be apportioned amongst the Improvement Committees of Salford, Pendleton, and Broughton.

In the year ending 25th March, 1880, the quantity of gas made at the works was, 818,805,000 cubic feet. The average illuminating power was equal to 19·31 standard sperm candles. The length of mains laid to that date was 200 miles and 1,303 yards. The price of gas within the borough of Salford is higher than that of the city of Manchester, being 3s. 1d. per thousand cubic feet, as compared with 2s. 8d. in Manchester. It will be noticed, however, that in Salford as well as Manchester, a handsome sum is realised from the gas profits for the benefit of the ratepayers. Both the Manchester and Salford works supply a considerable number of outlying townships with gas, for which, according to distance, a higher price is charged.

THE POLICE FORCE.

What the condition of society would be without "our guardians of the peace" may be much better imagined than described, but it is pretty certain that, in a vast city like Manchester, no greater calamity could well happen than for the community to be deprived of their services for one short week. When the varied and complex duties they discharge, many of them of a most onerous and disagreeably risky character, are considered, it must surely be admitted that no class of men are more deserving of sympathy, or are more entitled to respect and consideration. What chaos and confusion, and accidents, personal and vehicular, there would be at all the chief centres of traffic in the city, and at the street junctions, if there happened to be no policemen there to regulate the movements of drivers and carters. Their presence at public meetings, at places of amusement, and certain places of worship, is most valuable and acceptable, inasmuch as it both secures order and ensures peace and comfort.

In no city in this kingdom is the force more civil, respectful, or obliging than in Manchester and Salford. It is often puzzling how policemen generally, considering the diversity of their duties, and in many instances the continual worry to which they are subjected, can be so civil and ready to render assistance. Certainly, it speaks well for the Manchester police authorities that they have succeeded in filling the ranks of the force with men of the right stamp, and endowed with the best qualities for the proper fulfilment of the important duties entrusted to them. The strength of the City Police for the year ending 20th September, 1887, was 904, which comprised the Head Constable, 5 superintendents, 39 inspectors, 70 sergeants, 777 constables, and 12 clerks, and out of this large body of men there were but nine dismissed in the course of the year, a fact which is deserving of notice. The total number of resignations only amounted to twenty-seven, another creditable fact. The force at the date mentioned consisted of 679 married men, and only 225 single, so that the married men were slightly over three to one of the single ones. The average height of the men, in four out of the five police divisions of the city, is 5 feet 9½ inches, and in the fifth division, 5 feet 8¾ inches, this last section including the clerks and detective officers. It is thus evident that the members of the city force throughout are men of superior stature.

The Salford police numbers just 300 strong, and is composed of the Chief Constable, 2 superintendents, 11 inspectors, 32 sergeants, and 254 constables. The average height of the men (for the year 1880) was 5 feet 10 inches. It fully sustains the same high character in all respects as does the Manchester force.

From the foregoing figures it will be seen that the aggregate strength of the Manchester and Salford police is 1,204, and considering the vast population of the two places, and the enormous value of property of all kinds contained within their precincts, these numbers would appear to be small in proportion. At all events, it is a matter for congratulation, and it speaks highly for Manchester and Salford, that such a mere handful of police should be found sufficient to keep the peace, and to protect the lives and property of the inhabitants.

Church of the Holy Name.

FIRE BRIGADES.

Having spoken of the police of Manchester and Salford, another invaluable body of men, of whom it is almost impossible to speak in terms of too high praise, may be referred to, viz., the fire brigades of the city of Manchester and borough of Salford. These brigades are not to be excelled, for experience and ability, by those belonging to any other city in Her Majesty's dominions, and they are equipped in the most complete manner. Unfortunately their services are in much too frequent request to allow of their becoming inexpert in their profession; but, independent of this, the members of the force are thoroughly trained and drilled in every branch of the business, and the result is that in very many cases fires which at first have threatened to spread so as to become vast conflagrations, have by the skill, presence of mind, and energy of the firemen, either been quickly subdued or confined within comparatively small limits. Indeed, it is not an exaggeration to say that almost every man belonging to either brigade is an expert in the art of fire extinguishing, and, when actually engaged in that highly dangerous and difficult occupation, they one and all display a coolness and a courage which, to the uninitiated and terrified observer, often appears little short of recklessness or madness.

The authorised strength of the Manchester Fire Brigade is fifty-one, namely, one superintendent, one assistant superintendent, one steam engineer, four engineers in charge of stations, forty-three firemen, and one horse-keeper. There are three steam fire-engines, and four hand-worked engines, some sixteen hose-carts and fire-escapes combined, besides tenders, ambulances, &c., and there are sixteen horses. These horses, however, are likewise utilised for conveying the prison vans.

During the year ending 29th September, 1887, there were 507 "turn outs" to supposed fires. Of this number 420 were fires, 31 of which were classed as serious; 389 were slight fires, and the remaining 87 were false or chimney fire alarms. The total loss arising from these fires was estimated at £116,000, whereas the assessed value of the property at risk was £2,170,000. The chief fire station in Manchester is at Jackson's Row, and there are branch stations at Boond Street, Pollard Street, Ancoats; Great Jackson Street, Hulme; Gouldon Street, Rochdale Road; Royal Infirmary, Piccadilly; back of St. George's Church, Chester Road; Ardwick Green, Assize Courts, Strangeways; Hulme Town Hall, Stretford Road; and at all the police stations. There is a Volunteer Fire Brigade, consisting of a captain and seven men, whose station is at Monmouth Street, Rusholme, and they are ever ready to render assistance to the regular brigade in case of need. The Salford Brigade for the year ending 29th September, 1886, consisted of one superintendent, two engineers, one horse-keeper, and six firemen; but in addition to this force there are three branchmen and eighteen firemen who perform ordinary police duty, and who attend fires when called upon. The number of "turn outs" to supposed fires was 77, of which number 73 were actual fires, and the other four false alarms. The total loss from fires was estimated at £137,000 and £448,000 was supposed to be at risk. There is one steam fire-engine and several hand-worked engines,

THE FREE TRADE HALL.

besides fire-escapes and all the other apparatus requisite to meet all exigencies, and there are seven horses kept for the service of the brigade. The chief fire station is at the Salford Town Hall, and the two branch stations are at Broughton Town Hall and Pendleton Town Hall. When one considers the vast piles of warehouses in Manchester and Salford, some of them of enormous height and filled from basement to roof with merchandise of a most inflammable nature, and the number of mills there are where machinery is used which is driven at a high rate of speed, which is calculated, unless special care is used, to produce ignition, the wonder is that so few fires take place. But what is matter for greater surprise and, it should be added, congratulation, is how, when such places actually take fire, they are so frequently saved from becoming total wrecks. Nothing short of consummate tact, practical experience of the action of fire when brought into contact with different descriptions of liquids and substances, coupled with indomitable energy and unflinching courage, could ever successfully grapple with conflagrations in such establishments. Firemen, in places like Manchester, have to possess all these qualifications, and that they do possess them is evidenced at every great fire where their services are brought into requisition.

The brave and self-sacrificing men of our fire brigades ought, consequently, to be treated with great liberality, and not, as is generally the case, in a manner totally incommensurate with the onerous and important duties they have to perform, and the risk both of life and limb they so frequently incur.

MANCHESTER ROYAL EXCHANGE.

There was an Exchange in Manchester as long ago as 1729. A little more than five-and-twenty years ago the old Exchange was rebuilt on a very handsome scale. The floor of the room occupied a space of nearly 1,700 square yards, but even that amount of accommodation proved to be insufficient. It is a local tradition that when the Queen paid her memorable visit this floor was covered with a new carpet woven expressly for the occasion, and that the first words of Her Majesty were, "What a magnificent room!" On the following day the "Manchester Exchange" became the "Manchester Royal Exchange" by special permission. In 1865 and 1866 the complaints of the merchants who used the Exchange became so loud and so persistent that it was evident that something would have to be done. A scheme for another Exchange in a more convenient and central situation was mooted, and for a time it seemed possible that something of the sort might be established. The proprietors of the existing building were, however equal to the occasion, and obtained an Act of Parliament under which they were enabled to take up a very large plot of land, to evict the then tenants, and to commence the erection of what is probably the biggest building of the kind in Europe. The architects, Messrs. Mills and Murgatroyd, were not fettered as to cost, and the result is that the Exchange, as well as being big, is decidedly ornamental. The core is, of course, of brick, but the building is entirely faced with stone. Its principal entrance is in Cross Street, and consists of an exceedingly imposing portico of twelve columns, each 35 feet in height. The large room of the Exchange occupies about 4,405 square yards, and is raised about nine feet above the level of the street. Underneath is a restaurant of the best class, and round the building are shops and offices on a level with the street. At each corner is a species of pavilion containing staircases which lead to offices on the upper floors, whilst at the corner of Market Street and Exchange Street there is a tower 180 feet high, with a clock and its usual adjuncts. The Great Room of the Exchange is really a magnificent chamber. It consists of a nave and four aisles 206 feet long and 192 feet in width. The aisles are 28 feet in height, and the nave is nearly 100 feet wide in a single span. The lighting is effected by three domes, by which the building will be recognised in our bird's-eye view. These domes are in one case 60 feet and in the others 45 feet in diameter, and from the floor to the crown of the highest the height is 125 feet. Every convenience that can be desired is to be found in the building, so that the 7,000 subscribers to the Exchange have ample value for the £20,000 a year or more which pays the handsome dividend on the capital of the undertaking. It may be worth while to add a few figures from a pamphlet by the courteous and accomplished master of the Exchange, Mr. Edwin Simpson—a gentleman who is not merely an admirable man of business, but also one of the most competent and fearless of dramatic critics. The length of the new room is 206 feet; width, 192 feet; clear width of central area, 96 feet; height from floor to summit of dome, 125 feet. Westminster Hall is 228 feet long, 66 feet wide, and 22 feet from the floor to the ridge of the roof. In other words, the open space of the Manchester Exchange contains about 5,000 square feet more than Westminster Hall, while the entire floor space, including the aisles, is considerably more than double that of the same building. The annual subscription to the Royal Exchange is £3 3s., which must be paid on or before the 31st of January, otherwise an additional charge of 10s. 6d. is made. Subscribers are entitled to the use of the Great Room, which is fully supplied with telegrams of the Exchange Telegraph Co. and the Press Association, including a complete service of Reuter's foreign news, and the transactions in the most important markets. The Liverpool cotton reports and New York "Future" telegrams are received by special wire from the secretary of the Liverpool Cotton Association, and copies are posted on the news stands in the Large Room. The Reading Gallery is furnished with a large selection of London, foreign, country, and local newspapers, including the illustrated journals; and the Magazine and Review Room is supplied with the leading reviews and periodicals; and at the bar and in its immediate vicinity are kept files of all the newspapers, directories, railway guides, &c.

There are within the building rooms for the sale of cotton by sample, also telegraph and telephone offices, and on the main floor there are lavatories and other conveniences. In short, there is not a want which the board of management have not anticipated.

The present governing body consists of the following gentlemen; James Jardine, chairman; Joseph Broome, Edward Hardcastle, M.P., Abraham Haworth, Duncan Matheson, and Thomas Sowler; treasurer, R. F. Ainsworth, M.D.; master and secretary, Edwin Simpson.

Near at hand is the

STOCK EXCHANGE,

an unpretending yet handsome and convenient building, with a commodious room for the purposes indicated by its title. This room is, of course, much smaller than that of the Royal Exchange, but it is not every provincial town which can boast a Stock Exchange 66 feet long and 40½ feet wide. The Manchester Stock Exchange was established in the year 1836, and is worked on the same principle as the London and Liverpool Exchanges. The members number about a hundred, and the rules of admission are exceedingly strict and are rigidly enforced. No person is admitted to membership unless recommended by an existing member, and the committee of the Exchange must be satisfied both as to character and capital ere the applicant is elected a member. One advantage enjoyed by the Manchester Stock Exchange over others is this, that it is in direct telegraphic communication with the London Stock Exchange, and is worked in combination therewith, a privilege which can be only fully appreciated by persons engaged in the stock and share business. The extent of the business done in Manchester in stocks and share is something enormous.

The business hours are from 11 A.M. to 4 P.M., Saturdays 11 A.M. to 1 P.M. The premises are at 15, Cross Street, within a stone's throw of the Royal Exchange. The chairman and treasurer is Mr. W. C. Watterson, the deputy-chairman Mr. George Norbury, and the secretary Mr. John N. Cain.

CORN EXCHANGE.

Next in order comes the Manchester Corn Exchange, which is situated in Hanging Ditch. This building was opened in January, 1837, so that it has just completed a career of half a century.

The large room where those engaged in the corn trade assemble, has a floor-space area of 600 square yards, and it is sometimes used for public meetings, being admirably adapted for the purpose, more than two thousand four hundred people being able to find standing room within its walls. The corn market is held on Thursdays, from 11 A.M. to 2 P.M. The building is likewise used on Tuesdays as the general produce and grocery market, the hours being from 11 A.M. to 2·30 P.M. The chairman and treasurer of the Corn Exchange is Mr. Thomas Johnson, and Mr. James Bonnett is the secretary.

THE COTTON WASTE DEALERS' EXCHANGE.

The cotton-waste trade in Manchester is one of very considerable magnitude and importance, and so far back as the year 1869 the cotton-waste dealers established their exchange.

Previously to this the trade used to meet and transact their business in the roadway in High Street, much to their own as well as to other peoples' inconvenience. The undertaking is conducted by the Manchester Cotton-waste Dealers' Exchange Company, Limited, and the number of members is about one hundred and eighty. The Exchange is situated in the Market Place and comprises several convenient apartments, besides what is called the "Exchange Room," which has a floor-space of 60 feet by 26 feet, and is 30 feet high.

The "change" days are Tuesday and Friday, and it is "high change" from 11 to 1 on Tuesday.

There is a news-room in the building open to members every day. The property belongs to the Corporation of Manchester. Mr. Ellis Taylor, of Oldham, is the chairman of directors, and Mr. Eli Sowerbutts the secretary. In the same building is held the—

MANCHESTER COAL EXCHANGE.

This is an association which was established in the year 1880, and it numbers some four hundred and fifty members. The members embrace three classes, namely, first, colliery proprietors and agents; second, sundry traders, such as timber merchants, waggon-builders, and steel rail manufacturers, &c., in the habit of supplying colliery plant; third, coal merchants or dealers.

The rate of annual subscription varies in the order in which we have named them, the colliery proprietors and agents paying the higher scale of subscription. Before their exchange was established, the coal trade, &c., met in "the open," in and about Bull's Head Court, close by.

The Coal Exchange is open on Tuesdays from 2 to 4·30 P.M., and a very large amount of business is transacted in a very short time. The right of use of the rooms is obtained from the Cotton-waste Exchange Company, and the members of the Coal Exchange enjoy the same privileges as those of the Cotton-waste Exchange in regard to the use of the news-room.

The president of the Coal Exchange is Mr. Edgar Storey, of Wigan, the treasurer Mr. Ralph Peters, of Tyldesley, and the secretary Mr. Thomas W. Sowerbutts.

FREE TRADE HALL.

No description of the public buildings of Manchester would be complete without mention of the Free Trade Hall. It is situated in Peter Street, and only a very short distance from the handsome and well-known church of St. Peter, which stands in what is called St. Peter's Square. The present building, however, must not be confounded with the Free Trade Hall which existed prior to the

BUILDINGS OF OWENS COLLEGE, MANCHESTER.

repeal of the corn laws in 1846, although it occupies the same site. The original hall was opened on the 30th of January, 1843, when what is known as the Anti Corn Law Banquet took place, which was attended by a large gathering of M.P.'s from all parts of the country.

The dimensions of the old hall were: length, 135 feet 8 inches; breadth, 102 feet 6 inches, containing an area of 14,000 square feet. This was the celebrated hall in which successive gatherings took place to agitate for corn law repeal, and which will always be associated with the names of Richard Cobden and John Bright, the great champions of free trade.

A musical festival, which began on 23rd January, 1852, and which lasted five days, was the last occasion on which the old Free Trade Hall was used, previous to its being pulled down to make way for the massive structure which now exists. The present Free Trade Hall was inaugurated on the 8th of October, 1856. The cost of the building was £40,000. It is perhaps second only to St. George's Hall, Liverpool, amongst the public halls in the north of England, and is vastly superior to that building in its acoustic properties. It is the favourite place of meeting for all classes of politicians on important occasions, and there can scarcely be named a great political leader, who has lived during the last thirty years, who has not, at one time or other, figured within its walls. The late Lord Derby, Cobden, Bright, Disraeli (afterwards Lord Beaconsfield), W. E. Gladstone, Lord Granville, and Lord Salisbury, have all spoken (some of them more than once) from its platform, besides scores of other great men renowned not only in politics, but in science, art, manufactures, literature, philanthropy, and religion. In short, the Free Trade Hall of to-day is ready to open its doors and does open them, to all parties.

Manchester, as is well known, is a very musical place, and as the acoustic properties of the great room in which public meetings are held, are excellent, it is very frequently used for concerts. The concerts given here by Mr. Charles Hallé (which are decidedly the best out of London) are always numerously attended, and draw together the very *élite* of Manchester society.

The building altogether is of great magnitude, and it is admirably adapted for balls or other entertainments as well as for large meetings, conveniences of every description in the shape of lecture-rooms, anterooms, &c., &c., being provided. The hall is also constantly patronised for holding religious services. The interior is handsome and imposing, whilst its external appearance is noble and attractive.

The Great Meeting Room before referred to is galleried all

round, contains a magnificent organ, and can accommodate many thousands of persons.

Very near to the Free Trade Hall is another building, known as the

GENTLEMEN'S CONCERT HALL,

which is the property of a society of 600 members, something after the model of the London Philharmonic Society. The concerts are of the very highest excellence, and tickets for them are eagerly sought after. The popularity of these concerts may be gauged by the crowds of ladies in evening dress who are content to shiver under the portico on concert nights for a quarter of an hour whilst awaiting the opening of the doors. Besides this society, there are a considerable number of choral unions, glee clubs, &c., which hold their meetings in various suburban town halls and school rooms. For those who are dramatically inclined there are several theatres, in the immediate neighbourhood of the Free Trade and Concert Halls, and in Bridge Street, &c.

THE THEATRE ROYAL

is a somewhat modern building, of considerable size and architectural pretensions. At one time the management was not remarkably successful, but of late years things have greatly improved, and the great capabilities of the building are fully developed. The entrance to the building is imposing, and the auditorium large and handsomely decorated. The stage is one of the largest out of London, being 33 ft. wide and 37 ft. high, and having a depth of 68 ft. and a total width of 64 ft. Pantomime is produced here on a most elaborate scale. The theatre is the property of the Theatre Royal Company, Limited, and the lessee is Captain R. B. Bainbridge..

THE PRINCE'S THEATRE,

which is close by, is a little smaller than the Royal, and a much plainer building externally. The interior is, however, unquestionably one of the finest, if not the very finest, for its size in the kingdom, and is adorned with a remarkably beautiful tympanum

South-West View of Assize Courts.

by Mr. H. S. Marks, A.R.A. The performances here are of the very best kind. It is under the management of Mr. J. C. Smith, one of the most popular men in theatrical circles in this country, whose untiring enterprise and striking liberality are always noticeable in providing for the people of Manchester the best possible talent to be obtained. Pantomime is produced here also on a scale of remarkable splendour and costliness, and popular appreciation of it is sufficiently vouched for by the fact that this entertainment usually runs from Christmas to Easter. In the autumn both theatres are occupied for several weeks by the various London companies who make provincial tours.

THE COMEDY THEATRE,

(or the Amphitheatre as it is likewise called), is in Peter Street, opposite the Theatre Royal, and is one of the best patronized places of entertainment in the city. Like the "Royal" and the "Prince's" it is noted for pantomime. The proprietors are the "Manchester Comedy Theatre Company, Limited," and the manager is Mr. John Heslop.

In Bridge Street stands another theatre—the Queen's, which caters for a somewhat different class of patrons, but is well conducted. It is here the autumn performances of Italian opera usually take place. The manager of this theatre is Mr. Richard Mansell.

The other noted places of amusement are, the Folly Theatre of Varieties, Peter Street, Mr. Edward Garcia, lessee; the St. James's Theatre, Oxford Street, St. Peter's, Mr. J. C. Emerson, manager; the Prince of Wales Theatre, Liverpool Street, Salford, Mr. John Price, lessee; the Grand Circus, Peter Street, Mr. Edward Garcia, proprietor; the People's Concert Hall, Lower Mosley Street, Mr. Thos. B. Burton, proprietor; the St. James's Hall, Oxford Street, St. Peter's, Mr. James Reilly, proprietor; the Star Music Hall, in Pollard Street, Ancoats, and the Circus in Chepstow Street, Oxford Street. It is therefore evident that, as regards places of amusement, Manchester is abundantly supplied.

CLUB HOUSES AND CLUBS.

Manchester is, as might be expected, exceedingly well provided with clubs. The principal and the oldest of these institutions is the "Union," in Mosley Street, which is housed in a building that would do no discredit to Pall Mall. It numbers are limited to four hundred, and the entrance fee is forty guineas, the annual subscription being seven guineas. For this sum, however, the members obtain as much comfort and attention as they could have at the best of London clubs. The rooms are large and lofty, the service excellent, and the *cuisine* irreproachable. The club was established in 1825, and the house in Mosley Street was opened in 1836. The "Clarendon" is likewise in Mosley Street, close to St. Peter's church, and is of much the same character as the Union, though of more modest pretensions. The "Brasenose Club" in Brazennose Street, is a social club of men of letters, barristers and solicitors, actors, artists, and amateurs, and is very popular with visitors to Manchester, who are always welcomed with the frankest courtesy by the members.

The Freemasons' Club is in Cooper Street, at the Freemasons' Hall, and is exclusively composed of Freemasons. It is a handsome and commodious building, well furnished, and numbers some two hundred members.

REFORM CLUB BUILDING, KING STREET.

The German community of Manchester have a club of their own called the "Schiller Anstalt," situated in Nelson Street, off Oxford Road, about a mile and a half from the Exchange. The present club-house is a fine structure, and was formally opened by the Mayor of Manchester, Mr. Alderman Goldschmidt, in December, 1885. It is a remarkably popular institution, the members exercising a hospitality which is not of the kind usually associated in English minds with such places. At one time the club occupied the mansion formerly tenanted by Mr. Pinto Leite. There is a popular and well-supported club in St. Peter's Square, called the Anglo-French Club, which is of comparatively recent origin. Another very distinguished institution is The Arts Club, in Albert

Square, which was founded in 1879. It numbers about four hundred members, and is an association of men who are, or have been, authors, journalists, artists, actors, musicians, scientists, or men intimately connected with art, literature, music, and science. The club is most influentially supported, the president being the Earl of Crawford and Balcarres, LL.D., F.R.S., F.R.A.S.; and amongst the vice-presidents we notice the names of the Right Honourable Arthur J. Balfour, M.P., Chief Secretary for Ireland; Jacob Bright, M.P.; Sir W. Cunliffe Brooks, Bart., M.P.; Hon. Alan de Tatton Egerton, M.P.; W. H. Holdsworth, M.P.; J. W. Maclure, M.P., F.R.G.S.; C. E. Schwann, M.P.; and Henry Irving. The entrance fee is £2 2s., and the annual subscription is £3 3s.; but country members resident ten miles and upwards away, and having no place of business in Manchester, pay only an annual subscription of £1 1s., without entrance fee. The secretary is Mr. Robert Edward Johnson, F.C.A. There is likewise the Trafford Club in Peter Street, of a social character; and the ladies have club-rooms at 73A, King Street. The three principal political clubs are the Reform Club, the Conservative Club, and the Carlton Club. The Reform Club is a building of very superior architectural pretensions, and its internal arrangements are as complete and perfect as those of any other similar establishment in the provinces. It occupies a most eligible position at the top of King Street, and has a very noble appearance. It numbers many hundreds of members, comprising the *élite* of the Liberal party of Manchester and the neighbourhood, and of course is the Liberal headquarters for this district. Mr. Isaac Watts, Ph.D., is the secretary. The Conservative Club occupies a site at the corner of St. Ann's Street and Cross Street, and not far from the Royal Exchange. It is a handsome building, faced with Yorkshire stone in the Italian style of architecture, and was built from the joint designs of Mr. Robert Walker and Messrs. Horton & Bridgford. It

THE MANCHESTER CONSERVATIVE CLUB HOUSE.

contains a dining-room nearly a hundred feet in length, and of proportionate width, which is entered through a glazed ornamental screen, direct from the principal staircase. It reaches the whole length of the Cross Street frontage, and is on the first floor. There is also on this floor a luncheon and serving-room, and a spacious library, which is lighted on two sides. On the second-floor are two billiard-rooms (each containing two tables), several private dining-rooms, with still and service rooms at the back. Within the building are also the members' dressing-rooms, bath-rooms, cloak-rooms, lavatories, &c.; and on the third floor is the kitchen department, replete with every requisite, and fitted up in the most improved style, being provided likewise with a hoist from the basement, and also a separate staircase. There are also rooms for the use of the committee, and the steward's private rooms, &c. The cost of the ground and the building was £92,000, and the furnishing cost another £18,000, making altogether, £110,000. The club house has been occupied since 1876, when it was opened by the present Viscount Cross, K.C.B., who was then known as Mr. R. Assheton Cross, M.P., and held the office of Home Secretary. The present number of members is about eleven hundred, and the entrance fee is £3 3s., and the annual subscription £6 6s. There are, doubtless, other club-houses in the provinces of equal or even greater size, but there are none which excel it in comfort, completeness, or excellence of general management. The secretary is Mr. Robert Edward Johnson, who also holds the secretaryship of the Art's Club. The Conservative Club is the headquarters of the Conservative party in this part of Lancashire.

The Carlton Club was formerly known under the style of the Junior Conservative Club, but changed its title about ten years ago. It is located in Spring Gardens, and not far from the Reform Club, and though of a much more modest character than either of the other two political clubs, has a very numerous and influential membership. It numbers about four hundred members, and at Election times turns out some of the most ardent and energetic workers to be found in the ranks of the Conservatives of Manchester and district. It is not a rival of, but a worker with, the older and wealthier club in St. Ann's Street and Cross Street. The Carlton is handsomely and comfortably fitted up and furnished, and it is admirably conducted. The secretary is Mr. Thomas Johnston.

There are numerous other clubs of various descriptions in and around Manchester, which are far too numerous to be here enumerated individually, for every ward, in both Manchester and Salford, has its political club, both Liberal and Conservative. Then come some score of clubs connected with the Working Men's Club Association, whose headquarters are at Oxford Chambers, Oxford Street; and besides these there are chess clubs, swimming clubs, lawn-tennis and racquet clubs, bowling clubs, cricket clubs, rowing clubs, football clubs, and bicycling clubs. Then there are vast numbers of clubs connected with the different places of worship; and finally come those belonging to friendly societies, such as the Oddfellows, &c. When it is recollected that all these clubs form in themselves centres of thought and activity, and moreover that most of them are engaged in furthering some good, useful, or laudable end, it cannot be wondered at that Manchester should

View from Blackfriars Bridge.

hold politically, educationally, and socially the prominent and influential position it does amongst the leading cities of this great empire.

THE ART GALLERY,

situated in Mosley Street, was formerly known as the Royal Institution. It was established for the promotion of literature, science, and art, and was originally projected by one Thomas Dodd, an auctioneer and connoisseur. The building was begun in 1825 and completed in 1830, and Sir Charles Barry was the architect. It cost £30,000. In 1881 the governors of the institution resolved to accept the terms offered them by the Corporation, with reference to the transfer to the latter body, in trust for the use of the public, of the building and it contents, and in 1882 the transfer was legalised by Act of Parliament. The expenditure of £2,000 annually by the Corporation upon works of art is guaranteed for a period of twenty years. The managing committee consists of two-thirds members of the Corporation and one-third representatives of the Royal Institution.

It contains a permanent gallery of works of art of various descriptions, which bears witness to the liberality and good taste of the men of Manchester, past and present. The great feature of the institution is its annual exhibition, at which the local artists exhibit, and to which a considerable number of the pictures which have adorned the walls of the Royal Academy during the preceding season are lent by the artists or by purchasers. Lectures on music and other branches of art are delivered in the theatre during the winter months.

Next to the Royal Institution is the

MANCHESTER ATHENÆUM,

built in 1837 by the architect of the former edifice—the late Sir Charles Barry. This serves not only the usual purposes indicated by its name, but also as a club for the use of persons of all ages and of both sexes engaged in the innumerable offices and warehouses in the neighbourhood. There is an excellent library; a reading-room amply provided with the London and local daily and weekly papers; and classes of various kinds have been established, all of which are well attended, and are doing good work by the opportunities which they afford the members for self-improvement. Perhaps there is no institution of the kind in England which has more fully answered the expectations and intentions of its founders. The city of Manchester is, however, especially fortunate in the character of its young men. Of course there are exceptions to the rule, but it is a very gratifying fact that an unusually large proportion of the young men engaged in the trade of the district devote no inconsiderable part of their leisure to self-improvement, whilst an equally large class devote their leisure to religious and charitable work. Their employers have liberally seconded their efforts in both directions. To them belongs the honour of first taking advantage of the Public Libraries Act, and the liberality which was then manifested has never since flagged. The library contains some twenty thousand volumes. According to the annual report for the year ending 1886, the exact number of volumes in the library is 20,692. These embrace every class of literature: theology and philosophy, history, biography and correspondence, voyages and travels, jurisprudence, political and social economy, &c., science and the arts, education, works in foreign languages, collected works, miscellaneous literature and periodicals, poetry and the drama, works of fiction, and books of reference. During the year named (1886), the library being open 299 days, the total number of volumes issued was 90,177, giving an average of 301 per day. The number of members is over three thousand.

View of the Royal Exchange.

The subscription to the Athenæum is 24s. per annum, or 6s. 6d. per quarter; and for junior members, under twenty years of age, 16s. per annum, or 5s. per quarter; ladies, 10s. 6d. per annum, or 3s. per quarter. In connection with the institution are the following clubs and societies: Lecture and Debating Society, Dramatic Reading Society, Musical Society, French Conversational Society, German Conversational Society, Italian Conversational Society, Chess Club, and Graphic Club. Members of the Athenæum have the privilege of joining any of the foregoing on payment of very moderate fees. The evening classes embrace the French, Portuguese, German, Spanish, and Italian languages, the fees for attending any one of which do not exceed 5s. per term. The Athenæum is provided with dining, coffee, billiard, chess and smoking-rooms, admissible only to members of the institution.

PUBLIC FREE LIBRARIES.

The city of Manchester is well to the front in the matter of free libraries. The chief one is the Free Reference Library, in King Street. This library was first established at Campfield, Deansgate, in September 1852, and was continued there until March, 1877, when it was removed to its present home, the Old Town Hall,

King Street. For some months the books were simply stored here, as the King Street premises were not opened until February, 1878. This library is not only the largest in Manchester, but perhaps in the provinces, as the following figures will show. It contains 6,934 volumes on theology and philosophy; 21,416 on history travels, &c.; 14,525 on politics and commerce; 13,348 on science and arts; 23,319 on literature and polygraphy; 4,522 on specifications of patents; a grand total of 84,064 volumes.

The library is open daily from 9 A.M. to 10 P.M. on week-days, and from 2 to 9 P.M. on Sundays. The daily average attendance of readers for the year 1886-7, was, week-days 689, Sundays 180, and the total number of readers for the year was, week-days 192 762, Sundays 8,673, showing an aggregate of 201 435.

The whole extent of the Old Town Hall is appropriated to the purposes of the library, and the large reading-room is one of the finest in the United Kingdom. The people of Manchester are indeed fortunate in possessing such a magnificent and valuable reference library. The branch lending libraries are six in number, namely, Deansgate, Hulme, Ancoats, Rochdale Road, Chorlton, and Ardwick and Chetham, and amongst them they have up-

Interior View of the Royal Exchange

wards of 100,000 volumes, embracing works of every kind calculated to interest enlighten and instruct all classes of the community. The number of volumes lent by these libraries for home use for the year 1886-7 was 737,800. The number of volumes used in the reading-rooms attached to them was, week-days 70,992, Sundays 5,910; and in the reading-rooms set apart for boys, the number of volumes used was, week-days 250,300, Sundays 91,405; so that the total number of volumes in use during the year at home and in the reading-rooms amounted to 1,165 506, or a daily average of 3 265. A news-room is attached to each lending library, and is free to the public for the use of newspapers and periodicals from 8.30 A.M. till 10 P.M. on week-days, and on Sundays from 2 to 9 P.M., and reading-rooms for boys are open at all the branches from 6 to 9 every evening. Borrowers can obtain books from 8.30 to 9 P.M. every week-day except Saturday, when the issue ceases at 5 P.M.

In addition to these six lending libraries, there have been two reading-rooms recently opened within the borough, one at Bradford and the other at Harpurhey, and a third will shortly be opened for Ardwick and district. Each of these new rooms is supplied with magazines and newspapers, and with about 500 volumes of books for use on the premises. The number of visits made by the public during the year 1886-7 to the several establishments to which reference has been made, reached an aggregate of nearly four millions and a quarter. These facts and figures are eloquent and convincing proof of the utility of these institutions, and the important work which they perform in the social economy of the city.

All these free libraries and reading-rooms are most admirably fitted-up and arranged, and they are managed in a way which not only does infinite credit to the entire staff, from the highest to the lowest, but which redounds to the honour of the Corporation.

In the sister borough of Salford there are four libraries, similar in character to those of Manchester, namely, the one at Peel Park (attached to the Museum and Art Gallery), and the Greengate, Regent Road, and Pendleton Branch Libraries. They are as well equipped and managed as the Manchester Libraries, and equally as well patronised.

THE ROYAL INFIRMARY

is one of the most conspicuous objects on entering the town from London. The site which this building occupies is perhaps unequalled in the kingdom. A large open space surrounds the handsome and well-proportioned hospital, around which are clustured a number of immense and imposing warehouses. On each side is one of the most important commercial thoroughfares, and all around are evidences of wealth and industry of no ordinary kind. In days gone by the space in front of the Infirmary was occupied by a pond, which was anciently the place in which scolding wives were ducked under that "primitive discipline" which is now out of fashion. Until recently, however, the "ducking stool" was in existence. When the Infirmary was built the pond was fenced in, and fountains were erected in it. All this is now altered. When Her Majesty paid her memorable visit to Manchester in October, 1851, the pond was still in existence. Within a very few years, however, it was found to have become, as large pieces of water in the middle of great towns are very apt to be, a most serious nuisance, whilst the space which it occupied was too valuable to be lost in a busy place like Manchester. It was accordingly filled in and flagged over, and since that time the open space has been adorned with sundry sculptures. At the Portland Street end of the flags is a memorial to the Duke of Wellington by Mr. Noble, which is far more successful than the majority of huge allegorical structures usually are, and at the opposite end is a

Exterior View of the Royal Institution of Fine Arts.

corresponding memorial to Sir Robert Peel, upon which the same verdict may be passed. Besides these works of high art there are two simpler memorials, one a bronze copy of Chantrey's vigorous statue of John Dalton, the celebrated Manchester chemist, and the other a statue of James Watt, by Mr. Theed.

The Infirmary itself is a building of various dates, but of harmonious and fairly satisfactory plan. It forms three sides of a quadrangle, but the open space at the rear of the buildings is now pretty well filled up with new erections. Each of the three parts is adorned with a portico, and over that, on the Piccadilly side, is a cupola, which was erected some twenty years ago to supply the want of a clock tower in the neighbourhood, then much felt. The wing on the west side, oddly called the "North Wing," is a standing memorial to the kindly disposition of the late Madame Lind-Goldschmidt, who gave two concerts in the Free Trade Hall for the benefit of the Infirmary, by which a sum of no less than £2,500 was realised. The Infirmary has indeed been peculiarly rich in magnificent bequests. The late Mr. Robert Barnes, a local millionaire of great celebrity for his charitable disposition and munificent answers to every appeal made to him on charitable grounds, was a liberal benefactor. Finding that in too many cases patients lost nearly all the benefit they had derived from their stay in the Infirmary through leaving it for their poverty-stricken homes before their recovery was completed, he started the idea of a "House of Recovery" for the use of fever and small-pox patients, and subscribed a sum of £9,000 for this purpose. Another Convalescent Home had been in existence at Cheadle Hall (about six miles from the Infirmary) for some years past, and had rendered infinite service to patients recovering from non-infectious diseases. Mr. Barnes fully recognised the value of this institution, and a short time before his lamented death he presented a sum of £26,000 to the managers of the Infirmary for the erection of the "Barnes Convalescent Home." This money, supplemented by other sums of smaller amount, has been well laid out. A magnificent building, with accommodation for a large number of patients and their medical and other attendants, was erected under the personal care and superintendence of the accomplished and indefatigable Dr. Reid, the then Resident Physician of the Infirmary, who gave an amount of time, labour, and care to this work which has hardly been adequately recognised. The leading feature of the establishment is a very beautiful winter garden, which has been constructed in the open space formed by the two wings, and in which the convalescents can enjoy all the advantages of gentle open-air exercise with perfect immunity from its dangers. This part of the work is entirely due to Dr. Reid, and has been carried out in a most admirable and efficient manner.

In the early part of the year 1887, the rules of the Infirmary were revised. Before that time the management of the institution was principally controlled by a weekly board, of which, according to the rules, every trustee was a member. Since the revision of the rules the management has been placed in the hands of a board of twenty-one members, elected by the trustees from the general body, with power to divide themselves into committees to superintend the various departments. Ten years have elapsed since this change was made, and in instituting a comparison betwixt the year 1876-7 and the year 1886-7, as regards the position of the institution, the number of cases relieved, and the cost of maintenance, the results are eminently satisfactory. In the former year (1876-7) the total number of persons treated at the Infirmary and at the Convalescent Hospital amounted to 21,061 and the cost was £25,116. In the latter year (1886-7) the number of patients treated was 37,518 and the cost was only £22,596; thus, whilst the increase in the number of patients amounted to over 78 per cent., the actual expenditure absolutely decreased £2,520, or 10 per cent. Another comparison shows that while in 1876-7 the cost per occupied bed at the Infirmary was £71 13s. 8d., in 1886-7 it was only £12 4s. 2d. These great results, however, have not been obtained at the expense of the inmates, for there has been no diminution in their comforts, and no parsimonious system of management has been introduced. There has simply been maintained a wise economy, and the funds of the charity have been carefully and prudently administered.

The enormous benefits conferred on the community by this noble institution are abundantly proved by the number of patients of all sorts received therein, or treated by its eminent professional staff. For the year ending 1886-7 there were in-patients, 4,508; out-patients, 30,362; home-patients, 1,399; fever patients, 1,755; while 1,279 have received benefit at the Barnes Convalescent Hospital, Cheadle, making a grand total of 39,303. The Monsall Fever Hospital and the Convalescent Hospital just referred to are, although the accounts are kept separate, worked in connection with the Infirmary, and the expenditure upon each for the year 1886-7 was as follows: Royal Infirmary, £16,976; Monsall Fever Hospital, £7,598; Convalescent Hospital, £5,620; total £30,194. The beds in each number: Royal Infirmary, 298; Monsall Fever Hospital, 136; Convalescent Hospital, 238; total, 672. The total number of patients admitted since the first opening of the Infirmary, A.D. 1752, to June 25th, 1887, was 1,781,321. When it is borne in mind that the Royal Infirmary and the other two institutions mentioned in connection with it were built and have ever been maintained by donations and voluntary contributions, chiefly from residents of Manchester and its immediate vicinity, it may well be said that of all her public buildings and noble institutions those which reflect the greatest credit upon her citizens are the Royal Infirmary and its auxiliary branches. The Infirmary is under the patronage of Her Majesty the Queen, and the Earl of Derby, K.G., is the president. The medical staff is very numerous, and includes the most eminent physicians, surgeons, and apothecaries in Manchester and the district.

CHETHAM LIBRARY, INTERIOR VIEW.

The Royal Infirmary is, however, by no means the only hospital nor are its Convalescent Homes the only establishments for the relief of distress. Far from such being the case there are an immense number of

OTHER CHARITIES

scattered over the town, concerning which, owing to the exigencies of space, we must confine ourselves to little more than a mere enumeration. In Mill Street and Kirby Street, Ancoats, stands a very handsome Gothic building, erected and endowed by the late Miss Atherton, of Kersal Cell. This is the Ardwick and Ancoats Dispensary, at which establishment many hundreds of patients are relieved every week. At the further end of the Stretford Road, close to the junction of that thoroughfare with the City Road, stands a building commonly known as Henshaw's Blind Asylum, from the name of its founder. Mr. Henshaw died in 1810, and left some £20,000 for asylum purposes. For a while the trust was in abeyance, but when the original bequest had doubled itself a subscription, by which £0,000 was eventually raised, was got up for building purposes. At the same time the Committee of the Deaf and Dumb School were on the eve of building, and the two charities having secured adjoining sites a partial amalgamation was decided upon. The result is that the two buildings adjoin, and have one chapel in common, which is one of the sights of the place. Full cathedral service is performed therein twice every Sunday, the blind pupils forming the choir. A part of the Town Hall of the township of Chorlton-on-Medlock is given up for the purposes of a local dispensary, where several hundred patients are weekly relieved, and where accidents meet with ready attention. In Park Place, Chetham Hill—a quiet *cul-de-sac* at the side of one of the Jewish synagogues—is an admirable charity known as the Clinical Hospital. Here the diseases of women and children are specially treated. In-patients and out-patients are both dealt with. In Oxford Street, corner of Nelson Street, is an Eye Hospital, supported by voluntary contributions, and doing good work amongst the poor. The oculists of Manchester are men of more than local celebrity, and their labours here have been remarkably successful—a fact which is evidenced by the rapidly increasing number of the patients treated. Besides these hospitals and dispensaries there may be mentioned the Hospital for Sick Children, established in 1830; the Southern Hospital, for diseases of women and children, which is also the Manchester Maternity Hospital, Clifford Street, Chorlton-upon-Medlock (established 1866); the Hospital for Consumption and Diseases of the Throat, Hardman Street, Deansgate and Bowdon Cheshire (established 1875); the Skin Disease and Cancer Hospital, 35, Hyde Road, Ardwick; the Victoria Dental Hospital, 98, Grosvenor Street; and the Wilton Fever Hospital, Cross Lane, Salford. The believers in homœopathy are not behind their rivals in good works who protest against the heresy of globules. They maintain two hospitals in poor parts of the town, where some thousands of patients receive relief annually. In Lower Mosley Street is an Hospital for Diseases of the Ear. Near at hand is a "Night Refuge" for the destitute poor. In Quay Street, still in the same neighbourhood, is the St. Mary's Hospital and Dispensary, which is, next to the Infirmary, the largest and oldest establishment of the kind in the city. Here some 13,000 patients receive treatment every year, obstetric surgery being especially studied. About a mile and a half away, Salford and Pendleton have combined for the erection of an hospital and dispensary, which, although a comparatively recent foundation, is rapidly assuming very large proportions. The thickly-populated district around, and the hazardous nature of the occupations of many of the people, afford a guarantee that patients will seldom be lacking. Besides all these, the township of Hulme possesses its dispensary, founded and largely sustained by private munificence; there are a Penitentiary and a "Home" for Fallen Women, and a Nurse-training Institution, which is known to have done an almost incredible amount of good. It cannot, of course, be pretended that the foregoing is a complete list of the charities of the place, but it may be taken as representing with approximate accuracy those to which the epithet "public" may fairly be applied. Of private charities, provident societies, institutions designed for the benefit of poor women and children it may be said that their name is legion. Every church and chapel has one or two such societies connected with it—many have more—and it is no small testimony to the character of the people and excellence of the general administration that, so far as an impartial observer can say, there does not seem to be any pauperisation of the masses. Such associations and institutions as those which we have mentioned, together with the numerous parks and places of public recreation provided partly by the municipal authorities and partly by private munificence, are unquestionably civilising agents of no mean value. The

PUBLIC PARKS,

which are ten in number, are somewhat remarkable specimens of the art of gardening under difficulties. From the multitude of chimneys and the proximity of chemical and other works of a similar kind to the town, it is by no means easy to grow much in the open air. The wealthy merchant or manufacturer who can afford to pay for hot-houses and conservatories may, of course, always command a supply of flowers for his table, but the working man, or his immediate superior in the hierarchy of labour, finds it difficult in the extreme to wring from an ungenial soil, and still more ungenial atmosphere, anything worthy of consideration in the way of flowers or fruit. In the Manchester parks, however, a tolerably successful attempt has been made to overcome these difficulties. The Alexandra Park at Moss Side, to the south of the city, is 60 acres in extent, is a remarkably pretty place, and is very popular as a promenade. There are not many full-grown trees. In point of fact it would be difficult to say where, in the immediate neighbourhood of the town, much wood is to be found. But, if trees are wanting, their place is not altogether ill supplied by the admirably laid-out flower beds, the pretty lake, and the large open spaces allotted by the Corporation for cricket, gymnastics, &c. Close to this park was the Aquarium, an admirably managed institution, which for size stood probably about third in the kingdom. Peel Park, Salford, is a much more picturesque, and infinitely more imposing, place of resort than the Alexandra Park on the opposite side of the town. It is 37 acres in extent, and were it not for the omnipresent chimneys which mar every prospect in the manufacturing district, it would be easy to get up a good deal of enthusiasm about the beauty of this place, looking as it does over the valley of the Irwell towards the comparatively high ground of Kersal Moor. It is entered from the main road by an exceedingly handsome arch erected by a subscription of the working men to commemorate the Queen's visit in 1857. The iron gates which fill this arch were the gift of Mr. E. R. Langworthy, to whose liberality the place is indebted for the Langworthy wing of the Peel Park Museum, which contains a reading-room and picture gallery, as well as much of the interesting contents of the Museum and Library, which stands just within the park gates. This Museum was originated by the late Mr. Brotherton, and is a worthy competitor with the many other libraries and museums to be found in the capital of the North. Like them, it is wholly free, Manchester not having as yet discovered the beauty of the system so much patronised in certain places of making a charge of a few pence for the privilege of seeing the national property. In Peel Park, besides the unusual attraction of a goodly number of fine trees, are statues to Sir Robert Peel (after whom the place is named), to the Queen, and to Mr. Joseph Brotherton, whilst in various parts of the gardens surrounding the museum are to be found a number of interesting natural curiosities. The other parks of Manchester and Salford do not call for much remark. They are not very large, and are of too recent construction to offer much in the way of either natural or artificial beauty. Nevertheless, they are one and all well laid out, and are extensively patronised by those for whose special benefit they were intended, and they have proved immense boons to the community at large. The Queen's Park, conveniently located on the north-east of the city, is beautifully laid out, and during the summer season is a most popular place of public resort. It is thirty acres in extent, and, like the Peel Park, contains a splendid free museum and an art gallery, the contents of which are of great comprehensiveness, value, and attraction. The names and acreage of the others are as follow: Philip's Park (which is rather romantically situated on the left bank of the Medlock at Bradford, and, like the Queen's Park, is reached by tramcar from Market Street) 31 acres; Ardwick Park, 4 acres; Cheetham Park, 5 acres; Birch Fields, 29 acres; Albert Park, Salford, 16 acres; Ordsall Park, 15 acres; Seedley Park, 13 acres. To these parks must be added a number of open spaces and recreation grounds, some of them of considerable extent, and which answer a most useful purpose in their several localities. The total area of the parks and open spaces of Manchester and Salford is 267¼ acres.

THE BELLE VUE ZOOLOGICAL GARDENS,

which are now the only institution of their class in connection

PICCADILLY, AND THE INFIRMARY FROM MARKET STREET.

with the city, are much resorted to at holiday seasons. These gardens are well situated on the south side of the town. The zoological collections are among the most extensive and important in the British Isles. The gardens are probably known by reputation to many thousands of people who have never been within a hundred miles of Manchester, from the fact that they are owned and managed by one of the most practical business firms in the kingdom, whose skill and capability as caterers have been very often amply attested at Wimbledon. Instances have not been uncommon of their receiving and feeding at Easter and Whitsuntide some 20,000 or 30,000 guests without a hitch of any kind, whilst once or twice it has happened that they have been called upon to provide a meal for as many as 15,000 persons at once. Thus it has come about that there is no excursion more popular than one to the Zoological Gardens at Belle Vue. On such occasions as the Brass Band Contests, and when special attractions are announced for Easter and Whitsun weeks, the railway companies find it worth while to run trains to the Belle Vue Station from all parts of Lancashire, Cheshire, and the West and North Ridings. For the use of such excursion trains a special platform has been built by the London and North Western Railway, which is about half as long again as the arrival platform at Euston Station, London. Belle Vue Gardens were established in 1836 by the late Mr. John Jennison, who died in 1869. In the face of many difficulties that gentleman worked on, by degrees enlarging and beautifying the grounds and increasing his zoological collection, until he succeeded in making them second only to the Zoological Gardens in London. Messrs. Jennison & Company, the present proprietors, leave nothing

ndone, and spare no expense to add to the attractiveness of the Gardens and to provide amusement for the masses. The splendid collection of wild beasts and other animals, together with the curiosities exhibited in the museum, afford to the visitors a treat to be found in no other city in the provinces. That the gardens are very popular is conclusively proved by the immense number of people frequenting them. Messrs. Jennison & Company's gardens are well worth visiting, and they are conducted in a manner which cannot fail to ensure public confidence. Hitherto we have said nothing of

THE NEWSPAPER PRESS OF MANCHESTER,

but before concluding it is obviously necessary to refer to a factor which exercises so important an influence over the life of the people. Party spirit, as has been said, does from time to time run very high in the place, both upon religious and upon political questions. Both are, in fact, treated not as matters for the amusement of an idle hour, but as subjects of the deepest and most serious interest. The result is that the journals of Manchester are

View in Portland Street, Manchester.

written and worked with an air of conviction and fervour which is not always to be found in religious and political organs. The various editors and contributors are adepts in the art of "calling a spade a spade," though it must be admitted that they generally contrive to do their work with a commendable avoidance of personality. As much cannot always be said for the correspondence which appears in the columns of those journals, but some allowance must be made for the difficulties of journalists who find themselves obliged to use letters from influential supporters of their journal or of their party under heavy social or financial penalties. The newspapers themselves exhibit a commendable reticence with regard to each other. The traditional Eatanswill is, in fact, very generally extinct in England, and in Manchester the press exhibits a thoroughly metropolitan tone—except perhaps occasionally at election times. Popular interest in political affairs may perhaps best be estimated by the fact that no fewer than five daily papers are now published in Manchester alone, all of which are thriving and prosperous undertakings. The *Manchester Guardian* is perhaps at the head of English provincial newspapers. It has been long established as a daily paper, and is admirably conducted. It has always been a Liberal organ; recent political controversies in the governing councils of the kingdom have had a slight effect upon its original tone, and now like a good many contemporaries it inclines to the Gladstonian programme. The *Guardian* does not, however, depend wholly upon its political articles. Its general information is admirably condensed; its London correspondence generally excellent of its kind, and its fine art criticism brilliant and interesting. Following close upon the heels of the *Guardian* comes the *Manchester Courier*, the organ of the Conservative party. It had long held a more than respectable position as a weekly paper when, in 1864, the daily issue commenced. The then editor was the brother of the present proprietor, and was a member of the bar and a political speaker of no inconsiderable local celebrity. In 1867 failing health induced him to retire from the arduous duties of his post, but the prosperity of the paper, thanks to the exceedingly able management of its present proprietor, has shown no symptoms of diminution. Its commercial information is simply unrivalled—a fact which is proved by the constant quotations from its columns in the most influential organs of the London Press;' the leading articles faithfully reflect, where they do not lead, the political opinion of the Conservatives of the district; the London correspondence is decidedly piquant; and the dramatic and fine art criticism unusually excellent in quality. The *Examiner* is a well-conducted and well-written paper in the interests of the advanced section of the Liberal party. Its leading articles are clear and vigorous in style, and display very superior talent. It has a large circulation. There is also a print called *The Sporting Chronicle*, which is published daily.

THE DAILY EVENING PAPERS

are two in number. The *Evening News* is a halfpenny sheet, which was started during the by-election of 1867, in order that Mr. Mitchell Henry, who was then an independent Liberal Conservative candidate for the representation of the city, might obtain greater advantages of publicity than were accorded by the daily press. It was first got up in the offices of the *Manchester Guardian*, but soon became strong enough to run alone, and is now a by no means uninfluential or unprofitable property. The *Evening Mail* is a distinctly Conservative organ, and an offshoot of the *Courier*. It was established so far back as 1874, and it runs its Liberal rival hard, and judging from the number of its advertisements is a very thriving undertaking.

The local press also includes twenty-six

WEEKLY NEWSPAPERS.

Chief amongst these must be mentioned the *Manchester Weekly Times*, which claims to be, with its *Literary Supplement*, the largest penny weekly paper in the kingdom. It contains an amount of matter equal to eighty columns of the London *Times*, and gives full and accurate accounts of local and general occurrences, a digest of public events, parliamentary intelligence, commercial and market reports, foreign news, &c., whilst the *Literary Supplement* consists of original and selected articles, tales, poetry, hints for the household, ladies' column, gardening, social topics, and copious and interesting extracts from the leading reviews, magazines, &c. It enjoys an enormous circulation all over the north of England. The *Manchester City News* may be named next, and as its title implies, it devotes a considerable portion of its space to the municipal affairs of Manchester and Salford, although it contains excellent general matter.

There are likewise the *Salford Chronicle*, the *Salford Weekly News*, the *Alliance News*, the *Co-operative News*, the *Manchester Weekly Courier*, the *Manchester Weekly Post*, the *Sunday Chronicle*, the *Unitarian Herald*, the *Catholic Times*, *Ben Brierly's Journal*, the *Athletic News*, the *British Architect*, *Industries*, the *South Manchester Gazette*, the *Swinton and Pendlebury Times*, the *Umpire*, the *Halfpenny Novelette*, the *Cotton Factory Times*, the *Manchester Mercantile Gazette*, the *Mechanical World*, the *Pendleton, Salford, and Broughton Reporter*, the *National Commercial Agency Gazette*, t *Cotton-Spinners' and Textile Manufacturers' Diary*, and *The Wee* In addition to these daily and weekly papers there is the *Cred Drapers' Gazette*, which is a useful trade journal, published fort nightly by George Woodhead & Co., 3, Mason Street, Mancheste and 13, Bow Lane, London, E.C.

This does not, however, exhaust the list of Manchester litera productions, for there are published monthly, the *Catholic Firesid Delving and Diving*, *Health Journal*, *Insurance News*, *Iron and Co Trade Review*, *The Ironmonger*, *Journal of the Society of Chemic Industries*, *Journal of the Society of Dyers and Colourists*, *L'Ingenie Mechanicien*, *Onward Magazine*, *Onward Reciter*, the *Primiti Methodist World*, *The Sugar Cane*, *Textile Recorder*, *Textile Manu facturer and Trade Journal*, and though last, not least, the *Women Suffrage Journal*. It will thus be seen that, altogether, there a printed in Manchester and Salford close upon fifty distinct publica tions, of one description or another, in the course of each month.

It can scarcely be doubted that there is no other place, excep London, which can show such an amount of literary effort, very large proportion of which is of a remarkably high order excellence.

It is unnecessary to describe, separately, the character of a these publications, but with reference to the "weeklies," it evident that whilst some of them are merely a summary of th week's news, with a little entertaining and amusing matter adde others likewise discuss politics from the Conservative, Liberal, Radical standpoint, but as a rule with great moderation. Other again, like the *Alliance News*, are the advocates of particula social reforms, and some are devoted to the interests of particul trades, businesses, or professions, like *Industries*, the *Mechanic World*, the *Cotton Factory Times*, or the *British Architect*. The are one or two almost purely mercantile papers, like the *Mercanti Gazette*. Several are the organs of particular religious denom nations, such as the *Catholic Times*, and the *Unitarian Herald*; an then by way of contrast, we have papers of a somewhat light character, like the *Athletic News*, and the *Halfpenny Novelette*. Th same remarks to a great extent apply to the "monthlies," onl that the *Women's Suffrage Journal* (which is most cleverly edited b a lady), is entitled to special mention. Indeed, the ladies of Ma chester are to be congratulated upon possessing such an ably-co ducted and influential organ to advocate their cause. Alike in th field of literature and manufactures, Manchester, it is clear, occu pies a pre-eminent position in the country.

MANCHESTER MEN

are popularly supposed to be of so very different a class from th rest of their race, that a few words with reference to them may n be out of place.

A local proverb divides the people of Southern Lancashire in four classes. There are, we are told, "Liverpool gentlemen, Ma chester men, Oldham fellows, and Bolton chaps." That there a certain humour in this descriptive category may at once admitted, but that it is strictly accurate is open to a good deal question. The merchants of Liverpool are, without doub cultivated, refined, and gentleman-like, but so also are the men Manchester. A few years ago it is no doubt perfectly true th there were a good many amongst the manufacturers and merchan who still retained, to some small extent, the tradition of those da to which reference has already been made, when master, famil and apprentices sat at the same board and lived as it we *en famille*. But those days have vanished, and their hero have gone with them. In a few of the outlying districts, suc the suburbs of Bolton, Oldham, or Blackburn, something the kind may possibly yet be found, but no one is likely think or to speak of those quiet, enterprising, and highly-ucated men who may be found any day on the Manchester xchange with other feelings than those of respect and regard. ie explanation is simple enough. The last generation of anchester men had the practical wisdom to see that the world daily advancing, and that no efforts of theirs were likely to event its progress. And so they gave to their sons that which ey themselves, in many instances, had lacked. The boys were nt to good schools, if not always to public ones, and they followed their school trainings with a residence at one or other of the iiversities or a course of foreign travel—sometimes with both. did not invariably happen of course that the results of the process re satisfactory. Crœsus the Younger sometimes came back from ford little better in certain respects than he was when he went ther, and in other instances he returned from his Continental tour ving acquired habits of which he would never have dreamed at ne. On the whole, however, the effect has been decidedly advantage-s. The new generation has the merits of the old—its hospitality, idliness, liberality, and public spirit—upon which is superadded amount of intelligence and refinement which is not universally isidered to be synonymous with the name of Manchester. The e of the people for general culture is sufficiently evidenced by magnificent liberality which has given to the town some of the est free libraries and public schools in the country; while the preciation of art amongst the wealthy is notorious. Gentlemen o write in those dreary compilations known as "comic papers" nk it funny to talk about Manchester and shoddy as convertible ms, and to repeat the well-worn joke about the *nouveau riche* o ordered so many yards of books for his library and so many are feet of pictures for his drawing-room. But he who wants to w what is the truth about Manchester appreciation of art will well to ask the rising generation of English painters. Any mber of that body will tell him that his most appreciative patrons n odious word by the way—are to be found amongst the men of tonopolis, and that no more welcome sound can meet his ears n the name of a Manchester "plutocrat" announced as about visit his studio. The reason is not merely that he is sure of ting with a liberal purchaser, but that the buyer is tolerably e to be an appreciative one. The result may readily be under-d. Within a radius of twenty miles around the Manchester change it is probable that, if an accurate census could be made, should find more good pictures than in any similar space in ope, if public collections are left out of account. It would, ed, be difficult to find many specimens of the "old masters" he houses of Manchester merchants, but of the best periods of English school there are abundant examples. The smoky, gy, and apocryphal antiques of Wardour Street and the second-salerooms are no longer manufactured for home consumption. trade in them still goes on, but the demand comes from across Atlantic rather than from the manufacturing districts. What "Cotton Lord" of to-day does, as a rule, is to commission ures from one or other of our modern painters. Such com-sions are liberally paid, but it happens not unfrequently that picture proves one of the most profitable investments of capital ch could have been made. Within the last few years three at collections—those of Mr. John Pender, M.P., of Mr. Sam adel, and of Mr. F. P. Rickards—have been dispersed under auctioneer's hammer, and at each sale the sums realised were he majority of instances considerably in advance of those origi-y received by the artist. Several minor gatherings of paintings e been sold in a similar way and to similar purpose. It must not, however, be imagined that Manchester purchasers of pictures are invariably actuated by the trading spirit. Some few collectors do, indeed, sell off their stocks from time to time, but the majority seem anxious to treat the works which they buy as heirlooms, and to vindicate for themselves the character of enlightened votaries of the fine arts. Articles of *virtu* and *bric-à-brac* generally also find a ready market in Manchester, and there are few houses which do not exhibit abundant evidences of good taste and artistic feeling on the part of their possessors. One of the finest known sets of the *Liber Studiorum* is the property of a Manchester man, whose partner in business possesses an almost unequalled collection of the Reynolds mezzotints.

Of the public spirit and conduct of the men of Manchester, it is probable that enough has already been said. It would seem, indeed, that as regards money, it is only necessary to prove that an object is a deserving one to secure for it munificent support, whilst those who know the place are aware that the amount of time given up to public duty by the men of Manchester is simply astonishing. Men whose time is, in the truest sense of the term, literally money, willingly and ungrudgingly give up hours of the most valuable part of the day to sit on the magisterial bench, to assist at municipal councils and committees, to serve on the boards of charitable institutions, or to assist in the deliberations of the Chamber of Commerce, or of the associations connected with the political party with which they have cast in their lot.

We see the consequences. Our world-renowned city is rapidly rivalling the metropolis in external beauty and splendour, is setting an example of municipal administration which Londoners can only envy without the hope of copying it, and has a life of its own which points to a magnificent future. The climate may be depressing, the atmosphere heavy, the surroundings of the city unlovely, but all these things count for little when the spirit of the people is so high. A late election afforded the population an opportunity of displaying its mettle and its temper, and the result is surely something of which to be proud. The spirit which sends more than 40,000 adult males in responsible positions to the polling-booths, there to put on enduring record their political convictions, is not one to be despised. Whether outsiders like or dislike the choice of Parliamentary representatives which was finally made, they cannot refuse to admit that the spirit displayed on both sides was laudable in no ordinary degree, and eminently worthy of that great community which with so much reason boasts itself not merely the "Capital of Cotton," but also the second city of the Empire.

MANCHESTER SHIP CANAL.

Before closing our brief history of the growth and importance of Manchester's progress, mention must be made of a subject that has given rise to lengthy discussions in the governing councils of the kingdom, and which has engaged the most earnest attention of our financial and commercial speculators. In the ingenuity and extent of its manufactures, and in the production of every kind of machinery applicable to their perfection, the head-quarters of the cotton trade stands unrivalled in the world. It has long been in navigable communication with Liverpool, through the medium of the Irk and Medlock joining the Irwell, which, after pursuing a course of seven miles below the city, becomes a tributary of the Mersey, thereby forming communication with Liverpool. Besides these advantages Manchester possesses that of an inland navigation extending by means of numerous canals and their ramifications to every principal town; and by railroad, it is safe to say, that it has facilities superior to any other place in the kingdom. By these various channels Manchester receives raw materials for its manufactures, coal, building requisites, and every article of consumption not supplied by its own immediate neighbourhood, and it distributes to all parts of the commercial world the productions of its combined ingenuity, capital, and labour. Its relations with Liverpool have always been of the most friendly nature; indeed, the flourishing state of the one means the prosperity of the other, and "Liverpool gentlemen" with "Manchester men" constitute a body whose influence in the commercial interests of Great Britain has been fully recognised in all the mercantile councils of the world. Recently, however, the men of Manchester have given their attention to a project which, if carried out, will prove invaluable to the commercial interests of the city, while it may result unfavourably to parties who have made large investments in Liverpool to promote the best interests of that port. Strenuous efforts have been made within the last few years to obtain an Act of Parliament to connect Manchester with the sea by means of a ship canal, and in this way allow some of our ocean-going steamers to come direct to Manchester instead of di charging their cargoes at Liverpool. The bill was twice rejecto once by a committee of the House of Lords, and afterwards by committee of the House of Commons. It is needless to say th the strenuous efforts of the promoters were most energetically an systematically opposed by men involved in vast enterprises Liverpool as well as by the various railway companies who traffic would be largely affected by the success of so daring project as the Manchester Ship Canal. The promoters were n however discouraged by these reverses, and eventually succeed in realising their most sanguine hopes, when in the session of 18 Parliament extended the right to them to construct a canal.

DEVELOPMENTS SINCE THE PASSING OF THE ACT.

Since the Manchester Ship Canal Act became law, by the roy assent being given on August 6th, 1885, the record of its develo ments has been very eventful. The victory obtained after the mo prolonged struggle in the history of private bill legislation, was marked with great rejoicings by the inhabitants of Manchester and the district interested. Several extensive public demonstrations were made in honour of the successful result of the arduous parliamentary campaign. A great meeting of the subscribers to the parliamentary fund of £100,000 was held in the Town Hall, Manchester, on August 19th, 1885. A great demonstration took place at Eccles, a suburb of Manchester, on Monday, August 31st, 1885, at which nearly one hundred thousand persons were present. Soon afterwards, in October, there were three important celebrations in connection with the passing of the Ship Canal Act. On October 3rd there was a great public procession from Albert Square, Manchester, to the Belle Vue Gardens, of the trade societies of the district, in which sixty thousand members took part. An influential meeting of friends of the movement was held in the Great Free Trade Hall, on October 5th. On the next day, October 6th, a banquet was given to the promoters of the great enterprise by the Mayor and Corporation of Manchester, in honour of the passing of the Act in the Town Hall.

THE MANCHESTER SHIP CANAL: CUTTING FIRST SODS.

On October 8th a private preliminary prospectus was issued, l the Manchester Ship Canal Company. The subscription, howeve owing to the company having no power to pay interest out capital during construction, was not sufficient to meet the requir ments of the undertaking. To overcome this difficulty a furth application was made to Parliament, and resulted in an act auth rising the payment by the Manchester Ship Canal Company interest at the rate of four per cent. per annum to shareholde during the construction of works. This Act received the ro assent on 26th June, 1886. The sanction of Parliament havi thus been obtained, Messrs. N. M. Rothschild & Sons were auth rised to receive subscriptions for the balance of the capital of t company. The subscription lists were opened on Tuesday, Ju 20th, 1886, and closed on Friday, July 23rd. As, however, t full amount required was not subscribed, the issue was withdraw

After this disappointment a committee of influential gentlem largely identified with the trade of the district, was formed und the auspices of the Mayor of Manchester (Mr. Alderman Gol hmidt), to investigate into the whole bearings of the various iestions involved in the project. This committee, which was iown as the Consultative Committee, consisted of twenty-ree gentlemen, whose status, competency, and integrity were iexceptionable, many of whom started the investigation with isgivings as to the commercial prospects of the undertaking. fter, however, a thorough scrutiny into every detail, the Consultive Committee *unanimously* arrived at the conviction that within ro years of the opening of the canal, it would not pay less than a per cent. dividend, in addition to a handsome surplus equal to an lditional one per cent.

This estimate of the Consultative Committee will be seen to be very moderate one when it is explained that it is based upon ily three-fourths of the traffic which they had fully made up their inds would use the great waterway in the second year. Being sirous of putting forward an estimate in which the keenest criticism would be at fault in endeavouring to suggest the slightest exaggeration of the statement of the probable business and dividend of the undertaking, the Consultative Committee deducted from their estimate of traffic one-fourth of the quantity to anticipate the possibility of unforeseen contingencies. As a matter of fact, the volume of business which the Consultative Committee had arrived at, as the result of an exhaustive inquiry, would pay eight per cent., or three per cent. more than the modest judgment which they pronounced in their valuable report. The report of the Consultative Committee was signed on November 26th, 1886. On Thursday, December 9th, 1886, a meeting convened by and presided over by the Mayor of Manchester (Mr. Alderman Curtis), was held in order to receive the report of the Consultative Committee. There was a large and influential attendance. After the report had been read, an enthusiastic vote of thanks was accorded to the Consultative Committee for their arduous labours and great

THE NEW MANCHESTER SHIP CANAL. WORKS AT EASTHAM: LIVERPOOL END OF CANAL.

ervices in presenting their valuable report to the citizens. The eport of the Consultative Committee produced a very favourable npression, and greatly increased public confidence in the under-iking.

On March 18th, 1887, the directors of the Manchester Ship Canal 'ompany issued a private circular, making an appeal to the inhabi-ints of Manchester to subscribe one-half of the required capital f £8,000,000. If the first £4,000,000 were subscribed locally, the irectors were assured that the remaining £4,000,000 would be ound by London capitalists. On April 27th, a great public meet-ig convened by and presided over by the Mayor of Manchester Mr. Alderman Curtis) was held in the Town Hall, Manchester, to onsider the best means of assisting the Manchester Ship Canal 'ompany to raise the balance of its required capital, the bulk of he £4,000,000 required from Manchester and its immediate locality aving been subscribed. An extensive committee was formed at he meeting, with power to add to their number, to exert their est endeavours in obtaining subscriptions to complete the required alance. On June 8th 1887, the Manchester Ship Canal Preference Shares Bill was read the first time in the House of Commons. The object of this Bill was to divide the share capital of £8,000,000 into £4,000,000 of £5 per cent. Perpetual Preference shares and £4,000,000 of ordinary shares, ranking for dividend after the preference shares; the preference shares not to receive five per cent. until after the construction of the canal, preference and ordinary shares receiving four per cent. alike until the Ship Canal is in operation. The Preference Shares Bill was read a second time in the House of Commons on June 14th. After being remitted to a select committee, the third reading of the Bill in the House of Commons took place on June 27th, 1887, and the same evening the Preference Shares Bill was read the first time in the House of Lords. The second reading took place on July 5th; having been remitted to a select committee of the House of Lords, it was read a third time on July 11th, and received the royal assent on July 12th, 1887. Immediately after the special Act sanctioning the preference shares had been obtained, Messrs. Baring Brothers & Co., and Messrs. N. M. Rothschild & Sons, were authorised to receive subscriptions for £4,000,000 of Perpetual Five per Cent.

Preference Shares. The lists opened on July 19th and closed on July 21st.

The Ship Canal Company were required by the Act to raise £5,000,000 of its share capital, in addition to the purchase money of the Bridgewater Canal and the Mersey and Irwell Navigation, amounting to £1,710,000. The whole of this £6,710,000 required to be subscribed within two years of the passing of the Act. On August 4th, 1887, the Board of Trade duly certified that these conditions had been complied with by the company.

The actual commencement of the Manchester Ship Canal works took place by the cutting of the first sod, without any formal ceremony, by the chairman of the Ship Canal Company, Lord Egerton of Tatton, on Friday, November 11th, 1887, in the presence of the Board and some of the leading officials, at Eastham, where the entrance locks of the canal will be constructed.

The canal will be 35 miles in length, with five sets of locks, at Eastham, Latchford, Irlam, Barton, and Manchester. Each of these sets will consist of three parallel locks, the dimensions of which are designed to accommodate the different sizes of vessels. The largest lock in each series will be 600 feet in length and 65 feet wide. The large tidal lock at Eastham will be 80 feet wide. For smaller vessels an intermediate lock will be provided in each set. The dimensions will be 300 feet in length and 40 feet in width. The smallest-sized lock in each set will be for the accommodation of small coasting vessels and barges. The dimensions will be 100 feet in length and 20 feet in width. The minimum depth of the canal will be 26 feet. The minimum bottom width will be 120 feet, that of the Suez Canal being only 72 feet. The bottom width between Barton and Manchester, 3½ miles, will be 170 feet. Commodious docks will be provided at Manchester, Salford, and Warrington, and the canal will afford much better facilities for vessels entering or leaving the Runcorn and Western Point Docks, which are now the property of the Manchester Ship Canal Company. The Duke's Dock at Liverpool is also the property of the Ship Canal Company, being part of the interest acquired with the Bridgewater Canals.

The promoters claim that the project will enormously stimulate not only the trade of Manchester and the surrounding towns, but will largely develop the industries of South Lancashire, Cheshire, the West Riding of Yorkshire, and those of Derbyshire, Staffordshire, and Nottinghamshire. The population within six miles of the Manchester Royal Exchange, at the census of 1881, was 897,000 and the increase calculated to 1891, in which year the canal will be completed, will make the population in that year exceed 1,000,000. The population within twelve miles of Manchester Royal Exchange was over 1,800,000 in 1881, and in 1891 will be 2,100,000. Within twenty miles of the Manchester Royal Exchange the population in 1881 was 2,900,000, and in 1891 will be 3,500,000. It was established before the select committee of the House of Commons (session 1885), without any criticism on the part of opponents, that the Manchester Ship Canal, which will virtually be a continuous dock 35 miles in length, will afford the most convenient port accommodation for large ocean steamers to a population of 7,400,000, inhabiting an area of 7,500 square miles. The normal increase of the population will make the population of this Ship Canal area at least 9,000,000 in 1891, in which year the canal will be in active operation.

MARKETS.

As might naturally be expected in regard to a place of such magnitude and importance as Manchester, the city is well provided with market accommodation. It is not, however, so generally known as it ought to be, that, excluding London, the Manchester markets are the finest in the kingdom. The chief one is named "Smithfield," after the celebrated London Smithfield, and though at one period it was a market for the sale of live stock, it has ceased to be such for a considerable number of years, and is now a great fruit and vegetable market, covering an enormous area, and filled to overflowing with both home and foreign produce. This market, however, is more popularly known as Shudehill Market, from the circumstance that it is located close to that well-known thoroughfare, and it is seldom called by any other name. It is said to be the largest covered market extant, and is built of iron, the roof being formed on the principle of railway station roofs, covered with rough sheet glass and black Welsh slates, and so much glass has been introduced that the building is perfectly lighted. It has on three sides a verandah, under which it is open. On the closed side are a number of shops which look into the market and really form part of it. The entire market space is considerably over four acres, more than two-thirds of which is covered with a roof, as described. But even this extensive space is sometimes found inadequate, and in the height of the summer, when fruit and vegetables abound, the sides of the streets adjacent to the market are permitted to be used for market purposes. In the year 1846 the Manchester Corporation purchased the markets and manorial rights from the lord of the manor (the late Sir Oswald Mosley, Bart.), for the sum of £200,000, but at that time the Shudehill, or Smithfield, market was only about one-fourth of its present size, and it was entirely open to the weather. Then the market days were Tuesday, Thursday, and Saturday, and on the other three week-days little or no business was transacted. But now every day is a market day, and Friday the most important of them all, as it is on that day the dealers from all the populous towns around Manchester fetch their supplies for delivery to their customers on the following day. The market area is apportioned or assigned for special purposes: thus, there is a purely wholesale square where not less than certain quantities are permitted to be sold. There is a place for salesmen, and another for hucksters, and there are two covered spaces, beside large areas of uncovered space, which are reserved when required for growers, who are permitted to sell either large or small quantities as they choose. Until recently this market was dependent upon Cheshire and the Lancashire bank of the Mersey for its supplies of fresh vegetables and fruits, but the abolition of duties, coupled with the wonderful development of the railway system and steam navigation, has altered all this, and now Shudehill Market gets its supplies from all parts of the kingdom and from all quarters of the globe. Both as a vegetable and fruit market, Shudehill holds a pre-eminent position amongst the provincial markets of the United Kingdom.

Mr. John Page, the able superintendent of the Manchester markets, in his accurate and exhaustive essay on their sources of supply, says that during the first three months of the year broccoli or cauliflowers, to the extent of twenty tons a day, are received from Cornwall, and, as the season advances, large quantities are sent from the Midlands, the best coming from the neighbourhood of Northampton. Early radishes come from the Vale of Evesham, Worcestershire, and Wallasey, Cheshire. Watercress, of which many tons per day are sold at Shudehill, is chiefly procured from Oxfordshire, where it is much cultivated. Forty-five years ago, the only supply of this article in the city markets was what was gathered by two men from the Cheshire ditches. Spring cabbages come from Evesham, the districts round London, Lincolnshire, and Cheshire. Asparagus, the consumption of which has greatly increased within recent years, comes principally from Evesham and Northamptonshire. The first green peas come from Algeria, Spain, and France, Evesham and Nottinghamshire being the earliest English productive centres. The sale of these in Manchester markets is enormous, one salesman having sold as many as fifteen hundred sacks in one day. The first new potatoes come from France; in May, Cornwall and the Scilly Isles furnish their quota, and these are followed by Jersey. The demand for new potatoes has greatly increased during the last decade, and in proof of this it may be stated that one salesman in the city has sold as much as forty tons of them in a single day. Vast quantities of potatoes are also received from Lincolnshire, Yorkshire, Lancashire, Scotland, and Ireland. France is first in the markets with carrots, and is closely followed by Holland and the Midland counties. Turnips are almost entirely supplied by the districts lying round the city. Christmas-time brings the first forced rhubarb, which is mostly grown at Kirkstall, near Leeds, where its cultivation is made a leading speciality with gardeners and others. The forced is soon followed by the naturally grown article, the consumption of which is simply enormous. Celery makes its appearance in the middle of July, and comes chiefly from Ashton-under-Lyne, Sale, Ashton-upon-Mersey, Timperley, Retford, and Lincolnshire. Onions, of which eighty tons have been pitched in the city markets in one week from Bedfordshire alone, come from the Midlands and all parts of the Continent. Cucumbers are, for the most part, grown in Bedfordshire, and an idea of the demand for them may be formed from a statement of the fact that as much as one hundred and twenty tons of them have

THE MANCHESTER SHIP CANAL. PROPOSED LOCKS ON SHIP CANAL.

in one week been poured into the city markets. Apples are supplied from all parts of these islands, the Continent of Europe, especially France, and immense quantities are annually imported from the United States and Canada; France, Belgium, and the home growers are the principal contributors to the Manchester supply of these invaluable articles of food. Jersey and France and home producers take the first rank in the supply of pears. Strawberries are extensively grown around Ashton-upon-Mersey, Baguley, Sale, and Timperley for the Manchester markets, to which the Channel Isles and France also send large consignments. Cherries, plums, currants, gooseberries, and bilberries are almost entirely supplied from Kent, Worcestershire, Cambridge, and Cheshire, France and Germany being the chief Continental contributors in these lines.

There is still a market in what is called the Market Place, just off Market Street and opposite to the Royal Exchange, and through the spring and summer this locality presents a picturesque and somewhat novel appearance. It is occupied with roofed wooden stands or stalls, which line each side of the open space, and which are filled with flowers, plants, shrubs, and trees, in addition to choice fruit of all kinds. The stall keepers, however, do a good business all the year round, in whatever fruit and vegetables happen to be in season, and as the market-place is in the very heart of the city, it is always a source of great attraction to strangers, as well as to ordinary residents. Adjoining the Shudehill Market stands the Wholesale Fish Market, a large and handsome structure, built of brick and stone, and having an area of 3,538 square yards. It was opened in the year 1873 by the then Mayor (Mr. William Booth), but since that time has been greatly enlarged. It is both lofty and well-lighted, and is admirably adapted to meet the requirements of the wholesale dealers in fish, game, and poultry. In close proximity to the wholesale market is the Retail Fish Market, a comparatively modern building, fitted up in excellent style, of good extent (area 793 square yards), and well tenanted. That there should be a necessity for two such extensive markets affords conclusive evidence of the vast trade carried on in Manchester in fish, poultry, &c. Situate in the neighbourhood of Victoria Street there is another important market, which occupies a position partly in and partly betwixt that leading thoroughfare and the Market Place. Here are to be seen a number of retail fish, game, &c., establishments of a first-class character; indeed, it is doubtful that such a display can be met with anywhere, except in London. These establishments are patronised by the *élite* of the city and its environs. In 1885 the Corporation erected in Oak Street, at considerable cost, a market expressly for the use of second-hand clothes dealers, so that these tradesmen may now be said to have an "Exchange" of their own. The other markets of Manchester and Salford are the Campfield Market, in Deansgate and Liverpool Road. This is a noble covered erection in two sections, with open sides, and, altogether, occupies an area of 7,084 square yards; it was opened in 1878. It is now used as a mart for the sale of goods, both new and second-hand, and also contains some butchers' stalls. The other marts of the city are: Trinity Market, Chapel Street, Salford, crockery, clothes, and hardware; Abattoir and Carcass Market, Water Street, Bridge Street; Hay and Straw Market, Tonman Street, Deansgate; Hide and Skin Markets, Water Street and Chapel Street; Cattle Market, Cross Lane, Salford; and Pig Market, Water Street, Bridge Street. The celebrated Salford Cattle Market is situated in Cross Lane, and is the most important live stock market out of London. According to the annual report presented by the superintendent of the market to the Markets Committee, for the year ending March, 1886, tolls were collected upon the following live stock:—

Bulls	3,519
Beasts	161,158
Sheep and Lambs	587,776
Calves	12,017
Pigs	2,709
Total animals	767,179

Most of the beasts come from Ireland, as may be seen from the following figures:—

From Ireland	121,697	beasts
" North of England	11,850	"
" Holland	9,230	"
" Canada	12,050	"
" Home	9,850	"

The returns of 1887 show a considerable increase upon those of the previous year. At one time a very large number of cattle were imported from Spain, and many of them found their way to the Salford Market; but the restriction as to the slaughtering of cattle sent from foreign countries at the port of landing has put an end to the supply from that country. There is an extensive potato market on the premises of the Lancashire and Yorkshire Railway Company, in Oldham Road. This market is in the hands of the railway company, who pay the Corporation of Manchester £1,500 per annum for the privilege of holding it. Under the agreement, potatoes and carrots only are permitted to be sold there, and those only which arrive by the company's line. The market-days in Manchester for manufacturers, &c., are Tuesday and Friday (Tuesday being the principal); for corn, Tuesday and Saturday; for cattle, Tuesday; and for provisions and general produce, Thursday and Saturday.

THE POST OFFICE.

Manchester is abundantly provided for in regard to postal accommodation. Indeed, its enormous population, and the gigantic commercial operations carried on in the city and neighbourhood, render a liberal postal service a matter of absolute necessity and of the first importance.

When letters passing through the chief office have to be reckoned by millions in the course of a week, and parcels by tons of thousands, it is certain there must be proper facilities afforded for dealing with them with the utmost expedition, so as to obviate inconvenience and irregularities, and to protect the public from loss.

Some dozen years ago the Manchester Chamber of Commerce found it desirable to appoint a deputation to wait upon the Chancellor of the Exchequer, to call attention to the defective post office accommodation then existing. This was in 1875, and it was explained that whereas in 1861 the weekly delivery of letters was 401,000 and the number posted 485,000, in that year (1875) the weekly delivery was 927,000 and the number posted 1,134,000; the money orders had also increased from 295,000 to 364,000. It was further pointed out that when the Post Office then in use was erected (in 1840), the population of Manchester and Salford and their suburbs was but about 200,000, whereas, according to the census of 1871, it had risen to be over 500,000. There can be no doubt that the deputation did a good service to Manchester, for, in the following year, an Act of Parliament was passed "to enable her Majesty's Postmaster-General to acquire a site for the extension of the Manchester General Post Office." It was not, however, until eight years afterwards that the new General Post Office was completed and ready for occupation. A site had been selected in Brown Street, adjoining the old Post Office, a magnificent edifice erected thereon, and in September, 1884, the business was transferred from the old to the new premises.

The building was erected from the designs of Mr. Williams, the surveyor to Her Majesty's Board of Works, at a cost of about £120,000, and it is certainly one of the most imposing structures in the city. It is in the modern classical style, with separate fronts, one in Spring Gardens and the other in Brown Street. The external walls are of Portland stone, relieved at intervals by elaborate carvings. The extreme length is 246 feet, breadth 122 feet, and the area 3,334 square yards. The height of the building is about 78 feet. The principal front is to Spring Gardens. On this side there is a granite portico supported by massive Corinthian fluted pillars, some 30 feet high. In the basement are the delivery room, engineers' room, battery-room, general clerks' retiring room, &c. On the ground floor is the sorting-office, to which reference is made further on. On this floor there are also private bag-rooms, a registered letter office, postmaster's office, the telegraph office, boxes for the postage of letters, &c. On the first floor, which is reached by means of a broad stone staircase, are the enquiry office, inspector's room, general dining-room, &c. On the second floor is the telegraphic instrument department, located in a room 142 feet by 117 feet, dining-rooms, &c. There are letter receiving boxes both in Spring Gardens and Brown Street. It is an edifice in all respects worthy of the city it adorns, though by no means too extensive for the growing requirements of Manchester.

The site is an admirable one, and in this respect the mercantile community of Manchester are much more fortunate than those of

Liverpool, as the General Post Office in the latter city is in anything but a central or convenient position, either as regards the commercial classes or general public. There are, in Manchester, six deliveries daily (except Sunday) in the central district, from the head office, namely, at 7 and 10.45 A.M., 12 noon, 1.30, 4.15, and 7 P.M. And there are five deliveries in the other districts, namely, at 7 A.M., 12 noon, and at 2, 4.45, and 7.30 P.M. On Sundays there is only one early delivery throughout the district. In the matter of branch post offices, receiving offices, and pillar-boxes, both Manchester and Salford are well supplied, for there are five branch offices with telegraph and money order offices attached, about twenty receiving offices with similar accommodation, and about fifty receiving offices with money order offices *only* attached; and, in addition to these, there are upwards of one hundred and thirty pillar letter boxes throughout the postal district. In the aggregate the working staff employed is very large.

About a year ago there appeared in the *Manchester Guardian* a most interesting and instructive article headed "The Work of the Manchester Post Office," and as the facts and figures therein quoted may be relied upon as authentic, we select a few for the information of our readers. At that time (March, 1887) there were in the Manchester postal and telegraph departments no fewer than 1,511 persons. Of this number 777 were clerks, sorting-clerks, stampers, porters, and letter-carriers, engaged in the first-named department, while the number of telegraphists (male and female) and messengers in the second was 734. In 1876 the number of letters posted in the Manchester district every week averaged 1,367,326, and 974,065 delivered, besides which there

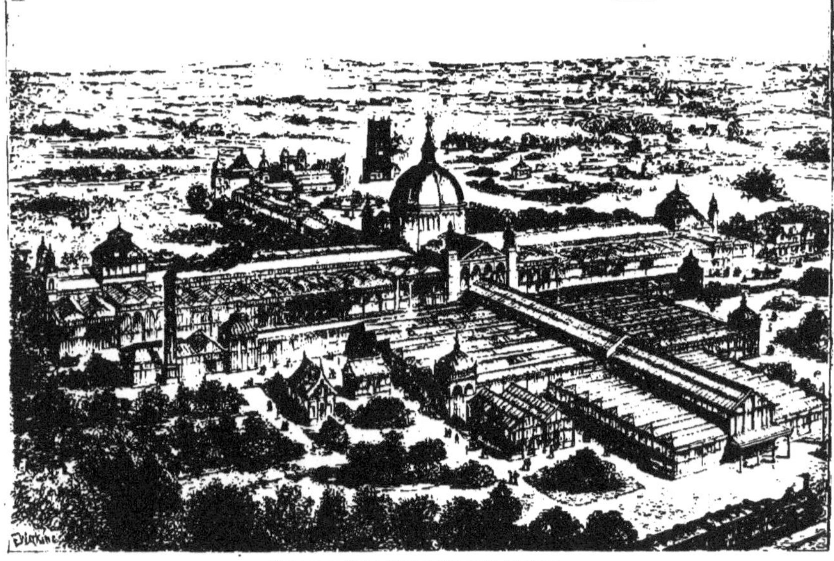

MANCHESTER ROYAL JUBILEE EXHIBITION BUILDINGS.

were 393,736 letters passing through; such, for instance, as letters posted at Leeds for Bristol, which would go through the Manchester office. In 1886 (though the ten years intervening were for the most part marked by great commercial depression) the figures still showed an increase, for the weekly average was: letters posted 1,861,025, letters delivered 1,394,889, and the number passing through amounted to 491,322. It will readily be understood that to deal with this enormous mass of correspondence the most complete organisation and precision are necessary, inasmuch as any hitch would lead to serious consequences. But the thorough efficiency of the system may be judged by the fact that even on such occasions as Christmas and New Year's eve, and St. Valentine's eve, when the work of the office is greatly increased, the dispatch and delivery of letters are got through satisfactorily, and the public are in no way inconvenienced. The principal work in connection with the receipt and despatch of the mails is carried on in a room 202 feet long and in the widest part 82 feet across, and it is lighted at night by parallel lines of gas jets extending from end to end. The number of letter bags despatched daily from the Manchester Post Office amounted in 1886 to 955, and the number received to 1,399. It may be stated that the rural postal district of Manchester is very wide, and the manipulation of letters for places within this area constitutes a very heavy part of the work of the office. It is well-known that all letters passing through the Post Office are stamped with the name of the Post Office, and again, to mark the stamp. It will, perhaps, surprise many to learn that this stamping process can be effected by hand, by expert stampers, at the rate of 165 per minute, and by a machine (the invention of Mr. Pearson Hill, a son of Sir Rowland Hill, the founder of the penny postal system), at the rate of upwards of 190 per minute. To an accomplished "sorter" the worst calligraphy presents no obstacles, and whilst an average sorter will dispose of 65 letters per minute, an expert will master between 70 and 80. One of the most remarkable departments in connection with the Manchester Post Office is that styled the "Dead Letter Office," which, in other words, means letters in regard to which the postal authorities are unable to discover the persons to whom they are addressed. Letters of this character, from nearly all the Post Offices from the Potteries to the border on the western side of England, are sent to Manchester to be disposed of. They are taken to a large apartment in the upper part of the building in the General Post Office, where they are opened by a staff of young ladies, and a register taken of them. In 1886 the number of "dead letters" which came into the hands of these fair Government officials reached the enormous number of 946,852, and the value of the property found in them amounted to £30,000. Property so discovered, principally money orders, stamps, &c., is kept for a given period in the event of a claimant appearing, but, should no one assert a right to it, it is ultimately paid into the Treasury. The arrangements for the loading and unloading of the mail carts are most ingenious and complete. This is conducted at the Market Street end of the Post Office, under a glass-covered roof. The doors of the sorting office, before described, are some feet above the level of the roadway, and are reached by a couple of platforms, which can be raised or lowered by hydraulic power as required. Upon the arrival of a mail van a truck is run out from the office on to the platform, which is at once lowered to the level of the floor of the van. In a few moments the bags are placed upon the truck, the platform is raised, and the truck wheeled into the sorting room. The vans are loaded by a similar process. These facts regarding the Manchester Post Office and the extent of its business prove its immense utility, and bear eloquent evidence to its systematic and perfect organisation.

ROYAL JUBILEE EXHIBITION.

It would be unjust to Manchester to omit from our pages all mention of the great "Jubilee Exhibition," which will ever rank as one of the most successful undertakings with which the name of the city has been associated. The energy and enterprise of Manchester men are known all over the world, and if no further proof could be adduced than their management of this marvellous exhibition, it would fully justify their eminent reputation for organisation, integrity, and commercial ability of the highest order.

On referring to the annals of Manchester it is seen that the great event of the year 1857 was the Exhibition of Art Treasures of the United Kingdom, at Old Trafford, which (as has truly been observed) "demonstrated the wealth of the British artistic possessions." That exhibition, like the recent one, was a great success, and reflected honour upon Manchester. It was opened by the late Prince Consort, on Tuesday, the 5th of May, the Prince on that occasion being the guest of James Watts, Esq., at Abney Hall. On the following day, May 6th, the Prince visited Peel Park, and there inaugurated Noble's statue of Queen Victoria. On Tuesday the 30th June following, Her Majesty the Queen visited the exhibition, being accompanied by the Prince Consort, the Prince of Wales, Prince Alfred (now Duke of Edinburgh), the Princess Royal, the Princess Alice, and Prince Frederick William of Prussia, now Crown Prince of Germany and the husband of the Princess Royal.

On the following day (1st July), the Queen and the other royal personages again visited the exhibition, privately, and on this occasion the public was rigidly excluded. The Queen, during her stay in this neighbourhood, was the guest of the Earl and Countess of Ellesmere, at Worsley Hall, near Manchester.

At later periods the exhibition was visited by a great number of royal and illustrious personages, including the late King of the Belgians and the Princess Marie Charlotte (afterwards the consort of the ill-fated Emperor Maximilian of Mexico), the Comte de Flanders (the present King of the Belgians), the late Queen of the Netherlands, the Duchess of Cambridge, the Princess Mary (now Duchess of Teck), the Duke of Cambridge, the Comte de Paris, the Duc de Nemours, Prince Napoleon, and many others.

There were exhibited in this exhibition 5,812 pictorial works of art, comprising 1,173 ancient pictures, 689 modern pictures, 386 portraits, 969 water-colour drawings, 260 sketches and original drawings, 1,475 engravings, 500 miniatures, 597 photographs, and 63 architectural drawings. In addition to these, there were 160 pieces of sculpture, besides 10,000 objects of art in the general museum, making a grand total of 15,972.

The historian records the fact that visitors came from all parts of the world to see the art treasures, and also that the exhibition gave rise to an extensive literature. A tolerably complete collection of the books relating to this exhibition, including some in the Lancashire dialect, are to be found in the Manchester Free Reference Library.

The exhibition of 1857 was closed on the 17th October, having been open one hundred and forty-two days, of which two, the opening day and that of the public visit of Her Majesty the Queen, were reserved for the holders of two-guinea season tickets. The total number of paying visitors during the season was 1,053,538, of ticket holders 283,177, making a total of 1,336,715. The receipts were £110,588 9s. 8d., being £304 14s. 4d. over the expenditure.

It is true that the numbers which attended the exhibition of 1857 are small when compared with the numbers that have attended that of 1887, and it is also probable that the profits of the 1857 exhibition will appear ridiculously small when compared with those which are confidently anticipated from the last one; still it must be borne in mind that the first exhibition was on an infinitely smaller scale, and it was confined to works of art. On that occasion there was no display of machinery in motion, there were no exhibits of the thousand and one specimens of British trades and manufactures, no illuminated gardens, fairy fountains, or representations of "Ancient Manchester and Salford," to interest and attract the masses from both far and near; it was purely, as its name described it, an "Art Treasures Exhibition," and, as such, it achieved a most wonderful success.

The Manchester Exhibition, to commemorate the Jubilee of Her Majesty Queen Victoria's reign, styled "The Royal Jubilee Exhibition," was opened at Old Trafford on May 3rd by the Prince and Princess of Wales. An address by the Corporation was presented to the Prince and Princess on their arrival in Manchester, after which the procession passed through some of the principal streets of the city to the exhibition, when the opening ceremony took place. The day was observed as a general holiday, and on the evenings of the 3rd and 4th of May the municipal buildings and many other institutions and warehouses were brilliantly illuminated.

On May 4th the Prince and Princess paid a second visit to the Exhibition, and then proceeded through Salford. Before their departure they were entertained at luncheon at the Manchester Town Hall. During their visit they were the guests of Lord and Lady Egerton of Tutton, at Tutton Park.

From the day of opening to that of its closing it may with truth be said that the exhibition enjoyed a season of uninterrupted prosperity. A number of things contributed to this:—the contents of the Exhibition itself, which were of the most attractive and interesting character possible, the excellent musical and other entertainments provided both indoors and in the grounds outside; the cheap and abundant railway facilities, &c.; glorious weather, and, though last, not least, energetic and able management. It is scarcely possible to give a description of the vast collection of wonderful productions of all kinds which were brought together under the exhibition roof. They comprised everything which could illustrate the progress which this country has made in every branch of art, science, trade, and manufactures during the reign of Queen Victoria.

Such a display of machinery, at rest and in motion, was perhaps never before witnessed, and the vast building was literally crammed with objects of wondrous workmanship and design. The picture galleries were of immense extent, no less than thirteen rooms (running parallel) being fitted up as galleries. Of these one was about 90 feet square, five more were 100 feet by 30 feet, and the other seven were 90 feet by 30 feet. The five larger rooms were hung with oil paintings by living artists, four of the smaller ones contained oil paintings by deceased artists; a fifth, water-colour drawings, drawings in black and white, engravings, and etchings; the sixth, water-colour drawings by living artists; the seventh, water-colour drawings by deceased artists; and the square room, or Central Hall, contained portraits of distinguished statesmen and others, and oil paintings by living artists. Altogether the pictures numbered over 2,100, and, without doubt, they formed the most attractive feature of the exhibition.

It may not be out of place here to mention the fact that at the exhibition of 1857 there were exhibited the works of all ages and

MANCHESTER ROYAL JUBILEE EXHIBITION. THE CENTRAL DOME.

countries, whereas at the last exhibition the pictures were modern and, with rare exceptions, by British artists, and painted in the reign of Queen Victoria; and, considered as such, the collection was matchless.

Not the least pleasing and noticeable circumstance in connection with the picture galleries was the fact that the interest of the working classes in viewing them was quite equal to that manifested by those of more exalted social rank.

The exhibition buildings were in two divisions, separated from each other by Talbot Road, but access from the one to the other was gained by means of a broad wooden covered bridge which crossed Talbot Road. The main building was erected in the grounds adjoining the Botanic Gardens, lying to the right of Talbot Road coming from Manchester, and in this portion were situated the sections devoted to industrial design and handicrafts, chemical and collateral industries Irish manufactures, &c., fine arts, photography, music, &c. In this division were also placed the kitchens and the principal refreshment rooms. The back opened into the grounds of the Botanic Gardens, where the models of "Old Manchester and Salford" were erected, including a church tower containing a full peal of bells. The gardens were beautifully arranged for the purposes of the exhibition, and every facility provided for the comfort, convenience, and amusement of visitors, in the shape of dining and tea rooms, refreshment bars, lavatories, and musical performances (of a very high order) whilst, after dusk, the gardens and lakes were magnificently illuminated with lamps, after the oriental style, besides which there was an immense fairy fountain, which threw up water, in constantly changing colours, to an immense height. The gardens—which are always laid out in admirable order, and contain conservatories, fern-houses, two extensive lakes, and numerous flower-beds, &c.—formed a superb promenade, and being abundantly supplied with seats and chairs, proved one of the greatest attractions connected with the exhibition. There were several band-stands erected in the grounds, and these were, throughout the whole season, occupied by the leading bands, military and civilian, from the Metropolis and all parts of the country. The gardens are situated betwixt Talbot Road and Chester Road, the main entrance to them being from the latter road, and visitors could obtain admittance to the exhibition through the gardens from Chester Road, as well as from Talbot Road. The "Royal Entrance" was constructed in Chester Road, and the Prince and Princess of Wales entered thereat, passing from thence into the exhibition down a grand avenue of flowers, foliage, and sculpture. The exhibition contained a magnificent music-room, provided with a spacious orchestra and a large and splendid organ, and frequent organ recitals and band performances were given daily. Coming now to the second division of the exhibition, on the other side of Talbot Road, there were the two vast sections devoted to machinery at rest and machinery in motion, which may, indeed, fairly be described as having formed an exhibition in themselves. This portion of the building excited the wonder and admiration of all beholders, young and old, and was always full of visitors. In this division was the third-class refreshment room. In the grounds adjoining this division were a number of open air exhibits of various descriptions—a creamery, a bakery, a switch-back railway, a tobogganning slide, a spacious cycling track, a band-stand, and a grand stand from which to view the performances of the cyclists, athletes, &c. From these grounds access was obtained to the platform of the Manchester South Junction and Altrincham Railway Company, which, in conjunction with the London and North-Western Railway Company, had erected a station at this point for the convenience of visitors to the exhibition from different parts of the country, who were thus brought within a few yards of the exhibition itself. There were, during the whole season, 'buses and other conveyances of all sorts incessantly plying to and from the exhibition, and putting down and taking up passengers, at both Talbot Road and Chester Road entrances, and the police arrangements, inside and outside the exhibition, were excellent. The exhibition was closed on the 10th of November, having been open 165 days. The total number of admissions from the opening, on May 3rd, was 4,765,137. The following were the six largest attendances during the period it was open: Saturday, October 15th, 74,595; Tuesday, June 21st (Jubilee Day), 70,141; Saturday, November 5th, 69,602; Monday, August 1st, 69,555; Saturday, October 22nd, 66,495; Saturday, October, 29th, 65,807. The smallest attendance was on Friday, August 26th, when the numbers were 14,171. With the single exception of the Colonial Exhibition, held in London in 1886, and which, of course, being a national affair, attracted visitors from all parts of the world, the Manchester Exhibition has eclipsed all exhibitions held in recent years as regards the number of visitors, as may be seen from the following figures: "Colonial" (1886), 5,540,336; Manchester (1887), 4,765,137; "Health," London (1884), 4,153,390; "Inventions," London (1885), 3,760,581; Edinburgh (1886), 2,769,632; "Fisheries," London (1883), 2,703,051; Liverpool (1886), 2,668,118; Newcastle-on-Tyne (1887), 2,092,273; Saltaire, 823,133. The figures relating to Manchester include the attendance of 40,000 season ticket holders, and 52,656 children who were admitted at reduced rates. On the day of closing Sir Joseph Lee, the chairman of the executive committee, stated that the guarantors might rest assured that the expenditure had been kept within proper and legitimate limits, and that at an early date they would be released from the liability they incurred in guaranteeing the sum of £140,000. According to a statement which appeared in the *Manchester Guardian*, the day after the closing, the receipts were put down in the aggregate at about a quarter of a million, towards which the exhibitors had contributed about £23,000, and the refreshment contractor about £40,000. It is highly probable, therefore, that there will be a handsome surplus announced when the accounts are published. The closing ceremony, on the 10th of November, was very numerously and influentially attended, and the proceedings most appropriately terminated with the singing of the Hallelujah Chorus and the National Anthem. The inhabitants of Manchester and Salford may justly feel proud at the splendid success which attended their Jubilee Exhibition; indeed, it would be strange if they did not, for, from first to last, everything connected with it prospered. Very great credit is justly due, for the gratifying result attained, to the members of the executive committee, with Sir Joseph Lee at their head, to the general manager, Mr. S. Lee Bapty, and to the secretary, Mr. A. A. Gillies. There can be no doubt, either, that the whole staff, from these gentlemen downwards, discharged their duties in a most able, diligent, and exemplary manner, and they are fully entitled to the credit and honour attending the brilliant achievements of their united, energetic, and enterprising efforts. With this we must close our historical and chronological sketch and leave future events to future publications. We now refer our readers to the following pages, which contain a review of leading establishments of Manchester, a careful perusal of which will be found interesting and instructive to all.

MARKET STREET AND TIB STREET, MANCHESTER.

Messrs. Rylands & Sons, Limited, Cotton Spinners, Manufacturers, Bleachers, Dyers, and Finishers, Manchester and London.—It is the privilege of almost every great commercial nation to take credit for the achievements of some firm whose name has become a practical synonym for the particular branch of mercantile or manufacturing undertaking in which it engages. Such a firm is, unquestionably, that whose world-renowned title appears at the head of this sketch. The distinguished and eminently representative house of Messrs. Rylands & Sons, Limited, has been no exception to the very general rule that has long obtained in connection with the inception of some of our most famous commercial and productive enterprises. It commenced its operations upon a decidedly modest scale, but from the proverbial "small beginnings" the similarly proverbial "great endings" have resulted, and the firm in question holds a position to-day which justifies in every sense their being entitled the monarchs of the cotton industry of England. This gigantic business, of which our present sketch must be necessarily concise, though it is hoped not greatly inadequate, dates virtually from the year 1819, and the following history of its foundation will be found interesting. When John Rylands joined his brother Joseph, he (John) undertook to travel, which he did throughout Shropshire, parts of Cheshire and North Wales, as well as Lancashire and Yorkshire, in order to sell their goods. He travelled on horseback, as was very general in those days, and carried his patterns in his saddle-bags. These journeys were very successful, and necessitated the rapid increase of their production of goods. Joseph Rylands attended to the manufacturing department and the execution of orders, &c., for which he was far better suited than for travelling, or for buying and selling. Finding his sons getting on so well, about the year 1819 Mr. Rylands, sen., asked them to join him, which they did at Wigan, and the firm then became what it is now, viz., Rylands & Sons. This business had been in existence for some years, and had made no inconsiderable success prior to the effecting of the partnership in question; but the latter event contributed in a very large measure to the extension of its scope. At first the house dealt principally with Chester, but Mr. John Rylands eventually proposed transferring those relations to the rapidly rising and progressive Manchester. This step was duly taken, and its immediate outcome was the opening of small premises in New High Street, in the latter city. On the site of this original location now stands the huge and magnificent structure of the firm's principal Manchester warehouse. The resources of the concern rapidly developed, and in 1824 two estates of good size were purchased near Wigan, and mills for dyeing, bleaching, and producing cotton and linen yarn were erected thereon and started in active operation. Here also was found a rich vein of coal, which the firm immediately began to mine, greatly to their own advantage, as may readily be imagined. In 1840 Mr. Joseph Rylands, jun., retired from the business, in 1847 Joseph Rylands, sen., died; and thus the entire control of the concern became vested in the one man who was of all others (as every record of the house tends to show) peculiarly fitted, by character and capacity, to become the head of a colossal industrial undertaking. Mr. John Rylands at once entered, fearlessly and entirely dependent now upon his own resources, upon the course of enterprise and ceaseless activity he has ever since pursued with such splendid and well-nigh unparalleled results. Mill after mill was bought, extended, or entirely erected; development followed development, departure succeeded departure; and by the year 1873 the concern had attained to such gigantic proportions as to be productive, doubtless, of no little anxiety to the one man whose sole efforts had been responsible for such a magnificent effect. Indeed, it is not difficult to believe that Mr. Rylands' position was in some measure analogous to that of Frankenstein—both had created a "monster" which became almost beyond individual control and management. At all events Mr. Rylands had every justification for accepting the relief offered from the strain of so exceptionally heavy a personal responsibility as the continued direction, unaided, of an enterprise of such stupendous magnitude; and there have been few projects of the kind more auspiciously mooted or more successfully realised than the formation fourteen years ago of the business of Rylands & Sons into a limited liability company, trading under the title given at the head of this review, retaining Mr. John Rylands himself as its governor, and inaugurating its career with the immense capital of £2,000,000 sterling, comprised in 100,000 shares of £20 each. Of this capital no less than £1,500,000 is paid up. The records of the house from that time onward are simply the history of industrial and commercial success—an amplification of prosperity that has had few parallels, and surely no superior, in the annals of mercantile England. The transactions of the firm, annually, are represented in millions; the yearly output of goods ranges in weight from 20,000 to 30,000 tons; the total force of hands employed is placed at close upon 12,000. Seventeen mills and factories are controlled, all in active operation; and the unique music arising from the almost ceaseless action of the 5,000 looms and 200,000 spindles that appertain to these immense hives of industry is a fitting accompaniment to the constant progress of an industry whose yearly income is positively in excess of that of many a State of recognised standing in the political world. The firm are immense importers, principally of raw cotton, which is for the most part spun and manufactured at their mills. In addition to this they draft into England from all parts of the world a well-nigh inexhaustible variety of commercial commodities of divers descriptions. They are merchants in the broadest and most cosmopolitan sense of the word. Their imports in cotton alone range from 5,000 to 6,000 tons in weight, and amount to upwards of £250,000 annually in value. The weight of their other imports aggregates about 2,000 tons per annum. In considering the exports of the Company, it is not difficult to imagine Mr. John Rylands in that happily-depicted character drawn by Oliver Wendell Holmes—the great merchant "sitting in his arm-chair in a velvet cap and flowered robe, with a globe by him to show the range of his commercial transactions;" for the operations of the house of which Mr. Rylands was practically the founder and is now the governor, extend to well-nigh every quarter of the world. Canada, Australasia, the United States, Europe generally, South Africa, the West Indies—all these are profitable markets, ever open to the commodities of the house; and a magnificent export trade is controlled despite the legislative restrictions of protective tariffs, which are characteristic of nearly all the countries named. It is far beyond the scope or capacity of this review to survey at any length the more particular features of this Company's industrial operations; but the firm's manufactures must be specified, and this can perhaps be in no way better accomplished within the space at our disposal than by a concise enumeration of the principal works of Messrs. Rylands, and a brief mention of the special products of the same. The chief factories of the house are situate and engaged as follows:—Gorton Mills, near Manchester—a fine brick building, enclosing three sides of a square, fitted with 1,550 looms, employing 1,350 hands, possessing engines of 2,000 indicated horse-power, and producing the firm's noted grey Dacca calicoes, sheetings, twills, and jeannettes. Gidlow Works, Wigan, a magnificent range of modern buildings, in every respect one of the foremost industrial features of the county, employing 1,300 hands, equipped with 1,600 looms, and engines of 2,000 horse-power (indicated), producing 300,000 to 400,000 yards weekly of superior Dacca calicoes for bleaching, twills for the celebrated finish of silesias, and cloth for printing. Mather Street Mills, Bolton, engines 700 horse-power, indicated, 600 Jacquard looms, 500 employés, making a large weekly production of dimities, satin

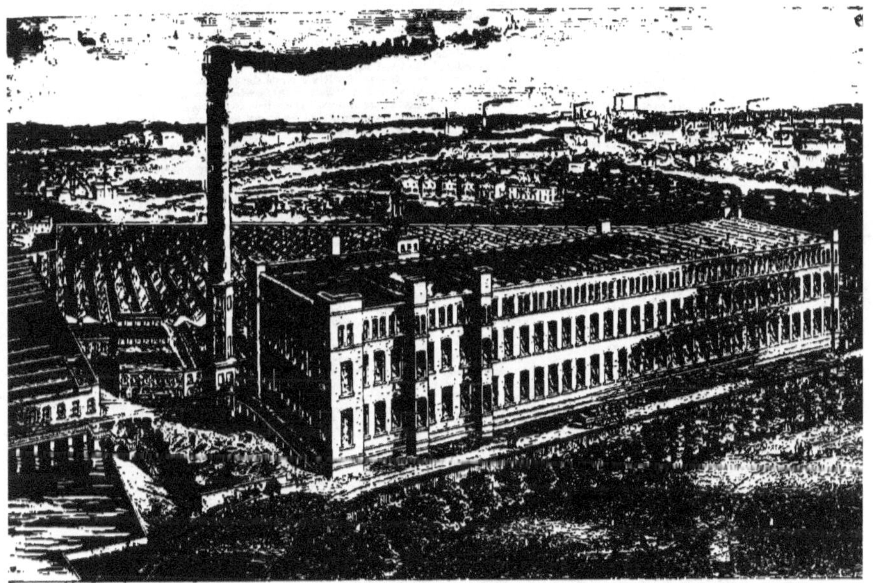

GIDLOW WORKS, WIGAN.

s) damasks, brocades, sattcens,
fancy novelties. The Swinton
great area of ground; engines
s, 800 employés, production in
Oxfords, Galateas, and coloured
The Heapy Bleach Works, near
lding, covering with the reserves,
leaching and dyeing, with water
about 2,000,000 gallons, engines
loyés. Floor Oil Cloth Works,
improved facilities; engines in-
; very large output of oil-cloths
Dacca Mills, Manchester, an im-
600 hands, fitted with engines of
ut great quantities of this noted
sewing cottons, India tapes, and
Longford Works, Manchester; a
block, of great range and dimen-
production of ready-made cloth-
stumes, corsets, shirts, under-cloth-
jackets, cloaks, dolmans, ulsters,
works for cabinet making, pack-
k, situate in Hulme Street. The
a large and commodious building
execution of letterpress and litho-
of pattern-cards and paper boxes.
blishments, it is safe to say, does
ntrol of any one house. Messrs.
magnificent warehouses in Man-
and Market Street (Bridgewater
itectural and mercantile features
tain enormous stocks of goods, as
for magnitude. The same words
perb London warehouses, situate
p Lane, E.C. The limits of our
s to mention the self-evident fact,
agement, the sound principles and
distinguished the conduct of this
sonal traits of its distinguished
or, still characterise the house, and
its every undertaking. We have
nt features of a concern regarding
l; and, in doing so, have surveyed,
out any exaggeration, be denomi-
an industry, than which there is
atial in the whole range of British

& Sons, Cotton Spinners
o.—In reviewing the great indus-
most importance must be assigned
of the country. These immense
ose the true source whence origi-
nation. A representative manufac-
is house of Messrs. Robert McClure
urers, whose works are known as
s at St. Peter's Square, Manchester.
this establishment may with every
t the principal trading stations of
is the natural result of a long and
productions of this house in cotton
y received as to result in a demand,
an almost unlimited extent. The
superior texture and high finish;
minent lead. The mills at Stock-
ng a conspicuous feature of the
n and effective machinery, and
ratives. The principals are Mr.
McClure, J.P. Mr. John McClure
been formerly Mayor of Stockport,
able position of Colonel of the 4th
are well known, widely respected,

mist, 81, Piccadilly.—This
the year 1828, by Mr. J. Lessey,
cher, Mr. Theophilus Lessey, and
or, Mr. R. L. Pickup, in the year
d roomy emporium, of attractive
d substantially furnished. There
ck-room. Mr. Pickup is the pro-
Eye Salve, an ointment that has an
ation all over the three kingdoms,
l. Pickup's Stomach Mixture is
nd its immediate neighbourhood,
d is daily becoming more widely
he usual drugs, toilet requisites,
and chemists' sundries. Mr. Pickup himself personally superintends the dispensing of all important prescriptions, and guarantees the absolute purity and perfection of all ingredients. A staff of fully qualified assistants is engaged behind the counters, and there is a branch post office located on the premises. The sole proprietor is Mr. R. L. Pickup, whose talent, experience, and ability, fully deserve the undoubted success the business has achieved.

T. Hayward & Co., Glass and China Dealers, 64, Deansgate.—This business was established in this city in the year 1811, by Mr. S. Armitt (succeeded by Mr. T. Harper), and eventually fell into the hands of Mr. J. Lownds, and gradually became known as one of the most important of its kind. The present proprietor has been in possession about ten years, and has done very much to add to the attractiveness and high-class character of the business. The display of glass, china, and art pottery is magnificent, and would appear to be a unique collection containing many pieces of almost priceless gems. Each year Messrs. Hayward & Co. make a special exhibition of the most exquisite productions of the year in the way of glass, porcelain, and pottery. Many choice examples of the finest works, from the Royal Worcester Porcelain Manufactory and from Messrs. Doulton's establishments, pieces of the celebrated Wedgwood ware and Minton china services, together with modern Spode and Derby, are shown. The whole collection is worthy a visit from connoisseurs and amateurs for many miles round. The premises consist of a most handsomely decorated and elegantly appointed shop of great size; the small frontage gives but little idea of its large proportions. The stock is enormous, and includes useful as well as ornamental goods; and the connection is high-class and extremely numerous. The managing partner is Mr. Thomas Hayward, a gentleman whose excellent taste and sound judgment are acknowledged and fully appreciated in this city.

Messrs. Stott & Sons, Consulting Engineers and Mill Architects, 60, Haworth's Buildings.—Engineering and architectural interests constitute a most important item in the commercial activity of Great Britain, and in no place in the world are its operations more perfected than in England. A prominent house in this department is that of Messrs. Stott & Sons, mill architects and consulting engineers, who, besides premises at the above location, have a branch office at 12, Clegg Street, Oldham. Established forty years ago, the firm changed to its present title of Stott & Sons about eight years since, and have occupied their present offices about three years, where, in addition to the businesses of architects and consulting engineers, an additional branch is carried on as surveyors and valuers for probate and legacy duty, &c., assessors for losses by fire for the insured only. The immense reputation enjoyed by this firm in mill architecture and consulting engineering shows itself by the erection of some twenty or thirty of the largest mills of modern date during a period of the past three or four years. In the engineering department the well-known practical experience of Messrs. Stott & Sons is very extensively sought for by capitalists, companies, and owners and managers of large works, and similar undertakings throughout the length and breadth of the kingdom. Messrs. Stott & Sons are the patentees of a system of fireproof flooring now largely used, and which, whilst giving greater stability, enables them to dispense with more than one half of the usual number of columns; and they have recently taken out a patent for an arrangement of triple expansion engine suitable to mill-driving. The premises in Haworth's Buildings comprise a magnificent suite of offices, elegantly fitted and furnished, and admirably adapted to the requirements of the establishment, and provides employment for a large staff of clerks, draughtsmen, and gentlemen of the highest professional abilities and greatest mechanical experience, whose advice and opinions are highly valued. The gentlemen representing the partnership are: Jesse Ainsworth Stott, and Abraham Henthorn Stott, junior, who are of the highest integrity and commercial status, well known and widely respected.

Glass, Witty & Co., Fine Art Dealers and Publishers 24 and 26, Millen Street.—Prominent among the great industries of the age, the interesting branch of business taken up by the fine arts and their accessories is one claiming a special notice, more particularly on account of its great public utility. A representative house in this line is Messrs. Glass, Witty & Co. Established in 1883, the growth of business has been very steady. The firm is noted as dealers in fine arts (oil paintings and water colours particularly); and as publishers they have acquired a sound reputation, the transactions in this department alone amounting to a large item. The business done is large and purely wholesale. The exports form an important feature, while the home trade is large. The premises comprise a bold five-storey building, utilised throughout its whole extent for trade purposes and stock. The stock is extensive, and includes the latest patterns in gilt and other mouldings of every kind. Modern frame-making in all its branches is carried on, as are also mount-cutting and the making of all kinds of moulds. As an index of the important operations of this firm, upwards of fifty skilled operatives find constant employment on these premises, and the machinery in use is fitted with all the latest improvements. The principals are gentlemen well known in artistic and literary circles.

The Commercial Union Assurance Co., Ltd., 47, Spring Gardens.—Where there is such enormous material wealth, in the shape of buildings and valuable merchandise packed into comparatively small area, there is an abundant field for insurance enterprise. The handsome building occupied by the Commercial Union Assurance Company, Limited, was especially constructed some seven years since to meet the growing requirements of this great company, for the conduct of its immense business in the district of which this city is the centre. The office has been established here for over a quarter of a century, having been originally located in Cheapside, and having removed to its present splendid offices on their completion in 1882. The Commercial Union is a complete and comprehensive office, taking every branch of business and every description of risk that can be enumerated, whether life, fire, or marine. Its annual income from all sources is upwards of twelve hundred thousand pounds, and its accumulated funds exceed two and a half millions, all most judiciously and safely invested on undeniable security, in addition to which there is a fully subscribed capital of two millions and a half. To enumerate all the descriptions of risk and insurance undertaken by the Commercial Union Assurance Company, Limited, would occupy needless space, but it may not be out of place to refer to some special features which serve to reveal the comprehensive nature of the undertaking, and to establish the fact that it is entitled to rank amongst the most complete insurance institutions yet developed. It insures rent of all buildings, whether payable or receivable, and in the Farm Stock department it pays for animals *killed by lightning*, if insured against fire. It insures pictures, prints, drawings, and sculpture, on exceptionally liberal terms and conditions. It offers special facilities for insurances in foreign countries and distant parts of the world, including ships and their cargoes lying in foreign and colonial ports, and it will quote rates (after survey, which will be made free of charge) for sugar refineries, biscuit bakeries, distilleries, musical instrument manufactories, cotton, flax, and hemp works, calico print works, rice and corn mills, saw mills, oil mills, woollen and worsted mills, and other hazardous risks, any of which can be insured by special agreement and on moderate terms. In the Life Department the rates of the Commercial Union Office are exceedingly favourable, as a very brief comparison with those of other good offices will at once establish. Being a proprietary company, with an enormous subscribed capital, and a wealthy and numerous body of shareholders, the Commercial Union offers elements of security to prospective insurers, which are by no means to be disregarded in making a selection. The business of this large and important branch establishment of the Commercial Union has been for more than twenty years under the management of Mr. J. V. C. Rivaz, who fulfils the functions both of secretary and underwriter, and who enjoys the assistance and support of a special board of directors, composed of gentlemen of the highest standing in the city. Everything about the offices in Spring Gardens, including the handsome erection, bespeaks the fact that here is a great enterprise most carefully and energetically conducted.

Henry Marriott & Co., Manufacturers of Ticks, Regattas, Fancy Shirtings, &c., Dyers and Bleachers, 23, Portland Street.—Under the heading of cotton goods comes a vast number of materials, and ticks, regattas and shirtings hold no unimportant place in the list. Manchester of course, is the head-quarters of the manufacture of these commodities, and a firm of good repute engaged is that of Messrs. Henry Marriott & Co., which was founded by Mr. Henry R. Marriott, who retired in 188[illegible]. This name is well-known in commercial and manufacturing circles all over the world. The business was formerly carried on in London, from 1825 till 1849, when manufacturing was commenced. The premises occupied consist of a fine four-storied building, large and commodious, the offices being on the ground floor, and the warehousing department on the remaining floors. The offices are well arranged and furnished, bearing an air thoroughly in accordance with the reputation and prosperity of the firm. The warehousing departments are very spacious, and contain an immense stock of cotton, union, and linen ticks, striped and checked regattas, fancy shirtings, dyed and printed twills, pocketings, black backs, and other similar commodities. The mills where these goods are manufactured are at Stockport, and are very extensive, the machinery and appliances being of the most moder pattern, and the hands employed numerous, experienced, and conjointl capable of turning out an enormous quantity of stuffs. The durabilit of the ticks, the tastefulness of the striped and checked regattas and fanc shirtings, dyed and printed twills, pocketings, &c., are remarkabl and are acknowledged qualities of the goods of this firm, and a ver heavy home and export trade is carried on. The firm's London agent are Messrs. C. Cole & Sons, 5, Red Lion Court, Watling Street, an Mr. B. Russell, 13, Lawrence Lane, E.C.; in Glasgow they are represente by Mr. J. H. Patterson, 51, Miller Street, and in Dublin by Mr. O'Brie 8, D'Olier Street.

G. F. Arden & Sons, Oil, Tallow, and Grease Manu facturers and Refiners, Albert Oil Works, Strangeways.—One attractiv and prominent feature in the development of modern industries is th great progress made in the manufacture of all descriptions of oils, tallow and grease. This business is ably represented in Manchester by the well known firm of Messrs. G. F. Arden & Sons, of Albert Oil Work Strangeways, Manchester, who have also extensive branch stores an offices in Cardiff and Liverpool; the business at the former shipping po being ably managed by Mr. G. M. P. Daniel, at 115, Bute Docks, an the latter by Mr. Walter Crawford, at 30, Brunswick Street, both the gentlemen being well known in the shipping world. The specialities fo which this firm are noted are the "Ardens' Lubricant for Land an Marine Steam Engine Cylinders," "Ardens' Marine Engine Oils," "Ardens' Compound Engine Oils," "Ardens' Matchless Gas Engin Oils," as supplied to her Majesty's Government, "Ardens' Boiler Com position, for preventing and removing Incrustation in Steam Boilers; machinery oils of every description; mill, railway, and colliery grease engine waste for steam ships, &c. Special double-refined tallow, whic is largely used by some of the best firms in the cotton trade for sizing, &c This business was founded some twenty years ago by Mr. George Frederic Arden, who died in September, 1886. Since that time it has bee carried on under the management of Mr. Frederick Victor Arden an Mr. Herbert Jackson Arden. The firm has established for itself reputation of the very highest order for the superior quality of the goods, the result of the many years' trading being that a most extensiv business has been established, the goods of this firm finding open marke in all the principal commercial centres of the United Kingdom, in additio to a large and valuable export trade. A special feature of this firm the extensive shipping business carried on at Cardiff and Liverpool, th concern being patronised by some of the best-known firms in the shippin trade in London, Cardiff, and Liverpool. The works at Strangeway comprise a large and substantial building, fitted with the most expensiv plant and high-class modern and most effective machinery for the pro duction and refining of the goods manufactured, and employing a larg number of highly skilled workmen, besides a large staff of traveller whose avocation takes them to all parts of the kingdom. The works Strangeways were built under the late Mr. Arden's personal supervisio and form in every respect a model oil refinery. In addition to the o business, this firm have also been established for the last thirty years the Blackley Dyewood Mills, near Manchester, as dyewood merchants an millers. They are large importers of Laguna, Honduras, and Jamaic logwood, madder roots, turmeric, myrabolanes, fustic, peachwood, an other dyestuffs, and have established a very extensive business with cotto and silk dyers and hat manufacturers. The first-class machinery of th Blackley Mill, which is turned by water, enables Messrs. Arden to com pete most successfully in these trades. The principals are gentlemen we known on the Manchester Exchange, and are widely esteemed an respected.

Messrs. Grundy & Smith, Ancient and Moder Printsellers, 4, Exchange Street.—In art, as well as in manufactures, Man chester it is well known stands prominent in the ever-advancing march o progress, and for nicety of discrimination and accuracy of judgment i art matters the connoisseurs of this city have the reputation of superiorit over many of their brethren in large art centres. The establishment o Messrs. Grundy & Smith, ancient and modern printsellers, the fashionabl resort of the élite of society interested in art matters, was founded at th close of the last century as Messrs. Grundy & Goadsby, then Messr Grundy & Fox, subsequently Mr. John Clowes Grundy alone until th year 1868, when the firm assumed its present title of Messrs. Grundy & Smith. Having under these different forms occupied the present premise since 1827 they have formed a gallery of pictures which is well worthy o their reputation and which is a source of delight and admiration to al who visit it. In this gallery many well-known and celebrated picture have been placed for inspection, the world-wide reputation of Messrs Grundy & Smith ensuring for artists a full measure of public attention It is perhaps to the untiring energy and indefatigable industry of th late Mr. John Clowes Grundy that this gallery owes no small amount o its excellence and success; this gentleman was not only well known, bu justly celebrated all over as a first-class judge of pictures, he was also on of the originators of the Art Treasures Exhibition of 1857. The appre ciation of the public for the selections of Messrs. Grundy & Smith is wel testified by the crowds of fashionably dressed and keenly discriminatin visitors who throng the gallery, and who continually express their appre ciation of the elevating and refining associations of the place.

Chatwood Safe Co., 11, Cross Street.—In the battle that is always raging between burglars in general and safe-makers in particular, the burglars seem, of late years, to be getting decidedly the worst of it. No doubt there are still instances of cases where "thieves do break through and steal," but their chances of success are very considerably modified by having to tackle one of Chatwood's safes. The foundation of the system on which safes are still made was laid by a Mr. Richard Scott in 1801. But very many improvements have been made since then, and at the present time these most valuable accessories, either to houses or offices, are made in a manner which is almost the height of perfection. There are many very important requirements in a safe. First, it must be fire-proof, of course; but, as a consequence of this requirement, it must also be proof against breakage by falling. In case of fire, the room containing the safe may be above the level of the ground, and should the building be burnt to a serious extent, the safe may be precipitated a very great distance. It is therefore of vital importance that it should be so constructed as to be in no danger of breakage by the fall. Again, it must be impregnable against the arts of the wily burglar, and as those gentlemen are not conspicuous for ignorance in their questionable craft, very special methods of construction have to be adopted. Chatwood's safes meet these requirements in a superlative degree, and the perfection to which the manufacture has been brought by Mr. Chatwood has placed his name at the very front of all firms engaged in this branch of trade. Mr. Samuel Chatwood, who is by profession a banker's engineer, established the business in 1865, but in 1883 it was formed into a company and now carries on its operations as the Chatwood Patent Safe and Lock Co., Limited. The works, which are very extensive, are at Bolton, and known as the Lancashire Safe Works. The firm have large depôts in London, Leeds, and Manchester, the offices in Manchester being at 11, Cross Street, and consisting of a large shop and office, where a considerable stock of safes is kept. The Company seem to have gained great superiority over other firms, although they have experienced some trouble in getting the due recognition of the fact. At the Inventions Exhibition a rival firm was granted the prize for safes, but this was proved afterwards to have been quite a mistake, Mr. Chatwood's exhibits having been in some most unaccountable manner overlooked. A correction was therefore made to some extent, and Mr. Chatwood granted a gold medal. The Universal Exhibition at Paris was more noted, perhaps, for the litigation it gave rise to, but here Mr. Chatwood obtained the only medal awarded for safes of British manufacture; and in the celebrated Safe Challenge Contest, Mr. Chatwood's safe was declared to be the best, and Mr. Chatwood entitled to receive the challenge stakes. At the Netherlands Exhibition, in 1879, Mr. Chatwood was elected president of the jury on safes, and this, of course, put his exhibits entirely out of court. As no one of the other exhibits fulfilled the required conditions, it was hinted that they were too severe. Mr. Chatwood proved that was not the case by subjecting the safe he originally entered to a series of public trials in accordance with the Exhibition requirements. The safe was burnt for one hour, then allowed to fall on one of its corners from a height of 20 feet on blocks of stone 15 inches thick (which it smashed), afterwards burnt another three hours, and then subjected to the burglars' test. A safe-maker was allowed four hours' time for his workmen to open the safe. But without avail. They rendered all the chisels useless, and at the end of the time had only managed to make sufficient space to admit a crowbar, but could not even then force the door, and eventually, on the third day (under Mr. Chatwood's instruction), powerful machines had to be used to obtain access to the safe. When opened the papers previously placed therein were found intact and undamaged. The superiority of the Chatwood safes cannot, after this, be a question of much doubt, though they have been even still further improved, a novel patented system of conically intersected steel having rendered them absolutely undrillable under any circumstances whatever. There are many other features peculiar to the Chatwood safes, such as the patent T frame, the patent "solid" flange lock case, dovetail claw bolts, patent curvilinear-edged doors, the "Invincible" unpickable, gunpowder-proof lock, which can be made of platinum and infusible acid-proof. All these improvements have made the Chatwood safes unrivalled for their general excellence, and their fame reaches far and wide. Many medals, diplomas of honour, and highest awards have been bestowed upon the clever inventor, Mr. Samuel Chatwood, and the firm, of which he is still the managing director, has an unsurpassed reputation, which, it is almost unnecessary to add, is well deserved.

Dearnaley and Orrell, Cotton Brokers, 17, St. Ann's Square.—Among the leading firms of cotton brokers and commission agents in Manchester, is that of Messrs. Dearnaley & Orrell. This business was established twenty years ago by W. T. Roldman, and was changed to its present title in 1880. The members of the firm have had long practical experience, and thoroughly understand the business in its every detail. Their connections are of a widespread and high-class character. Messrs. Dearnaley & Orrell deal principally in Egyptian cotton. They are agents for Messrs. G. Frauger & Co., one of the largest firms of shippers at Alexandria. Since the death of Mr. Dearnaley, in September last, the business has been carried on by Mr. Orrell. The firm does an extensive business throughout Lancashire with the principal mill-owners and manufacturers. Mr. John Orrell is well known for his energy and integrity, and highly respected in commercial circles, and the success he is meeting with is both substantial and well deserved.

Bryce Smith & Co., Calico Printers for the Home and Shipping Trade, 16, Nicholas Street.—Among the Manchester establishments engaged in calico printing for the home and shipping trade, a very good position may be fairly claimed for that of Messrs. Bryce Smith & Co., whose works are at Whalley, near Blackburn. This firm was established about forty years ago, and some thirteen years since purchased the calico printing works at Whalley, near Blackburn, and since that time has succeeded in obtaining a good and widespread connection among the largest home trade and shipping buyers of Manchester, London, and Glasgow. The headquarters at Nicholas Street are large and commodious, comprising offices and warehouses, the former fitted in a first-rate manner, and the latter containing a large and varied assortment of printed goods. The patterns are known as being tasteful and original in design, and the general quality excellent. The works at Whalley, near Blackburn, cover the extensive area of forty acres of ground, and the machinery, which includes twenty-five printing machines with all modern appliances used for calico printing, are the latest improvements and of the most powerful description. The hands employed, numbering about five hundred, are skilful and experienced and under able management. The trade done, upon the whole, is very heavy and rapidly increasing. The sole member of this flourishing house, trading as Bryce Smith & Co., is Mr. Bryce Smith, a man of great ability and experience in the trade, making strenuous efforts for its improvement. His management of the details of the business is perfect, and among the trade members he is well known and highly respected as a man of strict integrity and unswerving honour. With all classes of the community he is deservedly popular, whilst his house occupies a prominent place in the mercantile and industrial world.

John and William Bellhouse, Timber Merchants and Carriers, Eagle Quay Saw, Planing, and Moulding Mills.—In reviewing the various branches of industrial activity that have made Manchester the great manufacturing centre of the country, it is instructive and interesting to note the advances and improvements that have been made in each, and to ascertain exactly what has been accomplished by enterprise and capital. In looking over the field it is easy to see that the timber trade has been a most important factor in our commercial activity, and in this connection it is a pleasure to make prominent mention of such an old-established and thoroughly representative firm of timber merchants and carriers as that of Messrs. John and William Bellhouse, proprietors of the Eagle Quay Saw, Planing, and Moulding Mills, which are four acres in extent in the heart of the city; South Carriers Dock, Liverpool; and a large yard at Stockport. This business was founded about a century ago by David Bellhouse. It afterwards became D. Bellhouse and Sons, and subsequently as at present. From its very inception the business has enjoyed a prosperous career, and the house to-day is one of the largest and most important in the trade. The Eagle Quay Mills are of spacious dimensions, and equipped with the most improved modern machinery and appliances, employment being given to upwards of two hundred skilled hands. The firm's operations as lapping-board and case makers and lath-cleavers are very extensive, and a very large and rapidly increasing trade is done with builders and in the supply of warehouse fittings. The firm are owners of a large fleet of boats used for the transportation of timber, while their connections in all the great producing centres are of a character which enables them to offer special advantages to customers, and to execute the largest orders in the promptest and most satisfactory manner. The members of the firm are gentlemen whose enterprise and public spirit have won the respect and confidence of all classes, and their establishment is a credit to their capacity and the great industry it so ably represents.

J. & H. Patteson, Marble Merchants, 86, Oxford Street.—The widely known firm of J. and H. Patteson was established in Manchester more than half a century ago, and is entitled to rank as first and foremost amongst the marble merchants of that city. The extensive showrooms and works in Oxford Street bear eloquent testimony to the extent of the trade which is carried on; and the collection of British and foreign marbles, arranged in the spacious and well-lighted gallery, is a revelation in itself, showing as it does some of the most elegant specimens of workmanship and material it is possible to conceive. A speciality with Messrs. Patteson is their "Mosaic Adamant," a new system of flooring, which is at once inexpensive, artistic, and durable. This adamant is composed of pieces of various coloured marbles mixed with a specially prepared cement which bears a tensile strain of 2,000 lbs. to the 1½ inch square. It thus forms a very suitable pavement for churches, public buildings, entrance halls, conservatories, &c., and a notable fact in connection with it is that Messrs. Patteson were commissioned to lay down a large quantity at the new Owens College, which they performed to the satisfaction of all concerned. The popularity of the adamant is great, and Messrs. Patteson send their men to fix it in all parts of the country. They have recently completed the floors of the nave, transepts and choir aisles of the New Cathedral at Truro. They have also a very large and widespread connection in the general marble business, and supply an immense number of chimney pieces, in marble, wood and stone, grates, fenders, wall linings, tiles, memorial tablets, fonts, pedestals and other useful and ornamental items. Mr. H. Patteson, one of the partners, was mayor of Manchester in 1881.

A. F. Brook & Co., Dandelion Coffee Manufacturers, Coffee-Roasters and Merchants, Corporation Street.—The important firm known as that of A. F. Brook & Co. is one of the best known in the district of Manchester. It was originally established in 1850, and carried on a large business as wholesale tea and coffee dealers in Todmorden. The present firm in Manchester has been in existence about twelve years, and is solely in the hands of, and under the direction of, Mr. Ambrose Fielden Brook. The premises occupied are known as the Union Bridge Coffee Works, which are very completely fitted and where a considerable number of hands are employed, but the offices and sale-rooms are in Corporation Street, which is the postal address. This firm is widely noted for the excellence of its manufactures, and has a connection all over the country. *Taraxacum, or Dandelion Coffee.*—Taraxacum, in combination with podophylin, has come into general use as a medicine for restoring the action of a disordered liver. In its simplest form, that of dandelion tea, its valuable medicinal properties have been recognised and used for ages, and as a summer drink it is very popular throughout the countries where the root grows. But it is only within a recent period it has been manufactured in a form that not only makes it available in all seasons of the year and in all climates, but, in the form of Brook's dandelion coffee, it is coming into general use, supplanting ordinary coffee as an article of daily diet. Great care must, however, be exercised in the preparation of this mixture, otherwise the flavour is not acceptable. Moreover, the value of this new drink depends upon its strength and uniform quality, and it is only preparations manufactured by firms of good repute that can be depended upon. Now, as regards the mixture being pleasant and agreeable to the taste, a palatable preparation is manufactured by Messrs. A. F. Brook & Co., Corporation Street, Manchester, which is very popular, if the large sales effected may be taken as the basis of the assertion. In dandelion coffee the base of the article is coffee, and the dandelion gives it the medicinal tonic quality. Messrs. Brook impart this quality of the root to their mixture in a raw state, instead of roasting it as in the case of chicory. The dandelion is gradually dried in a temperature sufficiently high to retain its medicinal quality. In the ordinary process the root is dried at too high a temperature; in fact it is roasted, and thereby the pulpy and milky matter of the root loses its beneficial properties. The firm has just laid down extensive machinery to enable them to meet the increasing demands upon them. In a certificate of Dr. A. H. Hassall, analyst of the *Lancet* Sanitary Commission, it is stated that the dandelion coffee prepared by Messrs. A. F. Brook & Co., coffee-roasters, Manchester, is really composed of the ingredients stated by the proprietors to enter into its composition. The article manufactured by this firm can, therefore, be safely recommended to purchasers both at home and abroad. It is much cheaper than ordinary coffee, for its strength only requires a much smaller quantity to be used, and is thus within the reach of all persons; and being an agreeable and palatable beverage, it is available for general use, being an acceptable article of diet. The preparation being packed in tins, retains its freshness and aroma for a considerable time. Great care is required in the roasting of coffee, to develop its aroma, and enable it to be properly ground to powder. Too much heat destroys the qualities that should be preserved, and substitutes new and unpleasant ones, while too little heat destroys the flavour of the berry, and deteriorates the beverage made from it. Many important changes have been introduced in the method of coffee-roasting, this being the all-important part in the manufacture, and no firm has a better reputation for its success in this direction than Messrs. Brook & Co. They have introduced the latest mechanical and scientific improvements into their method of roasting and preparing, and this has produced a splendid quality of coffee which possesses very superior flavour. Gas and heated air are pumped in by means of a blast-pump, and 2 cwts. can be roasted at one operation. A powerful fan blows away all smoke, chaff, and refuse. Four grinding mills are kept running, each grinding at the rate of 3 lbs. per minute. There is also a fine mixer for mixing dandelions with the best ordinary coffee. The dandelion-mill, which is run at the rate of four thousand revolutions per minute, is, together with all the machinery, hoists, &c., driven by one of Crossley Bros.' latest improved gas engine of over six horse-power nominal. Many substitutes for coffee have been tried and recommended. Of all these Messrs. Brook & Co.'s speciality of dandelion coffee seems to have shown the best results, and this description of coffee has become very popular. Messrs. Brook & Co. have instituted a particular method of preparing this which has made their dandelion coffee widely noted, and a very large trade is done in this commodity. Messrs. Brook are also celebrated for the excellent class of teas they import, and their general reputation is so good that they have a very extensive connection, and do a large business. In connection with the coffee portion of their business the above firm have a large tin-box factory, in which they can manufacture many hundreds of gross of tin canisters per week of all sorts and sizes, a large number of huge presses, for cutting out, stamping, piercing, &c., being constantly at work—for even an ordinary tin-box has to pass through sixteen, and in some cases more, processes before it is finished. The economy of labour is here seen in considerable perfection, one machine cutting out the strip, another piercing it, a third raising it—that is to say, forming the groove for the top and bottom; another cutting and forming covers at one operation; another one stamping out bottoms for canisters, and of these a boy can make many thousands a day. A machine forms the bodies, and next is a large press that seams the tin up with one blow, and it is handed to another boy who puts it in a machine and the bottom is fastened on in a second and the tin is complete. A very ingenious machine is here seen: you insert a straight flat piece of tin, and it at once drops out in the form of a square tin. It is immediately fastened in the above-named seaming press, the cover is put on by hand, and the bottom securely fastened by another machine. We need scarcely add that the machinery and dies, &c., in this department are very costly, and represent a very considerable amount, one machine having cost upwards of £200. The mechanism is wonderful in the perfection of its operations; all the parts of a tin or canister are cut out by one stroke of a machine. They are united by other machines in a manner superior to soldering, and entirely finished in an incredibly short space of time. On the first-floor of the building the tin boxes are packed for shipment, while the basement is used for storage, and the top-floor for other purposes, and the whole factory is admirably placed almost in the heart of the city. The tin factory was commenced for the convenience of the firm, but the success secured has been so marked that many other houses now take advantage of the favourable terms offered them by Messrs. Brook & Co.

J. Milling & Co., Paper-hangings Company, 84, Victoria Street.—J. Milling & Co. (The Manchester Paper-hangings Company), is a well-known firm occupying extensive premises. Established over twenty years ago, under the same title as at present known, Messrs. Milling & Co. have occupied their present premises seventeen years, and possess a large shop which reaches a considerable distance towards the back part. Here they have one of the largest stocks of paper-hangings to be found either in Manchester or any other town or city. Piles upon piles of rolls, in all kinds of patterns, and with the widest range of prices, meet the eye at every turn. A great deal of this immense stock has been imported specially, including classes of paper which for many technical reasons it is impossible to manufacture here. Messrs. Milling & Co. also stock the celebrated "Lincrusta Walton Wall Paper." This is a very novel kind of wall decoration, presenting a very pleasing appearance, and is very serviceable, in many instances where the ordinary wall paper would be either entirely unfit, or at least out of place. A very large staff is engaged, as the trade of this firm has so increased that it in fact, comprises the principal part of the North of England. For over ten years Mr. Milling has been a member of the City Council in Manchester, and now represents the Exchange Ward, in which the firm's premises are situated. This alone speaks volumes for the ability, integrity, and commercial standing of Mr. Milling, who must feel highly gratified at the confidence reposed in him by his fellow-citizens. A business-like and straightforward system of dealing, sound commercial principles, and the exercise of the keenest ability have given this firm its present standing and its proprietors their honourable and well-deserved position among their fellow-men.

William Nelson & Co., Leather Factors, Scotland Bridge, Red Bank.—An historical review of the great mercantile and manufacturing interests of Manchester would be incomplete without mention of such an old-established and thoroughly representative firm of leather merchants as that of Messrs. William Nelson & Co. This house was founded over half a century ago, and from the very beginning has enjoyed a prosperous career, a fact which speaks well for the uniform quality and standard excellence of the firm's manufactures. The site on which their tannery is situated must have been used for manufacturing leather for many generations, not to say centuries, past, as in excavating a short time ago on the land contiguous, the wooden pits and alleys of a tanyard were discovered at a considerable depth below the surface. On their removal to obtain a foundation it was found necessary to dig down to the solid rock some feet from the surface, where pits were plainly visible cut out of the rock, and containing lime. The tannery of to-day is equipped with the most improved modern appliances. Their extensive warehouse is stocked with a large assortment of leather, for which this house is noted. The firm does a widespread wholesale trade. It is such houses as this that are the recognised exponents of the various branches of Manchester industrial activity, and they well deserve the prominent position which the enterprise and ability of their proprietors have achieved.

R. J. Lea, Wholesale and Retail Tobacconist, 45, Market Street, and 12, Market Place.—This well-known house was founded by the late Mr. R. J. Lea in the year 1857. By carefully studying the requirements of the smoking community, Mr. Lea soon acquired the reputation of being one of the best judges of high-class tobaccos in the North of England. Lea's Mixture and Fine Cut Cavendish became famous not only in Manchester but all over the United Kingdom. So great, indeed, was the success of these specialities, that they were soon supplemented by the celebrated "Mild and Cool" Boardman's Mixture, perhaps the finest mild mixture ever manufactured. The business rapidly increased, until, at the time of his death, three years ago, Mr. Lea was doing by far the largest retail tobacco business in the district. Since then the concern has been carried on by the executors, who have made great improvements in the old-fashioned frontages of the two shops, and by closer attention to the cigar and fancy goods trade, have made the old house as famous as a pipe and cigar warehouse as it always has been for its tobaccos.

Messrs. Samuel Gratrix, Junr., & Bror., Alport Town, Deansgate. Conspicuous among the commercial factors of the age, stand manufacturers of all kinds. The well-known firm of Messrs. Samuel Gratrix, Junr., & Bror., whose lead mills are situate at Bradford, Manchester, and whose productions are so well known throughout the whole trading community, is one of the most notable firms connected with Manchester. Established by Mr. Samuel Gratrix, in 1820, the career of his house has been one of long-continued prosperity and success. The specialities they manufacture are numerous and of the very highest value

WAREHOUSE AND SHOW-ROOMS, ALPORT TOWN.

to the many trades whose requirements are so amply and satisfactorily provided for with promptness and dispatch. One of the leading productions for which this house enjoys a wide fame is "Gratrix's patent solid drawn lead pipe"; this article has a reputation of the highest order, and is known as the acme of perfection in lead piping throughout all branches of the trade. Other distinctive features of this establishment comprise a superb stock of fancy chandeliers and artistic gas-fittings, in every size and pattern, and of the choicest designs. Lacquering and electro-plating are also carried on on an extensive scale; the magnificent show-rooms are filled with specimens of both these branches

LEAD WORKS, BRADFORD, MANCHESTER.

of industry, and contain a selection of such general utility that contractors and others make this establishment their source of supply and standard of selection for fittings of all kinds. The glass department is very extensive, embracing a large collection from plain to the most ornamental descriptions, and the sanitary stock is noted far and wide as the best and most complete throughout the district. The brass department is very comprehensive, and contains a well-arranged stock of all kinds of fittings used for gas, water, steam, household, sanitary, and hot-water purposes, and a very large stock is held of their own special water taps and fittings, which are in great demand by many of the leading gas and water works and engineers. Tools of all descriptions used by gas, water, and steam fitters form a good adjunct. The iron department has a very large stock of wrought-iron pipes and fittings; cast iron rain-water pipes, gutters, hot-water pipes, fittings, coil cases, &c., cisterns for hot and cold water in iron and slate; also a well-arranged show of baths of all kinds, from the plain cast-iron to the highly finished enamelled and decorated. In addition to their lead manufacturing, they are large merchants in metals—copper, brass, zinc, &c. The premises comprise extensive warehouses, filled with an enormous and exceedingly valuable stock. The show-rooms are a grand attraction in themselves, and the offices are well fitted and manned by a staff of experienced assistants and others. The lead mills are on a scale of great importance and magnitude. The combination of warehouse, show-rooms, and mills constitute in their capacity and completeness an establishment the most unique of its kind.

Laban Spencer, Estate and Insurance Agent, 12, Pall Mall.—This business has been established about twenty years, and is one of the best known and patronised in the city. Mr Spencer, who has been located in his present commodious offices for seven years, issues a monthly property list of twenty large pages, which has several features of interest. In addition to dry details of properties to sell or to let, there is a well-written article and other matter of an interesting nature, so that there is always some inducement to read and preserve the *Manchester and District Property List*, as Mr. Spencer has christened his well-printed publication. A glance over its pages proves conclusively that Mr. Spencer secures a very good share of the city's agency business, and confirmation of this is afforded by the industry displayed in all the various departments of his offices. Mr. Spencer himself is well known and extremely popular, both on account of his excellent qualifications and genial disposition.

Myer Kersh, Wholesale Clothier, 7, Dantzic Street.—The well-known house of Mr. M. Kersh, wholesale clothier, is one of the best of its kind, and thoroughly entitled to a foremost position in the ranks of its class. It is conducted upon the best and most commendable of commercial lines, and has been distinguished, from the date of its establishment, twenty years ago, by a management of all-round excellence and enterprise. Customers are afforded the maximum of satisfaction in every way. The goods are manufactured and supplied at a price that is moderate in the extreme, but which, by virtue of his extensive and valuable connection, Mr. Kersh is able, with satisfaction, to adhere to. The trade with Manchester and the surrounding towns is decidedly good, whilst the shipping department of the concern is rapidly increasing in importance. The special order department, of which Mr. M. Kersh is the founder, is the largest of its kind in Manchester. In this department special cutters and tailors are employed. Pattern books are continually supplied to the trade at every season of the year. This department enables clothiers in every part of the country to forward their measure orders and receive them back sooner than if made by their own tailors, and at prices which cannot be equalled. The premises are admirably appointed, four stories in height, and the warehouse always contains a comprehensive and good class stock of ready-made woollens, consisting of men's, youths', boys', and juvenile clothing. A large staff is kept in constant employment, and orders are attended to with the most praiseworthy promptitude and carefulness. Mr. Kersh caters in no half-hearted fashion for the patronage of the trade, and well deserves the widespread and cordial support that is accorded him.

William Wood, Cap Manufacturer, 10, Brewer Street, Port Street.—This business has been established fully twenty-five years. It was founded by the gentleman whose name it still bears, but has been conducted latterly by Mr. Henry Weight. The premises in Brewer Street consist of a fine range of lofty and convenient workrooms, and the busy hum of machinery indicates that a large working staff is actively employed. The trade is confined entirely to the large wholesale houses, the general warehousemen, and some of the shipping firms.

Christopher Wood, Calico Printer, 25, Portland Street. —This firm is one of the oldest in the trade, and was originally founded by the "Peels," to whom the late Christopher Wood succeeded in 1816. The present members of the firm are:—Wm. C. Wood, Joseph Wood, and R. J. Wood, who carry on the business under the original name, at Brinscall, near Chorley. The firm under the designation of W. C. Wood & Bros., are also large manufacturers at Birch and Heywood, where they employ a large number of hands.

Shanks & Co., Grosvenor Buildings, Deansgate.— Certainly not astonishing, but nevertheless remarkable, has been the impetus given by nineteenth-century civilization and scientific progress to the manufacture of sanitary appliances. It is only natural that growing intelligence should rebel against the deplorable unsanitary conditions of life that pervaded fifty years ago, and that the simple law of self preservation should induce man to free himself if possible from the dangers and horrors that surrounded him on every side. Colonel Waring, of New York, says, with reference to that well-known w.c., the pan closet:— "It very probably was not, but it certainly might have been, the invention of the devil." Those who are acquainted with such matters will know that the pan closet has a pan, and then it has a trunk or container, which certainly is a container, and very shortly becomes a fertile spot for the germs of those zymotic diseases which most terrify the human race. That this apparatus was the almost universal closet in use not so very many years ago, where there were closets at all, gives our readers an idea of the dense ignorance that prevailed amongst the masses of the people and the hidden dangers they harboured in their own homes. The pressing need for improvement which even yet exists has brought with it, although somewhat late in the day, the natural supply. In this as in other walks of manufacture, firms have arisen who have devoted their existence to the improvement and perfecting of sanitary appliances, and we are glad to find one of the front rank established in Manchester. We allude to the firm of Shanks & Co., Grosvenor Buildings, Deansgate, and it is our purpose here to give a short review of the progress of the firm and their manufactures. About thirty years ago Mr. John Shanks, senior partner of the firm, being by trade a plumber, and interested in sanitary matters, seeing the palpable defects that existed in the sanitary appliances of that day, turned the attention of his inventive and rather ingenious mind to the improvement of w.c.'s. The first production of importance was Shanks' patent flexible valve No. 4 water-closet. This was not received with favour at the outset, but ultimately they got a footing in the market, and since then the sale has been very large. At least 100,000 of these closets have been made and fitted up since their introduction, and even now the only objection to their use is the fact that they are not water waste preventers. This point was not of such importance twenty or thirty years ago, but now the water companies insist on appliances that measure a limited quantity of water. As an evidence of the superiority of this closet over the best closets of the time, we may mention a circumstance that found publicity in the pages of the *Lancet*. The serious illness of the Prince of Wales some years ago will be vividly within the recollection of our readers. The medical authorities rightly judged that the cause of the trouble was to be found in the sanitary, or rather unsanitary, appliances of the house. The arrangements were examined by experts, and it was then discovered that, with the exception of one closet, the servants' closet, all the others were in an unsatisfactory condition, and formed direct means of access from the sewer gas to the atmosphere of the house. The servants' closet was Shanks' patent No. 4. Since that time the business of the firm has made continued and steady progress, and now they are manufacturers of almost every conceivable kind of sanitary appliance, and water waste preventing and water supply apparatus. Since the supervision of water companies became so strict, closets have been almost entirely fixed with waste preventing supply cisterns. Closets of various forms have been used, and in many cases either the defective construction of the closet or the inadequacy of cistern resulted in a most unsanitary condition of things. Without alluding to many of the appliances which Messrs. Shanks have introduced, we shall simply refer to one or two forms of water closet which we have every reason to believe not only satisfy the restrictions of the water companies but give perfect results from a sanitary point of view. Shank's Patent Tubal Closet is made on what is known as the wash out principle. It is made in one solid piece of porcelain, or white enamelled fire-clay, constructed so that it may stand uncovered without any wood enclosure, and with a hinged mahogany seat, so that it serves the purpose not only of a closet but that of a slop sink and urinal. There are no valves or mechanism about it, and the patent combination of bottom stream and after flush chamber renders it a thorough washing out closet. It is supplied with Shanks' patent "Reliable" valveless syphon cistern, which we understand has received the prize medal at the Sanitary Congress of Great Britain, and various other awards at the large exhibitions. With this apparatus immunity from sewer gas is secured and perfect cleanliness is attained. The plague-spot of former years vanishes, and people have healthier houses, purer atmosphere, and enjoy that peace of mind which comes from the knowledge that insanitary danger is past. This closet has been fitted in many public and private buildings in Manchester, and in fact all over the world; and Messrs. Shanks & Co. assure us that a complaint is unknown with reference to this closet and cistern. Messrs. Shanks & Co. have also introduced a combination closet on exactly the same principle as the one first mentioned, with this difference, viz., that the cistern, instead of being overhead, is fixed just at the back of the closet, on a level with the top of the closet, and is actuated by a handle at side of cistern. The cistern is usually covered with a mahogany case, and the closet has a hinged seat to attain the same objects as the tubal closet. We have here a closet complete and self-contained, with the minimum of trouble and expense in fixing, and the maximum of sanitary efficiency. It might suggest itself to some that the absence of fall would so decrease the force of the flush as to render the closet inefficient; but the absence of fall is compensated for by the large size of the inlet, which is about six times the ordinary size, and admits the contents of the cistern into the closet so quickly that the basin and trap are thoroughly cleansed at every flush. The demand for this closet is so great that the manufacturers have difficulty in keeping up the supply. Fireclay trough closets, with automatic flushing tanks, for schools and public works, urinals of every description and of novel construction, on the best sanitary principles, we find among the manufactures of this firm. They have just introduced a most ingenious contrivance in the shape of a urinal for private houses. It has always been a difficulty to get a urinal that will not be an unsightly apparatus in a private room. Messrs. Shanks have overcome this by making a neat little urinal in a mahogany case, which at first glance has more the appearance of a telephone box, or something of that kind, than anything else. Lift the folding cover or lid and the urinal is disclosed, with water running all over the interior of the porcelain surface, which continues to run until the cover is let down. It has already had a considerable sale, and as it supplies a felt want, we have no doubt the sale will rapidly increase. Nothing has yet been said of what is really the most important branch of the firm's business, the manufacture of baths. As everyone knows, this is a rapidly increasing trade. Baths are being fitted into almost every respectable house nowadays, whereas in years gone by a bath was a luxury confined only to the rich. Messrs. Shanks have fostered and developed this important trade in quite a remarkable way, and now we believe they occupy the enviable position of being the largest bath makers in the world. Baths, with fittings and without fittings, cast-iron baths, sheet-iron baths, zinc baths, copper baths, porcelain baths, marble baths, silver-plated baths and nickel-plated baths of every style are turned out by this enterprising firm. These are made in various forms; and the bath that has, perhaps, contributed more to their fame as bath makers than any is their Imperial Combined Bath and fittings. This is a plunge bath enamelled, with hot, cold, and waste fittings fixed on a sunk shelf at the foot of bath, and covered with a porcelain slab, which has two commodious soap trays draining into waste pipe. It is finished with waste pipe and trap all in one self-contained piece, so that the trouble and cost of fixing is very small, and the arrangement as complete as possible. Many thousands of these baths have been turned out during the last few years, and the trade in them continues without abatement. Baths of a more luxurious type have also been brought before the public; and notice may be taken of that bath which Messrs. Shanks & Co. describe as the "acme of luxurious bathing." It is named the "Eureka" bath, and comprises a plunge bath of novel shape and construction—a spray, shower, douche, wave, and ascending spray and jet. The fittings are Shanks' patent Eureka fittings, by which it is possible to manipulate all these various baths with a remarkably small number of pipes, and to regulate the temperature of the water with the greatest ease. Many of these baths have been fitted up in the mansions of the nobility and in the residences of gentlemen, both at home and abroad. Examples of this bath were to be seen at the Manchester Exhibition and at the Newcastle Exhibition of 1887. Messrs. Shanks have a large cabinet department entirely devoted to the manufacture of cabinets for baths, lavatories, and sanitary appliances, and in many cases they send out complete suites of bath-room furniture, varying from the plainest to the most elaborate designs. Pages might be written descriptive of the various styles of baths, but it is not our object here to give a catalogue of the firm's manufactures, so we only mention the leading features. Shanks' patent lavatories have been hardly less successful than their baths. Their patent combined lavatories and fittings present an appearance that seems at once to confirm what is claimed for them. There is hardly any brasswork seen, no unseemly plug is seen in bottom of basin, waste pipe is in one solid piece with basin and table top, and the whole apparatus is, like the closets and baths, complete and self-contained. This is the principle which this firm has aimed at following, and we must say with considerable success. They believe that sanitary appliances and their connections should be no more hidden than the tables and chairs in a house, and that there should be none of those mysterious corners and enclosures which concealed nobody knew what, which nobody could reach for cleaning purposes, and which became receptacles for the accumulation of the filth of years. We notice that brass cocks and fittings are turned out by Messrs. Shanks of a very high quality. Cast iron, porcelain, and fireclay sinks form a large part of their business, and many other appliances which it is not necessary here to particularise. The extensive works of the firm, situated at Barrhead, near Glasgow, are very interesting, inasmuch as there are fourteen or fifteen different trades carried on within the gates. The success of such a firm must be interesting to the general public, as it touches so closely the amenities of every-day life. The engineer has the satisfaction of knowing at the end of his career that he has done his share in utilising the forces of nature for the good of his fellows, and the artist doubtless feels that he has impressed on the intellect of the world the idea that "a thing of beauty is a joy for ever," but to the sanitary reformer will come the simple but agreeable satisfaction that the world is not quite so dirty as when he entered it.

ightbown, Aspinall, & Co., Paper-hangings Manu-urers, Pendleton; also at 13, Pall Mall; 142, Queen Victoria Street, don E.C.; and 126, Ingram Street, Glasgow.—During the past few

Hayfield Mills, Pendleton, Manchester.

s marked improvement has been made, and is still being made, in the ufacture of paper-hangings, and some of the finest stocks in the try bear the imprint of Lancashire houses. A thoroughly represen-re house is that of Messrs. Lightbown, Aspinall, & Co., of Hayfield s, Pendleton, which has been in existence near half a century. The has established a reputation for the artistic merits of its manufacture. premises in the city, and those in London and Glasgow, are amply d and commodious, and are constantly supplied with stock from the works at Pendleton. These works are very extensive, and especially well adapted for this manufacture. Every mechanical appliance suitable has been pressed into service, and the hands employed are able and experienced. The paper-hangings of the firm are characterized by uniform good quality, elegant and original patterns, tasteful colourings, and among the stock are goods of the most choice and costly description. An extensive trade is done all over the country, the firm supplying the most noted merchants, decorators, upholsterers, &c., and at the same time has a large foreign trade. Mr. Lightbown, the proprietor, has a thorough knowledge of the requirements of the trade, having been connected with the business for about half a century. In the trade he is well known and respected, and his efforts to perfect this important manufacture are worthy of imitation.

John Hall (Limited), Quilting Manufacturer, 11, Mosley Street.—The manufacture of quiltings is perhaps the most difficult of all the various branches of weaving, and Messrs. John Hall's is undoubtedly the oldest existing firm of quilting manufacturers in England. From records in their possession it appears that the three brothers, Adam, John, and William Hall, were established at Gorsey Brow, near Bury, so far back as the year 1803, at which time they employed upwards of one hundred hand-loom weavers in that neighbourhood, so that they seem fairly entitled to claim that their firm is almost, if not quite, a century old. At this early epoch their only communication with Manchester, where their goods were disposed of, was by coach or on foot, and we believe the brothers Hall invariably chose the latter means, visiting the different hostelries and taverns, where they met and transacted their business with their customers. The various yarns used by them were obtained from Mr. George Cheetham, of Ashton-under-Lyne; Mr. James Clegg, of Heywood; and later from Mr. Richard Kay, of Heywood; and their cloth was bleached by Mr. Whitehead, of Elton, who delivered the pieces, as desired by Messrs. Hall, at the addresses of the purchasers in Manchester. In 1820 we find them located in a warehouse of their own in Newmarket Lane, from whence they shortly removed a few doors to 1, Sussex Street, which premises they were allowed by their landlord to occupy for more than thirty years at the same rental, and the first twenty of these years may be called the halcyon days of quilting manufacturing, for we know that they then employed about thirteen hundred hand-loom weavers, and the profits were reckoned not by so many pence per piece, but so many pence per yard. These hand-loom weavers were scattered over the townships of Tyldesley, Astley, Walmersley, Tottington, Haswood, Leigh, and Bolton, and many of them had to carry their pieces, or "cuts," as they called them, ten or a dozen miles after weaving them to appointed places, where a representative of the firm met them to pay them for the work done, and to provide them with the warp and weft required for the next pieces. In 1836 the Halls left Gorsey Brow and moved to Walmersley, near Bury, where they bought a small estate, called Naugreaves, and here they built a weaving-shed for power-looms, and later a spinning mill; and it is here that the present members of the firm of Messrs. John Hall (Limited) still carry on their process of manufacture, but with this difference, that in that year all their cloth was produced by hand, whereas they have now only one solitary hand-loom weaver left. The power-loom has, of course, undergone great improvement since its first introduction, but the Halls themselves and those associated with them—the Howarths and Nuttalls—were men of invention and adaptability, and they kept fully abreast with the times, also adding their full share to the list of improvements in the appliances for and the methods of weaving. Indeed it was often said that "John Hall" was the cleverest and best weaver in the whole of the civilised world. Amongst the improvements which sprung from Naugreaves, or were first used there, it must suffice to mention here the piano card-cutting machine, neutral sections, and an improved dwell for Bennett Woodcroft's tappets, pushers for Jacquard machines, oscillating tappets, and lastly a new taking-up motion, which for the manufacture of quiltings and other similar goods is undoubtedly the best motion known. For some years quiltings, having been out of fashion, have been under a cloud, but there has been a slight revival of late, and we understand that Messrs. Hall, whose warehouse is now at the above address, have established an agency at 12, Gutter Lane, Cheapside, London, that they are fairly busy, and are engaged at present in lighting up their sheds at Naugreaves with the electric light.

Messrs. Louis Behrens & Sons, Merchants and Shippers, 131, Portland Street.—In 1840 was established the well-known house now trading under the style of Messrs. Louis Behrens & Sons, manufacturers and merchants, dealing with most of the principal ports in the world, in Manchester cotton piece goods, and in silk plushes. The operations of the firm are not confined to shipping and export, as in 1871 a "home trade" was added, which has now assumed considerable proportions. The firm manufacture fustian and velvets largely for the United States, in which country they are represented by two of the brothers, Mr. Ernest and Mr. Walter Behrens, who reside permanently in New York, and who are in a position to deal with goods to any extent and value. The premises occupied comprise a large and well-built capacious warehouse of six storeys. The members of the partnership, Mr. Oscar H. Behrens, Emil A. Behrens, Ernest H. Behrens, are gentlemen well known and very widely respected.

Dowdall Brothers, Butter Shippers and Agents, 32, Hanging Ditch, (telegraphic address, Dowdall Brothers, Manchester).—This is a shipping agency of the first order of merit. The energetic proprietors, Messrs. James B. and Walter Dowdall, engage in a trade of considerable importance and enjoy a widespread and valuable connection, particularly in the line of butter exportation. Their trade transactions extend to all the great butter-producing countries of the northern hemisphere. Every Monday morning they receive batches of letters advising shipments and consignments from such distant countries as Denmark, Sweden, and even Finland in the north-east of Europe; from Holland, France, and Transalpine territory, as well as from all parts of Ireland. During the week not only are they advised by wire from the capitals of those kingdoms of the official changes in the quotations of butter, but also from New York and Chicago of what butter is doing on the American continent. Much valuable information is thus collected, and disseminated for the benefit of their clients, in their weekly publication entitled "Dowdall Brothers' Butter Review," the general report from which is copied into the commercial columns of the leading newspapers of Great Britain and Ireland. They were the founders and remain the sole agents of the Anglo-Irish Creameries Company, which has done so much to improve the quality of Irish butter; in fact, practically speaking they may be said to be the fathers of this movement in Ireland in a practical commercial sense, the other creameries introduced prior to their action only dealing with the cream brought in by farmers to a central depot. Their steam factory system treated the milk brought in fresh immediately after milking, on the Danish and Swedish centrifugal separating system, afterwards treating the cream throughout on a thoroughly scientific method. For this purpose they introduced into Ireland a staff of Danish and Swedish dairy experts, men and women, none of whom, with the exception of one, could speak a word of English on their first landing. Not confining those advantages to themselves, they specially fitted up for companies and private individuals in Ireland, and are prepared to do so in Great Britain, Ireland, or any part of the world, steam dairies on the most approved Danish or Swedish principles, furnishing dairy plans and estimates. They have in addition to their Manchester house establishments at Cork and Copenhagen, and employ a large staff, including travellers and agents all over the country. During the years that have elapsed since their establishment they have achieved a high reputation. Their method of management is one that commends itself in no unmistakable manner to the favour of practical minds, and they certainly afford their patrons many exceptional advantages and do the utmost in their power to give entire satisfaction to all who deal with them. Orders are executed to any extent without unnecessary delay, the goods supplied are unquestionably of a far superior quality, and the charges made are decidedly the reverse of exorbitant. The telegraphic address is, as already mentioned, Dowdall Brothers, Manchester.

The Atlas Assurance Company, Branch, 24, Booth Street. William Frevillier, Manager.—Prominent among the provident institutions of the age appear associations for the assurance of lives and for providing against loss by fire. These institutions must be ranked among the very noblest organisations of the day, the success of which is noted with great interest, and forms a guide to the great thrift and commercial progress of the age. The capital invested in business transactions of the leading assurance associations of civilised countries is a matter for such special consideration to the commercial mind that it leads to the formation of an accurate notion of the extent of progress made by the nation. A representative type of this branch of national industry is the well-known and universally patronised Atlas Assurance Company, one of the oldest and most reliable offices in existence, and enjoying a reputation second to none. Established so long ago as 1808, this Company has always enjoyed a large amount of public confidence and support. With a capital of £1,200,000, and invested funds of £1,804,539, the assets of the Atlas Assurance rank high in public estimation. The Company's branch office in Manchester is situated at 24, Booth Street, Cooper Street, under the very able and spirited management of Mr. Wm. Frevillier, a gentleman whose extensive experience and business qualifications are of that order which effectively conveys the assurance to the local public mind that the affairs of the Company, so far as relates to their branch at Manchester, could not be entrusted to better hands. Mr. Frevillier combines the business of land agent, &c., with the management of the branch office at 24, Booth Street, Cooper Street, thus offering the benefits of a large experience to those in the position of landed proprietors and assurers conjointly. Originally established in Princes Street in 1868, Mr. Frevillier subsequently removed to his address in Booth Street. The premises of the Atlas Company present a noble appearance, the offices being large and well fitted, and most admirably adapted to the conduct of the very large business which this association transacts. Assisted by an efficient staff of clerks and assistants of good business ability, the utmost facilities are at once afforded for the rapid and successful effecting of insurances. The Company's chief office is at 92, Cheapside, London, and a glance at their prospectus at once reveals on the list of directors the names of gentlemen of the highest integrity and social position, affording a guarantee of the very high commercial status of this association. The business of the Atlas Assurance Company has always been of the most elastic and widespread nature, being at the same time remarkable for its stability and the amount of public confidence it has continued to enjoy. Prosperous as have been the affairs of the Company in the past, the future holds out promise of still greater results, as the natural consequence of a long career combined with first-class management.

Messrs. R. Phillips & Son, Shoe Manufacturers, 73, Deansgate.—In reviewing the great trade industries of the city of Manchester and district, a very important position is taken by manufacturers of clothing, boots, &c. A representative centre in the boot and shoe-making trades is the well-known and far-famed establishment of R. Phillips & Son, shoe manufacturers, whose premises are situated in a choice and highly favourable position for business. The premises occupied consist of a large and well-fitted shop with plate-glass front, most admirably arranged and thoroughly adapted for carrying on the large and very important daily business of the firm, and affording employment to an adequate staff of competent assistants. Established in 1850, the reputation of this noted old and well-tried house for first-class boots and shoes is second to none in the city. A speciality in this business is, the goods are chiefly hand-sewn, and guaranteed to be made of the very best quality of leather, combined with the highest possible class of workmanship. It is a noted fact that none but the very best workmen are employed at this establishment. The result of the thoroughly good system of management is an immense and ever-increasing stream of business, the public confidence is obtained, and the highest possible success must of necessity result. The head of the firm is Mr. Richard E. Phillips, a gentleman well known originally at St. Mary's Gate, and now for fourteen years at the present address. Mr. Phillips had a widespread reputation at St. Mary's Gate, and is generally known as a thoroughly practical man of business, of high integrity and widely respected.

Godfrey Woodhead & Son, Victoria Tea Warehouse and Supply Stores, 28, Victoria Street.—This well-known and old-established concern—a credit to its proprietor, a boon to the public, and one of the distinct features of its kind in Manchester—was originally established as far back as 1831, by the late Mr. Godfrey Woodhead, who commenced business in premises near Victoria Bridge. These premises were pulled down when Victoria Street was cut through, and the business was removed in 1837 to the premises now occupied in Victoria Street. Since this date considerable progress has been made. Enterprise, unlimited energy, and careful management have long been the characteristics of the concern. Its connection is now a splendid and a widespread one, and its business and popularity may safely be said to be increasing every day. This happy state of things affords a convincing proof that a large proportion at least of the public have the common sense and inclination to give their earnest support to those who serve them well. At both of the handsomely appointed and large establishments known as the Victoria Tea Warehouse and Supply Stores, 28, Victoria Street, Manchester, and 48, Sankey Street, Warrington, a comprehensive and high class stock of goods may be obtained. In combination with this business a great speciality is made of scientific dairying. The firm have a model dairy, and from this they supply daily a large quantity of cream, possessing the triple qualities of purity, richness, and genuine thickness. The cream is separated from the new milk by means of the valuable invention known as De Laval's Separator, and is then packed in specially made registered-shape earthenware jars, holding $\frac{1}{4}$ pint, $\frac{1}{2}$ pint, 1 pint, and 1 quart each. The firm have also a reputation for a special quality in fresh sweet cream butter. All the operations at the dairy are carried on with scrupulous cleanliness, and all the water used is filtered. The present sole proprietor, Mr. Samuel Benson Woodhead, being also a partner with Mr. Wm. Baker, in the Daisy Bank Dairy Company, of Weaste, near Manchester, is able to afford his numerous customers many peculiar advantages that cannot be equalled elsewhere in the town. The firm is connected with the telephone exchange, the number being 928, and a private wire is laid on to the dairy, thus giving great facilities for prompt despatch of orders. As may be imagined from the foregoing, every possible care is taken to afford customers the maximum of satisfaction with the best of goods at a moderate outlay. These are the watchwords of Mr. Woodhead's extensive business, and, to buyer and seller alike they have proved the best and most beneficial in every way.

J. H. Hasler, Underwriter, &c., Swiss-German Marine Insurance Association, Bridgewater Buildings, Albert Square.—The marine insurance business of Manchester is very valuable, and the agents and underwriters are a talented and influential body. A very fine business in this line is that known as the Swiss-German Marine Insurance Association, comprising "The Federal Marine Insurance Company of Zurich" and "The German Lloyd Marine Insurance Company of Berlin." The company was established by Mr. J. H. Hasler six years ago at the foregoing address. The offices are large and commodious, and an adequate clerical staff is employed. In all kinds of marine insurance Mr. J. H. Hasler is thoroughly experienced, and he carries on a very lucrative business, having a first-class connection in the shipping trade. Business is transacted in a prompt manner. Mr. J. H. Hasler is well known in the shipping world, and greatly esteemed for his honourable business methods, talent, and courtesy, and owing to his efforts the "Swiss-German Marine Insurance Association" holds an important and influential place in the insurance business of Manchester.

The Lancashire and Yorkshire Accident Insurance Company, Limited, Head Office, 37, Princess Street. Charles McBride, Manager and Secretary.—The Lancashire and Yorkshire Accident Insurance Company, Limited, which insures against accidents of all kinds, has been established ten years, and few companies have in the same length of time made more substantial progress. It is well known that amongst insurance companies, of all kinds, there is a certain amount of competition going on, just as in other businesses; but the success which has attended the Lancashire and Yorkshire Accident Insurance Company, Limited, is due solely to good management, which has produced unlimited public confidence. A perusal of the tables of rates issued by this company discloses the fact that for a remarkably small annual premium the large sum of £1,000 may be assured in case of death from accident, and smaller amounts at correspondingly lower premiums. For instance, persons coming within the category of Class 1 (which embraces all whose occupations do not necessarily render them extra liable to accidents) may, for an annual premium of £3, secure £1,000 in case of death from accident, and £6 a week during entire disablement, the premiums for hazardous occupations being slightly higher. Again, the same class of persons may secure £100 in case of death from accident, and 15s. per week during entire disablement, for an annual premium of 12s. The company likewise issue insurance policies for "accidental death only," at about half the foregoing rates, and for "compensation for disablement only." Thus, for an annual premium of £2, the sum of £6 per week is secured in cases of entire disablement, whilst £1 a week may be secured by an annual premium of 12s. In hazardous cases the premiums would be a little higher. The company will also issue policies for "railway accidents only," securing £1,000 in case of death, and £6 per week during entire disablement, for an annual premium of 15s., whilst £100 in case of death and £1 a week during entire disablement may be secured by an annual premium of 5s. But, in addition to these policies, the company undertake marine insurances, by which passengers, captains, or other superior officers and pilots may be insured against death by shipwreck or accident whilst at sea at a very moderate rate of premium. That all people are liable to accidents is an indisputable fact, whatever their calling or occupation, or whether engaged in business or pleasure: and inasmuch as accidents are mostly unpreventable, it is the duty, as well as the interest, of every one to provide against them, and certainly there could not be any better method than that provided by an insurance company like the one now under notice. The Board of Directors of the Lancashire and Yorkshire Accident Insurance Company are gentlemen of the most extensive experience combined with high character and attainments, nearly every one of them occupying positions of great trust and responsibility in connection with leading insurance offices in Manchester and the neighbourhood. This circumstance of itself is quite sufficient to strengthen the position of the concern and to inspire the confidence of the proprietary; but, after all, the annual balance-sheet is what both shareholders and assurers alike attach most importance to, and the last one, dated 31st January, 1887, proved eminently satisfactory, for it showed the premium income for 1886 to be £30,082 11s. 11d., whilst the invested and other funds of the company amounted to no less a sum than £57,764 13s. We ought to explain that the capital is £100,000 (20,000 shares of £5 each); but of this sum only £30,000, or £1 10s. per share, has been paid up; consequently the £57,764 13s is in addition to the uncalled capital of £70,000, which, it may be remarked, is subscribed by a numerous and wealthy proprietary. When we state that last year (1886) the Company paid a dividend to the shareholders of 10 per cent. and returned a bonus of £1,918 17s. to the assurers, besides making the fullest provision for "contingencies," we think we have said quite enough to demonstrate the prosperous and gratifying condition of the Company's finances, which is fully confirmed by the most recent quotations of the shares on the Manchester Stock Exchange. Nor must we omit to mention that the Company are prepared to relieve all employers of their responsibilities under the "Employers' Liability Act of 1880," as well as the legal costs incurred in defending claims, on payment of an annual premium based upon the amount of wages paid; and we feel sure that an insurance of this character, which must necessarily save an employer so much risk, trouble, and expense, will at once commend itself to all parties affected by the Act in question. There is nothing in our opinion which is more calculated to add to the reputation of an insurance company, and, as a consequence, extend its business, than prompt settlement of claims, and the Company under review have ever been both liberal and prompt in meeting all legitimate claims upon the offices. The exact rate for any insurance will be supplied by the Company on receiving a proposal form with full particulars. Before bringing our remarks to a conclusion, we ought to mention the fact that the first chairman of the company was the late Richard Howarth, Esq., a gentleman of the very highest social position in Manchester, and whose name was in itself a guarantee for the genuine character of the undertaking; whilst in Mr. Charles McBride, the active and energetic manager and secretary, the Company secured the services of a most indefatigable, experienced, and able man of business, admirably suited for the important position he occupies. The Company's progress from its inception has been steady and uninterrupted, and its future career bids fair to be one of great usefulness and prosperity. We will only add that the Company have branch offices at Bank Chambers, 3, Cook Street, Liverpool, and at 42, Renfield Street, Glasgow, and at these branches, as well as at the chief office, 37, Princess Street, Manchester, the Company keep a large and highly efficient staff.

The Lancashire Fire and Life Insurance Company, Exchange Street.—This company was established in the year 1852 by a numerous and influential body of merchants and manufacturers resident chiefly in Manchester, London, Liverpool, and Glasgow. It has a capital of three millions, and an annual income of over seven hundred thousand pounds, with reserve funds of one million sterling. The excellent system of management pursued by the Lancashire Insurance Company has been made the subject of the highest encomiums by no less a financial authority than Mr. Gladstone, the ex-premier. Speaking upon the management of its funds Mr. Gladstone said that he placed the "Lancashire" amongst the "highest class" of Insurance Companies; and that to show accumulated reserves of about four times its premium income was a condition of affairs "very satisfactory." Admirably managed as is this company in all details its expenses are yet kept within exceptionally moderate limits, and for years now have not reached twelve per cent. of the premium income, whereas twenty-five or even thirty per cent. is not uncommon in even good-class offices. The scales of premiums are arranged upon a liberal basis, and the directors offer inducements for joint assurances of husband and wife, and to persons travelling to any part of the globe. By the careful management hinted at above, the directors find it possible from time to time to gratify their clients by awarding substantial bonuses. The company have now in addition to the handsome offices in Exchange Street, where a very large staff of clerks is engaged, commodious branches in London, Liverpool, Birmingham, Bristol, Glasgow, Edinburgh, Dublin, and other populous centres.

James Woolley, Sons, & Co., Manufacturing Pharmaceutical Chemists, 60, Market Street.—This old-established house still retains its leading position amongst the wholesale druggists in the North of England. Founded in 1796, it passed about the year 1842 into the hands of the late James Woolley; after whose death, in 1858, the business was carried on by G. S. Woolley, till 1872, when the present members of the firm were admitted into partnership, and the title became James Woolley, Sons, & Co. In 1873 the manufacturing department was removed from Market Street to Knowsley Street, Cheetham, where laboratories and drug mills were erected, the city warehouse being at the same time considerably enlarged by the addition of premises in Swan Court. In 1879 the expansion of the firm's trade necessitated the extension of the works at Cheetham, another laboratory being built and additional machinery being put down. The city house devotes itself to supplying pharmacists, hospitals, and other public institutions with drugs, medicines, and surgical appliances, and to meeting the demand for chemical reagents and products used in analysis, photography, and the arts. An important branch of the business is the chemical and scientific apparatus department. The operations carried on at Knowsley Street, Cheetham, consist in grinding drugs and chemicals and manufacturing medicinal preparations of every description. A large staff of fully qualified pharmacists and chemists is retained, and the firm employs about one hundred and forty persons.

A. & G. Murray, Limited, Fine Spinners, Murray Street, Ancoats.—The firm of A. & G. Murray, fine spinners, is one of the oldest and most important in this country, and dates back to the beginning of the century. Some few years ago the firm became a limited company, but it is believed that the shares are all held by members of the Murray family. Mr. George Murray, one of the original partners, resided for many years and until his death at Ancoat's Hall. He was succeeded by two of his sons. There is now only one member of the family residing in Manchester (a grandson of Mr. George Murray), Mr. George R. Murray, who, together with Mr. Herbert Dixon, is responsible for the management of this large and increasing concern. During recent years the mills and machinery have undergone a complete remodelling, and the internal arrangements are upon the most modern and approved principle. This determination on the part of the old firm to keep up with the times has not only enabled it to maintain its reputation as one of the most able and successful spinning concerns, but to forge ahead of many much more modern and recently-constructed establishments. The Murrays' mills are situated in Murray Street, Ancoats, and during a continued period of stagnation in the cotton-spinning industry for some years they have enjoyed the fortunate reputation of having never worked short time. The mills contain about 120,000 spindles, with full preparation, and about 500 hands are employed.

William H. L. Cameron, Shirt Manufacturer, 4, Portland Street.—Shirt manufacture has become a speciality of considerable importance of late years in many parts of the country—more particularly since the introduction of sewing machines, which have effected a great alteration and improvement in this branch of industry, which formerly was carried on under conditions by no means creditable to those concerned. The shirtmaking establishment of Mr. W. H. L. Cameron, whose manufactory is at Macclesfield, is open to none of the objections referred to. Before making any reference to the emporium in Portland Street, we will speak of the manufactory at Macclesfield. It is a brick building of great magnitude, but only one story in height, standing upon three-quarters of an acre of ground, and it is of good elevation. The factory proper may be described as one immense apartment, having no windows, but lighted from the roof, which is divided into six spans (each about 18 feet wide) and composed partly of wood and slates and partly of plate-glass, resting upon iron framework, and supported by five rows of strong cast-iron pillars, each row being twenty in number. The lights in the roof are arranged so that they all have a northerly aspect—the result of this is that the light thrown into the building is the best it is possible to obtain. The roof is firmly put together, and is impervious alike to wind and water. The place is splendidly ventilated, and in connection with this subject it may be stated that a steam fan has been fixed which is capable of discharging all the air of the whole building in about fifteen minutes. The establishment is heated by circulating high-pressure steam conveyed through iron pipes. At night the building is lighted with the Wenham patent lamp, which produces a light at once bright, white, and soft, and not hurtful or dazzling to the eyes. On the premises there are about 160 sewing machines, each working at about 1,400 stitches per minute. To every machine there is attached a bobbin containing six miles of cotton. There are, also, twenty button-hole machines, which make 800 revolutions per minute and work six buttonholes per minute, and the buttonholes are made in a superior manner to anything that can be accomplished by hand, unless much time is taken and considerable care is expended. The whole of the machines are driven by steam, so that the girls working them have not to undergo the labour and fatigue of the treadle; nevertheless, they are able to stop their machines instantly and start them with the greatest ease and promptness. The buttons have to be sewn upon the shirts by hand, and a long row of girls may be observed engaged in this particular occupation. The cloth store contains about 4,000 pieces. They include every variety of material used for shirtmaking, and in all colours, to suit all tastes, and adapted for wear in all climates; but they are chiefly cottons, woollens, and flannelettes, and the prices range from 3d. up to 3s. 6d. per yard, and the pieces are so arranged that every one of them can be plainly seen. The great bulk of the cutting-out is done by a band-knife machine, revolving at a high speed, capable of cutting through from forty to sixty folds of cloth, &c. There is what is styled "an examiner" to every forty girls, whose duty it is to superintend their operations and examine their work when executed. There is a sorting and packing-room, from which goods are forwarded to their several destinations, and a large stock of every kind is always kept on hand to enable orders to be executed forthwith. Gentlemen's pyjama suits and drawers are also manufactured here and can be seen in every variety. The engine and boiler are fixed at a distance from the main building, and the shafting which is connected with the various machines runs along the floor of the factory, and is so placed as to prevent accidents to the hands employed therein. Everything about the establishment appears to have been designed with the object of making it a thoroughly model concern, and such it really is. The comfort, health, convenience and safety of the employés have been the primary object of the proprietor, and to a visitor this is self-evident. Tea-rooms have been provided for the workers, fitted up with a patent steam kettle which always insures a plentiful supply of boiling water; there are, also, lavatories and conveniences of all sorts. Shirt manufacturing is a new branch of trade in Macclesfield, and consequently, when Mr. Cameron commenced business here, three years ago, he had to train all his hands and initiate them in the art; and we believe he encountered very considerable opposition and annoyance for his having made what was considered an innovation upon the silk trade of Macclesfield. However, his establishment is going on most prosperously, and is affording employment to some two hundred hands, which, of course, is a direct advantage to the town. Before closing these remarks in respect to this concern it may be added that what is particularly noticeable about the manufactory, is the splendid order and system everywhere introduced. It may justly be said that there is a place for everything, and that everything is in its place. Indeed, if the premises had not been specially built, and designed, and fitted up with this object in view, it would have been next to impossible to conduct it in the present admirable style. With regard to the workpeople, it may be observed that a cleaner, neater, better attired or more respectable body of employés could not be found at any establishment in the kingdom. The depôt in Portland Street, Manchester, contains a splendid assortment of Mr. Cameron's best manufactures, and these include every description of shirt that can be mentioned, in every variety of sizes, colours, and qualities of material. Mr. Cameron has carried the art of shirtmaking to the highest degree of perfection, and his manufactures have acquired a much more than local reputation, as the extent and ramifications of his business fully testify, for he has an agency in London, at 15, Fore Street, E.C. (Mr. James Ridley, agent), and another at 28, Tarleton Street, Liverpool.

Messrs. Dickson, Brown & Tait, Seed Merchants to H.R.H. the Prince of Wales, 43 and 45, Corporation Street, Manchester.—In very few branches of business in any way connected with agriculture has there been of late years more improvement than in the seed trade. Twenty-five years ago little reliance could be placed on the purity and vitality of a great many of the seeds sold by even the leading firms, and a great deal of disappointment and loss to purchasers were the consequent result. Fortunately for agriculturists, a great change for the better has been brought about owing to some of our leading firms having adopted methods which prevent anything but seeds of the highest germinating power and purity from being offered by them. Prominent among the great seed firms who have been instrumental in bringing this about is that of Messrs. Dickson, Brown & Tait, whose head-quarters are in Manchester, but whose operations extend all over the kingdom. This well-known firm was established in Manchester about half a century ago. Their offices and garden-seed establishment are situated at 43 and 45, Corporation Street, and their large and extensive farm-seed warehouse is in Park Street, Cheetham Hill. If some of our agricultural friends could visit the latter establishment any time from the middle of February until the middle or end of April, they would be astonished at the large quantities of clover and rye grass seeds, also permanent pasture grasses, &c., which daily leave here for all parts of the country. From our opening remarks it naturally occurs to one, how can such large quantities of seeds all be known to possess the highest germinating powers, not to mention their freedom from all seeds of a foreign nature, weeds, &c.? A glance behind the scenes will, however, convince one that this is the case. Every sample of seed submitted to this firm by the growers is, in the first place, carefully analysed, and, if pure of its kind, it then undergoes the testing experiment as to its germination, and if this proves satisfactory, if purchased by them, the stock, on its arrival in their warehouses, undergoes the most careful scrutiny, and is again subjected to the testing process before the purchase is completed, and if found inferior to the original sample, it is at once rejected. To any one unacquainted with the trade, it would be astonishing to see the large numbers—many hundreds—of samples yearly rejected by the firm, owing to their inferiority. These inferior seeds are no doubt sold by firms without ever being tested, and most likely at low prices. It will readily occur to the reader how foolish it is on the part of farmers to buy these second-rate and impure seeds simply because they happen to be a penny or twopence a pound cheaper. We certainly think they act unwisely in doing so; by saving twenty shillings in the price of the seeds they purchase, they lose oftentimes five or even ten times that sum in the crop, not to mention the trouble and expense they are at in removing the weeds which are too prone to grow if sown with seeds. Agriculturists would act to their own advantage if they were more careful to consider quality than price when purchasing their season's supply of seeds. Of course they must not pay more than market price for a first-class article, and which can only be procured from such worthy firms as the one we refer to. Messrs. Dickson, Brown & Tait have for many years carefully tested the productiveness and feeding qualities of all the various kinds of swedes, common turnips, and mangolds, and have discarded all but the very best kinds. We learn that they have now in hand a new variety of purple-top swede which for weight of produce and excellence of quality is unsurpassed, it having produced five tons per acre more than any variety they had growing in their trial grounds last year. It will be some time before they will have sufficient stock of seed to enable them to offer it to their customers. In writing about the agricultural seed department of Messrs. Dickson, we must not forget the vegetable seed one. The name of this firm is associated with several of the most popular varieties of vegetables, such as their famous Eclipse Cauliflower, All the Year Round Lettuce, Best of all Melon, &c. Few firms, if any, import and retail so many Dutch and French flowering bulbs. Had our space permitted, we might have gone more fully into the merits of this firm; but, from what we have stated, we trust we have given sufficient evidence of the most anxious desire on the part of Messrs. Dickson, Brown & Tait to do everything in their power to supply the public with the best seeds of their respective kinds which nature annually produces.

T. Thomason & Co., Ecclesiastical and Domestic Metal Workers, &c., 76 and 78, Cross Street.—The extent to which ecclesiastical and domestic artistic metal work is used all over the world has within recent years made the trade therein of great and growing importance. A noted firm in this branch of industry is Messrs. T. Thomason & Co., who have offices in Cross Street. The headquarters and works, which are of very great extent, are in Birmingham. The firm is one of the oldest in this line, being established about forty years. Its stock and trade are second to only one house in the trade, and this only in extent; for, from the artistic point of view, the various productions of the concern are unsurpassed. The trade of the establishment embraces all parts of the country, and many customers abroad confer their patronage on the firm, whose goods where known are highly prized for their excellence and economy. An idea of the operations of the firm may be gleaned from the fact that they employ a staff of a hundred and fifty men in their works at Birmingham. One of the founders of the house was formerly a member of the Birmingham Town Council, and Messrs. Geo. A. Thomason, J. F. Thomason, and T. H. Thomason are all gentlemen of the highest integrity and social status.

Browne & Murray, Shirt Manufacturers, 4, Pump Street. The firm of Messrs. Browne & Murray, Shirt Manufacturers, is one of e largest in the trade. The business was established about ten years ro by Mr. Robert Mitchell Browne, in a comparatively small way, and ur years later he was joined by Mr. Dunbar Murray. By their united ideavours these energetic gentlemen have so extended their trade that ey now employ over five hundred hands at their factory in Pump Street. hree years ago, seeing clearly that, through competition, a severe ruggle was imminent in their trade, they cleared out, at a great sacri- e, all old machinery, and had their entire factory fitted up with the ost modern machinery run by power. This bold change had the anti- pated effect, as, by the mechanical superiority, they were enabled to rn out thirty per cent. more work without materially increasing their penses. The quantity of shirts sent out by this firm annually is ormous. And this can be well understood when it is known they have ade a careful study of the exact requirements of every market to which ritish goods are shipped, and that they have given special attention to veltics and new ideas. In their sample rooms are on show from two ousand to three thousand styles of shirts, from which selections could made to suit all tastes, from those of the savage to that of the most stidious at home. Messrs. Browne and Murray have, by their skilful anagement, earned and do maintain a high reputation, and are con- lered the leading firm in their branch of the trade in this city. They e to be congratulated on the success that has attended their efforts, and ust be highly gratified at the result.

H. S. Attia & Bros., Shipping Merchants and Planters, and 31, Barton Arcade, Manchester.—This firm, the only one of the name the United Kingdom, was established at the present address some seven years ago. The principal business is with the West Coast of Africa, to all the States of which Messrs. Attia ship large quantities of Manchester, Leeds, & Bradford goods, as well as cutlery, jewellery, steel toys, beads, and small fancy goods of Sheffield and Birmingham manufacture, and from which they import native produce, particularly dye woods and offee. The coffee-plant is an evergreen shrub, and a native of Liberia d Arabia. It grows in Liberia in a wild state to the height of from 16 to feet, and the leaves are of a bright green colour. The blossoms are of a rilliant white, and very like the jasmine flower; they expand so abun- antly as to hide the leaves, and a coffee plantation in full blossom is a eautiful sight to see, giving out at the same time a most pleasant, elicious, and fragrant aroma. The most suitable time for planting coffee Liberia is from the beginning of June to the end of July. The Libe- ian coffee-tree grows equally well in the immediate neighbourhood of the a and at considerable distances from it, and an estate of 20 or 30 acres ell looked after would yield as much coffee as an estate of 200 or 300 cres of Coffee Arabica, or Ceylon, or any other coffee. Coffee-berries are ke plums, and as big; the berries are allowed to ripen, and are then aken off, a mat being put underneath to receive them; they are then ried in the sun, crushed by a stone roller, and the seeds picked out. ometimes the berries are plucked off, then dried in the sun, bruised in a ill, the pulp or husk washed away, and the seeds dried. They are then f a greenish yellow colour, and when thoroughly dried they are packed barrels or bags and consigned to different parts of the world for sale. Before they are fit for use the berries should be roasted in an earthenware an over a slow fire, and great care is required in this operation. They re then put into a coffee grinder and ground into a powder, and are then eady for use. Coffee has been used as an article of food for more than wo centuries in its own native land, Liberia (formerly called the Grain Coast), and other parts. Coffee is now largely used as an article of food, and exhilarating and refreshing coffee-houses are now universal. The irst in London was erected A.D. 1652, and at the present day the coffee- houses are numerous and are increasing daily; and owing to its increased demand, coffee has doubled itself in price within the last nine months. Messrs Attia have a plantation of 75,000 coffee-plants, situated eight miles from Grand Bassa, Liberia. Cam wood is also imported (Messrs. Attia being the largest importers in the world, Edina being the port from which it is supplied) for dyeing purposes, the whole of the New York market being supplied by them. Messrs. Attia were the first to cultivate the coffee-plant in Liberia and bring the berry into the market, where it s considered a great acquisition, both from its superiority in size and its aromatic flavour. Palm-oil is also largely imported by this firm, and distributed throughout the whole world. The premises at Barton Arcade are a handsome suite of commodious offices that are extremely well furnished and appointed, and fitted with all the recent modern business appliances. The Messrs. Attia enjoy a first-class reputation in the commercial world; they are well-known members of the Exchange, and they are never appealed to in vain in support of deserving public movements.

Premises at GRAND BASSA.

W. H. Williamson, Manufacturer of the Victoria Baking Powder &c., "Victoria Works," 13 and 15, Mayes Street, 51, Dantzic Street, and the Arch Pickle Works, Red Bank.—A principal place among the many branches of industry carried on in Manchester is held by the manufacture of baking powder, custard powder, pickles, sauce, starch, enamel, and quinine wine, and it is in the highest state of perfection. A house well known in all parts of the country is that of Mr. William Henry Williamson, which was founded in 1868. Mr. W. H. Williamson is noted as the manufacturer of the "Victoria Baking Powder," which, with his other productions, has been wrought to the highest state of excellence, and was awarded three gold medals at the New Zealand Exhibition of 1882, and a prize medal at the London Annual International Exhibition of 1873. The premises, consisting of warehouse and works, comprise a spacious, commodious, four-storied building, splendidly fitted up with the most modern machinery and apparatus for grinding, &c., and a large force of skilled hands is employed in manufacturing the famous "Victoria" baking powder, custard powder, pickles, sauce, starch, enamel, and quinine wine. The materials are of the highest qualities, the processes are the result of experience, patience, and talent, and the goods produced under the trade mark of the firm, "Victoria," are highly esteemed in all parts. Mr. William Henry Williamson carries on a most extensive trade in all parts of the United Kingdom, and manages with enterprise and ability. The works at Red Bank cover an area of four thousand square yards, and there may be seen thousands of barrels of goods in different stages of manufacture. The great demand for the goods, and the gaining of the medals, testify to their excellence. In the commercial and industrial world no member is more highly respected than Mr. W. H. Williamson.

John Wainwright, Land and Estate Agent, Valuer, Surveyor, Arbitrator, &c., Old Bank Chambers, 87, Market Street.—Established over five-and-twenty years, this business is amongst the most important in the North of England. In addition to the ordinary connection for the management, sale, and purchase of estates, shop, house, and warehouse property, Mr. Wainwright has a very extensive and valuable connection amongst barristers, solicitors, millowners, manufacturers, and others, so that his time is largely occupied in valuations and arbitrations. He is the founder and principal secretary of the North of England Fire Insurance Company, Limited, a flourishing concern, with offices in Manchester, London, Liverpool, Leeds, and Glasgow, and representatives in the principal towns of Great Britain; and also the secretary of other important commercial enterprises. With so much important business to transact, commodious and large suites of offices and many clerks are absolutely necessary, and in fact there are few firms in Manchester which employ so large and able a staff. Mr. Wainwright is a well-known Manchester man, and an employer of labour in connection with this and other large business undertakings.

British Equitable Assurance Company, W. R. Simmons, District Superintendent, 21, Cannon Street, Manchester.—The life insurance system has been for many years a positive force in the progress of modern civilisation and the accumulation of national wealth. It has been an important factor in the education of every community which it has influenced in habits of economy and prudence. One of the leading and most successful companies in the United Kingdom is the British Equitable Assurance Company, whose head office is at 4, Queen Street Place, London, E.C. This society was established in 1854, and from the very beginning has enjoyed a prosperous career, a fact which speaks more than volumes for the sound judgment and honourable methods which have always characterised its management. The Company is a purely Life Office, and assures English lives only. Its policy holders are taken from the classes of temperate, thrifty, and industrious habits, in fact from among the most desirable class in the community. Since the beginning of its career the Company has paid over one million pounds for death claims. Its accumulated funds amount also to upwards of one million and a quarter sterling. The constitution of the company gives the full advantage of mutual insurance without the possibility of personal liability. The principle of equity is carried out in its rates of premium, in the values given for the surrender of policies, and in its loans on policies, and in its prompt payment of claims. Add to this the fact that the administration is by a body of men who are largely concerned in the management of some of the most important benevolent institutions of the day, and are well known throughout the country as men of business distinguished for their ability, prudence, and honour. The Company has a large and steadily increasing number of policy holders in Manchester and vicinity. The local superintendent of this office is Mr. W. R. Simmons, a gentleman eminently qualified by more than thirty years' experience and well-proved ability for the important position.

Middleton, Jones & Co., Limited, Manufacturers, &c., 6, Chorlton Street.—Prominent among the great industries of Manchester and district are the large manufacturers, mills, factories, &c. These constitute the nucleus of the great wealth and prosperity of the city and its inhabitants. The house of Middleton, Jones & Co., Limited, manufacturers of velvets and velveteens, is a high representative centre of the manufacturing industry. Established in 1875, this house has long maintained a high reputation for its superior productions, and as a result there is a large and valuable trade, the firm having large business connections in most of the principal trading centres of the globe, and the well-known fine quality of its velvets and velveteens, dyed, as they are, by the world-famed dyers, I. and I. M. Worrall, commanding open markets and large sales at very satisfactory quotations. The home trade extends to most of the best buying houses of London, Glasgow, Birmingham, Bradford, &c., large operations being continually carried through by the firm, who, by their manufacturing facilities, and devoting the whole of their time and large experience to the production of these goods only, are well able to place their customers on especially favourable terms.

The premises occupied comprise a large and handsome warehouse of new and recent construction, very well appointed, and admirably arranged for the transaction of the large business of the house, and filled with a choice and costly assortment of very valuable stock, and affording employment to a large staff of well-qualified assistants, warehousemen, and others. Attached to the premises are a handsome suite of offices, well fitted and furnished and adequately provided with a staff of clerks, &c., for the prompt transaction of the counting-house business of the establishment. The whole aspect of the house is orderly and shows to the observing business man that nothing is wanting and no expense spared to make this what it appears to be, a high-class wholesale city house.

E. Goodall & Co. (R. M. Esplin, Proprietor), Carpet Warehousemen, Upholsterers, Cabinet-makers, &c., 15, King Street.—One of the most important business interests in Manchester is the carpet, upholstery, and cabinet-making trade, and it employs many establishments, whose attractive appearance is one of the chief business sights of the city. A well-known house, and one which is the oldest in Manchester, is that trading as Messrs. E. Goodall & Co. (proprietor, Mr. R. M. Esplin), which was established in 1827. The premises, eligibly situated on a corner site, and comprising a handsome block of buildings, form a spacious five-storied building, which is fully fitted and furnished for stock accommodation and display. The stock, which makes a magnificent display, is very extensive, and comprises furniture of the most costly nature and of elegant and original designs—carpets from the most noted looms, fittings for libraries, clubs, banks, offices, &c., joinery of great artistic merit, chimney-pieces of beauty and uniqueness in design, over-mantels, dados, panelling, parquetry, tiles, and other goods of an artistic nature for decorating and furnishing purposes. The works where the cabinet-making is carried on are in Cobden Street, Sussex Street, and are large and commodious, and admirably equipped, and the workmen experienced and skilful, as may be supposed from the costly work turned out. About two hundred hands are employed to meet the demands of the trade, which extends all over Great Britain, and is of a very high-class character. Travellers are employed, and Mr. R. M. Esplin, the proprietor of this splendid business, manages with ability and enterprise. He is well known in the trade, thoroughly understands all details, and enjoys the esteem and confidence of the many members and the community in general for his genuine qualities and the able manner in which he maintains the splendid name of a house which is the oldest in the trade, and has exercised an influence therein of a most salutary character.

The Hayfield Printing Co., Calico Printers, 52, Mosley Street.—This business was commenced in the year 1857, and is now considered one of the leading firms in its line. The premises consist of a handsome and commodious warehouse of four floors, with a suite of spacious offices. The print works are at Hayfield, in Derbyshire; and they cover an extensive area, furnishing employment for a large number of hands. The machinery and plant are all of modern construction, and
the entire premises are fitted up in
Company, determined to be forem
preparation in design, &c., and hav
ing and for novel and safe colourin

John H. Gartside & Co
and Manufacturers, Bleachers
Manufacturers of Bookbinders'
the most important and extensive
country is cotton spinning and its
printing, and it employs hundreds
is the centre of this district, and a
houses in the city, an important p
H. Gartside & Co., Limited, who
have extensive mills for spinning
Dukinfield, Hollingworth, and Ar
works at Buckton Vale, near Sta
city are large and commodious, co
offices and sale rooms, and a sta
warehouse, which is massively bui
large and varied stock of bleache
for home and foreign markets, all
dyed, and printed at the mills and
works are replete with the most mo
large number of hands, estimated
goods produced are of splendid qua
H. Gartside and Co., Limited, carr
establishment in France; and th
could be desired. The directors of
thorough knowledge of the cotton
ness early in life; and are well kn
industrial, and commercial world.
house has done much to advance t
producing power represented by
quadrupled in that period.

The Clayton Aniline Co
manufacture of aniline and dyes is
country, and among the cities enga
nificant place. A thoroughly repr
Clayton Aniline Company, Limit
established twelve years. The co
Charles Dreyfus, during its existe
holds a prominent place in the ind
very extensively and completely fit
the most modern construction for t
hands are employed in the manufa
used are of superior quality, th
advanced, consequently the articl
pure. Mr. Charles Dreyfus super
his untiring efforts the company
trade in all parts is carried on;
the business is increasing. The co
raw materials, on a very large s
largest producers of aniline oil and
in the world. These two articles
largely used for dyeing and prin
company is the best of any make
known in industrial and commerci
well defined, and through its tale
done much to perfect this importa

John Whitaker, 22, Bl
and varied application of electricit
ances and apparatus an importan
for the extent of her business in
typical house in this trade is that
experienced electrician, who rem
smaller premises to his present ad
his removal. The premises consis
the shop will be found a good s
apparatus, including bells, batt
speaking-tubes, philosophical and
parts and materials for the const
Mr. Whitaker manufactures his
and scientific principles. He al
principles, all work in connection
fire alarms, speaking-tubes, medi
the fitting of electric bells to bar
Whitaker's is the repairing of el
information will be hailed with j
had to send their repairs to Londo
a thorough scientific knowledge of
workmen, and having tools, &c.,
is enabled to please the most fastid
a good business in Manchester and
stand every branch of his busine
to his talent, business energy, a
known in business circles, where h

& Co., Manufacturers of Tarpaulins,
g Purposes, &c., 17, Palace Street.—Prominent
industry for which Manchester is famous is the
ns, oil-cloth, and patent packing, and other similar
rely in the packing of general goods to India,
n countries; and this branch of industry, by the
ie many members engaged, has been brought to
ection. A noted firm in this line is that trading
vell & Co. (Mr. John Blackwell, sole member).
he year 1811 by the late Mr. Henry Leicester, a
and highly respected, with whom Mr. Blackwell
rds of twenty-one years, the business in 1873
Blackwell and further developed in his own name.
works are at Collyhurst, and are extensive, and
d as regards modern machinery, appliances, and
methods of hand labour have been superseded by

ted by Mr. Blackwell, and protected by royal
and well-trained staff is engaged in manufactured methods the goods above enumerated, which
rial, and splendid workmanship. The Manchester
acious warehouse, recently rebuilt and enlarged,
nsive stock of oil-cloth of all kinds for packing
g, hessians, twill, sackings, &c. An efficient staff
Agencies of long standing are at Glasgow,
at London, 41, Allen's Buildings, Leonard Street,
xes. Mr. John Blackwell has brought his pro-
pitch of excellence, and they take a leading place
ries on a very considerable local and widespread
increasing under his able management and the
l travellers. Mr. John Blackwell is a gentleman
l aptitude for his trade, and he is well known and
ndustrial and commercial world, whilst the status
igh and well defined.

, Wine and Spirit Merchant, St. Ann's
, established forty years ago under the style of
ith central cellars and office in Hunts Bank, has,
steadily extended its circle of customers, until at
a select and high-class connection, not only in and
spread over every part of the United Kingdom.
hment in Hunts Bank, branches were opened in all
nufacturing towns in the North of England, and
ndon and the South. In 1871 the business having
proportions, the late Mr. W. M. Simmons took
oncern, his partner, Mr. Knowles, retiring. Mr.
ting his attention more especially on the Man-
siness, took very extensive cellarage accommoda-
nchester Royal Exchange, in which building he
en these cellars, large as they were, very soon
his ever-increasing business, and he therefore
e of offices and cellars, part of which the old firm
, in St. Ann's Square, to which he again removed
ock some five years ago. These cellars which the
the basement of three of the largest buildings in
in the rear as far as Barton Square. The bin
which contains a range of bins not to be sur-
the kingdom, are especially interesting, not only
models of order and symmetry, but also on account
e are to be found bins of priceless value, contain-
st noted vintages, ports, sherries, clarets, hocks,
ate Mr. Simmons having always felt that keen
ears feel in securing whatever is choice and rare;
the finest collections of rare and curious old wines
ever got together in one cellar. Mr. Simmons was also noted for the study he made of Scotch whiskey, and he produced, as a speciality, a fully matured blend of the choicest productions of the most noted Highland stills, and now known all over England as W. M. Simmons's "Special" Scotch whiskey. But no more need be said on this head, the whiskey in question being too well known and appreciated to need any further comment on our part. In both offices and cellars a capable and experienced staff is employed, and a steady trade is done the year round. For many years there has existed on the part of the public generally, and especially of private families, a great and steadily increasing demand for a light, high-class malt liquor, which, while perfectly free from the headiness of ordinary beers, shall at the same time possess the sparkling, pleasing, and nutritious qualities of a true pale ale. Mr. Simmons has fully satisfied this demand in introducing to the public of Manchester a beverage appropriately named "Gem" ale, brewed by Messrs. Lucas, Blackwell, and Arkwright, of Leamington. We are told the water from which the ale is brewed is drawn direct from the rock, and has been pronounced to be of "exceptional purity;" and the finest malt and hops are used in its production, whilst by a peculiar process of fermentation, that sparkling effervescent character is given to the ale, which forms so leading an element in the favourite beverages of the day. The keeping properties of the "Gem" ale will be found to be unrivalled, age simply serving to render its vinous qualities more marked and apparent. The "Gem" ale is supplied in casks of nine, eighteen, and thirty-six gallons, at the rate of one shilling per gallon. Mr. Simmons having lately died, the business is for the present being carried on temporarily by the executors. Arrangements have, however, been made by which it will be very shortly transferred to Mr. Simmons's two sons, Messrs. E. A. and H. S. Simmons, both of whom have had considerable experience of the trade, not only in this country but on the Continent. We understand they intend continuing the firm still under the style of W. M. Simmons.

Messrs. Nathan Smallpage & Sons, Manufacturers & Warehousemen, 86, George Street.—In the trade and industries of Manchester and district, a thoroughly representative establishment, and one well worthy of prominent mention, is the well-known house of Messrs. Nathan Smallpage & Sons, who control the large works at Kelbrook and Bridge Mills, near Colne, and manufacture all sorts of fancy coloured goods, such as American regattas, denims, diagonals, ticks, fancy and plain drills, ginghams, Harvards, Oxfords, twills, and every description of cloths, both for the home trade and export. Established now over thirty years, this house has always maintained a high reputation as one of the leading warehouses of the city. Its business operations are on a most extensive scale, including large consignments to all the South American, West Indian, the Cape, and Australian shipping houses, as well as the leading London, Glasgow, and Belfast warehousemen. The goods of the firm are well known, not only for their novelty and originality of design, but for the fastness of all the colours introduced into their various makes, and find ready and open markets at all seasons and at favourable quotations. The works are most compact, consisting of two large weaving mills, containing nearly one thousand looms, specially constructed for the large variety of their productions. The firm have also extensive dyeing and bleaching plant in connection with the mills, and are the oldest makers of coloured goods in East Lancashire. The premises in Manchester comprise a lofty and conspicuous building of five stories, thoroughly adapted to the many requirements of the business of the firm, and necessitating the assistance of a considerable number of employés, clerks and others. The stocks held are very large, consisting of fancy coloured woven goods, both for the home trade and foreign markets, all admirably arranged, and representing a large equivalent in capital. The stock-rooms are in every way adapted for the purpose of storage and display. The principals comprising the partnership are Mr. Nathan Smallpage, Mr. James Smallpage, and Mr. Richard Smallpage, gentlemen of high commercial status and of the strictest integrity.

Hulme Bros., Timber Merchants, Withington Street, Broad Street, Pendleton, and Quay Street, Deansgate.—There are some very extensive and substantial firms engaged in the timber trade of Manchester. One of the most notable of these is that known as Hulme Brothers. This establishment was started in 1840 by Mr. W. C. Hulme, who has since retired from the business. In 1876 the firm, as it now exists, was established. The partners are Messrs. Sam. (retired September last), John, and Alfred Hulme. The business, for extent and value, is equalled by few concerns in the same line in the district. The premises owned by the firm comprise timber yards, quays, and offices, at all of which a large staff of men is continually occupied. The stock of timber held is very large, and embraces ash, beech, birch, baywood, boxwood, cedar, elm, ebony, hornbeam, mahogany, maple, oak, pollard, oak and Dantzic, poplar, pine in log and deal, pitch pine, rosewood, spruce deals, sycamore, walnut, and all kinds of veneers. The firm is said to hold the largest stock of sycamore for special purposes possessed by any concern in this kingdom. Every part of the establishment is kept in perfect order, and the management of the whole concern is of the most energetic and faultless kind. The connections of the house cover all parts of the country. The partners enjoy the respect and confidence of the commercial community.

Samuel McLardy, Tobacco Pipe Manufacturer, and Importer of Tobacconists' Fancy Goods, Miller Street.

MAKING TOBACCO-PIPES AT NEWTON HEATH.

Twenty millions of clay pipes. Take breath for a moment, and see if you can realize such astounding numbers. Twenty millions a year of clay pipes are being manufactured by one firm alone, and that a Manchester one! And—alas for the hopes of the Anti-Tobacco-League—the manufacture is steadily increasing. Is Manchester going to the dogs? Not exactly. The croakers have no idea of what is being done in and around their own city. They do not know how one industry after another is quietly settling itself within our precincts, without noise, bustle, or ostentation; flourishing like a green bay tree under apparently adverse circumstances; seemingly without either rhyme or reason—except that in this vigorous soil and atmosphere of Lancashire, it seems only necessary to plant a tiny seed of a trade, and it immediately becomes a great tree with branches which overshadow the whole earth. This clay-pipe making is a curious instance in point. One would naturally suppose that the English headquarters of such an industry would be, almost of necessity, in that district which we call the "Potteries." But no; here in our midst, hundreds of miles away from the mines of raw material, suffering under disadvantages in the way of carriage which nothing but the Ship Canal is likely to remove, we find has grown up within the last twenty years or so the largest clay pipe manufactory in England, (perhaps in the world) competing with and exporting to well-nigh all countries. This is something to ponder upon. Mark Twain, in a sermon to anti-tobaccoites, says: "I don't want any of your statistics. I took your whole batch and lit my pipe with it. I hate your kind of people. You never try to find out how much solid comfort, relaxation, and enjoyment a man derives from smoking in the course of a life-time (which is worth ten times the money he would save by letting it alone); nor the appalling aggregate of happiness lost in a life-time by your kind of people from *not* smoking." Another writer opines that for good thinking the pipe is preferable to the cigar, and most certainly so for good reading. And we believe, (having had a little experience) that a long clay pipe, a veritable "churchwarden," is the best pipe of all. Two hundred years since, and until comparatively recent times, the best clay pipes were imported from Holland; but at last the introduction of our Devonshire white clay enabled us successfully to compete with the Dutch, and even to surpass them. Glasgow was for many years considered to be the chief pipe-making place, and large quantities are still made there; but our local manufacturer, Mr. Samuel McLardy, of Miller Street Manchester, and Newton Heath, has by the magnitude of his operations put himself at the head of all. The extensive works of Mr. McLardy are at Newton Heath, and thither we betake ourselves to examine the curious although apparently simple operations connected with the manufacture of clay pipes. The making of wooden pipes, meerschaums, and the like is an entirely different trade and is not carried on here, although this class of goods forms a large and increasing portion of Mr. McLardy's business. On arrival at the works, we find ourselves at once in the midst of heaps of pipes, stacks of filled boxes, and racks of metal moulds. Our first care is to see the clay. This so-called white clay all comes from the Devonshire mines in lumps about twice the size of one's head; and is greyish in tint in its unbaked state, but burns perfectly white. It is brought by ship to Runcorn, thence by canal to Manchester. In the clay-store we find perhaps three to four boat-loads of about thirty tons each piled up in lumps as described, waiting its turn to be prepared for service. About five hundred tons are used annually. The first thing to be done is to get the lumps dried, and this is effected by stacking them around the outside of the circular kilns, and in a chamber built for the purpose over the long steam boiler, which will accommodate about twelve tons. When dried (not baked) the lumps are broken up with a hammer into small pieces and put into great iron tanks about fourteen feet long, to be wetted down; various qualities of the clay being mixed together in careful proportion, according to the purpose desired. After it has become well soaked and softened, it is dug out of the tanks and thoroughly mixed and tempered by the spade of the workman, much after the manner of mortar mixing, and is thus prepared for the pug-mill—an upright cylinder, in which the final grinding and mixing processes are performed—from the foot whereof it is discharged in a perfect condition. The clay is now in what a sculptor would consider a delightful condition; it is indeed sold largely to sculptors for modelling purposes, among others the well-known sculptor here, Mr. Swinnerton, having it sent to his studio in Rome, there being nothing equal to it obtainable over there. It is soft, smooth, tenacious, pleasant to the touch, without a trace of grit or harshness, and our fingers itch to be modelling therewith. The pug-mill is driven by steam power, and is the only thing which requires it; all other operations being performed by hand. From the grinding and tempering mill we follow the clay into the moulding-room. This has a very peculiar appearance, and would—if anything could—gladden the hearts of some of our melancholy painters, who look upon the whole creation as one vast sink of greyness and "tone." There is plenty of greyness here, plenty of tone, but hardly a spark of colour. It is a great, long, well-lighted room, fitted with about fifteen or sixteen work-benches, each having space for four workmen. Room, floor, roof, benches, and workmen are all of one pervading tint of grey clay. From all the benches stick up short wooden arms or levers, connected with small presses used by the moulders; and there is a continual clicking going on as these are pulled down. We should mention before going further that here, as everywhere else in these days, subdivision of labour is carried out to its fullest extent. No man by himself makes a pipe; the man who works on short pipes cannot work on long ones, and each man devotes himself for ever and ever to his own speciality. Now let us watch the workers and see how a pipe is made in the rough. A man sits at the low work-bench with a lump of clay at his right hand, from which he from time to time pinches off a bit. The only tool he uses is a flat bit of board about six inches by four. Watching him, you might fancy him to be a pie-maker rolling out bits of dough for the ornamentation of the top crust. He takes the pinched bit of clay and rolls it out on the table with his hands to the length of the pipe required, using occasionally the flat bit of wood also as a roller, until the clay assumes the appearance of a kind of big tadpole, the head being intended for the bowl, and the long tail for the stem. These he lays together in dozens upon a narrow board or tray; and thus his connection with the making terminates. From him these embryos go into a room heated by steam pipes, where they are partially dried to give them stiffness sufficient for the next operation, in which they are made to assume their destined shape by the hands of the moulder. And now comes the solution of a puzzle which has mystified us all our life long. We never could conceive how the hole was made down the stem of a long pipe, say a "churchwarden," from twenty-one to twenty-seven inches long. One explanation given has been that you took a long hole and stuck some clag round it; but that never seemed particularly easy to be achieved. When seen, it is just the simplest thing imaginable, to look at. The operator takes the long clay tadpole in his left hand, a bright wire in his right, and jauntily draws the clay upon the wire, beginning at the extreme end of the tail, just as easy as a gentle piscatorian draws a worm upon a hook, or a skilful housewife runs a bodkin through the top casing-hem of a pinafore. It looks as easy as sneezing; but we have our doubts. When the tadpole has got itself threaded, it is laid (with the wire still within it) in a metal mould (which opens in the middle something like the two halves of an ordinary pipe case), and placed in the groove of a small press fixed on the bench. The wooden arm or lever before mentioned, to which a metal plunger is attached, is then pulled down and forms the hollow of the bowl, squeezing out at the same time the superfluous clay, which is trimmed off with a thin broad blade. The mould is then opened, the wire withdrawn, after being by a quick and almost imperceptible movement rammed home into the bowl, and you have a pipe completely formed. All refuse clay is collected, put into a hopper, and sent down below to be worked up again in the pug mill. In the moulding-room men only are employed; but the next workshop we visit, the "finishing room," is tenanted only by women and girls of all ages, from the wrinkled old lady down to the girl in her teens. They are respectable-looking and neat, and each one wears a great white apron as she sits at work at the table. Their occupation is to finish and trim up the pipes after coming from the moulds and being partially hardened in the drying-room. It is light, dainty work, and it is a pleasure to watch their wonderful, quick, deft movements. Each woman has a little wooden block fixed upon the table before her, and upon this is laid the stem of the pipe—the bowl being carefully held between finger and thumb—whilst with little tools she quickly takes off the seam left by the joining of the mould, and polishes up the surface. A wire is run up the stem to perfectly clear it out, the bowl is trimmed up wherever necessary, and a bit of damp sponge is run round the edges. Some pipes have a device imprinted on the sides with a hand stamp, and others require a fancy curve in the stem which is achieved with marvellous ease and quickness. There is, of course, much diversity of talent amongst these fair workers; and some very tender, highly-finished, short pipes, of best clay, can only be handled or worked by very few of them. Of course the wages they earn are in proportion to their ability and quickness, all being paid by piecework. As the pipes are finished they are laid carefully upon boards in rows and taken again to the hot drying-room, there to undergo a preliminary baking for about a day, before being transferred to the kilns to be burnt thoroughly hard. The kilns and furnaces are of novel construction and circular in shape, the kilns for the short pipes being altogether different from the furnaces in which the long ones are burnt. Before being placed in the kilns the short pipes are arranged in circular "seggars," or pots of fire-clay, about twelve inches in diameter and nine in depth, each one holding about three gross. These are piled in heaps one upon another in the kiln from floor to crown to the number of 360, and baked twelve hours. The heat is furnished by four fires ranged round at equal distances, communicating with underground flues having regulating dampers, by means of which the heat is regulated and allowed to ascend through the floor to the seggars, at discretion. The furnaces for burning the long pipes are entirely different. They are circular in shape, and are built round inside in steps, each step being larger in circumference than the one immediately below it. In the centre is a clay standard supporting an inverted fire-clay mug, or cap, upon which are laid, all round and close together, the pipes to be burned, the ends of all the stems pointing to the centre. When ranged round they are covered with very thin sheets of clay backed with paper, as a protection. Another cap is then fitted on, another range of pipes laid round, and so on until the furnace is filled, by which time it contains about one hundred and fifty gross. The fires are underneath, and the most elaborate precautions are taken to ensure uniformity of graduated heat, and to prevent damage to the quality of the pipe. Burning is a very critical operation, and does much to make or mar the finished goods. If too soft they are too brittle, and if over hard and flinty they are unpleasant to smoke. Much of the superiority claimed for our own clay pipes over those of French make is attributed to the better burning. In these kilns the pipes are burnt, or baked rather, during fourteen to sixteen hours. In the same building with these furnaces is a peculiar stove arrangement for vitrifying the coloured enamel on the ends of certain of the pipes. Those we saw being operated upon had the ends coated with what appeared to be red paint, but which, when burnt, came out as a beautiful green enamelling. From the kilns we follow the pipes to the "painting room," where we find many women and girls at work upon numerous varieties, the major portion being short clays of one kind or other. Wherever there is room, piles of seggars just fresh up from the kilns are standing about, their contents waiting to be operated upon by the artists. The "painters," however, are mostly glazers, who give the final touching up and sometimes impart a tint. It is the business of some to bring out a fine smooth surface with sandpaper, after which the pipes are handed to other girls who sit at the tables, each with a little pot of liquid glazing material before her, which she applies all over the surface with a soft camel-hair brush. This glazing has no gloss until after the pipes have been placed in an oven and heated for some time, whereby the gloss is developed. Some painting is certainly done here by our lady artists, such as the touching up of the moulded designs and figures which ornament many of the pipes. For this purpose the finest of colours are used, which are afterwards burnt in. The varieties of these short pipes are almost endless, old types continually falling into the rear and becoming unsaleable, whilst new fashions are for ever coming forward. One particular kind (Calcined), of which large quantities are manufactured, is a short clay which on a casual inspection might deceive the unwary into the notion that it was a meerschaum, so excellently are the colour and general appearance imitated. This deceptive appearance is given by girls sitting at tables each with a small spirit lamp before her. The pipes, after being well scoured and polished with sandpaper, have a glaze applied to the surface, are well dried, and are then brought to the girls with the lamps, who, by passing them through the flame, produce any tint desired, from the most delicate cream to the richest brown of the coloured meerschaum. The process looks simple enough, but requires very skilful hands to perform it well and artistically. There is a secret, moreover, in the glazing. Another speciality here, the "Gordon," is a registered pipe designed to prevent the passage of nicotine along the stem. This is fitted with a clay plug in the bowl, and a hole is pierced through the bottom and through the nipple, upon which a little movable metal cap is fixed which receives the tobacco-juice as it drains down. A fanciful toy in the shape of a short pipe produced at these works is one which has a serpent coiled round the stem, whose eyes are composed of tiny microscopic lenses which show, when looked through, a photograph of magnificent landscape scenery. We need not attempt to describe further the hosts of different designs. They are now before us by hundreds in almost every conceivable shape—straight, curved, sloped, or upright—adorned with all kinds of groups, and figures, and heads. Here we have a dolphin, there a fowl's head; sometimes a group of racers, sometimes a bicyclist; and of grotesques, they are simply endless in number. Our work is finished when we have had a glance at the packing and dispatching-room, which is piled to the top with immense heaps of filled boxes ready to be sent to various places at home and abroad. One great heap is going to Canada; another to Africa, to Lagos; others go to Australia and to America. In fact there are few places where clay pipes are known at all to which they do not go. A striking feature about these works has been their rapid growth, they having been started only in 1865, with half-a-dozen hands; whereas now Mr. McLardy finds employment for about one hundred and fifty of both sexes, who are kept steadily at work and receive good wages.—*Manchester City News*, April 9th, 1887.

Samuel McLardy & Co., Wholesale Jewellers, and London, Birmingham, and Sheffield Warehousemen; 14, Miller Street.—This well-known firm commenced business in the year 1877. Their trade is of a varied and comprehensive character. They are London, Birmingham, and Sheffield Warehousemen; importers of English and foreign china, glass, earthenware, toys, etc. The premises they occupy are extensive, handsomely fitted up, and well arranged, and are very attractive externally and internally. They are five stories high, and cover a considerable area; and the organization of the establishment is complete and efficient, down to the smallest details. On the ground floor are to be found jewellery, watches and clocks, gold and silver goods, cutlery, leather goods, albums, purses, stationery, and fancy goods. On the first floor, cabinet and hardware; musical instruments, concertinas, accordeons, desks, workboxes, etc.; ironmongery and general goods. On the second floor, china, glass, and earthenware; tea and dinner services, flint and fancy glass. And the third and fourth floors are devoted chiefly to English and foreign toys, of which they make a grand display. It would occupy a good-sized volume to particularize Messrs. McLardy & Co's enormous stock, but, taken altogether, it may truly be said of it that it is the largest and finest in the provinces. There are ladies and gentlemen's watches of English, Swiss, and American manufacture, and in an almost endless variety of style and make. Japanese ware, including cups and saucers, fans, plaques, and numerous other specimens of Japanese art and invention; and the collection of jewellery, English and foreign glass ware, London, Birmingham, and Sheffield goods of every description, is quite unique. Few establishments in the kingdom can make a finer display, or one that is more interesting and inviting; and this observation particularly applies to the stock of English and foreign china which form specialities of their business. Their trade (which is strictly a wholesale one) is conducted on the most admirable lines, and in a way which has won for them the confidence and esteem of their clients in all parts of the kingdom. The firm are in a position to compete successfully with any other house in the provinces, either for the sale of watches, jewellery, London, Birmingham, and Sheffield goods or fancy wares; and we may add, that the establishment is well worthy of a visit, either from lovers of the artistic, the beautiful, the curious, or the rare, as well as from those who require the more useful and substantial articles of commerce. In conclusion, we may observe that the proprietors are gentlemen of great energy, ability, and enterprise; they are much respected, and their commercial reputation is second to none in the city of Manchester.

The "Economic" Life Assurance Society, 27, Princess Street, Albert Square.—The Economic Life Assurance Society bears an honourable and enviable record of usefulness and high success. It was established in the year 1823, and has thus been a going concern for over sixty-three years. The funds now in hand, being the accumulation of premiums and interest, after the settlement of all claims, amount to over three and a half millions sterling, while the extent of its operations is very considerable, the sums insured up to the present reaching the splendid total of over nine and a half millions. Claims have been paid to the amount of over eight millions. In accordance with the mutual lines upon which the concern is worked, the directors are themselves members, and the management of the society is conducted under their orders solely in the interests of their fellow policy-holders, there being no shareholders to participate in the profits, whilst the assured are expressly exempt from the inconvenience of individual liability. The rates of premium of the "Economic" are considerably below the average of those usually charged for assurances with early participation of profits, thereby securing the immediate advantage of a larger original assurance than may be obtained elsewhere for the same payment. Policies are issued only on first-class lives, and no proposal is for a moment entertained where the personal condition or family history of the life proposed would necessitate payment of a premium higher than the tabular rate. This society has also a most satisfactorily "equitable and compound" bonus system. The method of apportioning the surplus is a factor of great importance in estimating the merits of different offices. Before selecting an office intending assurers should first of all ascertain whether the bonuses are apportioned on the compound system or on the original sums assured alone. Policies in the "Economic" not only increase in participation at each succeeding division, in proportion to the increased age of the assured, but the additions are also calculated on the original sums assured and previous bonuses. Notwithstanding the very low rates of premium charged, the profits are not reserved for the exclusive benefit of the "long livers," or of any select class of policy-holders, but are divided amongst all with profit policies in force at each investigation, the bonuses vesting after payment of the fifth year's premiums. As a result of the admirable management of this society, the bonuses declared since its commencement have been most remarkable—amounting in fact to the grand total of £4,153,000. In some instances policies have actually been trebled in amount by means of the accrued bonuses. Additional advantages are found in that the "Economic" gives intermediate bonuses, while the member has the privilege of option with regard to the application of the said bonuses. Immediate payment of claims is guaranteed upon the production of the necessary proof of death and title; and the directors of the society make every endeavour, in the various prospectuses issued, to give all information, thus enabling the public to judge of the merits of the office and the great advantages it offers in securing to policy-holders the largest possible return in proportion to the premiums paid, an "Economic" policy being not only a reliable family provision but an increasingly valuable investment. The office at 41, Brown Street, has been occupied since the establishment of this branch in Manchester. The business, however, has, on account of its increasing importance (and thanks to the hard-working and energetic district manager, Mr. W. Smith), now been removed to more commodious premises at 27, Princess Street, Albert Square. The head office of this flourishing society is situated at 6, New Bridge Street, Blackfriars, London, E.C.

Arnold, Constable, & Co., Shippers, 41, Lower Mosley Street.—One of the principal countries with which the Manchester trade is carried on is the United States, and among the American firms with houses in Manchester a leading position is held by that of Messrs. Arnold, Constable, & Co. It was originally founded at Chancery Lane in 1860, and subsequently removed to present address. The premises occupied are large and commodious. The firm is engaged in shipping British fabrics, such as cottons, woollens, silks, and linens to their New York house. These goods are shipped in immense quantities, and are obtained from the leading manufacturers in the United Kingdom. The firm has houses at Paris, 21, Rue D'Hauteville, and Lyons, 8, Quai St. Clair; and is well known in all markets for the satisfactory manner in which it conducts its extensive business, which ranks amongst the foremost in the country.

W. G. Thompson & Co., Aniline Dye Manufacturers, 5, Cooper Street. Messrs. W. G. Thompson & Co. are engaged largely in the manufacture of these celebrated dyes. Their works are at Middleton, and their warehouse and offices at the above address. An efficient staff is engaged in Manchester, and a large number of chemists and workmen at the works. The business was established soon after the introduction of aniline colours, about thirty years ago, and is one of the oldest firms in the trade. An enormous business is done, the trade extending all over the United Kingdom, and also abroad. A large staff of travellers is kept, and in every branch great energy and ability are displayed in the management. A leading position in Manchester trade has been maintained by this firm, and great success achieved in their manufactures. By the term Aniline Dyes is designated a large number of dye stuffs, which, though not necessarily made from aniline are all originally derived from one common source, viz., the products obtained by the dry distillation of coal. In 1856 Perkin prepared mauve, the first colouring matter belonging to this group, and his discovery was soon followed by that of rose aniline, and aniline black, the latter by Lightfoot (Accrington), in 1863. A noteworthy fact in the history of the aniline dyes is the preparation of aliganin (the basis of madder), from anthracene. This was effected in 1869, and the discovery is remarkable as being the first instance of a vegetable dye made by artificial means. A vast number of different aniline dyes have been prepared during the last twenty years, and their number is daily increasing. The quantity annually produced is enormous, and their manufacture forms a most important branch of industry, both in England and abroad. They comprise every possible shade, from the most brilliant to the quietest hues, and contrary to popular belief are in many cases as fast, or even faster, to light and soap than the most stable of vegetable dyes. The fear of employing these colouring matters, on account of their poisonous properties, is most

unwarrantable, seeing that scarcely one out of several hundred actually can be termed in any way dangerous to health. It may safely be predicted that the employment of aniline dyes will become more and more general, for in addition to the advantages above cited their cost of production is comparatively so small that any other class of dye stuff cannot well compete with them.

Prudential Assurance Company, 82, King Street.—The necessity of making provision for one's family in case of death, through the medium of life insurance, has become so obvious to all prudent men that the only question to be determined is which is the best company to insure in. This question is satisfactorily answered by the Prudential Assurance Co., Limited, whose Manchester office is at the above location. This company, which is empowered by Act of Parliament, was founded in 1848, and has enjoyed a phenomenally successful career; a fact which speaks well for the sound judgment and honourable methods which have always characterised its management. It furnishes life assurance at premiums slightly exceeding the actual cost, and is the largest and most popular organisation of its kind in the world. It has over seven million policies in force in its Industrial Branch, in addition to upwards of one hundred thousand policies in its Ordinary Branch. The annual premium income of the Industrial Branch exceeds £3,000,000, this vast sum being collected in weekly premiums by the agents of the Company; and since its establishment ten million pounds sterling have been paid in this branch in settlement of claims, including 18,861 deaths from accident during the five years ending December, 1886. In the Ordinary Branch a general business is transacted, policies being issued for any amount from £50 to £10,000. The annual premium of this branch exceeds £500,000. The funds of both branches are invested in very high-class securities, and the expenses of management have been reduced to a minimum. The Manchester office of the Company is at 82, King Street, Mr. John Moon being the district inspector. In this city the Prudential has an immense number [illegible] and [illegible]

John Kirkham, Timber and Mahogany Merchant, Lancashire Veneer Saw Mills, Clowes Street, Chapel Street, Salford.—The above is one of the oldest hardwood firms in England, having been established early in the present century. They are the largest veneer cutters and merchants in the district, and hold very extensive stocks of all the principal foreign hardwoods used in cabinet making, railway, coach, and steamboat fitting, and sewing machine manufacturing, &c., &c., Mr. Kirkham, Senr., being well known as a buyer and importer of these woods, whose judgment and experience are unsurpassed. The firm conducts an extensive wholesale business, especially in American black walnut, and American satin walnut, in which they do a large trade, disposing of many thousands of cubic feet annually, sawn and in the log, and they are the most extensive holders of these woods amongst the timber merchants. Here may also be seen some of the finest stocks of satinwood, mahogany, bird-eyed maple, sycamore, brown oak, &c., &c., both solid and in veneer, comprising many hundreds of thousands of feet. They have also very large stocks of billet oak, rosewood, baywood (including railway coach panels), birch, American ash, cypress (or canary-coloured whitewood), and cherrywood, &c., and, in fact, for all the principal foreign hardwoods they cannot be equalled, not to say surpassed. There are a number of horizontal saws cutting mahogany panels and other valuable woods, also circular veneer saws from ten to twelve feet and upwards in diameter, cutting veneers of less than one-sixteenth of an inch in thickness from one to three feet wide. There may also be seen large quantities of most valuable veneers which are not more than one-thirtieth of an inch in thickness. The premises are the most centrally situated in the city, being only five minutes from the Royal Exchange, and Exchange and New Bailey Street stations, respectively, eight minutes from Victoria, and about fifteen minutes from the Central, London Road, and Oxford Road stations. The business is carried on by the son Mr. W. H. Kirkham and nephew of Mr. J. H. Ashton, the founder, who have been the sole managers and proprietors of the same for several years past. Their telegraphic address is "Mahogany, Manchester."

Dickson & Robinson, Seed Merchants and Nursery-
men, 12, Old Millgate.—There are few trades that possess a greater iterest for all classes of the community than that of a seedsman, and when e consider the amount of knowledge necessary to become familiar, not nly with the seeds sold, but with the time of sowing the same, and the eneral appearance of the plants they produce, we feel confident our eaders will place the seedsman in the first rank of professions. There re seedsmen and seedsmen, as there are plants and plants; but to efine our meaning, we do not include in the category all who sell seeds—rocers, chemists, even stationers and others, whose meagre business causes ime to hang heavily on their hands for lack of customers, and who then 1 the season add seeds to their motley stock, and append seedsmen to heir bills; of such there are too many in every town. Not one in one undred of these self-styled seedsmen would know the appearance of the undredth part of the grains that are sown annually, much less the prouce; it is only those who have by time and careful study qualified themelves to deserve the appellation. This digression was prompted by oticing the establishment of Messrs. Dickson & Robinson during our eregrinations in search of enterprise. Being an old-established firm of ndoubted respectability and resources, and from the activity displayed t the time of observation, evidently possessed of a good trade, we extended ur inquiries, which resulted in our obtaining information of a trustworthy ature. It was the period of the seedsman's harvest, when every possessor f a plot of land considered it time to think about cropping it. Dickson : Robinson's business must be placed in the first rank of seedsmen, ecause they are elevated to that position by assiduity, energy, and usiness capacities to be participators of the patronage of our Queen, I.R.H. the Prince of Wales, most of the leading nobility and gentry in he United Kingdom, the public parks of Manchester and Salford, and last ut not the least, that influential body, the Manchester Botanical Society. 'hese facts speak volumes for enterprise, accuracy, and detail, for without hose essentials confidence would not be reposed in them, and a retrograde usiness the result. The kitchen garden, the flower garden, and the field re all treated with the spirit necessary in these days of progress. The ewest productions of the gardener's skill in improvements can be proured here, be it cabbage, cauliflower, pea, or potato; seeds of the choicest owers, new and old, that careful hands can save; or the best Swedes and iangolds for the farmer's stock; nor is this the limit to the vast knowedge requisite in such a firm as this. All readers of agricultural journals re periodically greeted with "the best grasses for all soils," or some ther equally attractive form of advertisement, setting forth or implying hat only "there" are *the best* to be had; our clients, *for the time being*, re not irrational enough to assume that they alone command "the best," ut their judgment leads them to the principal sources for such pure seeds, nd the natural result is that a very large and rapidly increasing trade is nnually done in laying down grass lands. In confirmation of these emarks we need only refer to the excellent lawn laid down by Messrs.)ickson & Robinson in the grounds of the Royal Jubilee Exhibition—we articularly allude to that portion immediately adjoining the Switch-back tailway, on the south-eastern side, which, although only sown after the pening ceremony, has throughout a most trying season maintained a ichness of verdure rarely seen under such circumstances. After being eceived from the growers, grasses, clovers, and in fact all farm seeds, are ecleaned, and the germinating power carefully tested to enable them to o offered with a guarantee that they grow a certain per centage, and his test is applied to all vegetable, and to the principal portion of the lower seeds sent out of the place. In autumn an immense trade is done a Dutch flower roots, such as hyacinths, narcissus, tulips, crocus, &c., nd thousands of clumps and crowns of lily of the valley, and other uitable plants for forcing for winter and spring conservatory decoraion, are annually imported from Germany, France, and Holland. All he subjects enumerated above are set forth fully and in detail in the lescriptive priced catalogues for each department published by this firm, vho are always willing to send them free of charge to any one who pplies. As nurserymen, Dickson & Robinson should be regarded with reat interest, for their planting on the lawn (Botanical Gardens) of the loyal Jubilee Exhibition was a charming example of judgment and good aste, and attracted considerable notice. Bidding adieu to this most nteresting and cultured business we can only express a hope that our ew words on the subject will bear fruit to our readers by introducing to heir notice where civility, attention, and good articles, at a fair market alue, can be obtained.

Beaumont Brothers, Woollens, Tailors' Trimmings,
se., 15, Cannon and 40, Corporation Streets; and Branch, 26, Whitehapel, Liverpool.—Prominent among the representative mercantile iouses of Manchester is that of Messrs. Beaumont Brothers, whose exensive warehouse is at the above address. This house was founded bout sixty years ago by George Beaumont, subsequently becoming ieorge Beaumont & Son. The present firm conduct an extensive wholeale business, the retail department being carried on under the firm's name f John & George Beaumont. The premises occupied consist of a substanial building of spacious dimensions, admirably arranged, and equipped rith every facility and convenience for the transaction of business. The ntrance to the retail department is at 40, Corporation Street, the wholeale department being at 15, Cannon Street. Throughout the entire estabishment there prevails a perfect system of organization, which facilitates the transaction of business and makes the house a pleasant one to deal with. There are many distinct departments, each of which is stocked with the best and most desirable goods in the market. These include every description of woollens, fancy worsted coatings, Scotch and Welsh tweeds, fancy trouserings and suitings, woollen and Bedford cords, naps, beavers, and pilots, livery cloths and trimmings, ladies' mantle cloths, carriage cloths, laces and trimmings, billiard cloths, calicoes, fustians, dyed goods, linens, flannels, tailors' trimmings, buttons, braids, velvets, &c. In fact this is a recognised headquarters for tailors' supplies of every description. It is so well known and has retained its old customers for so long a time that its reputation for honourable and liberal dealing is established beyond the requirements of praise.

Francis Carroll, Iron and Tin-Plate Worker, 18, Goulden Street, and 96, Tib Street.—Prominent among the old-established and well-known iron and tin-plate working establishments of Manchester, is that of Francis Carroll. This business was established in 1835 by the late Francis Carroll, and from a comparatively small beginning its operations have steadily developed and increased. Mr. Carroll died in 1886, after a long and honourable career, and since his death the business has been conducted by his family. The manufactory is of spacious dimensions, well arranged, and equipped throughout with the most improved machinery and appliances, employment being given to about one hundred skilled hands. Among the articles manufactured are oak and japanned iron trunks and bonnet boxes, galvanised buckets, coal boxes, baths, and all kinds of domestic hardware, kitchen, parlour, and bedroom fenders, fire-irons, ash-pans, bars, stands, and castings of all varieties, iron saucepans, and kettles, tinned, enamel, and cast frypans, stamped drippers, bowls, dishes, etc.; and all descriptions of stampings, wood ware, pegs, tubs, knife boxes, and similar articles are kept in stock, also specialities in confectioners' and bakers' materials. The articles manufactured by this firm have a standard reputation in the trade, being made from the best materials in the most skilful manner. With the manufacturing facilities possessed by this establishment it can offer every advantage to customers and can execute all orders in the promptest manner. It supplies a large home trade, and it is so well known, and has so well sustained its eminent reputation, that it enjoys widespread support of the very best class, of which, it may be added, it is thoroughly worthy. Special attention has of late years been given to the development of the shipping trade, a large and increasing demand having sprung up for all kinds of trunks, &c., which are used to take the place of our domestic furniture in those portions of the globe where civilisation has not yet completed its sway, many thousands of them have found their way into the great Dark Continent.

John Walkden & Co., West African Merchants, 4, Minshull Street.—With all parts of the world, Manchester carries on an enormous trade, and Africa comes in for no small amount of attention on the part of the numerous mercantile firms. A capital example of a firm trading with this productive region is that of Messrs. John Walkden and Co., which was originally founded at 31, Church Street, in 1867, by William Nuttall, upon whose death Mr. Walkden took over the management for the mother, and was afterwards admitted as a partner, for some years trading as Nuttall and Walkden. In 1880 he became sole proprietor, and gave the firm its present title. The present premises have been occupied since November, 1886. They are extensive and consist of offices and storage departments, the former being furnished in a substantial and superior manner and employing an adequate clerical staff. Messrs. John Walkden & Co. are engaged in trading with the West Coast of Africa only, and carry on operations on a large scale. They undertake all sorts of commissions on the most moderate terms and with dispatch. The goods traded in are of the greatest variety, and from the leading manufacturers in the country, and Messrs. John Walkden and Co. evince a sound and deep knowledge of the industries and commerce of the country. In all their transactions they exercise discretion, judgment, and dispatch, and their talent and honourable business methods are of the highest order, considering they have worked up their fine trade in about seven years. The business is now a very influential one, and it has been made such during the last seven years by its energetic proprietors. Messrs. John Walkden and Co. are gentlemen whose status in the industrial and mercantile world is high and well defined, and who are looked upon with great respect by all business men, and are in all respects typical West African Merchants.

Leigh, Buchanan & Co., Calico Printers, 57, George Street.—This business, though but comparatively recently established, has already achieved a very marked success. The works are located at Oakenshaw, near Accrington. The connection is mostly among the leading shipping houses, and such manufacturers as get up goods for foreign markets. Messrs. Leigh, Buchanan & Co. are already noted for their excellence of design, their artistic colouring, and for durability of their printing, and the firm are making great efforts not merely to sustain their reputation, but, if possible, enhance it.

Edward Williams, Fire Brick and Tile Works, Ashton New Road, Bradford.—The history of this well-known and flourishing concern extends over a considerable period of time; it is some thirty-five years since Mr. Robert Williams, uncle of the present proprietor, Mr. Edward Williams, opened this fine premises in Ashton New Road for the manufacture on improved lines of fire bricks and tiles. The present proprietor succeeded to the business about twenty-two years ago and many improvements have been made in the concern during this time. Throughout a marked progress, stimulated by an energetic and capable management, has been distinctly observable; the connection enjoyed has gradually grown in size and importance, and to-day it is one of the best that any firm of the kind can boast of, drawn together, too, by the force of sheer and unequivocal merit. The premises are large, admirably fitted up, and filled with a comprehensive and exceedingly interesting stock of goods used in the building trade. Amongst the specialities may be mentioned the class of bricks, tiles, &c., used by chemical and vitriol manufacturers all over the kingdom. The material used is got below the surface in the same manner as coal is got, forming the under strata of the coal seams, and is all manipulated and manufactured on the premises into goods both ornamental and useful. There is scarcely any form of terra-cotta manufacure that is not made here, and some really beautiful and artistic work is turned out. The staff employed is a thoroughly capable and well-organized one. The firm is well known by all contractors and builders, and Mr. Williams has a large circle of friends and acquaintances by whom he is highly respected. He is a member of the Manchester City Council, representing the interests of Bradford; he has been chairman of the Conservative organisation in Bradford for well-nigh twenty years; he is also a member of the Prestwich Board of Guardians, and has been for twenty-two years a member of the Manchester Literary Society; he is the author of several works, both historical and local, among which we may specially mention, "*The History of Clayton Hall and its Surroundings,*" published about twelve months ago; "*Freedom and Restraint;*" "*Moral Culture, the Basis of National Greatness;*" and "*Relics of the Chetham Family.*" The terms offered by Mr. Williams are most reasonable, and intending customers may rely upon perfect satisfaction at his hands.

J. B. Harrison, Corset & Stay Manufacturer, Granby Row.—In a large and commodious building at the corner of Sackville Street and Granby Row, is situated the well-known Stay & Corset Factory of Mr. James Bown Harrison. The business was originally commenced in 1845, by Mr. Joseph Buxton, who carried on with success the manufacture of a superior class of stays for many years, and retired in 1875, when he was succeeded by the present head of the firm. Mr. J. B. Harrison was for some years previously connected with the firm of Williams, Son, & Brookes, manufacturers of coloured cotton goods, at Stanley Mill, Whitefield, thereby obtaining an intimate practical knowledge of all kinds of cloth, and the various modes of making and finishing the same, which has been of great advantage to him in his present position. The business has been carried on for about three years in the present premises, which are admirably adapted for the purpose, being fitted throughout with the best machinery and appliances which could be obtained. The power is furnished by one of Messrs. Crossley's "Otto" Gas Engines, directly driving a long main shaft, from which it is taken by rope driving to the centre of each machine bench, and also to the various cutting and other machines in use. The sewing machines are of different kinds according to class of work required, but are all of most recent construction, and are placed in a large and lofty room in the upper part of the building, and so arranged that the light either from windows or gas falls without shadow upon the work. The stock-rooms, departments for storage of material, cutting, steam moulding, and other processes, are all well arranged to facilitate the quick and clean manufacture of the various classes of goods. There is also due regard for the comfort and health of the workpeople; a well-appointed kitchen with extensive cooking arrangements being provided upon the premises. Mr. Harrison takes the entire responsibility and superintendence of a large and increasing business, which is carried on with most of the best wholesale houses in Manchester and elsewhere, in all classes of stays and nearly every kind of corset, and has gradually built up, with energy and careful attention, a business which may be considered, of its kind, one of the most successful in the North of England.

Mitchell's Emery Wheel Co., Mill Street, Bradford, Manchester.—This Emery Wheel Company is a concern of which the proprietors may well be proud. The business carried on in the manufacture of emery-wheels, emery-wheel machines, emery, etc., is very extensive and important, in point of fact, one of the largest and best of its kind. The work turned out by the firm has a widespread reputation for its general and particular excellence, and commands a ready sale throughout the country. The concern is admirably managed by thoroughly competent men; the machinery in use is of the latest and most approved description, whilst the staff employed is a large one. Looking back into the past history of the firm, one is almost astonished at the really wonderful progress that has been made. Nothing but the best, most consistent, and most careful of managements, could have succeeded in bringing about such a satisfactory state of things; and it is due to Messrs. William and James William Mitchell, the managing proprietors, to say that for this they are in the main responsible. Messrs. Mitchell are gentlemen thoroughly versed in all the technicalities of their interesting business, never disappointing a customer, and who command the respect of all their employés. It was as far back as 1860 that this well-to-do firm was originally established; but the future yet before it is evidently a bright one.

Thomas Emmott & Sons, Cotton Spinners and Manufacturers, 38, George Street.—The industries of Manchester and district are conspicuous in the great manufactories, mills, and other evidences of activity on all sides. A representative concern is the well-known house of Messrs. Thomas Emmott & Sons, cotton spinners and manufacturers of improved fast pile velvets and velveteens, patent velvets, velveteens, cords, nankeens, twills, &c.; works, Vale Mills, Clegg Street; Albion Mills, Rock Street; Clegg Street Mill; Greaves Street Mill; Diamond Mill, Lewis Street; and Commercial Mill Shed, Falcon Street, Oldham. Established in the early part of the present century, the reputation achieved by this business house is very great and widespread, with the result that a business connection of a very high character has been formed. They do a large home trade in grey velvets and velveteens, fast pile velvets, cords, sheetings, twills, nankeens. These goods are known and find ready markets at all seasons at all the largest buying houses of London and Manchester. The firm have lately altered and rearranged their various mills. They have erected a large new spinning-mill, containing the latest improvements in spinning machinery. This mill is exclusively devoted to the spinning of combed and carded Egyptian cotton, and of the finest kinds of American cotton which are required in the construction of velveteens.

Messrs. Lomas & Gyte and Lomas & Slater, Corn and Flour Merchants, 102 and 104, Oxford Street, and 6, Ardwick Green.—The corn and flour trade of Manchester takes a prominent position among the industries of the city. About the oldest established and best known houses in this line are those under notice, they having been founded by Mr. George Lomas, senior, upwards of eighty years ago, on the site where the London Road Station now stands. Mr. Thomas Lomas commenced business on Ardwick Green about 1835, eventually establishing the present business in Oxford Street in 1847, the former concern being carried on under the style of Messrs. Lomas & Slater, and the latter under the style of Lomas & Gyte. The commercial antecedents of Mr. George Gyte date back to business transactions by his grandfather as a corndealer in Chapel Street, London Road, upwards of eighty years ago, and the present partnership was formed about the year 1860. The partners of the firms are well-known members of the Manchester Corn Exchange, Mr. Lomas having been such since 1847. The business of the joint firms are on a most extensive scale, and the houses are well reputed for the general excellence of their flours, grain, provender, &c. Many large orders for the supply of corn and flour, &c., both in the city and for many miles out in the surrounding districts, are taken up and carried through to the entire satisfaction of all parties concerned, by Messrs. Lomas & Slater and Messrs. Lomas & Gyte from their respective establishments. Being very heavy buyers and members of the Corn Exchange every advantage is taken of the "market fluctuations," placing the firm in the very best position to afford full advantages in price, &c., to their numerous customers. The premises at Ardwick Green, which are of modern construction, are very extensive, and exceedingly well arranged and appointed for the prompt transaction of the large business of the firm; whilst the establishment at Oxford Street is both commodious and conveniently situated. The stocks held are very large, representing a considerable equivalent, and there is also a considerable staff of hands employed on the two premises. The partners of the firms are gentlemen with the very highest and best associations in the corn trade, and of the strictest integrity, and widely respected.

Illingworth, Ingham & Co., Timber Importers, &c., 61, Gloucester Street, Oxford Street.—The timber trade of Manchester is of great magnitude and value, and employs many firms. A well-known firm engaged is that of Messrs. Illingworth, Ingham & Co., whose head-quarters are at Leeds, and who also have extensive yards and mills in Goole. The firm has been established in Manchester for a number of years, and bears a fine reputation for the quality of the timber. The premises occupied are of ample dimensions, comprising stores and yards, admirably arranged and fitted for the reception of timber. Messrs. Illingworth, Ingham & Co., manufacture mouldings, flooring, match-board, spouts, etc., making these prepared goods the speciality. There is a splendid stock of all kinds, including valuable woods, dry wainscot, oak, walnut, mahogany, baywood, etc., and also of the above-mentioned prepared goods. The timber is well seasoned and in fine condition throughout; it is imported direct from the leading sources, and a finer stock cannot be seen in the city. Messrs. Illingworth, Ingham & Co., carry on a very heavy and wide-spread trade, having a large connection among builders, coach-builders, cabinet-makers, and others using valuable woods. An ample staff is employed, orders are promptly executed, and the management throughout is able and enterprising. Messrs. Illingworth, Ingham & Co., are well-known in the timber trade and the mercantile and industrial world generally, and are highly honoured for their strict integrity, their knowledge of the business and courteous demeanour, whilst their house is not surpassed by any similar contemporary concern.

Chisnall & Co., Tailors for Ladies and Gentlemen, 4, St. Ann's square, and 3, Barton Square.—This business has been established for upwards of thirty years, under the same title and in the same premises. The shop is extremely large and very handsome. It is most beautifully decorated, handsomely furnished, and elegantly fitted up. The work-rooms are on the premises, where all the cutting and work are done. The connection is entirely a bespoke trade of the very highest class. The leading speciality is ladies' riding habits and tailor-made costumes. The stock is extremely good, and includes ranges of all the very finest makes of West of England, Scotch, Yorkshire, and French woollen goods. There are many ranges of patterns which are the exclusive property of the firm, and almost all are reserved. The leading speciality of the firm is *ladies' tailoring*; in this line they keep English and Austrian cutters, and a staff of two hundred workmen of the greatest skill constantly engaged in the making of costumes, jackets, cloaks, riding habits, &c. The trade, though largely supported by the Manchester district, is, nevertheless wide-spread and extensive. Many old and valued customers, who have gone to reside in distant places, still send their orders to this justly celebrated firm. Mr. James Chisnall is now sole partner. He is a gentleman of excellent judgment and cultivated taste, with a most correct eye, and a quick perception of the best points in all new fashions and styles. His judgment is almost unfailingly correct.

J. & E. W. Jackson, Commercial Printers, Stationers, &c., 62, Corporation Street.—Messrs. J. & E. W. Jackson have been established at their present premises for a period of no less than thirty-five years. Their concern, therefore, on account of its high-class character, is one of the principal features of this locality. As commercial stationers, general printers by steam power, engravers, and lithographers, they hold a high position in the neighbourhood, and have achieved a reputation of which they may well be proud. Their works are fitted up with the latest and most approved machinery, appliances, type, &c., and the utmost care is exercised in the execution of all orders, so that no work is turned out of an inferior description. The management everywhere observable in connection with this concern is in every way admirable, and the spirit of enterprise that has marked its progress are points and recommendations well deserving of attention. It is gratifying to state that Messrs. Jackson enjoy such a valuable and influential patronage, that their works are constantly the scene of great business activity. The firm shows manifest signs of ever-increased vitality and success in the immediate future.

The Decorators' Supply Company, (Showroom) 105, Deansgate; (Warehouses) 2 and 4, South King Street.—There is scarcely to be found in the annals of commercial enterprise a parallel to the success which has attended the operations of the extensive establishment known as the "Decorators' Supply Company." This well-known firm carries on business in extensive premises, occupying a splendid corner position at the above address, comprising show-rooms, large basements, and warehouses and stores; and a large warehouse at 2 and 4 South King Street, adjoining; the whole forming a most extensive and commodious establishment admirably adapted in every way to the requirements of the trade. This company occupies a position of importance and usefulness which is duly appreciated by decorators and artists all over the United Kingdom. In the showrooms a very extensive and most attractive stock of goods is displayed, comprising paper-hangings in most artistic and beautifully executed designs, the Lincrusta-Walton, the Tyne-Castle tapestry, and Japanese leather paper, for which the Company are sole agents for Messrs. Rottmann, Stromo & Co., Yokohama, Japan, as well as a large stock of flat brushes, ground brushes, tools, white lead, oil, colours, and varnishes, &c. The Japanese leather paper is a speciality of this company, and has been introduced by them with great success; it forms a beautiful, durable, and most artistic wall covering; it is altogether novel, and is rapidly gaining great popular favour. This business in every department is conducted in a most spirited and enterprising manner; Mr. George Heighway, the able manager of the Company, is a gentleman whose artistic talent is undoubted, and whose well-known integrity and untiring energy have gained the esteem and confidence of a very extensive and ever-increasing connection.

John Nesbitt, (late F. P. Walker), **Manufacturer of every description of Wrap Reels and Testing Machinery,** 42, Market Street.—The manufactures of Mr. John Nesbitt enjoy, on account of their rare excellence of workmanship and material, a world-wide popularity. The present proprietor of this firm has enjoyed the control thereof since 1873, but the business was originally started in 1784, by Mr. Francis P. Walker, whose name is still retained in the imprint. The mechanical appliances on view in the handsomely appointed warehouse are large in number and most valuable; but the speciality of the firm will be found in their wrap reels and yarn testers, which, although remarkably moderate in price, are nevertheless produced with unusual care and consideration for the increased requirements of the times. Wrap reel "No. 1, bot," for instance, is positively a marvel at the cost, and a most ingenious and interesting contrivance even from the point of view of one not specially interested in the business, in the improvement of which the house is playing so conspicuous a part. Constructed for the purpose of ascertaining the length of cotton, silk, or woollen yarns, from either cops, bobbins, swift or barrel stand, they serve their purpose admirably well. They are fitted on French stands of polished baywood, with double self-acting spreading motion, and having elaborately finished iron pillars and shaft, together with fancy brass arms and wheels, polished and lacquered. They are fitted with a dial and striking apparatus which records every one hundred and twenty yards wound. By the arrangement of this clever invention, the cops and bobbins travel with the spreading motion, by which the threads are controlled and guided directly opposite to the glass eye-piece, thereby securing the great advantage afforded by an equal distribution in the motion, which insures the exact length being wound off the cop or bobbin. The price for the reel specified is but £7 10s. Machines may be had of Mr. Nesbitt at rates considerably lower than this, and although these are somewhat inferior in scope, their manufacture is of a particularly high standard. Worthy of special mention is the "Vertical Lever Yarn Tester," a contrivance for testing the strength and elasticity of a lea of yarn; a machine which is handsomely mounted and well fitted with all the latest improvements, and of reasonably moderate price. In addition to the foregoing, ironmongery is carried on in all its branches, a large staff being employed in the fitting up of bells, speaking-tubes, etc., etc. Spinners, manufacturers, and the yarn trade generally would do well to give the most careful consideration to the many improvements which Mr. Nesbitt has recently made in his machinery. The house at the above address, in fact, is noted for the all-round excellence of its output, and any orders received (it may be thoroughly relied upon) will be executed with that accuracy and dispatch which a long and special experience so well enables the manufacturer to ensure.

John James, Wholesale Tobacconist, 24, Old Millgate.—A very well-known house of business is that conducted under the title of John James, and trading as wholesale and retail tobacconist. It was established in 1836, and is carried on in first-class premises. The trade is mostly done in the locality, but is nevertheless very extensive, and necessitates the employment of a very considerable staff. Mr. James keeps a very good stock, and is particularly noted for the excellent quality of his tobacco and cigars. The amount of controversy on the use of tobacco has been something overwhelming, and no agreement seems ever to come of it. Dr. Richardson in a very excellent pamphlet sums it up that smoking is only injurious when carried to excess. He says, "It is innocuous as compared with alcohol, it does infinitely less harm than opium, it is in no sense worse than tea, and by the side of high living altogether it contrasts most favourably." Another writer says that "snuffing is probably the least injurious form in which to take tobacco" (though the propriety of the habit is a matter of opinion), "and chewing the most deleterious;" yet cannot help noticing that sailors, who can generally chew any amount, are usually men in vigorous health. Dr. Arnott, in the *Lancet*, notices the case of a man, formerly a sailor, sixty-four years of age, in the very best of health, who for years had not merely chewed, but *eaten*, a quarter of a pound of strong tobacco every five days. A deal depends perhaps on the quality, and in this respect the class of tobacco sold by Mr. James is especially good. The house has long been known as the only one that keeps the "Long Churchwarden Clay Pipes." It is a common occurrence, when the old man at home is writing his son to spend such a holiday as Christmas with him, to tell him "not to forget to call at James's for 'one of them thear long clay pipes,' so as aw con hauve a gradely smooke on Christmas day." The firm is therefore widely noted, and is doing one of the most extensive trades in this line in the district.

James Gray & Co., Sunnyside Mills, Regent Road, Salford.—The business carried on at Sunnyside Mills, Salford, under the title of James Gray and Co., wire polishers, reed and heald manufacturers and general wire rollers, is one of the oldest in the district. It was established in 1822 by Mr. John Chapman, and afterwards carried on by his nephew, Mr. Gatenby, and Mr. James Pass, till 1863, when it became Pass & Co. till 1873; then it was changed to James Gray & Co. By these it was conducted till 1885, when it was purchased by the present tenant, Mr. George Metcalf, who has carried on the concern in a most energetic and successful manner for two years, adding not a little by his business capacity and excellent management to the high reputation previously enjoyed by the firm. The trade is to a large extent confined to the locality, and is very brisk. The workmanship reaches a high degree of excellence, and the patronage of late has been largely on the increase.

Kendall & Co., Horse and Cattle Condiment Manufacturers, Sahara Mills, Blackburn Street, Salford.—This important business continues to increase. The works, which are about to be enlarged, are known as the Sahara Mills, and are replete with every requisite to carry on a large and successful business. The specialities of manufacture are the Horse and Cattle Condiments that have made the firm so well known, and for which the demand is constantly increasing. Messrs. Kendall & Co., in the manufacture of their goods, use, as raw materials, none but the best articles to be procured in the market, and can say with pride a complaint is almost unknown to them. A clever staff of travellers is always on the road. The concern is one of the most successful businesses in the neighbourhood.

Messrs. Cottrill & Co., Spinners and Manufacturers, 23, Bridgewater Place, High Street.—The trade industries of Manchester and district are exemplified in the very highest degree in its great manufactories, mills, and workshops. A representative house is that of Messrs. Cottrill & Co., spinners and manufacturers of ticks, regattas, checks, &c., whose city warehouse is situated at the above address, and who control the large mills known as "The Britannia Mills," Whit Lane, Pendleton. Established in 1846, the business operations of this firm have always been on a very large and extended scale, and embrace a list of patrons which may be classed amongst the largest and best buying houses not only of the United Kingdom but of the whole civilised world. Their specialities in regattas have for a quarter of a century been leading and specially quoted articles in the exchanges of Hamburg, Amsterdam, Rotterdam, and other continental centres of commerce, and the name of the firm is plainly branded on each of the pieces exported to these markets, without which the buyers would not be satisfied as to their genuineness. The mills at Pendleton consist of an extensive brick-built lofty structure, used solely for cotton spinning; this forms a very conspicuous object for a very considerable distance around. There is also an extensive weaving shed, and the four-storey buildings adjoining are occupied for winding, warping, and beaming, yarn stores, cloth warehouses, and making-up rooms. The premises also comprise dyeing and bleach works, which not only provide for the wants of the firm, but do a considerable amount of "outside work" for other manufacturers whose operations do not extend to this branch; the whole are fitted with a vast complication of the best, most modern, and highly expensive and efficient machinery, of great productive power, and affording constant employment to about seven hundred skilled operatives. The products of this house find open markets throughout all leading commercial centres, at very favourable quotations; the well-known high reputation of the firm is sufficient guarantee of their high characteristic qualities. The premises in Bridgewater Place, Manchester, though unpretending and unostentatious as regards situation and general appearance, comprise a well-built, substantial-looking warehouse, containing a large and valuable stock of the productions of the mills well arranged, and affording employment to an adequate staff of warehousemen and clerks. The gentlemen comprising the partnership are of the highest commercial status, well known, and widely respected.

T. Hepplestone, Gun and Rifle Maker, 25, Shudehill.—The firm of gun and rifle manufacturers, so well known as Thomas Hepplestone and originally established in 1864, has been growing in reputation from that day to this. The warehouse of the firm contains an immense variety of fire-arms of almost every known make and description of good repute. In addition to the large and excellent display of specialities of the firm's own manufacture, for the protection of which several patents have been taken out, the stock of sporting guns, rifles and revolvers here displayed is to every sportsman well worth coming from a distance to inspect. This stock includes patent hammerless guns, double and single express rifles, small bore match rifles, military rifles, Webley's and other revolvers, in great variety. The firm, in addition to their large and private connection and business, are extensive contractors for small arms with our own and foreign governments, and devote a considerable amount of attention to this branch of business, for which their great facilities and large experience and practical acquaintance with the process of manufacture eminently qualify them. They are also purveyors, on a large scale, of every description of ammunition and other sporting requisites usually to be found at similar establishments; so that it may truly be said, that everything required by the sportsman or the soldier in the way of fire-arms and their adjuncts and accessories, may be had at the warehouse or ordered through the travellers of the firm of Thomas Hepplestone, which is one of the most reputable and comprehensive of its kind in the country.

A. L. Bostock, & Co., Sewing Cotton Manufacturers, Eagle Mills, Hunt Street, Oxford Street.—Prominent among the great industries of the age are these great and widespread manufacturing interests, forming in themselves the very vitality of commercial enterprise, and the centre from which every other branch of commerce must of necessity take its origin. A most representative establishment is that of Messrs. A. L. Bostock & Co., sewing cotton manufacturers, controlling the large and widely renowned Eagle Mills, Hunt Street, Oxford Street, and affording employment to some hundred highly skilled operatives. This business was established fully a quarter of a century ago. The premises comprise a very large factory of bold and lofty exterior, fitted throughout with very expensive modern and powerful machinery for the production and manufacture of all kinds of fine and coarse sewing cottons in 2, 3, 6 cord, &c., on reels, in balls and skeins, principally for the export trade, for the excellent qualities and textures of which this house is highly renowned. The development of this house is very rapid, and the system of business most commendable for great care and completeness in every detail. The firm is liberally supported by the best and most eminent firms in the foreign shipping trade, the widespread reputation of the house extending to all parts of the universe. The business transactions of this house are in every sense of the word of first-class character and the most solid footing. The principals are gentlemen of the very highest integrity, well known and widely respected.

W. Scott Hayward & Co., Jet Ornament Manufacturers and Jet Cameo Cutters, "The Whitby and Scarborough Jet Depôt," 59, Deansgate.—Jet ornaments are very popular in this country, and the manufacture is an artistic and advanced branch of industry. Manchester carries on a very heavy trade in these goods, although there is only one manufacturing firm in the city, in fact, the whole of Lancashire. The firm is that known as Messrs. W. Scott Hayward & Co. (the only member being Mr. W. Scott Hayward), which was founded in the district fourteen years ago, and has occupied the present premises seven years. Mr. W. Scott Hayward has wholesale offices in the city, at 78, Barton Arcade; a depôt at 59, Deansgate; one at Liverpool, Bold Street; one at Paris, 19, Rue D'Antin; and at Leipzig, Markt, 3A. He also carries on business as importer of Roman and French pearls. The works are at Whitby, Scarborough, and Manchester, and agents are established at New York, Port Elizabeth, Dis and Paris. The Deansgate premises, known as "The Whitby and Scarborough Jet Depôt," consist of a moderately sized, attractive looking, and elegantly fitted shop, having a splendid display of jet ornaments and cameos of exquisite beauty, many of them having gained prizes at different exhibitions. The ornaments are made from the genuine Whitby jet, by able and experienced workmen, at the various works, and for beauty could not be surpassed. Through his depôts and agencies Mr. W. Scott Hayward carries on a heavy trade all over the world. He is thoroughly acquainted with the business, designs all the patterns for which this firm is so noted and for which they have gained so many prizes, and is known in all industrial and commercial circles. He is deeply esteemed for his sterling qualities.

Twiss & Robinson, Silk Merchants, &c., 14, Piccadilly.—The silk trade in Manchester is one of considerable importance, and a large capital is embarked in it. A firm well established in this line is that of Twiss & Co., 14, Piccadilly, which was founded about 1859 by Walter Twiss and Walter F. Robinson. The latter gentleman having died in 1874, Mr. Twiss became sole proprietor, and he has carried on the business most successfully. The premises, consisting of suites of offices extending into Gore Street, were built by Mr. Twiss in 1677. He bestowed much care on the construction and fitting up of those portions designed for his own occupancy. There are spacious well-furnished offices and warerooms, an efficient staff of employés, and a very valuable stock. Besides the firm's own specialities, there are also to be found here specialities in silk goods from all the principal foreign sources of manufacture. Twiss & Co. thoroughly understand their business. Their status is of the highest; they have large facilities for upholding their reputation, and they are greatly honoured for their strict integrity and courteous demeanour. This house is not excelled by any contemporary concern.

T. P. Tyas & Son, Manufacturers and Importers of Artificial Flowers and Feathers, Beads, &c., 24, Turner Street, and 27, Church Street.—The manufacture and importation of artificial flowers and feathers, beads, and general fancy goods, form an important business in Manchester, and among the establishments engaged a prominent place is held by that of Messrs. T. P. Tyas & Son. This firm was founded thirty-five years ago, and since that date has made great headway. The premises occupied are large and commodious. The spacious show-rooms are at 24, Turner Street, and are heavily stocked with artificial flowers of great beauty and naturalness, feathers, beads, and general fancy goods, the latter being in great variety. These goods are manufactured by experienced female operatives, on the most advanced methods under Messrs. T. P. Tyas & Son's talented supervision, and are also imported from the leading sources. In both cases the goods are perfect in every respect and in great demand. A very noteworthy feature in connection with the business is that the firm is the only one in the city possessing a special bead warehouse. This is located at 27, Church Street, and the varied and beautiful stock held is unrivalled outside the metropolis. Messrs. T. P. Tyas & Son's trade is very considerable, chiefly in Manchester, and under their ability and enterprise it is rapidly increasing. Mr. Walter Hy. Tyas is the only member of the firm, and a gentleman who has devoted his whole talent and energy to the perfection of the productions dealt in by the house, and has been eminently successful. In commercial and industrial circles he is well-known and received with the great respect he deserves, and his house without doubt is a leader in its branch of industry.

John Sandbach & Sons, Wine and Spirit Merchants, 22, St. Ann's Square, and at 227, Oxford Street.—The wine trade of Manchester is of great magnitude and extent, and for excellence will compare most favourably with that of other large cities. A first-class and well-known firm of wine and spirit merchants is that of Messrs. John Sandbach & Sons, which was established in 1816, and has a reputation for the reliability and purity of its wines and spirits. The offices occupied are centrally located, and the stores contain an extensive stock of the best brands and choicest vintages. The firm has a branch at 31, Nevill Street, Southport, and the trade done altogether is very considerable, a splendid connection being enjoyed among the gentry of the city and its vicinity. Messrs. John Sandbach & Sons are excellent judges of wine, and are gentlemen of high financial, social, and business standing.

W. Batty & Son, Watch Makers & Jewellers, 9, Market Street, and 1, Cross Street.—This eminent establishment, founded so far back as the year 1837, enjoys a great and growing reputation for the excellence of its watch and jewelry manufactures of all kinds. There are two establishments, one at 9, Market Street, the other at the corner of Cross Street, in the same great thoroughfare, in addition to which there is a branch establishment at 125, Lord Street, Southport. The handsome edifice at the corner of Cross Street, opposite the principal entrance to the Exchange, has exceedingly well-stocked windows on the ground floor. The stock of manufactures includes gold and silver lever, hunting, and keyless watches of the best material and workmanship; ladies' Albert chains of the newest patterns; gem betrothal rings, for which Messrs. Batty & Son have obtained a wide celebrity; fine gold and diamond set bracelets, brooches, lockets, and earrings; broad necklets, necklets set with diamonds and pearls, all the newest styles and designs in silver jewelry; gentlemen's gold Albert chains, seals, lockets, and compasses; diamond, signet, and all kinds of gold rings, scarf pins and rings, studs, links, and solitaires; all kinds of silver and electro-plate for wedding, anniversary, christening, and other presentation purposes, including tea and coffee services; Tantalus spirit frames, salad bowls, trowels, oak mounted; Devonshire, Worcester, Crown Derby, and Doulton ware; writing and dressing-cases and bags, artistic inkstands and candlesticks in all descriptions of mount, as well as an endless variety of designs in clocks, timepieces, bronzes, and side ornaments. The establishment at 9, Market Street, contains a handsome shop and a fine show-room on the first-floor (and workrooms in the floors above, in which the firm gives constant occupation to a large staff of the most skilled English and foreign artisans), and is equally replete with a choice and varied selection of Messrs. Batty's productions. The specialities for which they are so well known, and in which they have attained such a high degree of excellence in good workmanship, variety, and beauty of design, are the gold and silver keyless watches, and their beautiful gem betrothal rings, which are mounted under their own personal inspection in a style of high artistic merit and beauty. The firm was founded in 1837 by Mr. William Batty, and became W. Batty & Son in 1873, when Mr. James Batty was taken into partnership by his father. Under this style it has since been carried on and expanded to its present extensive dimensions. The senior partner, Mr. W. Batty, stands in deservedly high esteem amongst his fellow-citizens of Manchester. He was elected to the Town Council in 1868, to the Aldermanic Bench in 1884. He is also a Magistrate of the city, in the public life of which he has always taken a most useful and important part.

Dixon & Co., Provision Merchants, &c., 18, Hanging Ditch.—It is a matter of vital importance to the commercial interests of the country and to the benefit of the vast working population of this country, that the provision trade should be in a most perfect condition as regards the excellence and general quality of the goods. Manchester takes a most eminent place among the cities of the world for the extent of her trade in this direction, and her firms are known in all parts of the country. That the trade is rapidly increasing can be seen by the number of firms that have been established during the past three or four years, one of the chief being that of Messrs. Dixon & Co. This firm has only a four years' existence; but such have been the energy and ability displayed in the management of affairs, that it has built up a very wide-spread trade, has earned a sound reputation, and is looked upon by the business men of the city as a flourishing concern. The premises are admirably adapted for the proper working of the business, the offices being large and commodious, substantially furnished, and the stores very extensive and spacious. An ample staff of clerks, travellers, and other hands are employed, and the organization of the business is complete in all details. The spacious stores contain an immense stock of general provisions, including ham, bacon, butter, lard, cheese, &c., all of the finest brands, and imported directly by the firm. This house devotes special attention to the trade in American hams. They deal most extensively in the famous Crown brand of Messrs. Jas. Wright & Co., packed by Messrs. Fowler Bros., at Chicago, Ill. These goods are cured from the finest young hogs, specially for the English market. All over the country the trade of Messrs. Dixon & Co. extends, and their name is familiar to nearly every provision salesman of any standing. Messrs. John William Dixon and Thomas Bincham are the individual members, and their ability and energy are plainly apparent in their surprising success. They devote the strictest attention to the business, and from the first they have taken a position of eminence in the trading world. In the cheese market they are represented by the principal buyer in New York, and their position is one of considerable and growing eminence. Honourable, sincere, and genial, Messrs. Dixon and Bincham own a business which for excellence is unsurpassed.

Barratt & Co., Corn, Flour, and Cheese Factors, 7, Todd Street.—A trade in Manchester which represents an immense capital is that of corn, flour, and cheese, and among the establishments engaged an important place is held by the firm trading as Messrs. Barratt & Co. (Mr. Frank Barratt being the only member). This firm holds its eminent place owing to excellent management, and the fact that it was established one hundred years ago.

Walter Merrall (late J. and W. Merrall), General Furnishing Ironmonger, &c., 286, Deansgate.—The ironmongery trade of Manchester is of considerable magnitude, and is one of the chief business interests of the city. An important house in this line is that of Mr. Walter Merrall. This fine business was originally established fifty-six years ago by Mr. Joseph Merrall, it was subsequently altered to Messrs. J. & W. Merrall, and at the present time the sole proprietor is Mr. Walter Merrall. The premises occupied consist of a large, spacious, three-storied building, of substantial and attractive appearance, and which is admirably fitted and furnished with the appliances and fixtures proper to the trade. The stock is very heavy and extensive, and comprises builders' ironmongery, such as sash weights, fasteners, nails, locks, lock furniture, ranges, grates, and usual appendages, rain-water pipes, guttering, &c.; household ironmongery comprising every requisite for bedroom, drawing-room, and culinary utensils; mill furnishing ironmongery, tools and appliances for millwrights, iron-founders, plumbers, tinsmiths, masons, bricklayers, plasterers, joiners, coopers, &c., and other ironmongery goods too numerous to particularise. It will suffice to say that in every department the stock is complete, admirably arranged, and is purchased from the leading manufacturers. Mr. Walter Merrall carries on a heavy wholesale and retail trade, and his travelling staff and able management are meeting with gratifying results. He also undertakes lock smithing, bell hanging, gas fitting and plumbing in all its branches, the work being executed with promptness and efficiency by an ample staff of experienced hands, and the connection for this work is of long standing and widespread. As before mentioned Mr. Walter Merrall manages his extensive business with ability and enterprise, and evinces a sound knowledge of the trade in all its branches. He is very popular and deeply esteemed, he is likewise in high favour with the community at large, and he maintains the fifty-six years' reputation of his house in an admirable manner.

Seelig Jacobson, Manufacturer of the Patent Fustian Interlined Stays & Corsets, 22, Bradshaw Street, Shudehill.—The manufacture of stays and corsets is an important branch of Manchester industry, of late years great improvement has been made in these useful articles. The market contains a large variety of stays and corsets, each claiming special merits, and among the number, an honourable place must be assigned to the Patent Fustian Interlined Stays and Corsets manufactured by Mr. Seelig Jacobson. The business was founded by the proprietor forty years ago, and he has gradually worked up a fine home and shipping trade. His goods are protected by Royal Letters Patent, are in great demand, and for excellence of workmanship and quality of material are unrivalled in the market. The factory is a large, spacious, three-storied building, eligibly situated, with a fine frontage, and completely equipped with special machinery and appliances for manufacturing the patent articles. Employment is also given to about fifty skilful hands. Travellers are engaged and the trade done—home and shipping—is very considerable and rapidly increasing, such is the splendid reputation of the patent fustian interlined stays and corsets. Mr. Seelig Jacobson devotes all his energy and ability to his manufacture, and bears the highest reputation for his sterling qualities. He is well known in the manufacturing and commercial world, and his house holds an eminent position in this special branch of industry.

R. Schloesser & Sons, 14, Charlotte Street.—The manufacture of colours and chemicals is a very important branch of industry, necessitating great ability and judgment on the part of the management. Manchester, for the extent and excellence of its trade in this direction, is second to none, and a well-known firm, engaged as merchants, importers, and manufacturers, is that of Messrs. R. Schloesser & Sons, which was founded nearly thirty years ago. Their premises comprise offices and works, both being well managed with commercial and scientific ability. In addition to its own products, which are principally in the region of colours, lakes, sizes, &c., the firm has extensive connections abroad, importing such chemical products for which this market depends upon foreign countries, and by means of which it is carrying on a large and ever-increasing trade with the various Lancashire and Yorkshire industries. Messrs. Schloesser, the members of this enterprising firm, have made themselves worthy representatives of the Manchester chemical industry.

James G. Holden & Co., Wholesale and Export Stationers, 9, Dantzic Street.—This business has been established upwards of forty years, and occupies a most important position in the trade. The premises consist of a large and convenient warehouse, with a capital suite of commodious offices, well furnished and fitted. The specialities of the trade are mainly printing papers, of which Messrs. Holden & Co. keep a large and varied stock. They do also a considerable trade in pattern card papers for which they have a speciality; they are sole agents for this district for Messrs. Gilton and Company, printing ink manufacturers. The firm is well represented. The sole proprietor is Mr. H. W. Simpson, a gentleman who may safely claim to be considered an expert in all branches of the stationery trade, having been in the business for thirty-three years. He takes an active interest in all local public matters and is an active supporter of the Manchester Ship Canal.

Thomas Hudson's Executors, Hardware Merchants, &c., 63 and 17, Shude Hill, and 6, Bradshaw Street.—The hardware and ironmongery and furniture trade of Manchester is of immense value and importance, in a perfect condition, and the establishments engaged are very numerous. A thoroughly representative house in this line, and the largest in the city, is that carried on by the executors of Thomas Hudson, which was founded in 1820. This business is carried on by executors, in the interest of the Hudson family, and on every side the trade is steadily increasing. The premises occupied consist of spacious attractive shops and warehouses. 63, Shude Hill is the hardware warehouse, comprising the following departments: cutlery, electro-plate, brassfoundery, builders' ironmongery, joiners' tools, scales, brushes, lamps, japanned goods, fenders, fire-irons, coal-vases, wire goods, coffin furniture. This department employs about eighty hands, and the manager has been with the firm for twenty-three years. 17, Shude Hill is the furniture warehouse, comprising the following departments: drawing and dining-room suites, also kitchen furniture of every description, oilcloths, carpets, bedsteads, bedding, and clocks, and fancy goods. Upholstery is done on the premises by first-class workmen. 6, Bradshaw Street is the warehouse for kitchen ranges, register grates, mantelpieces in marble, slab, and iron, gas, coal, and oil stoves, chandeliers, rain, water, steam, and gas pipes. All the goods are of superior quality by the leading manufacturers, and every department is most complete in its stock. An enormous local and widespread trade is carried on, and some idea of its extent can be formed from the fact that about one hundred hands are employed. The executors carry on the business in an able and energetic manner. The house under their control is the principal of its kind in the city, and the name of Hudson is a household word.

E. G. Archer, Tarpaulin and Oilcloth Manufacturer, Blossom Street Works, Ancoats (Telephone No. 107).—Of late years the trade in tarpaulin and oilcloth has greatly increased, and the manufacture is carried on more rapidly and economically; hence the cost of production is considerably lessened, to the advantage of all concerned. Manchester does the most extensive business, and goods of this kind bearing the stamp of her establishments are used in all parts of the country. A well-known firm engaged in this industry is that of Mr. E. G. Archer, whose works are at Ancoats, and which was founded about 1868 by the present proprietor's father. Mr. E. G. Archer has carried on the concern himself for the last four years, and at the present time the business has almost doubled itself. As a practical manufacturer he has no superior, and the promptness and fidelity with which he carries out large orders have gained him influential patronage. The premises consist of two ample-sized buildings for appliances, machinery, and arrangements, a model of perfection, in every way suitable for the business carried on. A large force of men are constantly employed in manufacturing tarpaulins and oilcloth of every description, and for other purposes. These goods are of the finest workmanship, remarkable for durability, and the trade done extends to all parts of the country. The travellers employed, four in number, are continually opening fresh ground. Mr. E. G. Archer throws all his energy and ability into his manufacture, and is looked upon by the members of the trade as one of the foremost in their ranks. Mr. E. G. Archer conducts his establishment in a manner which is worthy of imitation, and it fully deserves its high place in the manufacturing world.

W. Aronsberg, F. R. Met. Soc., **Optician and Instrument Maker to Her Majesty's Government,** 12, Victoria Street.—This well-known concern forms one of the prominent and most important features of the neighbourhood of Victoria Street, and its reputation has extended not only throughout the length and breadth of Lancashire, but all over the country and abroad. The talented and enterprising proprietor (who, it may be mentioned, has occupied the position of magistrate for a period of eleven years), besides dealing in all descriptions of mathematical instruments, magic lanterns, and so on, among which he has introduced a large number of popular novelties of his own, makes a great speciality of everything connected with the eye. His skill as an optician has, more than anything else perhaps, caused his name to become so widely known, and his efforts on behalf of suffering humanity so generally appreciated. A short while back, Mr. Aronsberg published a concise, but most interesting and erudite, treatise on the eye, and this has enjoyed a wide circulation everywhere, and been pronounced—as the author's spectacles and other optical aids and appliances have been pronounced—by the press and the public alike, to be very valuable indeed. Mr. Aronsberg has the privilege of attaching the royal arms to his publications and premises, as being optician and instrument maker to her Majesty's Government, and his finely stocked and palatial establishment at 12, Victoria Street, is well worthy a visit by all interested in the trade. The stock always on hand is positively unique of its kind, and would be very difficult to equal elsewhere. The business has been flourishing for about thirty years. Mr. Aronsberg affords his customers exceptional satisfaction, and so much ability does he throw into his work, together with the very best of management, that his many patrons find absolutely nothing left undone by him that could well be desired. At his establishment may be obtained the very best of everything in the line followed at the very lowest of prices. Mr. Aronsberg has worked hard and steadfastly for public favour, and has obtained and is still enjoying his just reward.

H. Statham & Co., India-Rubber, &c., 9—11, Corporation Street.—This is one of the oldest and best-known firms in the city of Manchester, and it has furthermore the distinction of being, with only one exception, the oldest in the trade. It was established under the name of H. Statham & Co. so far back as the year 1847, in the same premises which it now occupies. The shop and showrooms are a prominent and attractive feature in the busy thoroughfare known as Corporation Street, and comprise Nos. 9, 10, and 11. Here is to be found a stock which is remarkable for its great extent and variety, and which is a revelation in itself, so far as it gives an insight into the multifarious uses to which India-rubber and Gutta-percha can be applied. In domestic as well as in business and manufacturing appliances, these materials play a most prominent part, and every development of their use can be seen at Messrs. Statham's. Waterproof coats, capes, and leggings, suits for hunting, driving, and boating, fishing boots and garments, ladies' capes, paletots, and ulsters, waterproof sheets, portable baths, invalid beds—these are a few of the articles to be noted on what may be termed the domestic side. Nor must we omit to mention the celebrated "Porous Elastic Bandage," which has been for so many years a speciality with the firm. This is an admirable invention for the cure of ulcers, varicose affections and other diseases of the leg, and its value has been testified by some of the most eminent medical men of the day, as well as by the thousands who have made practical use of them. Turning to the other departments, an immense trade is done in India-rubber and Gutta-percha belting for engineering, mining, and mechanical purposes. These are perfect substitutes for leather, and can be run in damp places or exposed to the weather without injury. There is also a large demand for vulcanised tubing, which has many pronounced advantages over other kinds. It is largely used by brewers, gardeners, chemical manufacturers, and others. All those valuable applications of India-rubber and Gutta-percha have stood the test of years. They have answered every expectation, and that they are appreciated by the public is proved by the immense demand which Messrs. Statham have daily to supply.

J. Schofield & Sons, Dyers, &c., Cornbrook.—This firm was established more than seventy years ago, and has gone on extending its boundaries and prospering ever since, until at present it has few equals in its own branches in the whole district. The works cover a large area and the working staff is seldom less than three hundred hands. The business of the firm is comprehensive. Starting as dyers, the Messrs. Schofield soon saw the necessity of preparing their own dyes if they were to be successful beyond the average. To this end plant was erected for preparation of dyewood liquors, &c.; then, in order that certain improvements and inventions in machinery might be properly carried out, an engineer's shop was equipped; and this branch prospering extremely well, the firm established for themselves a reputation as clever machinists. The excellence of their dyeing was thus assured and the success of the firm was commensurate with the great labour bestowed upon the preliminaries. The trade connection includes most makers of high class goods in this district, whilst their machinery is exported to all parts of the globe. The amount of work turned out is only limited by the capacity of the premises. The partners are Mr. Thomas Schofield, Mr. John Schofield, Mr. John Wood Schofield, and Mr. John Alexander Schofield, and under their able management the firm cannot but progress and prosper.

The Clydesdale Oil Company, Limited, 41, Corporation Street.—In a review of the trades and industries of this country, written with the object of presenting in a short and concise form the history and commercial standing of the principal mercantile establishments, our attention is naturally first directed towards firms of old standing and extensive commercial relations, and in these connections the large and well-known business of the Clydesdale Oil Company, Limited, importers and refiners of oils and tallow, has special claims upon our consideration and attention. The business of this company has been established in Manchester over thirty years, and the same firm, under the title of Messrs. W. B. Dick & Co., Limited, have establishments in London, Liverpool, Glasgow, Newcastle-on-Tyne, and Barrow-in-Furness. A speciality of this firm is the new cylinder oil, which they have recently introduced under the name of "Kylindrosine." This valuable lubricant possesses many advantages, it being a pure hydro-carbon oil, remains perfectly neutral when exposed to the action of steam; at high pressure it will not saponify when brought into contact with the chemical salts present in the water in the boiler, as is the case with animal or vegetable lubricants, thus preventing the excessive priming frequently caused by the latter. Being perfectly free from acid and remaining so under all conditions, all corrosion is prevented, and no deposit left in the cylinders; and from its great "body" and consequent durability, it is much more economical than the ordinary cylinder oils offered in the market. Spindle, loom, and engine and shafting oils, also marine engine oils of the best quality, are made and sold in immense quantities at rates that cannot be beaten by any firm in the trade. This firm is conducted in a most energetic and enterprising manner, having travellers and agents all over Great Britain. The manager of the company in Manchester, Mr. S. Armstrong Graham, is a gentleman who has had great experience in this business, and by his well-known integrity and uniform courtesy has gained the esteem of all who know him, and possesses the entire confidence of the company.

Isaac Chorlton & Co., Sole Patentees and Manufacturers of the "Excelsior" and other Chain and Spring and Woven Wire Mattresses, Mattress Bedsteads, Ships' Berths, and Invalid Furniture, 19, Blackfriars Street. This firm, originally known as Chorlton and Dugdale, commenced business in the year 1875, and has had an unusually successful career. The head office and show-rooms of the firm are at 19, Blackfriars Street, Manchester, where neatness and order of course prevail as much as at their works, Water Street, Salford. Other offices, and show-rooms also, are maintained in London and Paris. On perusing the illustrated catalogue of Messrs. Chorlton & Co., one cannot but be struck with the careful attention they pay both to design and to utility in the manufacture of their goods; but, to fully appreciate the results of this careful attention, it is necessary to enter one or other of the show-rooms, where all the varieties of bedsteads, mattresses, &c., they produce are on view. Reverting for a moment to the works, we must mention that in order to meet the growing demand for their specialities, the firm have made large extensions in the various departments of their factory; the working capacity of the mattress department, for instance, has been so increased, that they are now in a position to turn out in a finished state six or seven hundred mattresses per week, either separately or in combination with bedsteads. The space occupied for the making of their invalid couches and other cabinet-work is located on floor No. 1, and is 80 feet in length. There are seven other rooms in the establishment, which are as follows: No. 2, "Excelsior" chain-mattress room; No. 3, packing-room and stockroom; No. 4, bedsteads, ship's berth, and tubular frame-making room; No. 5, room for wire-weaving and for creeling and adjusting the frames; No. 6, room used for storing couch and cabinet timber and for seasoning purposes; No. 7, pattern and designing-room; and No. 8, polishing and drying-room. Several large store arches and cellars in separate buildings are occupied with iron and timber, together with finished work. The rapidly-increasing demand—proof of the high estimation in which the manufactures are held by the

INTEGRITY
TRADE I.C.&Co. MARK
RELIABILITY

public—necessitates a heavy stock being kept in readiness, so that prompt delivery can always be relied upon. By a strict observance of due proportion, the firm secure strength and durability, not only to the "Excelsior" chain mattress, but also to their other chain and woven wire spring mattresses, whether in combination with composite frames, or with metallic frames made with tubular sides. The composite frames, we should mention, are constructed with iron or steel end angles, and with sides of wood; in the construction of the tubular ones wood is entirely discarded. All these frames are so made as to allow the spring surface of the mattress to retain a uniformity of elasticity under constant and long wear, thus greatly enhancing the value of the goods as articles of domestic use. By adopting also a uniform measurement, many of the parts of the different frames are made interchangeable, and will fit into one another without the slightest trouble. The firm are working on what is understood in the mechanical world as the "Whitworth" principle, which secures duplicate fits to important parts of their productions. The great speciality of the trade is the "Excelsior" Patent Spring Mattress, which was the first chain and spring mattress introduced to the public; and which has steadily held its own in public

estimation, notwithstanding the many others which have been patented by various inventors. In addition Messrs. Chorlton & Co. manufacture several of the favourite patterns of woven wire and other spring mattresses, and are prepared to manufacture seats for railway carriages and berths for ships of the same materials and on the same principles as the "Excelsior" and other descriptions of mattresses. One of the most striking of the firm's novelties, and one we must by no means pass by without mention, is their invalid appliance bed, specially adapted for hospitals, asylums, and the sick chamber generally, which by means of its mechanical arrangement for raising the patient to any angle, gives absolute security from accident. In addition, however, to bedsteads and mattresses, they have on view in their show-rooms at 19, Blackfriars Street, some valuable sanitary adjuncts, such as folding-stretchers, metallic camp folding beds, invalid spring couches and bed-rests, and ship's berth mattresses. There is also exhibited a patent double-tier or treble-tier ship's berth, specially designed with a view to comfort, and yet so constructed that every part can easily be detached and again put together. The facility gained by the use of this invention will be found highly advantageous when fitting up ships for troops or other passengers, or when afterwards dismantling them for cargo. It is also applicable for dormitories where space is valuable. We might say much more concerning the numerous appliances of the firm for promoting hygienic and domestic comfort did space permit. The benefit of their many unique and practical designs has been deservedly secured to the firm by Royal Letters Patent. It is impossible to inspect their iron bedstead show-room, with all its varieties of patent goods, and to consider that within the last four years they have taken out some thirty or more patents, without feeling convinced that Messrs. Chorlton & Co. are determined by constant energy and activity to keep fully abreast of the times. From the character of their goods, also, the inference may be drawn that they are not disposed to sacrifice the personal comfort of the user for the sake of gain to themselves. Their great aim appears to be to unite strength with simplicity and lasting value in their manufactures, and, while adding to the comfort of the public, to keep sanitary advantages steadily in view. Their trade connection extends all over England and requires the services of a number of efficient travellers.

Samuel Knowles & Co., Calico Printers and Yarn Bleachers, 66, Mosley Street.—The well-known firm of Samuel Knowles & Co., of which Mr. Samuel Knowles is now the principal, was established in 1854, succeeding the firm of Nelson Knowles & Co. As calico printers they have done much to give an impetus to trade and to introduce new and successful ventures and improvements into that branch of commercial activity with which they are connected. Enterprise and excellence of management, combined with workmanship of a very superior kind, have been their distinguishing characteristics; and their popularity and influence are undoubtedly increasing. They conduct a widespread trade. In all their departments there is manifest exceptional briskness and order, and especially with regard to their speciality—printing and bleaching on shipper's own material. The extensive print works, known as the Tottington and Kirklees Mills, are situated in close proximity to the important town of Bury; and their bleaching establishment, also of handsome proportions, occupies a prominent position in the locality of Radisher, near Ramsbottom, and which is likely soon to become more important; the warehouse and offices are at 66, Mosley Street. So admirably is it appointed in every way, customers may always rely upon receiving the utmost courtesy from the firm or any of its officials; and those who require productions of the kind mentioned, and who have not patronised the concern, should do so. We believe that constant custom and satisfaction will thereby result.

Isaac Bentley & Co., Oil Manufacturers, Refiners, &c., Adelphi Oil Works, Salford.—This old-established and important business occupies a leading position in this district, and its history is one of continuous progress and success. The works situated in Blackburn Street, Salford, and known as the Adelphi Oil Works, cover a very considerable area, and have been fitted up and furnished at great cost with the best modern plant and machinery. The specialities of production are machinery oils, the principal items being refined sperm oil, neatsfoot oil, spindle, cylinder, wool, and loom oils, of various degrees of refinement; mineral lubricating oils, refined Gallipoli oil, olive oil, and a variety of other vegetable oils. The connection of the firm is very large and widespread, being scattered over the whole of the United Kingdom, and requiring the services of a staff of capable and active commercial travellers. At the works Messrs. Bentley & Co. employ a large number of hands in addition to a considerable staff of clerks, travellers, and managers. The town address is 19, Corporation Street, City, where a representative of the firm is in attendance on market days (Tuesdays and Fridays) from eleven to five, for the convenience of country manufacturers attending the Exchange.

Mitchell & Co., Cutlers and Ironmongers, 50, Market Street.—This business has been established considerably over forty years, and has always been known by the same title—Mitchell & Co. The firm was originally located at 80, Market Street, but moved to its present address some eight years ago. The premises consist of a large handsome shop and the rooms over. The whole are unusually well furnished and fitted up, and there is abundant means for doing a very large turnover. The specialities for which Messrs. Mitchell & Co. are most renowned are LAWN TENNIS AND FISHING TACKLE; as a consequence, the show-rooms in Market Street are much visited by athletic amateurs, and a capital business is done. In addition to these particular lines, however, the firm works steadily at DOMESTIC IRONMONGERY, CUTLERY, and similar goods. Indeed, Mitchell's CUTLERY has long been esteemed in this city. The trade connection is drawn as much almost from country visitors and their friends as from the population resident in the immediate neighbourhood. The sole partner is Mr. John Mitchell Croisdale, a gentleman well known in the city, and highly respected in all commercial circles.

Ellis & Newsome, Hop Merchants (Dealers in Patent Malt), 7, Sansome Street, Worcester, and 96, Corporation Street.—In a country like England, where the test of time is always looked upon as the proof of stability, and where the keenness of competition brings so strongly into prominence the business abilities of the merchant, a house which has had a successful career of nearly forty years has undoubtedly strong claims on public attention. The firm of Messrs. Ellis & Newsome has thus, by a long and successful course, established for themselves that confidence in the public mind which is only attained by long experience and the exercise of that uprightness, integrity, and fair dealing which has for such a length of time so strongly characterized all their business transactions. This firm, originally founded by Mr. John Newsome, has gradually and steadily developed until its present enormous proportions have been attained. Under the present title of Messrs. Ellis & Newsome the firm has long occupied the premises in Corporation Street, which, together with a branch establishment at 7, Sansome Street, Worcester, form one of the most extensive and complete emporiums for the stowage and distribution of hops (English and foreign) and patent malt in the north of England. The warehouses and stores in Manchester consist of capacious buildings both in Corporation Street and Ducie Street, London Road, with extensive floor area, and replete with every convenience for the careful storing of their immense stocks. Through Lancashire and Yorkshire, and the whole north of England, this firm conducts a large and continually increasing business; their name is always a guarantee of the excellence of their goods, and the care and attention bestowed on their selection, and the prompt dispatch of orders, have placed them in the prominent position which they now occupy.

W. Heywood & Co., Machinists, Ellesmere Street, Hulme.—This well-known firm has attained an important position in its particular line. It has been established for upwards of thirty-five years. Mr. Wm. Heywood, previous to commencing business on his own account, was the leading foreman to the late Richard Roberts, C.E., the eminent engineer and inventor. The principal specialities manufactured by the firm are machines used by paper-stainers and wall-paper manufacturers — such as printing machines, staining or grounding machines, suspending or drying machines for drying paper while in the fold; paper-polishing and reeling and elastic braid and cord manufacturing machines are also made. Other features of the firm's operations are the manufacture of colour-grinding and mixing mills, book-paging machines, horizontal and vertical engines, millwrights' requisites, and similar productions of every description. These are all noted for excellent material and finish, and have won for the firm a first-class reputation among machinery users, and in the commercial world generally.

George Newton, Umbrella and Parasol Manufacturer, 31, Dale Street.—The premises consist of a very extensive warehouse, with suitable offices well fitted for the rapid transaction of business, but the greater part of the premises is used as a factory for manufacturing umbrellas and parasols. All one flat is used by a large number of mechanics making frames, and another flat is occupied by girls, either working sewing machines or finishing goods. The connection seems both large and varied, as they make goods suitable for all nations—India, China, Japan, South America, and the Continent, as well as doing a large home trade. All the cotton goods are got round from the grey cloth, and dyed the various colours required. It is not at all unusual to turn out upwards of one thousand dozen in a week, at all prices, varying from a few shillings per dozen to many pounds. The working staff is necessarily large, their trade being with large cities where wholesale business is done. The firm had a stall in the "Old Manchester" section of the Exhibition, in which they showed the whole process of making umbrellas and parasols. Three young girls, dressed in Marie Stuart costume, and a man in ancient dress, worked at a lathe, exemplifying the various operations. The sole partner now is Mr. Newton, a man of good taste, ingenuity, and good business capacity, who devotes the whole of his time to the business, but at the same time subscribes to most of the local schemes intended to promote the welfare of the city.

Jas. Travis & Co., Cork Merchants and Manufacturers, 77, Corporation Street, and 9 & 11, Redfern Street, Miller Street, Manchester.—During late years marked improvements have been made in cork manufacture, and owing to its utilisation in many new ways the demand has greatly increased, a fact which has tended to almost double the price of the raw material. Manchester enjoys a widespread reputation for the extent and excellence of her trade in this direction, and among the many establishments engaged in the manufacture of corks a leading place is held by that trading under the name of James Travis & Co. It was originated under the name of E. Avern in 1824, and subsequently changed hands until 1855, when it came into the possession of Messrs. Travis and Hibbert, the present proprietor of the house being Mr. James Pierpoint. The works and warehouse at 9 and 11, Redfern Street, Miller Street, are extensive and commodious, fitted with all the appliances used in the trade, the machinery employed being of the best and most perfect description, and employing a good number of hands. The cork is imported from the most noted sources, and the work turned out comprises every description of corks. The warehouse contains a very large stock of corks, corkwood, and almost every requisite connected with the brewing, wine, spirit, ale, and mineral water bottling trades, as well as the least, but not the least important, corks for the medicine bottles. The shop at 77, Corporation Street is of ample dimensions and attractive appearance, and very near and convenient to the market, Victoria and Exchange railway stations, and it contains a large stock of corks, &c. The trade done is very extensive, and extends to all parts of the country; two travellers are employed, and the connection is rapidly increasing. Mr. James Pierpoint manages the business in an able and energetic manner, and is well known among the trade members. He is thoroughly conversant with the trade, and the house has exercised beneficial influence in it.

Messrs. Robert Fielding & Son, Albert Works, Sycamore Street, Oldham Road. Office, 15a, York Street.—In reviewing the industries of Manchester, the business of Messrs. Robert Fielding & Son, designers and card cutters for Jacquard weaving, &c., of Albert Works, Sycamore Street, is worthy of particular notice. Established now many years in Manchester, the reputation of this house is very widespread. The business is of the most intricate nature, and, to acquire a complete knowledge of it, it is necessary to understand the companion industry of Jacquard weaving, and to be thoroughly conversant with the prevailing styles demanded by fashion in all classes of Jacquard fabrics. The work done is very considerable and extensive, as Messrs. Robert Fielding & Son design and cut cards for silk, cotton, and mixed dress goods, handkerchiefs, damasks, table covers, quilts, furnitures, and all kinds of goods woven by the Jacquard machine. Success in the sale of figured goods greatly depends upon the design and cards being carried out with great precision and exactness in every detail. The works at Oldham Road comprise a fair-sized building, admirably arranged and appointed, and fitted with all the latest machinery for the successful and prompt conduct of the business, and affording employment to a well-trained and highly skilled staff of assistants. The machinery in use by the firm is of the most modern description. They have two of Devoge's self-acting repeaters, each of which cuts forty cards per minute, so they can supply manufacturers with repeated cards in an exceedingly short space of time. The principals have recently taken a town office at 15a, York Street, where one of the members of the firm can be seen during business hours. The Messrs. Fielding are well known as thoroughly practical men in their department, and are much respected.

The Cornbrook Brewery Co. (Limited), Chester Road, Hulme.—The foundation of this justly celebrated business was laid very many years ago by Mr. L. O'Neill, who was in the course of time succeeded by Mr. Weld Blundell. Afterwards came the Cornbrook Brewery Company, which, in the year 1884, availed itself of the provisions of the Limited Liability Acts. The Cornbrook Brewery is now a very extensive concern, and the large staff of a hundred hands is constantly employed. The buildings are for the most part well designed and thoroughly adapted for the purposes intended, and there is a fine suite of offices handsomely furnished and most completely fitted up. The brewing plant and machinery are of the most improved and modern construction; and what is of most vital importance, there is an excellent and plentiful supply of pure water. The trade connection is most extensive, and there is a vast circle of private customers, as the "Cornbrook Ales" are in great request wherever they are known. A competent staff of commercial travellers is constantly upon the road; and the managing director and secretary are gentlemen of great personal influence in the city, as well as most capable men of business. The Cornbrook Brewery Co., Limited, has the reputation of being a good paying concern.

Meggitt & Co., Merchant Tailors, 22, Cross Street.—In a review of the commercial enterprises of Manchester it will be observable that some houses possess advantages over others in the same line of business, the result in some cases of longer experience, and in others of a greater natural aptitude for the particular trade. In the merchant tailoring trade, Messrs. Meggitt & Co. may be said to have attained their reputation as makers of fashionable garments from both of the essentials above mentioned. This firm has been established seven years, and from the very beginning has enjoyed prosperity. An extensive knowledge of what constitutes symmetry and elegance of design in wearing apparel, has given the firm a proficiency obtained by few of their competitors, and the truth of this is exemplified in the widespread and influential patronage which they now enjoy. The premises occupied are commodious, and are stocked with a large and carefully selected assortment of the finest and most desirable fabrics from the leading British and Continental manufacturers. Messrs. Meggitt & Co. have an excellent name as makers of ladies' riding habits, court uniforms, ecclesiastical robes, servants' liveries, naval and military outfits, &c. The firm employs the best and most experienced hands, and the work turned out is unexcelled for fit, finish, and fashionable elegance. The principal, Mr. Elijah Meggitt, is a gentleman whose enterprise and sound business principles have won the respect and confidence of all with whom he has had dealings.

John Allen & Co., Provision Merchants, 26, Victoria reet.—Occupying an enviable position amongst the more prominent isiness houses in Manchester, the different establishments of John Allen Co., provision merchants, at whose principal shop a remarkably brisk ade is being carried on, are conducted on strictly first-class lines. This ell-known concern was established thirty years ago as Allen & Briggs, Market Street. About five years after this date the title changed to hn Allen, and the house has been under its present designation for period of sixteen years. Branch establishments will be found in a ost thriving condition at Market Street, in this town; at Withington, ar Manchester; and at Blackpool. Whilst the enormous and increasing ade which is carried on at the several places above enumerated is to a eat extent local, the wide popularity which John Allen & Co. have quired is borne out by the large number of packages made up and forarded to all parts of the country, including London. The public, in ct, has been taught by a long and steady experience to place the utmost nfidence in this provision company, and all may rely upon obtaining full return for their monetary outlay, buy they in small quantities or large.

J. W. Seddon, Brace and Belt Manufacturer, 36 and , Lever Street.—Braces and belts, comparatively speaking, are somehat humble articles of manufacture, and comparatively of recent birth in is district, and we fully believe cannot date back now more than thirty ars. Nevertheless, as the yearly increasing demand argues, they are sential, and numerous improvements in their manufacture have been ade during the last few years to increase that demand. Amongst the ore prominent of the various makers who have distinguished themselves this branch of industry by means of the fertility of their invention in the ay of useful and novel designs, is Mr. John W. Seddon. Through the gency of such gentlemen as Mr. Seddon the once simple occupation of ace-making has especially undergone a change, and in its higher deartment indeed requires that skilful and artistic men and women should employed. At the establishment just alluded to the output in the ape of braces is very large, whilst the quality of the material used, d the excellence of the workmanship, are deserving of the highest aise; the chief characteristic being the durability of both material and orkmanship. Mr. Seddon has been established since 1870, and from at date up to the present time has enjoyed the most unqualified success. is speciality in the shape of web-cloth reflects upon him the highest edit, as used in the manufacture of belts, braces, suspenders, &c. here are also, in addition, numerous patents, which we have not space characterize in detail, but which have secured to the house a permanent putation, and has gained a wide popularity, being bought, to a very rge extent, both at home and abroad, the rising local trade being conderably improved and promising for the future. The chief aim of all r. Seddon's inventions is to give the general public the benefit of a urable and reliable article, while at the same time due regard is given to e principles of economy, so essential to the development of a strong holesale manufacturing business, for which Manchester has long maintained its now historical businesslike reputation. All orders are attended by Mr. Seddon with the utmost alacrity. Courtesy to customers is one the leading features of this well-known firm, and satisfaction may in ery way be confidently relied upon.

John Lees & Brother, Manufacturers of Oxfords, larvards, Regattas, Lustres, Zephyrs, Ticks, Denims, &c., 10, hœnix Street, Fountain Street.—During recent years great improvements have been made in the manufacture of coloured cotton goods, nd one of the principal houses engaged in this trade, and enjoying a putation for general excellence, is that of Messrs. John Lees & Brother. t was established by its present proprietors at Spring Gardens, 1863, but e trade having increased to a great extent it was found necessary, in 870, to move to the present address. The premises occupied are very onvenient as to position, size, and general arrangement, and consist of ffices and warehouse, which are suitably furnished for the convenient espatch of business. A full assortment of all goods of their manuacture is here kept, and conveniently arranged for inspection. The orks (lately purchased by the firm) are situated at Openshaw, and nown as Victoria Mill. These premises (which being of recent contruction, include all modern improvements) are large, and the achinery and appliances used throughout the manufacture are of the ost approved description, and by the best makers, whilst the hands mployed are able and experienced. The individual members of this ell-established firm are Messrs. John and James Lees, gentlemen of bility and experience, who conduct their establishment in an honourable nd upright manner. They are thoroughly conversant with the details f their manufacture, and have a keen judgment of the wants of the arket. Well known and highly esteemed in commercial and manufacuring circles Messrs. John Lees & Brother conduct (by direct personal upervision) a concern in every respect thoroughly sound and reliable.

Edward Schunck, Bleacher of Sewing and Knitting lottons, &c., 24, Corporation Street.—This business was established hirty-five years ago by Dr. Edward Schunck, Ph.D., and its history is ne of steady and uniform prosperity and success. The works are located at Wicken Hall, New Hey, near Rochdale. They cover a very large area, and are well engined and fitted with the best and most modern machinery, and employ something like one hundred and fifty hands. The trade is mainly the bleaching of sewing and knitting cotton, twist, and similar goods. The bulk of the trade is a foreign one, done through most of the large shipping houses, but there is also a large amount done with the makers of sewing, darning and knitting cottons, lamp-wick manufacturers, &c. The works are solely carried on by Mr. J. E. Schunck, who resides at Wicken Hall, and is well known in general commercial circles.

Denis Lee, Timber Merchant, 7, City Road.—Mr. Denis Lee occupies a fair-sized yard, where he carries on the business of a timber merchant and has a very large and valuable stock. An enormous quantity of timber is imported into this country every year, principally from Sweden, Norway, Russia, and other districts round the Baltic, and a very large amount into Lancashire from British North America, especially hewn, sawn, and planed firs. There is also a large quantity of mahogany imported from Honduras, Mexico, Cuba, and St. Domingo. The many kinds of wood dealt in by Mr. Lee embrace mahogany, cedar, oak, ash, birch, walnut, cherrywood, whitewood, pine, pitch pine, spruce, &c., and are sold in logs or sawn, in form of boards and planks. Another feature in the business is the sale of all kinds of veneers. For these and the varied woods above mentioned this firm has a well-known reputation, and a considerable amount of business is done with the cabinet and joinery trades. Mr. Lee having now been a number of years in business, has, by his skilful and efficient method of dealing, established a very thriving trade in Manchester and the neighbouring locality.

Ellis Tootill, Engraver, Lithographer and Letterpress Printer, Account Book and Stationery Manufacturers, 9, Minshull Street.—Established thirty-one years ago, Mr. Tootill has one of the very best businesses of its kind in this city. The firm has long been distinguished for the excellent taste displayed in all designs, lithographic, copperplate, and letterpress printing turned out of its commodious offices. All descriptions of high class work are undertaken; and, generally speaking, the name Tootill is held to be synonymous with whatever is excellent in the way of printing and paper. Mr. Tootill finds an able representative in the person of his son, Mr. John S. Tootill, upon whom devolves all the outside work of the firm. The business connection lies mainly amongst the city warehouses; and a very large trade is done in fancy chromo tickets for the ornamentation of finished goods, such as prints, velveteens, regattas, and other Manchester fabrics. In the designing of such ornaments, Mr. Ellis Tootill is extremely clever and happy; and a glance through the pattern-books of the firm reveals an amount of originality, inventiveness, and ingenuity very unusual indeed. Mr. Tootill has on several occasions been specially selected to prepare representative designs.

Burbie Brothers, Lard Refiners, &c., Springfield Lane, Salford.—This business was established in the year 1882. The premises in Springfield Lane consist of a modern built and commodious works, capacious stores, and a fine suite of excellent offices, handsomely furnished and fitted with the latest and most approved appliances for the rapid dispatch of business. The speciality of the trade is lard refining. They hold enormous stocks of pure, refined lard, the produce of Canada and the United States, from which they import in very large quantities. The connection is extensive and wide-spread, there being customers in all parts of England, although a large proportion of the trade is done within fifty miles of the Royal Exchange. A staff of some four or five experienced and clever travellers is constantly on the road, and in addition to clerks, book-keepers, and correspondents, the firm employs a considerable number of hands at the works and depôt. The firm have just opened a new refinery at Liverpool, where they will eventually remove their entire business. The premises have been specially built for them, and are elaborately fitted with pans, coolers, hydraulic presses, and various machinery and appliances; they are capable of turning out a hundred tons per week. The proprietors are Mr. Hugh Burbie, and Mr. James Burbie, gentlemen of experience in the provision trade, well known in the Liverpool and other produce markets, and everywhere highly esteemed as clever, reliable, and strictly honourable business men.

Watts & Taylor, Drysalters, Mansfield Chambers, St. Anne's Square.—This is the Manchester house of the well-known firm whose London branch is in Corn Exchange Avenue, Seething Lane. The business is principally in gums, dye-stuffs, shellac, and general foreign produce used by colour mixers, dyers, and paper, paint, and varnish manufacturers. The business premises in St. Anne's Square are of ample extent, but most of the orders are executed from Goole, Garston, Runcorn, and London stores. The offices are exceedingly neat and tastefully furnished. The sole proprietors are Messrs. John H. Watts and J. V. Taylor, who are also part proprietors of the Churnet Valley Colour Works, and are gentlemen of sound business experience and of unrivalled knowledge of drugs and chemicals.

Messrs. Broadhead & Co., Sign and Glass Writers and Gilders, &c., 82, Thomas Street, 17, Tib Street, and 102, London Road.—In reviewing the great and leading industries of the age, a special feature presents itself for observation in the house decorating branch, appropriately represented by the well-known firm of Broadhead & Co., Sign & Glass Writers, Gilders & General Decorators, whose establishments are admirably situated at the above addresses. Established in 1848, this firm has for many years carried on a very extensive business in sign and glass writing, and gilding, &c.; the well-known reputation of Messrs. Broadhead & Co. being second to none in the trade. In sign writing, some of the finest specimens to be seen in the city are the productions of this establishment, and many of the handsome and artistic designs on glass, both in writing and gilding, which form such a leading feature in the decoration of business houses, shops, and offices, are also specimens of their skill and handicraft. The decorative department receives the personal superintendence of the principals, and some very large contracts have been secured by this house. A reputation for excellency of design and dispatch in execution adds very materially to the world-wide fame of the firm. The premises occupied consist of large works in Thomas Street, Tib Street, and London Road, in which are fitted a most expensive and modern plant and accessories for the firm's business, and affording constant employment to a large number of highly skilled artisans and tradesmen. The business transactions of the firm are necessarily on a large and important scale, and comprise much of the best work in the city. The principals of the partnership are gentlemen well known as practically acquainted with their business in its every detail, of the highest integrity and widely respected.

Lowthian, Williamson, & Co., Dress Goods Manufacturers, 58, Portland Street.—The great manufacturing firm of Lowthian, Williamson, & Co., has now been established for upwards of ten years, its existence dating from the early part of the year 1877. The members of the firm as at present constituted are, Mr. Thomas Henry Lowthian and Mr. Edgar Williamson, trading under the title of Lowthian, Williamson, & Co., successors to the firm of Lowthian, Fairlie, & Co., of Manchester and Carlisle, established nearly 100 years ago, manufacturers by hand and power-loom of various descriptions of Manchester goods, including silk dress, worsted, linen, cotton, and mixed dress goods, ginghams, Oxfords, drills, zephyrs, shirtings, sateens, &c., &c. The manufactures of Lowthian, Williamson, & Co. in these specialities are exceedingly large, they having acquired a world-wide celebrity and doing an enormous home and foreign trade in them. This is entirely owing to the excellent value of their goods, which are all turned out in such superior style and with so superb a finish as to command attention in every market for which they are adapted. Messrs. Lowthian, Williamson, & Co., have acquired a great name for their various manufactures, but they have done much to earn it. A vast amount of taste, skill, technical knowledge, and the most painstaking and careful supervision are brought to bear on every part of the process. All the newest and most approved machinery and appliances only are employed. They have recently added a new department under able management for the production of dyed sateens, lace stripes, fancy dyed and white goods. The warehouse of the firm in Portland Street is a very handsome erection of four stories, being exceptionally lofty and well lighted, and consequently adapted for the storage and display of goods in a very superior manner.

Michael Nairn & Co., Floorcloths, Linoleums, &c., Manchester Warehouse, 4, Canal Street, Minshull Street.—The representative firm of floorcloth and linoleum manufacturers in the United Kingdom is that of Messrs. Michael Nairn & Co., whose extensive works are at Kirkcaldy, Scotland. The Manchester warehouse has been established eight years. It is a substantial four-story and basement building in Canal Street, and is equipped throughout with every facility and convenience for the transaction of business. An immense stock of the firm's world-famed floorcloths and linoleums is kept, including all the latest and most desirable patterns and styles. These goods are unexcelled for beauty and originality of design, superiority of workmanship, finish, and durability. They have been awarded the highest prizes at the following International Exhibitions: Paris 1867 and 1878, Philadelphia 1876, Sydney 1879, Frankfort 1881, Cork 1883, and Edinburgh 1886. The firm has also large warehouses in London, Glasgow, and Paris, and its home and export trade is fully in keeping with the large capital embarked in the enterprise of those responsible for its management. The individual members of the firm are, Mr. Michael B. Nairn, Mr. John Nairn, and Mr. John Forrester. They are gentlemen whose integrity and sound business methods have won the respect and confidence of the commercial world. Their great establishment is a credit alike to their enterprise and the important industry it so ably represents.

A. F. Pope, Ship, Marine, and Fire Insurance Broker, 11 & 12, Barton House, Deansgate.—In a city of such commercial importance as Manchester, whose annual exports reach an almost incredible figure, the business of an insurance broker is of considerable importance and (if properly and persistently followed) profit. This is
the line to which Mr. A. F. Po
established for many years, and
man is better known or more po
and his promptitude and integrit
support. He represents some o
and those covering fire risks also
Merchants' Marine, Globe Mari
and many other insurance corpo
writers both at home and abroa
do also most of the leading fir
ments Mr. Pope is widely know
being of the steadiest and best k
ship and property owners of the

John Chorlton & So
Piccadilly.—This most importan
Chorlton in the year 1845, and w
Street. In 1869 Messrs. Joseph
by their father, and the title chan
a removal was made to the pr
Chorlton, three years afterward
under the same title. The offi
nished, and are well adapted f
special line of the firm is the p
personal connection of the Mes
and capitalists, brings a large a
Their most important branch is
property, and collecting rents, a
creasing business. Messrs. Chorl
insurance business, and they a
Insurance Co., the Yorkshire Fi
Temperance and General Provide
Plate Glass Co. The partners a
Chorlton, gentlemen highly resp
professional circles.

J. J. Rigby, Oil Press
bank Works, Comus Street, Re
operations in the procuring of
manufacturers of soaps, candles,
ing, and this branch of industry
The manufactures of Manchester
important place must be assigned
very notable house in this directi
Sunnybank Works, Comus Stre
Since that date Mr. John Jos
gratifying extent in the district,
of the place, the energy and a
reason to believe that it will ex
tions. The works known as Sun
and planned and arranged spec
refining. The machinery applia
improvements, and the hands em
are conducted on the most advan
oil produced and the tallow refi
quality, and are much sought a
others interested in the district
practical and expert refiner, and
He is well known in the city an
financial and industrial status;
he has achieved a success in his b
of Manchester men for marked a

Messrs. Mountain, Ho
93, Corporation Street.—The w
Horsley & Co. was established,
subsequently it passed into the h
their joining Mr. Mountain, the s
Horsley & Co. The present title
Mr. S. H. Mountain and Me
The method of business adopt
of the generous patronage accor
best of quality is supplied to cus
care. The premises are well wo
lent example of what such a co
large and thoroughly organized.
tain, Horsley & Co. have their h
Borough, London. The busines
and generous lines that have bee
from its commencement. This fi
from every standpoint its reputati
and the future before Messrs. M
most abundant promise of even g
enced heretofore.

Charles Midgley, Dispensing Chemist, 28, St. Ann's Square.—Manchester is behind no other provincial city in the empire for the extent and excellence of her pharmacy business, and the members of the profession engaged therein are a highly educated, thoroughly qualified and influential body. An excellent representative house in this line is that of Mr. Charles Midgley, which was founded by Mr. T. H. Taylor, as far back as the year 1833; consequently it has survived a period of over half a century. Mr. Midgley has been the proprietor for fifteen years, and the business has been conducted in the present premises for the past nine years. The establishment is large and well appointed, and is situated in the very heart of the city, being close to the Exchange Buildings. Mr. Midgley's stock embraces all the multifarious articles dealt in by first-class pharmaceutical chemists, and his connection is both influential and substantial. He does a superior dispensing business, and enjoys the confidence of his clients and of the local medical practitioners. Amongst his specialities we may mention the "Improved Spray Producer," designed to allow the accurate use of concentrated solutions of cocaine hydrochlorate, morphia, &c. This invention is of the greatest value and utility, and has, consequently, become widely patronised by the medical and surgical professions. We may likewise name, as specialities, "Capsicum ointment," and "Taylor's Boil Plasters," which are held in great repute in all parts of the country. We will only add that Mr. Midgley is well known in Manchester and is popular and respected.

Abm. Pemberton, Paper Manufacturer, 23, Booth Street, Piccadilly,—This business has been established upwards of nineteen years, and has become one of the most important of its kind in the city. The premises consist of a capital warehouse, with commodious, handsomely furnished offices attached. The main specialities are brown, glazed, and manilla casings, skipping, backing and sampling papers, in use by the mills, hat manufacturers, and warehouses of the district. In addition Mr. Pemberton has a paper bag making department, which is always actively engaged, and he does a very considerable trade in rope, twine, and cotton band. A strong staff of salesmen, clerks, book-keepers, correspondents, warehousemen, and packers are engaged. The trade connection, though largely local, is not entirely so, as the firm has many customers in distant parts of the empire. Mr. A. Pemberton, the founder of the business, is still the sole partner. He is a gentleman with troops of friends throughout the district. He is a familiar figure upon the Royal Exchange, and is said to know all that there is to know in reference to the paper trade. Mr. Pemberton is looked upon as a generous employer and a willing supporter of all beneficent movements intended to ameliorate the condition of the less successful members of the community. His ready purse is never closed against deserving objects, and he himself is held in the highest esteem and regard.

R. Ward & Co., Manufacturers of Moles, Cords, Velveteens, Patent Velveteens, &c., 11, Stevenson Square.—For the extent and excellence of her manufacture of moles, cords, velveteens, patent velveteens, &c., Manchester bears a world-wide reputation, and among the many firms engaged therein an eminent place is held by that trading as Messrs. R. Ward & Co., which was founded over twenty years ago by Messrs. Robert, James, and John Ward, and is now carried on by them. Three storeys of a large building are occupied by this business, and as regards dimensions, fittings, and arrangements, the premises are all that could be desired. There is a very heavy stock of moles, cords, velveteens, patent velveteens, and such-like goods, which are manufactured by able and experienced workmen on the most approved principles. For durability, excellence of material, and general finished appearance these goods are equal to anything produced, and no expense is spared by the firm in keeping up this high state of perfection. The trade done is of great value, is local, and South African and Australian shipping; and owing to the energy of the partners, who travel at intervals, it is steadily increasing. The management throughout is all that could be desired, and the largest orders are executed with a dispatch that speaks volumes for the perfect organisation. Messrs. Robert and John Ward are gentlemen of the highest commercial and industrial status, well known and highly respected in leading business circles.

James McMillan & Co., Account Book Makers and Wholesale and Export Stationers, 10, Cannon Street.—This is one of the very best known firms of its kind in England, and has been established a great many years. The firm is old established, and the premises have the merit of being very large and very conveniently situated. Messrs. James McMillan & Co. have acquired a reputation for excellence of material and workmanship; while their manufactured account books are turned out in a substantial and finished manner. Their connection is a very extensive one. They employ a number of travellers, and at home a goodly array of assistants, salesmen, porters, and packers. A few years' training in this establishment appears to be regarded by other wholesale stationers as a guarantee of efficiency on the part of assistants, judging by the eagerness with which they snap them up. The entire turn-over is very considerable. The members of the firm are amongst the best known gentlemen in their trade.

J. M. Irving & Co., Chemical & Colour Merchants, 17A, Dickenson Street, Cooper Street.—This eminent firm of chemical and colour merchants has since its establishment in Dickenson Street, made remarkable progress. It was originally founded by Mr. James M. Irving, who still continues at the head of the management, and to his exceptional energy and business capacity is undoubtedly owing a great part of the success which has attended the operations of the firm. The specialities for which Messrs. Irving & Co. have already become so well known are both numerous and important, including many articles of the highest value in connection with the staple industry of the city, particularly for dyeing, calico printers, and paper-stainers. Messrs. Irving & Co. are purveyors of and agents for a great variety of special chemicals and colours used by calico printers, dyers, lithographers, and others, which are not elsewhere obtainable, at any rate in the same degree of purity and efficiency, as that in which they come from the hands of this firm. A fact like this has an important bearing on the success of the operations in which these chemicals are employed, and fully accounts for the large amount of support the firm now receives, as well as promises a very great expansion in the future. They keep themselves thoroughly posted in all matters pertaining to colouring, &c. Messrs. Irving & Co. test chemical colouring preparations of every description, as well as being importers of foreign chemicals for home use, and are also exporters of all kinds of general drysalteries to the various markets of the world in which there is a demand for them. Their business is therefore in every way an important and extensive one, capable of almost unlimited development, and almost certain under the present able and enterprising management to expand into dimensions for which the present warehouse accommodation, although by no means insignificant, will be found totally inadequate. It is already stocked very heavily, although the excellence of the arrangements prevents anything like a hitch in the dispatch of business.

Standard Manufacturing Company (Limited), 29 to 35, Blossom Street, Great Ancoats.—The manufacture of frilling is an important branch of Manchester industry, and during the past few years great improvement has taken place in the operation, considerably lowering the cost of production. A well-known firm carrying on business as frilling manufacturers is that known as the Standard Manufacturing Company (Limited), which was originally established as Hadwen & Co., but assumed its present title in 1882. The premises occupied consist of a spacious building completely fitted with the most modern machinery and appliances, and about four hundred experienced hands are employed. All kinds of frilling are turned out by the Company, the material used being of the finest quality, the workmanship excellent, and the patterns elegant and original; hence these productions hold a good place in the market, and are greatly in demand. A heavy trade is done, the Company supplying the warehouses in the City, and also in London, Glasgow, &c. The satisfactory state of this establishment, the excellence of the manufacture, are entirely due to the energy and ability of Mr. John MacCallum. A more practical or experienced man, thoroughly conversant with all branches of the manufacture, it would be difficult to find. He is respected by all classes of the community.

J. Pickup & Co., Manufacturers of Holland and Diaper Pinafores, Aprons, Underclothing, &c, 58, Liver Street.—The manufacture of holland and diaper goods is carried on to a great extent in Manchester, and the city is the centre of the trade for the United Kingdom. A well-known firm engaged in this important manufacture is that known as Messrs. J. Pickup & Co., which was originally founded at 17, Tib Street. The premises occupied are large and commodious, comprising manufacturing department and warehouse, the former being admirably fitted with the most modern machinery and appliances used in the trade. Over sixty hands are constantly employed in making holland and diaper pinafores, aprons, infants' gowns, underclothing, &c.

Thomas Davenport & Co., Makers-up and Packers, 4, Minshull Street.—Established over half a century, this business has enjoyed almost uninterrupted prosperity. The premises consist of exceedingly fine modern-built packing warehouses, with capital well-furnished offices, fitted with the telephone and all the latest and most approved appliances for the rapid dispatch of business. The packing-room contains a range of powerful hydraulic presses, capable of turning out the largest bales required by any shipping house in the city. The pumps are of the best known construction, and are worked by steam power; and there is every requisite and appliance to facilitate all operations in connection with their extensive business. The warehouse is most conveniently situated for the reception and dispatch of goods. The connection includes all the tenants in the block of buildings, No. 4, Minshull Street, and a large proportion of the shippers in the immediate neighbourhood. Messrs. Davenport & Co. employ an unusually numerous staff of working makers-up and packers, as well as an efficient office staff. The members of the firm are themselves extremely well known amongst the shippers and merchants of the city, and they have each a strong personal connection. The firm is especially noted for its prompt attention and quick dispatch.

The Guardian Plate Glass Insurance Company (Ltd.), 49, Spring Gardens.—Among the divers important institutions in existence in this country for the insurance of plate and other glass, the Guardian Plate Glass Insurance holds an honoured position in the front rank. It was founded in 1863, just a quarter of a century ago, and its progress since has been of a steady and profitable kind. The board of directors is made up of gentlemen honoured in both the commercial and professional walks of life and of the highest capacity and intelligence—not to speak of integrity. Another advantage from a local point of view is that they are all interested in Manchester affairs, and most of them reside in its suburbs. The head office of the corporation is located in a central and commanding position, and consists of spacious and elaborately fitted premises, and employs a numerous staff. Other branches exist at Hamburg, Bei St. Anuen; London, 71, Fleet Street; and Copenhagen, Ned Stranden, 2. In addition to these over eight hundred branch agencies are in full working order. From this the enormous trade done by the Company may be inferred. All kinds of plate, ornamental and other glass, is insured against malicious or accidental damage. The advantages offered by the Company are, (1) ample security, (2) moderate premiums, (3) policies covering all damage except from fire, (4) prompt settlement of losses. Already the Society has paid the large sum of over £110,000 in compensation for losses. The capital of the Company is £25,000, and this is fully subscribed. An extensive growing and lucrative business is the result of active, methodical, and judicious management. The present secretary of the Company is Mr. Thomas Harris. The Company has a large invested capital and a reserve fund to meet all contingencies.

James Watson & Sons, General Printing & Lithographic Works, 31, Tib Street, Market Street.—Over twenty years ago the well-known house of Messrs. James Watson & Sons was founded by its senior partner, Mr. James Watson. The premises occupied at the above address comprise a very large, handsome and lofty building of considerable architectural pretensions, and forming a very conspicuous feature of the locality; it is excellently laid out and contains a large number of first-class modern and valuable lithographic, letterpress and other machines necessary for the carrying on of the varied character of their business. Messrs. James Watson & Sons are engaged very largely in the manufacture of plain and fancy ornamental trade marks, labels, bands, and tickets, which are sent, on manufactured cotton, woollen, and silk piece goods, &c., to all parts of the world. They not only supply an enormous quantity of trade mark labels, but also keep many millions of fancy labels in stock and ready for immediate use. In addition to the label trade, they supply large quantities of counting-house stationery and printed forms for every class of business, price lists, catalogues, show cards, day books, ledgers, and all the varieties of books in use, and which require manufacturing to special patterns. Their establishment is noted for the excellency of its work, and the good character of its productions are very widely known; they keep a large staff of the best workmen and skilled artists; the result is a high-class and extensive business. The connections of the house are of a very wide-spread character, and the admirable order of every department of this establishment bespeaks the high-class character of its management.

George Davies, C.E., F.I.P.A., Patent Agent, &c., 4, St. Ann's Square.—Mr. John Davies established himself professionally in this city in the year 1835, and in the year 1862, having taken his son into partnership, Mr. Davies altered the style of the firm to John Davies & Son. Thus it remained, however, for no more than six years, as in 1868 the style of the firm became, as at present, George Davies. The firm has occupied the present premises since 1850. The offices at St. Ann's Square are a handsome suite of rooms, capitally furnished, having an extensive collection of books of reference, and appointed and fitted up with all the modern appliances for the rapid transaction of business. Mr. Davies is himself a fully qualified civil engineer, and a fellow of the Institute of Patent Agents, and a member of various learned and scientific societies. He has a very large circle of influential and wealthy personal friends, and a lucrative business finds its way to his offices from inventors and intending patentees anxious to obtain the advantage of his unrivalled experience, his ripe judgment, and his keen perception. Mr. Davies undertakes the registration of designs and trade marks in this and all foreign countries. He has influential agents in London, in all foreign countries where patents can be obtained, and no man is better known in his profession. He has published several excellent little works on the patent laws: "Self-help to New Patent Laws," and "Colonial and Foreign Patent Laws," being perhaps the most useful.

John Marsden, Floor Cloth Manufacturer, Varley Street, Oldham Road.—The attention that has been directed to the production of floor cloths, in this country, during recent years, has developed the fact that British enterprise and manufacturing skill are quite as successful in this department, as they have proved in many others. In this connection it is a pleasure to make prominent mention of one of the largest and most thoroughly representative establishments in the trade. We refer to that of Mr. John Marsden. This business, which bears ar evidence of enterprise and good management, was established in 1 and its career furnishes a good illustration of what can be accompli by well-directed energies and sound business principles. From a c paratively small beginning the trade of the house has grown to pro tions of great magnitude, its operations extending throughout all par the United Kingdom. The factory is a substantial six-storey buil covering a large area of ground; it was built in 1864 and is equi throughout with the most improved modern machinery and appliar employment being given to about one hundred hands. The floor clo &c. manufactured by this house are unexcelled for beauty and originalit design, superiority of workmanship, finish and durability. These g have a standard reputation in the trade, and Mr. Marsden is effici represented in all parts of the country by a staff of commercial travel He is well known and highly respected in commercial circles for enterprise and integrity.

F. P. Armstrong, Manufacturing Stationer, &c., Piccadilly.—This thriving business was established in the year 1880, its history is one of rapid and continuous progress. The premises co of a handsome shop of attractive appearance, and several lofty light convenient work-rooms and warehouses. The office is substanti furnished and is fitted up in the most perfect manner for the quick disp of a brisk business. The specialities of manufacture are plain and o mental show cards, window bills, catalogues, reports, balance sh prices current, invoices, statements, circulars, cards, delivery and me notes, account books ruled and printed to special patterns, and bookb ing in all styles. A very fine assortment of india-rubber stamps and is also held for sale, as is also the Simplex type writer, in which the h does a good business. All sorts of American notions and noveltie which there is a large stock, copying presses, &c., are dealt in, and establishment contains an extensive selection of a great many arti of general utility. The printing offices are supplied with an exce assortment of modern and antique type, first-rate machinery and powerful lithographic and other presses; and the bookbinding departm and the account book making branch are each furnished with everyth requisite to turn out work in the best possible style. Mr. Armstron also the proprietor, editor, and publisher of *Armstrong's Family Journa* publication of great merit and widely read. Its stories and gen literary contents are of high merit, and such as may be put into the ha of any member of the household with the best results. Her Majesty been graciously pleased to accept a copy of the journal, which is wor of widespread support. The connection is already important and ext sive. An increasing business as booking agent for the leading ste ship lines to all parts of the world is also done. Mr. Armstrong incl amongst his customers many of the leading merchants and warehouse of the city and district.

Forsyth Bros., Musical Instrument Showrooms a Warehouse, 122 & 124, Deansgate.—The love of music, alway prominent feature in the character of all civilised nations through the globe, has never within the whole history of time had such gr opportunities for its gratification as at present. Nothing adds much to the pleasing and soul-stirring effect of rich harmony as American Organ, a superb stock of which instruments are always view at the elegant showrooms of Messrs. Forsyth Bros. Their mat less stock of musical instruments and sheet music is about the lar in the kingdom, and offers a selection of American organs, manu tured by that well-known and justly celebrated firm, The Domin Organ Company, of Bowmanville, Ontario, Canada; a name so known for the excellence of the instruments turned out, as to need comment. The selection of instruments to be seen at Messrs. For Bros.' comprises specimens of all kinds and sizes, from the Villa Gem truly charming adjunct to the drawing-room or library, to the mag ficent, grand and imposing-looking two-manual bass organ, a fit accessory for either church, chapel, hall or mansion, at such astonishin reasonable prices as to produce a feeling of surprise how such substanti good and exceedingly pleasing and satisfying instruments can be p duced for the money. Such are now the facilities offered by Mes Forsyth Bros. for the acquisition of one of these charming instrume that no home need be without a parlour organ. The musical reader c not do better than obtain a catalogue of the immense and varied stock pianoforte music always in stock, from easy lessons for the beginner to full and orchestral productions of the great masters; any and all of most choice and leading compositions of both ancient and modern arti are to be obtained at this establishment at a minute's notice. The Mes Forsyth have been established in their capacious showrooms and wa house over thirty years, and such is the magnitude of the display organs, pianofortes, and musical accessories, that the spectator is bewilde at the long lines of costly and superb pianos of the highest finish quality, backed up by the still more elegantly finished cases and gilt p tops of the organs. Messrs. Forsyth Bros. have the largest piano-tun connection in the North of England, their reputation for sending none but the most skilful tuners being well known. The purchaser either piano, organ, or music of any kind will omit a grand opportun should he not decide to visit the above showrooms before making purchase.

Charles Bromhall, Umbrella Manufacturer, 8, Stevenson's Square.—Umbrella manufacturing in this city dates back many years, but up to a comparatively recent date its manufacturers have been voted principally for low and heavy umbrellas made of cottons and Bradford goods, great quantities of which have been shipped to all parts of the world; and for its better goods, including silks, &c., they have had to take second place, owing to the reputation of the London manufacturers. It has only been by steady perseverance and determination that they are

now able to compete with the southerners, not only in their own city, but in the North and Midland counties. The umbrella manufactory carried on by Mr. C. Bromhall has been established now on a sure foundation for several years, and its productions are daily growing in demand and reputation. Already Mr. Bromhall has succeeded in establishing himself amongst the best houses in the trade, and his umbrellas are beginning to acquire a more than local celebrity for excellence of material, neatness of finish, strength and durability. These satisfactory results have not been brought about without a great deal of painstaking labour on the part of Mr. Bromhall, whose devotion to business and study of everything calculated to improve the quality and appearance of his manufactures, has been very great. Mr. Bromhall has done much to improve the manufacture of umbrellas, both in material and design. The influence of his efforts may be seen in the neat and compact appearance of his Unique, which is the lightest and one of the smallest-folding umbrellas made. All these umbrellas are made with Mr. Bromhall's patent canes, which are guaranteed to resist

most severe storms and will not warp nor swell with rain. The best business qualifications, Mr. Bromhall possesses in a high degree, and he may therefore be relied on not merely to produce an article in the shape of umbrellas at a moderate price and of first rate quality, but to take measures to ensure the public's being everywhere able to obtain it. The progress already made in this difficult branch of business may be seen at Mr. Bromhall's establishment, where unmistakeable indications of a sound and rapidly increasing business are abundant and evident.

P. J. Villy & Co., Continental Merchants, 100, Portland Street.—Manchester has many firms of different nationalities, and among them an important place is occupied by the French. A well-known firm is that of Messrs. P. J. Villy & Co., which was established by the present head, Mr. P. J. Villy, in [illegible]. The firm is engaged in shipping Manchester goods to the Continent, having a house at Paris. The Paris premises are large and commodious, comprising offices, and stock and sample-rooms; the former well furnished and presenting a busy appearance. The stock-rooms are large and spacious, and contain a fair assortment of Manchester goods of every description. These goods are selected from the warehouses of the most noted manufacturers, and the trade is very large. The arrangements in Manchester for dispatch are perfect, and large and valuable cargoes are regularly consigned to the Paris house. English hands are employed in Manchester, and a very large number in Paris. Mr. P. J. Villy, the head member and founder of this old firm is well known at home and abroad, and bears the highest reputation for honour and integrity. Ably and enterprisingly managed, the house is an important factor in the Home and Continental trading world.

Geo. Thomas & Co., Engineers, &c., 28, Deansgate.—Doing an extensive home and export trade, the firm of Geo. Thomas & Co. is one of the most influential of the many large business houses in this town. Messrs. G. Thomas & Co. supply and contract for the fitting up and setting to work of any description of plant for textile and engineering establishments, and correspond in all languages. They are engineers, contractors, and exporters of all classes of machinery for spinning and weaving cotton, wool, worsted, shoddy, flax, hemp, jute, silk-waste, &c., bleaching, dyeing, printing, finishing, and their accessories. They supply specialities in the shape of copper rollers, metals, chemical products, dye-stuffs, oils, &c., furnishing mills with the necessary gearing and shafting. They do a large trade in boiler and steam engines, and manufacture machinery of almost every conceivable kind. They are the sole agents for the following well-known and established firms: Dobson & Barlow, Bolton (for Sweden, Norway, and Denmark), makers of cotton-spinning machinery, established 1790; Joseph Sykes, Bros., Lindley (for the Continent, except Russia), makers of card clothing, established 1795; Hudswell, Clarke, & Co., Leeds (for Alsace and the Vosges, Scandinavia, and Switzerland): Rodger's patent wrought-iron pulleys; Holden & Brook, Limited, Salford (for Europe), "Influx" and "Exhaust" injectors; and Blackman's Air Propeller Ventilating Co., Limited, London (for Sweden, Norway, Alsace, and Switzerland). Messrs. Thomas & Co. are also proprietors of Staub's patent universal yarn-assorting balance, and makers of patent American and other cotton and hair belting, which is ninety per cent. stronger than leather. When it is added that the firm has representatives in Mulhouse, Vienna, Leipzig, France, Spain, Portugal, Sweden, Norway, and the United States of America, some definite idea of this enormous and comprehensive trading concern may be arrived at, but samples, prices, and all further information may be had on application. The quality of the manufactures are unimpeachable; the prices charged are most reasonable, and the wide popularity which they enjoy testifies to the admirable and satisfactory manner in which Messrs. Thomas & Co. cater for the patronage of their ever-increasing circle of customers.

Craven & Whitehurst, Eagle Mills, Hunt Street.—In reviewing the various industries that have made Manchester the great manufacturing centre of the kingdom, it is instructive and interesting to note the advances and improvements that have been made in each, and to ascertain exactly what has been accomplished by energy and capital. In looking over the field, it is easy to see that the manufacture of braid and kindred products has kept pace with every other industry, and in this connection special mention should be made of the Eagle Mills, of which Messrs. Craven & Whitehurst are the enterprising proprietors. This business was established in 1878, and from its very inception has enjoyed a prosperous career, owing to the uniform quality and standard excellence of its manufacture, as well as the enterprising manner in which the business has always been conducted. The mills in Hunt Street are of spacious dimensions, admirably arranged, and equipped with every facility for the transaction of business, with a large number of skilled hands. Every description of ladies' dress braids in military, alpaca, mohair, and llama, also of shoe laces, elastic braids and cords, and window lines, &c., &c., is manufactured, and the goods turned out are unexcelled for quality, finish, and durability. The firm is efficiently represented in all parts of the country by first-class agents, and with the superior facilities at its command, is enabled to offer special advantages to customers and to execute all orders in the promptest and most satisfactory manner. The individual partners—Mr. William Craven and Mr. Jesse Whitehurst—are enterprising and thoroughly capable business men.

Ashley & Dumville, Coal and Coke Merchants, 105A, Market Street.—Moderate charges, combined with a quality which no one can, with fairness, do other than praise, are recommendations not always found where coal and coke merchants are concerned. Good coal is often as difficult to obtain as a good horse, when one's purse is not unfathomable or one's banking account not unlimited. Experience, however, has taught all customers of Messrs. Ashley & Dumville, Coal & Coke Merchants, that from the latter firm their household wants in the fuel line may be supplied at a cost most reasonable and satisfactory. In fact, during the whole of the six years which Messrs Ashley & Dumville have been established, they have enjoyed public favour in a most marked degree.

The "Hellewell" Rubber Co., 15, 17, 19, and 21, Corporation Street.—The growth of Manchester as a great mercantile and manufacturing centre has not only been very rapid during the last fifty years, but its entire history is one of advanced strides towards the position now so creditably maintained. Every branch of trade represented in our midst has kept pace with this remarkable growth, and to-day are to be seen the results of the ability and enterprise of our citizens. An establishment which is a credit to Manchester, and a successful exponent of its special industry, is that of the Hellewell Rubber Co. This business was established upwards of forty years ago as Hellewell & Co., they being succeeded by the present concern in 1871. From its very inception the business has prospered and grown apace, and it is to-day one of the most important in its line in the country. The company do a large wholesale and retail business in every description of waterproof, airproof, surgical, hospital, and general india rubber goods, a speciality being made in waterproof wearing apparel, which they manufacture largely, and cannot be surpassed for style and durability. The mechanical department consists of india rubber sheets, valves, buffers, washers, packings; india rubber, cotton, leather, and hair beltings; india rubber cord, tubing, brewery, suction, and delivery hose, hose for fire brigades, &c.; gutta percha sheet, carboys, buckets, tubing, and numerous other articles. Their stock is one of the largest and most complete to be found, and with their superior facilities they are enabled to offer special advantages to customers, and to execute all orders in the promptest and most satisfactory manner. Their trade extends to all parts of the country, and their productions have a standard reputation for durability and superior finish.

Messrs. John Ashton & Son, Leather Merchants, Curriers, &c., 36, Withy Grove.—In reviewing historically the trades and industries of Manchester and its vicinity, it is most interesting and gratifying to meet with such an old-established and well-known firm as that of Messrs. John Ashton & Son, and to give to this important business that prominence and consideration in our review which its high standing and extensive commercial relations so justly merit. This business was established over a hundred years ago, and for some time was carried on under the name of Messrs. John Curtis & Co. Subsequently the late Alderman John Ashton succeeded, and under the present title of Messrs. John Ashton & Son the business has attained that importance which it now possesses. The works are situated at Hyde Road, Gorton. These are well recognised as the largest and most complete in Manchester, employing constantly a large staff and manufacturing all kinds of leather goods—as single and double strapping wire, hemp or lace-sewn, of all widths; strap butts; brown, green, and oak-tanned leather bands, leather pickers, buffalo pickers, laces, roller skins, leather delivery and suction hose, fire buckets, buffalo skips, &c. In every department this extensive business is conducted with great energy and enterprise, the works and warehouse presenting a scene of great activity and animation, and forming together one of those representative establishments which play such an important part in the commerce and prosperity of Lancashire. The late Alderman John Ashton, the father of the present proprietor, was a gentleman very widely known and highly respected, and for many years a member of the City Council, and took an active part in the municipal government of the city of Manchester. Mr. John Ed. Ashton, the sole proprietor of this extensive business, is a gentleman who has been long and honourably connected with the commerce of Manchester, and occupies the very highest position in commercial circles. The extent and magnitude of the operations of this firm place it amongst the largest and most influential mercantile houses in the North of England.

H. & L. Slater, Paper Manufacturers, Dantzic Street.—An enormous consumption of paper takes place annually in Manchester and district, and many very influential firms are catering to the growing demand for this useful and indispensable commodity. One of the principal of these is Messrs. Henry & Leigh Slater, whose city offices are located in Dantzic Street, and are very commodious and elaborately fitted. The firm was started thirty years ago by the present partners and is still directed by its founders. The warehouse and offices comprise a noble building of five stories, in which vast stocks of all sorts of paper are held. White and coloured enamel papers and tin-foil paper are the principal lines to which attention is devoted. The mills are located at Bollington, near Macclesfield, and are one of the chief sources of employment for the locality. They are very extensive, imposing in appearance, and about the most complete in equipment of their kind in England. The partners are highly capable gentlemen, and are extremely popular in commercial circles.

Mr. James C. Norbury, Chromo-Lithographer, 49 and 51, Faulkner Street.—In a review of the trades and industries of Manchester and its vicinity, written with the object of presenting in a short and concise form the history and commercial standing of the various business establishments, our attention is naturally first directed to firms of old standing and extensive commercial relations, and in these connections the well-known firm of Mr. James C. Norbury, chromo-lithographer,
has special claims upon our co
was established in the year 1848
modious premises, comprising
work-rooms of large dimensio
machinery and appliances know
experienced workmen are emplo
many splendid specimens of t
harmony of colours, and superi
testimony to the skill and tale
James C. Norbury has had a lo
business, occupies a very hig
possesses the esteem and confid

**John Ryde & Co., Ma
and Importers of China Cla**
Street, Oxford Road Station, a
Blue Lias Lime, Yorkshire Lim
A branch of trade that is very
district is that of manufacturing
whiting. One of the leading
Ryde & Co., whose foundation
first known as Birch and Ryde,
fifteen years ago, when the prese
been located fifteen years at the
the best known in their parti
spacious, well arranged, and fit
machinery and appliances for t
business. Blue Lias lime, Yo
Roman cements, plaster of P
barytes, gypsum, colours, &c.,
premises at the works in Grea
the Stores, 49, Lower Mosley
hold. The firm has an office
devoted to the coal trade, in wh
demand, owing to their excellen
are constantly employed, and a
transacted with the Company's
prietor, Mr. Harry Ryde, is a g
much respected for his high int

**Duncan & Foster, B
Confectioners**, 61 and 63, Oxf
known firms in its line in this
year 1834, by Mr. G. Foster,
in 1838, when the firm becam
Subsequently changes occurred,
form, Duncan & Foster. The
shops, 61 and 63, Oxford Stre
Victoria Buildings, Victoria St
Street, Chorlton-on-Medlock.
enviable, but well-deserved rep
and biscuits; the extreme del
and the absolute purity of the
amongst the very first firms in
bread-making; and spotless c
consideration in their manufac
confectioners, and bakers, are
at each sale shop there is th
lady assistants. The trade co
the best families in Mancheste
parcels of sweets and confection

**Sam. F. Armitage &
and Cotton Ticks, Satteens,
Fancy Union and Cotton Shi**
worth, and Kearsley, near Bolt
of Manchester stuff goods is in
is almost needless to remark tha
chester firms is of enormous m
and well-known firm is that of
premises occupied are large and
tains an immense stock of Manc
and about thirty hands are e
at the firm's works, Farnworth
admirably equipped with all m
business carried on, and several
goods turned out are varied and
is spared in the maintaining of
mous trade is carried on in all pa
Messrs. Samuel F. Armitage &
most influential places in the
gentlemen respected by all; an
great and beneficial influence
firm is devoted.

and Outfitter, 77, Market
ss in the year 1850, but have
more than four years. There is
rket Place, which Mr. Wallis has
The Market Street shop is of
rable size. It is extremely well
ed, there being, indeed, but few
that can at all compare with it.
in the Deansgate shop, and his
57, Piccadilly, and another at 56,
is "Wallis's 'True Fit' Shirts,"
ellent material and good sewing,
rom 3s. 6d. to 6s. 6d. each. The
quired in gentlemen's outfitting,
atest possible care and the most
ugh for the most part local, is not
arrival make a point of purchasing
re from the well-lined shelves of
an active part in the business;
trade circles, and is ever ready to
humbler classes.

---

fic Instrument Maker,
founded about seventy years ago
ucceeded by his son, Mr. Joshua
ent proprietor, Mr. Casartelli, who
dest and most important firm of its
equal out of London. The main
urveying, mining, and engineering
pecially mentioned miners' dials,
ine indicators, a portable hydraulic
tor. The firm have secured gold
orkmanship and accuracy of con-
und worthy of the "highest words
upplies Journal) can give them;"
, surveyors, and scientific men
ionials of the very highest class.
he mining and manufacturing dis-
rland, Durham, and South Wales;
the world is maintained through
netropolis. The business in Market
lerooms, warehouse, offices, and
considerable staff is employed.
nce Street, Cheetham Hill, half a
re admirably arranged, and fitted
ratus. Mr. Casartelli is one of the
ers, and is held in the highest pos-
l and business men; while profes-
more than content to acknowledge
ty, inventive faculty, and fruitful

---

cal Instrument Makers,
Mr. Daniel Lynch in 1791, when
ghfare only a few yards wide, this
own amongst the chemists of Man-
by his son, Mr. James Rockcliffe
r many years. In 1861 Mr. Bate-
irm, which was conducted jointly
Mr. Bateman then became sole
ss until 1882, when he sold it, and
o manufacture of surgical instru-
ons in the workshops of the firm.
eman have an enviable reputation
broad, and for everything sold by
equivalent to excellence. Hence
e. The present sole partner is Mr.
ccomplished surgical mechanician,

---

of Calico, Silk, Woollen
ser, "Adelphi Dyeing and Finish-
st perfect and valuable branches of
trade of Manchester is embossing,
gaged are very numerous. A well-
Isaac Bury, "Adelphi Dyeing and
s been in existence for a consider-
nsive, and are fitted up in a most
chinery and apparatus, and there
the business. About four hundred
employed in dyeing, embossing,
conducted on the most advanced
energy and patience, has rendered
expense is spared in maintaining
t employment of a large number
of hands and the animated appearance of the works testify to the extent and value of the trade carried on, and Mr. Isaac Bury has offices at 49, Princess Street, Manchester. This extensive concern is under the entire control of Mr. Pollitt, who has been with the firm during the last forty years. The success attending his management is eminent testimony to his commercial ability, and he is well known and highly honoured in the commercial and industrial world, for his unswerving honour, talent, and courtesy; he is undoubtedly popular with his numerous hands, and his house is one of the most important in the dyeing, embossing, and finishing trade of Manchester.

Skegg & Co., Manufacturers of Ladies' and Children's Mantles and Costumes, 35, Lever Street.—The manufacture of ladies' and children's costumes is an important branch of industry in Manchester, and it is in the highest state of perfection. A thoroughly representative concern is that trading as Messrs. Skegg & Co., which was founded in 1880, and is now carried on by Miss Skegg. The premises occupied are large and commodious, of attractive appearance, fitted up in a superior manner with the necessary appliances and fixtures for stock accommodation and display, and for the manufactures carried on. There is a splendid stock of ladies' and children's costumes in the best material and in the latest and most fashionable styles, and employment is provided for about fifty able and experienced hands. The goods manufactured by the firm are of excellent quality and workmanship, and a very fine wholesale trade is conducted. The management throughout is able and enterprising, and the travellers employed are continually opening new accounts. Miss Skegg, the only member of the firm, is a lady well known in this branch of industry, and highly respected. She is a thorough, practical, business woman, and enjoys the esteem and confidence of all who have transactions with her.

Robert Kitching, Hardware Merchant, 100 & 109, Shudehill.—The trade in hardware in Manchester is of considerable extent and importance, and among the establishments engaged, a chief place is occupied by that of Mr. Robert Kitching which was founded by Mr. R. Hudson some thirty-five years ago, and purchased by the present proprietor fourteen years since. He has worked up a considerable wholesale and retail trade in the city, and owing to the strict personal attention he has given during that period to the requirements of his customers, he has earned a fine reputation. The shop is of ample proportions, admirably suited for the business carried on, and fitted with all appliances and fixtures in a superior style. The stock is heavy and complete, comprising all kinds of hardware and French and German merchandise. The hardware is obtained from the best Sheffield and Birmingham houses, and the foreign merchandise is imported from the leading merchants and manufacturers. Mr. Robert Kitching manages his business in an enterprising and energetic manner. He thoroughly understands the trade, and exercises judgment and ability in the selection of the stock, purchasing no goods of an inferior character. In the trade he is well known and highly respected, and his house is fully worthy of the patronage accorded to it.

W. S. Ogden, Architect, 8, Spring Gardens.—The architects practising in Manchester are second to none, and there is probably no city in the kingdom where so many of the profession have been called on to design and erect large and important buildings in the metropolis and elsewhere. Mr. Waterhouse, as the architect of the Town Hall, Assize Courts, Strangeways Prison, Owen's College and numerous churches, schools, and public buildings in Manchester and surrounding towns, has also erected in London the splendid Natural History Museum, Kensington; National Liberal Club, Westminster; and many other clubs, chambers, and business premises, besides colleges and churches at Oxford, Liverpool, Birmingham, &c. Mr. Crowther is probably the most accomplished master of Gothic architecture living, as witness his fine and most beautiful churches. He is now engaged in the restoration of Manchester Cathedral, and when completed it is likely to prove the only satisfactory restoration that somewhat unfortunate building has ever experienced. Amongst other architects of great ability we may mention the names of Messrs. Mills & Murgatroyd, who built the New Royal Exchange, and many banks, schools, and warehouses. Messrs. Clegg & Knowles have also erected some hundreds of large and splendid warehouses, apparently making a speciality of this class of building. To these we may justly add the name of Mr. W. S. Ogden, whose ability as an architect of vigour and originality is well known, and the numerous buildings he has erected are admirable examples of picturesque design. Mr. Ogden's work on "Mercantile Architecture," published a few years ago, has had a wide influence on modern architecture, and we are glad to see it has recently reached a second edition; his other works on art are also well esteemed. We are told he is now engaged in preparing a series of illustrations of antique furniture for the press from hitherto unpublished sources. The work is to be called "Examples of Antique Furniture." Mr. Ogden is also an indefatigable antiquarian, and his residence and offices contain many fine examples of old paintings and ancient furniture, &c. These are a few amongst the many architects in extensive practice, and whose works promise to make Manchester a city of buildings without a rival.

John Harrop, Importer, General Merchant, and Manufacturer, 56, Dantzic Street, and 89 and 91, Piccadilly.—Some of the general merchants of Manchester carry on establishments of great extent and commercial importance. It may, however, be doubted whether any of them surpass, either in extent or importance, the splendid business concern owned and ably conducted by Mr. John Harrop. This gentleman is a native of Manchester, and began his commercial work in a very small way in 1876, and from the commencement, on account of his exertions and industry, he met with nothing but success of the most marked kind. Various articles of Continental manufacture, such as regulator clocks and clocks of all kinds, bronzes, watches, organs, pianos, and musical and floral albums, are imported by him in large quantities. Able and energetic management soon caused the business to assume wide dimensions. The result of this is that branches of the house now exist at Nottingham, Birmingham, Blackburn, Oldham, Rochdale, Liverpool, and Stockport. At the last mentioned place there are two establishments, shops 17 & 19, Lower Hillgate, and factory, Bury Street Mills, which is acknowledged one of the largest manufactories of its kind in the Manchester district, where are manufactured bassinettes and bath-chairs of all kinds, all kinds of furniture by steam power, beds and bedding, and picture framing, and where about one hundred workpeople are kept in executing the important work ordered from his various houses, besides doing a large wholesale trade. The mounting and publishing of pictures is a very special feature of the firm's business, and in it the house has won considerable repute; picture-frames and mouldings of artistic, plain, costly, and cheap design, mouldings being imported direct from Germany and America. One of the great specialities of the firm is bassinettes of all kinds, to which, perhaps, more attention is paid than anything else, in which an extensive trade is transacted in each line on the wholesale, retail, and hire-purchase system. Many men of ability and energy are engaged in each of the above houses and in travelling for the house, and a steady and lucrative trade is the result. Mr. Harrop is the guiding spirit, and he does all the business from the head office at 56, Dantzic Street, where a large staff of clerks carry on the routine part of the work. The success won is the best eulogium of Mr. Harrop's abilities as a man of business.

T. Seymour Mead & Co., Wholesale and Retail Grocers and Italian Warehousemen, 7, Piccadilly, and Branches.—One of the most active, enterprising, and deservedly successful firms in the wholesale and retail tea, coffee, and grocery trade of Manchester is that of Messrs. T. Seymour Mead & Co. Even in this era of giant enterprises the business of this firm is pre-eminent among the vast operations of many houses in the United Kingdom. Started a quarter of a century ago in a comparatively small way, it is a standing monument of what an energetic business man can accomplish, resolutely pursuing a course of honourable and fair dealing. The entire business has, in fact, become a series of establishments for a huge system of food distribution, primarily supplying the wants of the congested population of South-East Lancashire. Far away beyond this, however, the name of the firm has become a synonym for pure, unadulterated tea, coffee, and general groceries, and we understand we are well within the limit of facts when we state that there is scarcely a county in the United Kingdom that does not contribute its quota of orders to swell the gigantic transactions of the firm. No stronger testimony of the general appreciation of the efforts of the firm could be supplied than the large and increasing permanent patronage of the best classes of the cash-paying public. Tea is, of course, the great speciality of the firm. The vast dimensions of their trade may be estimated by the fact that the tea-room, as it is called, is 46ft. 6in. long by 32ft. wide, with a height of 19ft. from floor to ceiling. Teas of every kind, from India, China, Japan, Ceylon, are here stored. The firm make their clearances from bond once a week, and the duty which they pay, even according to the present tariff, is something fabulous. The mills form a sight in themselves. In one machine, termed an equaliser, the tea is sieved, the whole passing over an inclined perforated plate, through which the smaller leaves drop into a large drawer. The larger pass on into an honeycombed apparatus, by which they are cut to an equal size. In a larger mill the mixing and blending of the various and ever-increasing growths take place. This machine can mix six hundred pounds in four minutes. Yet it takes nearly two days to mix all the tea sold by T. Seymour Mead & Co. in one week! The cylinder in which this process takes place empties itself, when the operation is completed, by the removal of a slide, into what we should call a tank, but which is really a vast box upon wheels. From this it is transferred by means of polished scoops into clean canvas bags for distribution to the Manchester shops of the firm, and into metal canisters of large dimensions to those outside the city. An old unused hand-worked tea-mixer, which stands against the wall, looks quite antique beside its gigantic brother, necessarily driven by mechanical power. Another feature of the firm's business, of which the outside public can know but little, is the constant stream of orders, principally for tea, received by post from all parts of the country. In almost every instance a remittance accompanies the order, but when such is not the case the invoice is sent awaiting remittance, which is certainly a very safe and sure method of doing business. We were privileged to look over a number of these orders, and we were much struck by the evident esteem in which this tea is held by correspondents of the firm. In the wholesale department we noticed one order for over one hundred packages of tea to be cleared from bond, with a remittance of £590. We were informed that this was from a wholesale firm for whom T. S. Mead & Co. have for many years bought tea on commission. Each establishment is a model of perfect equipment for the rapid transaction of business, and is completely stocked with the choicest teas, coffees, spices, and family groceries of all kinds. Only the purest and most reliable goods are dealt in, and every article is sold at the lowest possible price consistent with quality and fair dealing. Mr. Thomas Seymour Mead, the head of the house, is one of Manchester's self-made business men. He is held in the highest esteem in commercial circles for his integrity and personal worth, and the success he has achieved is as substantial as it is well deserved.

Edward Makin, Jr., & Company, Manufacturers of Shirting and Shirts, 3 and 5, Broom Street, Withy Grove.—The Manchester establishments engaged in the manufacture of material for shirtings are numerous and in able and experienced hands, one of the most prominent and best-known firms engaged being that of Messrs. E. Makin, Junior, and Company. It was founded about twenty years ago and enjoys a splendid reputation for its shirtings. Besides manufacturing the material, Messrs. Makin, Jr., & Company, also make up shirts, employing altogether about three hundred hands. The offices are large and commodious, well furnished, and give employment to an adequate staff of clerks. The mills, situated at Holly Bank, Radcliffe, and Garden Mill, Boothtown, are very extensive and completely fitted with the most modern machinery and appliances used, and the hands employed are able and experienced. A very heavy trade is done in all parts of the United Kingdom, and it is rapidly increasing. The principals of the firm are Mr. E. Makin and H. W. Makin, who manage their extensive business in an admirable manner. They are both thoroughly conversant with the details of their manufacture, and are well known and highly esteemed as honourable and courteous gentlemen, whilst their house holds an eminent position in the trade and the mercantile world.

Joseph Franks, Oculist and Optician, 44, Market Street.—This business was established in the year 1795, the title being the same as at present. The premises in Market Street consist of an elegantly fitted and most conveniently arranged shop, in every way suited for the transaction of business. Mr. Franks enjoys a great reputation as an oculist, and is consulted by patients from far and near. So celebrated is this establishment that unprincipled persons have from time to time been tempted to practise in Mr. Franks' name, calling at houses in Manchester and neighbourhood, representing themselves as connected with him, and offering goods for sale; indeed, to such an extent has this been done that Mr. Franks has been compelled to advertise the fact on more than one occasion. It is pleasing to notice that Mr. Franks does not confine his special knowledge to that class only who can pay for his experience, but with true philanthropic feeling he places those talents with which he is so eminently endowed at the disposal of the poorest of his fellow-citizens, and he may be consulted at any time free of charge, a fact which cannot be too widely known, and must ever redound to the credit of this enterprising and successful oculist and optician. The stock, besides every variety of spectacles and eyeglasses, includes telescopes, opera, field, and marine glasses, pedometers, compasses, barometers, and all the usual miscellaneous stock of an optician. The connection is extensive and wide-spread, and the business transacted very considerable, and we must say most deservedly so. The only address is 44, Market Street, where Mr. Franks can always be seen from ten till six o'clock.

T. Kingsford & Son, Oswego Starch Manufacturers, 8, Dantzic Street.—Messrs. Kingsford & Son the manufacturers of the celebrated Oswego Pure and Silver Gloss Starch, have been established in this city upwards of ten years. The premises in Dantzic Street consist of a warehouse of several floors. There is a suite of roomy offices, handsomely furnished and most completely fitted up. The speciality of the trade is the Oswego Pure Silver Gloss Starch, which is in great demand by manufacturers, calico printers and bleachers, Oswego Prepared Corn for blanc-mange and invalids' food (the original of all corn flours) sold by all the best grocers. The trade connection is very extensive, and includes the majority of the cotton manufacturers of Lancashire and Yorkshire, Cheshire and North Staffordshire; and the calico printing firms, the dyers and bleachers dependent upon them. The depôt at Dantzic Street is the headquarters of the firm for the whole of the United Kingdom. A speciality of first-class soaps for all domestic purposes is a feature of the business. These include Castile Soap, Patent Premier, White Windsor and Carbolic; and all are in great demand. The stock is extremely heavy, and is frequently renewed. Messrs. Kingsford & Son are represented in this country by Mr. J. Holden; and in addition to a number of travellers, there is a full staff of clerks and correspondents, warehousemen and packers. Mr. Holden has a very large personal connection amongst starch buyers for manufacturing purposes. He is extremely well known in the city, and is looked upon as an exceptionally thriving business man.

Devoge & Co., Jacquard Works, 462, Oldham Road, and 15A, York Street.—This is the oldest Jacquard machine manufacturing firm in the world, and probably the largest. The business was commenced by Mr. Devoge, a native of Lyons, while Jacquard, the inventor of the machine, was still alive. The establishment has a world-wide reputation, its machines being found in every part of the world where Jacquard weaving is carried on. They make single lifts, double lifts, double machines, compounds for cross border work, &c. (see illustration), machines for giving a rising and falling shed, and every variety of Jacquard machines. They also make every variety of Jacquard harnesses, piano and card-cutting machines, table repeaters with vertical railway presses, self-acting repeaters which cut forty cards per minute, and card-cutting plates and punches. Jacquard machinery being so intricate and important, the most skilled labour only can be employed

with success in its manufacture. The works of the firm are very extensive and are fitted up with the most perfect machinery, while a very large staff is constantly employed in manufacturing the machines and sundries for which the firm is noted. The city office in York Street has been recently opened to meet the demands of city and other customers. The works are divided into departments for the making of Jacquard machines, card-cutting machinery, harnessing and wire and lingoe making. The firm does an immense trade and is continually spreading its connection. Its resources are such that it is enabled to offer special advantages in the shape of perfect machines and sundries at lowest prices to customers, and to execute their orders in the most satisfactory manner. The firm is justly regarded as the most important and influential of its class.

David Reid & Co., Merchants and General Contractors, 71, Oldham Street.—This well-known concern carries on a widespread business of a comprehensive and very important character. The company trades as ironmongers, dealers in safes, whitesmiths, locksmiths, bell-hangers, gas and water fitters, copper and tinsmiths, wire netting makers, and general wire workers, dealers in cordage, ropes, lines, &c., merchants and contractors. Each department is conducted upon the best of commercial lines, the public being afforded the utmost satisfaction. The business of the first department mentioned has to do with ironmongery for domestic, furnishing, and building purposes, tools, cutlery, and similar goods. The stock always on hand of thief and fire resisting safes by all the best makers is in reality a splendid and most interesting one. Both new and second-hand safes for parchment, jewellery, plate, and bullion are dealt in, and the company in addition exchange all varieties. Should, then, your safe be too small or not secure enough to meet present wants, they can offer you the best market for it and advise you what other kind to have. They are not agents for any safe company, and can therefore recommend an article without bias, and by selling all qualities and kinds are especially enabled to suit foreign and export markets. Parchment and deed chests; cash, paper, and despatch boxes; bullion depositories; plate and jewel safes; gunpowder magazines (by Milner, Chatwood, Whitfield, Chubb, Price, &c.) are supplied; and D. Reid & Co. invite builders, architects, mill and warehouse proprietors to consult them for full particulars of their iron doors for strong rooms, sliding doors for factories, and many others of their specialities. Perfect satisfaction is guaranteed. Adjoined to this department is the one for the sale of nets and nettings which they manufacture, and which are made for use in inland fisheries, deep-sea and coast fisheries, for the preservation of game, rabbits, pheasants, poultry, &c., for aviaries, the garden, agricultural and horticultural purposes, lawn tennis, and various other sports. The goods which the firm manufactures are immense in quantity, and for variety, effectiveness, and economy may safely challenge competition in the North of England. The sale and netting branches are the leading features of the business. The remaining department—likewise an excellent and very attractive one—is devoted to cordage of all descriptions, fishing tackle, fishing lines, sea-fishing gear, ropemakers' ironwork, hooks, thimbles, roofing, and other felts, wire work, pulley blocks, hoisting apparatus, &c. The firm was established in 1848, and its progress since that date has been rapid and substantial in every way. The premises, as may easily be imagined, are large and handsomely appointed. The staff employed is numerous, and thoroughly competent; orders are attended to with praiseworthy promptitude and carefulness, and the connection enjoyed is valuable in the extreme.

E. B. Warner & Son, Account Book Manufacturers, 15, Spring Gardens.—The demand in Manchester for account books is very considerable, and it is a matter of great importance that these articles should be made of the best materials, and bound in a durable manner, sufficient to stand the wear and tear of a busy office. A well-known firm engaged in manufacturing account books, answering to the above conditions, is that of E. B. Warner & Son, which was founded by Mr. E. B. Warner thirty-eight years ago, and the present premises have been occupied for the last fifteen years. Since the date of its inception, Mr. Warner has built up an extensive trade, and during the past six years has been ably assisted by his son, whom he has taken into partnership. The premises are large and commodious, and completely fitted with the appliances used in the trade; and the hands employed are numerous, able, and experienced, and have the advantage of careful and talented overlooking. The materials used—paper, cloth, leather, &c.—are selected and examined with great care, and all inferior stuff is discarded. The trade done is heavy, the firm having a splendid connection of long standing among the leading merchants, manufacturers, business men and professional bodies in the city and its vicinity. Messrs. E. B. Warner & Son are well known in mercantile and manufacturing circles, and are looked upon as gentlemen of ability, enterprise, honour, and courtesy, enjoying the esteem and confidence of all who know them, and ably sustaining the reputation of the account book manufacture.

Thomas Oxley, Wholesale Ironmonger, &c., 48, 50, and 52, Port Street.—This business was founded in the year 1820, and is to-day one of the most important of its kind in this city. The premises consist of large and convenient sale-shop and warehouse, with extensive stores and stock-rooms. The proprietor is reported to be the oldest file cutter and mill furnisher in the city. The present proprietor is Mr. Edwin Oxley, and in the machinists' tool department he trades in this name. The firm some years ago introduced a new form of grindstone and trough that has had a very large and ready sale. These grindstones are of excellent, indeed unsurpassed, quality, and tons of them are exported to all parts of the world. They have supplied the leading railway companies, engineers, and machine makers since the commencement. They may be had in all varieties and for every purpose. In addition to these, however, Mr. Oxley keeps an enormous and representative stock of the tools and general machinery required in engineers' and other workshops, mills, &c., such as lathes, planing, slotting, shaping, drilling, screwing, boring, punching, and shearing machines, slide rests, patent chucks, and similar tools, crabs, jacks, fans, vices, circular-saw benches, small steam or gas engines, boiler bears, tube expanders, &c., &c. The machinists' tool department includes some remarkable specialities and foreign patents. The trade connection is extremely large, and includes many buyers from every part of the north of England. The present proprietor is Mr. Edwin J. Oxley, the son of the founder of the firm. A staff of workmen, including file cutters, are employed the whole year round. Mr. Oxley is a gentleman extremely well-known in the iron and ironmongery trades. He has a most intimate knowledge of all that pertains to his business, and a wide experience amongst the members of his particular trade.

David Moore & Co., Woollen Manufacturers, 9, Red Lion Street.—This business has been established about twenty years, and has enjoyed a very large share of success and prosperity. The premises include a most commodious warehouse of several very spacious floors admirably adapted for the purposes of very large trade. The factories are located at Bury, Rochdale, and Yorkshire, and provide constant employment for many hundreds of hands. For the convenience of their numerous customers, Messrs. Moore and Co. keep a large stock of their various manufactures at the Red Lion Street warehouse. Amongst them may be mentioned Witney, cloth and grey blankets, blue and green and Oriental quilts, Yorkshire and other flannels, plaidings, shirtings, kerseys, serges, unions, scarlet paddings, linseys, collar checks, sagathies, scourers, &c. The trade connection includes many of the leading shipping houses, the wholesale firms, and the general Manchester warehousemen, in London, Glasgow, Belfast, and Dublin. Mr David Moore is the sole proprietor. He is a gentleman well known in the woollen trade, and of great experience and business ability.

Burgon & Company, Wood and Cardboard Box Manufacturers, Atlas Box Works, 75, Sackville Street.—The manufacture of wood and cardboard boxes forms a most important branch of Manchester's industry; and of late years great improvements have been made in the machinery connected therewith, thereby lessening the cost of production. A leading firm engaged in this line is Messrs. Burgon and Co., of the Atlas Box Works (Telephone 434). This business was established by Mr. William Burgon twenty years ago; since the year 1875—when that gentleman died—it has been carried on by his son, Mr. Anthony Burgon, who is the sole proprietor. Since 1875 the trade has become a most extensive one, embracing all parts of the country, and it is still progressing. Messrs. Burgon & Co. recently obtained a patent for manufacturing hat and bonnet boxes entirely by machinery, whereas, formerly, they have been made nearly entirely by hand. We may also note that they are commencing a new branch of business, namely, the manufacture of cigar-boxes, which is evidently to be a speciality with them, and in which they are taking the lead, for, up to the present time, cigar-boxes have never been made in Manchester; and, we may also add, they are sparing no pains nor expense in special machinery and all special appliances necessary for making this department an unqualified success, and, we have no doubt, they will in this as in their other departments, be able to maintain their well-earned repute for the prompt despatch of all orders entrusted to them. The foregoing facts go to prove that Mr. Burgon is a gentleman of talent and enterprise, and it is only reasonable to anticipate that his energies will be crowned with success. The premises in Sackville Street consist of a large and attractive five-storey building, their own property, specially designed and built for the purpose, and comprising saw-mill, factory, and warehouse. The saw-mill and factory are admirably equipped with patent machinery, and with all appliances necessary for carrying on the business. The hands employed average about one hundred. The spacious warehouse contains a large and valuable stock of wood, cardboard, and all necessary materials for the manufacture of every kind of wood and cardboard plain and fancy boxes, suitable for packing velvet, plush, costumes, haberdashery, soap, perfumery, and all other fancy goods and articles, and for which purposes they are extensively supplied by this firm to manufacturers, merchants, shippers, &c. The business of Messrs. Burgon & Co., under the personal supervision of its head, and assisted by an able staff, is conducted with energy and ability, and, whilst the firm enjoys the confidence of its clients, in Manchester and elsewhere, it may also be said that its commercial status is well known to be thoroughly sound and reliable.

Thomas Rushworth & Son, Bristle, Bass, Fibre, and Brush Makers' Materials of all kinds, also Brush Manufacturers, 55, Shudehill.—Established so far back as the year 1830 the firm of Thomas Rushworth & Son, wholesale and export brush manufacturers, still continues to more than hold its own, both in the home and export markets. Its speciality may be summed up in one word, "Brushes," although that one word includes an almost infinite variety, amongst which may be enumerated: round oil or blacking brushes, scouring brushes, laundry brushes, furniture brushes, horse, dandy, spoke, water and harness brushes, hair, cloth, nail, tooth, shaving, jewellers', fancy, hearth, toy, dust, venetian blind, and whisk brushes, blacklead brushes and shoe brushes, whitewash brushes, ground paint brushes, and brush stails, bristle brooms, bristle bannisters, yard brooms, bristle carpet bannisters, Italian and French whisk carpet bannisters, Italian and French whisk carpet brooms, Victoria and Albert carpet brooms, and flat and oval carpet brooms, shaped mats, brush and chain mats and bordered mats, matting, &c., not excluding even sweeps' machine brushes, and all kinds of mill and machine brushes. This is only a selection from the list of goods to be found in the warehouse of Thos. Rushworth & Son, of which it may truly be said that it contains an assortment of brushes, brooms, and mats, about the most complete in the world. The warehouse in which this immense assortment is stored is a very large one, and the showrooms are all well lighted and arranged for its display. Messrs. Rushworth & Son do a very large wholesale trade throughout the United Kingdom, and the export of their goods to the various markets of the world, by themselves and others, amounts in the aggregate to something enormous. They import material from Russia, Germany, China, and other parts of the world. In addition to these branches of business they also do a very large retail trade, thus combining every conceivable department of commerce under one most efficient, and at the same time most economical, management. Mr. Thos. Rushworth, the sole surviving member of the firm, is a man well known in the city, and much respected by all with whom he comes in contact.

Jackson & Smithies, Yarn Agents, and Merchants, 70, Deansgate.—The trade done in yarn and similar goods in Manchester is of enormous and widespread value and extent. Numerous firms of great stability and repute in the commercial world are engaged in the business, and one such is that of which Messrs. John Jackson and David Smithies are the respected heads. This concern was started in 1868, and took possession of a suite of offices, admirably located, well fitted, and completely managed. In connection with the offices, in the rear of the building, the warehouse and sample rooms are located. The former is fully stocked with all sorts of yarns, is of ample dimensions, and well arranged. The trade of the house is of a local and export character, and is established on a very solid basis among the best class of merchants and manufacturers. The partners are noted among their compeers for energy and integrity, and the consequence is that their business is one of the most popular in its line.

Mallinson & Eckersley, Timber Merchants, Tin and Wood Packing Case Makers, &c., Palatine Saw Mills, Stevenson Square.—The timber trade and the making of packing cases and lap boards form a business in Manchester which is noted for its great magnitude and value, and it is in many hands. A thoroughly representative firm in this direction is that of Messrs. Mallinson & Eckersley, of Palatine Saw Mills, which was originated by the present members over twenty years ago. The Mills are spacious and are fitted up in a most complete manner with saws and machinery for timber sawing and for manufacturing tin and wood packing cases and lap boards. In this connection they have bought the business of Mr. Thomas Fildes, packing case maker, and the firm now maintains a high reputation as being one of the largest packing case and lap board makers in the city. A full force of men is employed in these operations, and the tin and wood cases are made of carefully selected and tested materials, and of excellent and durable manufacture, suitable for rough and heavy usage, and for all climes. Messrs. Mallinson & Eckersley have a splendid stock of timber of all kinds, including high-class wood in capital, well-seasoned condition, and from the leading sources, the bulk of which, for want of space at the Palatine Saw Mills, is stored in large quantities at their branch, Queen Street, Gravel Lane, Salford, which is connected with their Palatine Saw Mills, Stevenson Square, by private telephone. In both departments of the establishment a very heavy local trade is carried on. The management throughout is all that could be desired, and Messrs. Mallinson & Eckersley have the pleasure of noting a steady increase in their business. Their knowledge of the trade is undoubted; they are gentlemen of strict integrity and courteous demeanour, popular with the community, of high general business status, and they rank among the principal timber merchants and packing case and lap board makers of Manchester.

H. R. Freeborn, General Outfitter, Commercial Buildings, 13, Cross Street.—Fifty years ago was founded the well-known and world-renowned business of Mr. H. R. Freeborn, gentlemen's general outfitter, glover, and maker of the Corazza shirt. The well-known celebrity of this house entitles it to a high position as a representative centre of a branch of commerce of the very first importance, occupying a position second to none among the great industries of the age. The extraordinary reputation of this establishment has secured for it a business of truly fabulous proportions. Here can be obtained at a short notice complete outfits for travellers to any part of the world, every detail of which is carefully studied and supplied ready for any distance or climate. The other specialities of this firm are numerous, and consist of the Corazza shirts, a most unique article made of various qualities at corresponding prices and unequalled for fit; gentlemen's dressing-gowns, the largest stock in the city, embracing elegance with comfort; and specialities in overcoats in Melton and tweed, water repellants, braces, umbrellas, athletic clothing, high-class hosiery, travelling bags, portmanteaus, railway wraps, Scotch mauds, &c., &c., in great variety. The tailoring department contains every novelty in business suits, dress suits, servants' liveries, and ladies' riding-habits, hunting belts, &c. The circular of Mr. H. R. Freeborn reveals the fact that no article, consistent with the business of outfitter, can be applied for but will be found in stock or made to order with all despatch, and at terms which bear most favourable comparison with those of any other establishment in the kingdom. The premises comprise a large shop literally filled with a most valuable stock consisting of goods of every possible description, with showrooms and warehouse, and four storeys above, some portions of which are devoted to stock. The principal, Mr. H. R. Freeborn, is a gentleman of high business reputation, great integrity, well known, and widely respected.

Robert W. Trenbath & Co., Manufacturers of Shirts, Fronts, Collars, Scarfs, &c., 3, Union Street, Church Street.—This business has been established upwards of thirty-four years. Messrs. Trenbath & Co. manufacture shirts, fronts, collars, cravats, &c., for both home and shipping trade. The leading feature of their business is the trade in gentlemen's scarf goods, in which the firm enjoys a national reputation. Another speciality is white cotton shirts with linen fittings. Of these goods, which are sent all over the kingdom, the firm turn out hundreds of grosses per week. Another important line is in men's regattas and Oxfords; while of ordinary and common woollen shirts an enormous stock is manufactured during the season. A staff of some five-and-twenty hands are employed; but in the workrooms are several hundred machinists and finishers, while the out-door hands are extremely numerous. The firm has representatives in all parts of England and Wales, and does an enormous trade. The sole partner, Mr. Robert W. Trenbath, trading as R. W. Trenbath & Co., a gentleman who has had great experience in this business, and is deservedly popular in commercial circles on account of his ability and inflexible integrity.

[...]n Noble, Manufacturer of Calicoes, &c., 11, Picca[dilly, Ma]nchester.—Manchester has a world-wide reputation for the [magnitu]de and excellence of her trade in calicoes and all Manchester goods, [and man]y hands are employed in the trade and the manufacture. Among [the nume]rous firms engaged a prominent place is held by that of Mr. John [Noble, w]hich was founded by this gentleman in 1870. The premises occupied consist of a spacious, commodious six-storey building, used as a warehousing department and counting-house. The latter, which is very commodious, situated on the fourth floor, is fitted and furnished in a most superior manner, and employment is provided for an ample clerical staff. The warehousing department affords great storing capacity, and it is strained to its utmost with an immense stock of calicoes and Manchester goods of every description. Mr. John Noble makes calicoes his speciality, and the quality of these and their moderate price are renowned all over the world, under the trade mark of "Sterling Value." Over one hundred hands are employed, and the supervision is detailed and talented. Mr. John Noble has an office at 19 and 21, Henry Street, Belfast, and he carries on a very considerable home and export trade in calicoes and Manchester goods,

[...] immense quantities of calicoes, especially the renowned "Ster[ling Val]ue" and "Sovereign" makes, forwarding them to all parts of [the Unit]ed Kingdom, and most foreign markets. Throughout this [...] business the management is able and enterprising, and [orders ar]e despatched with promptitude. Mr. John Noble was amongst [the first] producers on a large scale to introduce dealing direct with [the cons]umers, thus affording the latter the opportunity of saving all [middlem]en's profits. Many thousands of ladies all over the United [Kingdom have] availed themselves of the opportunity of purchasing calicoes [direct fr]om the manufacturer, and were so pleased with the excel[lence of] Mr. Noble's goods and system of business that the inquiries for [other cla]sses of goods became so numerous that department after depart[ment ha]s been added for the purpose of procuring direct from the best [manufact]urers all kinds of flannels, dress materials, woollen cloths, [and supp]lying them to the public in any quantity at wholesale prices. [Manufact]uring underclothing and baby linen on a large scale has been [...] with Mr. Noble, as ladies find that they can buy [...] ready-made for little more than the cost of the material, whilst [the style] and fit are very much superior to that of home-made garments. [The cu]tting has been made a special study and is done on anatomical [principle]s and the garments made by experienced workwomen in well-[ventilate]d and light and airy workrooms in large quantities. The dress [departme]nt, too, occupying the whole of the ground-floor, is a very im[portant b]ranch of John Noble's large and ever-increasing business. In [this dep]artment will be found a truly remarkable collection of fabrics, [gathered] from all the great centres of manufacture, including many [novelties], and special makes in ladies' dress fabrics not to be obtained [elsewhere]. The ranges of cashmeres in black and all colours have [made a] name for themselves in all parts of the globe for their sterling [quality] of finish and wearing qualities, and the Royal Yacht Club [serges ar]e not left behind in the race for supremacy, being manufactured [on impro]ved principles, so that they are almost endless in wear, and [the colo]urs are absolutely unmovable. It would be impossible to [enumerate] here the various fabrics for ladies' wear, in which Mr John [Noble hold]s a prominent place, but it would be almost an impossibility [for a lad]y to fail in finding something to suit her taste from so large and [varied a] selection of novelties in fashionable dress fabrics as his dress [departme]nt contains. The woollen cloth and tailoring departments also [show tha]t John Noble takes a lively interest in clothing his fellow-men, as [there will] be found a collection of suitings in every conceivable style, which [can be p]urchased in cut lengths, or garments made to measure, to suit [custo]mers' convenience, while the prices are so reasonable that dress[ing] is reduced to a very small cost in comparison with the prices [usually] charged by retail firms. Mr. John Noble sends post-free to [all parts] of the world patterns and price-lists of every class of goods, so [that those] in the country should have no hesitation in writing to Mr [Noble st]ating their requirements, and they will soon find the pleasure [and conv]enience of purchasing at the wholesale price from large whole[sale] patterns without the trouble and annoyance of shopping excur[sions. A]ll letters received by Mr. Noble's firm, whether containing [orders or] inquiries, receive immediate and careful attention. It is well-[know]n that nearly all the drapery goods used in the country come from [Manchest]er in the first place, either direct to local drapers or through [wholesale] warehouses, so that consumers may well be pleased to obtain [their sup]plies direct, satisfied that no extra cost is incurred in their dis[tribution], either in the way of extra carriage or intermediate profits. [The succe]ss of Mr. Noble's business and the huge volumes kept in his [office de]partment containing the names of his regular customers in every [town, vil]lage, and hamlet all over the United Kingdom, prove the appre[ciation b]y the public of this new method of distribution. The proprietor is well known in the industrial and commercial world, and is highly respected therein for his talent, honourable business methods, and courtesy, whilst his house has exercised great influence, of a most salutary character, in the manufacture of calicoes and other fabrics.

The City of London Fire Insurance Company, Limited, 40, Spring Gardens.—The fire insurance business of Manchester is very considerable, and a very fair share is taken by the branch of the City of London Fire Insurance Company, Limited. It was established in the city in 1881, under the district managership of Mr. William Heap, who held the post till 1886, when he was succeeded by the present district manager, Mr. G. M. Bland, who was formerly in the London office, 101, Cheapside, E.C. The large subscribed capital of £2,000,000, the reserve fund of £50,000, and the influential position of the directorate afford absolute security to insurers, and enable the company to deal liberally with their policy holders. The rates of insurance for houses, shops, farming stock, and rent are very moderate, and special risks are insured by agreement. All damages to property by lightning or explosion of gas is made good, careful consideration is given to the cases of properties in which the electric light is used, and all claims are settled with liberality and promptitude. Many of the leading manufacturers, merchants, tradesmen, and private individuals in the city and its vicinity hold policies from the company, and the connection is daily increasing. Mr. G. M. Bland manages the business in an admirable manner, is well known and highly respected in the commercial and industrial world for his integrity, courtesy, and ability, and the company is regarded as one of the most prominent in the city.

Harry B. Wood, Agent for Chemicals and Foreign Produce, Argyll Buildings, 45, Hanging Ditch.—Amongst proprietors of paper-mills, manure merchants, soap-makers, and manufacturing chemists this somewhat juvenile but well-known concern has an excellent reputation. Mr. Harry Bland Wood, the enterprising proprietor, only started the business in 1881, but in the comparatively short space of time that has elapsed since that period he has succeeded in drawing together a particularly healthy and remunerative connection. He is the sole agent for the following leading firms:—William Pilkington & Son, of Widnes (manufacturers of bleaching powder, white and cream caustic sodas, muriatic acid, &c.); G. & L. Pilkington, of Liverpool (ditto); Golding, Davis, & Co., Limited, Widnes (bleaching powder, salt cake, cake alum); the Hven Wood Pulp Works, of Norway (moist and dry pine-wood pulp); the Skien Cellulose Fabrik, Norway (strong white sulphite wood pulp); Koch & Co., of Groningen, Holland (oat, wheat, rye, and barley straw in hydraulically compressed bales); Heymann & Co., near Brussels (rags, ropes, bagging, flax waste, &c., in pressed bales), and H. E. Bell, of Lille, France (flax and jute waste). As will be seen, Mr. Wood's business is a comprehensive one, but it is admirably managed. He employs no travellers, affords his customers every satisfaction, and his price list, which is an extremely moderate one, should be carefully consulted by all whom his business affects. In addition, Mr. Wood disposes of considerable quantities of artificial manures (superphosphate of lime, dissolved bones, turnip and mangold manure) on behalf of Messrs. W. Pilkington & Son, who manufacture these goods extensively in connection with their old-established alkali works at Widnes.

Mr. James Mason, Florist, &c., 6, Victoria Street.—Nothing is more attractive to the general public than a well-arranged and tasteful display of flowers and fruit. All classes of the community experience a pleasurable sensation whilst viewing the varied and magnificent products of nature, assisted by art; those who cater for them in this direction are always sure of handsome recognition. Such has been the experience of Mr. James Mason, who for ten years past has occupied a leading position amongst the florists and fruiterers of Manchester. His extensive establishment is one of the best known and most popular in the city. The handsome and well-fitted shop, bright and attractive in appearance, is filled from season to season with the most magnificent specimens of the floricultural art, and presents a brilliant combination of colour and perfume, such as cannot be surpassed at any other establishment. From the lowliest plant to the loveliest rose or the most expensive orchid, every variety of flower finds a representative in this vast and attractive display, whose beauty of blossom and luxuriance of foliage render it one of the most magnificent sights in the neighbourhood. Every variety of home-grown and imported fruit is also to be found here in its appropriate season; and for the provision of elegant table decorations or the most appetising desserts, Mr. Mason's establishment is unsurpassed, both as regards beauty, quality, and reasonable charges. The highest awards, including two gold medals, have been taken by Mr Mason for flowers and fruits in competitions open to the world. He also took the first-class Jubilee gold medal at the Manchester Royal Botanical Jubilee Show for bouquets and designs in flowers. Mr. Mason, who employs a large staff of skilled and experienced assistants, is a gentleman who has made flowers and fruit the study of a lifetime. His business connection is both large and widespread, and by his method of trade, backed up by energy and perseverance, he has won for himself a place in the front rank of his profession.

Jno. Heywood, Printer, Publisher, Wholesale Bookseller, Stationer, Account Book Manufacturer, and Church and School Furniture Manufacturer, 121—129, Deansgate.—Of those carrying on the important business of manufacturing stationers, printers, and booksellers, the Heywoods stand, without dispute, in Manchester, in the front rank and in the most honoured position. John Heywood's establishment is admirably located in a magnificent block of buildings, extending from 121 to 129, Deansgate, without doubt, the best business location within the city boundaries for a wholesale trade. The premises are exteriorly and interiorly attractive, and in the latter respect neatly and elaborately fitted and stocked. A wholesale bookseller's and stationer's business is done, and in a manner unrivalled by any other house in the trade in the city. Many works of great importance, and which have met with the greatest success, have been printed and published by the house. In addition to this line the manufacture of account books and stationery of all kinds is extensively carried on. In all branches the industry and ability of those conducting the establishment have brought about that most desired of all results—a large and profitable trade, the number of hands employed being upwards of 1,200; and the kindness and generosity of Mr. Heywood are such that seldom is there the slightest disagreement or misunderstanding. The business is one of the oldest and most widely known as well as the most stable and lucrative of the kind in the North.

John Jaffrey & Co., Plumbers & Glaziers, 27, Booth Street.—Few industries have attained greater perfection or a more deserved reputation in Manchester than that of plumbing and sanitary engineering, and in this connection it is a pleasure to make prominent mention of an old-established and thoroughly representative firm of plumbers and glaziers like that of Messrs. John Jaffrey & Co. This business was established in 1845, and from its very inception has enjoyed an uninterrupted career of prosperity. The firm does an extensive business, employing a large force of skilled workmen, and has executed many important contracts in Manchester and throughout the country. Mr. John Jaffrey is an expert and thoroughly practical plumber, &c., in all branches. In fact, he is so well known and has retained his old customers for so long a time, that his reputation for integrity and first-class work is established beyond the requirements of praise. Mr. Jaffrey is president of the Manchester Master Plumbers' Association. He is an enterprising and thoroughly reliable business man, and thoroughly deserves the esteem and respect in which he is held by all classes.

Anthony White, Wholesale Jeweller, Cutler, &c., 111, Oldham Street.—This business was founded in the year 1848 by its present proprietor; the firm is of high repute in the city, and the trade is very extensive. The premises consist of extensive departments, wholesale and retail, with many show and stock rooms; all of which are substantially furnished and fitted up. The trade connection includes a large number of the retail shopkeepers of the city, the neighbouring towns and country districts, as well as a large proportion of the Manchester merchant shippers. In the retail sales department the customers are drawn from the various parts of the city and neighbourhood. Mr. White issues a comprehensive price list, which gives some idea of the enormous and varied stocks of electro-plated goods, cutlery, jewellery, and miscellaneous articles, which are held in the Oldham Street warehouses. A large, experienced and competent staff of assistants and packers is constantly and actively employed, and Mr. White gives active and personal supervision to the whole. Mr. White is well known throughout the wholesale and retail trades, and is everywhere highly respected and esteemed.

John McKenzie & Co., Calico Printers.—One of the oldest and best-known print works is the Foxhill Bank Works, at Church, near Accrington, now in the occupation of Messrs. John McKenzie & Co. We believe these works were begun by the Peel family about the middle of last century. In the year 1814 they were leased by the late Mr. James Simpson, and since then the works have passed through various hands. These works are remarkable for the excellence of quality of their productions, and newness of design, and moderation in cost. Their goods find a ready market not only in the kingdom, but in all parts of the world, a very large shipping business being done by the firm. They are well supplied with the most approved machinery and appliances, and give employment to a large number of hands. The Manchester warehouse is at 29, George Street.

Turnbull & Bunyan, Watch and Clock Makers, Railway Clock Contractors, Corporation Chambers, 19, Corporation Street.—One of the important, valuable, and advanced branches of industry in Manchester is the making of watches and clocks, and the establishments engaged therein are very numerous. A capital and old-established business in this line is that known as Messrs. Turnbull & Bunyan, Corporation Street, and the sole member is Mr. John Speirs Turnbull. The business was originally founded by Mr. Thomas Morton and Mr. Thomas Bunyan fifty-two years ago, and has been in the present ownership sixteen years. The premises occupied are of adequate proportions. A well-trained indoor and outdoor staff is employed in manufacturing clocks and watches, and repairing these articles for the trade. The productions of this firm are excellent in material, of the most perfect mechanism, and the workmanship in every detail is first-class. The like excellence pervades the repairing work, and the firm makes a speciality of railway clock contracting. Mr. Turnbull has an establishment at Barnes Green, Blackley, and his management is able and enterprising. No member of the trade is better known than Mr. John Speirs Turnbull, and he is highly respected for his strict integrity and ability. We may add that Mr. Turnbull was selected to report (on behalf of the Society for the Promotion of Scientific Industry) on watches and clocks exhibited at the Vienna Exhibition of 1873 (*vide* "Artisans' Reports upon the Vienna Exhibition," Simpkin & Marshall, London).

J. F. Walker, Pattern Card and Book Maker, 85, Spring Gardens.—This business was established by its present proprietor in the year 1882, and has so far achieved a most decided success. The premises consist of a number of large, lofty, well-lighted, and convenient workrooms, and a suite of fine offices, handsomely furnished and most completely fitted up. The principal business is that of pattern-card, and pattern-book making, which, in a city like Manchester, with its thousands of firms connected with the manufacture or sale of textile fabrics, is a matter of first-rate importance. In addition, Mr. Walker has opened departments for engraving, letterpress and lithographic printing, book-binding, fancy box making, and the manufacture of all classes of account books. The successful pursuit of all these trades necessitates the employment of a very large staff of hands, controlled by experienced managers and foremen. The excellence of the work turned out by Mr. Walker is sufficiently attested by the fact that an almost purely local connection is all that is necessary to keep the works fully employed, while a glance through the pattern-books of the firm reveals a very unusual wealth of design, richness of colouring, and cultivated taste in the colour and chromo-printing of show cards and labels. Mr. Walker is himself a gentleman of keen artistic perception, and his judgment seldom errs in the selection of designs appropriate for particular purposes or special classes of goods.

A. Franks, Manufacturing Optician and Electrician, 2, King Street.—This business was established in a shop in the Deansgate, in the year 1798, and is the very oldest firm of the kind in the city. The business rapidly increasing, a removal was made to enormous premises in the present commanding position, the corner of King Street and Deansgate. The shop is of noble proportions and extremely handsome appearance. It is decorated in good style, and is furnished and fitted in the most solid and substantial manner. The speciality of the business is spectacles. In this city, at any rate, the name Franks is held to be a perfect guarantee of excellence; and no other firm in the district has a reputation at all comparable with Mr. Aubrey Franks for perfect adaptability and adjustment to suit all sights. The connection extends all over the United Kingdom, and many cases of goods are sent abroad. The stock of the King Street warehouse is extremely heavy and comprehensive and includes, in addition to spectacles and eye-glasses, microscopes, telescopes, scientific instruments, magic-lanterns, opera-glasses, and a variety of useful and ornamental articles. Two neat and flourishing branch establishments are conducted—one at Hull, and the other at Southport. The sole proprietor is Mr. A. Franks, an optician of great skill and repute, well known and respected in the city and justly considered a most prosperous man of business.

Messrs. Burgon & Co., Supply Stores, Ackers Street.—Forty years ago was established the well-known house of "Messrs. Burgon & Co.," with branches throughout the city: and at Salford, Bolton and Oldham—a truly representative establishment of its class. This vast concern, with its branches, stands second to none in the Kingdom and from the great variety of goods of every denomination on sale, the spirited proprietors may well be styled "Universal Providers." The business of supply stores has during the last quarter of a century become of such public importance and benefit, that they may with justice be termed a National Institution of Commerce. The supply stores, dealing as they do with nearly all branches of trade, offer great inducements to householders, the heads of large establishments, hotel-keepers, and all large consumers to become patrons, from the very fact, obvious to all large buyers, of the immensely superior system upon which the business is conducted. The maxim pursued is the popular and modern business one of small profits and large returns. This system is one which has grown thoroughly into public favour; the result is, the "supply stores" lead the way and occupy a high position. The premises of Messrs. Burgon & Co. comprise a noble, lofty, double-fronted building of striking architectural features, large dimensions, most commanding exterior, and in every way adapted for the prompt transaction of the very large daily influx of business, to meet the requirements of which a large and efficient staff of assistants is engaged. The proprietors are gentlemen with a long mercantile reputation of very high standing, and much esteemed as employers. Large as the business of this establishment has been in past years, it is easy to foretell a still larger development in the future.

J. Hunter & Co., Wholesale and Export Cabinet Makers and Upholsterers, 20, 16, and 12, St. Mary's Parsonage.—It would be extremely difficult to name a branch of business more important in its relations to other lines of trade and industry than that devoted to the manufacture and sale of furniture and upholstery. In this connection special mention should be made of the well-known and thoroughly representative firm of Messrs. J. Hunter & Co., wholesale and export cabinet makers and upholsterers. This business was established originally about forty years ago, being a branch of the London house, and from its very inception has enjoyed a prosperous career. The premises occupied are of spacious dimensions, admirably arranged and equipped with every facility and convenience for the transaction of business. A large and valuable stock of fine cabinet and art furniture is kept, including many specialities in all the prevailing styles. Mr. Hunter was the first, and is to-day the largest importer of American and Austrian bentwood chairs, the establishment being a recognised head-quarters for these popular novelties. The firm does a large export trade to the colonies and the West Coast of Africa. It is such houses as this that are the recognised exponents of the various branches of Manchester trade, and it well deserves the prominent position which the enterprise and ability of its proprietors have so unerringly attained.

S. Marsden & Son, Bolt and Nut Works, London Road.—The business now known under the title of Messrs. S. Marsden & Son was originally established in the year 1845 by Mr. Samuel Marsden, and is one of the best-known firms engaged in the manufacture of bolts, nuts, &c. Some idea of the immense business done by this house may be gained from the fact that five hundred tons of bolts, nuts, &c., are always kept in stock, and that two hundred hands are constantly employed. Messrs. Marsden have made quite a revolution in this branch of trade, having brought out a number of patents and other improvements in the machinery. Passing first on to the nut-forging department, a number of specially-designed machines attract attention. These marvellous labour-saving appliances turn out square nuts, forged and ready for tapping, at the rate of 45 to 80 per minute. These are known as Marsden's patent square nut making machines, and are extremely simple in their action; the nuts require no hammering or fraizing after leaving the machines, and one youth only is required to feed the heated bars into a machine, whilst the tools, being plain straight pieces of steel, are very durable and inexpensive. Another special machine is also a patented invention of Messrs. Marsden, in this instance for making hexagon nuts, and in working this no skilled labour is required. This machine, besides manufacturing the nuts so true to shape and size, also effects a great saving of material, the hexagon nuts being made without wasting the four angular corners, and with only one-fourth of the waste in punching the hole, by which means the waste of material is under ten per cent., and from three to five tons, according to the class of work, is turned out by one of these machines per week. In this section of the works there are altogether about a dozen specially designed machines expressly for nut-making, and passing on to the bolt forging department this is fitted up with about twice this number of special machines, the whole of which have been designed and patented by Messrs. Marsden. These include a very large machine, weighing about 12 tons, for making bolts from 1 inch up to $1\frac{1}{2}$ inch diameter; this machine takes the heated bar of iron, forges the head up out of the solid, and cuts the bolts off to the required length at the same heat. The construction of this machine is shown in the annexed illustration. Bolts of any length with square, hexagon, cheese, cup, or countersunk heads, with square, oblong, or round necks can be made by this machine from the plain round bar iron at the rate of from ten to twenty gross per day, according to the size. By recent improvements the machine will also make hexagon and square nuts without waste. The nuts are formed on the end of the heated bar in the same way that the bolt heads are made, then the hole is punched at the same heat, leaving the punching out of the hole on the end of the bar, which goes to form part of the next nut, and from 10 to 15 gross of nuts can be made per day according to size. One important feature of the machine is that the square or hexagon bolts or nuts are finished perfect without any hand dressing being required. Three different sizes of these machines are at work, the medium size making $\frac{3}{4}$ to 1 in. diameter, and the small machine $\frac{3}{8}$ in. to $\frac{5}{8}$ in. The firm has also patented machinery for the manufacture of railway wagon bolts, and in the forging department the machinery is of the most perfect order. The motive power for the works is supplied by a pair of compound horizontal engines of 100 horse-power. The firm is well known throughout the kingdom, and the technical skill displayed in the manufacture, the business ability and energy brought to bear on the management, and the universally acknowledged sound principles on which everything is conducted have combined to place this house in the very front rank of the trade in every quarter of the globe.

Consolidated Marine Insurance Cos. of Berlin and Dresden, 22, Booth Street (E. W. Muller, Underwriter).—This insurance office was established in Manchester and London in the year 1872, when Mr. Muller first conceived the idea of uniting three of the most powerful and successful German marine insurance companies, viz. the "Transatlantic Marine of Berlin," the "General Marine of Dresden," and the "Saxonian Reinsurance Company" (the three together embracing a capital of £495,000) under the above title, after having obtained their sanction for this step, and their powers of attorney, by which they covenanted from henceforth to mutually guarantee each other on the policies issued by him for their account and in their name. The business, which also extends to the negociation of fire insurances in Transatlantic and other distant states, commenced in Manchester, where its growth was so rapid and so decided that soon after it was resolved to start a branch in London, at 72, Cornhill, for which purpose Mr. Muller removed to that city, and for nearly ten years managed the two establishments conjointly, the London office assuming by degrees such large proportions that it is now looked upon as the head office of the said companies for England. By mutual agreement some five years ago, Mr. Müller returned to Manchester in order to again devote himself exclusively to this branch, whilst the London office was placed under the sole care of his son, Mr. Frederick Muller, as agent and underwriter, under whose management it has continued to enjoy a most remarkable and ever increasing success, its security being acknowledged and willingly accepted by all the leading banks of the city as equal to that of the best English companies. Mr. Müller, senior, has now been a resident in Manchester for more than forty years, and has taken a lively and consistent interest in all that concerns the welfare of the town and the trade of the district. He is looked upon as a kind and considerate employer.

Wilson Brothers, Bobbin Manufacturers, Cornholme Mill, Todmorden, and 14, Market Place.—The almost universal demand for superior and more uniformly balanced bobbins, owing to the great improvements recently effected in spinning and doubling machinery, for the production of single and doubled yarns for sewing cotton and manufactured goods, in the use of which, in great variety, these articles are necessary, is daily on the increase. It is in carrying on this important business that Messrs. Wilson Brothers are engaged. Their bobbin mills are located at Todmorden. The firm is a very old one, having been established in 1823, by the late Lawrence Wilson. Upon the death of Mr. Wilson the concern was continued by his sons, who now manage the business with great energy and success. The works at Cornholme, Todmorden, are very extensive, and are substantially built; they are supplied with all the most improved modern labour-saving machinery requisite for the perfect manufacture of their productions. The connection of the firm covers the whole of the textile manufacturing districts of the United Kingdom, and every country where English machinery is found. The management is marked by skill, energy and ability, and to it is principally due the success attained by this firm. They are proprietors of no fewer than ten patents for improvements, and have obtained six highest prize medals at recent exhibitions.

Luke Eastwood & Sons, Timber Dealers, Joiners, Builders, Packing-case Makers, &c., Charles Street Saw Mills. The timber trade and packing-case making of Manchester are of considerable extent and magnitude, and the establishments engaged are numerous. A representative firm in this line is that trading under the name of Messrs. Luke Eastwood & Sons, which was founded in 1835, over half a century ago, and is now owned by Mrs. Mary Ann Carr grand-daughter of the founder of the firm. The mills are large and extensive, completely equipped with steam saws of all kinds and other appliances for carrying on the business. There is a fine large stock of timber, and the firm has a good reputation for the variety and excellence of the stock. A good staff is employed in sawing timber and making packing-cases of every description for foreign shippers and manufacturers and merchants wishing to protect goods from heat, damp, &c. All kinds of joinery and building work are undertaken and carried out with dispatch, and in a first-class manner. Upon the whole, a very lucrative trade is carried on in the district, and the management of the business is such as to maintain the reputation of half a century's standing.

Thompson & Capper, Manufacturing Homœopathic Chemists, 51, Piccadilly, and 39, Deansgate.—Manchester is behind no other city in the country for the extent and excellence of her Homœopathic business, and among the manufacturing firms an important place is held by that of Messrs. Thompson & Capper. This firm was originally established as Messrs. Henry Turner & Co., in 1842, and carried on as such until 1878, when it came into the possession of the present proprietors, who have been established in Liverpool since 1843. The premises occupied are large and commodious, the shops are elegantly and completely fitted up with the necessary fixtures and appliances, and their general appearance is most attractive and pleasing. They contain a very large and perfect stock of homœopathical preparations, which are manufactured in the laboratory of the firm. Goods bearing the trade-mark of this firm are noted for their absolute purity and strength, and no efforts are spared in keeping up this high state of excellence. One of the specialities of the house is "Dentifrice Water," in which, as in homœopathical preparations, a very heavy wholesale and retail trade is done. Messrs. Thompson & Capper have establishments at Liverpool, Sheffield, &c. Messrs. Isaac Cooke Thompson and Samuel James Capper are gentlemen of great talent and experience in homœopathy, and they are well-known in Liverpool and Manchester, and enjoy the esteem and confidence of the community at large, whilst their house has done much to forward the cause of homœopathy.

Gault & Son, Tailors and Costumiers, 10, St. Ann's Square.—This business was established by Mr. Isaac Gault more than half a century ago. For the last ten years the firm has been known as Gault & Son, and has occupied the present premises the same length of time. The premises comprise reception and fitting-rooms equipped with every facility for the transaction of business. The work-rooms are commodious, light, and well ventilated. The great speciality of the firm is "cut" in trousers. Messrs. Gault & Son have been at very great pains and trouble to secure exceptionally good ranges of tweeds, fine cloths, and mixtures, and have now such a variety of patterns as cannot be surpassed by any house in the trade. The connection is almost entirely amongst the merchants and professional gentlemen of the city and neighbourhood. The sole partner is now Mr. Thomas Russell Gault, a gentleman extremely well known in Manchester and highly esteemed for his great abilities and his genial character.

Thomas Tomlinson & Son, Commercial Agents for Essential Oils, &c., Arbitrators and Valuers of Chemists' and other Stocks, 9, New Cannon Street.—There is no branch of industry or commerce that has not an agency system attached, and in an important city like Manchester, this department is most perfect and of great utility. The establishment of Messrs. Thomas Tomlinson & Son, which is connected with the essential oils trade, has been in existence, progressing and prospering, for ten years. The firm enjoys a special reputation for the prompt and liberal manner in which the business is conducted, and for the splendid quality of the goods. The premises are of ample proportions, and in every way adapted for this purpose. A very good trade is carried on in such commodities as essential oils and drysalteries, Messrs. Tomlinson & Son having a fine connection in Lancashire and neighbouring counties. Mr. Thomas Tomlinson and his son, Thomas Conway Tomlinson, are the partners in this flourishing concern, and they are thoroughly acquainted with the trade, and Mr. Tomlinson, Senior, having been connected with the trade for the last forty years, manages with ability and energy. He is well known and highly respected in the mercantile world, he being the oldest and most experienced chemists' valuer and arbitrator in this country; and his business is a worthy and able representative of the agency system.

F. H. Cheetham & Co., Stationers and Account Book Makers, 99, Market Street.—Prominent among the great industries of the age, and one which calls for special notice, is the stationery, account-book making and printing business, at once a branch of commerce of the very highest importance, and one upon which nearly every other commercial undertaking must depend in a more or less marked degree. The establishment of Messrs. F. H. Cheetham & Co. is a representative house in this class of trade and stands high among its compeers, claiming, as it does, to be the oldest established printing office of the district. The fame of this establishment has continued to spread itself and the result is, as might be reasonably expected, a large and influential connection, and a trade of the first magnitude. The premises occupy a bold and central position, and have been known under the title of James Cheetham about forty years. The business, which is very large and important, embraces every article on demand at such establishments, and being well conducted, enjoys such a favourable reputation, as always to command a large public support. A speciality which is worth a trial is Cheetham's celebrated and world-renowned *extra strong copying ink*, and fine cream-wove copying paper, orders for which come in from all parts of the world. It is also much appreciated and in daily demand by most of the merchants and business people at home. Some of the advantages are: the ink writes *black* at once, will take *six copies* at one impression, and will copy seven days after writing. The stock comprises every article in account-books, stationery, commercial stamps, forms, collecting-books, &c., &c., and is of such great variety that the most intricate orders can be executed with a punctuality and completeness not to be excelled by any similar establishment. Mr. James Cheetham is a gentleman widely known and highly respected by a very large circle of friends, and the public generally; and his long and successful career, added to his great reputation as a man of business has insured to him a very liberal support during the past, and no doubt can exist that the future augurs well for the still greater development of this old-established business.

John Shaw & Co., Nurserymen and Seedsmen, Landscape Gardeners, and Garden Architects, Horticultural Valuers, &c., also F.R.H.S., 29 to 31, Oxford Street.—The horticultural business of John Shaw & Co. was established nearly half a century ago—namely, in the year 1810, and it is now the oldest concern of the kind in Manchester. Mr. Shaw is the sole proprietor, and it is only right to record the fact that he has been for fifty years one of the leading landscape gardeners and garden architects in this country. He has also been extensively employed all over the kingdom as horticultural valuer, and he has, in addition, been an active promoter and worker in every branch of gardening. Mr. Shaw is an Honorary Life Fellow of the Royal Horticultural Society of London, and was many years secretary of the Manchester Botanical Society, and inspector of Public Parks. He has long been known as an extensive grower and exhibitor of orchids, coniferæ, and other plants. He was the inventor of the horticultural shading, Shaw's tiffany and elastic netting, and a patentee of hot water boilers, vineries, ventilators, and other useful articles connected with gardening. He has nurseries at Bowdon, near Manchester, which are seventeen acres in extent, and which enjoy a national reputation for the superiority of their choice plants and flowers, in which Mr. Shaw does an immense business. He is a new plant and bulb importer and seed merchant, and has a connection which extends all over the kingdom. Mr. Shaw's City office and depot is situated at Nos. 29 to 31, Oxford Street.

William Owen, A.I.B.A., Architect and Surveyor, 134, Deansgate.—This business was established in this city about seventeen years ago, under the title of O. Edwards. In 1877 Mr. Owen entered into partnership with O. Edwards, and the firm became known as Edwards and Owen; three years afterwards the partnership was dissolved and the present style, William Owen, was adopted. The premises consist of a capital suite of rooms, lofty, light, and exceedingly cheerful. They are handsomely furnished and thoroughly well equipped in everyway. Mr. Owen has a large and influential professional connection amongst property owners and capitalists; and thus a great deal of work finds its way to his offices. He was chosen architect for the buildings required for the Rhyl Winter Gardens; he built the new post-office at Knutsford, the Baptist Chapel, Bowdon, the Presbyterian Church, Denbigh, and many other important public and private buildings, including churches, chapels, manufactories, and villa residences. In all these Mr. Owen has shown not merely genuine constructive skill, but much ingenuity, inventiveness and resource; and a most perfect knowledge of all the leading schools of architecture, both ancient and modern, with an adaptability worthy of the highest commendation. Mr. Owen is assisted by several clerks and pupils, but to all his commissions he gives the most active personal attention. He is very well known in the professional and commercial circles of the city, and is much respected. Mr. Owen takes rank as one of the city's most successful professional gentlemen. In 1874 Mr. Owen carried off the gold medal annually awarded by South Kensington for the best architectural design of the year.

Manchester Sand-blast Company, 41, City Road.—The Manchester Sand-blast Company are extensively engaged in the business of decorating and lettering all kinds of glass. Few people are aware that the use of glass is comparatively modern, while the discovery of it is very obscure, and is generally attributed to accident. The earliest accounts represent glass as being made by the inhabitants of Tyre and Sidon, and the first Europeans who excelled in the manufacture were the Venetians. Its use is now familiar to everyone, and has given rise to the art of glass-decorating. It is in this business that the Manchester Sand-blast Company are engaged, their sphere of operations extending to engraving mirrors, lettering, decorating lamp-glasses, reproducing architects' own designs, and making ceiling lights, panels, conservatory decorations, &c. A special feature in the business is making glass advertising tablets for affixing to shop windows; these are duplicated by some process which is a secret. Another process carried on is that called etching or painting on glass, by which the most beautiful effect is obtained. The premises occupied by this firm are situated at the above address, where a large staff is employed. The business is under the management of Mr. A. W. Cramer, who has invented and adapted a number of ingenious processes in glass decoration, and who was the actual pioneer in this particular branch of business in Manchester; and several travellers are employed all over the country. The connection is very widespread, this firm having steadily increased during the eight years of its establishment. The present premises have only been occupied lately, the business having been originally carried on in Green Lane. In every branch of this industry the company has met with great success. Their methods, aided by the use of the best modern machinery, have produced results, attractive and artistic, at a cheaper rate than formerly. A very large business is done, and the company is well known all over the north of England.

Wm. Kleinertz, Chromo Printer, &c., 8, Fountain Street.—A skilful and reliable printer who can combine excellence of workmanship with moderation in charges is one of the best servants which the community can possess. Such a one is to be found in Mr. William Kleinertz, who has for fifteen years carried on a most successful business in Manchester. For ten years of that time Mr. Kleinertz has occupied extensive premises at the above address, and now he has one of the best fitted and well managed offices that can be found in the district. Capacious and well-lighted rooms are supplied with every requisite in the shape of machinery which are needed by a large trade, and the chromo-lithograph department is particularly well "found" in every respect, the work produced being of the most artistic and praiseworthy character. Show cards, labels, tickets, billheads, invoices, circulars, and all kinds of commercial work are turned out with the utmost neatness and dispatch; and Mr. Kleinertz has the pleasure of working for some of the largest and best firms in the city. He is a thoroughly practical and experienced gentleman who devotes constant personal attention to all the work which he undertakes, and the excellence and quality of his productions, together with the moderate prices which he charges, have placed him amongst the leading and most successful printers of the town.

George Pescott (late W. Maude), **Bags, Trunks, Portmanteaus, Sample Cases,** 119, Market Street, Manchester.—The manufacture of bags, trunks, portmanteaus, &c., constitutes a most important branch of industrial activity in Manchester; and among the leading exponents of the trade is Mr. George Pescott, whose spacious and well-stocked establishment at the above address was founded over thirty years ago by W. Maude, and has been conducted by its present proprietor for several years. The premises occupied are of spacious dimensions, admirably arranged, and fitted up with every facility and convenience for the transaction of business, employment being given to a staff of skilled assistants. The stock kept is large and varied, and includes all the specialities for which this house has been so long noted. These are emigration trunks, regulation cabin trunks, state room portmanteaus, dress suit cases, and hat boxes. Mr. Pescott is maker of the celebrated G. P. sample-bags, suitable for all trades, and also of the improved Hold-All and Carry-All. Ladies' travelling baskets, ladies' dress trunks, overland trunks for India and Australia, dressing bags, gentlemen's and ladies' hand bags, portmanteaus, commercial travellers' sample cases, writing folios, purses, satchels, pocket-books, card cases, letter cases, hunting equipments, bags, gun cases, flasks, &c., and hundreds of useful articles suitable for presents; every requisite for schoolboys' outfit in portmanteaus, boxes, bags, writing cases, &c. Every article is made on the premises, under Mr. Pescott's own supervision, from the best materials in the most skilful manner, and can be relied upon to give perfect satisfaction. He is enabled to offer special advantages to customers and to execute all orders in the most prompt and satisfactory manner. His trade is of a widespread and high-class character, and his establishment is a credit alike to Manchester and the important industry it so ably represents.

Wright & Barnaby, Pharmaceutical Chemists, 228, Oxford Street.—This business was founded in the year 1831 by Mr. C. Wright, who in the year 1870 took into partnership his son-in-law, Mr. Francis Barnaby, when the firm became known as Wright & Barnaby. Mr. Wright was a gentleman extremely well known in his profession, and was indeed one of the founders of the Pharmaceutical Society. He died in the year 1871. Mr. Barnaby has since that time conducted the business on his own account entirely, though without altering the title of the firm. The trade connection is for the most part amongst the best families in the surrounding neighbourhood. The premises consist of a handsome shop, elegantly fitted and furnished. The stock is admirably selected, and most attractively displayed, and all drugs and medicines supplied are of guaranteed tested purity. Mr. Barnaby himself prepares a list of useful medicines, which are of great repute amongst his patrons, and whose sale is very considerable. He is assisted by a capable staff of qualified chemists and dispensers, and the system of dealing with physicians' prescriptions renders it next to impossible for any mistake to occur in dispensing.

Messrs. Crosby & Walker, Wholesale Drapers and Milliners, 84, 86, 88, Oldham Street.—Prominent among the industries of Manchester are its large and thriving drapery establishments. A representative centre in this respect is the well-known house of Messrs. Crosby & Walker, mantle and costume manufacturers, wholesale drapers, milliners, silk mercers, &c. Established in Manchester eight years, this house enjoys a first-class reputation as a thoroughly good business concern, and takes rank among the largest establishments of its kind in the city. The business operations are very large and widely extended. In addition to the unceasing daily retail trade, the firm have a very extensive wholesale connection, and many of the large retail houses are their best customers. The premises occupied consist of a magnificent range of lofty and pretentious exterior, with considerable frontage, elegantly fitted up and appointed in the best manner, regardless of cost, presenting the appearance of a high-class and most substantial business house, and affording employment to a large staff of well-trained assistants, male and female. The stocks held are very large, and comprise an assortment of every kind of article in requisition in an establishment of this kind, and representing a very large capital. The firm's patent twilled black velveteen has acquired a world-wide reputation for its many points of excellence in manufacture and material. It has received the highest praise from the most competent judges in the textile trade and the commercial press, and is in daily increasing demand. The wholesale department is a distinctive feature, and is under the control of a well-organized special staff retaining a separate branch of the establishment, arranged and thoroughly adapted for the efficient conduct of this important line. The principals are Mr. Henry O. Crosby and Mr. Frederick Walker, gentlemen well known as of the highest commercial status, strictest integrity, and widely respected, who, previously to commencing business in Oldham Street, were connected with the manufacturing and wholesale trades. They left Messrs. Rylands & Sons nearly nine years ago to try a commercial experiment, viz., to supply the public direct from the manufacturer at wholesale prices. As might have been expected, it has proved a great success, the public having been quick to avail themselves of the great advantages offered by this firm over many of their rivals.

Messrs. John Boyd & Co., Fancy Goods Warehousemen, Mason Street, Swan Street.—In reviewing the trade industries of Manchester and district, a branch calling for especial notice and observation is the fancy goods importer, &c., fully illustrated by the well-known house of John Boyd & Co., wholesale London, Birmingham, Sheffield, and foreign fancy goods warehousemen. Established now some thirty years under the title of John Boyd & Co., this business has always maintained a very high reputation as a first-class importing house, with a great renown for its varied and excellent stock. The different apartments comprise jewellery, leather goods, &c., combs and brushes, cutlery, hardware, stationery and perfumery, glass and china, toys and dinner goods, very large stocks of all of which are held, and the importations amount to and represent immense amounts annually. The premises occupied comprise a large and lofty warehouse of four stories of elegant and neat architectural appearance, with handsome shop and offices on ground floor admirably fitted and adapted to the requirements of the large business of the establishment, and affording employment to a numerous staff of well-trained assistants and warehousemen. The stocks held are very large, comprising an immense variety in clocks and watches, English and foreign musical boxes, meerschaum and other pipes, pocket and side combs, table and dessert knives, tea and coffee-pots, spoons, &c., in Britannia metal, electro-plate, and nickel silver; note paper and envelopes, lustres and vases, English and foreign games, dolls, and many other such items. The business transactions are on a very extensive scale, the house being well known as one of the most reliable and best class fancy warehouses in the north of England. The principals are gentlemen well known as holding a very high position in commercial circles, and of the strictest integrity.

Mr. John G. Wilson, Practical Mechanical Engineer, Draughtsman, and Patent Agent, 55, Market Street. To the inventor and man of genius labouring to bring out some important creation of his own ingenuity, there is no more important institution than the Patent Office and Registry of Designs, where he can protect and make secure the results of his labours. At the offices of Mr. John G. Wilson is established the British and Foreign Patent Office, Trade Marks and Designs Registry. Mr. Wilson, having had twenty-five years' experience in this business, is able to decide or advise upon the practical utility or otherwise of any invention, thus saving intending patentees an immense amount of time and money. As a practical mechanical engineer, Mr. John G. Wilson enjoys a high reputation in this city, and has a large practice. The business of his firm in connection with British and foreign patents extends to all parts of the world. He has had a long and honourable connection with this city, and possesses the esteem and confidence of a very extensive and valuable connection.

[illegible] of industry.

Charles Gibbs & Co., Cotton Doublers, [illegible]

[illegible] Bros., Manufacturers of Engine-cleaning Cotton Waste, Sponge and Carriage Cloths, [illegible]

G. W. Chadwick, Paper and Twine Manufacturer, [illegible]

Hugo Shaw, Earthenware Manufacturer, [illegible]

Burgess, Ledward & Co., Manufacturers, [illegible]

usical Instrument Empo-
inly one of the most flourishing
articles of merchandise as musical
a branch at 56, Church Street,
ndsome and well-appointed esta-
pianofortes, harmoniums, Ame-
ty of material and workmanship.
gent in Lancashire and Cheshire
nofortes, in which connection he
has been established for thirty
al patronage, particularly in the
s business is by no means confined
struments, new and of the first
Meller, but those who have given
ave been afforded the most un-
nts, it may be added, are lent out
hire or purchase are remarkably
tainly be relied upon by all who
m.

cking Company, 27, Ex-
appliance of absolute necessity
king, and of late years many
a perfect material, that is, one
d does not burn or char. This
ter firm known as The Frictionless Engine Packing Company,
which was founded in 1881 by
Mr. H. G. Small. This packing
is universally acknowledged to
be perfect, fulfilling all the necessary conditions, needs no oil
or tallow, never hardens or chars,
stands any pressure of steam and
degree of heat, wears entirely
out, and lasts longer than any
other packing, and has received
flattering testimonials from leading engineers, manufacturers,
and others. In the *Engineer*,
Mechanical World, and *Machinery
Market* its merits are discussed
and the first place for perfection
accorded to it, and finally it is
used in nearly every mill and
factory, and by nearly every
machinery user in the United
Kingdom and in all parts. Besides this packing Messrs. Small
and Parkes also manufacture
" Hull's Pneumatic Engine
Speed and Blast Pressure Re-
ers patent and specially designed
yal Commission on Accidents in
he report: "In order to ensure
entrusted with the working of
a regular record of the speed of
attached to the engine of such
ed of the ventilator, and also the
-cast shaft or fan-drift." That
answers may be seen from the
firm from colliery owners and
it is in use in all parts of the
ier patent manufacture of this
india-rubber and asbestos mill-
superior, and in great demand
l manufacturers. The works at
pecial machinery and appliances,
re employed in manufacturing
Small and G. W. Parkes are pro-
Frictionless Engine Packing Co.,"
lity in the manufacturing world,
eir famous patent productions.

Merchants, 28, Fountain
ces is one of the most important
rominent among these who are
urst & Co. This firm has been
or nearly the whole of that time
above address, where they occupy
warerooms are well and hand-
a large stock of the calicoes for
spread reputation. The superior
aused them to be much-sought-
nt demand for them necessitates
eeping up the supply. By their
the firm have built up a business
r success, and which has obtained

H. Sotheran & Co., Booksellers, 49, Cross Street.—There are few bibliographers or booksellers in the kingdom who are not acquainted with the firm of Henry Sotheran & Co., and who do not regard it as one of the best and most enterprising in the country. Established many years ago by Mr. Henry Sotheran, the firm has two extensive establishments in London, one in Piccadilly and the other in the Strand; and for the last seven years it has had a flourishing branch in Manchester. This is at 49, Cross Street, in premises for thirty years identified with the bookselling trade; and here, in an elegant and well-filled shop and show-room, there is a splendid collection of books of the very highest class, comprising editions *de luxe* of all the principal English and foreign authors, historical and critical works, and scientific writings by the most eminent men. A speciality of the business is fine art books, and in the stock there are some of the finest specimens of this class of work which ever made the heart of bibliographer glad: whilst in antique and rare volumes the resources of the firm are almost unequalled. The firm have upwards of 200,000 volumes on sale. Scarce and precious first editions are enumerated in the periodical catalogues to a marvellous extent; and a brisk trade is carried on with all parts of the country. Large quantities of books are also exported to the colonies and America, where the firm is well known to collectors and others as one of the largest and most enterprising in the mother country.

Herbert Johnson, Watch Manufacturer, Goldsmith, & Jeweller, 29, King Street.—Manchester holds her own ground with dignity as regards the watch manufacture and jewellery trade; the establishments engaged therein are numerous and under able and experienced management. An admirable example of a business of this sort is that of Mr. Herbert Johnson, which was originally established half a century ago by Mr. Henry Whittington, Senior. The shop occupied is spacious, of attractive appearance, and fitted up in a most elegant and superior manner with the necessary trade fixtures and appointments for the display of stock and convenience of patrons. There is a splendid, admirably displayed and valuable stock of jewellery of all kinds, rings, gem and plain gold; pins, brooches, chains, necklaces, bracelets, &c., of unique patterns and artistic workmanship, watches in gold and silver of splendid manufacture and of latest improvements, and gold and silver work of every description of beautiful and original design are among the items on hand. A finer stock could scarcely be seen, and Mr. Herbert Johnson takes all means to keep it up to its strength and excellence. He carries on a very fine trade, having a connection of long standing and high-class character. The hands employed are able and experienced, and all work is executed under Mr. Herbert Johnson's supervision. This gentleman is one of the most important members of the trade, and to him, to a great extent, is due its fine reputation. He fully deserves the patronage accorded to his business.

John Stephenson, Umbrella Manufacturer, 24 and 26, Blossom Street Ancoats.—There is probably no other branch of industry in which so marked an improvement has been made during recent years as in the manufacture of umbrellas. Manchester has a good reputation for her business in this line, in which a well-known house is that of Mr. John Stephenson, which was established by the present proprietor in 1875. Mr. John Stephenson is one of the most expert and experienced umbrella manufacturers in the city. The factory is very spacious and commodious, and admirably fitted up with every possible appliance for the carrying on of the business. A force of from eighty to one hundred well-trained hands, as well as a large number of out-door workers, are employed in manufacturing umbrellas and parasols for ladies and gentlemen; and it is well known that the silk and other material, frames and sticks, are carefully selected and tested before being passed into the hands of the workmen, and the handles are fashioned in an elegant and tasteful manner. The factory turns out a very large number of these articles, chiefly for export trade. Mr. Stephenson also does a large business in working canes for the umbrella trade. The management of the establishment reflects the greatest possible credit upon Mr. John Stephenson, whose financial, social, and business status in the community is very well defined among the leading business men of the city.

J. B. Stansfield, Surveyor and Valuer, 14, St. Ann's Square.—It is seven years since Mr. Stansfield established himself professionally, and already he has secured an especially valuable and numerous *clientèle*. The offices are a capital suite of rooms, admirably situated and well adapted for professional purposes. They are handsomely furnished and fitted with all the usual modern appliances for the rapid transaction of business. Mr. Stansfield has a large circle of influential and wealthy personal friends, who are glad to avail themselves of his professional assistance. He is retained by an important insurance company, and is often appointed valuer and arbitrator in cases of dispute or settlement. His high character and unswerving integrity, combined with unrivalled experience and sound judgment, gives especial weight to his decisions; and the confidence reposed in them is itself a great compliment to his undoubted probity. Mr. Stansfield is supported by a competent staff of assistants. He is well known throughout the city, and takes a warm interest in all that concerns the welfare of the municipality or the community.

Oliver Whittle, Engineer, Cathedral Steps, Victoria Street, Manchester, and **Whittle & Adam,** 7, Wapping, Liverpool. – The most important patent of modern times is the "Lucigen," light, which is capable of yielding an illumination of 200 to 12,000 candle power at the ridiculously low cost of threepence per hour. The "Lucigen" supersedes the electric light for out-door purposes in a most marked manner, the flame giving a large, broad glow, which does not cast those inconvenient and undesirable black shadows so inseparable from the electric light, so that men can work by its aid with equal ease on the side of the job away from the light. Moreover, the cost of the plant is only one-fourth of that required for electric lighting, a considerable consideration where contractors, iron founders, colliery proprietors, engineers, ship-builders, steamship owners, railway companies, and others, are concerned. The light is specially adapted for both the open air or under cover. It is produced by burning heavy hydro-carbon oils in a special form of burner by means of compressed air or steam. The oil is thus consumed in the form of an extremely fine spray, and yields an intensely brilliant light, giving off no smoke or smell, and illuminating a radius of 300 yards around each burner with perfect clearness. The "Lucigen" requires no lantern, and burns equally well in a gale of wind or under heavy rain. The oil required is to a large extent practically a waste product of chemical manufacturers, gas and oil works, &c., so that the cost is but nominal; but the company provide a special preparation on most liberal terms. The "Lucigen" is sold in several varieties specially adapted for the requirements of particular work. The Manchester Jubilee Exhibition was built by its aid. The company are constantly receiving testimonials couched in the highest terms of praise from their ever-increasing circle of customers; and they publish a formidable list (which embraces a large number of the most important companies and firms in Great Britain) of those who use their patent light "Lucigen." The Aintree goods yard of the L. & Y. Railway, consisting of twenty-six miles of sidings, is lighted by ten "Lucigens," the farthest lamp being one and a-half miles from the engine and oil supply. Admiral Inglefield's yachts are being fitted with this light, with the object of illuminating during fogs and darkness. Among the numerous specialities in which Messrs. Whittle & Adam do an extensive business, the "Anti-Fouling Electroyd" takes prominent rank. This is a patent composition used for the painting of ships' bottoms, and the most incontrovertible proofs of its efficacy and superiority over other compositions used for the same purpose have been given. The famous yacht "Thistle," which competed last year for the America Cup, was coated with this "Anti-Fouling Electroyd." When docked after her trip across the Atlantic, her bottom was found to be in perfect condition and quite clean —no mean testimony to the efficacy of the composition. The same company are also patentees of the "Bathymeter," an invention for taking flying soundings at sea. Vessels going at the rate of sixteen knots per hour can take correct soundings, without having to slacken speed. Several of the great ocean racers are already provided with this ingenious instrument. Among other novelties, the Hannay's Patents Company offer an "Electroyd Enamel," for enamelling structures of all kinds—stone, brick, cement, iron, or steel thoroughly protecting them from the action of the atmosphere. Also, a patent "Coating Oil," for dipping iron tubes, &c., to protect them from rust and corrosion; and a patent "Oil-resisting Paint and Jointing," which is invaluable to engineers for covering portions of machinery which are to be exposed to the action of oil. The three last-named inventions are, as might well be expected, of the most practical utility, and reflect the highest credit upon the firm that produces them.

Lindley & Jones, Embroiderers & Manufacturers, Grosvenor Street.—Prominent among the many firms in Grosvenor Street, and especially in its own particular line, the firm of Messrs. Lindley & Jones, manufacturers and embroiderers, is particularly worthy of notice. Within their handsome premises will be found much to please the eye and tempt the intending buyer. In the embroidery departments an infinite variety of goods will be found of the most superior kind, wonderfully moderate in price; and, with regard to the other branches of this flourishing concern, a fine stock of plain and fancy handkerchiefs is always on hand. Throughout, the principle acted upon is one of small profits and quick returns. All orders are seen to and carried out with the utmost dispatch, and satisfaction is obtained by all who have transactions with this well-known firm. Messrs. Lindley & Jones have now been established for a period of about forty years; their works are large and always busy; their warehouses are roomy and always well filled with novelties in goods of the very best description; and they keep (on the average), about two hundred hands in constant employment; and, in addition to these qualifications, Messrs. Lindley and Jones may justifiably pride themselves upon occupying an almost unique position in that expansive industry, to the advancement and improvement of which they have so long played a conspicuous and creditable part.

Aspell & Sons, Manufacturers of Manchester Goods, 6, Marsden Square.—Amongst the various firms engaged in the manufacture of what are known all the world over as "Manchester goods," none are better known than Messrs. Aspell & Sons. The enviable reputation which this firm so justly enjoys is the result of years of careful attention to the requirements of both home and foreign markets. Nu[m]berless experiments in the production of new fabrics, and countless tri[als] of novel combinations of design and colour, have contributed to the we[ll] merited success and aided the establishment of a reputation which h[as] scarcely a rival in the country. It is only natural to suppose that no[ne] but roomy and commodious premises would suffice for the conduct of su[ch] a business. Accordingly we find that the warehouse in Marsden Squa[re] is five storeys high, and in addition to a considerable frontage extend[s a] long way to the rear. The manufacturing premises attached to the fi[rm] are located in the outskirts of the city, and are of commensurate exte[nt]. Messrs. Aspell are greatly respected as manufacturers and employer[s], and we may likewise add that in their capacity as citizens they pe[r]form more than their routine duties, for there are few charitable [or] benevolent movements set on foot in which they do not take an active a[nd] warm interest.

Davies & Kendall, Cheese Factors, &c., 41, Hangi[ng] Ditch.—This well known commercial concern was established thirty yea[rs] ago by Messrs. Hussey and Tickle, who were succeeded in 1879 by t[he] present proprietors, Messrs. Nathaniel Davies and William Dods Kendall. The business carried on is that of cheese factors. It is of [a] widespread character, and includes not only an important home conne[c]tion, but a considerable export trade as well. The management [is] thorough—all, in fact, that could well be desired; and the splendid po[si]tion occupied by the firm enables Messrs. Davies and Kendall to add [to] their already exceptional reputation, and to afford their patrons ma[ny] advantages that would be difficult to equal elsewhere. The premises [are] fitted up in first-class style, and the stock kept is very extensive—co[n]sisting mainly of prime Cheshire cheese—and invariably of a good qualit[y]. A successful branch establishment has been opened at 21A, Victo[ria] Street, Liverpool, and here a widespread connection of a very influent[ial] and substantial nature indeed has been formed, chiefly for Americ[an] cheese. A good staff is kept in regular employment at both establis[h]ments, and the concern, as a whole, is one of the first of its kind, a[nd] commends itself strongly to the provision trade generally.

John Chadwick, Spice and Fruit Merchant, &c., 2[...] Hanging Ditch.—Manchester does a very heavy trade in all parts of t[he] country in seeds, spices, fruit, tea and coffee, &c., and among the fir[ms] engaged a prominent place is held by that of Mr. John Chadwick, whi[ch] was founded thirty years ago, and enjoys a widespread reputation. T[he] premises occupied are very extensive, admirably arranged for the prop[er] carrying on of the business, and comprise offices and stores. The sto[res] are large and spacious, and contain a vast stock of goods, such as musta[rd], spices, seeds, and fruits of every description, teas, coffees, chicory, coc[oa], rice-flour, soaps, candles, household and domestic materials, drysalte[ries], peas, beans, &c., and tinned goods of every description. These goo[ds] are highly esteemed for their general excellence, and those articl[es] so difficult to obtain, thoroughly genuine. The spices are ground [on] the premises by the most perfect and powerful machinery; the r[aw] material is imported from the choicest plantations, and the operations [are] carried out on the most improved principles. These valuable and use[ful] commodities are guaranteed unadulterated and absolutely genuine. M[r.] John Chadwick is sole agent for Nestle's Swiss milk and milk foo[d], employs a number of travellers, an ample clerical staff and other han[ds] and does a trade extending all over the country. He possesses unus[ual] facilities for obtaining the best goods, and is also enabled to deal gen[er]ously with his widespread connection. Promptness, ability, and enterpr[ise] are the leading features of his management, and he is of high commerc[ial] and social standing. This gentleman enjoys the esteem and confidence [of] the mercantile members of the city, and his house is of considerabl[e] influence in the trade.

F. Bosshardt & Co., Patent Office, Carlisle Chamber[s], 4, Corporation Street.—One of the leading and most reliable firms [of] patent agents in Manchester is that of Messrs. F. Bosshardt & C[o]. This business was established in 1879 and was removed to the prese[nt] offices in 1880. Mr. Bosshardt, the sole principal, is a mechanical a[nd] consulting engineer and draughtsman of recognised talent and abilit[y], and his long practical experience and sound judgment will be found [of] great value to inventors and parties seeking patents. His connections [in] all parts of the world are of a superior character, enabling him to offer sp[e]cial advantages to customers, and to execute all commissions in the prompte[st] and most satisfactory manner. He possesses special facilities for introdu[c]ing working, and selling inventions of merit, whether at home or abroa[d], and he has hitherto been most successful in this branch of busine[ss], which may be regarded as one of his specialities. Another branch [of] his business is devoted to foreign translations, all business being execut[ed] in an accurate style. Mr. Bosshardt is an enterprising and thorough[ly] reliable business man, and the success which is rewarding his efforts [is] both substantial and well deserved. It may be mentioned in conclusio[n] that all work connected with the patent business is invariably execut[ed] within the precincts of Mr. Bosshardt's own offices, which is an adva[n]tage of no small moment to those interested.

Bennett, Brotherton, & Co., West and South-west African Merchants, 31, Major Street. The mercantile firms of Manchester are known all over the world, the amount of business done representing millions of money, and the members are a very influential body. A well-known shipping firm is that of Messrs. Bennett, Brotherton, & Co., which was originally founded a number of years ago. The premises occupied consist of commodious offices and warerooms and extensive cellarage wherein the goods are packed by machinery. The warerooms contain a heavy stock of Manchester goods, and an ample staff is employed. Messrs. Bennett and Brotherton, the only members of the firm, are engaged in shipping Manchester goods from this house, and hard-

ware, earthenware, and general merchandise from the Liverpool house, to the west and south-west coasts of Africa, where Messrs. Bennett and Brotherton are necessarily thoroughly acquainted with the requirements of the markets, having had considerable personal experience on the coast, carrying on a good trade with the principal markets. The firm fully understand the requirements of the west and south-west coasts, and the goods dispatched are of superior quality, and bear their own stamp and trade mark. A keen judgment in all their buying transactions is exercised, and a deep knowledge of British industry is shown by Messrs. Bennett & Brotherton. These gentlemen manage with energy and enterprise, and they are well known and highly respected in the commercial and industrial world. Their status therein is of considerable eminence, and their house holds an influential place in the African trade of Manchester.

Pitt & Leete, Paper Merchants, 31 and 35, Fountain Street.—Messrs. Pitt & Leete are proprietors of a very large business as wholesale paper merchants and dealers, and occupy extensive premises. The house has been established some years, and a steady and increasing business is done. The manufacture of paper is so ancient that its origin cannot be traced at all, though the first record of cotton paper appears to have been written about the year 1050. Some persons have credited China with having originated the art. Certain it is that the production of paper was known there very long before it was ever manufactured in Europe; and even to this day their production of this article shows very great ingenuity of device, both in texture and art. Great improvements have been made in this trade, and the strides taken in the invention of different kinds of machinery have given considerable aid to the production of paper. A Mr. Joynson was one of the first to discover the method of giving writing-papers the finish they now possess. His suggestions were carried out by a Mr. Dewdney, owner of a paper-mill at Cullompton, Devon, who, after rendering valuable assistance to the manufacture of paper, met with a terrible death almost at the same spot where years before he had erected his engine for this trade. An express train killed him instantly. Messrs. Pitt & Leete deal in every kind of paper that modern machinery can make. Moreover, any special description required is made to order. The firm is managed by the two partners, Messrs. Charles Pitt and Thomas A. Leete, who keep a large stock and employ an efficient staff, and in every department is shown a thoroughly sound system of management. Messrs. Pitt & Leete have devoted considerable attention to the requirements of the trade, have earned considerable repute, and own a very flourishing business both at home and abroad.

J. M. Leigh & Son, General Ironmongers, 67, Deansgate.—In reviewing the trades and industries carried on in Manchester and the vicinity, the old-established and well-known firm of Messrs. J. M. Leigh & Son comes prominently under notice, as having for many years been closely associated with the commerce of this busy city. The general ironmongery establishment of Messrs. Leigh & Son forms one of the largest and most attractive premises in the busy thoroughfare of Deansgate. Formerly Mr. J. M. Leigh carried on business in Market Street for many years, when, owing to the increasing development of trade, he removed to the more extensive and commodious premises in Deansgate; these are admirably situated and well-adapted to the extensive trade carried on. Messrs. J. M. Leigh & Son hold one of the largest stocks in Manchester of general ironmongery, comprising a great variety of household requisites, as ranges, stoves, cooking apparatus, fenders and irons, chimney pieces, heating apparatus, culinary utensils, &c. This business in every department is conducted in a most spirited and enterprising manner, and employs a large staff of experienced workmen. Messrs. Leigh & Son have been long and honourably connected with this city, and by their well-known integrity have gained the esteem and confidence of a very high class and extensive connection.

J. O'Donnell, Umbrella Manufacturer, 173, Stretford Road.—Among the many branches of industry common to all cities, an important place is held by the manufacture of umbrellas. In Manchester this branch of industry is of considerable value, in an excellent condition, and employs many establishments. A most representative house in this line is that of Mr. J. O'Donnell, which has been in existence since 1852. The shop is spacious, the fittings are complete and in first-class style, and the general appearance is most attractive. All goods sold at this house are manufactured under the proprietor's personal supervision. There is a very extensive and fine display of umbrellas, ladies' and gentlemen's, and walking-sticks, the latter articles being in various woods and styles, and richly mounted, and a stock of ivories—the finest in Manchester. The wholesale branch is at 1, Milk Street, Phœnix Street, Fountain Street, where, in the busy season, a hundred and fifty hands are employed. The umbrellas are manufactured by able and experienced hands, and every care is taken in the selection of the material for all classes of umbrellas, from the cheapest to the most expensive. Mr. J. O'Donnell's specialty is "Indus Cloth," a material for covering umbrellas, and which has been proved to be most enduring. Mr. J. O'Donnell undertakes the re-covering and repairing of umbrellas and mounting of sticks, and he executes all work in a prompt and first-class manner. Extremely large stocks are held in all lines. He carries on a very fine local and extensive shipping trade of a good class character, and under his energetic management it is rapidly increasing. Mr. John O'Donnell, without doubt, is a most expert and proficient manufacturer, and since his first establishment has given universal satisfaction. He is deeply honoured for his admirable qualities; in fact, he is one of the most popular tradesmen in the district, and his house occupies a most honourable and commanding position in the umbrella trade of this country.

Henry Geo. Stephenson, The Barton Arcade China and Glass Shop, Deansgate and St. Ann's Square.—The Barton Arcade China and Glass Shop, Deansgate and St. Ann's Square, is the leading and most thoroughly representative establishment of its kind in Manchester. It was founded eleven years ago, by its present proprietor, and from its very inception has enjoyed a prosperous career. The premises occupied consist of a large and handsome shop, which is admirably arranged and equipped with every facility and convenience for the transaction of business, packing rooms in the basement, and an immense warehouse in the sub-basement, extending both under the Arcade and the Deansgate shops. An immense stock is kept. It includes every description of china and glass ware, including the finest and most artistic productions of the leading British and Continental manufacturers. Each department is stocked with the best and most desirable goods, affording a wide range for individual selection. Mr. Stephenson's connections and facilities are of a superior character, enabling him to promptly suit his customers in all their requirements. His patronage extends throughout all parts of the country. He does the largest business in the trade out of London, and giving it, as he does, the closest personal attention, those forming relations with him may rely upon receiving every advantage. It is such establishments as this that are the recognised exponents of the various branches of Manchester trade, and the success which Mr. Stephenson has achieved is unmistakable and well deserved.

T. H. Fitzsimmons, Manufacturer of Soluble Essences, &c., 97 & 99, Port Street.—Mr. T. H. Fitzsimmons has only been established here for the comparatively short period of two years, but he is now to be congratulated as the proprietor of a remarkably flourishing and highly creditable business concern. His well-known specialities in the shape of soluble essences, specially prepared for the mineral water trade, have become immensely popular, whilst, as an importer of essential oils, &c., and as a representative of Mr. Dan Rylands, of Barnsley, manufacturer of wire-bound boxes, Codd's patent soda-water bottles, and McEwen's patent soda-water machinery, Mr. Fitzsimmons also enjoys a very valuable connection. His premises in Port Street are fitted up in first class style, and the stock of goods on hand is invariably a large and unimpeachable one. Customers' orders receive prompt and careful attention, and a trial of this excellent establishment cannot result otherwise than in the unanimous verdict that it is a model of its kind and worthy of generous support.

Robert Andrews & Co., Manufacturers and Warehousemen of Velvets, Velveteens, &c., 83, Fountain Street.—Manchester is world-famous for her velvets, velveteens, and such-like goods, and the manufacture and trade employs thousands of hands. A well-known firm in this line is that of Messrs. Robert Andrews & Co., which was founded sixteen years ago and at once came to the front by obtaining an award of merit at the Exhibition of 1872, for the QUALITY and FINISH of their productions. Since that date the firm has built up a most extensive trade, and made their house one of the leading establishments in the city for genuine velveteens, which they have never disguised under coined names. The warehouse is centrally situated, well lighted, and a large stock is kept of black and coloured velvets and velveteens suitable for the home and export trade, although for the latter orders are usually received to dye and finish, often many months before the goods are required for shipment. Their fabrics possess great brilliancy of finish, softness, and durability, and the face pile is so much closer than French and German silk velvets that it is only natural the demand for these British-made goods should steadily increase. Messrs. Robert Andrews & Co.'s velvets and velveteens are used by drapers, dress and mantle makers, milliners and costumiers, children's costume makers, manufacturers of hats and bonnets, ladies' boots, boys' caps, jewel-case makers, wholesale clothiers, upholsterers, and many others. Consequently a very varied stock is necessary.

Messrs. Edward Cockshott & Co., 99A, Portland Street.—In reviewing the industries of Manchester, a branch of trade calling for especial notice is that carried on by the well-known house of Messrs. Edward Cockshott & Co., merchants and manufacturers, agents for plain and fancy grey goods, principally fine makes, &c. Established in 1861 by Mr. E. Cockshott, this house has always maintained a very high reputation, and is now recognised as one of the oldest established agencies in the city. The business operations are on a large scale; the products of many of the largest manufacturing houses of the north of England are on offer at the warehouse of the firm, whose connection is one of the best and most reliable, and includes the names of most of the best buying houses on its books. The premises occupied comprise a considerable-sized basement in which is held a large and valuable stock, and the trade conducted affords employment to an adequate staff of assistants and others, in addition to which there is a well-fitted office for the prompt transaction of the business of the firm. The whole concern exhibits an appearance of good order and management throughout. The business is now Mr. R. H. Berry's, he having taken it over at Mr. Cockshott's death, which occurred recently.

A. H. Alexander, Cotton Manufacturer, 14, Mulberry Street, Ridgefield.—This business was established more than thirty-five years ago by Messrs. Alexander & Veerers, and was located for many years at 57, Brown Street. The premises at Mulberry Street comprise a capital and spacious warehouse of five floors, and three roomy offices, handsomely furnished and fitted. The mills are at Bolton, some ten miles from this city. The specialities of manufacture are white and coloured lawns, jaconets, nainsooks, fancy muslins, and similar goods. The trade connection includes the leading shipping houses, the general Manchester warehousemen, and the best of the wholesale firms. A large amount of the goods manufactured by Mr. Alexander finds its way to India, China, Burmah, and other Eastern states. The sole proprietor is Mr. A. H. Alexander, a gentleman possessing a perfect knowledge of the trade, well known in commercial circles, and extremely popular on 'Change. Mr. Alexander is considered to be a liberal employer and a generous supporter of charitable and benevolent movements, especially such as are of local interest.

Richard Todd & Co., Merchants and Manufacturers, Silk and Cotton Embroideries, Mason Street, Swan Street.—The wholesale trade in English and foreign silk and cotton embroideries, constitutes a most important branch of commercial activity, and among the leading houses in this line is that of Messrs. Richard Todd & Co., merchants and manufacturers. From its very inception this business has enjoyed a prosperous career, a fact which speaks well for the enterprise and sound judgment displayed in its management. The warehouse and factory are of large dimensions, well arranged, and possess every facility for the transaction of business; a large staff of skilled hands is constantly employed. The warehouse contains a varied stock of English and foreign silk and cotton embroideries in process of manufacture, which for beauty of design and superiority of workmanship are unexcelled. The firm's home trade is of large proportions. Mr. Richard Todd, the head of the house, is a gentleman whose integrity and sound business principles have won the respect and confidence of the commercial community.

Messrs. Labrey & Walker, Wholesale Tea and Coffee Dealers, 10, Fennel Street.—In reviewing the great industries of the age, a branch which calls for especial notice is the wholesale tea and coffee trade, an industry of the highest possible importance and public interest. A leading house in this line is the well-known and far-famed establishment of Messrs. Labrey & Walker. Established in 1818, the business of this firm has been one of great extent and of a high class character for many years past. They enjoy a wide reputation for superiority of quality and general good management in all departments. The special features of attraction in the establishment of Messrs. Labrey & Walker, is the first-class brands of teas of India and China growths. Being large buyers, they have every opportunity of taking advantage of the fluctuations in the markets. In the department for coffees this firm are buyers of large parcels, consisting of fine East India, Costa Rica, and Ceylon and other well-known growths, the full benefit accruing from large and important transactions being fully participated in by their numerous patrons. The premises comprise large and attractive offices well fitted and arranged for the transaction of their extensive business. The stores are literally filled with a choice stock of teas, coffees, &c., representing considerable money. The firm employ many representatives, whose avocation takes them into several of the northern counties. The connection is widespread, the house of Labrey & Walker being well known in these counties. The sole partner is now Mr. Jonathan Walker, a gentleman well known and widely respected for high integrity and commercial probity.

Alfred M. Hind, Engraver, Steel, Copper-plate, and Lithographic Printer, Stationer, Bookbinder, &c., 44, Lloyd Street, Albert Square.—Lithographic printing, stationery, bookbinding, and account-book manufacturing form one of the most important businesses in connection with the internal economy of Manchester. It is very valuable, and among the many establishments engaged a principal place is held by that of Mr. Alfred M. Hind. This business was originated forty-five years ago, by Mr. J. C. Hind, the father of the present proprietor, who has proved himself a worthy successor, and has greatly increased the connection. The premises, consisting of offices and workrooms, are large and commodious, the former being well furnished and adequately manned. The workrooms are admirably equipped with the necessary machinery and appliances for lithographic, steel, and copper-plate printing, special attention being given to portrait and other work of this class, bookbinding, and account-book making, and an efficient staff is employed in these operations. The printing turned out is in every way first-class, the bookbinding is durable and handsome, and the account-books produced are noted for their first quality of paper and material and their suitability for rough wear and tear. There is a splendid stock of superior quality in general stationery, and Mr. Alfred M. Hind makes every effort to maintain the high reputation of his house. He carries on a very heavy local business, and the management throughout is all that could be desired. Mr. Alfred M. Hind is one of the most popular business men of the district, and bears the highest name for unfailing honour, courtesy, and talent.

G. W. Belshaw, Insurance Manager, 1, Cooper Street.—Mr. G. W. Belshaw occupies a large suite of offices, and is engaged as district representative for many large and important associations. This is probably a somewhat unique business. It was established in Spring Gardens in 1877, and removed to present offices subsequently. His business deals almost exclusively with insurance work, and of this he has such a quantity that he is compelled to keep a very large staff of clerks and assistants. His offices are very large and fitted up in a most superior style. Among the many important companies for which Mr. Belshaw is district secretary may be specially mentioned the Liverpool Plate Glass Insurance Company and the Glasgow and London Fire Insurance Company. He is also district manager for the important association known as the Scottish Employers' Liability and Accident Assurance Company. In all these and many others Mr. Belshaw does such an amount of business that his offices are among the best known in Manchester. The care with which the interests of the public are guarded by Mr. Belshaw has given this firm a splendid reputation, and the connection is continually on the increase.

William Lund & Co., Shipping and Forwarding Agents and Insurance Brokers, 28, Brunswick Street, Liverpool.—This firm was established in 1883, and in its line is one of the best known firms out of Manchester. The company are shipping and forwarding agents and insurance brokers, and have secured a first-class connection. They do a large business as contractors for the transport of machinery, railway material, bale and case goods, &c., &c., besides receiving and "clearing" all kinds of merchandise arriving from foreign ports. They possess extraordinary facilities for shipping heavy and bulky articles and materials, and are therefore largely patronised by railway contractors, engineers, &c. The head of the firm (Mr. William Lund) is a gentleman of energy and enterprise; consequently the business is conducted on the best lines, and shippers may rely on having their interest carefully looked after. The scale of charges is very moderate.

Julius Lazarus, Agent for Continental Fabrics, 89, Spring Gardens.—The trade in this country in Continental fabrics is very considerable, and among the Manchester houses engaged as agents in this direction a leading place is occupied by that of Mr. Julius Lazarus, at the above address.

Keeble Bros., Hay and Straw Merchants, 41, Corporation Street.—In reviewing the trade industries of Manchester and districts, a special branch calling for prominent notice and observation is the provender department. A representative centre in this interest is the well-known house of Messrs. Keeble Bros., at the above address, and controlling a large and important business of hay, straw, and chaff merchants at Peterborough. Established in Manchester some few years since, this house soon obtained a high reputation quite in consonance with that of its other well-known branch, and the result was a trade of rapid growth which quickly reached considerable proportions. The speciality of this house is high-class quality, for which the firm are already well known and noted throughout the city and suburbs. Being large buyers, the proprietors are enabled to offer very special advantages to the public and their patrons, not obtainable at most similar establishments. They supply finest old English meadow and clover hay of exceptional good quality in quantities to suit their customers, at prices bearing favourable comparison with any other houses. They also supply straw, chaff, oats, &c., &c. The premises in Manchester comprise a well-fitted office admirably arranged and adapted for the requirements of the business with necessary staff of employes. The manager, Mr. Edwin C. Frow, is a gentleman of high commercial status, well known and widely respected.

J. & T. Guerin, Copper and Brass Merchants, Steel and Iron Manufacturers, 61 & 69, Addington Street, Rochdale Road, and New Allen Street.—In a vast commercial centre such as Manchester, where machinery of the heaviest and most costly kind is so extensively in demand, the copper, brass, iron, and steel business is one that if properly conducted is almost certain to win prosperity. Such a business is that carried on by Messrs J. and T. Guerin. This notable concern was established in 1838, and its career since has been one of unqualified success. This is due to a variety of causes, the energy and well-directed and exercised ability of the owners being the chief factors. The partners have secured extensive and commodious premises, which are admirably arranged and fitted with the most improved and effective machinery. The warehouse, which is very spacious, is fully stocked with all sorts of copper and brass, steel and iron, in various conditions and in many items ready for immediate use. Sheets, bars, rods, angles, pipes, tubes, and the numerous copper and brass articles in general use by millowners and machinery users in general, may here be purchased in the very best qualities and at prices unsurpassed for moderation by any other similar establishment in the city. The trade of the firm is widespread, and among the soundest and most desirable classes of customers, at home and abroad. A numerous staff of skilled operatives is employed, both at the works and in the city warehouses and offices. The manager is very able and energetic, promptitude and liberality characterize all his transactions, and, taken all round, the firm is one of the most popular of its kind in our city.

W. Wilson & Son, Estate Agents, &c., 20, Fountain Street.—The prosperous and flourishing firm known as William Wilson & Co. was established in Manchester about forty years ago, and is one of the best known in the city. In about four years, the business had grown to such large proportions that it was found necessary to remove into more commodious premises; and the handsome building known as 20, Fountain Street, was accordingly selected for the purpose. The premises are very extensive, affording a great deal of accommodation, and the offices are well arranged and excellently fitted up and comfortably furnished. A very large and widespread business is done in the agency of estates, sales by auction, and valuing; and Messrs. Wilson have a long record of successful operations in this direction. Many of the finest properties in the county are placed in their hands for disposal by private contract or otherwise, and in every case the utmost care and diligence are shown to secure the satisfaction of both buyer and seller. As auctioneers, the firm has a high and well founded reputation, which extends far beyond the city of Manchester; and as valuers for assessment, probate, or other matters, their services have received frequent recognition at the hands of the best judges. They are largely employed as valuers and arbitrators in railway and compensation cases arising under the Land Clauses Consolidated Acts. Prompt and punctual in all their dealings, possessed of a high personal charact-r, and moderate in their charges, Messrs. Wilson have achieved a solid success, and have secured a commercial standing which is second to none.

Thomas Pattinson, Silk Merchant and Commission Agent, 11A, Piccadilly.—In reviewing the great industries of the age a prominent position is taken by the merchants and brokers of all commercial centres; they form at once the mainstay of business, and are the channels for the outlet of the vast productions of our manufacturing industries. A representative establishment in this branch of industry is the well-known house of Mr. Thomas Pattinson, silk merchant and commission agent for raw and thrown silk, as well as for manufactured goods. Established in 1857, the business has been for many years very extensive, and this firm has now become one of the largest in the raw and thrown silk trade. While the principal establishment of the firm is at Manchester, Mr. Pattinson has places of business at Old Broad Street, London; Market Street, Leek; and Park Green Mill, Macclesfield, besides representatives in other silk centres.

Messrs. B. Duckworth & Sons, Warehousemen, 48, George Street, and 16, Turner Street.—The warehousemen of Manchester rival in numbers and importance those of London. In their very front rank must in justice be placed the widely-known firm of B. Duckworth & Sons, whose spacious, commodious, and admirably arranged premises are prominent among those of the leading houses in the city. In 1863, Mr. Duckworth started in a small way as a fent dealer, and from the very inception of the business success attended his efforts. He occupied premises on the site of which Messrs. J. & N. Phillips's new premises have been built. Increase of business compelled a removal from there to Nicholas Croft, where the firm was located for some years. Trade still continued to improve and the new premises in Turner Street were erected, and there up till 1883 the operations of the concern were conducted with great energy by Mr. Duckworth and his sons. Shortly after taking possession of the Turner Street premises, the sons, each, took up a different branch of business, which consists of prints, cretones, furnitures, woven cotton goods, twill silesias, fancy coloured and printed linings, cotton italians and satteens, white and grey calicoes, dress stuffs and woollens, also a remnant department which contains all kinds of cotton, woollen, and stuff fents and patchwork. In this branch there are a large number of females constantly employed. Mr. Duckworth is assisted in the management of the concern by his sons Edward, Charles, Thomas, and Joseph.

John Owen & Co., Limited, Foreign Fancy Goods Importers, Bassinette Manufacturers, 49 & 51, Shudehill.—This extensive and well-known firm of fancy goods warehousemen and manufacturers was established in 1824, and carried on for many years by the late Mr. John Owen. Some few years since, greatly in consequence of the immense development the business was undergoing, it was converted into a limited liability company, under the title of John Owen & Company, Limited, since which change it has gone on enlarging its trade and extending its connections in the same rapid manner, until it has become the largest and most important undertaking of the kind throughout the whole of the north of England. The items stocked, all merit in connection with which may be claimed as entirely due to the firm, have attained to so high a reputation that no fewer than three prize medals have been accorded them. They include billiard-tables, bassinettes, rocking-horses, bath-chairs, merlin-chairs, and a variety of other articles of the same description, all the best of their kind that can be produced. Every improvement in material, construction, and shape that ingenuity has up to the present been able to devise has been freely introduced, with the most gratifying result. At the Globe Steam Works, Pendleton, where the manufacturing branch of the business is carried on, many hundred work-people are employed, and every mechanical appliance is brought to bear which can facilitate the despatch or improve the quality of the work. The warehouses of John Owen & Co., Limited, at 49 & 51, Shudehill are replete with an immense variety of stock, both of English and foreign manufacture, including French and German toys of all descriptions, portmonnaies, combs, brushes, and perfumery, purses, Gladstone bags, portmanteaus, writing desks, workboxes, concertinas, &c.; cutlery and jewellery, albums and inkstands, cricketing and archery requisites, electro-plated goods, &c., &c., all of the best quality and the most artistic patterns and designs. The firm have also a large magazine for fireworks situate at Clayton, where many tons of fireworks are stored. The firm employ travellers, but rather for the convenience of their customers in the transaction of present business than for the purpose of seeking fresh, their name having become so well and so favourably known as to bring them an abundance of support without putting them to the necessity of seeking it.

Hodson & Waddington, Upholsterers, 135, Great Ducie Street.—Everyone must be familiar with the splendid premises of Messrs. Hodson & Waddington. This firm was started in 1871 by Mr. Peter Hodson and Mr. Heman Waddington, the present proprietors. The business carried on is that of cabinet makers, upholsterers, and carpet warehousemen. In connection with this there is a very large manufactory in Trafalgar Street, Broughton, where workmen are employed in the many different branches of the trade with which this firm is connected. The show-rooms and warehouse in Great Ducie Street are of splendid appearance, and fitted out with a well-assorted stock. The appearance of these premises is very fine, and some handsome suites of furniture are here displayed. Messrs. Hodson & Waddington have a very extensive trade, and their business is a constantly increasing and prosperous one. The firm have executed some very large orders in the supply of furniture, and they are noted for the sound manner in which every article is manufactured. Due regard is paid not only to the appearance but to the question of strength and durability, an important consideration in this class of goods. Estimates are given for the entire furnishing of large houses, and are always carried out in the most complete and artistic manner. A great deal of business is done in the way of furniture removing. Messrs. Hodson & Waddington have some very large vans, and are enabled to remove large quantities of furniture without the inconvenience of packing. These vans are to be seen all over the district. Altogether the firm is very prosperous, a result due greatly to business-like and skilful management.

J. Fryer, Wholesale Druggist, Drysalter, and General Merchant, 103, Shudehill.—A trade in Manchester of considerable magnitude, special importance, and in the highest state of excellence, is that of drugs, drysaltery, and general merchandise. The members of the trade are a body enjoying universal respect, and exercising no small influence in the commercial interests of the city. An admirable example of a house in this trade is that of Mr. J. Fryer, which is the oldest-established business of its class in the city of Manchester. Mr. J. Fryer has built up a very fine trade, and established a sound and healthy reputation. The premises occupied are extensive and commodious, fitted up in a complete and superior manner with the necessary appliances and fixtures for stock accommodation. There is a very large stock of drugs and drysaltery of the utmost purity and reliability, and general merchandise, such as meals, biscuits, butterine, candles, soaps, tinned meat, lobsters, sardines, salmons, vinegar, seeds, spices, groceries, staple and fancy confectionery, nuts, dried fruits, cigars, patent medicines, paints, oils, gunpowder, and an array of other goods for household and other purposes too numerous to particularise. His show of Christmas goods surpasses any we have seen. These goods are of superior quality throughout, and are selected from the leading sources, Mr. J. Fryer, by reason of his long and varied experience, being especially successful in this task. His catalogue and price-list contain a very great variety of goods, and Mr. J. Fryer has special facilities for procuring goods not in stock. He carries on a very considerable trade, his travellers calling at every town, village, &c., within a ten-mile radius of the city, and all goods are delivered by his own lurries, carts, &c., free of expense. Mr. J. Fryer's trade knowledge and experience, the judgment he exercises in stock buying, enable him to deal most liberally with his connection and those about to commence business. Over fifteen hands are employed in the business, and Mr. J. Fryer manages his establishment with ability and experience. His splendid business is proof of his talent and upright method of conducting his establishment, and he is well known and deeply esteemed in the trade.

Reade & Wall, Manufacturers of Plain & Fancy Muslins, Ginghams, &c., 97, Portland Street.—This establishment constitutes the warehouse department of the manufacturing business established, about the commencement of this century, by Messrs. Reade & Redfern, and carried on under the style of Reade & Wall since 1843, here and elsewhere, as manufacturers of plain and fancy muslins, ginghams, &c., on a very extensive scale. The mills are situated at Leyland, near Preston, and the firm have a branch warehouse at Bradford, Yorkshire, and another in Distaff Lane, London. The central warehouse, in Portland Street, is exceedingly commodious and well arranged in every respect, eminently adapting it for carrying on the large business which is here conducted. The stock kept here is a very large and heavy one, as may be judged from the fact that no fewer than thirty warehousemen and assistants are required to handle it. It embraces every variety of stuff that Messrs. Reade & Wall are engaged in producing, and in connection with which they have obtained an almost world wide celebrity. Their home trade extends over the whole of the United Kingdom, in the principal parts of which they are represented by their own travellers and agents. Of their foreign trade of course it is difficult to speak definitely, as it is not only carried on by themselves to a very large extent, but their various manufactures are purchased in the open market by shippers and the agents and representatives of many home and foreign houses. It is not going too far to say of this firm that there is no market, however distant, which their goods do not reach, and on which their name is not known as manufacturers of stuffs which are in every respect thoroughly reliable. Everything about the establishment in Portland Street, which may be characterized as the centre of their business operations, bears testimony alike to the extent of the ground they cover and the soundness of the principles on which they are conducted. The firm stands out conspicuously as an example of what a great English manufacturing and mercantile firm should be, a fact which is shown by the universal respect and esteem in which its members are held.

Messrs. Meglaughlin, Marshall & Co., Wholesale Provision Merchants, 3 and 4, Corn Exchange.—An important industry in Manchester is the large provision business ably represented by the well-known house of Messrs. Meglaughlin, Marshall & Co., provision merchants and importers of eggs, who have branch establishments at Liverpool, Limerick, Waterford, and Kilkenny. Established upwards of fifty years, the reputation of this firm is first-class and widespread; the business operations are on a very extensive scale, and may be said to comprise transactions with every commercial centre of note throughout the length and breadth of the kingdom. First-class American provisions, from the best curing establishments, are imported by this house in very considerable quantities, and form an item of great importance in its business transactions. Their speciality is the heavy trade in eggs; in this staple article of food this well-known importing house does a larger business annually than any similar establishment in the city, their supply being drawn from all parts of the Continent as well as from Ireland. There are several travellers in the employ of the firm, whose avocation takes them to all the chief commercial towns of note. These men do an extensive business among the best buying houses, all of whom are well acquainted with the system of business adopted by the firm. The premises occupied comprise offices and large stores, neatly fitted and arranged. The stores are thoroughly adapted to the purposes required, and contain a very large amount of high-class provisions of every description, representing a large equivalent in capital, and affording employment to a good staff of hands. This house, with its various branches, may justly be considered one of the largest and most important in this branch of trade in Great Britain. The gentlemen comprising the partnership are Messrs. John Meglaughlin, Isaac Honeyford, John Marshall, and Robert Barry, well known men, of the highest commercial status and widely respected.

G. P. Lee, Vernon Works, Longsight; Warehouse, 62, Tib Street.—Among the leading and most deservedly successful industrial enterprises in the vicinity of Manchester are the Vernon Works, Longsight, of which Mr. G. P. Lee is proprietor. This business was established about thirty years ago, and the annals of Manchester's commercial progress contain no more interesting example of well-directed energies and successful results than is to be found in the career of this concern. From a modest beginning the trade has steadily developed and increased, being to-day of large and prosperous proportions. The works are equipped with the most improved modern machinery and appliances, employment being given to upwards of 250 skilled hands. Mr. Lee is the manufacturer of a number of standard specialities including the "Ariel Bassinette," which obtained the highest and only award given for Perambulator Bodies, at the International Inventions Exhibition. It is unequalled for beauty and originality of design and superiority of workmanship. Being made of fluted steel, it always retains its perfect shape, each one being a fac-simile of the other. Ariel Bassinette Carriages can be had from all the principal makers in Great Britain and Ireland. Mr. Lee is also a manufacturer of Bessemer steel wire, Bessemer steel mattress chair and sofa springs, imitation hair seating, patent seating, patent glacé gimps, patent fancies, banding and carriage lace. These articles are made from the very best materials, in the most skilful manner, and have a standard reputation in the trade. With the unsurpassed manufacturing facilities at his command, Mr. Lee is enabled to offer special advantages to the trade, and to execute all orders in the promptest and most satisfactory manner. Such has been the success of the business that we understand Mr. Lee, at the invitation of many of his friends, has under consideration the formation of his business into a limited company, when the works will be greatly extended, owing to the increased facilities for the further development of the various branches of his business. It is such establishments as this that are the best exponents of the various branches of Manchester trade, and they well deserve the prominent position which the enterprise and ability of their proprietors have so unerringly attained. Mr. Lee is one of our most highly respected business men, and he has at all times been an active supporter of every movement having for its object the welfare of Manchester.

Cooper Bros., Cork Manufacturers, 12, Hanover Street, Shudehill, and Derby Mills, Long Millgate.—During recent years cork has been largely utilised, and a great variety of articles are fashioned out of this valuable substance. Manchester does a good trade in this direction, one of the best firms engaged being that of Messrs. Cooper Bros. It was founded by the present proprietors eight years ago, and since that time they have worked up a very large trade and earned a good reputation. These premises are large and commodious, consisting of a spacious three-storied building well stocked with cork, English and foreign corks, wood shives, vent-pegs, twine, and a large number of other articles. The works, known as "Derby Mills," at Long Millgate, are extensive, specially arranged for the business, and fitted in a complete manner with the most perfect machinery and appliances. The cork is imported from the best sources, and the hands employed able and experienced. A very good trade is carried on in the city and surrounding counties, and by the efforts of the travellers engaged, it is rapidly increasing. Messrs. Cooper Bros. are most expert and proficient in all branches of the manufacture, and pay great attention to its improvement.

Joseph Grave & Co., Merchants and Manufacturers, 39 and 41, Lloyd Street.—Prominent among the trade industries of Manchester and district, the operations of merchants and manufacturers call for especial notice. A representative establishment is the well-known house of Messrs. Joseph Grave & Co., leading merchants and manufacturers, founded nearly a quarter of a century ago under the same title. This house has from its very inception made a reputation of a high character, and the establishment ranks among the very foremost of its compeers. Conducted upon strictly modern business principles, the patrons are offered sterling advantages in the shape of high-class goods at very favourable quotations. The business transactions of the firm are upon a large scale. They hold large stocks of Hessians, sackings, and all kinds of jute and linen fabrics, and other packing materials. The premises occupied comprise a large and handsome warehouse, admirably arranged and adapted to the requirements of the business, with well-fitted offices on the ground floor, and afford employment to an adequate staff. The principals are gentlemen well known and of high commercial status and the strictest integrity.

Pool & Clewley, Manufacturers and Agents, 16, Faulk- Street.—This firm, being now well established, is doing a large and in- asing business. The premises consist of a commodious warehouse, and a te of convenient offices handsomely furnished and substantially fitted th the most approved apparatus for the rapid dispatch of business. The ncipal departments are devoted to bandanas, India corahs, fancy silk ndkerchiefs, ladies' scarfs, China shantungs, tussores, Madras handker- iefs, pongees handkerchiefs, black Brussels, China shawls, salampores, d similar goods. The trade connection is very considerable, though for most part local. It includes many of the leading shipping houses, general Manchester warehousemen, and the wholesale firms. At the rehouse a capable staff of salesmen, warehousemen, and clerks are em- yed for the transaction of their business. The sole partners are Mr. arles B. Clewley and Mr. Henry Pool. They are manufacturers specialities for the African, Indian, China, and South and Central nerican markets.

Wm. Prescott, Joiner and Packing-case Maker, rray Street, Blossom Street, Great Ancoats Street.—Considering the de of Manchester with home and foreign ports, it is easily understood w great must be the demand for packing-cases of all kinds. One of the ding houses devoted to the production of these commercial requisites is t of Wm. Prescott, in Murray Street. This concern was established hteen years ago by the present proprietor, who is an expert and actical man, and thoroughly *au fait* in all the details of the city quirements in this particular line. His factory and store rooms are cious, and in all respects suited for the extensive conducting of such a siness. They are possessed of all mechanical aids in the shape of steam ws, planing machines, and other appliances that can in any way save bour and expedite work. Vast numbers of packing-cases of every scription are made daily and find a ready sale to shippers, exporters, d manufacturers requiring such goods, and consigning to home and reign ports. Mr. Prescott has exhibited great talent and energy in e management of his concern, and his prosperity is the merited reward unflagging industry.

Mr. S. M. Rochead, Turkey Red Dyer, Cloth and arn and Handkerchief Printer, 27, Faulkner Street.—Prominent nong the industries of modern times is the scientific art of the dyer, a anch of the greatest possible public utility, and ranking high among mmercial enterprises of the day. The well-known house of Mr. Stuart . Rochead is a representative centre of this branch of trade, and is well own as a house standing high in public estimation, and enjoying a very eat reputation as being at the head of its department. Established any years ago, this firm has long been known as a first-class "shipping use," with a large and very widespread home trade. The specialities nsist of Turkey red dyer, cloth and yarn and handkerchief printer. ese two branches comprise special features in the art of dyeing and inting. The principal is a gentleman well known and of high com- ercial status, and highly respected by an ever-increasing circle of trons.

Earp, Son, & Hobbs, Architectural Sculptors, 63, ower Mosley Street.—One of the most valuable professions in Manches- r is that of the architectural sculptor, and the members are a highly lented and honoured body. A thoroughly representative house in this e is that of Messrs. Earp, Son, & Hobbs, which was founded in 1850. essrs. Earp, Son, & Hobbs are most talented sculptors, and they have orks at Little Canterbury Place, Lambeth Road, Lambeth, London. he premises are of moderate dimensions, ample for the calling; they are ll arranged, admirably fitted up, and there is a very fine stock of arble, alabaster, stone, and wood. Messrs. Earp, Son, & Hobbs carve redoses, fonts, pulpits, monuments, chimneypieces, &c., in any material, d fix the work in any part of the country; and they undertake the rving of churches and public buildings, employing thereat an experienced aff of carvers. Their work is of great beauty, of original and artistic sign, and some commissions recently executed—statue of the late Hugh rley, M.P., tomb for the late Bishop of Manchester, and carving for anchester Cathedral, are magnificent specimens of the craft. From all rts of the country the firm receives commissions for every branch of e profession, and a large staff of experienced and talented sculptors and rvers is employed. The members of the firm are Messrs. Thomas and rthur Earp and Edwin Hobbs, gentlemen who have in all parts of the untry splendid evidence of their talent and skill. In the artistic world d in business circles they are received with honour and esteem, and ey are generally recognised as masters in their profession of archi- tural sculptors.

John Wilkinson, late Manley & Wilkinson, Corn erchant & Flour Agent, 32, Hanging Ditch.—Messrs. Manley & ilkinson, corn merchants and flour agents, have been established in anchester for a period of about six years. The business is now rried on solely by Mr. John Wilkinson, and is of a thriving character, and the connection is extensive. He is agent for the following well- known and leading firms: Heinr. Haggenmacher (prize medal Hungarian flour), of Budapest; J. F. Milner, Woodside Mills, Elland; Edward Hutchinson, Mersey Mills, Liverpool; Cadge & Colman, millers, of Peterborough; R. Robinson & Son, oatmeal and groatine manufacturers, Annan, Scotland; and S. M. Macrory, Limavady, and Ardmore, Ireland. At 6, Bradshaw Street, Shudehill, Mr. Wilkinson has an establishment for picking peas, which affords employment to a large number of hands.

David Mayor, Chemist and Druggist, 83, Chancery Lane, Ardwick.—A most important and useful profession is that of the chemist and druggist, who dispenses the prescriptions of the physician and very often in some neighbourhoods does a great deal himself for the relief of pain in simple cases. The well-known establishment of Mr. David Mayor is one of very old standing and excellent reputation. It was originally founded in 1840, and has ever since been expanding and increasing in repute until it has reached its present large dimensions. It is now a handsome establishment, nicely fitted up in the best style with good taste, and is exceedingly well stocked with all the requisites which go to make up a first-rate dispensing chemist's establishment. Mr. Mayor's great experience and excellent professional training enable him to select with unerring judgment all the best drugs, chemicals, and other prepa- rations, and his establishment is renowned for the purity of everything dispensed from it, and for the thorough reliability and exactitude of its proprietor in the delicate and important operations of making up pre- scriptions. In consequence of this Mr. Mayor enjoys a very large amount of patronage amongst the most distinguished physicians of the neigh- hood. Prescriptions are often sent to him from distant places to make up, so great is the confidence placed in him, and so widely has his name become known as a dispenser. In addition to his chief establishment in Ardwick, Mr. Mayor has a branch one of considerable importance in Manchester, which is situated at 209, Great Ancoats Street. Here also a dispensing and prescribing business is done amongst the busy popula- tion of this important district. Mr. Mayor is greatly respected and esteemed for his kindness and skill in this locality, and both here and at Ardwick enjoys the respect of a very large circle to whom he has endeared himself by his uniform courtesy, attention, and readiness to oblige in all emergencies, and at any hour of the night, at whatever personal discomfort to himself. Throughout his long and honourable career Mr. Mayor has also distinguished himself by an unswerving in- tegrity and uprightness of conduct which have gained for him the universal respect of all around him.

Geo. Floyd, junior, Law and Wholesale Stationer, Lithographer, Printer, &c., 13, Norfolk Street, and 40, Kennedy Street. —Mr. George Floyd, junior, has been established for many years as a Law, Ornamental, and Lithographic Writer and Printer, and Wholesale Stationer. He occupies the basement of the building, 13, Norfolk Street, and also has a branch establishment in Kennedy Street. We have inspected specimens of Mr. Floyd's ornamental work, executed by work- men specially trained by himself, and for the purposes of Illuminated Ad- dresses, Testimonials, and other kinds of Artistic Penmanship, have not seen anything superior. For Law and all kinds of ordinary Copying and Engrossing Mr. Floyd employs a staff of competent writers, undertaking the copying singly or by lithography of any written or printed matter, and the addressing of circulars, envelopes, or wrappers on most reasonable terms, a fact little known to the public; and he especially excels in all kinds of Plan Work, which he will either copy, reduce, enlarge, or lithograph with the utmost accuracy, and we have reason to believe, from some books of plans, Conditions of Sale, and other matters to which our attention was called, that his work is of a very superior order; and one book containing letterpress, lithography, elaborate plan work, and also interspersed with numerous photographs, was an excellent example of tasteful arrange- ment, and we are surprised at the moderate cost of its production. Mr. Floyd has also launched into the Wholesale Stationery business, pur- chasing direct from the makers, and being content with very moderate profits; has transactions with some of the leading Commercial Firms in the district, supplying them with every article of plain and printed matter, such as note-paper, envelopes, invoices, statements, &c., giving his personal attention to the execution of this class of trade, in which we predict him a successful future, of which he is certainly deserving for his enterprise and painstaking attention to the minutest details of his business. We spent an interesting half-hour in Mr. Floyd's establish- ment, and wish him prosperity in all his undertakings.

William Mills & Co., Woollen Manufacturers and Merchants, 12, New Brown Street.—This well-known firm are noted for the excellence of their productions, and carry on a large business, princi- pally in the various classes of woollen goods, such as Bayeta de Glen Hilos, Frazadas, Pellons, saved-list baizes, flannels, blankets (white and dyed), striped fancy rugs, ponchos, &c., &c., suitable for the South and Central American, African, and other markets. The facilities possessed by this firm enables them to offer many special advantages to their clients.

F. Thompson & Son, Auctioneers, 1, St. Ann's Place.—One of the best-known firms of auctioneers, &c., in Manchester, is that of Messrs. Frederick Thompson & Son. This was established in 1871 as Frederick Thompson, and assumed its present title in 1881. The premises occupied have been in possession of the firm about ten years. The offices are very large and extend over two or three storeys, and a large staff of clerks is employed. The business embraces the usual branches of auctioneers' and valuers' work, with valuations for probate, legacy, transfer, &c., and is one of the most noted in the city. An auctioneer holds a very important position, undertaking as he does so many different varieties of business, and is responsible to his clients for skill and prudence. Very important duties in connection with legacies, transfers of businesses, &c., have to be fulfilled, and it is indispensable that an auctioneer and valuer should be eminently trustworthy. Messrs. Thompson & Son have a very first-class reputation throughout the district, and, with a widespread connection of the best order, there is no firm held in higher estimation by the Manchester public.

G. & W. Yates, Seed Merchants and Seed Growers, 28, Market Place.—The progress that has been made during the past few years in what is known as the seed trade has been simply marvellous. Seed merchants and seed growers have sprung up throughout the country with wonderful rapidity, and the seed industry is now a most important one. Amongst the foremost of the many firms engaged in it is that of Messrs. G. & W. Yates, which was started as long ago as 1826, and Messrs. Yates are the proprietors of one of the oldest and best-known commercial concerns in the city of Manchester. Their trial grounds at Heaton Norris are admirably arranged, and the seeds they supply are all tested ones. The business carried on is comprehensive in the extreme, and may be classed into the following departments: (1.) *That for vegetable seeds.*—Here some choice novelties are continually being successfully introduced in the shape of peas, beans, Brussels sprouts, broccoli, cabbages, cauliflowers, carrots, celery, cucumbers, lettuces, onions, radishes, turnips, seed potatoes, and so on. (2.) *Flower seeds.*—All the flower seeds are delivered carriage or post paid to any part of England, name, height, and colour being printed on each packet. The collections are composed of the most beautiful and effective flowers, so that amateurs who are unacquainted with the more recently introduced species and varieties may be furnished with such only as are calculated to maintain throughout the summer and autumn months a rich and gay floral display. Special collections are sold at moderate prices for sowing in gardens of various sizes, and a complete list is published and forwarded annually to their customers of such seeds as are most suitable for growing in the northern and midland counties. A large number of attractive novelties have been introduced in this department for 1888. The "Exhibition Victoria Aster," for instance, is one of the most beautiful in cultivation; the flowers are perfectly double, imbricated, globular, and of great size. Among other specialities are the "Exhibition Ten-Week Stock," "Phlox Drummondii grandiflora," "Pansy Trimardeau." "Virginian Stock (fairy queen)," &c. (3.) *Farm seeds* carefully selected by the most eminent English and Continental growers, form a separate department of their trade. The grasses and clovers are thoroughly cleaned from weeds by special machinery; Swede turnips and mangold have been improved by special selection at their seed trial grounds, and take prizes at the leading shows of the district. (4.) *Plants, trees, and shrubs.*—Their nurseries at Heaton Norris, covering fourteen acres, are well stocked with every variety of ornamental and fruit-trees, roses, greenhouse and other flowering plants. (5.) *Bulbs and other flowering roots.*—These, including hyacinths, tulips, crocuses, &c. are imported direct from Holland, France, and Germany in immense quantities, the demand for these beautiful harbingers of spring having enormously increased of late years. (6.) *Garden sundries.*—Of these a very superior stock is kept on hand, including lawn-mowers, garden-sticks and labels, insecticides, garden frames, implements, &c., of all descriptions for horticultural purposes. The management of the firm is first class, and the attention paid to customers all that could be desired. Messrs. Yates are now enjoying a widespread and valuable connection, and they certainly well merit the high estimation in which their concern is held.

J. Hothersall & Co., Cotton Manufacturers, 42, Corporation Street.—This firm has been established at this address for about ten years. Their factories are situated in Dutton Street, Manchester, also at Ramsbottom and Colne, and the London warehouse is at 5, Falcon Street, E.C. They have also agents in Belfast, Dublin, Glasgow, New York, Paris, and on the Continent, &c. Messrs. Hothersall & Co. manufacture large quantities of what are known generally as Manchester goods, such as Oxfords and Harvards, Checks, Towels, Fancy Cloths, Flannelettes, and all kinds of Dusters. They are the patentees and sole manufacturers of several articles known as "Hothersall's" specialities, including the Patent Chamois Leather Cloths, Ladies' Towels, Sanitas, &c. They are proprietors and manufacturers of the following registered goods: "Industry" and "Swansdown Dusters," &c., &c. They also carry on an extensive business in Dutton Street Mill as Engine Waste, Sponge Cloth, and Government and railway store contractors, having on their books Government, large home and colonial railways, engineers, &c. The business connection is very large and widespread, extending over the whole of the United Kingdom, while
a good many of the productions
tities by various city merchants. T
prise a handsome suite of three
houses, very well furnished and
clerks and salesmen finds steady a
members of the firm take leading
John Hothersall is sole partner.
thorough knowledge of the cotton
for his high character and abiliti
tending towards social improvem
schemes of technical and second
thoroughly with plans of municip

N. Thierry, Boot Make
the things which, with all our in
"they do better in France," is hi
leading tradesmen are compelled
have long ago ceased to buy any
Foremost in the trade may be
Thierry. The principal manufac
Mer, but there are several fine
places, while the splendidly situa
this city, is acknowledged to be th
in Manchester. The first consid
the firm since its foundation fo
perfectly easy though elegant fit,
and the best materials. Independ
measure, the firm has always bee
ment of ready-made boots. Mr.
great feature of his business to k
kind of boot and shoe *equal in qu*
over, having adopted a system o
some cases five, widths to each le
same sizes and kinds), the great
without any trouble or loss of tim
who through disappointment, or
fitted and get a good article at sh
commendable policy has been a
amount of business done; so th
hundred people, while the firm'
capital in Europe, the United St
round the well-filled cases in the
one that boot-making, as practise
ful art, and that in clothing th
display of great ingenuity and re
which a stock of not less than 10,
endless variety of styles, shapes, a
riding boots to the neatest walkin
shoe to the stout winter button or
shoes there is a unique display
required, walking, riding, shooti
wear. Every boot bears the impr
ably adapted to the purpose inten
and marked in plain figures on ea
is under able management, and all
patronage are sure to receive the
attention.

Mr. L. Kaufman, W
Goulden Street, and 50, Marsh
Manchester, the wholesale cabi
importance. This branch of t
well-known house of Mr. L. Ka
specialities of this concern are b
walnut, pitch pine, and painted, f
drawers, kitchen dressers and tab
lished now some years in Manc
business has made very rapid st
manufacturer of his goods, Mr.
positive accuracy to his patrons
well seasoned, &c., also to guar
largest furnishing establishments
scale, much of their best and gu
&c., are the product of this estab
keen-sighted and appreciative pu
an extensive warehouse of three s
exceedingly well arranged and a
first-rate highly skilled artisans, s
best journeymen cabinet-makers
held are very considerable, some
for polishing and sending out at s
house is that no rubbish is manuf
under any consideration whatever
reliable, and first-class. The mar
there is nothing in connection wit
obtain elsewhere. The principal
practical knowledge of his busines

Wm. Oram & Co., Steam and Hydraulic Engineers, eengate, Salford.—The manufacture of steam and hydraulic machinery a branch of industry, for the extent and perfection of which Man-ester enjoys a splendid reputation, and the firms engaged therein are y numerous. A capital house in this line is that known as Messrs. illiam Oram & Co. (the sole member being Mr. William Oram), Green-te, Salford, which was originated in 1827. The works are exten-e and are replete with the most powerfully constructed machinery d appliances for the business carried on. A force of skilled hands is ployed manufacturing steam engines for working presses; hydraulic

chinery for packing cotton, wool, hemp, jute, &c.; bowl presses for king callender bowls; presses for pressing oil out of cotton, linseed, .; lifts, &c. Well worthy of attention is Mr. Oram's new Patent uble-Action Hydraulic Packing Press, which possesses very great vantages over the ordinary packing press as used at present, its speed ing three to four times greater, with the same number and stroke of mps. This press is constructed with two rams, a large one and a all one, the small one, one-third diameter of large one, and when the ss is started, the water from the pumps acts upon the small ram (say ten in. diameter) only, until it attains a pressure of 3,000 lbs. per are inch. During that time, the large ram, which is being raised by small one, which gives a pressure of two tons per square inch, sup-es itself with water direct from the cistern, and then the pumps act on both rams together, giving a total pressure of an eighteen-inch n. The press is simple in its construction, not at all likely to get out order, and the improvements may be applied to existing presses of y description, valve motion connected to any of the ordinary stops in . The advantages gained by these presses are, that only one-third of water used is forced in by the pumps—less engine power and wear d tear. These machines are constructed with great care, are of any uired power, and in every detail the workmanship is excellent. Mr. illiam Oram carries on an extensive trade in all parts of the United ngdom, exports considerably, and manages his business with ability d enterprise. During his long establishment he has brought his ductions to the highest state of perfection, and has won the esteem d confidence of the entire commercial and industrial world, whilst house has done much to improve and advance the manufacture of draulic machinery. Mr. William Oram is the inventor of the Hydraulic rect-acting Crank Pumps and the Patent Valve Motion, for working a mber of presses without having to stop the pumps in changing the ssure from one press to another. He is also maker of horizontal ect-acting pumping engines, with pump plungers fixed to each end piston-rod for Hyde presses, and maker of horizontal high-pressure idensing steam engines, with Hartley's patent arrangements for nitting and shutting off the steam from the piston and cylinder of am engines according to the varying steam pressure, or load upon engines. Also an arrangement and construction of double-acting -pump in connection with a steam-engine condenser and hot-well, ereby the vapour-condensed steam and water can flow by their own vity, or, otherwise, from the condenser into the air-pump, without ring to pass through intermediate foot or other valves. Hence, by arrangement the ordinary foot-valves are dispensed with, and only ivery valves are required, through which the air-pump plunger-aket forces and delivers the condensed steam water and air into the t-well.

Hancock, Campbell, & Russell, Joiners and Packing-se Makers, 43, Granby Row.—One of the leading and most enter-sing firms of joiners and packing-case makers in Manchester is that Messrs. Hancock, Campbell, & Russell. This business was estab-hed thirty-six years ago, and from its very inception has enjoyed a sperous career. The firm do a widespread and permanent trade as ners and packing-case makers, turning out work of the best descrip-n. Among their patrons are many of the leading manufacturers and merchants of Manchester and district. They employ a staff of competent workmen, and as they give the closest personal supervision are enabled to offer special advantages to customers. Mr. John Campbell and Mr. Charles Russell, the members of the firm, are enterprising and thoroughly reliable business men, liberal and fair in all transactions, and well deserving of the substantial success which is rewarding their energetic efforts.

William Macpherson & Sons, Valuers and Auctioneers, Mechanical Engineers, &c., 35, Market Street.—There are but very few people indeed who have had any practical experience in the mercantile world who have not at one time or another felt the great importance of obtaining the services of a man who could give a correct estimate of value, &c., of mills and other works. Indeed, it requires considerable ability to carry out the functions of a valuer with success. The firm of William Macpherson & Sons, however, have, during the past twenty-two years, earned a high reputation for this class of work. The head of the firm is a mechanical engineer, and in that capacity has also distinguished himself. Added to these qualifications, William Macpherson & Sons have proved themselves most trustworthy and successful as auctioneers, and in this latter part of their business enjoy a very considerable patronage, particularly in the locality. It is almost needless to add that this popularity is well deserved, and that it is the result of ability and merit.

J. & D. Macnair & Co., Makers of Methylated Spirit, 29 and 31, Robert Street, Cheetham.—This business was founded in the year 1840, and has been carried on most successfully up to the present time. The premises consist of a spacious warehouse of two floors and a suite of offices, which are well fitted up. The firm possesses also a warehouse and works at Dalmarnock Road, Glasgow. The principal specialities of production and trade are methylated spirit, finish, shellac, button, garnet, and white lac, Arabic benzoin and other gums, wax of various kinds, glue, olive and other oils. The trade connection is very large and extremely widespread, covering indeed the entire kingdom and requiring the services of at least three commercial travellers. The sole proprietor is now Mr. Andrew D. Macnair, a gentleman who is thoroughly well experienced in the drug and drysalting trades, a chemist of considerable attainments, and a practical business man, who is everywhere highly respected and esteemed.

Richardson & Creighton, Yarn Agents, 8, New Cannon Street.—Great enterprise and ability is exercised in the agency business in connection with the Manchester yarn trade, and among the leading houses engaged in this agency, a prominent place is held by that of Messrs Richardson and Creighton, telegraphic address "Kriton". This well-known firm was established some seven or eight years ago, and since that date the energetic and able members have secured a very enviable connection, which is extending in a gratifying manner. A very good trade is carried on, the firm having a fine connection among manufacturers, spinners, and merchants, with whom it stands in high favour owing to promptitude shown in transacting the business, and the reliability of the various yarns supplied. Messrs Thomas Richardson and Charles A. Creighton, the members of this flourishing firm, are well known in the yarn trade, and thoroughly understand every detail. They pay every attention to their business and deal most advantageously with their influential connection. These gentlemen are highly esteemed in mercantile, social and industrial circles, and no house bears a higher reputation than that of Messrs Richardson and Creighton.

John Edmunds & Son, Estate Agents and Valuers, 29, Cannon Street.—Among the many estate and insurance agents of Manchester, an exceptionally prominent and lucrative position has been secured by Messrs. John Edmunds & Son. They began operations close on a half a century ago, in the year 1843. Mr. John Edmunds founded the business, and conducted it alone for many years. Afterwards his son William joined in the concern, and renewed vigour was infused into the management. The results of this were soon visible in the rapidly increasing stream of business with which the firm was favoured. Many years ago the founder died, and since that event Mr. William Edmunds, the son, has alone conducted the establishment on the old lines and with even more satisfactory results. The representation of the Royal Fire and Life, Edinboro' Life, and the North of England Fire Insurance Companies has been secured, and for each a highly profitable business is being done. The Ocean, Railway, and General Accident Guarantee Companies, Limited, of Mansion House Buildings, London, is one of the corporations represented, and others equally important have their interests attended to by Mr. William Edmunds. Both in the estate and insurance branches, the efforts of the house have met with more than average success, its long standing and the integrity of those responsible for its management being the best guarantee for fair dealing and prompt attention to all the interests confided to it. Personally Mr. William Edmunds is very popular, and this is only the just result of a blameless career.

Norwich Union Life Insurance Society, Branch Office, 1, Clarence Street, Albert Square.—The excellent institution known as the Norwich Union Life Assurance Society was established in 1808. It is conducted on the increasingly popular mutual principle, the whole of the profits belonging to the insured, and there being no proprietary to absorb the surplus. Guided by the experience of over three-quarters of a century, the directors offer the provident public every advantage of which life assurance admits, it is a significant fact that since the commencement of the society upwards of 49,000 policies have been issued. Claims have been paid amounting to eleven millions sterling—a sum, by-the-bye, which is exclusive of the policies issued by the Amicable Society, which ancient corporation, established by royal charter in the reign of Queen Anne, 1706, was in 1866 merged by Act of Parliament in the Norwich Union. In the New Series, the rates of premium, it is worthy of mention, do not, on comparison, exceed those of other societies making large early bonus additions to their policies. The profits are divided in proportion to the premiums paid between the periods of division, and the bonus to which each policy will be entitled will be then converted into its equivalent addition to the sum assured, or applied in extinction of premiums, according to a commendable and very satisfactory scale. Among other features of the society, bonuses standing to the credit of a policy may at any time be surrendered for an equitable equivalent in cash. Premiums may be paid yearly, half-yearly, or quarterly by a single payment, or by a limited number of payments. When the premiums are to be paid for whole life insurances by five, ten, fifteen, or twenty instalments, each instalment secures a proportionate part of the sum insured if further payments are discontinued. Such policies are non-forfeitable. A "half-credit" system is in force according to which one half of the first five annual premiums may remain unpaid as a charge upon policies of £300 and upwards granted for the whole duration of life (certain cases being, at the discretion of the directors, excepted). The debt thus incurred may be paid off at any time during the continuance of the policy, or it may be deducted from the amount paid to the representatives of the insured when the policy becomes a claim. Such policies are entitled to bonuses as if the full annual premiums were paid. Policies may also be effected under the "half premium" system without debt or interest, under which no arrears of premium are incurred. This society also issues policies of insurance where the amount is payable to a member on his attaining a specified age, or to his executors in the event of previous death. The premiums charged for such endowment assurances are exceptionally low, being less than those required by nearly every other life office. Policies conferring the same advantages as those just described are also issued with large guaranteed bonuses in addition, which have been managed so as to enhance to the utmost the investment element in the policies without unduly increasing the rates. To produce this result the bonuses have been payable only on the attainment of the given age. Thirty days of grace are allowed for the payment of premiums after they become due, and policies that have been forfeited by non-payment within the said thirty days may be revived by the directors at any time within twelve calendar months from the date at which the premium in arrear fell due, on the production of satisfactory evidence that the life is in good health, and on the payment of a small fine. With regard to foreign residence and travel, residence in time of peace in any part of Europe, Egypt north of the second cataract, the Holy Land, Malta, Madeira, the Canary Islands, Natal, Cape Colony, the Australian colonies "south of 25° of south latitude," and in every other part of the world (excepting Asia) "north of 33° of north latitude, or south of 30° of south latitude," and passage by sea between any places within the above limits, are allowed free of charge for extra premium to all persons not being engaged in any military, naval, or seafaring service, or in gold or diamond digging. But "whole-world" certificates cancelling all restrictions as to foreign travel and residence are granted at the date or during the first five years of the existence of a policy, on such terms as, according to circumstances, may be deemed fair and reasonable; whilst no additional premium is charged for insuring the lives of naval and military men, unless when called into active service, and no liability is incurred by serving in local militia or volunteer corps. With reference to the surrender of policies, it may be mentioned that values are allowed of whole-life policies on which not less than three annual premiums have been paid: but no surrender value is attached to half or third premium policies until the sixth annual premium has been paid, nor to policies for terms of years only. In lieu of a surrender value a free or paid-up non-profit policy for an equivalent sum, payable at death, may be obtained, subject to no further payment of premium. Payments of claims under policies are made three months after receipt of satisfactory proof of the death of the insured, but, the title being clear, they may be paid under discount before the expiration of the three months. No charge is made for entrance fees or policy stamps, and loans are granted on the security of policies to nearly the amount of the surrender value. The chief offices of the society are situated at Surrey Street, Norwich (secretary and actuary, J. J. W. Deuchar, Esq., F.I.A., F.F.A.), and in London at 50, Fleet Street, E.C. (manager, T. Muir Grant, Esq.); the treasurers being the well-known and much-respected firm of Messrs. Gurneys & Co., Norwich. Among the many highly successful branches and agencies that are scattered through the kingdom—notably at Manchester, Leeds, Liverpool, Newcastle-on-Tyne, Glasgow, Dublin, &c.—that at Manchester is undoubtedly one of the most important. Under the careful but no less capable superintendence of Mr. Charles Naismith, the energetic manager,
a large and influential business i
no small praise for the able man
accruing to his important and on
way in which he has placed befo
tional benefits belonging to m
Insurance Society. The society
sessing the services of such an o
discretion in the selection of th
valuable as it undoubtedly is fro
a very considerable portion of it
at 1, Clarence Street, Albert Sq
find that every courtesy will be
to insure him the best of all poss

William Allen, Hydr
Brass and Iron Founder, &c.
Ancoats; also Phœnix Iron W
Among the many branches of M
very important place, as in all la
The large quantity of powerful a
chester factories, workshops, &c.
engineering and other branch tr
advanced condition. Among th
a very good place may be fairly
Union Brass and Iron Works.
prietor over thirty years ago, an
extensive trade, extending all ov
ing on business as general engi
the manufacture of steam and h
fittings and appendages used
house are steam engines, steerin
pumps, and all kinds of pum
machinery of every description
tion it may be noted that the fir
engineering establishments of
being coeval with the birth of t
colour mixing, and drying mach
fire appliances of all sorts, and t
variety. In the last mentioned
manufacturers in the North of E
bodies in all parts of the worl
commenced on his own account
his indomitable pluck, energy,
his success is a bright exampl
severing efforts and honourab
superintends, now cover an area
them. He was an exhibitor at t
great strides have been made in t
been given to the manufacture o
Allen has not been slow in maki
approval. The premises occup
works, and warehouse. The
the most modern machinery and
ment being given to close upo
workmen. The warehouse is
goods, conveniently arranged a
venience of visitors and patrons.
the United Kingdom, is rapidly
energetic and pushing, the orde
Mr. W. Allen, the owner of this
ability and spares no efforts or
deserve the confidence of the pu
known and highly respected by
and acknowledged merit comma
have transactions with him and

Booth, Son & Co., Tea M
Place, and Hodson's Court, Cor
has been established about twen
its line in this district. The prem
and store-rooms, with the neces
latest improvements in applianc
The speciality is a capital ass
Booth, Son & Co. have a reput
trade, however, includes tea of
China, Java, and Japan. The
packet teas which have a well-
tion, although very comprehen
far beyond the city boundaries,
hundred miles of the Cathedral
sentatives of the firm. The staff
or six, and the whole are consta
house a brisk trade is done w
selection from stock. The s
blenders, and clerks. The mem
trade, and are as much at hom
Ditch, Manchester. It may be
special study.

, **Hotel**, 19, 21, and 23, to Manchester and residents of familiar with the Albion Hotel, on for such a business concern. lass houses in the city, and its ons confer upon it many advan-. The concern is very old-esta-ominently in the columns of the of *Cowdroy's Manchester Gazette*, Robert Wilson, a well-known proprietor, and the hotel was , and commercial magnates of it presents an attractive and of which there are about one

ing-rooms are furnished with ort and homeliness of visitors' ad of the best English and Con-of both, so that the substantial d viands of France and Italy are ent is of the most energetic and ccess attained, and the extensive et and homely establishment.

Pool Fold Chambers.—The Continent, colonies, and all parts o East, keeps the shippers whose with a profitable trade. Among e city is that of Mr. John N. tensive shipping trade in Man-and Mediterranean ports, com-He has been established over concluded that he is intimately onsignees to the ports named, and connection among the mer-ict, to whom his ability and the in his hands are perfectly well e in all business matters have l esteem.

ts: Flannels, Blankets, dens.—The woollen trade of this great importance, and Manchester, ss in this direction, enjoys a wide-merchants engaged in this trade is was established twenty-five years present premises, which are large and offices. The warehouse is valuable stock of woollen goods, es, felts, druggets, railway rugs, from the most noted manufac-ellence take a place in the market nsive, and the arrangements for all details. Mr. John Bell, the old-established firm, is a gentle-is highly esteemed for his un-

Timber Merchants and Mill- 11, Granby Row. This is one of the oldest and best-known firms in the packing-case trade in Manchester, and merchants, shippers, drysalters, drapers, confectioners, and all, in fact, requiring boxes either of wood, tin, or zinc, will find everything to suit their respective requirements upon application to Thos. Roebuck & Co. The trade carried on by them is considerable, and to a very large extent local, and excellence of manufacture, combined with moderate charges, may be depended upon. Besides the box-making branch of the business, an extensive trade is done in every department of joinery, and a speciality is the manufacture of lap and velvet boards. The firm has been established for about forty years, and the connection enjoyed is a remarkably good and steady one. The works, where a large number of hands are engaged, are kept going in a most satisfactory manner, and the superior degree of excellence attained in their manufactures is most commendable, and reflects the highest possible credit upon this well-managed and enterprising concern.

George Benson & Son, Estate Brokers, Valuers, and Accountants, 8, York Street.—The estate, brokerage, valuation, and accountancy business of Manchester is of very great value, engaging many establishments, and the members are a talented and highly respected body. A substantial house in this line is that of Messrs. George Benson & Son, which was originally founded twenty years ago by Mr. George Benson, taking its present designation in November, 1881. The offices are large and well furnished, and an adequate staff is employed. In all branches of the estate, brokerage, valuation, and accountancy business Messrs. G. Benson & Son are thoroughly proficient, and they have a large connection among estate and property owners, and in the industrial and commercial world. They carry out all commissions in a prompt and most satisfactory manner. Messrs. George Benson & Son, the only members, are gentlemen well known in the city, and deeply esteemed for their honourable business methods and courteous demeanour, and their status in the estate brokerage, valuation, and accountancy business of Manchester is most influential.

Mrs. Elizabeth Matilda Georgina Croxton, Florist, 6, Market Street.—This business was established in the year 1879 under the same title, and may fairly claim to be one of the most important of its class in the city. The business premises consist of a charmingly appointed and elegantly fitted sale shop, in the very best situation in Manchester; and the connection attached to it is of a very high-class character. The specialities consist of a very superior class of floral decorations, suitable for all occasions and every purpose, from the simple gentleman's button-hole to the most elaborate and proportionately costly table decorations for wedding breakfasts, ball suppers, and banquets, for church and altar decorations, and for the sadder and more melancholy occasions of death and burial. In the latter purposes Mrs. Croxton has a well-assorted stock of dried and artificial flowers, and a great variety of metal and porcelain wreaths and crosses, with the necessary glass shades and cases for their proper protection. Mrs. Croxton's floral displays are a great attraction to the fashionable residents of the city, and the exquisite taste invariably displayed in the arrangement of the various decorations and the making-up of bouquets is as uncommon as it is commendable.

John Taylor, Leather Merchant and Mill Furnisher, 84, Corporation Street.—Mr. John Taylor, leather merchant and mill furnisher, has been established in Manchester for about thirty years; his well-conducted concern is one of the oldest and best of its kind in that locality. Some five years ago, the growth of the business necessitated a removal to the present handsomely appointed premises. The trade carried on has been extended throughout the United Kingdom, and a fairly good shipping business is also transacted. The goods supplied by Mr. Taylor are comprehensive in kind, and of the first quality obtainable. Millowners particularly will derive much satisfaction from a visit to this well-known firm. Customers are treated with every courtesy, and their orders are attended to with the utmost care and despatch; his prices are moderate in the extreme. Small profits is evidently the motto of Mr. Taylor, whose enterprise and high-class management are deserving of more than passing praise.

J. E. Lawton & Co., 38, George Street (**Agents for Sir Richard Arkwright & Co.**, and others).—Many of the agents in Manchester, who represent leading firms, do a business of considerable magnitude. Such is true of Messrs. J. E. Lawton & Co., who act only for the concerns for which they are the accredited agents. Amongst these are some of the leading and oldest cotton spinning and manufacturing houses. Sir Richard Arkwright & Co. was established by the great inventor of the spinning jenny, in 1769, and the business has since been uninterruptedly carried on. The present members of the firm being Mr. Frederic Charles Arkwright, of Willersley Castle, the lineal descendant of the founder, now High Sheriff of Derbyshire, and Mr. J. E. Lawton, who acts as managing partner. Energy and limitless resource and tact in all branches of business have ample scope for their exercise. With what excellent results they are employed the position held by the firm of Arkwright & Co. best shows, and gives conclusive proof; and the same may be said of Messrs. J. E. Lawton & Co.

Lewis's, Market Street.—One of the most prominent landmarks of Manchester, from a business as well as architectural point of view, is Lewis's in Market Street. Lewis's magnificent house of business is as well known in Lancashire and the surrounding districts as the Bank of England is in London. Manchester is a city of warehouses, and as the acknowledged seat of the manufacturing drapery trade it is only to be expected one will find drapery establishments of gigantic proportions and of considerable architectural pretensions. Of all the Manchester warehouses, Lewis's stands out alone, holding a unique position, for it is at Lewis's that the experiment was first tried of devoting wholesale advantages to the supplying of retail wants. Established in 1879, it was so found that the original building (a fine specimen of the Italian style architecture) was but ill adapted to the rapid growth of trade whi Lewis's experienced from the very outset. Additional premises w acquired and rebuilt to suit the purposes of Lewis's business. The re is the magnificent pile of buildings, a splendid advertisement in its which cannot fail to catch the eye of every visitor to Manchester. Lewi business is a wonderful example of modern commercial progress. addition to Lewis's trade with the local population, Lewis's have acqui fame as the producers of what is now known all over the world

"Lewis's Wonderful Velveteen." Lewis's do not employ travellers or agents, who as a rule are extensive factors in the ordinary Manchester wholesale trade, but have relied on the power of the press and the postage stamp to bring their wares before the notice of the people. Lewis's have one speciality only, and that consists in making Lewis's *the* house of the district, and offering the buyer terms of such genuine advantage and v as to place all fears of competition out of the question. The heads of firm are gentlemen of high position, of great business abilities, amongst the leading representatives of the commercial interests of day.

The North of England Fire Insurance Co., Limited, Chief Office, 87, Market Street (Secretary, Mr. John Wainwright; Assistant Secretary, Mr. Edward S. Heap).—The importance of insuring houses and goods against fire was first brought home to the public mind by that dire calamity, the Great Fire of London, and in the following year (1667) we find the earliest record of an insurance against fire in London. It was, however, not until 1696 that the first regular insurance company was established, and from that time the business steadily increased and fresh companies entered into competition, until in 1800 it was calculated that the sums insured in the different offices amounted in the aggregate to over £200,000,000, and at the present day the insurance world is one of the most important and considerable interests of our commercial system. Whilst the principal share of the fire business has not unnaturally gravitated towards London, the chief provincial centres have not been backward in supplying their own needs in this direction, and amongst the offices which have been established to cater for the requirements of the great trading interests of the north, one of the most enterprising is the North of England Fire Insurance Company, Limited, whose last report and balance sheet, issued from the chief office at 87, Market Street, Manchester, furnishes abundant proof to the effect that the company is in a thoroughly sound and healthy condition and fully merits the cordial support of intending assurers. Without entering fully into actuarial details which must be dry and uninteresting to the general reader, it may be stated that it is satisfactory to find that, with a progressive and rapidly increasing premium income, the proportion of losses is each year less and less, whilst with characteristic caution and conscientiousness, the directors have set aside considerable amounts to expenses accounts and against unearned premiums. With an ample reserve fund and assets invested in thoroughly safe and well-recognised securities, the position of the company must be considered entirely satisfactory and worthy of confidence. Whilst the directors have very properly made it their first duty to build up the financial position of flourishing company, they have by no means neglected the task enhancing its reputation with the class of assurers from whom t business is chiefly derived. The fact that every year has shown a stea augmenting business arising from fire risks of the best kind is the su testimony that could be desired of the satisfaction and approval of company's customers. This gratifying and profitable result has been chi attained by attention to two points: firstly, the operations of the comp have been confined to fire risks of the best, that is the *safest*, class; the more speculative kinds of business, such as risks connected w cotton and woollen mills, &c., where the chances of a conflagratio any moment are necessarily constant and very great, have not b accepted under the head of the general business of the company. Secon or perhaps the matter should be more properly as of primary importa the directors have endeavoured by a prompt and liberal recognition of just claims placed before them in a bona-fide spirit to earn the support confidence of the commercial public. Special facilities have been affor in cases where, in the judgment of the directors, there was room for s little concessions, and the results of this liberality have been agree manifest in the accession of new business. The large and influen body representing the pawnbroking trade have been catered for in a wi considered and successful spirit of enterprise. For their great suc with this trade the directors are mainly indebted to the efforts and w known influence of their resident secretary in Liverpool, Mr. A. Hardal The board of direction comprises the names of gentlemen of influence substance whose gratifying success in the conduct of the business the company has added to their reputation as men of business abi and foresight. The company has established branches at 27, Nich Lane, London, at 1, Crosshall Street, Liverpool, and at 51, West Reg Street, Glasgow, and is further represented by an influential body agents in most of the principal towns in Great Britain.

Samuel Lawton & Sons, General Finishers, Waterers, and Embossers, 2, Stevenson Square.—This firm was established in the year 1866, by Mr. Samuel Lawton, who had previously occupied the position of foreman to the firms of Messrs. Brocklehurst, Macclesfield, and Messrs. Kemp, Hoyle & Co., Middleton, the latter firm giving up business in 1866, when Mr. Lawton decided to establish a business for himself, and the result has proved an eminent success. From 1866 to 1870 the business was largely developed, through Mr. Lawton's untiring energy and personal attention to all the various classes of dress goods which were continually passing through his hands, and during the first four years it was twice found necessary to remove to larger premises. In 1870 the convenient and extensive works called Cross Street Finishing Works, and situated at Middleton, were erected, and fitted with the most modern and improved machinery. The finishing of zephyrs, Oxfords, &c. &c., was added, and also the finishing of prints and batistes. In the latter class of goods, which previously were finished in Glasgow, Mr. Lawton soon acquired a reputation, which may be safely said to stand unequalled. In 1880 the business of embossing silks, satins, velveteens, silk velvets, plushes, &c., was added, and soon proved very successful. Within the last few years the watering of silks has been included, and we believe that this is the only firm in England which can do the moiré antique watering so fashionable at the present time. In 1885 Mr. S. Lawton died, and since that time the business has been carried on by his three sons, viz. Mr. Peter Lawton, Mr. Harry Lawton, and Mr. Tom Lawton, under the name of S. Lawton & Sons. The firm are also well laid out and largely engaged in the finishing of all kinds of upholstery and tapestry goods. The warehouse at 2, Stevenson Square, Manchester, is chiefly used as a receiving house for the purpose of taking in goods to be dealt with at Middleton, where Messrs. Lawton's finishing and embossing works are kept in constant employment in this peculiar but important part of our great staple industry. In this department Messrs. Lawton have acquired a reputation which may be said to be unequalled.

few others in the same line having had the advantages, both in respect of a practical acquaintance with every part of the many processes involved in "finishing," and of the experience resulting from having so large a quantity of different kinds of work continually passing through their hands. To how great a degree of perfection the art of "finishing" has been carried may be seen at a glance by those who have had the opportunity of comparing almost any kind of Manchester goods of the present day with the same class of goods produced fifty years ago. In this art, which may almost be termed a science, Messrs. Lawton & Sons may be said to have attained the highest degree of perfection, and the high position now occupied by them in the commercial world is but the just reward of an enterprising firm.

John Phethean & Co. (Limited), Spinners and Manufacturers, by power, of Cotton Sheets, Alhambra Quilts, White and Coloured Counterpanes, Toilets, &c., Royal Hotel Buildings, 126, Market Street, and 3, West Mosley Street.—Among the many branches of the cotton industry of Manchester a very important place is taken by that of the spinning and manufacture of what may be called household goods, such as sheets, Alhambra quilts, white and coloured counterpanes, toilets, &c. A well-known firm engaged in this industry is that of Messrs. John Phethean & Co. (Limited), which has the reputation of being one of the leading houses. It was established about sixty years ago, and has enjoyed a most prosperous career, and was turned into a Limited Liability Company in 1885, under the present name of Messrs. John Phethean & Co. The premises occupied by the firm for the last fifteen years are large and extensive, and comprise offices and warehouses. The offices are spacious and furnished in a first-rate style, employment being given to a good staff of clerks, whilst the warehouses are very commodious, and stocked with a vast number of quilts of every description, cotton sheets, white and coloured counterpanes, toilet covers, tapestry covers, and curtains in elaborate designs and colours, and a great many other similar articles. The works are at Moses Gate, near Bolton, and are very extensive, covering a large area of ground, and admirably equipped with the most powerful and modern machinery and appliances used in the manufacture, and a large number of able and experienced hands are employed. The trade done is very heavy and widespread, the house enjoying a reputation for quality and workmanship all over the kingdom, particularly for the China and Indian markets. The leading member of the firm, Mr. John Phethean, is a man of great ability and experience in the business, and manages the establishment in an admirable manner. He is well known in the manufacturing and commercial world, and is highly respected for his unswerving honour and undoubted abilities, whilst the house occupies a well-defined and leading position in the cotton industry.

J. Boothman, Wholesale Boot, Shoe, Upper, and Slipper Manufacturer and Leather Factor, 14 and 16, Dantzic Street, and Hooley Bridge Factory, Heywood.—Of the larger local firms, one of the best known is that of Mr. Jonathan Boothman, boot and shoe manufacturer, currier, and leather factor, whose imposing premises form quite an interesting feature of the locality, even from an architectural point of view. Mr. Boothman commenced business here about fourteen years ago, and the history of what is now a flourishing concern, is one of substantial progress, instituted by skilful management, and marked success. The goods produced by this firm have achieved a reputation throughout the midlands, the north, Scotland, and Ireland, for a general and particular excellence that would be somewhat difficult to beat; and the enterprising manner in which Mr. Boothman caters for his numerous customers well merits cordial commendation, and fully entitles that gentleman to a generous return. Mr. Boothman has recently opened a large boot factory at Hooley Bridge, Heywood, near Manchester, where he has commenced the manufacture of all kinds of boots, shoes, and slippers, and all descriptions of tennis shoes He has just returned from the

United States and Canada, where he has purchased a great variety of machinery for the manufacture of boots and shoes, and which is now being put in motion. This outlay is calculated to lessen the cost of production and to increase the output to an enormous extent. There is in this factory one machine of which Mr. Boothman has secured the patent right for the United Kingdom. This machine will rivet the soles on a thousand pairs of boots per day. This gives some idea of what can be done by this new and improved machinery which Mr. Boothman has introduced into the shoe trade. We may mention that this trade is quite a new industry in this part of Lancashire. It will prove of great value to the district, as many of the large cotton mills in this part of the country are entirely unable to run the machinery now in use for the production of cotton goods. They have consequently been closed, and a large number of the inhabitants have removed to districts where mills to accommodate such machinery have been built. This additional employment of labour must prove a great boon to the town of Heywood. We may add that Mr. Boothman has for some years given great attention to the export trade, and his goods are well known in most of the leading stores of South Africa.

John Hough, 5, Newton Street.—Amongst the representative commercial establishments of Manchester deserving of prominent mention in this historical review of the city's leading industries is that of Mr. John Hough. It was originally founded in 1856, by Paine, Bowden, & Hough, becoming Paine & Hough in 1863. From 1869 to the present time Mr. John Hough has been sole proprietor. From a comparatively small beginning the business of the house has steadily developed and increased, its growth being in keeping with the enterprise and sound principles which have always characterised its management. The warehouse in Newton Street is heavily stocked with a large assortment of goods, including Brussels, tapestry, and Kidderminster carpets, Axminster, tapestry, and velvet rugs, mattings, druggets, printed tablings, cabinet cloths, quilts, table covers, linoleums and floor-cloths, Oxford, Harvard, and Grandrill shirtings, shirts, white and coloured flannels, kerseys, serges, linseys, blankets, railway rugs, army cloths, Spanish stripes, and other woollen cloths, &c. Each department is replete with the best goods in the market, and taken altogether form probably the largest and certainly the best assorted and the most complete stock of its kind in Manchester. Mr. Hough's connections among manufacturers are of a superior character. He does a large home and export trade. This is one of the recognised exponents of the various branches of Manchester trade, and the success it has achieved is both substantial and well-deserved. Mr. Hough is one of our most respected merchants. He has always taken an active interest in every movement having for its object the permanent welfare and advancement of Manchester. He has been a magistrate for the city since 1879.

John Munn & Co., Grey Cloth and Yarn Agents, Fountain Street.—A conspicuous commercial establishment in Cottonopolis is the well-known house of Messrs. John Munn & Co., grey c and yarn agents. This business was founded about the beginning of present century, under the style of John Munn, grey cloth, &c., ag The business grew rapidly, and in 1820 his two sons, Robert and J became associated with him in the business, Robert being the fath the present Robert Whitaker Munn, the partner in the firm. The fi title was altered to John Munn & Co., which designation it has down to the present time. The present partners are Robert Whit. Munn, J.P., of Heath Hill, Stacksteads, Manchester, and James Hoo Shird Fold, Poynton, near Stockport. The premises are very large, form a lofty conspicuous block of buildings, and comprise warehouses offices, the former containing a large and most valuable stock of g cloths, yarns, &c., in every variety and texture, and by far the large its kind in the city. The offices are spacious, well fitted and furnis and an adequate staff of clerks and assistants is employed for the sp transaction of the business of the firm. The reputation of this hou world-wide. The name of John Munn & Co. is so thoroughly known by all the leading buyers of the United Kingdom, as to pas once for a trade mark or guarantee of sterling quality. The principa the firm are gentlemen well known and widely respected, Mr. M whose residence is Heath Hill, Stacksteads, near Manchester, holding a l position and being much respected as a prominent and influential citi

---

Coates, Brothers & Co., Printing Ink and Varn Manufacturers, and Lithographic Stone Importers, 20, M Street.—The manufacture of printing ink and varnish is an impor and advanced branch of industry extensively carried on in Manche and London, as well as several other large towns in this country. Manchester, for the value of her trade in these goods, is behind no o city. A thoroughly representative house in this line is that of Me Coates, Brothers & Co., which was founded in 1875. This house, u the management of Mr. George Bunyan, is the branch establishment this part. The headquarters are at London, 74, Fann Street, E.C. West Ham. The firm also has houses, conducted by agents, in mingham and Glasgow. Messrs. Coates, Brothers & Co., are also n as fine colour merchants and importers of lithographic stones and br powders. The Manchester premises are commodious and admir fitted up and heavily stocked with inks, printers' sundries, colours, Previous to the establishment of this house, travellers and agents cov this ground, but now Mr. George Bunyan is the sole representative. productions of this firm are simply perfect, and in all parts they ar great demand. Mr. G. Bunyan supplies the whole of the connection the northern counties, which means a trade of great value. Me Coates, Brothers & Co., are gentlemen who have, by untiring ene and honourable methods and undoubted talent brought their product to the highest state of perfection, and throughout the industrial commercial world the name of Coates, Brothers & Co. is well and hig respected, and looked upon as one of the principal printing ink varnish manufacturing firms in the United Kingdom.

Higginbottom & Co., Chemical Manufacture Agents, 116, Portland Street.—Among the many branches of indu carried on in Manchester, the manufacture of chemicals holds an portant place, by reason of its value and its perfection. A well-kn firm in this line is that known as Messrs. Higginbottom & Co., t graphic address, "Alkali," Manchester — established in 1870. T firm acts as the representatives of manufacturers in several impor branches of the chemical trade, and as a central agency for concen tion or distribution of a great variety of chemical products, they f a necessary link between manufacturers and consumers both at h and abroad. During a period of great commercial depression, in wh the chemical trade has undergone many changes, and especially respect of manufacturers' profits, Messrs. Higginbottom & Co. h recognised the signs of the times, and have made it their aim to red to a minimum the intermediate costs between manufacturers and c sumers. This policy has resulted in the establishment of wide busin connections, and the interests of producer and consumer are benefit thereby. Mr. H. Higginbottom, who conducts the business, is w known in Manchester circles, and thoroughly understands the tr with which he is connected. His firm bears a good reputation and h an influential place in the chemical trade of Manchester.

G. H. Marston & Co., Wholesale Furriers and Sk Merchants, 11, Mosley Street.—This business was established in year 1886 only, but has already given signs of great vitality and ultim success. The premises include a capital warehouse remarkably well fit up, and an office substantially furnished and supplied with all the lat and most approved appliances for the rapid dispatch of business. Th speciality is mainly expensive and very high-class made-up furs a dressed skins, but the peculiarity of their business lies in meeting t requirements of the wholesale trades in all the large centres of commer and at the same time making the highest class of goods, so as to specially adapted to the best trades of London, Manchester, Liverpo and Glasgow. The firm are well known both in London and Leipsi in fact, their produce is known throughout the world. The firm highly respected by the entire trade.

J. Robinson & Sons, Silk Mercers and Family Drapers, Funeral Requisites, and Dressmaking, 301 & 303, Oxford Street. This is a very old-established concern, having been started in the year 1835. In 1841 it was removed to 171, Oxford Street. At this address it was conducted until 1879, when the business was transferred to its present location. Here the shop and storerooms are very capacious, and afford adequate facilities for the storage of an extensive and varied stock. The workrooms are also large, and a staff of close on forty is therein usually occupied all the year round. The partners in this reputable establishment are Messrs. H. E. and L. F. Robinson, sons of the founder, and they manage the business with great ability. Its operations in the lines to which it is devoted are equalled by those of no other house in the southern part of the city. The stock comprises all sorts of silks, dress goods, costumes, skirts, shawls, mantles, furs, curtains, flannels, linens, sheetings, prints, hosiery, gloves, laces, flowers, ribbons, umbrellas, and the other branches of outfitting. These goods are held in great variety of colour, quality, and design, so that all sorts of customers can be satisfied. The partners are able business men, and their enterprise and integrity merit success.

Barrett's Country Bottling Company, Limited, Central Station Arches, Watson Street, Peter Street.—Among the great and leading industries of the age, a most important position is held by that devoted to food supply. In this department of trade a prominent firm is "Barrett's Country Bottling Company, Limited," ale and stout bottlers in screw stopper bottles, of the above address. This is a firm whose reputation is widespread and whose fame extends throughout the whole civilised world. Established in London about 1876, the business as beer bottlers so rapidly developed itself, and their new patent screw stopper bottle became at once so very popular, as speedily to necessitate the opening of branch establishments throughout the kingdom. The premises forming the Manchester depôt are large and commodious, and although not strictly speaking a building, are yet so well appointed and arranged for the conduct of the large business as to furnish every requisite facility, and thus enable the firm to execute the orders of this district from their own stores on the spot. Messrs. Barrett and Co. possess a valuable patent in their now well-known and highly approved screw stopper bottle, undoubtedly one of the greatest domestic and business improvements of the age. The saving of time and immunity from danger in drawing corks, places the screw stopper at once in the front of the most useful of modern improvements of general utility. The firm employ a large staff of experienced bottlers and others at Watson Street. Wirers and tiers, as in olden times, are not required. The facilities in beer opening proved by this patent are so great and yet simple as to have resulted in an immense amount of public support and demand, which large as it now is in extent, must of necessity be insignificant as compared to what future results must produce.

R. Ramsbottom, The Sportsman's Depot, 81, Market Street.—An historical review of the great mercantile and manufacturing interests of Manchester would be incomplete without a sketch of the well-known Sportsman's Depôt, of which Mr. R. Ramsbottom is the enterprising proprietor. He has been established thirty years, eleven of which have been at the present location. Conducted on enterprising and honourable lines, his business from its very inception has prospered and grown apace, and he is now a recognised leader in this branch of trade. The premises occupied are of spacious dimensions, admirably arranged and equipped with every facility and convenience for the transaction of business. The stock kept is the largest and most comprehensive in Manchester; it includes every requisite for shooting, fishing, cricket, croquet, lawn-tennis, fencing, football, boxing, archery, lacrosse, gymnasia, skating, &c. Each department is replete with the best and most reliable goods, which for quality and superior finish are unexcelled by those of any establishment in the country. Mr. Ramsbottom does a widespread trade, and his connections are of a strictly first-class character, embracing the leading clubs in all parts of the kingdom. Mr. Ramsbottom is an enterprising and thoroughly reliable business man, and much respected.

James Booth, Size, Varnish, and Colour Manufacturer, Clayton.—The applications of size, colour, and varnish are manifold and universal. For this reason many firms of standing and repute in the city are engaged in their production. One such establishment is that conducted by Mr. James Booth, whose business was commenced in 1866, and has been since continued by himself. The works are of moderate though ample dimensions, and their productive capacity, owing to the employment of the most effective machinery, is much greater than their proportions bespeak. All sorts of size, colour, varnish (including black, red, green, yellow, white, slate, blue, and stone), Brunswick black, quick iron black, wire varnish, and Prussian paste blue are prepared on the works and sold in large and ever-increasing quantities. The proportions of the trade are evenly balanced between home and export orders. The quality of the goods turned out is their highest and best recommendation, and the only one used by Mr. Booth to extend and fortify his trade.

D. A. Merrin, Royal Exchange Printing and Publishing House. The demand for truly artistic printing is rapidly increasing, and where a firm can be found to satisfy the educated requirements of the times in return for a reasonable outlay, it is certain to be rewarded by a generous custom. Such is the experience of Mr. D. Alexander Merrin, the proprietor of the Royal Exchange Printing Works. By judicious management, aided by a sound practical acquaintance with the many technicalities of his profession, this gentleman has succeeded in the comparatively short period of eight years in acquiring a handsome reputation, and now enjoys the patronage of a large and discriminating portion of the public. His premises are of a commodious description and fitted up with every modern improvement; whilst his stock of type, besides being very interesting and well selected, is a comprehensive one and always up to date. The workmanship he produces is calculated to ensure the most perfect satisfaction. A special feature of the establishment is the care which is taken to suit the inevitable variety of tastes. Mr. Merrin well deserves his success, and it is but fair to add that his price-list is a particularly moderate one. His success, too, has been none the less marked in connection with his scholastic publications and kindergarten appliances. But in these, as it is in every branch of trade, a man must place in the market a thing worth the having, and then he must advertise it well. These qualifications appear to be a study with Mr Merrin, as shown by his great success at the Manchester Jubilee Exhibition. His position there was an unique one. His was the only show of kindergarten appliances in that vast emporium, and the excellence of his exhibit was the admiration of all who saw it. Like the kindly humorist, Douglas Jerrold, we say, "Blessed be the hand that prepares a pleasure for a child," and wish Mr. Merrin every success in his commercial and publishing career.

Hague, Smith & Co., Yarn and Cloth Agents, 6, Dickinson Street.—The agency business of Manchester in connection with the yarn and cloth trade is of great value, and there can be no doubt of its utility in the industrial and commercial world. A thoroughly representative firm in this line is that carried on as Messrs. Hague, Smith & Co., which was originally founded by Messrs Simpson & Hague, twenty-five years ago. It then fell into the hands of Kemp & Hague, and finally the present members, Messrs. Hague & Smith, came into possession, and since the date of their inception they have greatly increased the business. The premises occupied consist of a spacious, substantial four-storied building of attractive appearance, which comprises many offices and affords great storing capacity. This capacity is strained to its utmost with a very extensive stock of yarn and cloth of superior quality, from the leading manufacturers. Their consignments consist mainly of goods for the great Eastern markets, and no other firm is so noted for its specialities in fancy goods for India. Besides these their goods comprise an unusually extensive and varied assortment, many of which will be found in no other warehouse in the city. Messrs. Hague, Smith & Co. fully understand the trade, are intimate with all its details, and their careful and sound judgment of the state of the markets is of great value to their connection. They carry on a very lucrative business, having a fine connection among the principal merchants and manufacturers, and their prompt and thorough manner of executing commissions is rapidly increasing it. Messrs. Hague & Smith, the only members of the firm, are gentlemen of mature judgment and deep trade knowledge, of great experience and special aptitude for the business. Their status in the industrial and commercial world is high and claims respect, and their house is one of the principal and best-known factors in the yarn and cloth trade of Manchester.

James Lythgoe & Sons, Law Stationers, 20, Booth Street.—This business, which was established in the year 1865, at an address in St. James's Square, was removed to present premises in 1876, where the business is now carried on under the personal superintendence of Mr. Lythgoe and his two sons. The offices are a handsome suite, very neatly furnished and fitted up, and are most conveniently situated for business. The stock includes every description of stationery, &c., required by solicitors, barristers, and other members of the legal profession. Attached to the offices is a staff of legal copyists and engrossers, and lithographic writers, and several clever writers of testimonial and address forms. There are also a few accomplished illuminators. Messrs. Lythgoe are thus able to execute orders for the very highest class of address or testimonial writing on vellum for presentation or otherwise. They are also able to execute any kind of lithographic or letterpress printing. Mr. Lythgoe is a gentleman of great experience in the business, understanding all the requirements of the most fastidious of his clients, energetic and most attentive to business, prompt, punctual, and deservedly successful.

Hulse & Company, Engineers and Tool Makers, Ordsal Works, Regent Road, Salford.—This well-known and highly-important firm was established in the year 1852, so that the concern has enjoyed a career of close upon forty years. The works are known as the "Ordsal Works," and are situated in Salford. The premises are extensive, and although space will not permit of our going into minute particulars, we may observe that the buildings comprise a lofty structure in three and a half bays of unequal dimensions. Three of the bays are used as erecting shops, and are fitted with overhead-power travellers and other cranes. At the rear of these erecting shops there is a large five-storey building, of which the three first floors are used as turning, fitting, and light erecting shops; whilst the floors above are used as stores for patterns, of which they have an enormous accumulation. At the north-eastern boundary of the works are placed the pattern-making shops, also the engines and boilers, and a commodious basement is used as general stores. Nearly all the machines in use on the works (with the exception of the plant in the pattern-making shops) have been made upon the premises, and they may be regarded as specialities of the firm's manufactures. The establishment turns out all kinds of lathes, of large and small dimensions; also planing, shaping, boring, drilling, screwing, slotting, and milling machines in great variety, together with steam hammers, cranes, &c. Much of the work is of a very heavy description, particularly the lathes and planing machines; some of the former have measured little short of 100 feet long, and some of the latter have weighed upwards of 100 tons. The tools made by Hulse & Co. can always be relied upon for strength and durability, which latter is due to the accuracy of workmanship and quality of the materials used. The firm do a large business with our own and many foreign Governments, and in almost all the leading engineering establishments, whether for marine, locomotive, ordnance, or general engineering work, Messrs. Hulse's machine tools are to be found. They employ some three hundred hands. At the International Exhibition, London, in 1862, highest honours were obtained; also a gold medal for exhibit of tools at the Bradford Exhibition of 1882. The firm likewise were awarded a gold medal at the Inventions Exhibition held in London in 1885 "for the excellence of the machine tools exhibited by them." In addition to the Exhibitions above referred to, their machine tools were to be seen at the Oldham Exhibition of a few years ago, and the Manchester and Newcastle exhibitions held last year. The two former were non-competitive, but at the latter the highest award, a silver medal, was obtained. We will only further observe with respect to Messrs. Hulse & Co. that they possess a commercial reputation of the very first order, that their trade is conducted upon the strictest lines of honour and probity, and that they occupy the very foremost place in the particular branches of the engineering business to which they have devoted their special attention and energies.

Robert Riddel & Sons, Manufacturers, &c., Chapel Square, Birchin Lane.—One of the oldest established and deservedly successful firms in Manchester is that of Messrs. Robert Riddel & Sons, manufacturers, &c. This house was established above forty years ago, by Kendal, Riddel, & Yates, afterwards Kendal, Riddel, & Co., and for the last eighteen years it has been conducted by Messrs. Robert Riddel & Sons. They are manufacturers of white and grey shirtings and dyed goods, and do principally a home trade. The premises occupied in Chapel Square are commodious and admirably arranged, and equipped throughout with every facility and convenience for the transaction of business. An extensive stock is kept, each department being replete with the best and most desirable goods. With its superior manufacturing facilities and connections, the firm is enabled to offer special advantages to customers. It is such houses as this that are the recognised exponents of the various branches of Manchester trade, and they well deserve the substantial success which the energy and ability of their proprietors have so unerringly attained. The members of the firm are gentlemen whose integrity and sound business principles have won the respect and confidence of our leading commercial circles.

Mr. E. F. Goulburn, Cured Fish Dealer, 47, Oxford Street.—An important feature of business is Mr. Goulburn's well-known establishment. He is an Italian warehouseman, dealer in all kinds of cured fish, kippered salmon, Kiel sprats, Dutch herrings, sardines, and the variously prepared anchovies.

> "To quicken appetite it will behove ye
> To feed courageously on good anchovie."—FLATMAN'S "Belly God," 1674.

The latter being one of the specialities of the business, whose general purpose is the supplying of the numerous exquisitely dainty morsels of a well-kept sideboard. This first-class business was opened by the proprietor in 1884, and from the very date of its inception it became a distinct success. It is worked in conjunction with his chief establishment in Millgate, which dates back to 1845, thus possessing a reputation of over forty years standing. It is noted far and wide for the superior quality of its Scotch haddock, which was honoured with the first-class medal at the Edinburgh Fisheries Exhibition. Fish lovers come from great distances for this delicious breakfast and tea relish. The method of curing adopted by Mr. Goulburn is also a speciality, imparting to the fish a peculiarly pleasant flavour much prized by epicures, which has assisted in no small degree in establishing the great popularity of his business. In addition, there is a considerable all-round trade done in large parcels of dried fish despatched to all parts of the country. The premises occupied in Oxford Street are well appointed and arranged, and fitted up in a most complete manner for the purposes of facilitating business, and is well filled with a high-class stock of cured and preserved fish and "kippered salmon," the latter being a rich and choice delicacy much admired; also the famous *pâté de foie gras* and caviare, two more exceedingly high-class and toothsome relishes. We have no hesitation in recommending the most exacting epicure to seek the gratification of his appetite out of the rich, abundant store of this efficiently conducted establishment. Mr. Goulburn's well-known establishment is now an important feature of the cured fish trade.

Joshua Hoyle & Sons, Limited, Cotton Spinners and Manufacturers, 41, Mosley Street.—This well-known firm was established in the year 1840, and its history is one of almost unexampled success. In the year 1873 the concern was formed into a limited liability company, but no outsiders were admitted or allotted shares, the intention being to give all the employés an interest in the business, and thus secure to them a full share in the profits. The mills are: Plantation Mill, Bacup, India Mills, Bacup, and Beech Mill, Bacup, Brooks Bottom Mills, Summerseat, and Freeholds Mill, Shawforth. In all, between two and three thousand hands are employed. The specialities of their manufacture are grey and bleached cotton cloths ranging in width from 20 to 120 inches, of high class. The trade connection is both home and shipping, and is, of course, of enormous extent. The warehouse in Mosley Street is very large, and the offices are a very fine suite of rooms, most handsomely furnished and fitted with all the latest and most approved appliances for the rapid transaction of business. The managing directors are Mr. Isaac Hoyle, M.P., and Mr. Edward Hoyle, J.P. These gentlemen are amongst the very best-known members of the cotton trade, and their active interest in all that concerns its immediate and future welfare is productive of the very best results.

William Carvell & Co., Lithographic Printers, 47, Mosley Street.—Printing of all kinds is very extensively carried on in Manchester, and a notable house in this connection is that conducted by Messrs. William Carvell & Co., whose foundation dates back many years. Their premises are centrally and suitably located, and well equipped with the necessary appliances for all sorts of lithographic and heraldic printing and embossing at the most moderate cost, and with a promptitude and fidelity unsurpassed by any other concern in the same line in the city. The connections of the house are widespread and of an influential character among the leading merchants, manufacturers, commercial corporations, and insurance companies. Everything is done in the best style and under the personal supervision of one of the principals, who make it a point to carry out exactly the minutest wish of every patron. Hence the well-merited popularity of the firm.

Geo. Battersby & Co., Grey Cloth Agents, 85, Mosley Street.—The agency business in Manchester in connection with the grey cloth trade is of considerable extent, and among the establishments engaged a good position is that occupied by the firm of Messrs. George Battersby & Co. It was established in 1880, and since that date the firm has worked up a very fine connection among the principal merchants and shippers. The premises occupied are large and commodious, comprising offices and warerooms of ample dimensions. The warerooms contain a large stock of cloth from the leading manufacturers, which for quality could not be excelled. Messrs. G. Battersby & Co. have a good reputation for the prompt and perfect manner in which they transact their business, and the special facilities they possess enable them to deal with great liberality towards the widespread connection. The individual members of the firm are Messrs. George Battersby and John H. Houghton, gentlemen well known in mercantile circles, and highly honoured for their strict rectitude and genial bearing. They are thoroughly conversant with all branches of the trade, in which their house is an able and worthy representative.

H. & J. Beales, Button Manufacturers, 25, Spear Street.—Prominent among the most successful firms engaged in the button trade is that of Messrs. H. & J. Beales, which was established in Manchester about fourteen years since. The large and extensive works of this firm are situate in Dyer Street, Chester Road, and the offices and warehouse are at the above address. The latter are also of a spacious and well-arranged character, and contain a wonderfully large stock of buttons of every description. Messrs. Beales are manufacturers of bone and wood buttons and wood moulds, the "Anchor" vest back-strap, also agents for pearl, paper, and other buttons, buckles, &c., and the superior quality and finish of their goods command for them a large and ready sale. The firm are also agents for Messrs. Player Brothers, of Birmingham, whose linen, metal, flexible, military, and other buttons and ornaments are so well known, and for Messrs. William Guest & Son, of Sheffield, the noted manufacturers of ivory buttons. Messrs. Beales also deal in pure bone manure, bones for case-hardening, &c. Their business is of a very extensive and widespread character, and is conducted throughout upon principles which have gained for the firm a very high and honourable position in the trade.

ompany, 20, Rook Street.—
ıg, at the Manchester Exhibition,
lied by the celebrated Rossendale
ting, which is the firm's speciality,
tability for main and other heavy
cement, coal, &c. The following
ny for their woven belting: (1) It
' leather; (2) it has greater biting
and will not stretch or slip, and
t. more work in a given time than
derably cheaper than leather. These
ches wide, and are guaranteed to
dynamos of the Anglo-American
e majority of the main drives at the
by these belts, and the Rossendale
most gratifying reports from Mr.
argo, the Anglo-American Brush
kson, the superintendent of the

Williamson, assistant electrician.
Belting Co.'s hair belts over other
by their patent Anti-Friction Edge,
rely the action of the strapfork, and
herto the great objection to woven
which were burnt some time since,
offices are now at 7, Meal Street.
cated in the vale of Rossendale.
hich are now in such great favour
or them a staff of one hundred and
r famous Hair Traces. These are
e that they are impervious to all
nger, and much more durable than
qualities are so manifest that the
argest and most important carriage
any has branch offices at London,
m, Newcastle-on-Tyne, Birming-
ow, and Dundee, and a Continental
brisk and rapidly-increasing busi-

—

Cotton Waste Merchant,
waste trade is one of the great busi-
orld-wide reputation; it represents
y hands. A well-known firm in this
h has a reputation of upwards of
his son. The premises occupied
ries, which affords excellent offices
ed with a large engine, and special
ton waste for all markets. Mr.
otton and cotton waste, the cotton
Mr. Mellor has special facili-
cotton waste, and during his fifty
name for reliability. He carries
lid connection among the leading
s. He has also representatives in
ell as agents in America, and does
s employed, and the organisation of
orders are executed with dispatch.
ancashire in the leading business
his admirable qualities, whilst he
n waste merchants of Manchester.

ine, Cotton Band and Net
t.—This business was established
as far back as the year 1826 under the same title as it bears at present, and has been located at 38, Corporation Street for upwards of thirty years. The sale shop is both large and convenient, well lighted and fitted; and in the rear are extensive stock-rooms and warehouse. The basement is used for storage purposes. The trade connection, though to a great extent local, includes many customers in the distant parts of the kingdom, and though no travellers are employed a considerable wholesale trade is carried on. The specialities of the firm are a very superior make of cotton mill banding, and their celebrated netting, suitable for every purpose required. The sole partner is Mr. Thomas Johnson, a gentleman of great experience in the rope and twine trade, and familiar with every detail of the manufacture. Mr. Johnson is well known on the Royal Exchange, and in commercial circles. He is a liberal employer and an ardent supporter of such public movements as are designed to benefit the community.

McLeod Bros., Manufacturers of Skirts, Children's Goods, &c., 23, China Lane.—This business has been in active operation upwards of ten years, and its success has been most marked. The premises consist of a very substantial building of many floors. The offices are a suite of convenient rooms, handsomely furnished and thoroughly well fitted up. The main specialities of manufacture are plain and fancy skirts of every kind of fashionable material. In addition, Messrs. McLeod Bros. do a very large trade in wadded bed quilts. They have also a separate department for children's goods, such as washing-dresses, skirts, pinafores, aprons, &c. The trade connection is purely wholesale, home trade and shipping. The machinists number upwards of two hundred and fifty indoor hands, and there is a very strong contingent of outdoor workers. The sole proprietors are Mr. James McLeod and Mr. Henry McLeod. These gentlemen are thoroughly well experienced in their business, and perfectly familiar with every detail of manufacture. They are extremely well known in commercial circles, and are most highly reputed for their sterling commercial reputation, for their sound business abilities, and their ready tact and judgment.

Donald Brothers, Cotton Manufacturers, 31, Spring Gardens.—This business has been established more than sixty years, but until 1854 the firm was known as John Ferguson & Co. The factories and headquarters of the firm are at Carlisle, the premises in Spring Gardens in this city being little more than town warehouse and office. Messrs. Donald Brothers manufacture a great variety of goods, such as checks, ginghams, romals, Madras handkerchiefs, striped Salempores, Florentines, Fodens, blue weft regattas, zephyrs, and stripes, no goods being offered by the firm except its own manufactures. The trade connection is very extensive, and includes all the merchant shippers, the wholesale trade, and general warehousemen in the city and the other important towns in the kingdom. The members of the firm are amongst the best-known gentlemen attending the Manchester exchanges. The firm, besides being liberal employers, devote every year a considerable sum to the advancement of popular and technical education; while no benevolent or charitable enterprise need ever lack their warm support.

Miss Bacon, Children's Outfitter, 45, Deansgate.—The public during the last twelve years have been taught to look for goods of a most superior description at this establishment, and have never been disappointed. Experience and careful study have sufficed to impart an exceptional knowledge to Miss Bacon, and this lady, knowing well what is expected from such concerns as that she is the proprietor of, spares no pains to afford her numerous patrons the maximum of all possible satisfaction. Her stock is always comprehensive and up to date, and, moreover, arranged with considerable taste, and as a first-class children's outfitter and a dealer in chaste lace and fancy goods, Miss Agnes Bacon enjoys a local connection of a very valuable character at her well-known and largely patronised establishment. Her terms are cash, but the best of quality and manufacture is guaranteed in return. Each day seems to add to the popularity of her admirably conducted business, and the public are becoming more and more alive to its claims upon their attention. Miss Bacon, therefore, is much to be congratulated upon the result of her persevering energy and enterprise, but she is in receipt of her best reward—the cordial and material approbation of those whose tastes and requirements she caters for so well.

Daber & Son, Valuers, Estate and Mortgage Agents, 2, Pall Mall.—In every large industrial and mercantile city the valuation and estate agency business is very considerable, and of great utility and importance. Manchester is behind no other city for the extent and excellence of her transactions in this direction, a well-known firm engaged therein being that of Messrs. Daber & Son. It was founded in 1855, and since that date the ability, energy, and judgment displayed have secured a very fine connection among house, estate, and property owners. Messrs. Daber & Son have occupied for fifteen years the present offices, presenting a very busy appearance and employing an adequate clerical staff. All valuations and inventories are prepared with promptitude and accuracy, mortgages are arranged; and neglected estates soon regain their market value under the able management of Messrs. Daber & Son. A very good business is done, and the utmost confidence is placed in the firm by their influential clients. Messrs. Daber & Son are gentlemen of the highest reputation for honour and integrity; they are well known in the agency business, and deeply esteemed by the community at large.

Messrs. S. Moore & Son, Bookbinders and Account-Book Makers, Letterpress and Lithographic Printers, Paper Rulers, Bankers' and Lawyers' Stationers and Engravers, 5, Duke Street.—The firm of Messrs. S. Moore & Son is one holding the very first rank in their special branches of trade, and this observation equally applies, whether regard be had to the extent of their business or their mercantile reputation and standing. In the year 1872 this firm acquired the large trade and connection of Mr. Hatton, who had conducted a successful bookbinding business in Manchester for half a century. The special feature of this house has always been high-class account-book making and bookbinding, but in addition to this rapidly developing trade the firm have added engraving and lithographic and letterpress printing in all its

branches. The premises are very extensive, covering a large area. The works and warehouse are contained in a handsome well-lighted building, and the offices and stock and sale rooms are fitted up in excellent style. Lately the basement has undergone considerable change; all the letterpress and litho machines have been moved into the cellar from the printing-room, which is now used as a packing-room and for composing (printers). More machinery being required to overtake the work in the printing department, new plant—embracing a new machine by J. Mann & Sons, Leeds, a double-demy litho machine and press, one of Payne's Wharfedale double-demy letterpress printing machines, and two Arab machines—has been put down. The ground floor is devoted to the public and private offices, the general warehouse, and the stock-room, and here are found all the various makes of hand-made writing and printing papers. Upon this floor also are the various specimens of bookbinding. The stock of leather used by this important bookbinding concern is most extensive and valuable, including calfs, russias, and moroccos; in fact, skins from the wilds of Russia to the plains of Manitoba, and the prices of which range from 1s. 6d. to £3 10s. per skin. The firm undertake the binding of all classes of library, publishers' and private works to pattern, and an idea may be formed of their stock when we state that in brown calfs alone there are to be found from twenty to thirty different shades. We may observe, in passing, that Messrs. Moore & Son pride themselves, in this branch of their business, in both the superiority of the materials used and the high class of workmanship, and certainly their work, if it be equalled, cannot possibly be surpassed either in Manchester or elsewhere. Upon the second floor is the letterpress and lithographic printing department, the composing-room being the chief feature. The machinery, from the smallest Arab up to the latest double-royals, is first-class, and bears the names of such houses as Messrs. Payne & Sons. The type, too, is of the newest and best description that is manufactured. The lithographic work of this house merits special attention, and the bank and public company work, including cheque, receipt, and order books, is all of the highest class. The bookbinding sections are most interesting. The work-rooms are healthy and well appointed, and cleanliness and neatness are observable everywhere. Every description of machinery necessary for carrying on this department of the business is found here, and we may add that the whole of it is of the best that mechanical science has yet devised. It is impossible in visiting this branch not to be struck with the splendid quality of the materials used by the firm, as well as the superb workmanship executed, for both are of the highest order. The house undertakes everything that is possible within itself, even to the marbling of paper used for end-sheets of the books. The next floor above is the women's bookbinding department (the rooms below being exclusively occupied by men), and this room is used for paper folding, paging, perforating, thread and wire stitching, envelope making, &c. Here are to be seen one of Salmon's 54-inch self-clamp machines, and seven of Salmon and Thompson's paging machines. Some of these machines will run up to 9,999,000 without being touched by the operator. The rolling, flattening, and perforating machinery is altogether unique, especially Brehmer's Yankee perforators and the wire-stitching machines, which bind pamphlets and other small books up to 1,500 an hour per machine. The top floor is occupied for paper-ruling and the finishing department of the bookbinding, and here may be observed four American double-ruling machines, which eclipse for swiftness, cleanliness, and accuracy British machinery. This room is splendidly lighted, and is lofty and well ventilated: in fact, the firm have evidently studied the health and comfort of all their *employés* to the fullest possible extent, and are deserving of the highest commendation. The firm employ close upon one hundred and fifty hands, and a more respectable, orderly, well-conducted body of workpeople, male and female, are not to be found in the United Kingdom. Messrs. Moore & Son had an exhibit at the Manchester Jubilee Exhibition (No. 128, Central Nave West), and their goods excited much attention, and elicited universal admiration. We may remark that this firm, in addition to the usual business of bookbinders and account-book makers, printers, stationers, and engravers, do a large trade in pattern-card making, which in a place like Manchester, where so many houses are engaged in the manufacture or sale of textile fabrics, are articles in enormous demand. Messrs. Moore & Son have produced many beautiful things in this line, and have quite taken the lead for taste and design; indeed their productions may fitly be described as "works of art." We must not omit to mention that the firm obtained a first-class prize medal at the London Exhibition of 1873 for excellence of workmanship. We ought just to state that the letterpress bookbinding department is replete with every appurtenance used by the modern bookbinder, including patent backing machines, imperial blocking machines for embossing work, and large and small presses. The firm employ a number of travellers, and their business extends far beyond the limits of either Manchester or the district, and we may further observe that it is daily becoming larger and more widespread. No house in the kingdom can produce better goods, or turn out superior work of whatever description, and their prices will at the same time bear favourable comparison with those of any establishment in the trade. The co-partnership consists of Mr. S. Moore and his son Mr. Harry Moore, and these gentlemen are well known in the city of Manchester and surrounding districts, and are esteemed and respected by all who have the privilege of their acquaintance.

F. W. Ashton & Co., Calico Printers, 59, Portland Street.—The growth of Manchester as the great manufacturing centre of the kingdom has not only been very rapid during the last twenty years, but its entire history has been one of steady advance towards the position it now so creditably occupies. Every branch of trade represented here has kept pace with this wonderful growth, and to-day are to be seen the colossal results of the enterprise and capacity of our business men. Among the old and well-known firms whose career is linked with the development of the city's trade is that of Messrs. F. W. Ashton & Co., calico printers, whose works are at Hyde, Cheshire. This house was founded in 1815, and its career furnishes a good illustration of what can be accomplished by British commercial enterprise and energy. The goods manufactured by the firm have a world-wide reputation, and are unsurpassed for beauty and originality of design, superiority of workmanship, finish, and durability. The firm's works are equipped with the most approved modern machinery and appliances. Calico of every description is here printed in all styles suitable for home and foreign trade.

Messrs. Stephenson, Routley & Co., Wine Merchants, 42, Cross Street.—Twenty-five years ago was established in Manchester the well-known business of Messrs. Stephenson, Routley & Co., a firm whose name is known throughout a large and widespread circle of patrons as second to none for a choice selection of foreign wines, spirits, &c. They also enjoy a very high reputation as Gaugers and Valuers to the trade. The premises comprise handsomely-fitted offices and sample rooms thoroughly adapted in every way for the proper conduct of the business of the firm, who employ an adequate staff of clerks and assistants. There are also extensive cellars in the basement in which are stored a large and highly superior stock of wines and spirits both in bottle and cask, comprising rare old ports by those well-known shippers, Thomson & Croft, Dow Sandeman, and others; also very superior pale and dry sherries in cask and bottle by Peter Domecq and other celebrated shippers; fine old brown sherries, East Indian, Madeiras, &c. The stock of duty-paid spirits comprises a valuable selection of old brandies, Scotch and Irish whiskies, old Jamaica rums, gins, &c. The firm's bonded stores are situated at Ancoats, Manchester, and contain a stock of wines and spirits for home consumption or exportation. The reputation of this house as valuers and gaugers extends over the whole of the North of England. The wine and spirit stocks of many of the principal hotels and retail houses have been valued for transfer by the firm. The firm acts as agent for Reid & Co., the celebrated stout brewers of London, and are sole owners of the "Glenray Blend" (registered) of fine Scotch whisky. The sole proprietor is Mr. Robert William Routley, a gentleman of high commercial status and widely respected.

James Neill & Sons, Cromo-Lithographic Printers ad Fancy Stationers, 59 and 61, Cumberland Street, Deansgate. A stinguished establishment in its line is that of Messrs. James Neill & Sons, hich was founded by the present firm members in 1858. The building cupied is of commanding appearance, and comprises six floors divided into orkshops, warehouses, and show-rooms, being exceedingly well fixtured r all trade and manufacturing purposes. The firm manufacture all kinds general, commercial, and fancy stationery, and execute all descriptions lithography, as well as importing foreign-made fancy goods, French d German prints, straw boards, &c. During the thirty years they have en in business, the improvements in the art of chromo-lithography have en little short of wonderful. The slow and costly hand printing press s entirely given way to the steam lithographic machine, which has orked a complete revolution in the trade. Messrs. James Neill & Sons ere the first to discard the old methods, and they still possess the first eam lithographic machine introduced into Manchester, and since then ey have not been slow to adopt the various improvements which have ide the steam printing machine of to-day what it is—a modern wonder.

e stocks held are of an exceptionally large nature, embracing al goods the best quality, and specially suited to the requirements of the rchants and shippers who export Manchester goods to every corner of globe. An important branch of their business is the sale of French German chromo prints, of which they hold the largest stock and most ied assortment out of London. These are mostly used in the orna-ntation of white and print goods and for pattern-cards, &c. The great ciality for which the firm are highly celebrated is the production of ir fancy embossed and perforated borders, corners, bands, and labels, , for velveteens and fancy box manufacturers. All their embossing chines are worked on the newest principles by steam-power, and are the largest and most powerful yet made. The highest repute is orded to the house for the perfect workmanship, high class finish, and ability of all materials used in the manufacture of the goods bearing name of the firm, a full working staff of over seventy hands is manently engaged in this branch of industry at these well-known ks. The trade is very extensive, five commercial gentlemen constantly ering the best ground of the English markets to promote its interests, which are purely of a wholesale nature, and particularly well established among the leading houses in the trade all over the United Kingdom. The firm members are Messrs. James Neill, James Neill, jun., and Jno. Neill, all of whom are gentlemen of the highest commercial integrity and status, as well as practical craftsmen, and their courtesy and prompt completion of all orders entrusted to their widely-known house secures for them the unqualified esteem and regard of their numerous patrons.

—

Mr. John Roberts, Carriage Builder, 6, Cavendish Street, Stretford Road. The well-known carriage-building establishment associated with the name of Mr. John Roberts is one of the oldest and most successful in the city of Manchester. It was founded as long ago as 1815 by Mr. John Roberts, sen., and the present head of the firm, Mr. John Roberts, jun., who succeeded his father in 1859, occupies a high position in municipal and parochial life, having been for five years a councillor in All Saints' ward, and for many years a member of the Chorlton Board of Guardians. The extensive works are situated at the above address, and are fitted with every requirement for the immense trade which is carried on. The factory, a well-arranged and commodious department, affords occupation to a large staff of men, and the capacious show-rooms are filled with the finest specimens of carriage work. Mr. Roberts has a peculiar aptitude for the construction of carriages which are light but exceedingly strong, and the vast number of testimonials he has received from all parts of the world are unanimous as to the excellence of his work. In addition to this, Mr. Roberts has been a constant exhibitor at international and other gatherings, and can point to a proud array of no less than sixty-two gold and silver medals which have been awarded him; among the more recent being a silver medal from the Liverpool Exhibition of last year for landaus with patent automatic head which can open and close with ease. This award also included the small circular-fronted brougham with patent springs. A very large proportion of these medals have been gained by the "Parisian Phaeton," a speciality of the firm. This elegant and popular vehicle is one of the marvels of carriage building. It has a long, easy, and graceful body, hung upon four elliptic springs of the latest finish and manufacture. There is an adjustable rumble-seat for the driver at the back, which can be removed at pleasure, and the general appearance of the phaeton is so attractive and pleasing that its success cannot be wondered at. The landaus, broughams, and other carriages turned out from the Stretford Road works have also won most favourable renown, and especially has this been the case with the dainty and elegant miniature phaetons, &c., which Mr. Roberts has provided for use in pantomimes at the well-known Prince's Theatre. These have been marvels of workmanship, and have received hearty recognition from the press and the public. Mr. Roberts is, in fact, one of the most famous and successful carriage-builders in the kingdom. He can always be depended upon for good workmanship, punctual fulfilment of engagements, and reasonable charges, and these are qualifications which the public require.

—

Executors of William Hargraves, Tobacco, Cigar, and Snuff Manufacturers, 44, Swan Street. The oldest and most thoroughly representative establishment in its line in Manchester is that of the late William Hargraves, tobacco and snuff manufacturer. This business was established in 1833, and from its very inception has enjoyed a prosperous career. The business is now and has been carried on for the last quarter of a century by the proprietor, Mr. H. J. Cundlin, under whose management there has been a large development of the trade and extension of the premises, which rank for size amongst the largest in the North of England. The manufactory gives constant employment to a large force of skilled hands, and the high standard of excellence and superior quality which the goods of the house possess is maintained by the use of the most approved machinery and the selection of the best materials the various markets of America, the Continent, and the East can offer. Its wholesale trade in Manchester and district is of such a character that the firm is known by reputation in all the leading towns of Lancashire and Yorkshire, the counties to which most attention is directed. By the superior facilities at its command, it is enabled to offer the greatest advantages to customers. Under the continued personal management of the proprietor and a devoted staff of assistants in all departments, this old and reliable house continues to meet with the success that has marked its career for over half a century.

—

W. T. Alexander, Maker of Methylated Spirits and Drysalter, Brown Street, Red Bank.—Established about seventeen years ago this firm is now extremely well known in the trade, and its reputation is of the highest class. In addition to the manufacture of methylated spirits, which is an important part of the business, Mr. Alexander does an extensive trade in the various aniline dyes and colours, and the drugs and chemicals used by bleachers, dyers, finishers, and calico printers, and wood-naphtha, shellac, gums and all requisites for French polishers, cabinet-makers, and hat manufacturers. The works in Brown Street are extremely compact, of modern construction and well arranged. The sole proprietor is Mr. William Taylor Alexander, who is a member of the City Exchange. The firm has a wide business connection, and is held in favorable estimation.

Robert Wilson, Manufacturer of Cocoa-nut Fibre Mats and Matting, Carpets and Floorcloths, 59, Cannon Street.—This business has been established over fifty years, and of its kind has become most extensive and important. The premises are spacious, and comprise a large well-stocked warehouse of six storeys, containing a large assortment of all goods for which this firm is celebrated. The speciality of the trade is the manufacture of cocoa-nut fibre mats and mattings, which, however, is not done upon the Cannon Street premises. There are also departments for Brussels, Tapestry, Kidder, and Dutch carpets floor oil-

cloths of all kinds; velvet-pile Axminster, heald, skin, and list rugs and mats; linoleum, corticine, and various other floor coverings. The trade connection includes many of the shipping houses and general Manchester warehousemen, and the best of the wholesale and retail houses of the district. Mr. Wilson employs a staff of experienced travellers, who cover all the chief towns of the United Kingdom. The sole proprietor is Mr. Robert Wilson, a gentleman extremely well known and highly respected in commercial circles. Mr. Wilson, besides being an excellent man of business, takes a very deep interest in municipal affairs, and all other matters affecting the good of the country generally, and is a great advocate of improved general and technical education for the masses.

Alfred Smith, Manufacturing Chemist and Drysalter, Bank Lane Chemical Works, Clayton.—These important works were established in 1856 by the late Mr. George Smith, who for many years conducted them with invariable and increasing success. On this gentleman's retirement the business was taken over by his son, Mr. Alfred Smith, the present proprietor. The works are extensive and of solid construction. A staff of men is constantly occupied in carrying on the various technical operations therein conducted. All sorts of chemicals and drysaltery goods are made and dealt in. Bisulphide of carbon, chloride of sulphur, carbolic acid, carbolic disinfecting powder, liquid ammonia, salammoniac, spirits of salts, black hypo, body black, caustic soda, farina, shellac, and seed lac, reclaimed indiarubber, indiarubber substitute, naphtha, French chalk, barytes, ground lime, borax, oxide of zinc, litharge, oils, greases, pigments, and the "Excelsior" boiler composition for preventing corrosion and scale in steam boilers, are prepared at the works and sold in considerable quantities and despatched to various parts of the world. Mr. Smith is a very worthy successor to his father, and those who remember that gentleman's honourable career require no further proof of his son's integrity and business ability.

Midland Counties Insurance Company, 17, St. Anne Square.—This old-established Company has been doing business in Manchester for over thirty years, and its stability has attracted a large number of insurers. For a long time the Directors gave their attention more particularly to the development of the Fire branch; latterly, however, they have joined the ranks of companies competing for Life business. The office was founded in 1851 in the city of Lincoln; since then Branches have been opened in London, Liverpool, Manchester, Edinburgh, Birmingham, and Bristol. The subscribed capital amounts to a quarter of a million; the Fire Reserve Fund, apart from the capital, through the wise restraint exercised by the Directors, now amounts to a sum considerably in excess of one year's Fire premiums, thus presenting a security which would be found ample to meet the most adverse trading. In the Life department four-fifths of the profits are allocated every five years to the participating policy-holders, the last valuation resulting in very satisfactory sums being thus divided. The Directors invite applications for agencies from gentlemen of influence.

Henry Vollmer, Manufacturers' Agent for and Importer of Buttons, Trimmings, Braids, Patent Novelties, &c., 41, Spear Street.—The agencies employed in connection with our great industries are manifold as well as important. There is a subdivision of labour which extends far beyond the manual and operative departments, and reaches every branch and every stage of the commercial handling as well as the manual. The manufacturers' agent is one of these and affords a striking illustration of it. The manufacturers' agency business conducted by Mr. Henry Vollmer has now been established for twenty years, Mr. Vollmer himself having been the founder of it. He represents foreign manufacturers and sells their goods to wholesale houses, buying also on his own account, with the result that at the present time he is one of the largest dealers in the kingdom in his own special lines. The specialities handled by Mr. Vollmer are buttons, trimmings, braids (for tailoring trade as well as for the drapery business), gimps, fringes, laces, &c., in connection with which a very large amount of business is done. Mr. Vollmer has been exceedingly fortunate during the period he has been engaged in the business in securing the confidence and connection of all the first-class wholesale houses. This has no doubt been owing in an eminent degree to his first-class business qualifications, hard work, and general tact and judgment, and there is little doubt that the reputation he has acquired has been most thoroughly earned by him. In addition to his establishment in Spear Street, which is the centre of his business operations, their enormous development has necessitated the opening of no fewer than four branch establishments, one in the metropolis, at 22, Nicholl Square, E.C., another at 62, Argyle Street, Glasgow, and at Belfast and Dublin, and he has an agent at Paris who conducts a large Continental business. Such extensive ramifications afford conclusive evidence of the great proportions Mr. Vollmer's transactions have assumed, covering as they do the whole face of the country from north to south, and embracing most of the important home and Continental markets. This direct representation at great centres is a characteristic and distinguishing feature of Mr. Vollmer's system of business, and is in strict keeping with the enterprising spirit which has carried him to his present eminent position in the commercial world. To that spirit of enterprise has been added an inflexible integrity and the strictest regard for honour and fair dealing, as well as a ceaseless endeavour to do the best for every interest confided to him. These qualifications, together with a liberal and enlightened mind, have gained for him the universal respect and esteem of all with whom he has been brought into contact.

Thomas Hassall, Salt Merchant, Drysaltery, Spice, and Moss Litter Merchant, Canal and Railway Wharf, Ducie Street, and London Road.—The salt trade of this country is of immense importance, not only to the inhabitants of these islands but to those of the whole world. In this branch of industry there are few firms more worthy of prominent and favourable mention in such an industrial work as "Manchester of To-Day" than the Eureka Salt Manufacturing Company. The business has been in active operation since 1810, and now occupies an exalted position in the estimation of those in the trade and salt consumers generally. The firm occupies capital offices, and large warehouses capable of storing an immense quantity of salt. The works of the firm are conveniently located at Anderton and Winnington, Northwich, conveniently situated for distribution either by rail or water. The specialities of the firm, which is ably represented in Manchester by Mr. Thomas Hassall, of Ducie Street, are the Eureka Table Salt and the Eureka Household Dairy Salt, which are sold in bags of from 14 lbs. to 2 cwt. Freezing, fishery, crystal, chemical, and rock salts are also sold in enormous quantities, and together with the two leading lines, are daily received by the public with greater favour. This is true of all parts of the world, as well as of these islands. Of the Dairy Salt, in 1883 close on two hundred thousand bags were sold, and it is now solely used in the royal dairy farms, from the director of which Mr. T. Hassall, Ducie Street, has received the most flattering testimony as to its value and efficacy in preserving the butyric ether in the butter globules. The firm's exhibit at the Manchester Exhibition, a salt model of the proposed aqueduct at Barton over the Manchester Canal, was much admired. The excellence of the Company's salt is universally admitted, and appreciated by steady support, the greater part of which, as far as Manchester and district are concerned, must be attributed to the able management of Mr. T. Hassall, who is highly respected in all commercial circles.

The Alpha Works, Philip's Park Road, Beswick.—The Alpha Works, Philip's Park Road, were originally established about twenty years ago by Mr. William Atherton. Since the decease of that gentleman they have been carried on by his executors in a style that reflects the very highest credit upon their business character and managerial skill. From its commencement this concern has been distinguished for general and particular excellence, being consistently conducted upon the most approved lines. The firm trades as engine and machine smiths. They undertake turning and boring, the manufacture of patterns, the production and finishing of castings, and so on. Their connection is extensive and of a valuable character, a fairly large working staff being kept in constant employment. The building in Philip's Park Road is of a superior kind, admirably fitted up and appointed. All orders taken by this firm are executed with the most scrupulous care, whilst punctuality, combined with moderate charges, are leading features of the concern.

George Reece, Wholesale and Export Boot and Slipper Manufacturer and Leather Dealer, 58, Marshall Street, Rochdale Road.—The boot and shoe trade in Manchester is, like the population, yearly on the increase. In this, one of the leading branches of industry in our city, a very prominent establishment is that conducted by Mr. George Reece, who is an extensive manufacturer of boots and shoes and slippers, and deals very largely in leather. The house cannot boast a very lengthened commercial existence, but what is better, during the time it has been established, energetic and competent management, goods of the very best quality and moderation in prices have secured for the concern a connection of wide extent and of a high class and steady character. The premises in which the business is conducted are of spacious dimensions, substantially fitted and completely stocked with an enormous and varied selection of boots, shoes, and slippers of every conceivable design, quality, and material. In one thing they are all alike, and that is excellence of quality, Mr. Reece storing none but the best and most durable and fashionable goods the respective prices charged will allow. His workshops are of ample extent, and afford accommodation to a large staff of men who are kept constantly employed in executing the orders received by the house. The trade is of very large and continually growing dimensions, the excellence of the goods, combined with Mr. Reece's ability and persevering energy in the management, having won for the firm a first-class reputation among retailers and shippers, with both of which branches a large business is transacted. Mr. Reece is a man of the utmost integrity, and few stand higher in the estimation of the trading community of our important city. He has agents at 12, Darville Road, Stoke Newington, London, N.; 140, Raeberry Street, Glasgow; 9, College Street, Belfast; St. George's Chambers, St. George's Street, Capetown, South Africa; and at Lagos, West Africa.

Darrand & Catlow, Calico Printers and General Merchants, 12, Faulkner Street.—This firm, formerly known as J. C. Darrand & Co., is doing a remunerative and extending business. The premises consist of a capital warehouse and a suite of convenient offices, well furnished, and fitted with the latest and most approved appliances for the rapid despatch of business. The principal department of business is calico printing, for which the firm has a very large connection. Messrs. Darrand & Catlow have very justly acquired the reputation of being unusually successful in producing permanent colours in addition to artistic and attractive designs, and they are consequently entrusted with orders for printing by many of the principal shipping houses, the leading manufacturers, and numerous home-trade firms. A good trade is also done as general merchants and importers of Havana and Mexican cigars; an extensive business is also carried on in mill furnishing, including hair and cotton belting, engine packing, indiarubber Busch' gas governors, and appliances of every description. The firm do not employ any travellers, as Messrs. Darrand & Catlow find their reputation so well established as to render travellers' assistance unnecessary. A capable staff of experienced salesmen, clerks, and book-keepers is retained at Faulkner Street. The sole proprietors are Messrs. H. Catlow and Mr. J. C. Darrand. These gentlemen are well known on 'Change and in commercial circles, and are considered thriving and prosperous business men.

Hime & Addison, Musical Instrument Manufacturers, Dealers, Tuners, and Repairers, 30 and 32, Victoria Street.—This well-known and popular concern (which still goes by the name of Hime & Addison, though the sole proprietor is now Mr. James Lowe), was originally established in Manchester in 1815, and at the present time occupies a prominent position as one of the oldest and best of its kind out of London. The connection enjoyed is widespread, custom coming from all parts of the world. The business carried on is that of music and musical instrument dealers and manufacturers on a comprehensive scale. The new and enlarged show-rooms at 30 and 32, Victoria Street, always contain an unrivalled collection of goods. Two hundred pianos, for instance, form the average in this line continually on hand; while, in addition to these, an immense stock of harmoniums, violins, guitars, flutes, &c., is kept. The famous "Pioneer" American organs, imported by this firm direct from the United States, and constructed according to their original registered designs and specifications, form one of the principal and most pleasing specialities of the firm, and are certainly marvels for the money asked for them. They are made at Worcester, Mass., U.S.A., and embody the practical results of the long experience, inventions, and improvements of Messrs. Hime & Addison. They are made now with entirely new combinations and musical effects, designed especially for the requirements of the English market; and, owing to a new mode of voicing the reeds, and a different method of conveying the wind, the most pipe-like tones are produced. The firm, which, it may here be mentioned, were the first to introduce American organs into this country, can now, owing to the improvements they have made and their special contracts, offer the public instruments of the most approved and superior construction, made of the best selected materials and seasoned timber, at such reasonable prices as to be within the reach of all, and which, it is confidently claimed, cannot be equalled by any other maker or dealer elsewhere. The organs are specially recommended, not only for their undoubted superiority of tone, special actions, and really exquisite finish, but also for their sound construction and great durability. The following varieties are offered: (1) The Cottage organ. This is in well-finished, solid American walnut case, varnished, with four sets of reeds (F to F), nine stops, tremolo, and two knee-swells. (2) The Popular organ, in American walnut case, with genuine oil finish, smooth-rubbed surface, bookcase top, vermin-proof pedals, and solid-cased bottom; four sets of reeds (F to F), nine stops, two knee-swells, and the improved vox humana. (3) The School organ. Case and finish same as Popular organ; five sets of reeds, octavo coupler, eleven stops, knee-swell and knee-pull organ, vox humana (F to F). (4) The Model organ, in best American walnut, high-class design and finish, hand-polished case and carved ornamentation, ebonised panels and book recesses, five octaves (F to F), six sets of reeds, thirteen stops, octave coupler, and two knee-swells. (5) The Chancel organ. In American walnut, with low top and dull polished case, panelled back and front; bottom of case entirely closed in, and blow-pedals with mice excluder; strongly made, durable, and powerful in tone; six sets of reeds, octave coupler, thirteen stops, and two knee-swells. (6) The Church organ, in best American walnut case, with best possible finish, low top and burr walnut panels in back and front; top panel and back hinged; great power and brilliancy, and remarkable quality of solo stops; sixteen stops, nine sets of reeds, sub-bass, octave coupler, vox humana, two knee-swells; five-octave compass (F to F). (7) The Drawing-room organ, in artistic case, with hand-carved ornamentation, best burr walnut panels, bookcase top, and extra high finish throughout; especially remarkable for its novel solo stops, the picco pipe, Cor Anglais, violina, &c.; compass, five octaves (F to F); nine sets of reeds; sixteen stops, octave coupler, vox humana, two knee-swells, and sub-bass; made in four styles, and positively the finest of the kind ever produced. With reference to the other special department of the firm, viz. their "Speciality" pianos, these obtain the best qualities of the foreign iron-framed instruments, combined with the sweet mellowness of the best English wood-frame pianos, and are, without doubt, "the best value in the world." The price list of the firm should be at once consulted by all in search of high-class instruments at a reasonably moderate figure. Their Pioneer model pipe organs are rapidly advancing in popular favour. They are the result of four years' labour, experiment, and thought, are of the very best quality in point of material, construction, and tone production, of a size enabling them to be placed in any room, and sold at a most moderate rate. Hime & Addison well merit their present popularity and deserve a long-continued and greatly increased success.

Mr. John Kennedy, Manufacturer of Knitted Hosiery, 6A, Union Street, Church Street.—Manchester and district, although principally famous for cotton goods, comprises amongst its many industries other important manufactures, not the least of which is that of hosiery, both woven and knitted. In connection with the manufacture of this latter kind, the well-known firm of Mr. John Kennedy has for many years occupied a most prominent position. His business is carried on in large and commodious premises, well situated, and admirably adapted to the requirements of the trade. This manufacture is principally done by women, about two dozen being continually engaged at the looms, besides others in the various departments of the business. The machinery in this factory is very fine, most ingenious in construction, and moreover exceedingly costly. The work of the house may be divided into two classes, viz. plain and ribbed hosiery. The former class comprises children's black, coloured, assorted, and striped socks; black hose, black drabs, brown drabs, and blue greys, with double knitted tops and spliced heels: women's black, white, violet, and maroon hose, black drab with rib tops and fashioned legs I H: men's drab, grey, grampian, and grey wheeling hose, in ribbed hosiery; black ribbed, black navy, cardinal and maroon with spliced heels; black and brown drab ribbed hose with double heels; women's ribbed hose and men's ribbed half hose; also men's Cardigan jackets. This business in all its branches is conducted in a most spirited and enterprising manner. Mr. John Kennedy occupies a high position in commercial circles, and by his well-known integrity and enterprise has gained the esteem and confidence of a large and valuable connection.

Green & Scott, Manufacturers of Moleskins, Cords and Velveteens, &c., 8, Mosley Buildings, Market Street.—This firm was founded some nine years ago, and has already achieved a most marked success. The premises consist of a warehouse of considerable size, extremely well stocked with goods, and a capital suite of offices handsomely furnished. The specialities of manufacture are moleskins, cords, velveteens and similar goods, jeans, twills, boot linings, Oxfords, lambskins, dyed goods, &c. The trade connection is extensive. Messrs. Green & Scott do a very considerable business with the Manchester shipping houses, the general Manchester warehousemen, the wholesale grindery stores, and the best buyers amongst the boot and shoe manufacturers At the Market Street warehouse a staff of experienced salesmen and clerks find plenty of active employment. The members of the firm are extremely well known in commercial circles, and they have each a very large personal connection amongst the buyers for the large houses. Messrs. Green & Scott take rank as one of the best firms in their own particular line. Combined with first-class general business ability the partners possess a thorough knowledge of all the details of the trade, and of the manufacture of the goods they produce. Liberal employers, they are also generous supporters of local charities.

Thomas Jackson, Manufacturing Chemist, Clayton and Bolton.—There is probably no other branch of industry in the country in which so much ability, skill, and judgment are required as in the manufacture of drugs and chemicals, and Manchester has a good reputation for the excellence of her productions in this direction. Among her firms a leading place is occupied by that of Mr. Thomas Jackson, Clayton, which was founded by this gentleman over seventeen years ago, and since that date he has built up a large trade, and placed himself in the front rank of manufacturing chemists. The works are eminently suited for the business, and are large and commodious, fitted up with every requisite appliance, and the operations are carried out on the most advanced principles. About twenty hands are employed in manufacturing chemicals, and as only the finest materials are used, the productions are of the best quality. Mr. Jackson's trade is rapidly increasing. He is well known in manufacturing circles. He is very popular among the local community, and is in every respect a representative manufacturing chemist. He takes an active part in all matters affecting the public weal, and his social position is of a high order. He is chairman of the Rural Sanitary authority and vice-chairman of the Ashton-under-Lyne Board of Guardians.

Stand Lane Mill Company's Cotton Goods, 28, Fountain Street.—The large and prosperous concern known as the Stand Lane Mill Company is one of the best known in the whole cotton industry. Established about twenty years since, the company has a town warehouse at the above address, to which it has recently removed from smaller premises at No 35 in the same thoroughfare. Handsome and well-fitted offices are here provided for the clerical staff, and there are ware and showrooms of an extensive character. In these are to be seen a splendid stock of all kinds of coloured cotton goods, such as cotton union and linen drills, printed and padded drills, trouserings, vestings, Oxford and Harvard shirtings, all kinds of bleached drills, ginghams, ticks, regattas, checkbacks, denims, &c. All these are of the newest designs, the finest finish, and the most reliable and durable material, and are celebrated far and wide for their superior quality. For such an extensive trade very large works are necessary, and those of the Stand Lane Company are to be found at Radcliffe, in the Allen Street Mill and the Canal Mill, and at Farnworth, in the Limefield Mill. These are very extensive, covering together a very large area, and are fitted with every mechanical appliance that science and experience can suggest. Over six hundred hands find employment in the production of the various goods for which the firm is noted, and the management is in the hands of skilled and experienced men. The fabrics of the Stand Lane Company are known and esteemed in all parts of the world, and as an undertaking it has achieved one of the highest positions in the commercial world

Thomas Kenyon, General Smith, &c., 23, Jackson's Row, Deansgate.—This is a local concern of considerable promise and of no inconsiderable importance. The energetic and enterprising proprietor, Mr. Thomas Kenyon, started business here in 1862 as a packing tool maker, locksmith, bell-hanger, and general smith, making a speciality of the manufacture of ironwork for fire-escapes and firemen's axes, &c. He is known as a workman of more than ordinary merit, and a rapidly increasing demand is now being made for the articles of his special make. His premises are admirably fitted up and well appointed with the many and various requirements of the busy trade that is being carried on. A good staff is kept in constant employment, and, judging from the present outlook, this compact little concern is likely to develop in the near future into a successful business house of decidedly more than ordinary influence. Mr. Kenyon spares no pains to ensure his numerous customers the very maximum of satisfaction, and he well deserves the generous patronage accorded him. He is well known in Manchester and neighbourhood and greatly respected.

Mr. Joseph Lingard, Patent and Sheet Wadding and Cotton Wool Manufacturer, 6, Church Street.—In the historical review of the manufactures and industries of Manchester and its vicinity, written with the object of presenting in a short and concise form the origin and history of the leading houses engaged therein, it is incumbent upon us to give special prominence to those firms which have for many years been identified with some particular branch of commerce or manufacture. For more than thirty years the well-known name of Mr. Joseph Lingard, patent and sheet wadding and cotton wool manufacturer, has been most intimately associated with the commerce of this city. This firm has very extensive works at Chapel-en-le-Frith, known as the Milton Mills, where the manufacture of the patent and sheet wadding, also the cotton wool, is carried on. These mills rank amongst the largest of their kind in the United Kingdom; they are replete with the best and most improved machinery and appliances, and turn out these goods in large quantities and of first class quality, and give employment to an efficient staff of workpeople. This firm is in every way a representative establishment, being not simply dealers, but manufacturers of their own goods. They send out travellers covering the whole of Great Britain and Ireland, and also do an extensive shipping trade, these goods finding a ready sale in all the markets of the world. The business in all its branches is conducted in a most spirited and enterprising manner, and is well recognised as one of the oldest and most extensive in the trade. Mr. Joseph Lingard has been long and honourably connected with this business, and has contributed in no small degree, by his energy and enterprise, to the development of this branch of commerce, and the prosperity of the neighbourhood where his works are situated. The firm occupies a high position in commercial circles, and is fully deserving of the success which it has attained.

C. F. Ryan, General Commission Merchant, 64, Corporation Street.—This firm has been established upwards of twenty-one years, and has occupied the present premises about two-thirds of the time. Mr. Ryan is sole agent for Messrs. W. J. Shaw & Sons, Limerick: Messrs. W. P. Sinclair & Co., Liverpool: Messrs. Thompson & Co., Hamburg, Assen, Holland: all firms connected with the provision trade. Also for James Clow & Sons, Millers, Emyvale, Ireland. The offices in Corporation Street are situated in the centre of the provision trade. The connection is most extensive, and includes many of the leading buyers in the Lancashire and Yorkshire towns. Mr. Ryan is himself a gentleman of experience in his business, and is accounted an excellent judge of qualities and values. His business abilities and character are well known in commercial circles.

James Dawson & Son, Manufacturers' Agents, 13, Dale Street.—The manufacturers' agents of Manchester form a very influential body in the commercial and industrial world, and the business represents very large financial interests. A thoroughly representative firm of manufacturers' agents is that of James Dawson & Son (Telephone 497), who represent various manufacturers in Scotland, England, and Germany, and the premises occupied by them are compact and spacious, comprising offices and warehouse. Mitchell's zephyrs, Schlottmann's shawls and jerseys, Campbell & McLennan's ponchos, and Preston's webs are so well introduced in the home and shipping trades that competitors have hard work in displacing them. J. Dawson & Son have the reputation of possessing great commercial and industrial experience, are well known and much respected as hard-working successful men, and their house (founded twenty years ago) is acknowledged to be one of the principal manufacturers' agency businesses of the city.

Lancashire and Cheshire Telephonic Exchange Com-any, Limited, 38, Faulkner Street.—It is an undoubted fact that the vention of the telephone forms one of the most remarkable landmarks of ientific progress in the present century. But it is nevertheless the fact, so, that people for the most part now are engaged, not so much in con-mplation with regard to the original invention itself as in wonder at its uly marvellous development. Commercial men in particular have much be thankful for in this direction, and one of the beneficial effects of the rowth referred to is to be seen in the number of companies and associa-ons that have been instituted throughout the country for bringing into mmunication distant centres of industry and other places of importance. he northern counties are especially well catered for in this regard; for stance, the Lancashire and Cheshire Telephonic Exchange Company, imited, one of the principal of the organisations referred to, enjoys a wide d most substantial popularity, proving thereby the appreciation of good commodation on the part of the public. It was established in 1879, upon sound basis, and the promise it held forth then has not gone unfulfilled. y diligent and persevering labour and enterprise its business has gradu-ly grown until its dimensions are now very large indeed, and its fluence very important. According to the Government licence granted to the company, its instruments are to be used for the purpose of enabling any person with whom the company agrees in that behalf to transmit direct from, and receive at, any office, to or from any person, telephonic messages relating to the business or private affairs of such persons respectively, or one of them. In Manchester, Liverpool, Blackburn, Preston, Bolton, Burnley, Oldham, and other towns within the range of its comprehensive district, public call stations are opened, where any one may converse, by telephone, not only with subscribers to the company's exchanges, but also with anybody who, by previous appointment between the parties concerned, has gone to some other call station to receive a message. Thus, two non-subscribers could, by previously arranging the time, hold a conversation at two different call stations, either in the same town or in any two towns joined up. If one of the parties was a sub-scriber he could, at any time, be "rung up" at his own office by his friend, from any call station in the various towns in Lancashire, Cheshire, and Yorkshire with which the company has connection. Special facilities are also provided for members of the Manchester Royal Exchange. The three call boxes formerly erected having proved insufficient to meet the increasing demands made upon them, a large call-room was recently opened at the south-west corner of "the boards." This room is fitted

ith a number of private boxes from which conversations may be held, y telephone, with the company's subscribers in Manchester, and also ith subscribers in any of the towns connected by trunk wires, full etails of which will be seen on the accompanying map. The charges made r these and, in fact, for all the many other exceptional advantages pro-ded by the company, are strictly moderate. It is obvious, then, that the . & C. T. Ex. Co., Ltd., is a great boon to commercial and business men of l kinds, and the amount of time and money saved annually by people avail-g themselves of its facilities reaches a very considerable item. The oard of directors is a particularly strong one, a remark that applies to the entire management; whilst the able secretary, Mr. Kenneth MacIver, is certainly to be complimented upon the satisfactory results that have followed his persevering industry. The chief offices of the company are situated at 38, Faulkner Street, a building of six storeys, handsomely furnished and appointed well in every particular. The staff employed is necessarily a large one. Improvements are daily being made in the work-ing arrangements; the patronage of the company is, undoubtedly, rapidly increasing, and the future before it should be useful in the extreme and crowned with complete success.

The Alliance Assurance Company, 10, Cross Street.—here is nothing which appeals so strongly to our minds as the desire to cure to ourselves or families a provision against unforeseen contingencies. n passing under review the numerous highly important institutions con-ected with fire and life insurance, the old-established "Alliance Assur-nce Company" has special claims upon our attention. The business of is Company was established in the year 1824 in London, and twenty ears ago the branch establishment at Manchester was opened, and it is is office which forms the subject of the present notice. The business ere is under the management of Mr. H. F. Cutler, and comprises the sual life and fire risks. The offices of the Company are well situated and admirably arranged. The Alliance Assurance Company possesses a capital of five millions sterling, and this, together with the large amount of its reserves and the high character of its investments, afford security of the highest order, and produce that confidence and stability which this Company so eminently enjoys. The rates of premium both in the fire and life departments are moderate, and the conditions most favourable to the assured. As a financial undertaking this Company has been throughout a brilliant success. The powerful and influential board of directors, with the Right Hon. Lord Rothschild as chairman, and the firm hold already obtained upon popular confidence, together with the advantages of a high class and sound security, assure for this Company a long continuation of the career of usefulness which it has already been its province to fulfil.

Dobson & Barlow, Makers of all Descriptions of Machinery for Preparing and Spinning Cotton and other Fibres, 2, St. Ann's Place.—The first notice we have of the importation of cotton into England is that from the Levant, and it was used chiefly for the manufacture of candle-wicks. Contrast that with the position of cotton manufacture in England at the present time, and an idea of the improvements made by machinery may be gained. Messrs. Dobson & Barlow are engaged in the manufacture of machinery for preparing and spinning cotton and other fibres, and own some gigantic works at Bolton. The establishment of this firm dates back to 1790, when the methods in vogue were very simple compared with those of the present day. It was only in 1760 that the manufacture of cotton in England was almost as simple as that of India, though the carding had been copied from the woollen manufacture, and the loom was a trifle superior. The first great improvement was the construction of a spinning jenny, and this is generally ascribed to James Hargreaves, a weaver in Lancashire, in 1767. It was in 1768 that Arkwright (formerly a Lancashire barber, and subsequently Sir Richard) invented his water spinning frame. In 1779 Samuel Crompton invented a machine that combined the principles of both Hargreave's and Arkwright's systems, and it was only eleven years after this when the above-mentioned firm of Messrs. Dobson & Barlow was originally established under the same title. What changes in machinery since then! How different the methods employed now! Again, what a revolution has been made by the introduction of steam power! The firm mentioned have seen all the many different modes of cotton manufacture, and supplied a great proportion of the machinery used. The present partners are Messrs. Thomas Henry Rushton and Benjamin Alfred Dobson, both justices of the peace in the district. The premises occupied in Manchester consist of a large suite of offices splendidly fitted, and employing a very efficient staff. At the works in Bolton some thousands of hands are engaged, and the factory is one of the principal industries of the town. Mr. Dobson is alderman of Bolton, and both partners occupy an important position. All kinds of machinery used for making cotton are constructed at these enormous works and many special patents are the sole property of the firm. Among these may be mentioned a self-acting mule for fine spinning, of which the firm are the patentees. It may be interesting to notice the career of the original inventor of the mule, namely, the Samuel Crompton mentioned above. Born in 1753, at the time of his invention, in 1779, he lived at a place called "Hall i' th' Wood" at Bolton. He did not patent the invention, which thereby, although it came into general use, did not give him any benefit. A grant of £5,000 was made, the whole of which he lost by misfortune. In 1825 a few of his friends bought him an annuity, but he only lived two years to enjoy it. Parliament, at the recommendation of Sir Robert Peel, granted a sum of £200 to his two sons and one daughter, in 1834; and finally in 1862 a bronze statue was erected to his memory by public subscription and placed in Nelson Square, Bolton. Messrs. Dobson & Barlow make all the most improved forms of gins, carding engines, combers, mules, fly frames, throstles, doublers, winding frames, and reels, &c., &c., and have special rights in the celebrated Heilmann combing machines, also combined draw frame and ribbon lap machine, with many other important machines incidental to this trade. The Manchester managing agent is Mr. Sam. Mason, junr. The firm have many agents all over the Continent, America, and many other parts. Hardly any idea can be conceived of the magnitude of the business done by this house. Their engines and all kinds of machinery are seen in every quarter of the civilised globe, and they enjoy an unsurpassed reputation in every branch of their business. It is almost superfluous to remark that the management is perfect. The wide-spread fame of this firm is familiar to most people even remotely connected with manufactures, and Messrs. Dobson & Barlow are to be congratulated on the success their efforts have met with, and the reputation they have always maintained.

W. Cowell, Manufacturers' Agent, 71, Mosley Street.—Few manufacturing firms, however large, can afford to have establishments of their own in all the commercial centres in which it is yet very necessary to their interests that they should be adequately represented. Hence the agent is called into requisition. The manufacturers' agency business of Mr. W. Cowell was established in the year 1861, previous to which Mr. Cowell was buyer to Rylands & Son, and Copestake, Moore, & Crampton. He afterwards represented Messrs. Yates, Brown, & Howat, of Glasgow, and still represents this firm, now D. G. Howat & Co., which connects him with the trade of Manchester during a period of fifty-two years. How deservedly high his reputation is, may be gathered from the names of the large manufacturing firms whose business in this city is entirely committed to his care. He represents Messrs. A. Baillon & Co., of Nottingham; Messrs. Kay & Richardson, Limited, of London; Alder, Rappolt, & Engler, of Switzerland, all of the same first-class character and extensive trade in plain and fancy muslins, lace curtains, nets, laces, crapes, Swiss embroideries, &c. These are a fair selection of the class of firms and description of goods with which Mr. Cowell has to do. The aggregate of his transactions for these houses totals up to a very large figure. All the qualifications that go to make up a thoroughly good manufacturers' agent he possesses in a high degree, and it is to this that is undoubtedly to be attributed the fact that he has secured the unbounded confidence reposed in him by so many shrewd commercial men. His strict honour and undeviating good faith and integrity afford the firmest assurance that this confidence has not in any instance been misplaced.

Rigg, Brothers, Cotton Spinners and Manufacturers, 6, Mosley Street.—Manchester, for the magnitude and excellence of her cotton industry, is unapproached by any other city in the world, and among the firms engaged in spinning and manufacturing, an important place is held by that of Messrs. Rigg, Brothers, 6, Mosley Street. It was established in 1840, and since that date the firm has worked up a very extensive trade. The premises occupied are commodious and central, comprising office and stock-rooms. The stock-room is well filled with goods manufactured by the firm, and are conveniently arranged for inspection. The works, known as Bleaklow Mills, situated at Tottington, near Bury, are extensive, and admirably equipped with the most modern machinery used in the spinning and manufacturing operations, and the hands employed are able and experienced, and most careful attention is insisted

upon in the making of cloth, *no bad work being allowed to pass*—viz. ring twist and weft spinning—and the broadest looms used in the trade, in which they manufacture "THE BEST SHEETINGS," so well known in all the leading retail establishments of this country, their speciality being *pure woven, free from any size or dressing whatever*, double warp, and made from the very best cottons that can be procured; also they are *warranted thoroughly shrunk*, in widest widths the shrinkage being as much as from fifteen to twenty inches. The productions of this firm are highly esteemed for their durability, texture, and general quality, and a heavy trade is done all over the United Kingdom. The individual members of the firm are Messrs. S. S. and W. R. Rigg, gentlemen of the highest reputation and much respected for the able and enterprising manner in which they conduct their business. They are well known in mercantile and manufacturing circles, and occupy a high position in the trade.

Giddings & Dacre, Junction Lead, Paint, Glass, and Brass Works, have extensive premises situated in Ducie Street, Whittle's Croft, and Mather Street, off London Road. This business has been in active operation for over forty years, and its history is one of steady prosperity. The business is carried on in three large works and warehouses, and consists of manufacturing of sheet lead, lead, water, and gas-pipes, paints, brass-finishing, lamp making and numerous other articles connected with the general plumber's trade. Besides the above, they keep a large stock of cast-iron rain and hot-water pipes, wrought-iron tubes, fittings, locomotive and boiler tubes; plate, sheet, embossed, and enamelled glass and leaded lights; oils, varnishes, colours; cisterns, boilers, cylinders, galvanized and copper; baths, pumps, globes, mirrors, gas cooking and heating stoves, chandeliers, brackets, hall lamps, &c. A great advance has been made by the firm in placing in the market special qualities in all colours of quick-drying varnish paints, and also enamel paint, the latter being suitable for ladies' use and home work. The trade connection is very extensive and widespread, many travellers being employed, and also a very large staff of hands. The sole proprietors are Mr. Alfred Giddings, Mr. George Dacre and Mr. Thomas Hartley who succeeded the founders of the firm on their retirement.

Midgley & Carr, Manufacturers, 26, Faulkner Street.—The widely known and flourishing firm of Midgley & Carr was established in Manchester so far back as the year 1851, and in the hands of the present proprietors, Messrs. Thomas and C. G. Ratcliffe, it maintains a high and honourable position in the city. The city offices and warehouses are well situated, as above. The ware-rooms are well stocked with a splendid collection of Angolas, satteens, royal ribs, reps, welts, quiltings, imperials, drills, ducks, twills, and other fancy cloths, remarkable for their superior quality in point of style, durability, and cheapness; and they are very much in demand not only in the home market, but for export to various parts of the world. The works of the firm are at Greenhill Mills, Colne, and are replete with the most improved machinery in every department. The result is that the manufactures of Messrs. Midgley & Carr enjoy a well-deserved popularity, and that in this particular and important branch of industry in Manchester, the firm has a reputation second to none.

John Hetherington & Sons, Cotton Machinery Manu-sturers, Vulcan Works. —One of the foremost industrial institu-ns of Manchester, both in magnitude and importance, is the distin-ished house of Messrs. John Hetherington & Sons, controllers of the ll-known Vulcan Works in that city. This representative firm has t completed the first half-century of a signally prosperous career, ving been founded in 1837, and the industry it controls to-day has ained to proportions which place it among the first in the kingdom. fty years have wrought a great and abiding change in the commercial tures of Manchester, and it is safe to say that one of the strongest ntrasts that have been effected in that period is that which would pre-nably exist between the Vulcan Works as they are to-day known oughout the whole of the cotton trade centre, and the establishment in ro Street, in which Messrs. Hetherington first opened in 1837. Still latter was destined to lay firmly and solidly the foundations of a ghty industry, and in it the business received that healthy impetus l development which ere long necessitated the building of the present extensive works. Nor did the growth of the industry pause at this point, as is shown in the subsequent erection of a large addition to the Vulcan Works as they were originally constructed, which addition is now devoted entirely to tool-making. The combined premises cover a great area of ground, and are replete with every mechanical requisite in improved plant; yet such are the rapid strides continually being made by the business of the house that further structural extensions are quite within the bounds of probability. The industrial operations of Messrs. Hetherington embrace the manufacture of all kinds of cotton opening, scutching, carding, preparing, spinning, and doubling machinery, and of tools of every description. In this way two fairly distinct departments have been constituted, giving rise to two titles for the firm, who trade in the cotton machinery department as John Hetherington & Sons, and in the tool department as Hetherington & Co. These distinctions are, however, merely to facilitate postal convenience in the receipt of orders and other communications respecting the two departments individually; in all other respects the house is one undivided concern, and the two

es are merged and identical. The great speciality of the firm, and largest and most important feature in their industry, is the manu-ture of cotton-spinning machinery. In this branch they have achieved world-wide renown, and their productions are in constantly increasing nand in almost every home and foreign centre of the cotton industry. ssrs. Hetherington were the first in England to make a machine for nbing cotton, and their invention in this respect has been the great hetype upon which all successors of a similar kind, by all other British kers, have been modelled. Their leading manufactures in cotton-nning and preparing plant now embrace the following well-known l highly appreciated machines: Crighton vertical beater openers; eupino beater openers; Derby doublers; lap machine for making laps combing machines; the Heilmann combing machine for long staple ton, and the Pinel, Lecœur, and Hetherington combing machine for yptian, American, and Surat cottons; ring throstle frames with bbeth or Booth-Sawyer spindles; flier throstle frames, with or without Ashworth long collar and drag-shell; self-acting mules and a patent machine of high efficacy for grinding and toning the leather covering of top rollers. To this list must be added scutchers, ring doubling frames and flier doubling frames, grinding machines and rollers, drawing, slubbing, intermediate, roving, and fine jack frames. They have made and patented many improvements in revolving flat cards and every description of cotton cards, together with a wide variety of other machinery and plant, large and small, applicable to all the purposes and requirements of the great industry of which Manchester is the universally renowned head-quarters. It is needless in these pages to dwell upon Messrs. Hetherington's productions in this department as regards their excellence and efficacy. Their many merits have been repeatedly proven by that best and most severe of all tests, practical use and experience; and we have only here to reiterate what is a well-known and admitted truism among cotton manufacturers, that the Hetherington machinery has never yet failed to give full satisfaction. In the second branch of their great industry Messrs. Hetherington & Sons are almost equally fam us. They engage here in the manufacture of all kinds of heavy plant, including power travelling

[**John Hetherington & Sons**] cranes, mill-gearing, hoists, &c., and in the making of every description of engineers' tools; and their success in each of these lines has been most complete and gratifying. The resources and capacities of their immense works are quite unsurpassed, every facility being possessed in multiplied form for the production of mechanical and engineering appliances and apparatus of all kinds. And it is noteworthy, as an example of the firm's capabilities in this respect that they were the manufacturers of the largest lathe ever made for the Portsmouth Dockyard up to the date of its production. The firm's industrial operations, in their entirety, are carried on upon a scale of great magnitude, and in the various departments of the Vulcan Works an enormous staff, numbering over 1,200 hands, is constantly employed. Every branch of this immense business is conducted upon the same lines of commercial integrity, enterprise, and energy which have raised it to its present high level of importance and eminence. The high reputation of the house and its valuable and influential connections are equally widespread, and the great trade controlled extends its ramifications throughout the entire United Kingdom and over a far-reaching circuit of foreign and colonial custom.

Felber, Jucker, & Co., Exporters of Machinery, &c., 60, Peter Street.- The exportation of machinery is extensively carried on in Manchester. An immense amount of capital is invested in the business, and many firms are engaged therein. One of the best-known and largest of these is that of Messrs. Felber, Jucker, & Co., which was established by the late Mr. J. Felber about 1860. The premises occupied are very extensive, affording great storing accommodation, and the offices are large, and furnished in a very superior manner. The firm carries on business on a very extensive scale, and it has branch establishments abroad. It exports to all parts of the world immense quantities of machinery for all kinds of industrial purposes, making a speciality of textile machinery, and the goods are obtained from the leading manufacturers. Over thirty engineers, travellers, and clerks are employed, and the organization of the business is all that could be desired. Messrs. Felber, Jucker, & Co. are also consulting engineers; they undertake the preparation of plans for all branches of engineering, and employ a large number of mechanical draughtsmen. Messrs. Felber, Jucker, & Co., always have their hands full of the most important commissions from all parts, and they are noted for the prompt manner in which they carry them out. Their plans are distinguished by great inventive power, and evince a thorough knowledge of all engineering matters. Messrs. Felber, Jucker, & Co. are gentlemen who are well known and highly respected in the mercantile and industrial world, and their status therein is of the highest; whilst as exporters of machinery and consulting engineers they have no superiors in the United Kingdom.

John Buckley, Mineral Water Manufacturer, Canal Street, Great Ancoats Street.—The manufacture of mineral waters is extensively carried on in Manchester; it is in the highest state of perfection, and the establishments engaged are numerous and under able management. A typical house in this line is that trading as John Buckley, which was established by that gentleman eight years ago, and is now carried on by his widow. The premises occupied are of ample dimensions, and comprise works with yard and office, the latter being suitably fitted up. The works are admirably adapted for the business, the machinery and apparatus are in every respect perfect and of modern construction, and a good staff of skilled hands is employed in manufacturing mineral waters of all kinds. The processes are carried out on the most advanced principles, and the mineral waters produced are unsurpassable for strength, flavour, and appetising properties. In proof thereof samples were submitted to Mr. G. H. Sharpe, F.C.S., of London, and this gentleman reported that he found them perfectly wholesome and entirely free from all injurious substances. Mrs. John Buckley carries on a very heavy local and district trade, which under her able and energetic management is steadily increasing. She is thoroughly acquainted with every detail of the manufacture, and is well and favourably known all over the city and district. Her honourable business methods have won the universal esteem and confidence of her customers, and her house is unexcelled by any contemporary concern in the city.

John Mark, Tea and Wine Merchant, Grocer, and Italian Warehouseman, 3 and 5, St. Ann's Square.—Among the mercantile establishments which have obtained well-deserved notoriety in what we may term modern Manchester, we must include the well-known house of Mr John Mark. It was founded in the year 1863 by Mr. Mark, and has remained continuously under his sole proprietorship, and its course has been one of prosperity and commercial success. We may remark, in passing, that Mr. Mark served a lengthy probation with the late extensive and eminent old firm of Messrs Richardson & Roebuck, of the Market Place, Manchester, in which he became a partner, and obtained a very thorough knowledge of all the details of a high-class family grocery and wine trade, in which he is now engaged. The experience thus acquired has enabled him to combine a natural capacity for business with enterprise, and to exercise prudence and sound judgment in his mercantile speculations; hence the good fortune which has attended his career. Mr. Mark was thus well known in Manchester when he first commenced business on his own account, and had already obtained a reputation in the city. He soon secured a large connection and influential patronag[e] which has never ceased to grow in extent and importance, not only [in] Manchester and vicinity, but in distant parts of the country. His pre[mises] in St. Ann's Square are very commodious, and his trade operatio[ns] carried on thereat are of a magnitude that command attention and pla[ce] the establishment upon a footing of equality with any other emporium [of] the kind in England. Originally, the business was chiefly confined [to] family groceries, including French and Italian specialities, with an exte[n]sive tea and coffee trade, in which important branches Mr. Mark did [a] large and high-class trade. His success emboldened him to add oth[er] branches of business, including especially those of a wine and spirit mer[]chant and dealer in Chinese and Japanese goods; and as a direct import[er] on a large scale of fine Havana cigars for the last twenty years, he ha[s] obtained a high reputation, and these additions now form leading featur[es] of his extensive commercial transactions. Mr. Mark holds splendid stoc[k] in each department of his miscellaneous business, and they are displaye[d] in his establishment in the most tasteful, convenient, and effective mann[er] possible. We can only attempt to give a sort of cursory review or sket[ch] of Mr. Mark's business premises, but we may state that externally the[y] have a commanding and attractive appearance, and are in a centr[al] position, close to the Royal Exchange. Internally the attractions a[re] still greater, for the stock throughout is at once seen to be of immen[se] extent and of high-class quality; a glance at the handsome sale an[d] show-rooms, which are numerous, clearly indicates that the establish[]ment is filled with a most valuable and varied description of merchandis[e] in the hands of a busy and smart-looking staff of salesmen and clerk[s]. Mr. Mark has a large grocery warehouse in Half Moon Street, ver[y] extensive wine cellars under the whole range of Mansfield Chamber[s] with entrance from St. Ann's Square, both of which are utilised for th[e] storage of reserve stocks, ready to supply the chief warehouse as re[]quired. Mr. Mark is an extensive importer in all the several lines [of] business in which he is engaged, dealing directly with the manufacture[rs] and the best home and foreign sources of supply, and constantly intro[]ducing to the notice of his patrons everything that is worthy of con[]sideration, either as a saleable novelty, or as a staple whose use [is] sanctioned by long-established custom. The high standard of excellenc[e] of quality that has been uniformly maintained from the outset of hi[s] career down to the present time, has won for this house a public confi[]dence, and the name of the house has come to be widely known fo[r] reliable quality of goods in every department, whilst the business itsel[f] has always been conducted on lines of the strictest probity and honou[r]. Higher praise than this cannot be accorded to any establishment; never[]theless, we have not travelled beyond the limits of truth and justic[e]. Mr. Mark exhibited at the Royal Jubilee Exhibition at Manchester[,] where he had two stands, one devoted to Chinese and Japanese good[s] and the other to choice Havannah cigars, and both commanded an[d] deserved general attention and admiration. As an importer of Chine[se] and Japanese articles, the name of Mr. Mark has become known both i[n] Manchester and the surrounding districts, and the superb display h[e] made at the recent exhibition was in every respect worthy of the reputa[]tion he enjoys in the city of his adoption. To suit the convenience an[d] meet the requirements of his many customers, Mr. Mark has quite recentl[y] opened an office at 32, Jermyn Street, London, W., for the sale of ciga[rs] and wine only. Mr. Mark has been, for many years past, a prominen[t] figure in the municipal and social life of Manchester. Ten years ago h[e] was induced to accept office as a representative in the City Council, fo[r] the wealthy and important ward of St. Ann's (wherein his own busine[ss] premises are situate), and he has ever since continued to represent th[at] noted constituency, having been three times in succession re-electe[d] without opposition, a fact which, of itself, testifies to the faithful an[d] satisfactory manner in which he has discharged the duties of the offic[e]. Mr. Mark has interested himself in various other enterprises affecting th[e] welfare of the city, such as the Ship Canal and the late most successfu[l] Jubilee Exhibition, and in both instances his earnest and practical sup[]port has met with an appreciation commensurate with its sterling wort[h]. As a citizen, and a thoroughly representative business man, Mr. Mar[k] has done good and effective service to Manchester, and his labours [in] the cause of social advancement and trade development will always b[e] remembered with appreciation by the residents of the city and distric[t]. We will only add that Mr. Mark enjoys the respect and esteem, not only [of] his fellow-citizens, but of all who have the privilege of his acquaintanc[e].

James Aspinall Turner & Co., Cotton Manufacturer[s], 37, Faulkner Street.—This is a very old-established firm, and its histo[ry] is one of great prosperity and success. The premises in Faulkner Stre[et] consist of a very handsome warehouse of four spacious floors. The offic[es] are a fine suite of commodious rooms, exceedingly well furnished, an[d] and fitted with the latest and most approved appliances for the rap[id] dispatch of business. The factories, known as Bankside Mills, a[re] located at Rochdale. The specialities of production are ginghams, check[s], stripes, ticks, Harvards, Oxfords, regattas, flannelettes, and similar good[s]. The connection is very extensive and includes practically all the leadi[ng] merchant shippers, the wholesale firms, and warehousemen. At th[e] mills some hundreds of hands are employed, while in Faulkner Stre[et] there is a strong contingent of clerks, bookkeepers, warehouse hands an[d] porters. The sole partner now is Mr. W. Fairhurst, a gentleman who [is] highly esteemed and respected in general commercial circles.

The Singer Manufacturing Company, 107, Market Street.—Among the most wonderful and beneficial inventions for which the present century is noted, the sewing machine must be accorded an honourable position. No mention of this industry can be complete without a reference to one firm whose name is familiar from end to end of the world, namely, The Singer Manufacturing Company, manufacturers of the celebrated "Singer's Sewing Machines." Good wine needs no bush, and the name of Singer requires no commendation to a public which knows so well the productions which are identified with it. Something exceeding half a million of machines bearing the trade name, "Singer," of this firm, are sent out into the world during a single twelvemonth. For more than twenty years The Singer Manufacturing Company have

had flourishing and successful branches in Manchester and its district, the most prominent among them being at the above address. Most extensive and handsomely fitted premises are devoted to the business of supplying and repairing the productions of the Company. Hand and treadle machines of every description are located here for selection. For one kind of family treadle machine, a marvel of simplicity and make, it is claimed that nearly four millions have been sold since its introduction in the year 1865. The adoption of the hire system has brought Singer's sewing machine within the reach of the poorest family in the country. The Company, whose European works at Kilbowie, Glasgow, cover the enormous area of forty-six acres, have branch offices all over the world, all under capable and skilled management, and the business which is daily transacted is of the most widespread and successful character.

Samuel Mills, Vauxhall Hat Works, Rochdale Road.—A most important branch of industrial and commercial activity in Man-

chester is the manufacture of hats, and in this connection it is a pleasure to make prominent mention of such an old-established and well-known concern as the Vauxhall Hat Works, of which Mr. Samuel Mills is proprietor. This business, which bears ample evidence of enterprise and good management, was established in 1850, and from a comparatively small beginning its operations have grown to the proportions of a large and eminently successful industry. The extensive works in Bronze Street, Rochdale Road, are equipped with the most improved appliances, employment being given to a large force of skilled hands. All sorts of hats, including ladies' riding hats, pullovers, and caps of every description, are made in great numbers. Mr. Mills' exhibits at the Manchester Exhibition were very favourably noticed by *The Railway Supplies Journal* of June 25th last. The hats manufactured at this establishment are unexcelled for beauty and originality of design, superiority of workmanship, finish, and durability. They are made from the best materials in the most skilful manner, and have a standard reputation in the trade both at home and abroad. With the superior facilities at its command, the firm is enabled to offer special advantages to customers, and to execute the largest orders in the promptest manner. Mr. Samuel Mills, the head of the house, is a gentleman whose enterprise and sound judgment have won the esteem and respect of the commercial community.

G. Wright & Sons, Manchester Dyers and Cleaners.—The densely populated area of which Manchester is the natural centre and mart, forms also the principal seat of the dyeing trade in this country. The best makers of dyeing utensils, the best dyes and soaps, the most skilled workmen, and water naturally soft and suitable for the work—these are all to be found in this locality; and although there are of course large dyeing concerns in other parts of the country the trade done does not represent a tithe of that turned out by the great works in this locality. The dyeing and cleaning art is also well represented, and one of the oldest and most widely known among these concerns is that of Messrs. G. Wright & Sons, of the City of Manchester and Great Northern Dye Works. The ramifications of this firm, which was founded in 1835, extend to all parts of England, there being branch establishments in London, Liverpool, Sheffield, Birmingham, and other large towns. In Manchester there are no less than five chief offices: 231, Oxford Road; 4, Clarendon Street; 61, Great Ducie Street; 183, Stretford Road, and Moss Lane; and a large number of agents in the city and its suburbs. Goods are collected and sent out by means of a well-equipped service of vans, and every day of the week has its appointed circuit, the vast amount of business entrusted to the firm necessitating this division of the district. The extensive works at Stockport were specially built for the trade when this firm removed their works from Manchester a few years ago, for more room and convenience, and they are unquestionably one of the largest and most carefully fitted up in the United Kingdom. Messrs Wright & Sons have had a lifelong experience of the trade, and every department is under the supervision of members of the firm, whilst every shop and office is frequently visited. So excellent are the arrangements that, notwithstanding the enormous number of consignments from all parts which reach the works, there is never any confusion, and every article is returned to its rightful owner. Rapidity, excellence, and cheapness are the keynotes of this gigantic concern, the merits of which have been recognised by the Queen herself; and in every respect nothing could be more correct than the statement that it is amongst the largest and most successful dyeing and cleaning works in the country.

T. Nelson & Co., Wholesale Furriers, Skin Merchants, and Fur Mantle Manufacturers, 9, Mosley Street.—This business was commenced in the year 1878, and has been very successful. The warehouse consists of several spacious rooms, and there is a capital suite of offices very handsomely furnished and thoroughly well fitted up. The specialities of the trade are furs and skins. In the former, a large business is done in seal jackets, dolmanettes, and visites; cashmere circulars or dolmans, lined with various kinds of fur, muffs, collarettes, for trimmings, &c.; fur sets and flouncings, fur carriage-wrappers, and skin hearthrugs. Messrs. Nelson bestow particular attention to the carrying out of the orders for specially made garments in the fur line; and no matter what measurement be required, or what alterations made, they are enabled to effect anything necessary, as they keep assistants who are experts for those very purposes. Nor does their business cease with the manufacture of the furs, or making and fitting the made-up garments, but their works are fitted with all the requisites to enable them to clean and renovate the furs, which they not only repair and re-line, but alter, while sealskin jackets can here be re-dyed, re-made, or lengthened. The connection includes a proportion of the shipping houses, but the bulk of the trade is done with the general Manchester warehousemen, the first-class drapery houses, and mantle manufacturers. Some two or three travellers are constantly on the road in the interests of the firm, and make a considerable turn-over. At Mosley Street the staff includes salesmen, stockkeepers, clerks, fur cutters, and fitters. Mr. Thomas Nelson is the sole proprietor and is well known amongst the fur buyers in the city.

G. I. Sidebottom & Co., Manufacturers of Dyed and Printed Silesias, &c., 19, Portland Street.—This well-known and important business was established in the very first year of the present century. The style of the firm was then Warren & Kershaw. In 1819 it became Lees & Millington; in 1824 Lees, Kershaw, & Calendar; in 1832 Lees, Kershaw, and Co.; in 1843 J. Lees, Kershaw, & Co.; in 1858 Kershaw, Sidebottom, & Berry; in 1869 Kershaw, Sidebottom, & Co.; and subsequently assumed the present title, G. I. Sidebottom & Co. The London address is 2 and 3, Honey Lane Market, Milk Street, E.C. The Glasgow address is 153, Queen Street. The specialities of manufacture are cotton goods, such as dyed and printed silesias, whites, greys, linen yards, regattas, and similar goods. The connection includes the principal shipping and home-trade houses. The members of the firm are all extremely well known on 'Change, and in commercial and business circles.

Queen's Hotel, Portland Street.—Amongst the many things for which Manchester has long been famous, in common justice the hotels must be included. There are several which rank very high, and there are beyond these a number which partake more of the character of commercial houses, and which are equal to any of their class in the provinces. There is one hotel, however, in Manchester which, from its long and notable career, historical associations, and splendid reputation commands the foremost place, viz. the "Queen's Hotel," which is situated at the

corner of Portland Street and Piccadilly. This hotel is known not only over the whole breadth of the United Kingdom, but throughout the world, and its patrons comprise the *élite* of all nationalities visiting the city. It would fill a volume to enumerate all the imperial, royal, noble, and otherwise distinguished personages who have, for longer or shorter periods, lodged beneath its hospitable roof, but it may not be amiss to name a few of them. They include the Emperor of Brazil, the late King of the Belgians, the King of Portugal, the Crown Prince of Austria, Prince Napoleon, ex-President Grant, Jeff Davis, late and present Earls of Derby, the Marquess of Salisbury, the Duchess of Montrose, Earl of Rosebery, Lord Brabourne, the late Lord Chief Justice Cockburn, Sir E. W. Watkins, Chairman of the M. T. & L. Railway and the S. E. Railway, Lord Colville, Chairman of the Great Northern, Mr. Thompson, Chairman of the Midland Railway, Val Prinsep, George Augustus Sala, Coutts Lindsay, Lady B. Coutts, Alma Tadema, the High Sheriff of the County, Charles Dickens, Thackeray, Charles Mathews, Mark Lemon, G. V. Brooke, Jenny Lind, Patti, Grisi, and Mario, Lablache, Rossini, Macready, Sims Reeves, C. Santley, Jullien, Mr. and Mrs. C. Kendal, J. L. Toole, Foli, Tom Taylor, Fred Archer, the Chinese Embassy, and the Siamese Embassy. In short, the Queen's Hotel possesses a charm for visitors of distinction, from whatever quarter of the globe they come, or to whatrank or profession they belong. In Axon's "Annals of Manchester" it is recorded, under date of 1867, "Lieutenant-Colonel C. G. Gordon, the famous 'Chinese' Gordon, was for a few months resident at the Queen's Hotel during the survey for the Redistribution Bill." The chronicler further adds, "He interested himself in the work of the Dark Lane Ragged School, and in the visitation of the slums of the City Mission." Some letters addressed by him to Mr. James Johnson, one of the missionaries, are printed in the "Report of the City Mission for 1884." In one he says, "Remember me to all my friends, the lads of Dark Lane." Perhaps no greater honour was ever conferred upon the "Queen's" than when this great and noble hero and philanthropist (the Martyr of Khartoum) lodged under its roof. The "Queen's" occupies decidedly the best position of any hotel in Manchester. It overlooks, from Portland Street, the grand open space in front of the Royal Infirmary, and commands a clear view of Piccadilly down to its junction with Mosley Street and Market Street. It is within five or six minutes' walk of all the railway stations, theatres, Town Hall, Exchange, and Cathedral; and within a few yards of it busses can be obtained for all parts of the city and suburbs. Externally the hotel has a neat but exceedingly handsome appearance. It is a square block of building, four stories in height—exclusive of basement and attics—with two frontages of considerable extent, one to Portland Street, and the other to Piccadilly; and there are spacious entrances from both thoroughfares. The fronts are coated with Roman cement, and as they are usually painted a light colour the hotel has always a clean and cheerful aspect. Internally the accommodation is most complete and superior. Prior to 1856 it was a comparatively small establishment, not numbering more than some fifty rooms, all told; but in that year it was considerably enlarged in view of the opening of the great "Art Treasures Exhibition," of 1857, and it then attained its present dimensions. The hotel contains about one hundred bedrooms, fourteen sitting-rooms, masonic rooms, rooms for banquets and weddings, table d'hôte and coffee-rooms, drawing-room, billiard and smoke rooms; and has all modern improvements, such as an American elevator, and baths, lavatories, &c., on every floor. It is furnished throughout in handsome style, everything being of the very best, and combining the elegant with the substantial. The hotel is celebrated for its home comforts, its good *cuisine*, excellent wine cellar, and also for its famous turtle, made from live fish, for invalids and dinner parties, which is sent over the whole country and has restored many to health and vigour. In the year 1851 the late Mr. Thomas Johnson, who had formerly been proprietor of the Albion Hotel, Manchester, became landlord of the Queen's, but in 1863 he was joined by Mr. Frederick Mehl, and the business was carried on thenceforward under the style of Thomas Johnson & Co. Mr. Johnson died in 1868, since which time Mr. Mehl has conducted the hotel on his own account, though he still trades under the former style. Mr. Mehl is a gentleman who is most extensively known in Manchester and elsewhere, and he is universally esteemed. Under his able and judicious management the "Queen's" has, if possible, increased its fame and popularity at home and abroad, and it now occupies a position of equality with the very first hotels in the kingdom.

Messrs. W. Singleton Birch & Sons, Limited, Merchants and Manufacturers of China Clay, Colours, Cement, Plaster of Paris, Ground Chalk, Whiting, &c., Upton Street.—One of the most notable of Manchester houses in respect of its wide-spread influence in British industrial circles, and of its own high individual importance as a commercial concern, is that of Messrs. W. Singleton Birch & Sons, Limited. This eminent firm of mineral merchants was originated as far back as the year 1815. Messrs. W. Singleton Birch & Sons, are known to-day throughout the entire United Kingdom as miners, manufacturers, and suppliers of china clay, ground chalk, ochre, colours, cement, plaster of Paris, mineral white, Paris white, and whiting; and control, in connection with their operations in these most important commodities, very extensive works in Devonshire, Lincolnshire, and Cornwall. In addition to this the firm have depôts at Runcorn, Fleetwood, Preston, and several other centres, conveniently located for purposes of rail and waterway shipment. At each of these depôts complete and very extensive stocks are held. Messrs. W. Singleton Birch & Sons, Limited, were the first to introduce into the Lancashire market the china clay, for which they are now so famous and of which many thousands of tons are annually used at the present time by paper makers, bleachers, calico-printers, and the textile industries generally. The value of the commodity to these branches of manufacture needs no accentuation here. Indeed, it is difficult to imagine the satisfactory operation of the industries in question, upon the advanced principles of modern times, *without* the indispensable aid of china clay in most of their pre-eminently important processes; and the service rendered by Messrs. Birch in first bringing it forward in the Lancashire district is unquestioned and indisputable. China clay now constitutes one of the great specialities of the house, and in it alone a trade of immense and continuously increasing magnitude is vigorously and successfully carried on. Messrs. W. Singleton Birch & Sons have thoroughly identified themselves with the supply of this invaluable substance, a fact which is evidenced even in the minute detail of their telegraphic address—"China," Manchester. The firm are also manufacturers, at their Lincolnshire works, of a very fine quality of whiting, which is most extensively used by manufacturers of mineral and aërated waters by reason of the exceptional quantity of carbonic acid gas it generates. And, in addition to China clay and whiting, cements, plaster of Paris, ground chalk, and barytes, are notable features in the stock of the house, and valuable specialities have been developed in mineral white, Paris white, ochre, and various mineral colours, in which large and important import operations are carried on. The entire business is one of the first order of mercantile and industrial influence. The connections maintained extend throughout the whole of Great Britain. All the characteristics of the concern are such as to peculiarly entitle it to prominent mention among the representative business institutions of modern Manchester.

Edward Evans & Son, Merchants, Warehousemen (Silesias, Cottons, Italians, &c.), 3, Back Street, York Street.—A thoroughly representative house in Manchester trade is that of Messrs. E. Evans & Son, which has held its eminent position in the mercantile world for fifty-five years. The present premises have been occupied for about thirty-five years. Messrs. E. Evans & Son make a speciality of battery calicoes and linings, and their storage department contains a large stock of these goods, and of cottons, Italians, and silesias. The firm carry on a very extensive trade in all parts of the country, and also export considerable quantities of these goods. The house is considered one of the leading concerns in the trade, and the principals are well known in the commercial world.

J. J. Meakin, Tea Merchant, 31, 33, and 35, Fennel reet.—This well-known firm has establishments in both London and anchester. In the former city, at 27, Great Tower Street, E.C.; in anchester, in Fennel Street. It has a history extending over a period twenty years—a history of rapid progress and substantial success. r. John James Meakin, the enterprising proprietor, a gentleman of arked managerial aptitude and business ability, is certainly very much be congratulated upon the manner in which he has built up, conducted, d still conducts, this admirable concern. Mr. Meakin's connection is despread and very valuable indeed, and in his spacious tasting and mple show rooms teas of every conceivable class and growth may be en, from the highest and most expensive kinds to prices which seem to incredibly low. Being extensive shippers of tea will no doubt account r the extent and magnitude of the business. It is interesting to add at Mr. Meakin has been an esteemed member of the Salford Town uncil since 1880, and is also one of her Majesty's Justices of the Peace. e employs a large number of hands, including several travellers, and s premises are handsomely appointed in every way.

The Ashbury Railway Carriage and Iron Company, mited, Railway Carriage, &c., Builders and Ironfounders, Openaw.—Manchester is noted for the magnitude and perfection of her manuəture of railway carriages and other similar plant, and among the firms engaged a principal place is held by the Ashbury Railway Carriage and on Company, Limited, Openshaw (Secretary, Mr. William Charlton). is firm was established about fifty years ago by Mr. John Ashbury, t was incorporated as a limited company in 1862. The works are very tensive, covering about twenty-two acres of ground, and the offices form fine building, opening in the Ashton Old Road, and the entrance hall s a very attractive tesselated pavement. Since the commencement velopment has followed development, until now over twenty-two acres of ound are covered and fifteen hundred men are employed. The works e chiefly divided into departments for the erection of railway waggons, th of wood and iron; railway passenger carriages; for carrying out neral engineering-work, and for bridge building. In the wood-workg department, it is observed that the arrangement of the place is such at the logs, &c., are brought into the mill from the line of the Manester, Sheffield, and Lincolnshire Railway, which forms the southern undary of the works, and the planks there cut are passed forward to e erecting-shops in due order, so that nothing is taken back when once has passed the saw-mill. In this last-named department, which occues three bays, there is a frame in which forty-three saws can be worked one time, and a log 20 inches square can be cut. Besides this, there e smaller frames and a number of circular saws. In the wood-mill, ich occupies two bays, there are some large planing-machines, some ving cutters of the ordinary type, and others having horizontally tating cutters. There is also an immense tenoning machine, designed iefly for the heavy frames of railway-waggons and coaches. The ecting-shops, of which there are several, are all of a substantial charac-r—airy, roomy, and well lighted. Their present capacity is equal to e hundred waggons and ten railway-carriages per week. The foundry cupies a spacious building in three bays, each of which is fitted with a werful overhead traveller. Three cupolas are employed, and the erage weekly consumption of pig iron is about one hundred tons. There also a brass foundry having five furnaces. The forge is equal to an tput of three hundred tons per week. There are two rolling-mills—e for rolling large sizes and the other for the small sizes. Five steammmers of various types, ranging in weight from three to five tons, are ntained in the building, and the whole of the plant is driven by an oldshioned but powerful beam-engine. The smithy comprises in all eight ys. It contains 150 fires, and is well-fitted with stamping-hammers d all needful tools. Passing into the wheel-shop, which is in three ys, it is ascertained that 160 sets of wheels and axles can be turned t per week. Hydraulic power is used for forcing the wheels on to the les. In the adjoining shop hydraulic power is also employed for rging the bosses upon the wheels, for which some costly plant has en recently laid down, comprising a hydraulic press capable of giving pressure equal to 2,000 tons, with suitable steam pumps and other pliances. The fitting shop is in four bays, and contains, as its name plies, necessary tools for fitting, &c. It is, however, only needful to ake mention of one tool, viz., a lathe used chiefly for turning locomotive rntables. The face-wheel, which works in a pit, is 16 feet in diameter, d is capable of taking work up to 18 feet 6 inches. Adjoining this partment are some large stores, and in near proximity is a good-sized op in one bay, which is used for a variety of purposes, according to essure of business. The painting-shop for both passenger coaches and aggons is also near at hand, and consists of two bays, one running at ght angles to the other. Here thirty coaches can be painted at one me. Railway tracks are laid throughout the works, and there is siding nnection with the Manchester, Sheffield, and Lincolnshire Railway. A comotive-engine and about 700 waggons are owned by the firm; out one-half of the latter are engaged directly in the service of this mpany. Wheels, axles, travelling and fixed cranes, water columns, nks and other general foundry goods, appliances, and apparatus are ade on the premises in immense quantities. The carriages, &c., of the m are of elegant design, and, in fact, all the productions are of first ality in material and superior manufacture, and in heavy demand. The huge army of hands is under the talented and energetic supervision of Mr. Robert Phillips, chairman and managing director. An enormous trade is carried on in all parts of the world; travellers and agents are employed, and the organisation is all that could be desired. The London offices are 5, Westminster Chambers, S.W. The status of the Ashbury Railway Carriage and Iron Company, Limited, in the general industrial and commercial world, is unexcellable, and no firm in the iron industry is better known, and it is one of the principal railway carriage building concerns in the world.

George Eastwood, Decorator, &c., 3 and 5, St. John Street, Deansgate.—One of the most eminent houses in its line in Manchester is that conducted by Mr. George Eastwood, which was originally founded in conjunction with Mr. Taylor, the firm erecting, in 1871, the spacious edifice now occupied. Subsequently the partnership was dissolved, and since that time Mr. Eastwood has been the sole proprietor. Both these gentlemen had valuable experience with the late Mr. Tyrer, to whose estate Mr. Eastwood was appointed executor. The premises are prominently situated in St. John Street, Deansgate, and consist of a handsome pile of three floors and a basement, commodiously arranged as offices, show-rooms, and warehouses, being well appointed in every respect throughout. The operations of the house are chiefly confined to artistic decorations, such as the fitting up of banquets, temporary wooden ballrooms, and bazaars with stalls, and generally decorating the same, in which difficult task exquisite taste and skill are invariably called into requisition. Private parties are also supplied with supper tables, rout forms, curtains, hollands, &c. Temporary pavilions are erected for similar purposes, and decorated and illuminated in the highest style of art. The celebrity of the house is well known for all its productions, but more especially is it noted for the picturesqueness of the stage scenery supplied for amateur dramatic performances, fairy fountains, &c., as well as numerous other entertainments of a unique description obtainable only at this establishment. Good organisation pervades every department of the business, a regular staff of efficient decorators being permanently employed, and the emporium is invariably the centre of considerable bustle and stirring industrial activity. The trade is of a very widespread nature, and thoroughly well established among the aristocracy, public bodies, and institutions associated with the time-honoured city of Manchester. The proprietor is a gentleman of the highest commercial integrity, and thoroughly acquainted with all the details of his business, being highly respected by his patrons for his courtesy to them and the prompt execution of all orders entrusted to his deservedly well-known house.

Walter Laverton & Co., Velveteen Manufacturers, 13, Chatham Street, Piccadilly.—This comparatively young house, established in January, 1882, under its present style, commenced practically a new business, although Mr. Walter Laverton had previously been connected with other firms, and has made for itself a name both at home and abroad; and by energy, activity, and business tact has attained a success reached by few in so short a time. The specialities of manufacture are certain makes of velvets and velveteens for ladies' wear; also heavier makes for clothiers, with a range of dyed and printed linings, cotton Italians, &c., of peculiar finish and fitness for their purpose, and of high reputation in the several markets where they are sent. These are all protected by registered names and marks distinguishing them from the crowd of imitations which their success was sure to bring out. Another branch supplies stay and corset manufacturers with the various fabrics used in their trade, and these are in high repute for their texture and finish, every piece being thoroughly examined and guaranteed perfect before leaving the warehouse. The hosiery trades of Nottingham and elsewhere are extensive buyers of this firm's products; and the beautiful satin finish of the linings, with the delicate and well-matched colours, is made a particular care of the department. Until the fancy sprung up for leather-lined boots and shoes, an immense trade was done in linings known as linen drills of various makes; these, with others, are still in constant demand, and Messrs. Walter Laverton & Co., always stock a considerable variety, and guarantee that many of their cloths shall long outlast much of the so-called "leather." A prominent feature in the business of this house is that some reserved marks and makes of goods are confined wholly to certain leading wholesale houses, who, under the protected trade mark, adopt the goods and advertise, truly enough, that no other house can supply them, thus creating monopolies for their own benefit. The trade connection, exclusively wholesale, is extensive and widespread, including, besides the prominent shipping-houses of this city, London and Glasgow, most of the Manchester and general warehousemen, and the large buyers amongst the metropolitan and provincial home-trade houses. The firm is represented in London by three distinct resident agents, undertaking different branches; and, besides agents stationed in various parts of the country, the travellers of the firm are pretty well known where wholesale houses exist. The Continental business is mostly confined to the shippers to more distant parts, where the reserved marks and makes have made themselves deservedly well known, and are in constant and increasing demand. Mr. Laverton is a native of Bristol, and commenced business in Manchester in 1866. The business belongs wholly to him, the "Company" having from the first been merely nominal.

G. B. Ollivant & Co., Shipping Merchants and Manufacturers, 3, Albert Street. This firm was established exactly thirty years ago in New Cannon Street. In 18[illegible] a move was made to 20, Lever Street, and in 1870 to the commodious premises now occupied. The principal business was, at first, as manufacturers of velvets, velveteens, cords, sateens, croydons, &c., but later a large general business began to develop itself in every description of goods suitable for the West Coast of Africa, which is now a large and increasing market with them, and they especially pride themselves upon the production from the grey of every description of finished goods, both bleached, dyed, and printed. They do besides a large business in prints for Africa. The firm has a first-class reputation, and great care is shown in the selection of material, the finish, and the various colourings. The requirements of the markets are attentively studied, and no firm in the shipping trade has a better assortment of goods suitable for the African market. The warehouse in Albert Street is a large well-lighted building, containing ample stocks of all goods in which the firm does business; the offices are an elegantly furnished suite of considerable size, and the staff comprises buyers, clerks,

packers, &c. The present sole partner is Alfred Ollivant, Esq., a gentleman thoroughly trained in the business, and an expert in his particular line. He is recognised as a keen man of business and a clever buyer.

A. Baumann & Co., Importers of Farina, Indian Corn, Wheat Starch, Gum Substitutes, and Colours, 40, Kennedy Street. —It requires no demonstration to clearly comprehend how great must be the trade in farina, corn starch, wheat starch, and colours, in and around a city so extensively engaged in the textile trade as Manchester. This is the branch of business to which Messrs. A. Baumann & Company are devoted. Indeed, in this line they are, though to the casual observer it would scarcely seem so, one of the leading establishments in the city. Their offices are situated in Kennedy Street, a leading business thoroughfare of the city, and have been established several years, during which they have worked up a widespread local trade in the commodities in which they are so favourably known. These include every kind of starch, home and foreign, and especially wheat starch crystals, which they import in very large quantities and rapidly sell, and the same may be said of farina. Both these commodities are extensively used in the various processes through which many of the fabrics manufactured in the district have to be put before being ready for the market. The firm enjoys a high-class reputation for the excellence of the goods it introduces, and its connection among the leading local houses is of the soundest and most regular order. The efforts of the principal and his staff are so directed that the number of patrons secured is well maintained and added to weekly. Probity and promptitude are characteristic of the firm's transactions, and have secured for Mr. Baumann, the sole partner, a large share of support and respect.

Wm. Watson & Co., Calico Printers, 60, George Street. —Calico printing is unquestionably one of the most important branches of Manchester industry. In the front rank of the leading firms devoted to this trade a prominent position is held by Messrs. Wm. Watson & Co., whose extensive and commodious city premises are centrally and conveniently located. This enterprising firm began operations about 1873. Mr. Watson, shortly after founding the firm, saw the necessity for cheapening the cost of production, and to effect this he, in conjunction with Mr. R. H. Scott, established a print works at Littleborough. These were fitted up in the most complete manner and equipped with modern machinery. A staff of the most skilled and experienced operatives was engaged. The result of this was soon perceptible in the widespread and influential patronage secured and the steady expansion of the trade done. The designs, patterns, and finish of all work turned out by the firm were and are remarkable for their originality, beauty, taste, and general excellence. The establishment at Littleborough is carried on under the style of the Gale Printing Company. Mr. Watson is now the sole partner in Messrs. Wm. Watson & Co., and has recently purchased the Handforth Printing Works, which he now carries on in conjunction with Mr. James A. Wilson, under the name of the Handforth Printing Company. These premises are of extensive dimensions and fully equipped for the execution of every description of extract and dyed printing work. They furnish employment to a numerous and efficient staff. Messrs. Wm. Watson & Co. do a large trade in all departments. Their satisfactory execution of all work has won for them a widespread, constantly increasing, and valuable *clientèle*, and a reputation of the highest order.

Sharp & Galloway, Sugar Refiners, &c., Salford, and 94, Corporation Street.—The well-known firm of Sharp & Galloway, sugar refiners of Salford, has a history that dates from 1861. The refinery at Salford is fitted up with the very best machinery and appliances. The staff employed is necessarily a large one, as they refine upwards of 180 tons of sugar per week. The management reflects the very highest credit upon all connected with it. The sugar and other similar products of the firm find a ready market throughout the kingdom.

Bednal Brothers, Commercial Stationers, Letter-ress and Lithographic Printers and Engravers, Paper-Rulers, ookbinders, Account-Book Manufacturers, &c., 128, Market Street. Vorks, 51, Tib Street.—This well-known house was established forty ears ago. The business is a comprehensive one, for the firm are commer-ial stationers letterpress and lithographic printers and engravers, book-inders, account-book manufacturers, paper-rulers, &c. The establishment ı Market Street is admirably situated. All miscellaneous wares, in the ape of fancy goods, which now adorn the first-class houses in this line f business are held in stock, a private telephone connecting this establish-

ıent with their works. The works, here represented, are situated in Tib treet (within a minute's walk of the Market Street establishment), and ey comprise a handsome block of buildings of four flats, each flat covering n area of about three hundred square yards. Here are to be found the ecessary plant and machinery for executing every description of work con-ected with the business. The works are supplied with adequate steam ower, and are admirably arranged and managed throughout, and they afford nployment to about sixty hands. The trade throughout is a first-class ne, and the firm's connection amongst the warehousemen and manufac-urers of Manchester and the district is extensive and influential. Messrs. Bednal Bros. are gentlemen of experience, energy, and enterprise, and are ell known and much respected in the city and neighbourhood.

John Burtinshaw, Tin Plate Worker, Lever Street.—'his business was established by its present proprietor in the year 1843, nd is one of the largest of its kind in this city. The premises consist of building of five storeys, used as workshops and stock-rooms, with a mall neatly-furnished office. Mr. Burtinshaw has a branch works, nown as the Park Tin Works, at Stockport; and another called the 'anal Tin Works, at Reddish. There is a workshop, also known as the

Ioward Street Plumbing Works. The main specialities of manufacture re wire curl, eyelet and middle traversers, ring guides, tin and steel tra-verse guides, tin throstle bobbins, stamped goods, tin rollers, Patent oil cans and canisters, round and square; he is also the inventor of a new patent self-sealing canister, the properties of which are most admirably adapted for tinning soap, grease and such-like substances; he is also sole maker of Broadhead's patent damping brush for bleachers and paper makers. In addition to these goods, Mr. Burtinshaw does a large business as tin lined packing-case maker, plumber, glazier, and gas fitter. The con-nection is amongst makers of cotton and woollen machinery, spinners, bleachers, manufacturers, and shippers, engineers, grocers, and others. Mr. Burtinshaw employs from fifty to sixty hands, and a brisk trade is carried on. He is a gentleman extremely well known and respected in Manchester business circles, and his great business abilities make him deservedly popular.

A. H. Sansom, Manufacturers' Agent, 30, Faulkner Street.—Mr. Sansom has now been established in this city for a consider-able period, and his business, while steadily increasing, gives tokens of being extremely remunerative in the not distant future. The premises include capacious stock and pattern rooms, and a most convenient office, handsomely furnished and fitted with the latest and most improved appli-ances for the rapid dispatch of business. As commission agent, Mr. Sansom represents the following firms: Messrs. Sansom, Coleman & Co., lace manufacturers, and Messrs. Hutchinson & Co. (late J. and H. Haddon), hosiery and smallware manufacturers, of Nottingham. The principal pro-ductions are lace curtains and hosiery, but the trade in trimming, laces, and smallwares is by no means inconsiderable. The connection being both home and foreign, includes the wholesale houses, the general Manchester warehousemen, and the leading shipping firms. At the Faulkner Street premises, Mr. Sansom has an efficient staff actively engaged. The sole proprietor of the business, Mr. Sansom, finds the whole of his time fully taken up. He is a gentleman of great experience, sound judgment, and capital business ability, and, it is generally conceded, fully deserving of his undoubted success.

James Carr & Sons, Manufacturers of Small-wares, &c., Clarence Mills, Clarence Street, Chester Road.—The manu-facture of smallwares forms a most important branch of trade in Manchester, and marked advances have been made during recent years in the articles usually included under the general definition "smallwares." To no firm in the district do these observations more directly apply than to Messrs. James Carr & Sons. This is an old-established concern, having been founded just forty years, and a thoroughly representative one. It is a leading house in this particular line, and enjoys a wide-spread reputation both for the excellence of its productions and the sound principles upon which the business is conducted. The mills are very extensive, covering a large area, and form a handsome and imposing block of buildings, and they afford employment to some three hundred workpeople. They are equipped with the most improved modern machinery and appliances. The articles manufactured by this firm embrace Cretonne and Tapestry Bindings, Float and Orris Lace, Fringes, Gimps, Cords, Worsted Bindings, Venetians, Londons, Carpet Bindings, Spindle Banding, Wire Ribbon, Window-Blind Cords, and Tapes of every description. Messrs. Carr & Sons are the original inventors of the celebrated "Woven Throughout Ladder Tapes," which have effected such a wonderful improvement in the appearance of Venetian window blinds, and which have almost altogether superseded the old-fashioned sewn tapes. It appears that owing to the pressure of com-petition the firm have found it desirable to manufacture several qualities of this article, but they still make the old distinct and superior quality which earned them their high reputation; and in order to protect the public against the possibility of fraud, and also to protect their own repute, this article is designated and stamped "Carr's Ladder Web." Messrs. Carr & Sons had an exhibit at the late Manchester Exhibition (1887), which proved both interesting and instructive to visitors. The firm do a large export trade in addition to their home business, and they are making substantial progress, and are constantly enlarging the sphere of their trade operations at home and abroad. Messrs. Carr & Sons have agencies both in London and Glasgow. At the former city their agent is Mr. J. Maygrove, 29, Jewin Crescent; and at the latter, Mr. D. McRae, 11, West Nile Street. The co-partnership consists of Messrs. James Carr (the father), John Lindley Carr and James Carr, junr. All these gentlemen are well known in Manchester and elsewhere, and are esteemed both as manufacturers and private citizens.

Thomas Schofield & Co., Cotton Manufacturers, 12, Marsden Street.—This is a very old-established and well-known firm, whose mills and factories are at Woodbottom, Walsden, Lobb, Todmorden, about eighteen miles from the city. The premises at Marsden Street serve as town warehouse and offices, and comprise very large stock-rooms, and a handsome suite of well-furnished general, clerks', and private offices, which the firm has occupied for about five years. Messrs. Schofield & Company are manufacturers of almost every principal class of cotton goods, including wigans, cambrics, satteens, shirtings, long cloths, domestics, and drills. Their reputation is un-surpassed. There is a steady demand for their productions. The mem-bers of the firm are all extremely well known on 'Change, and few gentle-men are more highly esteemed or respected in commercial and private circles.

Robert Neill & Sons, Builders and Contractors, Lower Broughton.—The firm of Robert Neill & Sons, builders and contractors, Broughton Lane, was established by the senior partner in 1846. Mr. Neill came to Manchester from the neighbourhood of Edinburgh in 1834. After several years as journeyman, and subsequently manager, he started the present business in Sherbourne Street, Strangeways, Manchester. In 1865 Mr. Neill took into partnership his two sons, Robert and Joseph Skidmore, both of whom continue to be active managers of the business, and have in their turn each a son in the offices of the firm. The firm have been much employed by the various railway companies. The New Exchange station, Manchester, has been built by them, and the other stations in the city, viz., the London Road, the Victoria, the Central, and the Salford have, from time to time during the last forty years, been in their hands for repairs and extensions. The firm are now erecting the new railway station and viaducts at Tithebarn Street, Liverpool, for the Lancashire and Yorkshire Railway Company; the new station at Blackburn, and smaller ones at Walkden and Wardley, on the new line to Hindley, a large goods warehouse at Chester, and one at Bangor, with stations at Thornton Green and Hooley Hill, for the London and North-Western Company. The principal business of the firm has, however, been in warehouses, houses, and other buildings in and around the city. They erected the new Prestwich County Asylum, the new asylum at Rainhill, just finished; and some years ago the very large asylum for South Yorkshire, at Wadsley, near Sheffield. Last year they finished the new Manchester Post Office and the renowned Manchester Exhibition Buildings, which covered about fourteen acres of ground, and it is worthy of remark that although the exhibition buildings were enlarged from time to time during the erection, until the value of the buildings, including "Old Manchester," was about two and a half times the amount originally contracted for, and notwithstanding the very short time allowed for the work, the whole were *absolutely complete* on the day of the opening. There is nothing on record of the kind, that we know of, to equal this feat in the building trade, unless it be the erection by the same firm, very recently, of the large edifice for Buffalo Bill (William Cody), on the Manchester race course. Mr. Salisbury, the managing partner in the Wild West Show, has said that even in America, where they do very big things quickly, he had seen nothing to beat the rapid and systematic completion of the work. Their offices in Broughton Lane, and staff of clerks, are quite in keeping with the rest of the establishment, the whole bears evidence of a regard for appearance as well as the substantial interests of the concern. Mr. Neill was mayor of Manchester twenty years ago, for two years, and he, as well as one of his sons, are justices of the peace for the city.

Messrs. John Royle & Co., Boot and Shoe Manufacturers, 36, Dantzic Street.—A prominent and influential name in the boot and shoe manufacturing industry of Manchester is that of the extensive house of Messrs. John Royle & Co. This business has been in existence for upwards of a quarter of a century, and was originally located at Shude Hill. Seven years ago the developing tendencies of the trade carried on warranted an extension of premises, and Messrs. Royle accordingly completed the purchase of their present large and commodious establishment in Dantzic Street. John Royle & Co.'s premises are prominent among the best structural features of Dantzic Street. The firm carry on a very large and important trade and industry in the manufacture and supply of all kinds of boots and shoes. Of late years an extensive and valuably connected shipping trade has been opened up. At 96, Shude Hill, a branch is conducted under the name of the Bristol Tanning Company. At this latter address the leather grindery and boot-upper trade is energetically carried on and is well known as a successful bespoke business, shoemakers being enabled to take a customer's measure, forward the same to this firm, and receive the "uppers" made to order within a few hours. Messrs. Royle & Co.'s business is ably and enterprisingly conducted in all departments, and ample provision is made for meeting the demands of a growing trade, the stock of boots and shoes held at the Dantzic Street warehouse being sufficient to shoe about one-third of the entire population of Manchester.

Murray's Manchester Railway Guide and Time Table.—This is perhaps the most useful, as it certainly is the most concise and handiest, of local compilations of this class. It was started about a decade ago by a member of the well-known Murray family, whose name is associated with the time tables of Scotland, the Metropolis, and all the great provincial centres. The publication in question is most accurate and full of very valuable information, which cause it to be in great demand. "Murray's Guide" has beyond a doubt the largest bespoke circulation in Manchester, which necessarily enhances its value as an advertising medium. It has recently been acquired by Messrs. George Woodhead & Co., the well-known printers and publishers, who have added considerably to its old attractive features by making many important improvements. Indeed, it is not too much to say that every possible modern improvement has been made. Its field for usefulness has thus been extended, as well as the area included in the compilations. "Murray's" was the first local guide to adopt the system of free insurance against railway accidents. The office for advertisements and general information concerning the "Guide" is 22, High Street.

Travers & Pierson, B
Road.—This business was founde
but since his demise in 1865, it h
of Mr. J. N. E. Pierson. It now
The premises are very extensive,
ing into Kenyon Street, close upo
stock, which fills every portion
enormous; in addition to which
railway stations and shipping p
line in Great Britain. It comprise
work, from the largest hampers to
chief trade is represented by ladie
market baskets, clothes-baskets, u
hundreds of dozens are sent off d
is done in artistic wickerwork i
materials, comprising chairs, tea-
linen baskets, tidies, &c., in whic
The firm is noted for the importa
description, whisk brooms, hand
nection is widespread, including b
dealers, tea dealers, bazaar keep
their way to all parts of the Unit
The partners are experienced in th
much respected in the neighbour
usually thriving and prosperous.

Percy Brothers, Gener
East Street, Lower Mosley Street.
year 1857, in Albert Street, by Mr
chased in 1876. In 1879 it was rem
tinued at that address until 188
increase of business and the nece
nery, the firm were compelled to
deciding on taking a part of the
Britannia Mills, formerly occupie
spinners. Being built in the m
building is admirably suited for a f
Brothers have filled their rooms w
firms of Payne & Sons, Dawson &
endless variety, and includes not
but also from Germany and Americ
commercial, and ornamental worl
graving, and music-printing, in bo
and they make a special feature o
logues. A glance through their
manship, and a very commendal
judgment. Their business has ext
of hands employed runs up to bet
nection, though to a large extent
parts of the country; and the fi
printers of the *Alliance News*, the
and satirical journal *The Parrot*.
respected throughout the trade.

The Jackson Street Spi
Prominent among the spinning e
chester so well known and famous,
Street Spinning Company. Thes
century by the philanthropist, Mr
into the possession of Mr. W. Ros
by whom they were very largely e
owner, Mr. Gerald Peel, has bee
seven years, and has made consid
newest machinery, suitable for the
the departments are roomy and w
for the comfort and convenience of
hundred and fifty to four hundred.
spinning of the finer counts of yar
counts spun extending from 80 to
are used for making lace and fin
largely in demand in Nottingham
personal supervision are given to
proprietor employs none but the
the various departments.

Madgwick Jefferis, Dr
water Place.—The dress goods tra
magnitude. A capital agency busi
wick Jefferis, which was founded
taken up by a large stock—manu
meres, twills, &c. Mr. Madgwic
supplying only Manchester wareho
trade, and exercises judgment an
is an honourable man of business,
the commercial world, and his hou
chester dress goods trade.

Messrs. Kino Bros., Court, Naval and Military ailors, 35 & 37, Market Street.—There is scarcely to be found in the ty of Manchester a more attractive or extensive establishment than that Messrs. Kino Bros., court, naval, and military tailors, and habit makers.

reviewing the various businesses carried on in this splendid and busy oroughfare it is incumbent upon us to give special prominence and conleration to a firm like this, which plays such an important part in the mmerce of the city of Manchester. It is impossible even for the casual server, in passing along Market Street, not to be struck with the splend display of goods so admirably and tastefully arranged in the two large ndows forming the façade of Messrs. Kino's establishment, comprising they do ladies' and gentlemen's costumes in every variety; gentleen's morning and evening dress suits, plain and fancy coats, trousers, d vests; tweed walking, shooting, and travelling suits: white or blue nnel or serge boating, cricketing, or fishing suits: hunting costumes, hitney or beaver overcoats, drab Devon overcoats, &c. &c. Ladies' stumes and jackets of every description; ladies' riding habits, for which tter Messrs. Kino Bros. have a speciality, and for excellence of fit and auty of material in that graceful costume cannot be excelled. Servants' eries and military uniforms constitute special features of this well-known m, and in the latter Messrs. Kino Bros. are by special appointment akers to the "King's Own" regiment. To carry on this extensive siness a large staff of skilled and experienced workmen is constantly ployed on the premises, and an immense quantity of work is also done outside tailors connected with the establishment. This business in all branches is conducted with great energy and enterprise. Messrs. Kino os. have also large establishments at 322, High Holborn, London, and No. 71, Boar Lane, Leeds; also at 4 and 6, Darley Street, Bradford. essrs. Kino Bros. have for many years been most honourably associated th this business, and have acquired a reputation and popularity enjoyed very few houses in the trade, and the extent and importance of their ansactions as merchant tailors, extending as they do all over the world, title them to rank with the largest and most influential of our great ercantile establishments.

James Henry, Wholesale Perambulator Manufacrer, 93 and 95, Port Street.—The industry of perambulator manufacre is now a most important one. During the past few years the ogress it has made has been remarkable, and among the foremost of the any fine firms engaged in it may be included that of Mr. James Henry, ose flourishing concern, which has now been established for a period of urteen years, bears a splendid reputation. Mr. Henry's manufactures marvels of neatness, usefulness, and general excellence as they are—ve the additional advantage of being always up to date. Accordingly, ey give general satisfaction, command a ready sale, and have achieved a widespread and valuable popularity. The leading characteristic of Mr. Henry's concern has from the first been energetic and well-directed enterprise. In fact, the manner in which the business has been conducted may be said to have afforded the public patronising it the utmost possible satisfaction. The premises are admirably suited for their purpose, being fitted up in handsome style, with the best of modern appliances. The stock in the store-rooms is kept to a superior average of excellence and will well repay a visit. With regard to the important consideration of price, nothing more truly economical in its way could be found than Mr. Henry's price list. The promptest attention is paid to all orders, and no pains are spared to give the patron every possible gratification. This firm is certainly well deserving of the most wide and generous support.

The General Life and Fire Assurance Co., 24, Cross Street.—In Cross Street is situated the local office of the General Life and Fire Assurance Company, an institution incorporated by Act of Parliament in the first year of the reign of our present Sovereign, and which has become one of the most successful of the many companies promoted at that time. Its directorate, funds, and character for prompt and liberal settlement of losses, place it in the foremost rank of similar associations, and it is one of those offices approved of by the Postmaster-General for the assurance of the lives of post-office officials. Looking through the record of its founders, we recognise the well-remembered names of Sir John Easthope, M.P.; Sir J. Pirie, Bart.; C. Hindley, M.P.; Sir Morton Peto; Alderman Sir Thomas Challis; the Rev. Edward Steane, D.D.; and many others. Well-known names, too, are to be found in the present prospectus, among them being Sir Andrew Lusk, Bart., Ald., the chairman; the Rt. Hon. C. P. Villiers, M.P., who has had a seat at the board from its foundation; Principal Angus, D.D.; the most Hon. the Marquis of Exeter; and two eminent local gentlemen, J. Pilkington, Esq., J.P.; and J. Bancroft, Esq., late deputy-chairman of the London and North-Western Railway. Steady and solid progress has characterised the career of the office, and beginning with a paid-up capital of but fifty thousand pounds its funds now considerably exceed a million, while its income is over three hundred thousand pounds. The uncalled capital is nine hundred and fifty thousand, fully subscribed by a substantial proprietary. The Board of Trade accounts disclose that for the five years ending 1882 the Company made a profit of £107,159 in the life department, which enabled the directors to declare a very favourable bonus to assurers on the participating tables (amounting in the case of old assurers to a return of 25 per cent. on the premiums paid during the quinquennium), and a dividend of 10 per cent. to the shareholders. The accounts also show that the valuation was based principally on the Institute of Actuaries' Hm. Table, which is a severe test of the condition of an office, compelling it to hold in hand larger reserves than would be required by some tables in use among assurance companies. The rates of premium are moderate, and give equal advantages to those guaranteed by similar institutions. Its policies, after a few years, are practically indisputable, and under certain circumstances the assured is allowed to reside in any part of the world, without the payment of extra premium. Liberal regulations are in force for the revival of lapsed policies, and generally its contracts appear to be as free from burdensome conditions as any that can be effected. No. 24, Cross Street, has been occupied as a branch for some fourteen years, the Company having bought the freehold in 1873, and rebuilt the premises at a total cost of about seventeen thousand pounds. The offices are commodious, and the business in connection with the insurance of some millions of property in the district, and the interest of several hundred life policy holders for a period of twenty-one years, have been confided to the careful management of Mr. G. J. Johnson, a gentleman thoroughly conversant with his work in all its branches, and who is highly esteemed by all who meet him for the urbanity and skill with which he conducts the affairs of the Company in Manchester and the immediate district.

A. Megson & Son, Wholesale and Retail Stationers, Commercial and Art Printers, Account Book Makers, 1, Fountain Street, Manchester.—The stationery, printing and account book making trade of Manchester is very considerable. A noted house devoted to the trade is that of Messrs. A. Megson and Son, which was established in 1846 at 107, Market Street, and removed in 1881 to the more commodious premises now occupied. The premises are completely stocked with a large assortment of stationery, account books, &c. The commercial and art printing department is in a very fine condition, the work turned out being characterised by excellent and artistic workmanship and first rate materials. The firm enjoy an unequalled reputation for durability and general excellence of their account books, whilst the manufacture of the Manifold Self-Copying and Commercial Traveller's Manifold Order Books is the largest in the United Kingdom. Both these are the inventions of Mr. Megson, and are extremely popular. The Manifold Order Book is made with double-jointed binding, so that the back can be turned back as a support to write upon without injuring the binding. The self-copying system is wonderfully simple, neat, and clear. In every department the most perfect arrangements exist for carrying on the business, and the hands (fifty in number) are able and experienced. The only member of this old-established and widely-known firm is Mr. Albert Henry Megson, who is possessed of great ability, and is well known and highly respected in manufacturing and mercantile circles.

Messrs. Wilson, McPherson & Co. (late William Mather), Cigar Importers and Manufacturers, 32, Corporation Street. —The above firm is one of the largest and most influential in the North of England in the cigar trade, having been established in the year 1831 by Mr James Mather, who carried on business at 69 and 70, High Street, Manchester, until he was succeeded by his son William, who continued the business there until the year 1874, when the premises were required for city improvements; he then removed to the extensive premises situated at 32, Corporation Street, until his death, which took place on March 1st, 1879, when he was succeeded by his cousin, Mr. Thomas Wilson, who successfully carried on the business. The trade having increased to such an extent as a merchant and importer he decided to manufacture, so that he could compete with any house in the kingdom, he therefore took into partnership Mr. Duncan McPherson, who had successfully manufactured for some years previously, and who had a large connection amongst the wholesale buyers in most parts of the country. This amalgamation has in every way proved satisfactory. Their warehouse at 32, Corporation Street, reminds one of a bonded warehouse, where every quality of Havana, Mexican, Manila, and British cigars may be inspected, as they hold one of the finest stocks in the kingdom, duty paid, and also a large stock in bond. This house may well be entitled, as regards cigars, the Universal Provider, as there is scarcely a brand of Havanna or Mexican which is not obtainable at their warehouse. The factory, which is situated at 10, Yorkshire Street, Salford, in close proximity to the bonded warehouse, consists of five floors

W. M.
TRADE MARK
ESTABLISHED 1831

and is indeed a model factory, the firm having provided every accommodation for their workpeople, who remind one of a hive of bees. The make and quality of their British cigars are steadily gaining favour with the general public, especially the following brands, viz.: Flor de Casilda, Lancashire Lass, Afamada, Candido, and their celebrated WM brand, which has gained a wide reputation, and is now a household word among smokers, and is without doubt one of the finest twopenny cigars ever smoked, and does the firm great credit. They supply tobacconists, wine merchants, brewers, hotel keepers, stores, and others.

Holden & Brooke, Limited.—It is only a few years since Mr. Robert Grundy Brooke, who was then superintending Messrs. Sharp, Stewart & Co.'s workshops at Dieppe, decided to enter into partnership with his friend, Mr. Harry Holden, who was then engaged as assistant manager at Messrs. Sharp, Stewart & Co.'s works at Manchester, after having been some time at Sir J. Witworth's works. Having taken the Saint Simon's Works in Salford they at once commenced the manufacture of various engineering requirements, amongst others of Borland's Patent Portable Boiler Drilling Machines; but soon they began to experiment with steam injectors for boiler feeding, an education in which they had previously received when with Messrs. Sharp, Stewart & Co., who were the first to make the original instrument under license from the patentee, Mr. Giffard. Messrs. Holden & Brooke continued their experiments so successfully that they produced an instrument so entirely original and efficient that of their success from this date it was impossible to doubt. Their Patent Influx Automatic Re-starting Injector soon became known and consequently popular. Then followed their Patent Exhaust Steam Injector, by means of which boilers are fed with water by the steam which we still see so frequently being wasted by being allowed to escape into the air. Fig. 1 illustrates their Patent Influx Injector, and Fig. 2 illustrates their Patent Exhaust Steam Automatic Re-starting Injector. Other valuable patents followed one after the other in quick succession until 1887, when Mr. Holden being desirous, owing to ill health, to have more leisure at his disposal than his position as partner in such a rising firm would justify, it was determined to convert the business into a private Limited Liability Company (consisting only of immediate friends of the partners); and Mr.

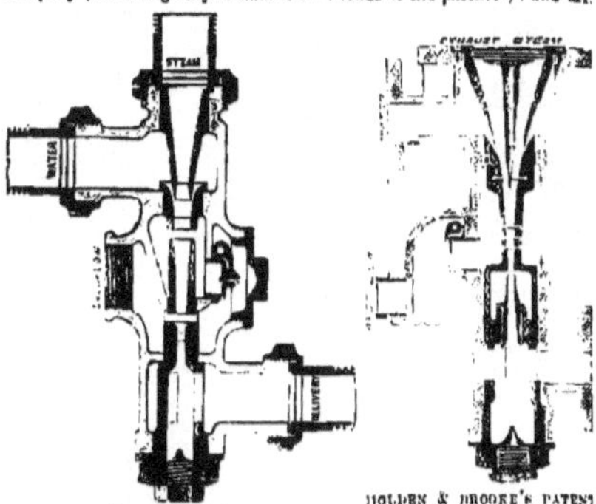

HOLDEN & BROOKE'S PATENT INFLUX INJECTOR.

HOLDEN & BROOKE'S PATENT EXHAUST STEAM AUTOMATIC INJECTOR.

Geo. F. G. Hooper, who was at this time assistant engineer in the commercial department of Messrs. Sharp, Stewart & Co., after having been several years at Messrs. Beyer, Peacock & Co.'s works at Gorton, was invited to join the new company, the active management of which was intrusted to Mr. Brooke and Mr. Hooper; and these gentlemen, aided by Mr. Holden, form the present directorate. It will be easily understood therefore, how Messrs. Holden & Brooke, Limited, are enabled to execute work of the finest description, where the greatest accuracy and delicacy are required, since the education of the managers has been in the hands of firms whose work is perhaps unrivalled. Since this date the company have by no means forfeited their title of inventors, as the patents which have been granted them for high pressure automatic exhaust steam injectors, valves and taps, &c., amply testify. The secret of their success undoubtedly is in their high standard of workmanship and design. Commencing business as these gentlemen did on the eve of an era of universal prosperity, to be almost immediately plunged into an epoch of trade depression utterly unparalleled in the annals of British commerce, it is interesting to note how they have succeeded, in spite of this, in forming for themselves a connection so valuable, substantial, and numerous (including as it does many Governments), that their prospects, always bright, are to-day, if possible, brighter, and we are sure that only a little time is required to make the firm of Messrs. Holden & Brooke, Limited, one of which any Manchester business man will be proud to speak.

Voss & Delius, Merchant Shippers, 3, Parsonage. —This business was established in the year 1852, and has had a career of great success. The premises consist of a fine spacious warehouse of many floors, and a suite of commodious offices. The trade is with the Continent and North America. The principal shipments are of cotton yarns, cotton-waste, and machinery. The machinery includes every description of plant for cotton spinning and weaving, steam engines and engineers' machine and hand tools. Messrs. Voss and Delius have a branch at Oldham which is devoted to the cotton-waste trade exclusively. The firm employs a large number of hands both at the Parsonage and Oldham. The partners are now Mr. E. Kyllmann, Mr. E. Goetz, and Mr. C. Collmann. All these gentlemen have had much experience in the trade and the special business carried on. They are respected members of the Royal Exchange, and are much esteemed in commercial and business circles. The firm takes high rank amongst the shipping houses of the city.

John Bennett & Sons, Calico Printers, 9A, St. Peter's Square.—The works of this enterprising and high-class firm are situated at Birch Vale, Derbyshire. As calico printers, dealing in both home and export trade, John Bennett & Sons have achieved a widespread and valuable reputation. The work they turn out is very superior; the best of machinery and a thoroughly well organised staff are employed in its production. The concern is managed throughout in that praiseworthy spirit that deserves success. The connection at present enjoyed is certainly a well-merited reward of able and energetic management. The Manchester warehouse is at No. 9A, St. Peter's Square.

Kissane & Co., Butter Merchants, 17, Fennel Street.—'ery few people have any idea of the importance of Manchester as a dis-ibutive centre for the food products of this country. The name is so 'ell known in connection with cotton spinning and weaving, bleaching nd printing, that a very general impression exists that Manchester is ntirely given up to these industries. Such is far from being the case, owever, and among a hundred industries that flourish in and around its orders, we find that here is the great distributing centre for the butter ade of this country. Though dairy farming has often been urged as a anacea for agricultural depression, the supply of English butter at any ate could never compete with the imported product. This latter is most rgely obtained from Ireland and Denmark, and the business itself ap-ears to be principally controlled by Irishmen. Naturally they possess spe-al qualifications for this business, and in connection with this we may ention the well-known firm of Messrs. Kissane & Co. Mr. Kissane, ie head of the firm, is a native of North Kerry, a district famous for the uality of its butter. His family have long been identified with the ounty, his grandfather being the well-known and daring huntsman, Mr. eremiah Murphy, whose benevolence and beneficence during the Irish amine is remembered to this day. His father, William Kissane, was member of the Listowel Union for many years, and his retirement from ie board of guardians, owing to declining years, was only accepted by ie people of Bally Conry with much regret and reluctance. The busi-ess was started in Manchester, some thirteen years ago, by Mr. Jere-iah Kissane, and a few years later he was joined in partnership by

Ir. M. J. Kenny, M.P., a gentleman who may be characterised as one of our coming men." This connection was terminated three years ago, owever, owing to Mr. Kenny's Parliamentary duties, and his being called the bar. The business since then has been carried on under the sole rection of Mr. Kissane, and through his energetic and capable manage-ent it has flourished in an unmistakable degree. All classes of Irish d foreign butters are kept in stock at the large stores situated in Fennel treet. A very large business is also done in butterine, or, as it is now lled, margarine. It was supposed that the Margarine Act would have nsiderably hampered this branch of the business, but it has not proved do so, as the publicity given in connection with the manufacture of this oduct has been most advantageous, proving beyond doubt that the utmost re is taken in its preparation, that the most extreme cleanliness is ob-rved, and that the result is a most economical and thoroughly reliable ticle of food. The ramifications of the firm extend through all the principal ovincial centres, and as an item of trade information it may be interest-g to know that it was this firm who first introduced the imitation Irish mp butterine into Manchester, of which there are now many thousand ckages imported every week. Mr. Kissane is very fortunate in possess-g a thoroughly practical knowledge of the business he controls, and as e management throughout is marked with the most straightforward inciples, we are not surprised to learn that he enjoys the confidence of large body of the trade, and a connection which is steadily increasing.

H. Sutcliffe & Co., Coppers and Tin-plate Workers, rocers' Canister Makers, Scale and Weighing Machine Manu-cturers, Coffee Mill and Paint Mill Depot, 49, 51, and 53, Thomas Street, and 110, Great Ancoats Street.—Established not far short of a century, no firm is better known amongst makers and users of weigh-ing machines, balances, or scales. The "Patent Movable Relieving Pillar Scale" is the latest novelty introduced by this enterprising firm. It is understood that by this invention the beam centres are preserved from damage, however rough may be the usage the scale may have to endure. The public has not been slow to recognise the merits of the new scale, and a great many pairs have been sent out. The works are in Great Ancoats and Thomas Streets, where upwards of a hundred hands are employed. The trade is not by any means local or even confined to this country, as large quantities of the firm's manufactures are sent abroad. Messrs. Sutcliffe & Co. are makers of Agate Scales, and a very large number of all descriptions of these highly finished and accu-rate instruments may be seen in stock. The firm also contracts for keep-ing scales and machines in order at a yearly fee. The sole partner at the present time is Mr. John Thompson, a gentleman whose ingenious faculties have been perfected by a careful mechanical and business training.

J. H. Parker & Co., Paper Canvas, Tarpaulin, Rope and Twine Manufacturers, 3A, Union Street.—Among the many branches of business devoted to the supply of what may be called the accessories of the staple trades of the city and locality generally, the manufacture of rope, twine, tarpaulin, and canvas takes prominent rank. In this important branch of industry a notable house is that of Messrs. J. H. Parker & Co. Their business is not one demanding extensive and imposing premises, still those now occupied are of ample dimensions to meet any development of the trade of the house. They manufacture paper and canvas of the best, and all descriptions of rope and twine for every purpose, and of tar-paulins and similar goods for all kinds of packing purposes, which is a special feature of the business and are making rapid strides into the favour of the most extensive local consumers of such commodities. Indeed, Messrs. Parker & Co.'s connection is for steadiness, soundness, and remu-nerativeness unsurpassed by that of any house in the same line in the city. Dispatch and fidelity to the desires of customers are the distinctive traits of the able management to which the house is subject. These and the superior quality of its goods render it and its proprietor extremely accept-able among all those requiring the commodities in which the firm deals.

William Fairweather, Embroiderer, &c., 67, Sackville Street.—Embroidering, fringing, and general sewing, is an important branch of Manchester industry, and among the establishments so engaged a leading place is occupied by that of Mr. William Fairweather, which was established thirty years ago. The works, known as Pyramid Works, are large and commodious, and fitted throughout with the most modern appliances and machinery, and the hundred hands engaged are able and experienced. The work done by the firm consists of embroidering, toilet and mat fringing, general sewing, hemming handkerchiefs, sheets, quilts, and all classes of hemming for the home and shipping trade, and the manufacture of grey and white allover tuckings, frillings, cordings quilted goods, white tucked skirt making, &c. The trade done is wide-spread. Merchants' own cloth is accepted for making up, and the work is executed with dispatch and efficiency. Mr. Fairweather, being a practical engineer, claims the advantage over his competitors in that he is able to adapt and make any new machinery or new mechanical appliances that may be required for his manufactory. The manage-ment throughout is able and enterprising. The proprietor is highly esteemed for his genial bearing and strict integrity.

Edward Pollock, Tobacco Pipe Manufacturer, 33, and 35, Gartside Street, Bridge Street, Deansgate.—A well-known house in the tobacco pipe trade is that of Mr. Edward Pollock, which was established by him in Fir Street, Oldham Road, in 1850, and removed to the present address in 1884. The building occupied is of large dimen-sions, and commodiously arranged into workshops, store-rooms, &c. All kinds of tobacco pipes are manufactured and extensive stocks are kept on hand, and any pattern of pipe can be made to order to meet the wishes of patrons. The working staff employed in this branch is over forty in number, and thorough organization is infused into the management of the business in every department. The pipes produced are celebrated for their uniqueness in design, smoothness in finish, and mild smoking pro-perties generally. No travellers are employed. The trade is exclusively wholesale, and well established among the leading trade houses of the city and neighbourhood. Mr. Pollock is well known as a gentleman practically acquainted with all the details of this branch of industrial enterprise, and highly respected by his customers for the courtesy and strict integrity he at all times extends to them in the conduct of his extensive business.

Cameron & Co., Drysalters, &c., 61, Faulkner Street.—The stores and warehouse are located at 55A, New Wakefield Street, Oxford Street. The specialities of the trade are the dye-stuffs, acids, gums, starch, and soda required by dyers, calico printers, &c. The trade connection includes a large proportion of the dyers and printers of the northern manufacturing districts. The sole proprietor now is Mr. Kenneth Cameron.

George Harrison, Corn Miller and Merchant, 67, Oldham Road.—The corn, flour, and provender trade of Manchester is very considerable in magnitude and value, giving employment directly and indirectly to many hands. A thoroughly representative business in this trade is that of Mr. George Harrison, which was originally founded at No. 65, Oldham Road, in the year 1836, by Mr. Robert Lomas, who, in 1870, transferred it to Mr. Harrison as a token of esteem for faithful services. The premises are close to the Lancashire and Yorkshire Railway Co., and the business has been developed to its present magnitude by Mr. Harrison. The premises now occupied, consisting of a spacious, imposing-looking building, having the advantage of a corner situation, were erected last November twelvemonth, and they consist of offices, warehouse, and grinding and splitting mills, the latter being fitted up with the most modern and powerful machinery for grinding and splitting operations, &c. The warehouse contains an immense stock of flour, hay, straw, meals, and general provender, the flour being ground from the choicest wheat, the

hay cut upon the premises, and the straw—in fact the whole of the goods supplied by Mr. George Harrison—is of the best quality, and could not be excelled in the market. An important feature in the conduct of this business is the fact that Mr. Harrison carries out all trade transactions upon a strict cash system, which enables him to buy in the best market and supply his numerous customers with superior class produce at moderate prices, and this has in no small degree been the means of building up the sound and flourishing concern of which he is the deserving proprietor. There are stables, models of cleanliness and comfort, for five horses, and a goodly number of hands are employed. Mr. Harrison carries on a very heavy local business, and under his able and energetic management, and the efforts of the travelling staff, it is greatly increasing. He is one of the most important members of the city trade, and he is highly esteemed for his strict integrity and courteous demeanour. He is unboundedly popular with the local community, and is one of the foremost men of business in the district.

W. Hill & Sons, Brick and Tile Manufacturers, 20A, St. Mary's Gate.—Messrs. Hill & Sons have a large business as brick, tile, and sanitary tube manufacturers. The business was established by Mr. William Hill as far back as 1852, but it has only been known by its present title since 1883. They have a suite of two offices and a depôt at Urmston, near Manchester, and trade all over England, Ireland, and the continent, especially Holland. Messrs. Hill & Sons have the advantage of the best machinery, and make a first-rate quality of bricks, in addition to the descriptions that are still made by hand. Another branch of Messrs Hill's manufacture is that of tiles and pipes, in which the clay has to be much purer and stronger. They have also agencies for building stone, and a large business is done in Welsh and Westmoreland slates, London and Rugby Portland cement, of which they keep a large stock always on hand at their depôts, Liverpool Road station and Castle Street, Deansgate, and for which they have large contracts with the various railway companies, corporations, &c. The trade of this firm is very extensive, and the good name Messrs. Hill & Sons have acquired is warranted by their superior methods of manufacture.

George White, Umbrella Manufacturer, 6, Exchange Street.—There is no more useful article of outfitting than the umbrella, and few in more general use. Hence the great number of important commercial concerns engaged in the making of these articles, to which they generally add the manufacture of sticks of all kinds. Among such firms a prominent position is held by the establishment of Mr. Geo. White. This is one of the oldest concerns in the trade, having been founded in 1816 by the late Mr. Goodfellow, from whom, about twenty years ago, it was taken over by Mr. Nicholson, who was succeeded by

Mr. Geo. White, the present pro
is one of the most attractive in M
and walking-sticks could with dif
ally are probably unsurpassed in
all sorts of figures and shapes for
wood, and divers sorts of stones
pletely master of all details in c
his guiding influence the future o
ful past.

J. Woodrow & Sons, 18,
the principal articles of a gentle
almost more than any other. It
in other respects, if wearing a con
appearance desired is wanting.
written by him and entitled "'Th
hat,' an 'eccentric hat,' nay, some
well when you are at the seasid
country, or making a tour abroa

crowded cities, and in paying visi
of esteem and respect, I don't thi
hat which, for the last century o
versal use among the great body
other than the old Spanish beaver-
of the best silk velvet nap, modifi
the capricious mutability of fashi
crown and breadth of brim; and
few years in brightness, elasticity,
procured from the very best mak
me." There is great difference
between different makes of hats,
one of the oldest-established firm
Kingdom, and have long been no
ness in quality of their silk and fe
ratum—the combination of ease, c
hats is made "easy-fitting" by th
forehead under the leather. The
amply vouched for in the facts
medals at the London and Paris Ex
and that they are, by special appoi
the Prince of Wales. Their pri
built by them specially for this
modern appliances for the producti
under their own personal supervisi
have branch retail establishments
Street, Liverpool; as well as the ab
Manchester; which is a handsom
and being opposite to the Excha
portion of Manchester, is most co
retail trade which is undoubtedly
the city. The specialities of the
from the finest silk plushes in the
Hats," in all the newest shades
"Zephyr," light felt hats, lined R
roughly ventilated—a luxury for
combining the appearance of a har
"Soft Felt Hats" of the finest te
pocket, travelling, lounging, and
stylish and comfortable hat for cour
opera folding hats, hunting, shootin
waterproofed and very durable; h
badges; "Caps" for the seaside a
and pattern; "Helmets," in pit
adapted by well-studied forms of
bicycling and for the country. Th
patent "Conformateur," which re
once taken is always available. T
ments are carefully packed and d
Kingdom. The firm are large s
Australia, Canada, and all other p
and the trade are supplied upon s
at any of their establishments.

Hodgson & Stead, Patentees and Manufacturers of Veighing Machinery, Egerton Iron Works, Windsor Street, Regent oad, Salford.—The high reputation of this well-known firm has xtended itself all over the civilised world. Messrs. Hodgson and Stead ave been established since 1852. Their splendid factory, which abuts n the railway in the vicinity of Cross Lane station, is one of the best nd most thoroughly furnished of its kind. A very large staff of workmen re constantly employed, and all orders are attended to with praiseworthy romptitude and careful attention. The machines are made of the very rst quality of materials and on the most approved lines, whilst they are raduated by the agency of special appliances to any national standard—unique and palpable advantage of considerable importance, and one hich enhances to no mean extent the value of the trade in the exporta-on of these machines to the Continent and other places abroad. The Platform" weighing machines turned out by this firm will be found valuable for the requirements of iron works, paper works, chemical orks, warehouses, storerooms, and manufactories of all kinds. They re strong, reliable, and particularly well finished, and possessing the dvantage of simplicity in their construction, are not liable to be put out f order. They can be mounted on wheels, and are also made with folding wings and back frame for cotton bales, waste bags, trusses, and other bulky articles, with wrought-iron cradles for bar iron, &c. When fitted with a front guard they will be found extremely useful machines for importers of canes, bamboos, rattans, &c. They are made to suit the special requirements of particular trades. The "dormant" variety of platform machines is specially adapted for gas and chemical works, railway, canal, and carriers' warehouses, &c. They are equal in every respect to the portable contrivances, but being constructed for fixing flush or level with the floor, are particularly convenient for weighing barrows, barrels, tierces, hand-trucks, and heavy articles difficult to raise by hand-power. Amongst the many other interesting novelties of this enterprising firm—who are ever abreast of the times—is one of their latest inventions in the shape of a patent (1886) self-indicating weighing machine. This is a distinct and marked advance upon anything which has previously been done in this department of manufacture, and one which is confidently recommended as meeting all the requirements of colliery work in a thoroughly efficient and satisfactory manner. The objections generally brought against machines of this class—that they are complicated, soon and often out of order, and difficult and expensive to repair—do not in any way apply to this clever

nvention, it having no springs, no wheels, no toothed rack and pinion, or, in fact, any loose weights. Throughout its mechanism is so simple, hat the machine may be described as one of the "steelyard" class, which ossesses, however, the distinctive merit of being able to indicate n an automatic manner the "correct weight." With reference to the nore elaborate and weighty machines made by Hodgson & Stead, hese are of admirable construction and of undoubted utility. "Self-contained" weighbridges for railway trucks and waggons were first introluced by this firm, and have proved themselves to be, for stability, strength, accuracy, and durability, superior to all others. The strong olid cast-iron frame with which they are enclosed and supported entirely supersedes masonry foundations, and in addition, insures exact and accurate fixing, the only pit required being one about three feet deep. The difficulty hitherto experienced in the matter of proper drainage is at once overcome, whilst the entire work of erection can be completed in a very few hours. These weighbridges, when needed, can be readily removed and refixed without the expense attending the laying of special masonry foundations. The stock of machinery kept by Hodgson & Stead is a most interesting one. The intending purchaser will find at their warehouses all that he could possibly require in this particular line, while the utmost courtesy will always be shown to him, and the most perfect satisfaction in every way may confidently be relied upon.

The Clayton Wire-Mattress Manufacturing Co., late **Slack, Chiswell & Co., Spring Mattress Manufacturers, and Inventors, Patentees, and Makers of Wringing and Mangling Machines,** Clayton.—In this age of luxury nothing can be of more importance than that which has for its object the perfecting of any arrangements affecting our domestic comfort. The manufacture, therefore, of spring mattresses and also of wringing and mangling machines, is of considerable importance. In the city of Manchester we find a representative house in this business to be that of The Clayton Wire-Mattress Co., whose works are situate at Clayton. This firm has been established some ten years, and has since its foundation grown in importance, and consequently in standing, year by year, till it has assumed the position of one of the leading houses in the trade. The sole representative of this house is Mr. G. H. Slack, whose experience at home and abroad has enabled him to keep abreast of the times in his manufactures. The works of this company are conveniently situated in the centre of the manufacturing district of Clayton, close to Manchester, and are of ample dimensions; they are being fitted with modern machinery, and every mechanical appliance of the latest kind and most approved pattern that can save and simplify labour and perfect the manufactures to which the house devotes its energies, and for which it is so deservedly noted. Here are turned out in large quantities the famous spring mattresses, specimens of which are to be found not only in the neighbourhood of Manchester but, we may say, in the houses of the inhabitants of almost every portion of England. Mr. Slack, however, does not content himself with the simple manufacture of the articles we have enumerated, but improves and invents others; and among these his fertile brain has conceived we find an article of domestic use, whose value it would be difficult to determine—namely, a wringing and mangling machine, which he has patented under the style of the "Patent Clayton Wringer," and which will of a certainty prove a boon to many a household—for no invention of the like kind has ever approached it in simplicity, durability, and the remarkable facility with which it can, when requisite, be repaired. Numerous certificates and prize awards have been secured by these inventions. It requires no great gift of prophecy to foretell that The Clayton Wire-Mattress Manufacturing Co. will, by pursuing their present energetic and pushing mode of business, attain that position which is the object of all honestly industrious concerns—that is, to be the leading house in their line of business. Of the proprietor, Mr. G. H. Slack, it is needless to say anything, for he is well-known not only in home markets and circles but also in foreign countries.

Thomas Isherwood, Spinner, Cotton Waste, &c., Irk Mills.—One of the best-known and most successful establishments connected with the cotton waste industry in Manchester and Heywood is that of which Mr. Thomas Isherwood is the proprietor. This concern was established about thirty years since. The Manchester branch, which is located at the Irk Mills, in Long Millgate, presents at all times a scene of business activity. The Irk Mills are large and commodious, and a numerous staff is employed. The waste warehouses at Heywood are situate in Ormerod Street and Schofield Street Mills. The Foundry Street and Railway Street Mills cover a very large space, and are replete with every mechanical appliance for spinning. Mr. Isherwood is well known in commercial circles and on 'Change as a gentleman of long experience and thorough business integrity.

Bagley & Wright, Cotton Spinners, Cannon Street.—Many of the firms engaged in the staple manufactures of Manchester and district enjoy a universal reputation for the excellence of their goods and the extent of their works and enterprise. Though Messrs. Bagley & Wright cannot strictly lay claim to a world-wide reputation, they can with justice aver that they enjoy a splendid name for the excellent quality of their sewing, crochet, and knitting cottons. They began business over twenty-five years ago as cotton-spinners and manufacturers, and their career since has been of the most successful and brilliant kind. They possess the splendid Wellington and Belgrave Mills at Oldham, the Cliviger Shed Mills at Burnley, Crooklands Bobbin Mill at Milnthorpe, Westmoreland; and in addition to these a spooling mill in Montreal, Canada, the latter having been commenced last year to avoid the heavy tariff placed upon cotton goods by the Canadian Government. The Belgrave Mills at Oldham form the chief seat of operations, and here the sewing cotton is made from the single yarn and

afterwards sent to be bleached or dyed upon the premises, the firm possessing a splendid dye-house where every imaginable colour is constantly being produced. It is afterwards spooled upon the regular small bobbins with which ladies are so familiar, packed up in one-dozen parcels, and afterwards in half-gross packets, and dispatched to almost every part of the habitable globe. The firm's productions have everywhere met with that approval which good cottons merit, and the demand for them has so rapidly increased that the firm have to-day four times the amount of machinery employed they had two years since. It used to be thought, and that within the last few years, that Scotland alone could produce good sewing cottons; but it is now proved beyond a doubt that Lancashire can not only produce the best sewing cotton, but also produce it much cheaper than Scotland, being better situated for obtaining single yarns, good machinery and skilled labour. Messrs. Bagley & Wright have already reaped some reward for their labour, and for the better prosecution of their trade have established a fine warehouse and suitable offices in the city. These are under competent management, and afford all requisite facilities for the prompt transactions of a brisk business. The warehouse is fitted and arranged in a substantial and neat manner, and is stocked to repletion with the various textile wares manufactured at the different mills. A strong staff manages the city business from the Cannon Street offices. The firm's connections embrace the wholesale and retail city establishments, and cover every part of the country. Branch warehouses in Glasgow and Belfast work the Scotch and Irish ground with success. The firm have also offices and hold stocks in Melbourne, Bombay, and Moscow, and from these distributing centres do a fair amount of trade; and this is only the just recompense of the energy and ability exercised in the conducting of the business by Messrs. Bagley & Wright.

Crouchley & Unsworth, Tea and Coffee Merchants, 30, Hanging Ditch.—This first-class firm of tea and coffee merchants is widely known, both in Manchester and the surrounding districts. They have been established many years and have a large connection, extending over the northern and midland counties, which necessitates the employment of a numerous staff of travellers. They deal chiefly in high class goods, and enjoy a splendid reputation, both for teas and coffees. Their coffee trade (of which they have made a speciality) is second to none in the provinces; in fact, few establishments have attained equal distinction in this branch of the business. Their premises in Hanging Ditch are spacious and commodious, and are situated in the heart of the grocery and provision trade, close to the Corn Exchange. Their stocks are of great extent and of unsurpassed excellence, and they are in a position to compete successfully with any other house. Their business, too, is conducted with energy and ability, and upon the lines of strict commercial probity, and the firm possess the confidence and respect of their numerous clients. The co-partnership consists of Messrs. Henry M. Crouchley and Walker Unsworth, gentlemen of great practical experience, who are highly esteemed, both in commercial and private life. We will only add that the firm employ a large staff, and their trade from year to year grows in magnitude and importance.

Ellen Taylor, Manufacturer of Upholsterers' Trimmings, 43, Cannon Street.—This business was founded more than a quarter of a century ago, and its history has been one of gradual and complete success. For upwards of twenty-five years it was carried on by Mr. George Beaumont Ward, the present proprietress purchasing the business some two years ago; the premises, including spacious and
capital work-rooms, business pu
furnished and fitted up in a man
trade. The speciality of these v
trimmings, any length, pattern, o
to harmonise with colourings and
of furnishing requirements, deco
nection the firm have many hand
customers, and in the show-roo
patterns of trimmings blended in c
in taste and of great artistic mer
best trimmings houses, leading u
furnishers of the city and distric
are employed in the work-rooms
of the various materials used i
rosettes, cords, and tassells, &c.,
is a lady endowed with sound ju
careful and discriminate superv
entrusted to her receives every
managers, and by this means ens
and steadily increasing trade.

William Smith & Co., J
and Merchants, 24, Dickinson
in the year 1860, and has enjoye
Messrs. Smith & Co. have an add
The specialities of the trade are
and packing purposes, and Scotc
similar goods. The trade conne
houses. No travellers are empl
so well established as to render
An efficient staff of clerks and s
ness is constantly going on.
Smith, a gentleman of very grea
and familiar with all the details c
well known in commercial circles

Hardy & Sons, Brewe
ter Road.—As an important bra
revenue to the country, the bre
industrial and commercial world.
city is that of Messrs. Hardy & S
established for a quarter of a cent
for the strength, purity, and gene
stout. The brewery is large and
model. The machinery and appl
ment and the most powerful desc
widespread, and is rapidly incre
wine and spirit trade. Messrs.
highest reputation for the honour
conduct their business. Their fir
question, and at no time of thei
more prosperous position.

Gleim, Brettauer & Co
Lower Mosley Street.—The Man
merchants are numerous, and the
and rapidly increasing. A thoro
tion is that of Messrs. Gleim, Br
1875. Since that date the firm h
gained a sound reputation. The
tions, comprising offices and war
employing an able clerical staff.
dious, and well stocked with goo
facturers. A very wide-spread
largely to West Africa. The lead
& Brettauer, are gentlemen of n
courteous manners, managing the
judgment. In commercial and in
deeply esteemed, and their house

Hugh L. McInnes, E
5 & 7, Mary Street, Cheetham.—Th
years ago by Mr. Hugh L. McInn
carried on by the former alone.
works and capital offices. The sp
the copper roller required by c
of velvets, leathers, &c. In this
thing depends upon the artistic sk
connection includes most of the
hood of Cheetham, Broughton, Sc
eighty clever and experienced em
tion to the clerical staff. The sole
a gentleman of great experience
for calico printing have been extr
a wide popularity.

W. H. & J. Maxfield, Shop Front Builders, Shop [fi]tters, and Show Case Makers (on the air-tight principle), Clare Street, [Te]mple Street, Chorlton-on-Medlock.—This business was established in [th]e year 1845, and is still carried on by the founders. The premises [co]nsist of a large roomy shop of most handsome appearance, elegantly [de]corated, and thoroughly well fitted and most perfectly appointed. The [off]ices are a capital suite of rooms, exceptionally well furnished and most [co]nveniently arranged. The works are of large size, and there is an [ex]tensive dry timber stores. The speciality of the business is the manu[fa]cture of air-tight show cases, counter-cases, and shop fittings. In all [th]ese Messrs. W. H. & J. Maxfield have a very high-class reputation. [S]pecial care is taken that none but the most perfectly seasoned mate[ri]als and best polished plate glass is used, and that everything is finished

[i]n a thoroughly workmanlike manner. Messrs. Maxfield also do a large [am]ount of general hardwood joinery, such as oak fittings for banks, [w]arehouses, churches, and other public buildings. The connection is [ex]tensive and widespread, and there are very few shows or exhibitions [th]at do not contain many cases manufactured by this firm for their [n]umerous clients. Hotel bars are completely fitted, and the polishing [an]d bevelling of plate glass shelves are undertaken. Silvering is also [ex]ecuted in a finished and skilled manner. Skilled workmen and experi[en]ced representatives are sent to all parts of the country. A permanent [st]aff of some fifty to sixty workpeople is engaged, and there are busy [se]asons when the number is more than double. The proprietors are [g]entlemen of experience and sound business principles, their great success [be]ing thoroughly well deserved.

The Oxford Street Packing Company (Manager, [A]rthur Vickers), Packers by Hydraulic Power, Chepstow Buildings, [O]xford Street.—One of the most useful businesses in connection with the [in]dustrial and commercial organisation of Manchester is packing by [h]ydraulic power. A well-known firm in this business is that of "The [O]xford Street Packing Company," which was founded in 1875, and is under [t]he management of Mr. Arthur Vickers. The premises occupied are [e]xtensive, and they are admirably equipped with hydraulic machinery. [H]ere are to be seen presses of extraordinary size, weight, and power, [w]orked by an accumulator of great capacity, in conjunction with powerful [h]igh-pressure pumps, the whole in marked contrast with the conditions [a]ppertaining to the laborious method of hand-pumping, in existence but [c]omparatively few years ago. Probably in no other department of [in]dustry, in this age of progress, has greater comparative development [ta]ken place than in the appliances and facilities afforded generally for [c]arrying on the important trade of packing. The reduction in bulk of [t]he goods packed, the saving in expense for freight, coupled with the [s]afety and general convenience attained, and combined also with the [e]lement of economy in favour of shippers, mark the value and utility of [th]ese operations. Mr. Vickers's management leaves nothing to be desired; [h]e is well known in the business world, and highly esteemed for his [g]enuine qualities and courtesy. In every respect he is an able manager in [a] business whose operations are of the first importance in connection with [t]he commerce of Manchester.

James Dyson, Muslin Manufacturer, Manchester [W]arehouse, 110, Portland Street.—A leading representative in Man[c]hester's staple industry is the well-known house of Mr. James Dyson, [m]uslin manufacturer, Alexandra Mills, Preston, whose city establishment [i]s situated at the above address. Established in 1864 by Mr. James Dyson, [th]e firm was known for some time as Emery & Dyson, but assumed the [t]itle of Mr. James Dyson, by which it is known to this day. This house [h]as a first-class reputation for its goods. The samples of muslin manufactured at the "Alexandra Mills" bear most favourable comparison with any other similar production in the market. The mills at Preston comprise a large and imposing-looking structure fitted with most expensive machinery, and employing a large staff of highly skilled artizans. The Manchester warehouse comprises a large brick building containing handsome offices on the ground floor. The upper floors are well arranged and fitted throughout for the reception of stock, of which there is a very large and high-class assortment, consisting of muslins of every well known quality and texture, and affording to buyers and the representatives of large houses a selection unequalled by any similar house. A considerable staff of well-experienced warehousemen, travellers and others, find employment on the premises. The principal, Mr. James Dyson, is a gentleman of the highest integrity, well known, and very highly respected.

Smith Bros. & Co., Manufacturers of Bleached Twills, Sheetings, Domestics, &c., 24, Dickinson Street.—This business was established about the year 1880, and now occupies an important position in the front rank of similar concerns. The premises include a capital roomy warehouse and a first-class suite of spacious offices, most handsomely and substantially furnished, and fitted up in the latest and most approved style, with every known appliance for the rapid transaction of business. The special items of manufacture are bleached twills, sheetings, indigo blue twills, domestics, &c.; while in the ordinary way the firm produces and prints angolas, imperials, and moleskins. The trade connection is both home and foreign, and includes the principal Manchester wholesale firms and the leading shipping houses. No travellers are engaged, but a numerous and efficient staff of salesmen, clerks, and warehousemen is actively employed. The sole proprietors are Mr. J. A. Smith and Mr. Charles Norton. Each of these gentlemen has had very considerable experience in the various details of cotton manufacture and calico printing. They are very well known and are everywhere held in the highest regard.

The Anchor Line of Transatlantic, Oriental, Mediterranean, and Peninsular Steamships. Messrs. Henderson, Bros., 7, York Street.—A highly prominent position amongst the travelling conveniences of the present progressive age is occupied by the great and highly important fleets of ocean-going steamships, unquestionably grown into a real necessity of the age. A great representative type of the ocean steamship service is the well-known and justly renowned "Anchor Line" of Messrs. Henderson, Bros., established in Glasgow upwards of thirty-five years ago, with branch in Manchester at the above address, and other branches at all the principal seaports and cities throughout the world. The "Anchor Line," celebrated for its magnificent fleet, comprising many of the largest, most powerful, and fastest vessels afloat, in which is included that finest and most popular steamer, *City of Rome*, has a reputation of being second to none in the inducements held out both for travelling or freight. The comfort for passenger traffic and the stowage capacity for cargoes are on a par with any other company in existence. This Company have fortnightly services to India and Mediterranean ports, sailing from Glasgow and Liverpool always punctually to date; weekly services between Glasgow and New York, and regular services between Liverpool and New York, London, Halifax, N.S., and Boston; a special feature being the round voyage, presenting a route of unequalled interest, by steamers from Glasgow, sailing every ten days for Lisbon, Gibraltar, Genoa, Leghorn, Naples, Messina, and Palermo, and back again to Gibraltar, from whence the steamers proceed to New York or other American ports. Passengers land at Gibraltar, and return to London or Liverpool by the steamers from India. Such is the estimation in which their vessels are held, that passengers have sometimes to wait their turn for a vacancy, the berths in the Company's steamships being taken up far in advance of the date of sailing. This line has enjoyed a singular immunity from accidents and losses. Whilst disasters of magnitude occasionally occur to ocean steamships, such occurrences are almost unknown to the "Anchor Line;" and so great is now the confidence inspired in the minds of the travelling section of society, that voyages to and fro are recommended and undertaken for the immediate object of change of air, upon the return-ticket principle, with as little hesitation as would at one time have taken place in organising a journey of a few miles or hours' duration. The steamers of this line are fitted up with every modern improvement to insure health and comfort, and give ample justification for their being called sumptuous floating hotels. This Company's Manchester branch is situated in an admirable position for the conduct of their large business. A staff of clerks and competent assistants are ready at all times to afford the fullest information.

Krönig & Siegler, Merchant Shippers, 5, Marsden Street.—This firm was established in the year 1875. Messrs. Krönig and Siegler are engaged in the general shipping trade, and have connections of an extensive character in all parts of the world. The premises consist of a large modern warehouse, and an extremely handsome suite of commodious offices. The working staff is very large. The partners are gentlemen well known in business circles. They are highly respected members of the Royal Exchange.

John Harding, Son & Co., Wholesale & Manufacturing Clothiers.—This is one of the oldest firms of manufacturing clothiers in the kingdom, sharing with but few others the distinction of being pioneers in the establishment and development of what must now be acknowledged one of the great industries of the country. From the very nature of the business, it will at once mercial enterprise alone could not avail of a people whose tastes become more ref of education. In meeting these demands, successful, as the high class character testifies. Messrs. John Harding, Son &

United Kingdom by a large staff of travellers of ability, and by resident agents in some of the large centres of population. The central offices and warehouses form an imposing structure, and are situate in New Brown Street, in the heart of the city of Manchester. Large and commodious factories in Dutton Street, Strangeways, Manchester, and the Barony, Nantwich (a quaint old town in Cheshire), have been erected and furnished on the most approved principles, modified and extended by the long practical experience of the firm, so as to meet its own specific requirements. This firm, which has attained such a prominent position in its own special branch of the clothing trade, has always good and satisfactory work done, the co do the work must be good. Hence in th utmost care has been taken to secure lofty tion, and agreeable warmth. This th comfort and well-being of the many hun about the factories will account, in some m ing that has characterised for so long employers with the employed.

The Union Plate Glass Company, Limited, 9, Gore Street, Piccadilly.—There are only four firms engaged in the manufacture of plate glass in the United Kingdom. One of the oldest and most substantial of these is the well-known "Union Plate Glass Company." The extensive works of this Company are situated at St. Helens, the head quarters of the British glass industry, and the furnaces, machinery, and appliances are of the most modern type. The works were built by the Company in 1836, and have been enlarged from time to time to meet the increasing demand for their products, which are known the world over and esteemed for quality and finish. As a consequence, the Company has had a prosperous career, having since its formation returned to the shareholders a very large sum in dividends. A home and shipping trade is done. The latter embraces in its range the Continent, United States, Canada, the colonies, and Japan, where this Company's glass is preferred, having recently, we understand, been selected by the Mikado to be exclusively used in the palace he is now building. The Company has also offices and representatives in London, Glasgow, and Birmingham. In concluding our short sketch of this Company, we may say that the position it has attained reflects great credit on the management.

Thos. Barnes & Co. (Limited), Cotton Spinners, 21, Marsden Square.—Improvements in the machinery for cotton spinning have followed each other as continuously and rapidly, and competition in these latter years has become so very keen, that none but the most modern mills, filled with the very newest class of machinery, have any chance of success. Old mills are being closed, pulled down, and rebuilt, solid but old-fashioned machinery is being constantly broken up; and amongst the cotton spinners of Lancashire, at any rate, the old order of things changeth rapidly. Amongst well-appointed mills of to-day's requirements are those belonging to the well-known firm of Messrs. Thos. Barnes & Co. (Limited). The Farnworth Cotton Mills are well designed, solidly built structures, of great size, and contain an enormous number of spindles. In these extensive premises the cotton manufacture may be seen in its every stage. Raw cotton as it is imported at Liverpool passes through all the various processes of its interesting manufacture—carding, spinning, doubling, weaving; and the range of finished goods comprises moles, cords, velveteens, and lambskins of all sorts and colours, and twills of all kinds. The company's mills employ an enormous number of hands, and the standard of excellence in the goods produced is so high that the firm is never short of orders or the machinery standing idle, even in the dullest times. Barnes's velveteens, moles, cords, and lambskins are known the world over. In the city offices and warehouses a full complement of clerks and salesmen are actively engaged.

Osborne Brothers, Brass Founders and Finishers, Commercial Brass Works, Commercial Street, Knot Mill.—Brass founding and finishing is an important branch of the metal industry of Manchester, and it is of considerable extent and magnitude. A firm of good repute engaged in this direction is that of Messrs. Osborne Brothers, Commercial Brass Works, Commercial Street, Knott Mill, which was founded by the present members two years ago, and since that date they have laid the foundation of an extensive trade. The excellently arranged for the business car modern machinery and appliances. A employed, and the work turned out con cups, suet cups, whistles, water-guages, marine, portable and stationary, lift and brass, gun-metal, and phosphor bronze c and every description of engineers' and goods are manufactured with the greatest excellence of workmanship are unrivalled. member of the firm, manages in a man status in the mercantile and industrial w

Atho Joannides & Co., Ship
—First and foremost among the many fi to the shipment of Manchester goods t stands that of Messrs. Atho Joannides & well-known and popular in commercial established thirty years ago, have hands offices at the foregoing location, and c Their special attention is devoted to that which includes Egypt, the Soudan, and t and with the leading merchants here they sending out very large consignments description, which meet a ready sale in th Joannides are well and favourably know turers in the Manchester district. Their with the strictest regularity and dispatch Manchester trade with the above markets

J. D. Mould, Architect and S
Chambers, 77, King Street. - The archite Manchester is of great value, and the me have no superiors in the world. A cap of Mr. J. D. Mould, which has been in exis is a thoroughly proficient and experienc the hon. secretaryship to the Manchester offices are large and commodious, admir Mr. Mould carries on a very varied busine commissions, including chapels and sch ton, Edenfield, Hampstead (London), Ch Whitefield, Bury, Spring Vale, &c. H buildings are of great beauty and origi and the buildings are the cause of much has his hands full of commissions, and l and master-like manner. There can be n for he is known and his services in dem In all business circles he is well know integrity, courtesy, and genius, and he architectural and surveying profession of

S. & J. Watts & Company, Manufacturers, Merchants, d General Warehousemen, Portland Street.—There are some estab- ıments scattered here and there over the United Kingdom which joy a reputation and a fame extending far beyond the limits of the trict where they are situated, or even the boundaries of the Queen's minions, and the firm of "S. & J. Watts & Company" is one of them. compile a work on the "Industries of Manchester," and to leave out mention of the palatial warehouse belonging to this firm, would be an pardonable omission; and yet, to do full justice to the establishment thin the limits of our publication is an impossibility. The emporium s no rival of its class in the Kingdom. The huge pile stands upon 00 square yards of land, and its length is 300 feet, its width 90 feet, d its height 100 feet. It is six storeys high, exclusive of the basement, windows of which are level with the street. The windows of each ry are different in character—thus imparting beauty as well as variety each. There are four towers, which are lighted by rose windows, liating from a central boss, and the roof has a series of bays in it, ed with ground plate glass, with the best possible light for examination of goods. The style of architecture may be de- ibed as the composite Italian, the Venetian being strongly repre- ıted. The basement is of solid granite, and above it is a massive ırse of stonework, inclining inwards like a pyramid, giving great idity to the appearance. The front and ends of the building are of lished Yorkshire stone. The following figures will give an idea of s colossal structure. There are 70,000 cubic feet, or about 550 tons stone in the building; 700 tons of iron, 40,000 cubic feet of timber, d 27,000 square feet of plate glass, exclusive of what is contained in internal fittings. The aggregate area of the united floors, measures 360 square yards, or about four acres. The land upon which the rehouse is built (including the old buildings that were on it), cost 9,000, or close upon £10 per square yard, and the warehouse itself and internal fittings about £80,000, so that the gross outlay on the land d building, was nearly £110,000 The site was purchased by the late . Samuel Watts, in 1855, and the warehouse took nearly two years to nplete, it being first opened to the customers on the 16th of March, 1858. has been truly observed, that Watts & Co.'s warehouse has more the ap- ırance of a royal palace than a place devoted to business. The interior magnificently fitted up, whilst all the arrangements for conducting the siness are most admirably and systematically planned and carried out. e main entrance, from Portland Street, is provided with sliding ors. The vestibule is paved with encaustic tiles, of neat design; and scending a flight of stone steps, the warehouse is entered through hogany and plate-glass folding doors, of which there are three pairs, d in front is a triple archway, supported by beautiful alabaster pillars. e grand staircase receives its light from the dome, and it is protected a balustrade of iron tracery work, of great lightness and elegance. e floors of each room are supported by Corinthian pillars tastefully d artistically painted. The building is provided with no less than five ists, four for goods and one for passengers, and on the premises are draulic presses, cranes, measuring machines, &c., which are worked a couple of steam engines. At the back of the warehouse is a fire- oof staircase, and at the top of the building is a large water cistern, d on each floors there are hose and other fire-extinguishing apparatus. e warehouse from top to bottom is stocked with Manchester goods of ery description, together with every conceivable article appertaining to e silk, mercery, drapery, hosiery, and haberdashery businesses. Messrs. 'atts & Co.'s connection is an enormous one. The firm employ a very rge staff to attend to the twenty-nine departments into which this lossal and unrivalled establishment is divided.

Bagnall & Co., Refiners and Manufacturers, Red Bank l Works.—This firm has been established very nearly thirty-five years, d enjoys a most enviable reputation in its particular line. Their great ciality is the oil known as "The Compo," and which is prepared pressly for lubricating the working part of spindles, looms, engines, and gh-speed machinery: also their brand of X. and XL. cylinder, valve, and rious burning oils which are well known and highly appreciated. ssrs. Bagnall & Co. have also a very considerable business in railway d colliery oils and greases. They are on the list of government con- ctors, and have a large connection amongst cotton and woollen manu- turers, machinists, collieries, forges, contractors, and railway companies. e works at Red Bank cover an extensive area, and the stock of oils, &c., extremely large. The city offices are at 22, Bull's Head Chambers, pwood Avenue. The sole proprietor is Mr. William Bagnall, an expert the oil trade, and as well known on the Liverpool and London markets at the Royal Exchange in this city; a thorough business man, a liberal ployer, and a generous supporter of every movement for the improve- ıt of the city or the benefit of the community.

John Cameron, Engineer, Oldfield Road Ironworks, ford.—Manchester can claim a very important place in the industrial rld for the extent and excellence of her engineering trade, a branch of lustry which employs many hands, and represents great wealth. A ll-known house is that of Mr. John Cameron, which was established as far back as 1852. The works are extensive, admirably arranged for the manufacture, and completely fitted with the most modern and powerful machinery. About three hundred and fifty hands are employed in manu- facturing general machinery and pumps, Mr. John Cameron making specialities of steam pumps of every description, patent cam and lever punching and shearing machines, horizontal punching machines, angle and bar cutters, plate-bending rolls, and planing machines, and other ship-yard tools. These productions are of splendid workmanship, and are in great favour in the industrial world. Mr. John Cameron carries on trade in all parts of the United Kingdom, and his London agents are Messrs. Price & Belsham, 52, Queen Victoria Street. Owing to the energy of the travelling staff and Mr. John Cameron's able management, the business is progressing favourably on all sides. There can be no doubt of Mr. John Cameron's talent, and he is deeply honoured for his strict integrity in the industrial world. His status therein is of considerable eminence, and he is one of the many engineers to whom Manchester owes much for her worldwide and splendid reputation in this branch of industry.

The Dee Oil Company, Haworth's Buildings, 5, Cross Street.—In the great industries of the age, a most prominent position is taken by the oil trade of the world, which forms a branch of industry of exceeding great magnitude, affecting every centre of commerce, and constituting in itself a staple commodity, the daily consumption of which reaches tens of thousands of gallons throughout the area of England alone. As a representative establishment in this great industry, the well-known and widely celebrated Dee Oil Company, manufacturers of patent cylinder and lubricating oils, Haworth's Buildings, stand in the front rank. Their large works are at Saltney, near Chester. This Company have been established in Manchester about fifteen years, but have occupied their present offices since 1885 only. The business career of the Company has been of extraordinary growth and popularity, and resulted in a connection extending throughout the whole civilised world. The reputation of The Dee Oil Company for patent cylinder and lubricating oils has reached a standard far exceeding the most sanguine hopes of its promoters. These oils are so well known as to command a sale every- where, and are pronounced by competent authorities to be without doubt the finest machinery oils produced. To cut down expenses the Company further erected its own sulphuric acid works, and will shortly put up its own stearin plant. Competition has thus been fought with its own weapons. At the Manchester Exhibition last year the samples of manu- facture exhibited comprised specimens of crude petroleum as taken from the American wells, refined petroleum, burning oils and residuum, which is a material used by this firm. From it are manufactured lubricating oils of different brands, cylinder oils, and a special class of oils termed "valvolines" sterling. They are oils for internal lubrication, and are said to be superior to even the best makes of cylinder oils. They are especially recommended for use with sight-feed lubricators and in all high-pressure steam cylinders. They are remarkable for a high flash point (510° to 550° Fahr.), a low setting point (under 32° Fahr.), and a great viscosity even when exposed to high temperatures. An entirely new method is used for their preparation, avoiding, it is said, distillation and treatment with acids and alkalies. Three grades were exhibited—"torpedo oil," for use on torpedo boats, launches, &c.; "dynamo oil," adapted for electric machines; "gas engine" and "ring spindle" oils. We observe also a preparation for therapeutic use, *oleum Deelous*, a most effective oil for skin diseases. The works of the firm at Saltney are on a prodigious scale, covering upwards of thirty acres of land, and fitted up with superb machinery of the latest, most modern and expensive character, and employing some five hundred operatives all the year round. The premises occupied in Manchester comprise an elegant suite of three offices, manned by a suitable staff of clerks for the prompt transaction of the Company's large business. The manager is a gentleman well acquainted with the nature of the business he controls. He is highly respected and much esteemed by a large and ever growing circle of friends.

The Scottish Imperial Insurance Company, 10, Kennedy Street.—Among the leading insurance companies in Manchester we find the Scottish Imperial Company, which confines itself solely to life assurance. The company was established for the transaction of all the varieties of life insurance business, and its subscribed capital amounts to half a million sterling, held in shares by a numerous and wealthy proprie- tary. The capital and funds on 31st December, 1886, were as follows: capital uncalled, £450,000; capital paid up, £50,000; shareholders' reserve fund, £12,361 5s. 7d.; life assurance fund, £224,169 9s. 10d.; total amount, £736,530, 15s. 6d. During the last six years the life assurance fund of this office has been almost doubled. The tables of rates for all classes of assurance are based on a very liberal scale. Assurances can be effected for short periods at moderate rates; thirty days of grace are allowed for the payment of the premiums after they become due; lapsed policies can be revived; surrender values and paid up assurances can be negotiated; loans on policies are granted; foreign residence is permitted upon mutual arrangement; all claims are paid with the utmost liberality and prompti- tude. This office has also a temperance section for abstainers. The directorate are composed of gentlemen of the very highest integrity and social status. The resident secretary of the Manchester branch is Mr. R. Scott Orr.

F. Steiner & Co., Turkey Red Dyers, &c., 34, York Street.—This old-established firm is one of the very best known in the trade. The premises consist of a fine warehouse of four floors, with spacious offices handsomely furnished, and fitted with all the most modern and approved appliances for the rapid dispatch of business. The Church Works, now known as the Church Turkey-Red Dye and Print Works, remained in the hands of the Peel family up to about the year 1830, when the estate was purchased by the late Mr. F. Steiner. A Frenchman by birth, Mr. Steiner came over to this country about the year 1817, when he was thirty years of age. His ability as a chemist had been made known to the proprietors of Broad Oak Works, and Mr. Dugdale was told off to London to engage him as manager of the chemical department at Broad Oak. Mr. Steiner only remained at Broad Oak a short time, and after a brief connection with Primrose Works, he removed to Church, where he commenced the chemical business in conjunction with Messrs. Howarth and Barnes. Leaving this concern, after a partnership extending over a few years, he turned his entire attention to Turkey-red dyeing, in which he had experimented during half his life-time, and by which he soon made his fortune. Up to about 1840, Mr. Steiner carried on a most successful business on his own account, but about that time he admitted as a partner Mr. J. Green, whose place, fifteen years later, was taken by his son, Mr. Robert Green. The business continued to be carried on more or less successfully until about the time of Mr. Steiner's death in 1869. For a few years prior to Mr. Steiner's decease, and during several subsequent years, the works were not conducted with such enterprise as they had been formerly, and during that period little or nothing was done in the way either of extension or improvement. Consequently, upon Mr. Robert Green's retirement in 1874, when the management of the concern devolved upon Mr. James Kerr, the works were, in some respects, in rather a backward state. During the next few years, however, after the admission of Mr. Kerr as a partner in the firm, the works became completely reorganised throughout, so much so that it would be difficult at the present moment to point out a single department conducted under the same conditions as it was ten years ago. One of the principal features of Mr. Kerr's management has been the foresight he has displayed in developing the business, and the boldness with which, even when times were at their worst, he laid out large sums of money in putting down new and improved machinery. The wisdom of this course has been rendered abundantly apparent by the marvellous success the firm has enjoyed during recent years. The Church Works to-day are second to none in regard to the quality of their machines and the nature of the principles upon which they are worked. As illustrative of the extraordinary development which has in recent years taken place in Messrs. Steiner & Co.'s business, it may be stated that ten or fifteen years ago the yearly production of manufactured goods was about 1,000,000 lbs. Now, with no great increase in the number of the hands employed, the out-turn is about 10,000,000 lbs., or 4,465 tons of manufactured goods annually. This represents at least 2¾ million pieces of 25 yards long, or about 39,000 miles—as much as would encircle the globe more than once and a half. The principal markets to which the goods are exported are Calcutta, Madras, Bombay, Kurrachee, Java ports, Macassar, Shanghai, Hong Kong, Japan, Persia, Algeria, and North Africa generally. The shipments to these places have within late years increased fivefold. The rapidity with which the works have grown is astonishing. A little over half a century ago Mr. Steiner carried on his business in a very few buildings, and with a small number of hands. Now there are no fewer than 113 buildings, comprising 33 separate departments. There is a row of large drying stoves in the works about a quarter of a mile in length, and the river Hyndburn, which flows through the works, is arched over for a similar distance. The works stand upon 14 acres of ground, enclosed by a wall 8 to 10 feet high. The number of hands employed is about 1,300, chiefly adult males. In 1850 the number of workpeople was about 300, and ten years later this number was more than doubled. At present Church Works, as just mentioned, finds employment for close upon 1,300 hands; but the actual development of the business, and the advances made in the quantities of manufactured goods produced, have, owing to the adoption of labour-saving machinery and the advance of chemical knowledge, been in far greater proportions than the figures given would appear to show. There are now in operation at the works 110 steam engines, large and small. These are supplied with steam from 35 Lancashire steam boilers, consuming about 3,000 tons of coal per month. The daily consumption of water is about 2½ million gallons, supplied from reservoirs in the neighbourhood belonging to the firm. But for the vast changes and improvements which have taken place throughout the works within the past ten years, the firm's present out-turn, as compared with what it was in 1874, when Mr. Kerr became managing partner, must have necessitated the employment of between 3,000 and 4,000 hands, instead of rather under 1,300, and the consumption of 15,000 tons instead of 3,000 tons of coals per month. Some idea of the extent of the capacity of the works may be gathered from the fact that they are fitted up to turn out, on an emergency, 160 miles of cloth per day. Although Messrs. Steiner & Co.'s principal business is Turkey-red dyeing, they are also extensive calico printers, and there are upon the works 15 printing machines, capable of printing on an average 7 colours each. One of these machines is the largest printing machine in the world, the circumference of the printing bowl being 41 feet 4 inches. This machine works upon the hopping off and on principle, for which the firm possess the patent rights, and which entirely obviates the necessity of printing with blocks, the machines working under this principle bein able to print side borders, cross bars, and centre fillings at one time, and wi much greater accuracy than could possibly be accomplished by block prin ing. Messrs. Steiner & Co. have 6 machines working under this patent principle, one of which is capable of printing 16 colours. By this las mentioned machine they can turn out as much work as would employ fewer than from 50 to 150 block printers, according to pattern. The accor plishment of this class of printing is a task which has occupied the attenti of the firm for a great number of years; much labour and much money h been expended upon its working out, and by none has the object been pu sued with more interest and determination than by Mr. Kerr. The comple success which has crowned his efforts amply repays all the risks undertake The invention is regarded by many as the greatest printing improveme of the present day. Besides these works at Church, where the firm dye a print cloth only, they have a large yarn works at Irwell Springs, ne Bacup, where several hundred hands are employed. And within the p year this enterprising firm have taken over the large and well-kno Sunnyside Print Works, in the Rossendale Valley, formerly run Messrs. Butterworth & Brooks. There are on these works no fewer th 25 printing machines, which, after standing idle for a few years (since t retirement of Messrs. Butterworth & Brooks from the printing busines are gradually one after another being made to revolve in the service of t busy firm who have taken the place in hand, and wakened once more t industries of Crawshawbooth, much to the advantage of that localit and let it be hoped that it may not be without some adequate reward their own activity and enterprise. The firm have offices and warehou at Manchester, London, and Glasgow, but Church is the headquarte where a staff of 45 clerks is employed. It is doubtful whether there is a private firm, and certainly there are but few except the largest and m important public corporations, so completely fitted up with fire apparat as Messrs. F. Steiner & Co. Their fire engine station, a large well-light and ventilated apartment, heated by steam piping, contains one Messrs. Shand, Mason & Co.'s No. 2 steam fire engines, capable pumping 670 gallons of water per minute; a large hand fire engine, w a pumping power of 150 gallons per minute; and another smaller ha fire engine, capable of pumping 110 gallons per minute. Besides th moveable engines, there are on the works 8 stationary steam fire engin capable of throwing in the aggregate 2,030 gallons per minute. Th are also 20 hydrants from the main water pipes, and 28 for steam pow For the working of these various apparatuses, Messrs. Steiner & Co. h a large and efficient fire brigade, composed of 20 able-bodied men belo ing to the works, most of whom occupy dwelling-houses, the property the firm, in the immediate neighbourhood of the works, so that, sho occasion arise, they may be summoned to duty at once. Each f man is supplied with a copy of the rules and regulations of brigade, in which the duties of every member are fully set forth explained; and in order the more thoroughly to fix in their mi the duties belonging to each, and to accustom them to the perfor ance thereof, they are called forth to drill and practice once ev month, when the captain sees that each man understands and perfo his exercises efficiently. The electric light has been introduced extended over all the principal departments of the works. Electricity made use of in other forms in the works, and photography in vari branches is also called into requisition. As bearing upon the imme advantage which cheaper transit and a nearer port would be to a firm Messrs. Steiner & Co., it is only necessary to mention that they s many thousand cases yearly to Liverpool, *viâ* Manchester, Messrs. Stei having upon their own works a case-making establishment capable producing 100 cases per day, which, however, represents nothing like quantity of their actual shipments. At Irwell Springs, near Bac Messrs. Steiner & Co. possess another works devoted exclusively to y dyeing. The firm has warehouses at Glasgow and London. The speciali of the business are cloth and yarn dyeing and calico printing. The tr connection is very large, and includes all the shipping houses in district, the general Manchester warehousemen, and the best of wholesale buyers. There are no commercial travellers engaged, as unrivalled reputation of the firm renders their assistance unnecessary. the mills and dyeworks very large numbers of hands are in constant c ployment, and at the York Street warehouse there are some forty peo engaged in addition to salesmen, clerks and correspondents. The memb of the firm are amongst the best-known gentlemen who frequent Exchange; and few firms are as highly respected as Messrs. Steiner & Co.

John Tuffnell & Co., Merchant Shippers, 12, Minsh Street.—This business, originally known as Hamel & Wright, established upwards of twenty years ago, the present proprietors succe ing in the year 1885. The premises consist of a fine suite of offices, there are several commodious ware-rooms in the rear. The firm manu ture dyed and printed linings of all descriptions. The shipments incl greys and whites, twills, checks, stripes, prints, muslins, cambrics zephyrs; linings, satins, velveteens, and, in fact, the entire range Manchester goods. In addition to their general trade Messrs. Tuffnel Co. have occasional orders for Leeds, Bradford, Huddersfield and Ba goods; Sheffield tools, Birmingham hardware, Leicester hosiery, N tingham lace, and Stoke pottery. The trade connection is mainly amon Continental buyers, and with North and South America. The firm h the reputation of being most excellent buyers, and the sterling integrity every transaction engaged in earns them the respect of their many patro

J. Veitch Wilson, Halliday & Co., Queen Street, Brad-d. Manchester.—There are few people throughout the length and adth of the United Kingdom who take any intelligent interest in use of lubricants who have not, at some time or other, heard Mr. Veitch Wilson's name mentioned in connection with that subject; ilst in Lancashire and Yorkshire, at any rate, the majority of the ers of oil are not only familiar with his name, but recognise the value his long-continued investigations and experiments, and of his rious contributions to popular knowledge of the subject, by the ding of papers and the publication of pamphlets, by which he has rly earned the reputation, which is accorded to him, of an authority on all matters affecting lubrication. From an interesting account of Messrs. J. Veitch Wilson, Halliday & Co.'s works and operations, which appeared in the *Mechanical World* for January 7, 1887, and from a notice, of a more personal nature, which appeared in the number of *Inventions* for November, 1885, as well as from notices and reviews in other papers, we have compiled the following notice of the firm's present business:—Mr. Veitch Wilson established his business in Glasgow in 1865, in a comparatively small way. He originally devoted his attention to Scotch mineral oils, and for some time confined his transactions to his own country. As he prospered in business he sought wider fields for his operations, and gradually extended them to England, to Ireland, and to the Continent. The increase of his business involved some changes in his arrangements, and for some years he carried on business under the firm of J. Veitch Wilson & Co. In 1881, in order to devote more atten-

ion to English, and more particularly to Lancashire trade, which had ow become an important feature in the business, Mr. Wilson took up is abode in Manchester, and in 1885, his old partnership having ex-ired, he sold his works in Glasgow, and, in conjunction with Mr. Ienry Hales Halliday of this city, established the firm of J. Veitch Vilson, Halliday & Co., and erected the works shown in the accom-anying sketch. From the description of these works given in the *Iechanical World*, under the appropriate title of "The Model Oil Vorks," we learn that as they are the newest they are also, probably, e most complete works of their kind in the country, and in extent ey are very capacious. In the warehouse, or stores, there is ample om for the necessary large stocks required to carry on the firm's ade, while in the refinery every provision is made for the refining, lending, filtering, and tankage of the numerous special oils manufac-ired by the firm. The whole of the plant, which is new, was made to Ir. Wilson's specifications, and erected under his personal superintend-nce. The pans, which play an important part in a work of this sort, ere specially designed and patented by Mr. Wilson, and the whole rrangement is such as to secure maximum efficiency and uniform excel-nce of quality by minimum outlay of capital, time, and labour. Besides n extensive business in the ordinary oils of commerce, *e.g.*, sperm, lard, live, colza, &c., &c., the firm manufactures a number of specialities, which are offered to the public under their well-known registered trade-mark (a mariner's compass) and brands. These include oils for marine engines and cylinders; for stationary, locomotive, and portable engines, cylinders, and valves; for engineers' and machinists' machinery and tools, and for every kind of textile machinery, *e.g.*, looms, spindles of all kinds, &c., &c. We notice also, special stainless spindle oils, and oils for ring spindles. The firm published an excellent catalogue in connection with the late Manchester Jubilee Exhibition, in which are shown illustrations of the most important specimens of textile machinery exhibited there, and full particulars are given of all the oils manufactured by the firm. We recommend all who are interested to obtain a copy of this catalogue, which we understand will be supplied gratis to *bona-fide* oil users. Messrs. J. Veitch Wilson, Halliday & Co. conduct their business partly through the intervention of a few local travellers, but mainly by means of agents in the leading manufacturing towns and ports of the kingdom, in most of which they are now represented. Among their customers they include several of the leading railway companies and steam-ship com-panies of the United Kingdom. They also ship oils to various foreign countries, including the East Indies, Africa, South and Central America, and elsewhere. With regard to their home trade, it is sufficient to say that their oils are to be found in use throughout Great Britain and Ireland.

Trevor & Pilling, Chartered Accountants, 2, Clarence uildings, Booth Street.—The business now so successfully conducted by Iessrs. Trevor & Pilling was established in 1867 by Messrs. Richardsons Trevor. In 1875 Messrs. Richardsons retired, and Mr. Trevor carried n the concern in his own name until December, 1880. In January, 1882, Ir. Pilling was taken into partnership (having previously been with the rm for eight years), this combination continuing, with most satisfactory results, down to the present time. Both partners are members of the Institute of Chartered Accountants in England and Wales, and also of the Manchester Chamber of Commerce. The connection they enjoy is very large and of a sound and responsible character. They possess the confidence of a large number of patrons, and their exceptional business qualifications render them exceedingly popular. Messrs. Trevor & Pilling have a branch establishment at Bury, and they employ a large and com-petent staff of clerks.

E. Heyworth, Cambric Manufacturer, 11, Norfolk Street. This business was established in the year 1863, when Mr. Eli Heyworth started as a cotton manufacturer at Audley Range Mill, Blackburn, and where he continued to work it until 1874. Up to 1870 the Audley Hall Mill was a little shed. It was built and originally worked by a co-operative society, and afterwards run by a private firm, but in both cases unsuccessfully. In 1871 Mr. Heyworth became the owner of the property, and rebuilt and enlarged it, but his business developing so rapidly it became necessary to further enlarge his premises. He built another mill alongside his first one, having now—instead of three hundred looms, in a small shed, with which he started in 1863—two thousand two hundred looms, two large well-appointed mills, designed and maintained with an eye to order, cleanliness, and the health and comfort of his twelve hundred workpeople. Few mills can compare in this respect with those owned by Mr. E. Heyworth. The most modern machinery is used, and Mr. Heyworth has taken advantage of the many patents modern ingenuity has invented. His works are most elaborately fitted up. This can be better understood when we mention that nearly every loom in his works can be converted to a different use, according to demand. He has Dobbies and Dhooties sateen looms, and various other contrivances, so that when occasion requires he can put nearly every loom in his two sheds on fancy work, and when this is not wanted they can all weave plains. An important branch of this business is the manufacture of white and coloured cotton handkerchiefs. These, while in the piece, are sent out to be bleached, then returned to the mill, where there is a department for cutting them up, hemming and folding them, and packing them in boxes ready for the drapers' counter or the dressing-room. Having markets in nearly every quarter of the globe, and an infinite variety of manufactured goods, Mr. Heyworth distributes his manufactures through the hands of merchants. The trade is a peculiar one that Mr. Heyworth has built up for himself by close application to business, and by the adaptation of his work to the requirements of the time. In all the different varieties of fabrics manufactured the firm has gained great renown for the superior quality and excellence of finish of the goods turned out. Mr. Heyworth does also a large business as agent for cotton manufacturers. A word or two of the gentleman who controls this flourishing business. In 1874 Mr. Heyworth was elected a member of the Blackburn Town Council, and since that time he has been in the front rank of the local Liberal party, having a seat in the executive and a voice in all the important decisions of the party. About twelve months ago Mr. Heyworth was unanimously elected to fill the dual post of Chairman of the executive and President of the Council of the Liberal Association. In 1874 he was appointed one of her Majesty's justices of the peace for the borough of Blackburn, and in 1880 for the county. Mr. Heyworth also devotes a considerable portion of his time for the benefit of his fellow-townsmen. He is a member of the committee having in hand the establishment of a technical school for Blackburn, and has contributed largely to the school fund. He is also a member of the Blackburn Chamber of Commerce, and is one of the original directors of the Lancashire and Cheshire Telephone Company, at present holding the position of vice-chairman. Mr. Heyworth gives his personal supervision to every department of his business, and fully maintains the old-established reputation of some twenty-eight years that the house has enjoyed. The Manchester office and warehouse are situate at 11, Norfolk Street, and consist of a well-fitted office and large warehouse. In both Blackburn and Manchester the telephone is fitted, and everything is done to advance the firm's interests, and at the same time to study the wishes of their very large *clientèle*.

Salt & Co., Brewers, Burton-upon-Trent. Branch, Great Bridgewater Street (D. Morris, Agent).—Notable amongst the great industries of the present age are the vast establishments for the production and perfection of the food and drink supply. A thoroughly representative house in this branch of commerce is the renowned firm of Messrs. Thomas Salt and Company, Brewers, Burton-upon-Trent, who have been established in that famous brewing centre for upwards of a century, and have ever maintained a reputation of the highest possible character. The specialities of this firm comprise Burton old ales, mild and pale or bitter ales, which are brewed from some of the finest well water which is tapped in that celebrated district, and the fame of which, in connection with Burton ales, is world-wide. The operations at Messrs. Salt & Co.'s brewery are on a gigantic scale, and a vast staff of workmen are employed there under the supervision of the brewer, whose duty it is to attend to and direct the whole process of the brewing. The brewer must, of necessity, be a practical chemist, as the several ingredients used for brewing have to be systematically subjected to analytical tests. It will thus be seen that a high responsibility attaches to the position. This fact, combined with the use of the very best ingredients and the employment of large capital, results in the production of a liquid food at once wholesome, palatable, agreeable, stimulative, and nutritious, forming the popular beverages known as mild and bitter ales. The excellence of this firm's productions is amply testified by their large and increasing business both at home and abroad. Their new brewery in High Street, Burton, is of the most complete character, the machinery, plant, and other appurtenances being of the most modern and improved description. The firm have, likewise, extensive premises in various parts of the town of Burton, including maltings, cooperage, &c., the whole of which are connected with the firm's private lines of rail, bringing them all into immediate connection with the great railway systems extending to all parts of the country, so that their ales can be forwarded direct from the brewery to the place of destination. Messrs. Salt & Co. were awarded the gold medal for excellence of quality at the International Health Exhibition of 1884, and at the Liverpool and Edinburgh Exhibitions of 1886. All the Burton ale—both bottle and draught—consumed at the recent Manchester Jubilee Exhibition was supplied by Messrs. Salt & Co., and obtained well-merited praise. The firm have branch establishments in every important town in the kingdom and on the Continent. The Manchester stores and office are situated in Great Bridgewater Street, where the firm always keep on hand a large stock, in casks, varying in size from nine to one hundred and eight gallons. The office (which is neatly and conveniently arranged), adjoins the stores, and the business of the Manchester district is ably conducted by their local representative, Mr. D. Morris.

E. H. Downs, Glass and China, 13, Exchange Street. Works, Regent Road, Salford.—The leading and most thoroughly representative establishment of its kind in Manchester is that of Mr. E. H. Downs, glass and china manufacturer. This business was founded thirty years ago, and from the very beginning, being conducted on enterprising and honourable lines, it steadily prospered. There is something more required in these days than the commendable qualities above named. To be successful it is necessary to excel in some particular, and this is what Mr. Downs has accomplished. With a natural artistic aptitude perfected by special training and matured experience, Mr. Downs early evinced an unusual discretion and taste in the production of original designs in fine cut glassware, china, &c.; and his specialities have won a national reputation for superiority of workmanship, finish, and artistic accuracy, in proof of which fact we may quote the following extracts from the press of various dates:—In the *Manchester City News* of July 18th, 1869, we find that Mr. Downs supplied the dinner service (which was in turquoise and gold) for the royal table; and on May 13th, 1871, the *Manchester Daily Courier* notices that he had on view some rare and magnificent specimens of Capo di Monte porcelain which was formerly in the collection of the King of Hanover. The *Manchester Examiner and Times*, dated September 11th, 1877, states that Mr. E. H. Downs had on view at his establishment a beautiful service of cut glass, manufactured by him for the Mayor and Corporation of Manchester, and that it was then on view, and could be seen until the period of its removal to the Town Hall for the use of the inaugural banquet. The premises occupied in Exchange Street are of spacious dimensions, admirably arranged and equipped with every facility and convenience for the transaction of business. A large and valuable stock is kept, embracing the most comprehensive assortment of glass and china figures, vases, and *objets d'art* to be found outside London. Each department is replete with the most beautiful goods, and throughout the entire establishment there prevails a perfect system of organisation which facilitates the transaction of business, and makes the house a pleasant one to deal with. Mr. Edwin H. Downs, the proprietor, is an enterprising and thoroughly capable business man, honourable and fair in all transactions and well deserving of the substantial success he is achieving.

Gregory & Ramsdale, Public Accountants, Auditors, &c., York Street Chambers, 8, York Street.—In a large industrial and commercial city like Manchester, a business that is bound to be very valuable is that of public accountancy, auditing and estate and insurance agency. Among the establishments so engaged a principal place is held by that of Messrs. Gregory & Ramsdale. This business was founded over twenty years ago and has occupied the present address for seventeen years. Messrs. Gregory & Ramsdale bear a high reputation for their skill in accountancy matters and the management of trust estates. As estate and insurance agents they also bear a like name, and their long experience and talent qualify them admirably to draw up policies and advise in all branches of insurance to suit individual cases.

Threlfall & Co., Manufacturers and Leather Merchants, 15, Fennel Street.—The boot and shoe trade of Manchester is one of great extent, and many houses of the first rank are engaged in the business. Among others a prominent position is held by Messrs. Threlfall & Co., who have extensive premises. These consist of offices and warehouses, both of which are very large and commodious, and are elaborately fitted. The concern was started in 1861, and the quarter of a century since elapsed has sufficed, under energetic management, to give the establishment a very firm hold locally and throughout the country. They carry on the business of boot, shoe, and upper manufacturers, and do only a wholesale trade in these lines. They also act as leather merchants and shoe mercers, and manufacture French Glycerine Ki[illegible] Reviver, Challenge Waterproof Dubbin, and Manchester (Paste) Blacking, all got up in decorated tin boxes, in which they do a very extensive and profitable trade among most boot and shoe houses and leather merchants. The sole partner is Mr. Thomas Threlfall, and his personal superintendence of all details in connection with the business has been the principal cause of its rapid development and success.

The Zoological Gardens, Belle Vue.—For many a year nchester and Belle Vue have been inseparable. Deprived of her mag- cent Zoological Gardens, Manchester would seem to have passed into a new and undesirable sphere of existence to nine-tenths of her at population, and would have lost one of her chief attractions to the t community of annual visitors and migratory sight-seers with which metropolis of the cotton trade, in common with the generality of re, handsome, and note-worthy cities, is not unpleasantly familiar. Belle Vue Gardens are in no danger of separation from Manchester, citizens and her visitors. They have been where they are for much re than half a century, and it is not at all improbable that they will nain in the same position, both geographically and in public affection, another half century to come; beyond that it would be unsafe in the sent remarkable age to prophecy or forecast concerning the stability nything. The establishment of Belle Vue Zoological Gardens dates k far into the last generation, when the energy, enterprise, and hing spirit of Mr. John Jennison and his noted coadjutor, Mr. Dan- , now both of them deceased, made the place famous for all time as a ular resort, and brought the Gardens to the front rank among British logical institutions. The founders have been succeeded in the manage- it by their sons and the success of Belle Vue Gardens grows greater r by year, for the present directorate seem to have inherited the full sure of capacity and energy requisite to continue the long lease of ularity and prosperity granted to the establishment by a beneficient ame at the very outset of its career. Opposition has come; some of as remained, some has passed away; all of it has been worthy of the stance of any great institution, and would have effected the *quietus* of e concerns of less solid foundation and unimpaired vitality than Belle Gardens. But Belle Vue Gardens have suffered little or nothing n rivalry or competition in any form. They are unique, for one thing; y are old-established and world-famous for another; and, above all,

BALL ROOM.

y have never fallen off in their constant putting forward of new and el and eminently pleasing attractions, and have thus won for themselves t most lasting of all popularity—the popularity which is stimulated new life year after year by public confidence and expectancy. Each son the Messrs. Jennison and the Messrs. Danson have fresh treats of ious kinds to offer to their patrons; and the people have come to re- d Belle Vue as a sort of inexhaustible mine of attractions, a Pandora's t of sights and sounds worth seeing and hearing, a peculiar species of ennial pleasure-plant, putting forth a different style of bud, blossom, l flower every year, each succeeding bloom surpassing in some extra- inary way anything of the kind ever known to have preceded it. Upon h a basis of existence as this Belle Vue is sure of an indefinite popu- ity. The Gardens are exceedingly well situated, and are most con- nient of access from all parts of Manchester and its environs. They lie ween the Hyde and Stockport turnpike roads, and have three main rances, one at each extremity, and one about the centre of the grounds. is latter entrance is in Hyde Road, and is approached from Manchester er by that road or by Ashton Road, the distance from the Manchester irmary being about two and a half miles. The Manchester Carriage npany's omnibuses and tramcars afford excellent means of communi- ion here, running to and fro every few minutes. The other entrances equally easy of access from various parts, the western entrance being se to the Longsight Station of the London and North-Western Rail- y, while the Gorton or eastern entrance, with its excellent hotel (opened elve years ago) is near the Belle Vue Station of the Midland Railway. th these means of access are obviously especially convenient for visitors ning in by rail. At the Gorton entrance, in connection with the hotel, been provided fine stable accommodation for several hundred horses, charge being made for stabling. In many ways the enterprise of the ssrs. Jennison has made the Gardens one of the most pleasant places public resort for purposes of recreation and relaxation in the United ngdom. Botanically and zoologically, Belle Vue is never otherwise than beautiful and interesting in the highest degree, and a host of other incidental attractions is ready at hand for the visitor who has satisfied himself in the matter of plants and flowers, birds, beasts, waterfowl, and reptiles. The great annual open-air picture, produced under the direction of Messrs. Danson Brothers, is the yearly *pièce de résistance* at the Gardens, and is looked forward to by the public with as much eager expectancy as is displayed by the average juvenile in his anticipation of the coming circus or the prospective pantomime. The Belle Vue picture is always a magnificent spectacle, a triumph of scenic and prospective art for the time of its existence, and would in itself alone be sufficient to well repay a visit to this delightful place. It is changed every year, and the Messrs. Danson and Jennison always manage to select a subject which "takes" the popular fancy and brings the public of town and country *en masse* to view the annual wonder, and renew their protestations of admiration for the enterprise and resource that can make such things possible and profitable. That no expense is spared in perfecting to the utmost the pleasing illusion of these vast scenic representations goes without saying. The public nowadays is notoriously fastidious in matters spectacular, and has come to expect from Messrs. Jennison and Messrs. Danson something that shall be of the very best exclusively. The expectation, it is safe to say, is as a rule more than realised. Topical occurrences, incidents, and impressions are usually treated in the annual picture at Belle Vue. In 1885, for instance, the subject, very appropriately, was Khartoum, the mournful scene of General Gordon's long beleaguerment and ultimate massacre. In 1886 the siege of San Sebastian by the British under Sir Thomas Graham was the subject, and afforded opportunities for a magnificent battle spectacle. In 1887 the management fittingly deferred to the pervading spirit of jubilee, and presented their patrons with a splendid view of the city of London, River Thames, St. Paul's, Westminster Abbey, and quaint Old London Bridge, all complete and wondrously faithful in semblance to the great original. The limited space at the disposal of this brief sketch quite precludes the possibility of any detail being given here of the host of attractions, great and small, with which the Belle Vue Gardens constantly abound. The birds, the animals, the grottoes, the waterfowl, and many curious aquatic creatures, the magnificent ferneries, hothouses, and conservatories—these to some will prove enough and to spare for one day's outing. But beyond all this is much more of a varied and comprehensive nature, for Belle Vue is a little world of amusement in itself. There are the lakes and the boating, the cricket and archery, the horse and velocipede rings, the enchanting and bewildering "Hampton Court maze," the dancing platform, the tennis lawn, the elephant and camel houses, the always popular monkey house, the deer paddock, the museum, and the bear pit. And when the "inner man," or the "inner woman," calls for attention, as it undoubtedly will from time to time even among such surroundings as these, there are the tea-rooms and refreshment rooms of every description, where the best of light refreshments are provided at the lowest possible prices. Messrs. Jennison have long recognised the vital importance of catering well to the requirements of this same "inner man," and many a place of popular resort might do much worse than take a leaf from their book in the matter of price and quality. For the rest, there is a large music-hall, and there are lavatories, parcel offices, cloak rooms, and every desirable convenience and accommodation that can tend to enhance the comfort and increase the general enjoyment of the visitor. Belle Vue Gardens are a species of Ranelagh, Vauxhall, and Marylebone rolled into one, refined in most ways, improved in many respects, and equal to practically every demand that can be made upon them in a hardworking but pleasure-loving age. They are emphatically one of the great institutions of Manchester; and brief and superficial as this sketch has undoubtedly been, its compilation has been necessary in order to complete the present review of the leading industrial, commercial, and, in this one instance, entertainment enterprises of the city.

Isaac Ades & Co., Shippers, 81, Peter Street.—A well-known firm of shippers of Manchester goods is that of Messrs. Isaac Ades & Co., which was originally founded in 1875, in Bond Street, under the title of Messrs. Andrea Ades & Co. Some time afterwards, it was removed to 6, Hall Street, the title changed to Ades, Dayan, & Co., and finally, under the present designation to the present address. The offices occupied are commodious, and furnished in a substantial manner. Messrs. Isaac Ades & Co. are employed in shipping Manchester, Glasgow, and Bradford goods to Syria, and they are one of the largest shippers to Aleppo. Messrs. Isaac Ades & Co. have under their control ample resources for any emergency, and are thoroughly conversant with the requirements of the Eastern markets. They are well known and respected in the mercantile and industrial world.

W. T. Sutcliffe & Co., Corn Merchants, 1, Fennel Street.—W. T. Sutcliffe & Co. have been established for a period of no less than twenty-five years. Their business is a widespread and very important one, the custom enjoyed being very extensive. No pains are spared to ensure patrons every satisfaction. This firm have many exceptional facilities. They are specially represented on the Liverpool Corn Exchange, and certainly occupy a position in the front rank of their class. They have acted continuously for the last twenty years as sole agents in the Liverpool and Manchester district for the sale of the celebrated Hungarian Crowns flour, manufactured by the Pannonia Steam Mills of Buda Pesth. The telegraphic address of the concern is—"Crowns," Manchester.

Geo. M. Bass & Son (Late T. and M. P. Bass), Timber Merchants, Joiners, and Packing-Case Makers, Importers of American Doors, Manufacturers of Moulds, Skirtings, Match Boards, &c., Saw Mills, Worsley Street, Salford, City Offices, Stanley Street, Manchester.—Comparatively few persons, even among the citizens themselves, have any idea of the great proportions attained in their midst by the timber and joinery trades of Manchester. Probably the reason of this is, that the extensive yards, premises, steam plant, &c., required by a few of the largest firms engaged in these industries are not, as a rule, visible from the principal traffic highways, but are nevertheless secluded, close at hand, in convenient nooks, down narrow side streets. Not a little surprising to the visitor is it to find that the great extent of space required by the largest of these establishments has been obtainable at all, where it has been secured. One might, and does, pass and repass hundreds of times without ever suspecting the presence of works so extensive, in localities apparently so out of the way, and yet so near to the active business centre. One of the oldest businesses of this kind in the Manchester district is that of Messrs. G. M. Bass & Son. This firm was established in the early part of the century. Originally it was known under the title of Lens & Bass, changing shortly afterwards to Bass, Lens & Bass, subsequently to T. & M. P. Bass, and finally, in 1886, to its present designation, G. M. Bass & Son. Messrs. Bass and Son have city offices and show-rooms for doors, mouldings, &c., in Stanley Street, Manchester. Their works are situated just out of the city boundary, along the opposite bank of the river, in Worsley Street, Salford, where the firm employs a large number of hands. The various departments and offices of the concern are all connected by telephone. We paid a visit to the works of Messrs. Bass a few days ago, and were considerably surprised, after passing through the gateway, at the unexpected extent of space occupied by them, between the entrance and their quay at the river side; at their vast stocks of timber, their numerous workshops, drying and seasoning sheds, and the indications all around of the evident magnitude of the business carried on there. In the great yard, lurries and carts were busily loading with packing-cases, deals, joinery, mouldings of all sorts, sizes, and descriptions. Timber was being removed to and from the drying rooms or the workshops, whilst the busy hum of the driving-gear and the steam-driven saws very demonstratively assailed the ear on every side. The stocks of timber first attracted our attention. As previously described, the yard extends to the river bank; thither from May to December arrive innumerable barges laden with timber from Quebec, from St. John's, from Swedish, from Russian and other ports. Among the timber importers of Liverpool, Hull, or Grimsby, few firms are better known than Messrs. Bass & Son. In the yard are long avenues of timber, arranged in great horizontal stacks, with apertures skilfully left for the better distribution of air-currents over their surfaces. Here are huge logs of mahogany, of baywood, of pine and pitch-pine, of oak and birch. It should be mentioned, however, that even the enormous quantities of timber seasoning here do not comprise anything like the actual amount of the firm's stock, a very large proportion of it having to lie at various wharves along the river and canal, whence it is carted as required by Messrs. Bass. From the open yards we pass to the covered sheds, and inspect the stocks of best class and expensive pine deals, of red deals and boards in all thicknesses, of picked deals for ladder and hat-box makers, of baywood sawn and ready for use, of material for mould-making (which stands for months before use), of spouting in red deal and pitch pine. Thence we go upstairs to another great shed filled with match boarding of spruce, red deal, and pitch-pine. Further on we notice a room filled with timber suitable for coach-builders and machinists' patterns. Another department contains hundreds of ready-made doors. During our inquisitive peregrinations through all sorts of manufactories, we are repeatedly confronted by the bugbear of foreign competition, and here we encounter it once again. Practically it is impossible for us to compete with the foreigner in the making of doors; these are made in America or in Sweden, brought here, and notwithstanding all the expense of carriage, the foreigner beats us in our own market. From what we have seen there can be no doubt that foreign doors are as well made as our own of nominally similar class, and can be sold for less money. Said we to our guide, "How do you find the Swedish doors compare with the American?" "We think the American are much better: not so skimped in design, fuller and bolder-looking." "You sell the American, then, chiefly?" "Well, we sell just whatever our customers require." We now leave the wood and go to have a look at the workshops, first of all paying a visit to the saw-sharpener, who is cheerily filing away in a room all by himself, and tells us that he sharpens from forty to forty-five saws in a day, and that there are frequently as many as forty saws at work at the same time. Then we have a casual look at the engines, one horizontal and one vertical, which can be worked either together or singly. Then we pass into a long mill in which are all sorts of saws, circular and otherwise, actively at work. Here is a great circular saw cutting up logs, yonder is a frame in which sometimes as many as thirty horizontal saws are in operation at once: in all cases the wood is carried to the saws by steam power. Then we pass to the great packing-case room, where are boxes of all sizes being made, from wine cases to the big packing-cases for abroad, some of them about the size of a cottage parlour. Another room is devoted to mould-making, all turned out of the machine as clean and smooth and finished as if they had been sand-papered and polished by hand. Elsewhere are the machines for floor-board, match-board, and skirting making. We look in at the long joiners'
shops, filled with carpenters' be
the boilers, inspect the elaborate
or extinction of fire, and so bring
their general joinery business M
manufacturing, and many specim
sent to the great exhibitions of
After the preceding description
connection of Messrs. Bass & Son
mouldings, doors, window frames
builders in the city and district
supplied to the principal shippi
reputation of the firm for the i
character, is sufficiently proved b
by the enormous extent and vari

Campbell Redmayne &
ham Street.—This firm was est
which are situated in Collyhurs
upon upwards of three and a h
River Irk and the new line of t
The present partners of this
Redmayne McLaine. The late
McLaine, the former retiring fro
1873, at the time leaving Peter M
he took as partner into the busin
ship the firm has since then exis
member of the firm, was apprenti
the founder of the firm), and in
years' experience of the various m
1860, when it became the fashi
McLaine was one of the first to
which the firm made thousands
houses as Rylands & Sons, Lin
head, and S. and J. Watts. Aft
by the steel used for the same pu
was encircled in an extensive
were then worn, of which they
gross weekly, for the home trade
formation of the original firm its
the making of packing materials,
cloths, patent packings, pitch pap
facture they have yearly increase
in this particular being circulated
have special agents in the most i
one of the most important firms i
owing to its constant, hard work
makers of rope and twine, humm
lines for a great number of years
one of their chief items. As an
experimenting, enabled themsel
makers, stay makers, and tailors,
fener Hessians: with this acco
with any opponent in the same b
Piccadilly, are mere town offic
are simply used as a town addr
very extensive and employ a ver
member of the firm is extreme
reputation of being an experienc
ness. The firm is accounted li
of charitable movements.

A. Bedell & Co., Cott
39, Fountain Street.—Messrs. A
turers of linen and cotton goo
Newton Heath, where they en
firm has a city office at the abov
staff and have been located abou
been in existence about thirty
great celebrity for the excellent
cial class of manufacture to whi
and linen ticks and union and
Union goods have much improv
years. The term is a general
composed of more than one mat
of flax and hemp, cotton and fl
qualities of this kind of goods
widely known. Tick, or tickin
covering of beds, mattresses, &
from a German source, and
of linen, but now cotton ent
Messrs. Bedell & Co. are very
description of goods also. Thei
with all the most modern ma
known in the northern district
county of Chester. The firm h
being sent all over the world.
of this important business.

Samuel Brooks, Cotton Machinist, Union Iron Works, Vest Gorton.—The extensive and important business of this firm was ommenced in the year 1859, and during the interval that has elapsed reat honours have been won at numerous exhibitions. Amongst the rize medals recently gained may be mentioned the gold medal of the nternational Inventions Exhibition, London; the gold medal of the Exposition Universelle, Antwerp; and the silver medal of the World's Fair, t New Orleans—all in the year 1885. The principal business of the irm is the making of all kinds of cotton machinery, such as drawing-rames, slubbing-frames, spinning-frames, doubling-frames, winding-rames, balling machines, loom temples of every description, &c., &c. arge departments are also devoted to the construction of heavy engineers' tools, such as punching and shearing machines, planing machines, rilling and slotting machines, screwing and shaping machines, &c., &c. One of the most important specialities of the firm is known as the ring ystem of spinning and doubling; of this speciality the average produc-ion is over six thousand spindles per week. The interests of the firm re looked after by a large staff of representatives at home, and residen-ial agents in every cotton-manufacturing country abroad. The firm ecently had the misfortune to lose its esteemed head and founder, the ate Mr. Samuel Brooks, whose long and honourable business career had arned him the esteem of all with whom he came in contact. His son, Mr. Samuel Herbert Brooks, has succeeded to the business in conjunction with other relatives, and owing to the energy displayed in every depart-ment considerable development has taken place since the death of the late Mr. Brooks, and at the present time the firm are filled with home and oreign orders which will fully employ them for many months to come. The city office is at 15, Market Street (opposite Royal Exchange), and he favourite position for the representatives on the Exchange is No. 4 Pillar, where they may always be found on 'Change days between and 3 p.m.

David Shaw & Co., Oil Manufacturers and Refiners, Clayton, near Manchester. Manchester offices, 35, Market Street.—One

f the most important and highly successful business concerns in Clayton, ear Manchester, is that of Messrs. David Shaw & Co., manufacturers nd refiners of oils, tallows, glue, sizes, manures, &c. At their large nd handsomely appointed works this firm gives constant employment o about one hundred and fifty men, and the various articles produced re widely known throughout the United Kingdom. The business was stablished twenty-seven years ago, and affords a striking example of apid and at the same time substantial progress. Besides carrying on an xtensive home trade, that to other countries is of very respectable dimen-ions. During the earlier portion of their career this firm devoted much ttention to the production of wool, cloth, and soap oils, and oleines, argely used by worsted spinners, and keeping abreast of the times by dopting improvements resulting from practical experiments, they deser-edly hold a position second to none in this branch. Tallow, a necessary ollateral industry with the foregoing, has grown with the increasing make by the woollen trade of the oils mentioned, until now tons of tons er week are turned out. In this article are various qualities suitable for ubrication and the sizing of cotton goods, and as they are made without he aid of acid or other chemical matter they are pure. Much is converted nto soap for scouring and other purposes. Messrs. David Shaw & Co. ncourage their clients who use soap to undertake the manufacture of it hemselves, and they are always ready to give such directions as are necessary to this end. This enterprising firm, some years ago, began the istillation and refinement of oils generally for machinery purposes, with which they supplied the trade, but finding the necessities of the times emanded it they determined to go direct to consumers, and the wisdom f their determination has been proved by the steady growth of their rade in spindle, loom, engine, cylinder, and machinery oils within the ast four or five years, as nearly as we can learn. On what might be termed an inquisitive inquiry as to the cause of this surprising success we find, as we think, the secret to be in the manner in which they laid hold of the condition of the market. Anticipating a fall, they appear to have made their calculations accordingly, and offered qualities at such prices—no doubt giving a fair working margin—as surprised and tempted consumers, and it is not to be wondered at that many of the largest cotton-spinning and manufacturing firms in these times of keen competition should lay hold of offers affecting their interests, and of upholding a firm producing and supplying an honest article at a fair price. This is admittedly the pace that will win the race. The firm is also well known as fur-nishing the following articles: hot and cold neck greases, cog and water-wheel greases, for which they have a large demand; also bone or glue size, extensively used in the production of dyed and printed calicoes. They are also extensive importers of oils, which are all carefully refined—such as olive, castor, gallipoli, lard, linseed (raw and boiled), rape, neatsfoot, and so on. Not satisfied with their attainments, Messrs. David Shaw & Co. added to their productions a few years back chemical manure manufactur-ing, and they appear to have made as rapid progress in this as in all they have undertaken, for thousands of tons every season are forwarded to all parts of the country, and with satisfactory results. The fertilising properties of these manures—if analysis be worth anything—cannot but go greatly to assist the agriculturist in obtaining the most his land will give. We do not pretend to understand the value of these commodities, but if comparisons are right they certainly do show a great advantage over manures of which we have some knowledge. We have been unable to touch minutely on many articles supplied by Messrs. David Shaw & Co., but we have been led to give expression to the result of our inquiries, prompted by the excellence of their exhibit at the Manchester Jubilee Exhibition, where was shown the interesting processes by which the finished articles were produced. In the future we hope to hear more of this firm, and so long as they confine themselves, as they are evidently now doing, to giving the buyer the article he requires at a reasonable charge, and in exercising their wonted foresight and care in all business transactions, this hope will be realised.

John Smith, Timber Merchant, and Packing-case Maker, Junction Saw Mills, Ducie Street, Piccadilly.—Few establishments engaged in the timber and packing-case trades of Manchester are more favourably known or more widely patronised than that conducted by Mr. John Smith, at the Junction Saw Mills, Ducie Street. This business dates its origin back to 1850, in which year it was founded by Mr. Joseph Moores. Upon the retirement of Mr. Moores, some years ago, Mr. Smith, who had been several years in the employment of the founder, succeeded to the business, under whose able and energetic management it rapidly as-sumed a position of great prominence. The premises are very extensive, and consist of a spacious timber yard, fine saw mills, and an ad-mirable suite of well arranged and comfort-ably furnished offices. The saw mills are fitted and equipped in the most complete manner with the most modern machinery. Log frame, deal frame, and powerful circular saws are prominent items in the mechanical equipment of the works, and the entire machinery is driven by steam power. A very large and judiciously selected stock of timber, suitable for every local and general requirement, is stacked on the premises. In this a valuable and rapidly increasing trade is done with the leading builders, joiners, cabinet-makers, machinists, and engineers. Under-takers' mahogany, birch, ash, whitewood, Stettin oak, black walnut, and pitch pine in the log, American oak in logs and planks, Dantzic oak billets, Staves, pine and spruce deals, are sold to the foregoing tradesmen not only in the city and suburbs but all over the North. Packing-case making is an important branch of Mr. Smith's operations, and his connection in this line is one of great extent and value among the principal shipping houses, the home trade, wholesale warehouses, engineers, and machinists. The offices of the establishment are in connection with the telephonic exchange, thereby securing promptitude and despatch in the execution of orders. In addition to his operations as a timber merchant and packing-case maker, Mr. Smith does a large business as a public sawyer, being patronised by the various timber merchants and others in the trade who do not possess the necessary facilities for the sawing and converting of their own timber. The general trade done is very extensive and steadily increasing. Mr. Smith's solicitude for the welfare of his employés is proved by the existence of a flourishing insurance fund in connection with the works, by which the operatives are insured against loss through any accident that may befall them while engaged on the premises. The staff numbers over thirty, and the house is efficiently represented by a number of capable and energetic representatives who are con-tinually on the road, extending its connections among the most desirable classes of custom. The business is on the whole one of the most important of its kind in the city, and its enterprising proprietor is justly esteemed and respected for his integrity and ability, and the liberal manner in which he treats his numerous and influential *clientèle*.

Messrs. E. Dean & Sons, Horse-Slaughterers, Manure Manufacturers, and Leather Dressers, Gibbon Street, Ashton New Road, Bradford.—One of the most extensive and important businesses of its kind in England is that carried on by the well-known house of Messrs. E. Dean & Sons, of Bradford, Manchester, who rank among the largest firms of horse-slaughterers, manure manufacturers, and leather dressers.

Their system of operations is indeed almost exceptionally comprehensive, comprising as it does an industry of very great magnitude in both its individual and collective characteristics; and the enterprising and energetic manner in which this industry has always been conducted—and especially during the past quarter of a century—has made the name of the firm notable in all parts of the United Kingdom. The house was founded as far back as 1825 by Mr. John Dean, and at his death, in 1832, passed into the hands of his brother, Mr. William Dean. The latter gentleman died in 1856, having contributed largely to the extension of a trade which had been well and firmly established by his brother. The business then became vested in the widow and sons of Mr. William Dean, and was by them carried on under the style of Esther Dean & Sons. Mrs. Dean is now deceased, but the concern is still personally conducted by her sons, who retain the title which heads this sketch, and administer all the affairs of the house in a characteristic spirit of progressive enterprise. In Gibbon Street, Ashton New Road, Bradford, near Manchester, the firm have very extensive industrial premises, covering a large area of ground, equipped with every facility for the efficient conduct of the manufacturing and productive branches they have so successfully specialized, and affording employment to a numerous force of hands. Branch establishments are also controlled at Parliament Street, Mile End, London, E., and in Manchester, Stockport, Oldham, &c. These are important as depôts for the sale of boiled horse-flesh as food for cats, dogs, and poultry; and in this department one of the greatest points of enterprise in connection with the transactions of the house becomes apparent. For three hundred years the trade in cats' and dogs' meat has had its great head-quarters in London, and the requirements of the provincial towns have been principally supplied from that centre. This state of things was manifestly inconsistent with the "go-ahead" characteristics of the large provincial communities, who seem every year to be making themselves more independent of the metropolis; and the energetic firm of Messrs. E. Dean & Sons by a bold stroke of adventure "cut adrift," so to speak, from the long-existent order of affairs, and effected a very considerable revolution in an important line of business by developing an immense trade system in boiled horse-flesh of their own preparation, and by supplying a numerous circle of provincial customers direct. The success of the departure has been distinct and unquestionable, and this branch constitutes to-day a leading feature in the operations of the house under notice. The firm have a most extensive horse-slaughtering yard near Manchester, and are in a position to carry on the business incidental to such an establishment upon a scale of the utmost magnitude. This, indeed, they are now doing, and every year marks an appreciable extension in the widespread connection they have opened up in all parts of the English provinces. Space forbids any extended detail regarding the nature of their undertakings as horse-slaughterers. They possess, as already indicated, the most complete facilities for such work, and an inspection of the establishment they control demonstrates the fact that the killing of the animals and the subsequent preparation of the horse-flesh are processes which here receive the best possible exemplification. Everything about the place works with the regularity and system of the traditional clockwork; and day by day many an old and worn-out horse, whose active and lively occupation in this world has come to a terminus, enters into a new sphere of inanimate utility, which amply illustrates the truth of the worthy Friar Laurence's speech in *Romeo and Juliet*—

"For nought so vile that on the earth doth live
But to the earth some special good doth give."

As horse-slaughterers, Messrs. Dean & Sons occupy a position of continuously increasing note and prominence, and in this department they have rapidly built up a trade of first-rate volume and importance. The exceptionally high fertilizing power of concentrated animal matter, bone, &c., for use in connection with grain crops, and the value of the same constituents with an admixture of superphosphates for the nourishment of root crops, have long been recognised. Messrs. Dean & Sons' productions in manurial agents, therefore, need no introduction here. The firm have devoted much attention to the preparation of special blood, bone, and animal manures of a high class, and have developed compounds of this character which have met with widespread and well-merited approval. This constitutes the second branch of their business, and is a feature of principal importance in their operations. Their manures have been prepared in various classes suitable for all crops, and they hold many testimonials from agricultural sources of the highest consideration, affirming in unequivocal terms their excellent fertilizing properties. As leather-dressers the firm supply all classes of strapping for machinery; oak-tanned and green leather picking bands; white, green, and oak-tanned laces, &c., and are also extensive dealers in plasterers' hair. For the development of both these last-named industries—manure manufacture and leather-dressing—the horse-slaughtering operations of the house pave the way; and it is readily apparent that every part of the animal from which any "special good" can be derived is utilized to the fullest extent in the three departments we have herein briefly referred to. It is quite impossible to give more than a concise and superficial sketch of the transactions of such a firm within the narrow limits of a necessarily slight commercial sketch. The house of Messrs. E. Dean & Sons is one of the most thoroughly representative concerns in its important line in any part of the kingdom, and its operations have from the first been conducted upon principles which have built up a trade of very great magnitude, established a connection of distinct value and influence, and laid securely the foundations of a lasting and well-deserved prosperity.

Wm. Flanagan, Wadding Manufacturer; Warehouse, 14, Union Street, Church Street.—The commodious warehouse of Mr. W. Flanagan, wadding manufacturer, forms the central depôt of a business which has now been established for several years, and has in that time attained to very large proportions indeed. As an indication of this the amount of work in Mr. Flanagan's warehouse necessitates the employment of nearly a score of hands. The manufactory in connection with this warehouse, and known by the name of "West End Mill," is situated at Mottram, and is likewise the scene of a large degree of business and activity. A very considerable number of hands are employed at West End Mill, which is fitted up with the best modern machinery and appliances devised for the manufacture and preparation of wadding for the infinite variety of purposes for which that article of commerce is now used. Mr. Flanagan's trade extends over a wide area, both at home and in many markets, to which his goods are consigned in very considerable bulk. His straightforwardness, combined with his consideration for the claims and interests of others, has secured Mr. Flanagan the esteem of his patrons and connections.

William P. Burnley & Co., Metal Merchants, &c., Red Bank.—This is the business formerly known as that of Carter & Company. Under the present proprietor the trade has been largely increased, various new departments having been added. Messrs. Burnley & Company manufacture an immense number of tinman's sundries and other making up goods; and they do a very large turn-over in founders' and moulders' requisites. The principal branch of trade carried on by Messrs. Burnley & Co. is bright-tinning sheet-iron, for which the firm is noted. This process has been conducted on their premises during the last thirty years, and the house is the only one in Manchester or neighbourhood that conducts this process. A prominent item in their stock is Howard's Tinning Solution, for tinning iron, copper, brass, and other metal. It prevents discoloration or oxydation of bright metals, effects a great saving of tin and solder, enables the solder to flow more freely from the soldering iron, and makes stronger, cleaner, and better work in less time than any other fluid used for the same purpose. It is sold at 6d. per bottle and 4s. the gallon. The firm sell immense quantities of this solution, and their business in tinning is very extensive and continually increasing, owing to their resources and superior workmanship. As metal merchants they keep a large and comprehensive stock of sheet brass, zinc, and copper; bar and hoop iron; black, tinned, galvanized, and terne-coated sheet iron, besides nails, screws, riddles, sieves, spades, and general ironmongery heavy goods. The works are of considerable size, fitted with modern plant and machinery. The offices are convenient and commodious, and the warehouse covers a large area. From thirty to forty hands are employed, and several able representatives travel the districts, the connection being widespread and increasing. The sole partner is Mr. William P. Burnley, a gentleman of very long experience in the metal trades, and as well known on the exchanges of Birmingham and Wolverhampton as in Market Street, Manchester.

W. T. Mitchell, Ship and Insurance Broker, 8, York Street.—This business was established in the year 1861. The offices are admirably situated. With ship brokerage Mr. Mitchell combines the business of forwarding and insurance agency. He represents in this city the Reliance Marine Insurance Company, whose offices are at Exchange Buildings East, Liverpool, and whose capital is £400,000, and also the well-known firm of Messrs. G. H. Fletcher & Co., steamship owners, of Mersey Chambers, Liverpool. Mr. Mitchell has a large personal connection amongst the leading shipping firms.

Robert Froehlich & Co., General Merchants, 84, ulkner Street.—No city in the world excels Manchester in the value of export trade, and no firms, taken collectively, exercise more influence the mercantile world than those of this famous city. A well-known m is that trading under the title of Messrs. Robert Froehlich & Co., iich was founded in 1868. The sole member now of the firm is Mr. bert Froehlich, who holds the Italian title of Cavaliere and K.C.I., d is the Italian Consul for the city of Manchester and district. The ite of offices occupied is spacious, handsomely furnished, and a good rical staff is employed. The firm carries on an extensive export and port trade with various parts. The goods exported are principally those Manchester production, while the imports mainly consist of raw aterials. Mr. Robert Froehlich, by virtue of his consular position, is ell known in leading circles, and his personal qualities command uni- rsal esteem, whilst his house holds a respected place in the business mmunity.

W. D. Sanderson, Hide and Leather Factor, 11, alf Moon Street.—This business was established as far back as the year 48, under the style Dennison, Sanderson & Son. In 1859 a limitation partnership took place, and it became known under its present title. 1885 Mr. W. D. Sanderson, senior, died, and the present proprietor ok over the business. His initials being the same as his predecessor's, change in the style of the firm was necessary. The present premises ve been occupied by the firm a little less than two years; they consist convenient offices and warehouse. Mr. Sanderson's connection is wide- read, as he has connections in every part of the United Kingdom d in many places on the continent of Europe. As a factor Mr. nderson enjoys the unlimited confidence of the tanners. He regularly tends the Leeds Leather Fair, and is equally at home at Bermondsey; s sterling integrity and fair dealing winning him universal respect and teem.

Bond & Riley, Cotton Manufacturers, 14, Calender reet, Palace Square. Also at 17, Lawrence Lane, Cheapside, London, C.—Founded more than sixty years ago, this firm is still in the front nk of the trade. The factories are located at Bolton, ten miles from the y, and are of very great extent. A large number of hands are con- ntly employed. The productions of the firm are toilet covers and ilts, honeycombs, alhambras, tapestry, and similar goods, and the excel- it make of all of them is so generally and fully recognised that the ms are never idle. Messrs. Bond & Riley display great enterprise in production of new patterns and styles, and are constantly placing velties upon the market. The warehouse is of very considerable size, d in addition to a handsome suite of offices, has a range of pattern and ck rooms. The connection extends throughout the United Kingdom, large foreign as well as home trade being done. The partners are r. Joseph Riley, Mr. Walter Bond, and Mr. John Thomas Bond, of whom are well known in commercial circles, and are highly teemed.

William Clemson & Co., Velvet Dyers, Printers, nbossers, &c., Horrock Dye and Print Works, Red Bank.—This ry important firm has been established upwards of eighty years, and cupies a leading position amongst velvet dyers and printers. At the esent time there are no fewer than four hundred hands, dyers and inters, in constant employment, and a staff of commercial travellers is quired to wait on the numerous customers of the firm. The works and ctories are very extensive. The whole of the plant and machinery has cently been entirely remodelled. Amongst many specialities for which ssrs. Clemson & Co. are so well known are certain new colours in dyes d printings of great permanency; and, in addition, their manufactures distinguished by durability, excellence of design, and skilful execution. e present partners are Mr. John Henry Clemson and Mr. Thomas illiam Clemson, both well known amongst Manchester merchants.

Joe Young & Co., Woollen Merchants, 39, York reet.—This business was established in the year 1880, and has proved ry successful. The premises consist of a capital roomy warehouse, ex- mely well-stocked, and a first-rate suite of offices that are handsomely nished and fitted with the most approved modern appliances for the pid dispatch of a brisk business. The specialities of the trade are eds coatings, Huddersfield trouserings, Dewsbury and Batley mantle ths, pilots, seals, and heavy coatings; and a large variety of Bradford ffs, dress materials, and worsteds; also cotton dress goods. The con- ction is extremely large, and includes most of the home trade houses, ne of the shippers, the mantle manufacturers, and certain of the best olesale clothiers and woollen warehousemen. The reputation of the m is now so well established that the services of commercial travellers unnecessary. A strong body of assistants, clerks, and bookkeepers actively engaged, and a capital trade is carried on. The sole partner Mr. Joe Young, a gentleman of inflexible integrity and well known Leeds, Huddersfield, on the Bradford Exchange, and in this city. capital man of business, Mr. Young is deservedly prosperous.

A. C. Brown & Co., Manchester Warehousemen, 15, Marsden Square.—This well-known firm has been established under various names for no less a period than half a century, and during the whole of that long period has enjoyed a high-class reputation for its special manufactures. Besides manufacturing on their own account certain classes of cotton fabrics known generally as Man- chester goods, Messrs. Brown & Co. have the exclusive sale of Messrs. Greenwood & Whittaker's water-twist shirtings, a class of cloth which is unrivalled in the trade. In addition to shirtings, Messrs. Brown & Co. do a large trade in linings, twills, sheetings, &c. The assortment of patterns and designs is most complete.

G. Roskill & Co., Merchant Shippers, Chepstow Street. —The business was originally a branch of the Bradford house, established in 1830 by Messrs. Semon, Siltzer, & Co. The premises in this city were opened in the year 1850, and the firm here was known as Messrs. John Siltzer & Co.; but in 1885, certain changes having occurred, the style of the firm became, as it stands at present, G. Roskill & Co. In 1875 the firm took over the extensive business of the late Sam Mendel, and from that time the trade enormously increased. The warehouse is very large and convenient. A very large staff is employed. Shipments are made to every port on the face of the globe. The members of the firm are pro- minent in all movements connected with the welfare of the city and the permanent improvement of its trade and commerce.

J. Jack, Insurance Broker, &c., 26, Pall Mall.— Although Mr. Jack has occupied his present premises for little more than two years, it is many years since he established himself professionally in this city. The offices are a handsome range of apartments, most con- veniently situated for business. Mr. Jack enjoys a high-class professional connection. He is well supported by mercantile offices, financial associa- tions, and by a number of the leading professional and other firms in the city and district. He is frequently consulted upon the policy of proposed investments, and advises clients and others upon the investment of trust moneys and other capital. As a general insurance broker he does a large business, and is connected with all the leading insurance offices. He is assisted by a fully competent staff of clerks. His clients justly repose the most perfect confidence in his judgment and integrity.

Lawrence Lord & Co., Cotton Manufacturers, &c., 10, Marble Street.—This business has been established upwards of thirty years. The firm have occupied their present premises since 1867. The warehouse is large and most comfortably arranged. The trade con- nection includes nearly all the city shipping houses and most of the wholesale home trade warehouses. The principal sorts which they sell are fine cloths, shirtings, printers, cambrics, drilletts, satins, twills, serges, Spanish cloths, &c.; such as are not manufactured by the firm being sold on account of the actual makers. A considerable number of clerks and warehousemen are constantly employed, as the firm hold a very large stock. The representatives of the firm are very well known and esteemed on 'Change.

M. Hertz & Co., Shippers, 42, Bloom Street.—The old established and well-known shipping house of M. Hertz & Company, of Bradford, is now also carrying on an extensive trade in Manchester. The merchandise taken in hand consists for the most part of Manchester manufactures—almost entirely, in fact. But the products of the Man- chester factories are numerous and varied, and open up a fine field for enterprise of which M. Hertz & Co. have not been slow to take advan- tage. Every opportunity has been improved upon, and the most careful management has placed this business among the very best of its kind. The firm is in the possession of facilities which enable it to give its customers unusual advantages, and guarantee the entire satisfaction in the execution.

Edward Wright (successor to C. H. Rickards), Paper Manufacturer, 11, New Brown Street.—This business was established over half a century ago under the style of C. H. Rickards, but for the last six years it has been carried on under the name of its present pro- prietor, Mr. Edward Wright. The reputation attaching to the firm is the result of steady and persistent effort on the part of the chief, aided by a well-trained experienced staff of assistants, many of whom have been with the firm almost from its foundation. In the country districts a number of travellers are constantly upon the road, in the interests of the firm. A very large trade is done in all makes of paper-packings, tissues and linings being specialities.

J. Middleton & Son, Corn and Flour Merchants, 35, Withy Grove.—A representative centre in the provender trade of Manchester is the well-known house of Messrs. J. Middleton & Son, corn and flour merchants. This firm was established in 1827, and its reputation stands second to none of its kind throughout the city.

Andrew Davidson, Woollen Manufacturers' Agent, 39, Piccadilly.—This business has been established a number of years, and occupies an important position in the woollen trade of this city. The premises consist of stock and pattern-room, and convenient offices. Mr. Davidson is the duly appointed agent for the following eminent firms:—Messrs. Booth Brothers, woollen manufacturers, Leeds; Messrs. Adam Wade & Co., manufacturers of printed meltons, &c., Millshaw Mills, near Leeds; Messrs. Edward S. Howgate & Co., woollen manufacturers, Mirfield and Dewsbury; Messrs. A. and J. T. Marshall, manufacturers of dress meltons and shawls, 20, Park Place, Leeds, and Yeadon; and one or two other firms. The connection is for the most part with the leading shipping houses, the wholesale woollen cloth merchants, wholesale clothiers, and the general warehousemen of the city; and a large turnover is effected. Mr. Davidson is making a speciality of Donegal homespun tweeds, the work of Irish cottagers. These fabrics are all made from pure wool and hand-woven. They were exhibited at the Manchester Jubilee Exhibition, and attracted more attention than any other exhibit. Mr. Davidson deserves every encouragement in his praiseworthy endeavours to help the struggling natives of Donegal to build up an industry which, besides its intrinsic claims to support owing to the excellence of the cloth produced, enables the cottagers to tide over seasons of hardship and distress, the result of causes over which they have no control. Mr. Davidson is extremely well known in all the commercial circles of the city, and is very highly esteemed by all those with whom business brings him into contact.

Maburn & Co., Manufacturers of Sol Petros Vegetable Boiler Fluid, Arlington Street, Salford.—This business was established in the year 1863, and has now reached very large proportions. The premises, known as the Sol Petros Works, are of very considerable size, and include a capital and spacious warehouse and a fine suite of offices, handsomely furnished and thoroughly well fitted up with the latest and most approved appliances for the rapid despatch of business. The speciality of manufacture is the celebrated Sol Petros Vegetable Boiler Fluid for removing and preventing incrustation in steam boilers. The Sol Petros is one of the very few out of the vast number of preparations before the public that is actually capable of doing what is claimed for it, and hence its great and constantly increasing success amongst the largest users of steam power in Great Britain. The trade connection is not confined to the United Kingdom, for large quantities of the fluid are shipped for use abroad. A staff of travellers is constantly on the road, and at the works Messrs. Maburn & Co. employ a considerable number of hands, in addition to clerks. The members of the firm are well known and esteemed in commercial circles.

Jno. Binns, Provision Merchant & Commission Agent, 15A, Fennel Street.—The great and growing population of Manchester and district renders the business of provision merchant one of great profit. It is in this branch of trade that Mr. John Binns is engaged. The premises occupied consist of offices and stores, which are neatly fitted. Mr. Binns acts as agent for Mr. Timothy Mangan, who carries on business at the same address, but has also another place at Tralee, in Kerry, Ireland, from which establishment the greater portion of the supplies for the Manchester house are sent. The goods consist of Irish butter, Cheshire cheese, eggs, and the other sundries that go to make up the stock of a first class provision merchant. A number of assistants are constantly employed. Mr. Binns attends to all details in person, and is favourably known to customers and clients of the house and to business men generally in the city.

Peterkin & Cooke, Agents, 2, Bridgewater Place.—The Manchester carpet trade is one of great magnitude and importance, and the largest portion of it is in the hands of manufacturers' agents. A thoroughly representative house of this class is that of Messrs. Peterkin & Cooke, of the above address. This business is the oldest of its kind in Manchester, having been founded upwards of thirty years ago. Messrs. Peterkin & Cooke represent leading manufacturers in all branches of the carpet trade, having agencies for the sale of Axminster, Wilton, Brussels, Tapestry, Kidderminster, felt, and jute carpets; all kinds of rugs and mats, cocoa and twine, mattings, linoleum, floor-cloths, &c., &c. Messrs. Peterkin & Cooke carry on a very large business, and it is managed with enterprise and ability. The house is well known in the industrial and commercial world, both in the home and foreign markets, and its long establishment, extensive trade, and splendid reputation, places this house in one of the most prominent and influential positions in the carpet trade of Manchester.

Michaelis, James & Co., Manufacturers and Finishers, 22, Fountain Street.—This well-known firm has been established for about thirty years. The premises, which have been occupied during the past fifteen years, are large and conveniently fitted up. They contain at all times a splendid stock of beetled twills and cambrics, printed silesias, printed and plain satins, printed and plain brocades, cotton merinos, casbans, pocketings, reversible and black back linings, Italian cloths, gloves and glazed finished shirtings, Jeannetts, furniture linings, cords, moleskins, lambskins, velvets, calicoes, &c., &c. The management of the different branches of the concern is conducted by the different partners, viz., R. James, J. T. Lewis and R. N. Michaelis, in a manner that reflects the highest possible credit.

Jones, Crewdson, & Youatt, Chartered Accountants, 5, Norfolk Street.—This highly esteemed professional firm was established in the year 1872 as a branch of the London firm of Theodore Jones & Co. of world-wide reputation, and was originally known as Theodore Jones, Crewdson & Co. In 1886 the style of the firm was altered to its present title, Jones, Crewdson, & Youatt. The present premises have been in the occupation of the firm for twelve years. They consist of a very handsome and commodious suite of convenient offices. The ordinary staff is numerous and fully qualified. In addition to the usual accountancy business, Messrs. Jones, Crewdson, & Youatt are the chosen auditors of several large companies and many important private firms, a speciality of their work being the arrangement of books to meet the requirements of different trades and manufactures. They are secretaries to many well-known societies, trading and philanthropic. The present partners are Theodore B. Jones, Esq., F.C.A., Ernest Crewdson, Esq., F.C.A., and John Youatt, Esq., F.C.A., all well known and held in the highest estimation in commercial circles.

Mr. D. Ginocchio, Mineral Water Manufacturer and Italian Warehouseman, Harris Street and 31, York Street.—The large and increasing quantity of mineral waters and effervescing beverages consumed by all classes of the community in this country has made their manufacture and sale one of the most important branches of native industry. Among the many firms who cater for the public in this direction, that of M. Dominic Ginocchio occupies a prominent position. This gentleman succeeded to the business carried on by P. H. Murat at Harris Street, Strangeways, and has here extensive works and stores. The former are capacious, and are fitted with the most approved machinery and appliances for the manufacture of lemonade, ginger beer, soda water, and other favourite drinks. These are prepared by skilful assistants, with the most careful attention to purity and quality. They are immensely popular with the public. Mr. Ginocchio has also an elegantly fitted up establishment at 34, York Street, Cheetham, which was founded fifty-nine years ago, where he carries on the business of an Italian warehouseman, and does undoubtedly as good a trade in this line as anyone in the neighbourhood. He does a large trade here in maccaroni, vanilla, and Italian star paste in great variety, besides foreign wines of all sorts, and is conducted under the style of D. Bertola, practical mineral water and essence maker. The business of the Harris Street Works is one of the soundest and most successful in the trade.

John Marsh, Cut Nail Manufacturer, Parker Street, Ashley Lane.—The nail-making trade of Manchester has of late years greatly increased, and amongst the best establishments engaged therein an excellent position is occupied by that of Mr. John Marsh. He has been established for some years, and he does a large trade, which embraces the manufacture of iron, copper, brass, steel, and zinc nails, also clout and tip nails, and tacks. The business is both extensive and wide-spread, and all his productions are first-class. The works are on a good scale, and the machinery and appliances in use are by the best makers. The warehouse contains a large stock of nails of all sizes and descriptions, and the trade is rapidly increasing. Mr. Marsh, the proprietor of this concern, is a gentleman of ability. In the industrial world he is well known and esteemed, and his establishment possesses a sound commercial reputation.

S. Dewhurst & Co., Limited, Bleachers, Dyers, and Finishers, Broughton Dye Works.—Among the most important branches of trade in connection with the staple industry of Manchester are bleaching, dyeing, and finishing. One well-known and thoroughly representative concern is that of Messrs. Samuel Dewhurst & Co., Limited, Broughton Dye Works, Salford. This house was founded by Mr. Samuel Dewhurst half a century ago, and is now carried on as a limited company. The works at Adelphi, Salford, are extensive, and are thoroughly equipped with the most improved machinery and apparatus for finishing, bleaching, and dyeing, and the water supply from wells and special reservoir is perfect. The operations are conducted on the most approved principles. The firm by talent, patience, and energy has brought this branch of industry to the highest state of perfection. In addition to the branches enumerated the firm are extensive manufacturers of bookbinders' cloth, label cloth, and beetled twills, besides the celebrated vellum tracing-cloth, used by architects and engineers all over the globe. The directorate of Messrs. Samuel Dewhurst & Co., Limited, are gentlemen who thoroughly understand the business, their commercial and industrial status is of the soundest, they are highly honoured by all, and their house stands in the front rank of the principal bleachers, dyers, and manufacturers of the United Kingdom.

J. Standring & Co., Manufacturers, 57, Newton Street. As one of the largest and oldest manufacturing concerns in the whole anty of Lancashire, the well known firm of John Standring & Co. have bieved a world-wide reputation. Established so long ago as the year 29 by Mr. John Standring, father of the present sole proprietor and incipal, the firm have for many years had their city offices and wareoms at No. 57, Newton Street. Here there are extensive and well-ranged premises, with excellently fitted up offices and a spacious and ell-lighted warehouse, in which is a large and representative stock of o materials for which the firm has so good a name. These include braids, ot-laces, crinoline steels, lines, window-cords, and smallwares of every de-ription, and the excellent make and quality of all these articles can be en at a glance. They are highly thought of by a very large army of holesale and retail houses, and the ramifications of the firm extend to all rts of the United Kingdom and the principal foreign and colonial arkets, where the excellence of their manufactures secure them ready coptance. The firm have two large factories in constant work, one at vesey Street Mills, Oldham Road, and the other at Lion Mills, Blackley. oth of these are of an extensive character, covering a large area, and are ted with the most improved machinery and appliances, finding constant nployment for several hundred hands. Their London warehouse is at 4, and 5, Maidenhead Court, Aldersgate Street, E.C. In every respect e firm of Standring & Co. is a worthy example of Lancashire industry d perseverance.

Booth & Fox, Bed Feather Purifiers, Curled Hair annufacturers, and Original Patentees of Real Down Quilts d Down Clothing, 9 and 11, Mark Lane.—The leading and most oroughly representative firm of bed feather purifiers, curled hair manu-turers, &c., in the United Kingdom is that of Messrs. Booth & Fox, hose Manchester warehouse is at the above address, the extensive anufactory being at Cork, Ireland. This firm was established in 1825, d were the original patentees of real down quilts and down clothing. heir specialities have world-wide reputa-on, and have been varded the highest emiums wherever hibited—at London chibition, 1862, Dub-, 1865 and 1882, rk, 1883, Melbourne, 81, Liverpool, 1886. ley do the largest siness as bed feather rifiers of any house the trade. As bed-ng and mattress anufacturers they so maintain an ex-llent reputation, aile their specialities real down quilts and wn clothing are the iest and most perfect ticles of the kind in e market. A large stock is kept at the Manchester branch factory and arehouse. Their spacious and finely equipped factory is at Cork, and ey have branches at Mark Lane, Manchester, 81, Hatton Garden, ondon, 14, Reade Street, New York. The affairs of this old, reliable use are conducted on a sound, well-balanced, and honourable basis, d the success it has achieved after over sixty years' existence is as bstantial as it is well merited.

Messrs. Salomon de Paris, Magasins de Chaussures rançaises, 21, King Street, Manchester.—The boot and shoe trade of anchester is of great magnitude. An old-established business in this ne is that of Messrs. Salomon de Paris, which has been in existence for lf a century. Messrs. Salomon de Paris are French and English boot akers, and for honourable business methods they have no superiors. The op occupied is spacious, elegantly fitted, and there is an extensive and mirably displayed stock of boots and shoes for ladies and children. ie order department for these goods, as well as all kinds of boots and oes, is in the hands of experienced men, under their talented supervision. etter boots, &c. could not be produced. Messrs. Salomon de Paris carry a very heavy business of a high-class nature, employ an ample staff, d their management is all that can be desired. Messrs. Salomon are also ents for Nathan and Sons, London, costumiers to H.R.H. the Prince of 'ales. Ladies', gentlemen's, and children's costumes for fancy dress lls are kept for sale or hire, and general satisfaction has always been ven in this department. Messrs. Salomon de Paris are well known in e city trade, and bear the highest reputation for honourable business ethods, talent, and courtesy, are popular with the community in gene-l, and their house is unexcelled by any contemporary concern.

Railton & Co., Manufacturers of Children's Clothing, , London Road.—Messrs. Railton & Co. have devoted themselves to a special branch of the manufacture of clothing, namely, the making of children's garments. Those articles, in the form of frocks, cloaks, tunics, pelisses, costumes; also infants' millinery, hoods, hats, and bonnets, are produced in all kinds of different materials, such as French merinos, Cashmeres, Musk, silk poplin, silks, satins, serge, cloth, velvet, &c.; also washing materials and piques. In these numerous branches Messrs. Railton do a very large business. The business has been established over fifty years, and is now under the able management of Mr. John Parr (sole partner), a gentleman of great practical ability and long experience in this branch of trade. A large number of hands are employed, there being over two hundred and fifty engaged in the mills alone. The trade and connection altogether are first-class, and extend far and wide, although no travellers are employed. Messrs. Railton carry on their immense business entirely on the recommendation of their well-known quality of manufacture. A special feature is made of merino goods. The introduction of merinos to this country is mainly due to George III., who, in 1786, imported a few merino sheep from Spain for the purpose of improving the wool of England. Many other countries, like Saxony and France, followed suit, and since that time great attention has been given to the production of this description of material. Messrs. Railton's goods in this class bear an excellent name in the trade, and the business in this line alone is very large. A very sound method of dealing with their customers is characteristic of this firm, and their energy and business ability have very considerably enhanced the renown of this old-established house.

Baxter, Woodhouse, & Taylor, late J. W. & F. Baxter, Manufacturers of Beetled Silesias, Printed Cambrics and Twills, Brocades, Casbans, Jeanetts, Wigans, Unions, and White Shirtings, 11, George Street.—This business has been in active operation since the year 1836, and has enjoyed a career of almost uninterrupted prosperity and success. The premises consist of a modern-built warehouse of four floors, conveniently arranged and supplied with everything necessity for carrying on a large trade. The specialities of manufacture are beetled silesias, printed cambrics and twills, dyed and printed brocades, casbans, jeanetts, dyed and white wigans, pocketings, unions, white shirtings, &c. The connection is amongst the leading shipping houses, the general Manchester warehousemen, and the wholesale buyers. In addition, Messrs. Baxter have several agents and an able staff of salesmen, clerks, and warehousemen. The partners are Mr. Fred. Baxter, jun., Mr. Robert Woodhouse, and Mr. J. C. Taylor, who succeeded to the business on the retirement of Mr. F. Baxter, sen. in 1887.)

Howarth Brothers, 273, 275, and 277, Stretford Road, **Architectural and Monumental Sculptors.**—The firm of Howarth Brothers is a comparatively new one, having been established only a few years. A large business is carried on by them in architectural carving, their name being connected with the ornamentation of most of the new churches and buildings which have been erected in the North of England. Their workmanship in marble, stone, alabaster, and wood is exceedingly fine, and their specialities are reredos, pulpits, and fonts, although, judging by the number of workmen who are engaged upon capitals, corbels, trusses, friezes, &c., a large business in general building carving must be carried on. This, the principal department in their business, is under the care of Mr. James Howarth, who gave us ample proof that for excellence of design and workmanship they cannot be surpassed, a fact which no doubt has contributed to their rapid success in forming a connection and establishing a reputation among the leading architects in this and other towns. We may add that in figure work they are also at the head, a group of figures (in Caen stone) representing the Apostles being about the finest we have ever seen, a special feature being the excellence of the drapery. As monumental sculptors, Messrs. Howarth Brothers execute some exceedingly fine work, and the expensive monuments in their extensive show-rooms are always rich in design and workmanship. We may add, in conclusion, that they are direct agents for the marble from the celebrated Carrara quarries in Italy, and also for the Swedish green granite.

J. S. Wood (late R. H. Chambers & Son), Wholesale Tea Merchant, 1, Sugar Lane.—This business was established in 1841 under the title of R. H. Chambers & Son, but in 1885 it was purchased by its present proprietor, J. S. Wood, Esq The trade is confined entirely to wholesale dealing in tea and coffee. The connection extends all over both Manchester and Salford, and includes many of the leading buyers in all the neighbouring towns and villages, and in Shropshire, North Wales, North Staffordshire, North of England, and South of England. The business premises at Sugar Lane include commodious modern-built warehouse, stores, and a suite of lofty and completely fitted offices, testing and sampling rooms, and sale rooms. Mr. J. S. Wood is sole partner. He is as well known on the Mincing Lane market as any tea-merchant in the country, is considered an excellent judge of quality and value, being possessed of a rare and discriminating palate. His commercial status is of the highest class, and his estimable personal qualities ensure for him the respect and esteem of all with whom business brings him into contact. He holds the sole right in Great Britain to sell the world-famed VAN DUNCK'S DUTCH COFFEE. This coffee is second to none in Europe, being twice the strength of any other, and having that rich aroma in which drinkers of fine coffee delight.

Thomas Horrocks, Tar Distiller and Manufacturing Chemist, Bradford.—This business was established about ten years ago by Messrs. John May & Co., but has latterly been carried on by its present proprietor, Mr. Thomas Horrocks. The works are of fair average size and are fitted up with entirely modern machinery of the very best construction. The principal items of manufacture are the highly valued products of tar distillation, and several preparations used by dyers and calico printers, &c. The leading lines are solvent naphtha, naphthaline, benzole, burning naphtha, carbolic anthracine, dyers' solutions, vegetable and lamp black, liquid ammonia, chloride of sulphur, carbon bisulphide, boiler composition, lubricating oils, creosote oil, pitch, and varnish. The trade connection is chiefly local, though a considerable quantity of the firm's production is shipped to the order of various city houses. A large working staff is constantly and actively employed. Mr. Thomas Horrocks is now sole proprietor. He is a gentleman of great experience in the chemical trade, and is well known and respected on the Manchester Exchange, and in the commercial circles of the city and district.

John Howe, Manufacturer of Machine Belting and Hose Pipes, Currier, &c., 2, Parsonage, Blackfriars, Deansgate.—This business has been established more than thirty years, but was commenced in a building a little distance away from the present address. Mr. Howe has occupied the new premises for eight years. There is a capital ground-floor warehouse and show-room and a first-rate office. The principal speciality of the business is a superior make of strapping for mill-gearing. The excellence of the strapping made on his premises is equalled by few if any firms in the trade, and is certainly excelled by none. Whether single or double none but the very best and properly seasoned leather is used; every stitch of sewing is perfectly done, and neither thread nor laces are used that are at all doubtful in quality; hence Howe's Mill Banding never fails. Howe's strapping is in great demand by the best engineers and mill-owners, and the trade connection includes all the important firms of the city and district.

Sillitoe & Seares, Packers of Cotton Waste, Mary Street, Strangeways.—The cotton industry is divided into a great many branches, that of cotton waste packing, &c., being of no small importance. Among the Manchester establishments so engaged the foremost place is held by that of Messrs. Sillitoe & Seares, which was founded by the present proprietors twenty-one years ago. This firm were the introducers of the present system of packing. The premises occupied are large and commodious, being built especially for the business. The spacious warehouse is well stocked with cotton waste, cleaning waste, &c., and the appliances and presses used in the packing operations are powerful and of the latest improvement. The work is carried out with promptness and efficiency, and the business done is heavy and rapidly increasing. The firm stands in high favour with the chief shippers and dealers in the city and its vicinity, and the management throughout is able and energetic. The partners are Messrs. James H. Sillitoe and Henry Seares, men of ability, integrity, and courtesy, and highly esteemed.

Jennings & Co., Safe Makers, &c., 44, Deansgate.—Amongst the many important industries carried on in Manchester and its vicinity that of Messrs Jennings & Co., safe makers, occupies a very prominent position. For more than eight years, this business has been conducted in the present handsome premises. In these are upwards of two hundred fire-proof and holdfast safes; in addition to their own manufacture, Messrs. Jennings & Co. have a large stock of Phillips & Son's extra strong safes, also Milner's and Perry's fire-resisting safes. This firm are also agents for Messrs. Humber and Co., bicycle and tricycle manufacturers, of 32, Holborn Viaduct, E.C., and Beeston, near Nottingham. Messrs. Jennings & Co. hold a large and varied stock of th "Genuine Humber" safety bicycles, the "Genuine Humber" tricycl and the "Genuine Humber" tandem. To amateurs or others who wan a really good and genuine machine, new or second-hand, a visit to thi establishment is well worth the time and trouble. Messrs. Jennings Co. have had a long and honourable connection with this business, an have by their well-known integrity and perseverance gained the confi dence of an extensive and valuable connection.

J. W. Pickstone & Co., Provision Merchants an Commission Agents, 6, Fennel Street.—The provision trade in Mar chester is one of the leading branches of commerce in the city, despite th latter's pre-eminence for textile manufactures. One of the principal firm that we noticed engaged in this business is that of Messrs. J. W. Pickston & Co. Messrs. J. W. Pickstone & Co. carry on the trade of provisio merchants and commission agents. The stock embraces hams, bacon butter, margarine, eggs, and the various other kinds of goods that go t make up the stock-in-trade of a first-class business. In the commissio line valuable consignments are received and quickly sold, whatever branc of the provision trade they belong to. The connections of the firm cove all parts of the city, and in the suburbs and surrounding district a soun and profitable trade is done. The travellers of the company are dail adding to its connections among the medium and high-class retail house and altogether the firm does a very sound and extensive business.

Matthew Stuttard & Bros., Cotton Spinners an Manufacturers, &c., 5A, Marsden Street.—Manchester is pre-eminentl the centre of the cotton trade, and the various branches in connectic therewith employ a large number of people. A well-known firm of cotto spinners, manufacturers, and warp sizers is that of Messrs. Matthe Stuttard & Bros. The firm has been established sixteen years, bu only opened the Manchester house a short time back. It is known, how ever, in all parts as a firm of high standing, and as the trade was rapidl increasing it was found imperative to found this branch. The warehou contains a valuable stock of cotton goods, &c., which is replenished fro the Knowlwood and Copperas House Mills, at Walsden, and Bridge Mil and Underbank Mills, at Whitworth, and Bridge Field Mill, Rochdal The mills are very large and fitted throughout with the most mode and powerful machinery and appliances. The goods manufactured b the firm are of the finest quality, coupled with the most skilful workma ship. Mr. Matthew Stuttard, the leading member of the firm, manag the business in an able and enterprising manner. He is thoroughly co versant with the trade and bears the highest reputation for honour ar integrity.

Edward Rushton & Son, Auctioneers, Valuers, an Fire Loss Assessors, 13, Norfolk Street.—A very important firm auctioneers and valuers is that of Messrs. Edward Rushton & Son, occu pying large and well-fitted offices at the above address, Manchester, an large sale-rooms and offices at Blackburn. This is one of the leadir houses engaged in the business in Manchester, and is worked on a ve large scale. Mr. Edward Rushton is a member of the Town Council Blackburn. The business has been in existence about thirty years. Th is the registered office of the New Bridge Lane Mill Company, Limite of Stockport. Messrs. Rushton's sphere of operations takes a very wi range, and embraces sales, either by auction or private treaty, of eve description of property. Messrs. Rushton are occupying a most pr minent position among the principal mill auctioneers and fire loss assure in Lancashire.

John Rothwell, Tin, Zinc, and Lead Packing-cas Manufacturer, 32, China Lane, Hilton Street.—This business, which h been in active operation for about ten years, has achieved a very mark success. The premises consist of a capital works and warehouse, with nicely-arranged office, neatly and suitably furnished for the rapid tran action of business. The speciality of the trade is the manufacture tin, zinc, and lead packing-cases; and in a business centre such as Ma chester, from which valuable goods are being constantly despatched f long sea voyages, there is a constant demand for air-tight metallic pac ing-cases. In addition to packing-case making, Mr. Rothwell does large business as a general iron, zinc, copper, and tin-plate worker, i cluding ventilators, biscuit tins, and general mill work. There is also department for stencil-plate cutting, &c. Mr. Rothwell also does an e tensive trade in patent speaking-tubes, electric bells, telephones, & The works are supplied with machinery by the best makers, and t plant is very complete. The trade connection includes a very large pr portion of the merchant shippers, general Manchester warehousome and the principal wholesale houses. A large staff of hands is constant employed, and some two or three travellers are upon the road in t interests of the firm. The sole proprietor is Mr. John Rothwell, a ge tleman extremely well known and most highly respected in the trad and in commercial circles generally.

S. Thomas & Sons, Needle Manufacturers, British Needle Mills, Redditch, near Birmingham.—The firm of S. Thomas & Sons, of Redditch, is one of the most noted in the United Kingdom for the manufacture of needles. It has been established upwards of half a century, and now enjoys a world-wide notoriety. The firm manufacture

S. THOMAS & SONS'

British Needle and Fish Hook Mills, Redditch.

TRADE BRITISH MARK

THE LARGEST AND MOST COMPLETE NEEDLE MANUFACTORY IN THE WORLD

needles of every description and for all purposes, and these range in size from the needle little thicker than a hair to others, for sailmaking and packing, of the dimensions of a small bayonet. Redditch, where Messrs. S. Thomas & Sons' works are situated, is a small picturesque town of some eight or nine thousand inhabitants, in the county of Worcester, and is in fact the head-quarters of the British needle trade. Nearly every man, woman, and child in the town of Redditch is connected, more or less, with the needle trade, and the bulk of the population find employment at one or other of the several manufactories in which the place abounds. No firm in the world manufacture a better or more highly finished article than Messrs. S. Thomas & Sons, and certainly no house in the needle trade enjoys a wider or a higher reputation in the commercial world; and the process of needle making is one of the most interesting and instructive that can be imagined, and it also reveals an amount of skill, scientific knowledge, and inventive genius which is alike creditable to those engaged therein, and to the progressive age in which we live. A visit to the manufactory of Messrs. S. Thomas & Sons affords a treat of the very highest order, and must prove instructive. The extensive plant and machinery is all of the most approved construction, and everything connected with this immense establishment is of the very first order of excellence. The workshops are most admirably arranged, and are spacious, well lighted, and well ventilated, and the general condition and appearance of the workpeople, both old and young, testifies conclusively to the care and considerate attention which is bestowed upon them by their employers. The firm do a very large foreign trade in addition to their gigantic home trade, but in no part of the British provinces do they execute larger orders, or have they a more influential and substantial connection, than in the Manchester district. Their business here is most ably conducted by Mr. J. J. Bristol, at their depôt, 13, Dale Street, Manchester. Notwithstanding the depression in trade during the last few years, Messrs. S. Thomas & Sons have maintained their output of needles, and are now offering a great novelty in the shape of needles ready threaded for use at the same cost as ordinary needles. They are also the sole manufacturers of the famous "agonic-eyed needles," which are pronounced to be the best in the market, and are so much appreciated by tailors and others who depend upon the work done by the needle for their livelihood. Vast as is the business now carried on by Messrs. S. Thomas & Sons, it still goes on increasing from month to month, so that the prospects of the concern are highly encouraging.

Beaver Packing House, 28, Dickinson Street.—A most important branch of industrial activity in Manchester is that devoted to the making-up and packing of manufactured goods. The leading establishment in this line is the Beaver Packing House, 3, Lloyd Street and Queen Street: having establishments at 26, 28, and 30, Dickinson Street; 83 and 85, St. James Street; 131, Portland Street, and 45, Oxford Street. It was established many years ago, and from its very inception has enjoyed prosperity. The premises occupied comprise a number of substantial buildings, which are well arranged and equipped throughout. Constant employment is given to upwards of a hundred skilled hands. The establishment numbers among its customers many of the leading manufacturers of Manchester, and with its unsurpassed facilities it is enabled to offer special advantages to shippers of Manchester goods, and to execute the largest orders in the promptest and most satisfactory manner. The entire business is controlled by Mr. Maybrick, whilst the shipping department is under the management of Mr. Van Thal. Mr. R. Atwood Beaver is the sole proprietor.

J. Berrie, Dyer, &c., 14, Oldham Street.—Mr. J. Berrie carries on one of the most extensive businesses of its kind in England. Dyeing, although a chemical process and therefore requiring an acquaintance with the properties of the elementary bodies, and the laws which regulate their combination, is sometimes unfortunately carried on by those who know little, if not absolutely nothing, of chemical science. The relations of dyeing with the principles of chemistry constitute the theory of the art, and require a knowledge of (1) The nature of the bodies which the process of dyeing bring into contact; (2) The circumstances in which they are brought together; (3) The phenomena during their action; and (4) The properties of the coloured combinations produced. Mr. Berrie, in his practical and theoretical knowledge, has managed to produce results in the art of dyeing which have placed his firm in the very first rank of the trade. The business was established by Mr. Alexander Draik in 1830, and bought by Mr. Berrie in 1849. The offices are at the above address, and the works, which are very large, are at Newton Heath, and are called the Monsall Works. Here, about two hundred hands are employed in dyeing and cleaning all kinds of fabrics. Every possible appliance is in use at these works, and the use of the most improved machinery, combined with the exercise of the best talent obtainable, enables Mr. Berrie to produce a class of work which is unsurpassed. A great speciality in this firm is what is known as French cleaning, or, as it is sometimes termed, dry cleaning. This is an invaluable process for gentlemen's clothing, stage and fancy dresses, curtains and tapestries, silk dresses, &c. In this department Mr. Berrie has achieved a wonderful reputation; his improved method producing the most astonishing results. As an instance of the really wonderful state of perfection to which machinery has been brought, it may be mentioned that by a special combination of recently introduced machinery, which has been completed by J. Berrie, curtains are made to enter at one end dirty, and come out at the other washed, starched, dried, and calendered. The speed at which this is done can hardly be imagined, and the cost is therefore proportionately low. The process of cotton and linen glazing many of the articles sent to this firm is one to which special attention is given; and it is evident that in all cases where articles are glazed, they must keep clean much longer. The trade of this firm is simply all over the kingdom. There are offices in London, Birmingham, Bristol, Liverpool, and many other large towns, and, added to that, nearly 1,500 agents in districts far and near. The great skill shown in every branch, the strict punctuality and despatch exercised in every detail of the business, and the generally energetic way in which this large firm is managed, are exceedingly creditable to all concerned, and there is no better known or more respected firm in the trade than that of J. Berrie. The firm has had an existence of continued prosperity which has been well merited in every respect.

Browett, Lindley & Co., Engineers, St. Simon Street, Salford.—This firm was established over fifty years ago, and was formerly known as Deakin, Parker & Co. The present proprietors took over the business in 1879, and in 1884 changed the title of the firm to identify themselves personally and more directly with their various patented specialities. The premises, known as "Sandon Works," occupy a very considerable ground space. The offices are convenient, and the buildings generally are of a substantial character, with a handsome frontage. The reputation of the firm is based upon the excellence of workmanship and soundness of material employed. Its principal manufactures are horizontal and vertical high-pressure and compound and condensing steam-engines, with or without patent automatic expansion gear. A very leading feature in the manufactures of this firm is that of special engines and driving gear in electric lighting machines. Messrs. Browett, Lindley & Co. make a speciality also of their patent high-speed "Acme Governors." Altogether they employ considerably over a hundred hands. Their trade extends over the whole of the United Kingdom, and they have an important shipping connection. The partners are influential gentlemen, well known on the city Exchange and in commercial circles, of unimpeachable business character and reputation.

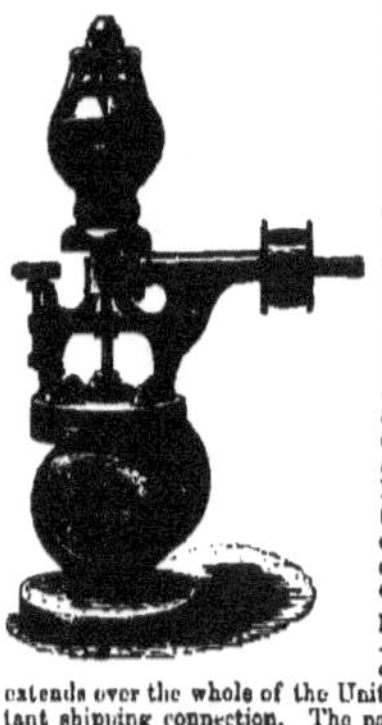

C. & W. Walmsley, 22, Booth Street, Mosley Street.——This firm has been engaged as cotton manufacturers and merchants over half a century. Works, Blackburn district.

George Wm. Pratt, Wholesale and Retail Druggist and Dentist, 41, Stretford Road.—The internal drug trade of Manchester is one of the most valuable businesses in the city. A typical business in this line is that of Mr. George W. Pratt, which has for a period of twenty years enjoyed public favour. Mr. G. W. Pratt also carries on business as a dentist; he is thoroughly proficient in the calling. The premises are completely and elegantly appointed. There is a heavy stock of drugs of all kinds, which are of absolute purity and reliability. A speciality of great repute is Pratt's Mississippi Hair Restorer, which has been pronounced by all who have tried it to be better than any yet brought before the public. It is a preparation of the highest quality, and is certainly cheaper and more efficacious than any other restorer, and thoroughly deserves the widespread demand it enjoys. The consulting rooms are admirably furnished, the dental apparatus and instruments are of modern construction, and Mr. George W. Pratt bears a fine reputation for his skill. He has a high-class practice, and is honorary dentist to the Day Nursery for the Children of Widows, 114, Bloomsbury. He carries on as druggist a very heavy local retail and wholesale trade. An efficient staff is employed. Mr. G. W. Pratt is well known in the trade and in the dental profession, and is highly respected.

Jacob Pareezer, Fashionable Tailor, 1, Greenwood Street, Corporation Street.—The tailoring trade of Manchester is, owing to the dense population, of great magnitude and value, and gives employment to thousands of hands. A very fine business in this line is that of Mr. Jacob Pareezer, which was founded eight years ago. The premises occupied are spacious, and situated at the top of a large building, and are fitted up in a very complete manner. Mr. Jacob Pareezer employs a large staff of skilled cutters and tailors in making clothes of every description, and the productions of the house are characterised by the latest and most fashionable style, first quality of material, and excellence of workmanship. He carries on a very heavy wholesale and retail trade, having a fine connection among clothiers and private persons, and he executes all orders with promptness. Mr. Pareezer manages his business with ability and enterprise, and there can be no doubt of his knowledge and experience. Honourable and courteous, he enjoys local esteem and confidence, and his house holds an influential place in the trade.

Thomas Elderkin, Bassinette Manufacturer, 371, Oxford Street.—This business was established in Burlington Street, in the year 1875, and was removed to the present address in the year 1881. The premises consist of a fine large front shop with extensive show rooms; and attached are convenient workshops. The main speciality is the manufacture and sale of infants' bassinettes and perambulators. These are made in every imaginable style of wood, wire, or wicker-work. Mr. Elderkin is noted for the excellent workmanship, good material, and durable painting and varnish of all carriages manufactured upon his premises. There is also a very first-rate stock of bicycles and tricycles of the approved makes in one of the show-rooms. Mr. Elderkin sells his productions upon most liberal terms. In domestic machinery there is a good assortment of the most approved styles of wringing and washing machines, and brass and iron bedsteads, and many household requisites. Mr. Thomas Elderkin is a clever man and gives great personal attention to the details of his highly successful business.

Mrs. Fred. Wilkinson, Artist, Mansfield Chambers, St. Ann's Square.—Since Mrs. Haweiss published her charming little work, "Art in the House," the internal decoration of our homes has received a very large share of attention, especially from those most nearly concerned—the ladies. The fashion styled "Æstheticism" did at least this permanent good—it directed attention towards, and did very much to improve, the style and quality of furniture, hangings, carpets, upholstery, and mural painting. Early recognising the need of classes for instruction in painting and kindred arts, Mrs. Fred. Wilkinson established herself, some six years ago, at Mansfield Chambers, and opened her studios for the study and practice of various branches of decorative art. Her success has been most marked; ladies belonging to the very best families in the neighbourhood have gladly availed themselves of the opportunities she afforded them. In addition to the rooms at Mansfield Chambers, Mrs. Wilkinson has a fine studio at 36, King Street, where she does a great amount of decorative and other work, and at the Art Repository, Bowdon. Friezes are her speciality, and these she executes with great harmony of colour and originality of design. Her terms, which are moderate, are reduced in the case of sisters.

William A. Danby, Fashionable Tailor and Breeches Maker, 100, Mosley Street.—Mr. William A. Danby has been established since 1878. Formerly he was with the well-known firm of H. Verity & Sons. As a fashionable tailor and breeches maker of the first grade he occupies a prominent position in the locality, and the connection he enjoys is large, influential, and nevertheless well deserved. The best of goods are to be obtained from his shop at remarkably moderate prices. The stock on hand is always up to date and of superior quality, whilst customers' special orders are attended to with promptitude and care; all garments being made under strict personal supervision and by hand labour.

R. H. Lees, Tailors' T
Street.—Mr. R. H. Lees has been
and carries on the business of a w
of goods required by the tailoring
largely used for coat linings, &c.,
blacks and colours. Black and
specially printed in *fast colours*,
clothing purposes. An assortm
buckrams, flax, French canvas, &
for tailors' use. There is also a
mohair braids, buttons, sewing
belonging to the trade. The p
several travellers are employed, a
done in the surrounding district
time, this firm has made very gre

Wm. Wilson, Inventor a
Electro-Magnetic Appliances,
St. Mary's Gate.—Electricity is
nature, but is now employed as a
upon the truth, "Electricity is l
rate electricity are worn to cur
human frame. A celebrated ap
as the "Wilsonia," invented a
who has been established eigh
appliances fit all parts of the bod
tages claimed for them are, that
that generate electricity and retai
that they are the only ventilated
stituents, acting by absorption,
and that they are quite comforta
child and weakest invalid. A
been sold. They are much estee
whole of the north of England,
received, testifying to their effica
consumption, bronchitis, paral
pleurisy, spinal weakness, nervou
affections of throat, liver, or kidn
has also written in flattering ter
commodious, and furnished in
assistant is engaged. Mr. Willi
enjoys the esteem and confidence

Thomas Carter, Bool
Power, &c., 7, Bridgewater Plac
binding, and machine ruling form
is of great magnitude. A well-k
Thomas Carter, which was found
large and commodious, and are ad
of eighty experienced hands is c
books and other stationery, mac
account books turned out are in
quality of material and soundness
is strong, durable, and in many
mented. The trade is rapidly ex
Martini, and thread and wire se
to do large orders of pamphlet a
any other trade house in the town
business circles, and bears a repu
ness man in the city.

T. R. Withecomb, Ciga
and 16 and 18, Victoria Street.—
enjoys is largely due to the immen
the "wide-bore pipe" has been r
Withecomb was the originator of t
it was this invention which first br
riety. The business was established
present proprietor. The new cig
reason of its unique and tasteful
novelties, and there was always a
inspecting the curious and eleg
tobacco-pouches. It is safe to sa
of tobacconists' goods had hithe
the same time many new things
goods, Mr. Withecomb soon too
ment in the choice of cigars
reliable, and his stock most var
Victoria Street depôt led to the o
Street, and the firm became kno
high-class tobaccos and cigars in
comb, the founder of the firm, r
known in the city, and his genial
with all who "love to blow a clo
cigar when they see it."

Macdonald's Free Dentorium, 29, Piccadilly.—It was ith the greatest pleasure we received the polite invitation of Mr. .mes Macdonald, of the Free Dentorium, to visit his well-known .d extensive establishment in that busy thoroughfare, combining as it oes the various processes, unique of their kind, in the production of rtificial dentures. Doubtless there is a largely growing demand for rtificial teeth amongst all classes, as, besides the appearance, they are ecessary for health. The hygienic laws show the absolute necessity for eeth to masticate the food and not give the stomach double work, which it is quite unable to perform for any lengthened period without producing serious consequences. These laws are becoming more understood by all classes, hence the growing demand. The "Free Dentorium," for as such it is now universally known, is the only first-class establishment where the working classes can have the experience and services of the ablest dentists in the extraction of teeth and manufacture of artificial dentals. The first department the courteous proprietor introduced us to was the large and luxuriously fitted waiting-room for patients, a sketch of which we give. No words of ours in description can overrate the elaborate arrangements made for their comfort. A rich-toned musical box is continually playing in the waiting-room, and charms, if it does not allay the pain of the patients. The second was the operating room (also illustrated), replete with all the latest improvements, apparatus for painless extraction, and all improved appliances for alleviating pain, of which we cannot speak too highly: indeed, the whole betokens plainly in every detail the great skill and indefatigable energy displayed throughout the establishment. The next, and to us the most important, was the workshops, the subjoined sketch giving a general idea of the rooms. Here are made the lately patented teeth, the result of years of thought and experience; teeth (prior to Mr. Macdonald's discovery) were made of a mineral compound not so natural, suitable, or durable as his patented vegetable ivory. The reasonable charges, combined with faultless workmanship, are showing to a marked degree the truth of the old adage, that a nimble penny is ever better than a sluggish pound, for where others complete small numbers, here may be seen turned out daily work that rivals in quantity and quality the largest establishments in Great Britain. We have no doubt that the great skill, reasonable charges, and general courtesy, have conduced to the unparalleled success of the "Free Dentorium." The great tendency of late years to save middlemen's profits has extended even to professions. The "Free Dentorium," manufacturing all its own materials, and having a large wholesale connection, is enabled to give the public the benefit of their wholesale prices. We may add, Mr. Macdonald shows himself a true philanthropist, not only in supplying teeth at such low prices, and extracting teeth free, which he does from six to eight o'clock daily, but indeed at any time to those unable to pay on producing a letter of recommendation from any doctor, clergyman, or magistrate, besides attending all public and charitable institutions free by appointment, thus meriting the support of the public. We feel assured no one regrets the confidence they place in him. We observed a lady in attendance, who (and indeed all in the establishment) evinced such kindly, courteous, and considerate demeanour, as to win the greatest respect and good wishes throughout his widespread connection.

WAITING ROOM

WORKSHOPS

Mr. Stubbs, Agent for Alexander Hadden & Sons, Worsted Spinners, Hosiers, and Carpet Bag Manufacturers, 30, Dale itreet, and at Aberdeen.—The agency conducted by Mr. Stubbs for the ld-established firm of Alexander Hadden & Sons, worsted spinners, hosiers, ınd carpet manufacturers, is one of a most important character. The irm was originally established some hundred and twenty years ago by Alexander Hadden. Since that time his sons, grandsons, and great-grandons in succession have continued the business, which is now carried on ınder the above style. The connection of the Hadden family as public nen with Aberdeen has extended over several generations. They have, ndeed, supplied the chief magistrate, or provost, more than once. They ıre important people also in Manchester, and are well known on the Continent, Canada, in the North and South Americas, Australia, and all he Colonies. Their specialities are worsted yarns, hosiery, and carpets, n the manufacture of which they have always had a good reputation. The warehouse is under the superintendence of Mr. Stubbs, as agent, and is very capacious, and contains a splendid assortment of the arpets, hosiery, and other productions of the manufactory amply ufficient to enable all who inspect them to judge for themselves as to the excellence of the manufactures which have rendered famous the name of Alexander Hadden & Sons, of Aberdeen.

Sotirios Hazzopulo & Co., Merchants, 5, Sussex Street. —The important business of this establishment was commenced here in 1858 by the eldest brother of the family, Mr. Z. D. Hazzopulo, who retired from this city to Constantinople in 1866, when the entire management of the business here was entrusted to Mr. Sotirios Hazzopulo. Afterwards Mr. Z. D. Hazzopulo took the helm of the entire business abroad, which up to the present time he holds. The business of the firm s carried on abroad—in Turkey, Egypt, Persia, and Bulgaria. The shipments made there are principally Manchester goods, the leading lines ›eing prints, greys, and yarns—more particularly extra hard yarns; also Yorkshire goods and Bradford stuff, and various other merchandise. Mr. S. Hazzopulo, the present guardian of the firm in Manchester, being very well known and highly popular in this city, was in 1881 elected a Councillor for St. John's Ward of the Salford Corporation, and held the office for three years. Shortly afterwards he was appointed Consul-General for Persia in Manchester, after which he was appointed Hellenic Consul of the first class by the Hellenic Government. He received from the Turkish Government the orders of Medjidie and Osmanie, and also obtained the Persian order of the Lion and Sun and the Tunisian Star from the respective rulers of these countries. In 1887 he had the honour of entertaining at his princely mansion, Bella Vista, Higher Broughton, the Crown Prince of Greece, Duke of Sparta, and suite, for which he received the thanks of his Majesty the King of the Hellenes, with the order of the Greek Gold Cross of the Saviour. The warehouse is a compact block very centrally situated, being near to the Post Office, and also very convenient to the Exchange. The arrangements of the establishment are of the best and most approved kind for the rapid transaction of business, the maxim of the firm being to let no dust remain upon merchandise in their possession. Consequently the whole place has a beehive appearance at all times with the rapid egress and ingress of goods, considerable employment being found for a good staff of employés, the greater number having been connected with the firm for a lengthened period of years. The members of the firm are gentlemen highly esteemed and respected in Manchester commercial circles and abroad.

Portheim & Co., Merchant Shippers, 7, Portland Street. —This firm, though of comparatively recent establishment (1883), is making steady and continuous progress. There is a branch of the firm at Belfast. The connections of the firm are scattered over the greater part of Europe and the United States. The shipments are largely made up of handkerchiefs, printed fabrics, and special goods for particular markets. The members of the firm are gentlemen extremely well known and highly respected in commercial circles and on the Royal Exchange.

George Haward Hyde, Stock and Share Broker, 4, St. Ann's Square.—The enormous increase of late years in the number and magnitude of joint-stock enterprises, is one of the most remarkable features of the times. Now-a-days everyone who has a few pounds to spare seeks a profitable investment for them, in preference to allowing his money to lie idle at home or at nominal interest in the banks. But just as there are enormous facilities for investing money in large or small sums, so it is important that investors should be well advised as to the direction in which they should operate. Never before has there been such need for a well-informed confidential stockbroker. His wary experience and astute management may save his clients enormous sums, while his reliable information, culled from all manner of sources, should enable him to secure handsome profits for those who put themselves under his guidance. In this connection in our city no more reliable man can be recommended than Mr. George Haward Hyde, who commenced business as a stock and share broker nearly twenty years ago. He has also an establishment at Southport, and at either address he is prepared to undertake commissions at a moderate rate of remuneration. He is assisted by a staff of experienced clerks, and publishes monthly lists showing not merely market prices but comparisons of former values and other useful information. He likewise issues daily circulars of interest to holders of mining and miscellaneous securities, and is the recognised medium for such business in Lancashire. Mr. Hyde enjoys the confidence of a large and influential *clientèle*, and is one of the best known brokers in the provinces.

Samuel Ralphs, Flint Glass Manufacturers, Prussia Street Works, Oldham Road.—This old-established business, formerly conducted by Andrew Ker & Co., changed hands in 1886, when Mr. Samuel Ralphs became the proprietor. The connection enjoyed by the concern is a widespread and very valuable one. The manufactures carried on consists of table and decorative glass of every description in flint and colours, show glasses for confectionery, gas globes in great variety of style, glasses for every make of colliers' lamps. No effort is spared to procure the services of the very best skill in every department of the trade, and the business as a whole is most comprehensive in its scope, and deservedly enjoys a high reputation for its artistic and useful productions. The staff employed is a very large one, and the premises are fitted up with the latest and most approved machinery and appliances. The firm have a fine set of show-rooms at the works, which are well deserving of a visit. The system of doing business is all that could be desired, and customers are afforded perfect satisfaction in every way.

Hawkins & Taylor, Shirting, &c., Manufacturers, 11, 13, Fountain Street.—The old-established and prosperous firm of Hawkins & Taylor is entitled to a very prominent position in the history of Manchester commerce. Founded in the early years of the present century, under the style of Todd & Coston, it was in the year 1837 that the business of the firm was removed to its present address; and forty years later it came into the possession of the present proprietors, who have well sustained the reputation of the concern. The workrooms are replete with every appliance which the industry requires. In the warehouse is always to be found a large and varied stock of shirtings and calicoes of every description, the like of which it would be difficult to find, so excellent are the various makes in texture and quality. The materials produced by Messrs. Hawkins & Taylor are well known all over the kingdom for their excellence and durability, and for the manner in which they meet the taste and requirements of all classes of the community. The principals, gentlemen of thorough business experience and acumen, spare no effort to maintain and increase the widespread popularity which their firm enjoys; and they are worthy and respected representatives of an important industry.

R. Graefinghoff, Foreign Agent, &c., 27, Brasennose Street.—The importation of foreign paper, colours, chemicals, &c., is one of the most important business undertakings of the day, and an active and energetic agent can always rely upon finding a ready market for his goods. Such an agent is to be found in Manchester in the person of Mr. R. Graefinghoff, who for the last six years has carried on a prosperous and successful business. Mr. Graefinghoff is the sole representative for the United Kingdom of the famous firm of Heyl, Bros. & Co., whose factory at Charlottenburg, near Berlin, is one of the largest in the German empire. The colours and chemicals manufactured by this firm are widely known throughout the world for their purity and quality; Mr. Graefinghoff is the representative of several well-known firms, and has secured a leading place in the trading community.

H. M. Addey & Co., 27, Portland Street.—This business, founded in 1870, has been exceptionally successful. The Portland Street premises consist of offices and warehouse well adapted to the rapid despatch of business. The members of the firm are well known and second to none in their own line, and their operations in the various classes of Irish and Scotch linen and jute goods, of which they are manufacturers and finishers, enable th
the most extensive kind. The m
the different canvases, sacking, a
trade and foreign; of linen and
textures for the clothing, and int
stay trades. The firm also deals
for milling cotton waste and c
linens, and buckrams for the u
advantages of selection from a l
their Manchester clients, they are
make to sample or specification, ei
market. Their close attention t
tion given, has caused the greate
the firm is in consequence unusua

Ancizar Bros. & Co.,
Produce Importers, 34, Prince
Bros. & Co., the well-known S
representatives in Manchester of
of great importance to many m
the British colonies have been v
value the vast and wealthy count
no such territory exists as Coloml
such a glorious country for natu
unexplored but enormous territor
Messrs. Ancizar Bros. & Co., wi
pointments, give the observer an
whole undertaking. The staff o
advent of the opening of the Pan
year or two, cannot fail to give
America as to place the whole of
the immediate notice of capitalist
Co. are to be congratulated upon
must of necessity shortly assume

Archibald D. Scott & Co
Tarpaulins, Linen and Cotton
—Manchester does an enormous
cotton oil cloth and such-like go
Messrs. A. D. Scott & Co., whos
been established for thirty years.
and warehouse, are extensive. T
Hessians, tarpaulins, linen and c
Messrs. Scott & Co. manufactu
The firm holds a prominent pos
world.

J. Johnson & Co., Pinaf
facturers, 63, Spear Street.—M
and underclothing manufacturers,
Mr. John Johnson, the energetic
marked business ability. The w
and ready sale. The firm's prices
they offer, are remarkably modera
what one of its kind should be. T
class, and all orders, both large a
exactitude and dispatch.

Messrs. Willcocks &
A representative house in Manche
ray, merchants and shippers, w
calicoes and sheetings. The busin
tation of this firm for white calico
trade. In addition to an importa
large consignments of goods are
buying establishments, both on th
The members of the firm are W
gentlemen of high commercial sta

J. H. Crosfield, Stone
Street.—This business was establ
Messrs. William and John Worth
spacious yard and canal wharf, w
from the boats. The lifting tack
overhead travelling cranes. Mr
quantities of ashlar and other st
and edgings; pipes, road sand, lin
rials required by builders, contrac
nection is principally local, and t
who do not find it convenient t
in Brewer Street. Mr. John Ha
He is a gentleman of great experie
member of the School Board.

Thomas Cottam, Mantle Manufacturer, 74 & 128, dham Street.—The manufacture of mantles has of late years become e of the most important branches of the outfitting trade. It is mostly rried on in the large cities, where female labour is so cheap on account its abundance. In this business Mr. Thomas Cottam, whose establish-ents in Oldham Street are well and widely known, is engaged. The isiness was started about ten years ago, and is now conducted by r. Cottam. The premises occupied are very spacious, neatly ordered, borately fitted, and fully stocked with all sorts of goods to the manu-cture and sale of which Mr. Cottam devotes attention. These include antles, dolmans, jackets, capes, woollens, silks, velvets, black cashmere, id crape goods. Trimmings of all kinds are also sold by the yard at holesale prices in retail or wholesale quantities. Special lines are made fur cloaks and capes, and some splendidly finished specimens of these e always on hand to meet the increasing demand for this class of goods. amily mourning is one of the departments in which the house has been id is most successful. The efforts of the house in every direction have on most energetic and judicious, and have met with due appreciation the part of the public, whose wants, in his own line, Mr. Cottam sup-ies in a prompt and economical manner, thereby making daily additions his already strong *clientèle*.

D. M. Stephens & Co., Discount Bank, 82, Cross Street.—a great commercial centre like Manchester, discounting facilities are dispensable. In this connection an important factor is the concern known Messrs. Stephens & Co., Discount Bank, which is admirably situated in e best part of Cross Street. The establishment was started twenty-five ars ago, and needless to say at once commanded attention and secured ccess. The premises occupied are very neat and of commodious dimen-ons, suitably fitted, and managed by a competent staff. The present oprietor of the business is Mr. J. H. Howard, a gentleman thoroughly rsed in all the financial details of such a business. The connection of e establishment lies chiefly among the best class of tradesmen and the ost select private residents. The principle upon which the business is orked are such that when due precaution is exercised (as it invariably) loss is impossible. The liberal and generous spirit in which Mr. oward treats his *clientèle* has made both himself and his house very pular, and secured an extensive and extending support of the best nd.

Mr. Duval, Photographer, 107, Oldham Street.—Mr. Duval tablished himself professionally at the above address some seven years go, and his success since the opening of the studio has been little less an phenomenal. The various reception, waiting, and dressing-rooms, id the operating-room are all handsomely furnished and elegantly fitted p, and every possible convenience has been provided for the comfort of sitors and sitters. In the reception rooms are many positively brilliant ecimens of Mr. Duval's beautiful art; and by examination of the amerous portraits of distinguished persons that ornament the walls, the sitor is encouraged to believe that in the skilful hands of the principal, e may expect to find his own presentment a work in which he may imself take pleasure. Mr. Duval has a branch studio at 19, Marsland's oad, Sale; and at this address a great deal of printing and finishing of ldham Street work is carried on. Considering the quality of the work, Ir. Duval's prices for all classes of portraits is extremely reasonable. A rge trade is the natural consequence, and as a fact the staff is never lle. Mr. Duval is well known in the city, and is much esteemed mongst artists and in general society.

John W. Greenup, Pattern Card and Book Maker, 1, George Street.—A very important branch of industry carried on in Ianchester, and which is of a most useful and progressive character, is attern card and book making, and, among the establishments engaged n important place is held by that of Mr. John William Greenup, which as originally founded by Mr. William Allin, who was succeeded in 882 by the present proprietor. Mr. John W. Greenup is a most expert anufacturer, and he is noted for his honourable business methods. The remises occupied consist of a spacious top floor, which is admirably tted up with patent machinery for cutting and binding and other opera-ons. A good staff of skilled hands, with the aid of the patent achinery, is employed in manufacturing pattern cards and books of very description, and these goods are of excellent and durable work-anship and splendid material. Mr. John William Greenup carries on a ery lucrative business, supplying the home and shipping trade, and he pares no expense in maintaining the high standard of excellence for which is productions are noted. An honourable, courteous, and talented man, Ir. John William Greenup is highly respected in the commercial world.

J. and A. Stott, Bleachers, Dyers, and Manufacturers f Linen, Union, Cotton, and Fancy Mattress Ticks, Sun Blind Ticks, eans, Coutils, Nankeens, Galateas, Regattas, White Twills and Plain alicoes, S Finish Imperial, R Finish, Shrunk Croydons, Heavy Collar loths, Sheetings, Staylings, and Lustres, 10, Faulkner Street, Manchester. nd 10, Foster Lane, Cheapside, London.—This important business was established in the year 1852, and continues to hold the leading position in the trade to which it attained many years ago. The premises include ware-house accommodation and a capital suite of first-rate offices handsomely furnished and most completely fitted up with all the appliances necessary for carrying on a large business. At the Faulkner Street warehouse and offices a numerous staff of clerks, salesmen, and warehousemen are actively employed and a very large business done. The works are located at Flixton, some five or six miles from the city. They are of very considerable size, and find employment for some hundreds of operatives. The London address is at 10, Foster Lane, Cheapside, E.C. The specia-lities of manufacture are linen, union, cotton, fancy mattress and blind ticks. For these goods Messrs. J. and A. Stott have a reputation which places them A1 throughout the entire trade. Other productions of the firm are coutils, nankeens, regattas, twills, calicoes, sheetings, and many similar goods. The trade connection is extremely extensive, and includes the large majority of the shipping houses, the wholesale firms, and the whole of the Manchester general warehousemen.

T. Vickers, Milliner and Mantle Maker, 155 and 157, Great Ducie Street (opposite the Assize Courts).—The millinery and mantle trade of Manchester is very considerable, and in a flourishing con-dition. Among the many establishments engaged a very good place is held by Mr. Thomas Vickers, which was established by the present pro-prietor twelve years ago, and since its inception he has created a very extensive trade which is rapidly increasing. The premises occupied are large and commodious, admirably arranged and furnished with all appli-ances for the display of his stock and for the convenience of the patrons. In the stock will be found mantles, dresses, jackets, cloaks, &c., in every kind of material, and in the latest and most fashionable styles, and a large assortment of rich trimmings, feathers, flowers, lace ribbons, and other similar commodities. The mourning department of this establishment is in a first-class condition, the goods being of the best quality, and the making-up characterized by elegance and originality. The trade done is very considerable, of a high class, gives employment to twenty assistants, and is rapidly increasing. Mr. Thomas Vickers, the proprietor of this lucra-tive business, possesses great ability and experience in the trade, has a detailed knowledge of the markets, and a sound judgment of the public taste. He is well known and highly respected by the members of the trade, and his integrity and courtesy have won the esteem of the com-munity, whilst his business ably sustains its long standing reputation.

Brown's Chop House and Day Hotel, 14, Corporation Street.—Among the old and well-known establishments in Manchester is "Brown's Chop House," which is eligibly situated. It was originally opened about forty years ago, and has been in the present premises upwards of fourteen years. It has a national reputation for the superior quality of the good cheer it supplies, and has always enjoyed a high-class patronage. The premises are of spacious dimensions, admirably arranged and fitted up in a neat and tasteful manner. To dine at "Brown's" is to partake of all that is best and most substantial in the culinary art. Mrs. Brown, the proprietress, has carried on the business since the death of her husband, about thirteen years ago, and the active management of the establishment is in experienced and thoroughly capable hands. "Brown's Chop House" maintains its old-time reputa-tion, and the success it is meeting with is well deserved.

Josephine Massey, Hosier, Glover, &c., 12, Victoria Street.—At the foregoing address, the premises of Miss Josephine Massey, trading as hosier, glover, shirt-maker, &c., we have well exemplified the maxim of "little and good." The shop is not large but the show is very good, and the stock is of the highest quality both in workmanship and material, and in addition to the window display the well-appointed storeroom at the basement contains an assortment of the most carefully selected goods. The business was established twenty-eight years ago as A. & S. J. Massey, assuming its present title some eighteen years since. A vigilant and discriminating eye is kept upon the buying and selecting of stock, and none but the best goods are offered to the public. So far, in fact, has this praiseworthy system been carried out in every particular that this shop has earned for itself a most enviable reputation throughout Manchester and the surrounding district.

D. Riley & Sons, Tailors & Drapers, 9, Deansgate.—The tailoring and drapery trade of Manchester is of considerable magni-tude, and of great importance in the interests of the city. A well-known firm engaged is that of Messrs. D. Riley & Sons, which has been esta-blished in the city for many years. Their premises are large and well adapted for the business. The stock is very extensive and complete, con-sisting of all makes of woollen goods from the best manufacturers. Sixty hands are employed in producing special high-class clothing, civil, military, and Court costumes, which are sent to all parts of England, the Colonies, and America. The Firm consists of Richard F. and Michael Riley, sons of the founder, Denis Riley, who died in May, 1887. Their commercial and financial status in the city is high and well defined, and their house occupies an honourable position in the mercantile world.

Mr. Frederick Rawcliffe, Furnishing and General Ironmonger, 203, Oxford Street.—Among the many industries of Manchester, the furnishing and general ironmongery is a branch of very considerable importance, and calls for special notice and remark. The well-known house of Mr. Frederick Rawcliffe, of 203, Oxford Street (opposite Owens College), furnishing and general ironmonger, is a fairly representative type of this branch of commercial enterprise. Established in 1847, it was carried on by Mr. W. Minshull, its founder, until 1875, when the business was succeeded to by its present proprietor, Mr. F. Rawcliffe. It has always maintained a high reputation, and is known as one of the best and cheapest depôts in the city for good cutlery and electro-plated spoons and forks, &c., and more particularly for all kinds of detail. Mr. Rawcliffe having had experience in London, Liverpool, the United States, and several other places, has gained such a practical knowledge of his business as is rarely met with, and we are informed that it is a very common occurrence for people who have unsuccessfully hunted for some particular article elsewhere to succeed here. The business operations are on an extensive scale. This depôt having a widespread reputation, large parcels are despatched from the house to customers in all parts of the kingdom. The premises occupied comprise a substantial house with well-appointed shop and warehouse, admirably arranged and adapted to the full requirements of the business, and affording employment to a moderate staff of experienced assistants. The stocks held are large and valuable, and comprise an immense assortment of furnishing and general ironmongery goods, &c., of every description and all of good quality. The proprietor is well known as a thoroughly practical business man.

Mr. Joseph Kidson, Tailor and Draper, 87, Piccadilly.—Prominent among the great industries of the age is the necessary and highly appreciated branch of commerce, the tailoring trade. As an appropriate and representative centre in this branch of trade, the well-known house of Mr. Joseph Kidson stands unrivalled. This far-famed establishment occupies a very excellent and prominent position. Established so far back as 1822, this house has from its very inception occupied a high position as a first-class concern. Originally founded by Mr. Joseph Kidson in 1822 in Market Street, it was removed to its present address in 1829. The reputation of this house is first-class and widespread; the business has the great advantage of being personally superintended by the principal, thereby insuring a more than usual amount of public confidence. The premises comprise a neat and well-appointed shop, with workrooms in which are employed numerous highly skilled workpeople. The stock on hand is very large, consisting of a variety of West of England broadcloths, doeskins, Scotch plaids, tweeds, mixtures, diagonals, fancy waistcoatings, flannels for athletic and boating suits, alpacas, and other fabrics of all patterns. A speciality about the business of this establishment is, it is very old-established and so well and creditably known that it enjoys a connection of the very highest order and of sterling value. No similar establishment in the city bears a higher reputation for excellence. Mr. Kidson has on his books now a customer who has dealt with him upwards of sixty years. The proprietor, Mr. Joseph Kidson, is a gentleman well known as an old and much respected citizen of Manchester, widely respected, and of very high repute.

John Barton, Manufacturer and Ladies' Outfitter, 72 and 76, Oldham Street.—It is somewhat hard to realise the fact that this flourishing concern has only been established for a period of fifteen years. The management that has brought it such speedy and substantial success has been no laggard one, and merits unqualified praise. In each of the departments a splendid stock is always kept on hand. Mantles, ulsters, waterproof cloaks, and costumes of every conceivable description are cut and fitted on the premises, under careful and attentive surveillance, by skilled hands. The mourning department calls for especial commendation, and here as elsewhere the goods offered to the customer are reasonable in price and of the latest and most approved designs. The factory, which is situate at 1, Warwick Street, is furnished with the best of machinery and appliances, and is certainly one of the first in the trade. A large staff is employed. The products of this house have achieved a widespread popularity. From the quality of the goods themselves to the manner of their manufacture, all is supplied that the most particular taste could desire. Mr. Barton is much to be congratulated upon his ability and enterprise; and, catering so well for public patronage, it is no wonder that he is awarded such generous support.

Charlesworth Bros., Engineers and Patentees, 45, Blackfriars Street.—The engineering business of Manchester is of very great value, and the establishments engaged are very numerous. A fine and well-known house engaged in this line is that trading as Messrs. Charlesworth Bros., which was founded in 1873. The sole member of the firm is Mr. Thomas Charlesworth, who is noted as the patentee and manufacturer of "The Improved Norton's Patent Self-Registering Turnstiles," which are made at his works, Bedford Leigh. The offices in Manchester, to which all his correspondence and orders are addressed, are large and commodious, well furnished, and a good clerical staff is employed. The turnstiles of Mr. Charlesworth are in every respect perfect; they are most useful inventions, and for effective action and accuracy are unrivalled. They are manufactured with great care by able and experienced hands under talented supervision, and have given every satisfaction wherever adopted. There were twenty-five in use at the Royal Jubilee Exhibition, Liverpool. Mr. Charlesworth carries on a very heavy trade in all parts of the United Kingdom, and his turnstiles are daily becoming more popular. Mr. Charlesworth, it is needless to say, is well known in engineering circles, and his talent is universally recognised. He bears the highest reputation for honour and courteous bearing, and his house has done much to uphold the dignity of British engineering.

E. Harrison, Tobacconist, 120, Market Street.—This is certainly one of the best-appointed and most popular tobacconists' in the city. The shop is particularly well stocked, the goods offered for sale are of first-class quality, and the charges made are most satisfactorily moderate, while the extensive trade carried on fully justifies the assertion that the public will always bestow their attention where a fair price is demanded for a fair article. THE UNRIVALLED BRITANNIA SMOKING MIXTURE sold here is very popular indeed amongst all classes in and around the city; whilst the most fastidious of smokers will find themselves admirably suited either where the "weed" itself is concerned or the necessary articles—pipes, &c., &c.—required for the enjoyment thereof. Cigarettes (Turkish, Virginian, Egyptian, &c.), can be seen in splendid variety, cigars of the choicest Havana brands, Manilla cigars and cheroots, Mexicans, AND THE CELEBRATED MONTEGO CONCHAS, and other British goods, are kept in stock of no mean size. Taddy's, Gawith's, and Wilson's famous snuffs are also sold, as are fancy goods in great variety. Repairs are executed with care, neatness, skill, and despatch, and the business well deserves the popularity which it has so long enjoyed, and which promises to be even greater in the future.

William Maben, Joiner, Contractor, &c., 29, Blantyre Street, Chester Road, Hulme, and at 12, Britannia Chambers, 74, Market Street.—This is one of the best concerns of the kind in the locality—admirably conducted, comprehensive, and undertakes special or general work with promptitude and thoroughness. Mr. William Maben started business some eleven years ago, and, as a joiner and contractor for all branches of work in the building trade of more than ordinary merit and ability, he has gained a widespread reputation. There is one branch of his business in addition to the repairing, &c., upon which a particularly large amount of attention is bestowed, *i.e.*, in connection with those two vital considerations, ventilation and sanitation. Upon these Mr. Maben is an acknowledged authority, being consulted by a very large circle of clients. For the convenience of such clients some little time since he opened a branch office at 12, Britannia Chambers, 71, Market Street. A competent staff of workmen is kept in constant employment. All orders are attended to with praiseworthy promptitude, and the concern throughout ensures the utmost satisfaction to the customer.

Provident Clerks' Associations.—These institutions are under one board of management, but they have entirely separate and distinct funds. The branch business of these associations is conducted under the management of Mr. F. Merriman, at 21, Booth Street, Manchester. The head offices are situated in Moorgate Street and Coleman Street, London, and the business consists of life insurance, accident and employers' liability insurance, and fidelity guarantees. **Life Branch.**—Originally started with a view of placing life insurance within the reach of persons with limited incomes, the life branch of the association now includes insurers of every class, attracted by the favourable rates charged in early and middle life, and the undoubted security afforded by a well-invested fund of over £1,100,000. **Fidelity Guarantees.**—This department, which is an offshoot from the life branch, enables persons holding situations of trust to give security for the fulfilment of their duties in a trustworthy manner, and has supplied a cheap and welcome alternative to the former system of "personal sureties." **Accident and Employers' Liability Insurance.**—To meet the requirements of a large body of the members in the above departments, an accident branch was started, which was extended in 1881 to the insurance of the risks imposed on employers of labour by the Employers' Liability Act, 1880.

Jno. Jenkinson, Grocer, Tea Dealer, 79, Great Ducie Street and 10, Higher Broughton.—Mr. Jno. Jenkinson is the proprietor of a first-class business as grocer and tea dealer. He established this twenty-five years ago, and by his ability and strict attention to the wants and requirements of the public in the locality, has succeeded in obtaining a first class connection and excellent reputation. His shop, which is of good appearance, is situated at the corner of Nightingale Street, Strangeways, and he has a very large stock of everything incidental to the trade. The articles supplied are of first-class quality, and Mr. Jenkinson is very expeditious in carrying out the orders of his numerous customers. His strictly conscientious method of business has greatly contributed to the fame of this shop, and the proprietor is to be congratulated on his successful efforts.

Manchester and Salford Equitable Co-operative ciety, Downing Street, Ardwick.—That the advantages of co-operation trading are daily becoming more fully recognised among the general blic is obvious. The system of conducting business in the present day s a decided tendency in favour of extensive dealings, and the larger ms and associations are taking the place of the small dealers. If a firm society, with almost unlimited capital at command, are purchasing ods of any description in the markets, it is evident that, by reason of eir extensive trade and financial circumstances, they can exercise free oice in their selection of commodities to a much greater extent than the all retail dealer. Again, by purchasing in such large quantities nearly ery class of goods may be obtained at a much less rate, and can, there- e, be sold to the public at a lower price. In the case of co-operative cieties, the trade is assured by the members themselves, and they are equally interested in the success of the society. No better illustration a really sound first-class co-operative society could exist than that of Manchester and Salford Equitable Co-operative Society, one of the gest and most admirably managed associations of this description in the United Kingdom. It was originally founded in 1859, with various objects intended for the benefit of the general public, among which may be mentioned that of providing a sound investment for capital, coupling the profits incidental to trading with the advantages of a bank. Other objects, such as providing means for social intercourse and literary study, and encouragement of the "cash" system of business, are included in the purposes of this society, which has been registered under the Industrial and Provident Societies Act. The society carry on all the business incidental to wholesale and retail dealers in grocery, provisions, coal, [illegible] bakers, butchers, tailors, ironmongers, to the buying and selling of land, and farming. Each member is charged a nominal entrance fee, and is compelled to hold one £1 share at least, for which payment may be made in instalments that cover the space of two years. Any number of shares may be held up to two hundred, but every member must have one. At the end of each quarter a dividend is paid upon these shares, and the balance of the profit gained by the society is divided among the members proportionally according to the amount of their purchases in the meantime. The system adopted for keeping account of these purchases is exceedingly simple,

W. Reynolds, Dyer and Cleaner, 295, Stretford Road. Steam Dyeing and Cleaning Works, Stretford Road, near Moss Lane.—Dyeing and cleaning is a very important and valuable branch of industry in Manchester. It is of great utility, in a perfect condition, and employing many establishments. A thoroughly representative house in this line is that of Mr. W. Reynolds, Dye Works, Stretford Road—one of the largest and best arranged works in the trade. Strict attention and rapidity in the execution of orders; moderate charges; goods cleaned in perfection by the dry process (*nettoyage à sec*), are the leading features. W. Reynolds' steam dyeing and cleaning works were founded fifteen years ago. Mr. W. Reynolds is a most expert and experienced dyer, cleaner, and finisher, and he has, for convenience of receiving goods, branches at 95, Stockport Road, 617, Rochdale Road, and 281, Regent Road, Salford; and a spacious shop and showrooms at 295, Stretford Road; he has also one hundred agents in Manchester and the suburbs who receive goods on commission. The works are very commodious and are fitted up in a most perfect manner with the most modern machinery and appliances. A large staff of skilled and practical workmen are employed under Mr. W. Reynolds's talented supervision and direction, in cleaning, dyeing, and finishing silk, poplin, satin, velvet, damask, and all kinds of costly fabrics and materials for ladies' and gentlemen's wear and household purposes. The processes are on the most advanced principles, including cleaning on the French dry system: no shrinking of goods, no unpicking required; all classes of goods are cleaned made-up. The works are fitted up with the best machinery and appliances for this branch of the business. The dry system of cleaning has great disinfecting properties; goods are best cleaned by the dry process before being laid by for any length of time. The chemicals and dyes used are of the best quality. In the showroom can be seen splendid specimens of work, proving that he has brought the operations to the highest state of perfection. Mr. W. Reynolds owns a number of vans which collect and deliver goods with dispatch, and orders by post are promptly attended to: in fact, the organisation of the establishment is simply perfect. Mr. W. Reynolds carries on a very heavy trade of an influential character; also carpet cleaning and beating by steam-power, and from five hundred to one thousand pairs of white and cream curtains are cleaned every week. Orders come from all parts throughout the city and suburbs. Mr. W. Reynolds is a practical dyer and cleaner: being in the business from his youth, he thoroughly understands the requirements of the present age in this special business; he is well known for his unbounded popularity with all classes, and he ranks among the principal dyers and cleaners of England.

William Righton, Dress Warehouse, 56, Stretford Road.—Of the various businesses conducted in most large cities, none are so prosperous or so ably managed as those devoted to the production and sale of ladies' dress and mantle materials. In the ranks of these establishments a prominent position is held in our city by that belonging to Mr. William Righton, who has been established for over seven years. His spacious premises are admirably fitted and located for the purpose of making a fine display, and this is done in a manner that wins the admiration of the regular and casual passing pedestrian. All sorts of ladies' dress materials in the latest and most fashionable styles, patterns, and materials are here on view, from the best and newest designs. A wide-spread trade of the most select order is done, and the house and its proprietor bear an excellent reputation for the quality, style, and finish of all materials procured from them.

W. Lindop, Ivory, Bone, and Hard-wood Turner, 69, Shudehill.—The manufactory of Mr. W. Lindop, ivory, bone, and hard-wood turner, and walking-stick maker, was established in 1855, and has since been conducted by the original founder without any change of management. Mr. Lindop has, since the commencement of his business, gone on gradually increasing it, until it has reached its present very respectable dimensions, and is now doing a very considerable amount of first-class business, both in the ivory, bone, and hard-wood turning, especial care being given to billiard-balls and bowling-green bowls, and the other speciality to which he has recently been giving his particular attention: this line is walking-sticks, on which he is bringing to bear a large amount of ingenuity in order to place before the public a first-class article at a very moderate price. So far his efforts in this direction have been exceedingly successful, and his stock contains some capital specimens which are likely to attract considerable attention and command a ready sale. Mr. Lindop holds a very large and choice assortment of walking-sticks of almost every description of material and variety of mount, in ivory, stag, and buffalo horn. He is also a maker of umbrellas, and supplies the trade with all kinds of umbrella material and sticks for the same. Mr. Lindop employs a number of workmen in his manufactory, and there is little doubt that with the energy and skill with which he is applying himself to the development of his walking-stick trade, his business will very considerably increase, both locally and in more distant markets.

John Smethurst, Tailor, 14, St. Ann's Square.—This firm was established in the year 1850 under the title of Andrews & Smethurst; in 1860 it became known as John Smethurst & Son, a name which was again altered in 1885 to John Smethurst, as at present. The premises consist of a very large shop, handsomely decorated, well furnished, and admirably fitted up with cutting-rooms at the back and work-rooms above. The stock is most varied and extensive; there are splendid ranges of all the best makes of the West of England, Scotch, Yorkshire, and French goods; many of the patterns are reserved, while the expensive quality of others places them beyond the reach of the lesser houses. The trade, which is bespoke and of the highest class, is by no means confined to the local gentry; the firm has customers all over the world, and has the good fortune of retaining them when once they are on the books. Especial attention is paid to cut, style, finish, and the class of material used; and the wishes of every customer are carefully studied. Mr. Smethurst is esteemed an artist in draping the figure, and all clothing turned out of his establishment carries with it its own recommendation. He is highly esteemed by a very large circle of friends and customers, and is at the head of his profession in this city.

A. Beckett & Sons, Fashionable Bootmakers, 49, Swan Street.—This business has been in active and continuous operation since 1821, and its history of nearly seventy years is one of steady and uniform success and prosperity. It was founded by the late Mr. Ambrose Beckett, and is now carried on by his sons. The premises consist of a handsome shop of attractive appearance, thoroughly well and substantially furnished and fitted up with great completeness. There are several capital show-rooms and comfortable fitting-rooms for ladies and gentlemen. A considerable portion of the trade is for good, serviceable, ready mades, which are supplied at very moderate prices; but there is a capital first-class bespoke trade in both ladies' and gentlemen's goods. Messrs. Beckett & Sons, for the convenience of their friends, keep a choice selection of ladies' boots by the most noted London bootmakers. There is a capital choice of slippers and various sundry articles, such as blacking, kid reviver, &c. A capable staff of first-class hands is employed on the premises, and there are numerous outdoor workers. In the shop several clever and courteous assistants are in attendance upon customers. The sole proprietors at present are Mr. Joseph Beckett and Mr. John Beckett, gentlemen having a perfect knowledge of the trade, and deservedly successful.

Robert Westbury, Surgeons' Machinist, 26, Old Millgate.—Mr. Westbury occupies premises at the above address consisting of sale shop on ground floor and workshops above and below for the manufacture of artificial limbs, trusses, and various appliances for deformity of different parts of the human body. He was an exhibitor at the Great International Exhibition of 1862 held in London, and was awarded a Prize Medal for excellence of workmanship and designs. Strange to say, deformities are more common among human being and domestic animals than among wild animals, or still less birds. To remedy these defects is the purpose of many branches of manufacture in which Mr. Westbury is engaged. Amongst these may be noticed appliances for curvature of the spine, of which there are two distinct kinds, namely lateral curvature and angular curvature; also, instruments for deformed legs and club-foot, the latter being a twisting of the foot by one or more of the tendons being contracted. In all these cases Mr. Westbury has constructed surgical appliances of the highest order of merit adapted to each special deformity; his efforts have proved eminently successful and he has acquired a world-wide reputation. Mr. Westbury is also the inventor and sole maker of an imperceptible curative truss for the cure of hernia, which is justly celebrated for its comfort and utility, and in this article he does an extensive trade. We may observe that as a manufacturer of the various appliances referred to, Mr. Westbury has been specially trained, and has had a business experience extending considerably over a quarter of a century at his present address. During this long time he has enjoyed the confidence of the medical profession generally as a thoughtful and skilful maker of the specialities peculiar to this particular business. We will only add that Mr. Westbury is one of the best-known tradesmen in Manchester; he is looked upon as a most honourable and upright citizen, and as such is highly popular and universally respected.

Benjamin Weekes Wood, Fustian Finisher, 8 Browncross Street, Salford.—This important business has been in active operation for nearly twenty years, and its history is one of steady and continuous prosperity. The works occupy a considerable area, and include a large mill thoroughly well fitted up with capital plant and machinery, a spacious and convenient warehouse and suitable offices, handsomely furnished and thoroughly equipped with the latest approved appliances for the rapid dispatch of business. The speciality of the trade is fustian finishing. The connection includes many of the leading shipping houses, the wholesale firms, the general Manchester warehousemen, and the principal manufacturers of fustians and velveteens of the city. An efficient staff is employed. Mr. Benjamin Weekes Wood is the founder of the business. He is a gentleman of very great experience in the trade, of sound judgment and considerable ingenuity, and has introduced very many improvements in the process of finishing. He is extremely well known in general commercial circles, and is looked upon as a thriving, prosperous, and enterprising business man.

…er & Methuen, Chemist.
…extent and importance in Man-
…lishments engaged therein are
…ly qualified body, enjoying the
…thoroughly representative house
… Methuen. This gentleman was
…ker (under the title of Messrs.
…siness in 1832. The shop occu-

…tive appearance, fitted with the
… superior manner, and is well
…d other pharmaceutical prepara-
…ventor, patentee, and preparer of
…he city as the "Oh, yes! Cough
…ies of patients, who, when asked,
…ost always, "Oh, yes!" Also
… in great demand by the Man-
…mited confidence in all prepara-
… The drugs supplied by Mr. R.
…ble, and he dispenses with skill
…carries on a very fine local trade,
…lity; his courtesy is reflected by
…own among the members of the
…pected, and he enjoys the esteem

…g and Insurance Agent,
… feature in the great industries
… These form an item of the very
…uth be regarded as the centre
…ree radiate. As a representative
… of Mr. W. H. Ingram, shipping
… into prominent notice. Estab-
…use has been one of steady and
…r. Ingram is agent in Manchester
…es of steamships and sailing ves-
…e civilised world. Amongst the
…y be mentioned Thomas Wilson,
…e & Co., Castle Mail Packet Co.,
… These and other lines are noted
…prising Continental and trading
…sages to the Continent, South
… house is large and widespread,
… and punctuality. The premises
…ces thoroughly adapted to the
…uate staff of clerks and assist-
…shipping and general commercial
…widening circle of patrons.

D. T. Batty, Dealer in Old Coins, Antiques, &c., 10, Cathedral Yard. Mr. Batty's well-appointed establishment at 10, Cathedral Yard is the oldest of its kind, and presents many attractions to numismatists and to the general antiquarian. Curiosity collectors will here find much to interest them. The proprietor himself has his whole heart in the work he so successfully carries on, and the splendid assortment of articles he has drawn together is of a particularly instructive character. A curiosity shop has always irresistible attractions for men of all minds. Gathered together at one of these places may be found relics of the past that serve alike to recall to the aged observer many pleasant memories and to give a fresh impetus to the younger but inquiring student of times and manners long gone by. Mr. Batty's courtesy to customers is well known. He has published a large and exhaustive work on the British and Colonial Copper Coinage from Elizabeth to the present time.

Mrs. M. A. Boulger, Milliner, Costumier, &c., Albion House, 176–178, Oldham Road.—Among the many trades in Manchester engaged in supplying the population with wearing apparel, no insignificant place is occupied by that devoted to the sale of millinery, mantles, costumes, and fancy goods. Many establishments are engaged therein, a leading one being that of Mrs. M. A. Boulger, Albion House, which was originally founded by W. Boulger, twenty years ago. The premises occupied consist of a large double shop fitted up in a superior and elegant manner with trade appliances and fixtures, and bearing a prosperous and substantial appearance. It is well stocked with mantles, millinery, costumes, &c., in the latest and most fashionable styles, and fancy articles of every description. Funerals are furnished throughout on the modern principle. A staff of experienced hands are employed in the business, and complete mourning can be supplied at a few hours' notice, so perfect are the resources at Mrs. M. A. Boulger's command. Every department of the business is in thorough order, and the management throughout is able and enterprising. A very fine local trade is carried on, and the excellence of the stock and the promptness and efficiency with which all work is carried out are doing much to extend the business. Mrs. M. A. Boulger is well known in the trade and is looked upon with great respect by the many members. Very popular also with the local community, Mrs. M. A. Boulger enjoys esteem and confidence, and maintains the twenty years' unsullied reputation of the business in an admirable manner. Dressmakers and milliners are sent to all parts of the country to wait upon ladies, if required.

Wilson, Hewson, & Co., Wholesale Confectioners, Factors for Manufacturing Confectioners, and Commission Agents, 5 and 7, Cannon Street.—This firm has now been established four years and has been unusually successful. The premises in Cannon Street are centrally situated, being close to the Corn Exchange, and admirably adapted for the varied business carried on by this enterprising firm. Messrs. Wilson, Hewson, & Co. have the justly-acquired reputation of supplying all goods of good quality, and attractive in appearance. The importation of wooden toys, and jewellery for lucky bags, and their great variety of fancy goods for the Christmas trade, are special features of their business. In addition to their own special business, Messrs. Wilson, Hewson, & Co. are sole agents for Messrs. McCall & Stephen, Adelphi Biscuit Factory, Glasgow. They also act as factors for several firms of high standing, and make a speciality of John Buchanan & Bros.', Glasgow, famed home-made marmalade. Their connection is extensive, including Lancashire, Yorkshire, Derbyshire, Shropshire, and North Wales. Their stock of lozenges, pipes, rocks, pan goods, gelatine productions, gum compounds, liquorice goods, jellies, fondants, mixtures, and everything in the confectionery line, is very seldom equalled. The members of the firm are justly respected in business circles, and are practically acquainted with every detail of the business which they have so successfully established.

John Wilkinson, Manufacturer, &c., 71, Mosley Street.—In the great and leading industries of Manchester and district, a most important position is held by such representative firms as Messrs. John Wilkinson, manufacturer of Oxfords, Harvards, zephyrs, ginghams, fancy dress goods, &c., whose premises are conveniently situated. The works are at Laurel Bank Mill, Nelson, and Union Mill, Skipton. Established many years, this firm enjoys a large and very widespread reputation for their goods, extending to every commercial centre of the civilised globe. The business done is very considerable, and includes consignments on an immense scale; the well-known quality of the products finds for them open and ready markets everywhere at quotations of a most satisfactory character, in addition to which large sales take place with most of the leading houses in the United Kingdom. The mills at Nelson and Skipton are fitted with costly machinery of the most modern construction and highest efficiency, employing large numbers of highly skilled artisans, and may be considered as taking rank amongst the foremost manufacturing establishments of the kingdom. The Manchester house comprises neat and well-fitted office admirably adapted for the transaction of the firm's business and of affording occupation for competent assistants, with stock-room for samples, &c. The sole proprietor is Mr. John Wilkinson, a gentleman well known in commercial circles.

M. Guttenberg, Photographer Royal, "Kensington House," 316, Oxford Road.—The art of photography is extensively carried on in Manchester; it is in the highest state of perfection, the establishments engaged are many, and the members are a talented and enterprising body. A well-known house in this line, and one of the principal in Manchester, is that of Mr. M. Guttenberg, of "Kensington House," which was founded in 1880. Mr. M. Guttenberg, however, was established in Bristol for sixteen years, and he is a most talented photographer. His fame may be judged from the fact that he has been patronised by Royalty, including H.M. the Queen, H.R.H. Prince Christian, H.R.H. Princess Mary of Teck, and Oriental potentates; the nobility, and gentry from all parts, bishops and clergy of all denominations, actors, and the mayors, aldermen, and councillors of the city. His premises are spacious, the studio on the ground-floor is simply perfect, and the waiting-rooms are handsomely furnished. The influential patronage of Mr. M. Guttenberg speaks for the beauty and perfection of his work, and he is also very talented in executing in water colours, or on porcelain and in monochrome. Mr. M. Guttenberg photographs invalids at their own residences, out-door groups by special arrangement, and the widespread and lucrative business carried on necessitates the employment of a large staff of assistants. Mr. M. Guttenberg is well known in the photographic world, and highly respected.

Wm. Siddeley, Hosier and Shirt Maker, &c., 16 and 18, Market Place.—The trade in hosiery and shirt making is of some considerable importance and influence in the commercial interests of Manchester, and the establishments engaged are many and under excellent management. A thoroughly representative house in this trade is that of Mr. William Siddeley, which has a reputation of twenty-five years' standing. The premises are large and commodious, comprising two large shops of elegant appearance, fitted up in a most superior style, and displaying a choice selection of goods in the window. A very heavy and complete assortment of hosiery, gloves, &c., is kept in stock, and it is frequently replenished from the warehouses of the best manufacturers; Mr. William Siddeley showing more than usual ability in this task. He is also a most practical and proficient shirt maker, putting in first-class workmanship and in the newest fashion. The trade done is considerable, of a local high-class nature, and rapidly increasing. Mr. William Siddeley also owns another shop at Llandudno, and altogether does a very lucrative business. He is very popular in the neighbourhood, is highly esteemed for his courtesy and sincerity, and his business holds an important place in the trade.

Pascal Nessi, Dealer in Fancy Goods, 79, Corporation Street.—This establishment is a particularly interesting one and well worthy of a visit of inspection. Pascal Nessi has been established for thirteen years, and has been at his present well-appointed premises for about ten. As a dealer in Italian pictures and paintings in water colours, and wholesale and export dealer in fancy leather and other goods of all descriptions, suitable for fancy stationers, bazaars, and fancy drapers, he occupies an honourable position amongst the very first of his class. The stock kept on hand is always above average merit, and the prices charged are particularly moderate. P. Nessi is an agent for Mr. William Pealling, the well-known writing-desk, workbox, tea-caddy, and cigar cabinet manufacturer, of 46 and 48, Harman Street, Kingsland Road, London, E. He is a gentleman thoroughly well versed in the many intricacies of his business and is in a position to afford his patrons the most perfect satisfaction. Mr. Nessi carries on a wonderfully flourishing and prosperous trade. He spares no pains to keep his premises well stocked with the latest novelties, and his method of business is in every way commendable, as all will find who pay him a visit.

Heywood & Jones, Tailors, 10, Exchange Street.—One of the leading and most thoroughly representative firms of merchant tailors in Manchester is that of Messrs. Heywood & Jones. This business was established forty years ago, and by a straightforward system of honourable dealing Messrs. Heywood & Jones built up a large and permanent patronage among the best classes of Manchester and vicinity. The premises occupied are spacious and commodious, admirably arranged, and equipped with every facility and convenience for the transaction of business, employment being given to a force of skilled and experienced workmen. The stock kept is large and carefully selected. It includes the best and most desirable goods from the leading British and Continental manufacturers. The firm have an excellent reputation for first-class and artistic work, and the garments made by them are unexcelled for fashionable cut, finish, and durability.

B. Lowe, Travelling Trunk Manufacturer, 11, 89, and 91, Great Ancoats Street.—This business was established in the year 1855, and has progressed very rapidly during the period of its existence. The premises consist of three handsome roomy shops, with commodious workshops, warehouse, and stock-rooms. The offices are substantially furnished. The main speciality of the business is the manufacture of steel and sheet-iron travelling trunks and bonnet-boxes, and as these are produced in a variety of useful sizes, shapes, and qualities, and are distinguished by careful construction and thoroughly good workmanship, they are sold in very large quantities. In addition, Mr. Lowe makes some fine ranges of grocers' canisters, artistically ornamented and thoroughly well finished; mills, scoops, scales and balances, with a large assortment of shop-fittings and sundry furnishings. The trade connection includes a large proportion of the ironmongers and furnishing houses of the city and district, and there are many country customers, especially for the trunks and bonnet-boxes. A number of experienced hands are employed the year round, additional workmen being engaged during the busy seasons. The sole proprietor is still Mr. B. Lowe, the founder of the firm, a clever business man, whose great success is thoroughly well deserved.

Bernard Markus, India-rubber and Waterproof Garment Manufacturer, 8, New Street, Bradshaw Street, Shudehill.—This business was established ten years ago, and has proved very successful. The premises include a capital warehouse of five floors, and a number of light, lofty, well-ventilated workrooms. The offices are convenient and well furnished, and suited for the rapid transaction of business. The specialities of manufacture are waterproof coats, cloaks, leggings, capes, imperials, and similar goods. The connection is very extensive, and though the local trade is very heavy, the firm has many customers in the more distant parts of the empire. A considerable shipping trade is done through the medium of the city merchants, and the firm has agencies and correspondents in most of the large commercial centres. A large staff of cutters and machinists is constantly employed the year round, and several commercial travellers are engaged in representing the interests of the firm. Mr. Bernard Markus remains the sole proprietor of the business. He is a gentleman of great experience in the manufacture of waterproof clothing, and has himself introduced many improvements connected therewith. He is well known in the city, and has a large personal connection amongst buyers. A liberal and considerate employer, he is considered a deservedly thriving business man.

J. Barnet Brugh & Co., Manufacturers and Agents, 17A, Dickinson Street.—This business was founded more than twenty years ago by Mr. Brugh, and its history is one of steady and uniform success and prosperity. The premises include a very capital basement warehouse, thoroughly well stocked, and a pair of offices neatly furnished and fitted with all the latest and most approved appliances for the rapid despatch of business. The specialities of the trade are cotton checks, stripes, ticks, figures, colourings, regattas, Harvards, Oxfords, ginghams, nankeens, and similar goods. Of some of these Messrs. Barnet Brugh & Co. are the manufacturers, while of others they are the makers' agents. The trade connection is as extensive as it is comprehensive, and includes all the leading shipping firms and wholesale houses. Messrs. Barnet Brugh & Co. have no travellers, but the working staff at Dickinson Street includes several competent salesmen, clerks, and correspondents, and a brisk business is constantly going on. Mr. Barnet Brugh is now the sole proprietor. He is a gentleman of varied and lengthy experience, a capital man of business, and extremely well known on 'Change and in general commercial circles.

J. Jefferies, 206, Stretford Road.—Watch and clockmaking and the jewellery trade in general in Manchester is in a very high state perfection, some of the ablest craftsmen in the kingdom being denizens of the city. A notable exemplification of the truth of this is to be found in the business of Mr. Joseph Jefferies, whose fine shops and work-rooms are situated at 206, Stretford Road, wherein silver and gold jewellery manufacture is carried on, from the smelting of the gold to the finished article. A complete staff of workmen is employed under the direct superintendence of the proprietor, who has also works and a manufactory at Vyse Street, Birmingham, and an extensive central establishment at 33, Market Street, in the city of Manchester, and is the only jewellery manufacturer who is himself a practical and finished workman, who exposes for sale goods made on his own premises; we know in the city his stock of diamonds and precious stones, mounted and unmounted, is a magnificent collection. His establishment was founded in 1872, and its gradual and certain extension from time to time is a sure proof of the satisfaction his manufactures give to the public, who intrust the most complicated designs and orders to his care. In connection with his business he has also a manufactory of English watches, for which he is celebrated, having repeatedly large orders from India and the Colonies, as well as from English railway companies and others. The establishment, which was founded fifteen years ago, is of ample dimensions and admirably fitted and arranged for work, storage, and effective display. Watches and clocks of the most complicated character and jewellery are repaired in a very first-class manner. Gems, and gold and silver for melting are purchased, and a good price given. The goods sold at this establishment are acknowledged to be splendid value for the price paid. A very extensive and increasing trade is the result, Mr. Jefferies having the confidence of a very large number of Manchester people.

John Thompson, Baker and Army Contractor, 350, [D]eansgate.—There is not a more important trade in connection with [the] internal economy of Manchester than that of bread. An old-esta[bli]shed house in this line is that of Mr. John Thompson, which was [ori]ginated thirty years ago. The premises consist of a fine commodious [sh]op, which is complete in its fittings and appointments, and bakehouse [of] ample dimensions. The bakehouse is eminently suitable for its purpose, [be]ing well ventilated and lighted, and the apparatus and appliances are [of] modern construction. The bread is made of the best flour by able and [sk]ilful hands under Mr. J. Thompson's superintendence, and it is per[fe]ctly pure and highly esteemed in the locality. The shop is well stocked, [an]d Mr. John Thompson carries on a very fine wholesale and retail trade [of] a good-class character, and his management is tending to the increase [of] business. Mr. John Thompson spares no trouble or expense in main[tai]ning the excellence of his bread, and has proved himself a perfect [ma]ster of his craft. He is a genuine, honourable, and courteous business [m]an.

John Massey, Chemist and Dentist, 280, Deansgate. [T]he pharmaceutical profession in Manchester ranks second to none in [the] kingdom for the extent of business done, and the general ability, [en]terprise, and talent of its members, more than one of whom has filled [the] civic chair with credit to the city. For many years the practice of [den]tistry has been carried on by a number of chemists, in conjunction with [ph]armacy, a thorough knowledge of the latter science being a valuable [au]xiliary to the former, chemistry and therapeutics forming a very essential [pa]rt of dentistry. A conspicuous example of the combined professions is [aff]orded in the case of Mr. John Massey, of 280, Deansgate, Manchester, [an]d Chester Road, Stretford. The business was originally founded by the

[lat]e Charles Moseley, Mr. Massey entering in 1846. The premises are [com]modious and fitted up in an elegant manner, and supplied with a com[ple]te stock of the purest drugs and the miscellaneous articles connected [wi]th the business of a chemist. As a dentist, Mr. Massey bears the repu[tat]ion of his being a most skilful and humane operator, having had a long [an]d extensive practice for over forty years, treating both surgical and [me]chanical cases with the greatest success, whilst his charges are most [mo]derate. As a tooth-extractor Mr. Massey has no rival, his reputation [be]ing world-wide, his patients numbering many thousands annually. [H]is dental surgery is replete with every modern appliance, both for [ex]tractions, fillings, and the manufacturing and fitting of artificial teeth, [&c]., the excellence of which are not surpassed in the profession. In [sh]ort, Mr. Massey's devoted and personal attention to business, and [hi]s urbanity and gentleness of manner in the treatment of his patients, [ha]s gained for him the esteem and patronage of a large *clientèle* not [on]ly in Manchester but also in the surrounding towns.

G. Wolstenholme, Cigar Merchant, 26, Piccadilly.—[M]r. G. Wolstenholme is the proprietor of a large tobacconist's and cigar [bu]siness. The firm was established in 1819 by the present proprietor's [pr]edecessor, and has a first-class local trade. The shop is a large one, [we]ll fitted, and contains a valuable stock, in which may be noted princi[pa]lly the varied assortments of meerschaum, briar, and other pipes, and [th]e numerous articles that are requisite to the smoker's enjoyment. Mr. [W]olstenholme has controlled the business during the last twelve years, and [ha]s a very fine stock of cigars, some of the foreign brands being especially [ch]oice. The quantity of tobacco used in this country has greatly in[cre]ased of late years, and in regard to the use of the fragrant weed so [gr]eat an authority as Mr. Layard says that among Oriental nations the [us]e of tobacco has gradually reduced the resort to intoxicating beverages; [an]d Mr. Crawford, in a paper on the "History and Consumption of To[ba]cco," remarked that simultaneously with the decrease in the use of spirits in Great Britain there was a corresponding increase in the use of tobacco. Mr. Wolstenholme keeps in stock the popular kinds of packet tobaccos made by Lambert & Butler, Wills, Hignett's, B. Morris & Sons, and other first-class firms. The first-named firm especially are just now selling a really splendid class of shag, which surpasses almost any other kind of shag before the public. The trade done by Mr. Wolstenholme is large and increasing.

J. Morton & Co., Brace Manufacturers, Manchester. —Among the different branches of manufacture more or less connected with what are termed Manchester goods, a very important position is taken by that devoted to making braces, and various descriptions of bands. One of the principal firms thus engaged is that of Messrs. John Morton and Co., who for many years have been established in Manchester. The premises are of considerable size and are fitted in superior style, all the most modern and improved appliances and machinery incidental to the trade having been adopted. Messrs. Morton and Co. employ a large number of hands, who are busily employed in manufacturing goods of a very superior quality. In this respect the firm has acquired a wide-spread reputation, and thus commands a very extensive business among the leading wholesale firms in all parts. The stock on hand comprises many varieties of bands and braces that, for durability of material and make, are unsurpassed by any similar firm in the trade. A great proportion of the business is done locally, the firm being held in the highest estimation throughout the district. A large and important business is however conducted in all parts of the United Kingdom, and the connection is both widespread and important. The business is very ably conducted in every department.

Thos. Mawdsley, Joiner and Contractor, 11, Minshull Street.—The joinery business is a very important one, in which a man who can guarantee a high quality of workmanship and promptitude is sure to secure a fair amount of patronage and profit. Mr. Thos. Mawdsley is precisely the sort of workman to whom one would refer for superior workmanship and careful attention. Mr. Mawdsley succeeded to this business nine years ago, which was established thirty years since, and throughout this period has enjoyed a very fair share of success. He soon made it manifest on his arrival in the neighbourhood that all work taken in hand by him would be conscientiously and thoroughly carried out, with the result that he soon had as many demands upon his time and facilities as he could well cope with or satisfy. His joinery work is of a high order, and the exemplary manner in which he attends to contracts of almost every kind is creditable in the extreme. His concern is now a flourishing one, and affords a striking instance of what may be brought about by a determination to please the public, and indomitable energy in the direction of superiority of workmanship.

C. H. Cooper, Commercial and General Printer and Stationer, 52, George Street.—The various and manifold requirements of such a commercial city as Manchester, in all things pertaining to printing, open up a fine field for the operations of the energetic and competent printer. Such a tradesman is Mr. Chas. H. Cooper, who has been established, on his own account, since 1884, and has, by dint of merit and perseverance, rapidly taken a commanding position among those of this important craft. He has from his inception, in the commercial sense, occupied his present commodious premises, which are of extensive dimensions and well fitted with the necessary machinery and mechanical appliances for the conducting of such an exacting business. The connection enjoyed is very widespread and valuable, and lies chiefly among the leading business houses, hotels, and institutions of the city and district. Their orders and the casual trade secured are of such dimensions that a staff of experienced printers is continually engaged on all descriptions of printing. Invoices, circulars, cards, bazaar announcements, programmes, price lists, menus, memos, &c., are all executed in the best and most artistic style, and at the lowest remunerative prices. Mr. C. H. Cooper is a man personally much respected and esteemed for his promptitude and integrity in all business transactions.

M. C. Thomson & Co., Flax, Hemp, and Jute Spinners and Manufacturers, Importers of Russian and Italian Hemps, Flax, Tows, &c., 22, Dantzic Street, and at Glasgow, Dundee, Liverpool, and London. Works, Wardmill, Arbroath. Telegrams, "Rope, Manchester."—Of its class this well-known concern is one of the oldest and best in the neighbourhood. It has a substantial local connection, and enjoys in addition the advantages of a widespread trade. The firm was originally established by Mr. M. C. Thomson, who carried it on for a number of years in a most successful manner. Since the formation of the company it must be admitted that the business has decidedly increased. The company trade as flax, hemp, and jute spinners and manufacturers. The firm have always on hand a large and varied assortment of Russian and Italian hemp, flax, and jute yarns, sewing twines, bleached yarns, tarpaulin canvas, hessians, &c. The flourishing position of the company enables them to proffer their customers many exceptional advantages, their supply is invariably of the best description, and their prices by no means immoderate. Branches have been opened at Glasgow, Dundee, Liverpool, and London.

William Mitchell & Son, Painters, General Decorators, and Wholesale and Retail Dealers in Paper Hangings, 265, Stretford Road, Hulme. The firm of William Mitchell & Son was established in the year 1847. As painters, sign writers, general decorators, and wholesale and retail dealers in paper hangings, Messrs. Mitchell & Son occupy one of the first positions in the important city of Manchester. The present partners are William Mitchell and Francis Voltaire Mitchell, and under their personal supervision a very large staff of skilled workmen is employed, so that nothing but the very highest class of painting, decorating, and workmanship in the other branches connected with the trade is turned out. The premises wherein the business is carried on are extensive, and a very large and choice stock of goods incidental to the large trade carried on by this firm is always kept on hand. The Messrs. Mitchell are not only high-class tradesmen and large employers of labour, but are gentlemen universally respected throughout their district. Mr. William Mitchell was the founder of the firm, and in the year 1878 he took into partnership his son, Mr. F. V. Mitchell, since which time he has to a large extent ceased to take an active part in the management and conduct of the business, and has on several occasions been elected by his fellow-citizens to represent them on the Board of Poor Law Guardians, where his business qualities and well-known sound principles have secured a local reputation that will no doubt live long after him. Mr. F. Voltaire Mitchell's high reputation as an artist should not be allowed to pass without mention, and we feel sure that he will continue to uphold, and may probably enhance the already enviable position attained by this firm.

M. Corrigan. General Printer, 34, Shudehill. — This business has been established nearly half a century, and the firm is eminently respectable. The premises consist of a capital front shop with composing and machine room in the rear. The trade connection is very extensive and of old standing. Indeed, it is a noteworthy feature of the business that it still retains a very large percentage of its original customers. The working staff numbers many old and faithful servants, and a large proportion of highly skilled and experienced compositors. The firm enjoys a capital reputation for its excellent style of displayed work, and the good taste which is invariably manifested in the selection of type and the inks employed. A glance through the firm's pattern-book shows that Mr. Corrigan has from time to time been engaged upon most important jobs; that no class of work—commercial, book, pamphlet, newspaper, circular, price list, catalogue or poster—comes amiss; and that throughout all there is abundant evidence of careful supervision and precise attention to the instructions of customers. The head of the firm is much respected in the neighbourhood and by the Manchester section of the printing trades; and there are few charitable movements that he does not warmly and actively support.

S. Taylor, Hair Cutter, Wigmaker, and Perfumer, 26 & 28, King Street.—Few tradesmen can boast that their labours are more generally in requisition or more thoroughly appreciated than the competent hairdresser and wigmaker. To this useful and respectable body Mr. Samuel Taylor belongs. He started his business nearly forty years ago, and it requires no demonstration to win belief for the fact that he enjoys an extensive and valuable patronage. His premises are admirably located, fitted and arranged in a tasteful and substantial manner. There is no business in which the comfort of the customer is of greater importance, and this fact has been well realised by Mr. Taylor, for the interior of his establishment is furnished in the most complete and one might almost say luxurious fashion. The goods stocked are very varied in character, and suited in all respects to the high-class trade done. Wig-making of all kinds is conducted on the premises. In this line the patronage of the highest class is secured, and the same may be said of the choice assortment of fancy and toilet articles held. A sound business of a very select kind is transacted in all departments.

J. Brownhill & Co., Paper and Paper Bag Manufacturers and Printers, and Shop Fitters, 66 & 68, Thomas Street.—This business was founded in the year 1878, and its history is one of steady and continuous prosperity. The premises include a handsome well-fitted front shop of attractive appearance, and many spacious well-lighted workrooms in the rear. The main speciality of the business is paper-bag making and general shop and tradesmen's printing. In these departments the workrooms are supplied with a considerable amount of most excellent machinery, and many founts of modern and antique type. In addition, Messrs. Brownhill & Co. do a very considerable trade as paper-makers' agents and as shop window fitting manufacturers. In the latter connection they supply all kinds of wax figures, costume stands, brass brackets, and in fact every article required by shopkeepers for the proper display of their goods. The trade connection is both home and foreign, and includes many of the leading shipping firms of the city. Many travellers are employed, and their united journeys cover a large part of the United Kingdom. In the various workrooms numbers of skilled hands are employed, and the weekly wages list amounts to a very formidable total. A special feature of the operations of the house is the complete furnishing of shops of all kinds with trade fixtures, particular attention being given to milliners', clothiers', and hatters' requirements. The members of the firm are gentlemen of great experience in the business, and the whole of the work turned out is characterised by great taste and excellent judgment.

Mr. W. H. Savery, Ironmonger, &c., 46, Stretford Road.—The busy commercial centre known as Stretford Road can boast of few more successful concerns than this. It was established at 70, Downing Street in the year 1874 by Mr. John Lister, who was succeeded by Mr. William H. Savery in 1880, who brought with him the wide experience he had gained during the fourteen years he was with Mr. Lister; and in the eight years which have elapsed he has got together a large connection. The business premises are commodious and well adapted to the trade, which is that of a wholesale and retail ironmonger. In the shop there is an excellent and varied stock of London, Birmingham, and Sheffield goods, for which there is a large demand, and which Mr. Savery supplies at very moderate prices. In addition, an extensive trade is done in kitchen ranges, grates, stoves, boilers, and other articles of a similar character required by builders and cabinet-makers, who find themselves so well served by Mr. Savery that they are continually making demands on the large stock which he always has on hand. This is selected from the best manufactories, and every care is taken to ensure that the make and quality are such as will commend themselves to those who purchase them. Mr. Savery takes the greatest personal interest in the working of the establishment, and its success is due in great measure to the experience and knowledge which he can bring to bear on its management.

G. Siddall, Importer of Produce, 256, Oldham Road.—More than twenty-five years have elapsed since Mr. George Siddall established himself in Manchester as an importer of Irish and American produce, and during that period he has achieved an extensive and widespread success. Mr. Siddall's wholesale warehouse is situate at the above address, and is admirably fitted for the purpose it is intended to serve, being spacious and well lighted. It contains a very large stock of provisions of all kinds, imported from the leading manufacturers in Ireland and the United States, with whom Mr. Siddall has a very extensive connection. In bacon, butter, cheese, and other produce he is enabled to supply the English consumer with some of the best that can possibly be secured, and great confidence is placed in his experienced selection by a very large circle of wholesale and retail customers. Mr. Siddall has two other establishments—one at Coop Street Avenue, Smithfield Market, and the other at 109, Portugal Street, and the same may be said of them as of the Oldham Road Store, that every article offered to the public is of the most superior quality, warranted to be genuine, and placed in the market at the lowest possible price. Mr. Siddall has had a long experience in this particular business, and his strenuous endeavours to meet the requirements of the trade and of the public have been rewarded with a most gratifying amount of success.

Thomas Stensby, Gun Maker, 11, Hanging Ditch.—Founded as far back as the year 1810, this highly respectable firm maintains its acknowledged lead in the gun trade. During the whole of the eighty years of its existence the firm has retained the original address card—quite an old-fashioned work of art, so much so that a copy of it was introduced as one of the illustrations in the descriptive guide to "Old Manchester and Salford," Manchester Jubilee Exhibition, and extremely interesting when placed beside the cards printed in these days. It is needless to say that the bulk of Mr. Stensby's trade is in sporting guns, fitted with the latest improvements and inventions, though it appears that he even yet describes himself as a "Gun, Pistol, and Crossbow Maker." His premises consist of shop, offices, and various workrooms. As none but the very best work is turned out, only experienced hands are employed; and as Mr. Stensby is perhaps the best known man connected with the trade in the city, there is no need for the employment of travellers. In addition to sporting guns he has a large and varied assortment of rifles and revolvers of the newest patterns. Repairs of every description may also be entrusted to him, and all requisites for a shooting outfit may be obtained at his establishment.

William H. Rothery, Heraldic Engraver, 9, Corporation Street.—Mr. Rothery established himself at the above address in the year 1858, and has been very successful. The speciality of the business is heraldic designing and engraving; but Mr. Rothery also undertakes a good deal of general draughtsman's commissions. As heraldic engraver and designer of monograms, Mr. Rothery has been extremely successful. He is well posted in heraldry and its technicalities, and may be relied upon in all matters concerning crests and coats-of-arms. He is frequently commissioned to search for arms, crests, mottoes, and monograms. As general draughtsman, Mr. Rothery has few equals in this city, his work being invariably distinguished by genuine artistic merit. Mr. Rothery's professional connection includes a large portion of the North of England.

J. Smedley & Co., Wholesale Mantle and Skirt anufacturers, 1, Auburn Street, Piccadilly.—This business was esta- shed in the year 1874, at Temple Street, Chorlton-upon-Medlock, and rht years afterwards was removed to the present address. The premises nsist of a handsome building of five floors and basement, and includes pital warehouse, light, airy, well-ventilated work-rooms, and a fine ite of commodious offices, handsomely furnished and fitted with all the ost approved modern appliances for the rapid transaction of business. ie specialities of the firm are a superior class of ladies' jackets and lmans braided by patent machinery; and children's braided coats, and ibroidered aprons. The general goods include ladies' ulsters, satin, felt, oth, alpaca, and cashmere skirts. The trade connection is very large d widespread, the firm having agents in London and Glasgow. The orking staff numbers considerably over a hundred machinists indoors, d some forty or fifty out-door hands. The sole partners are the essrs. Smedley Brothers, both well-known gentlemen in Manchester mmercial circles, and both highly esteemed and respected.

W. Fearnley, Ladies' and Gentlemen's Hair Dresser, , King Street.—The hair-dressing business of Manchester is of consider- ile magnitude and in the hands of able and experienced men, who form highly-respected and energetic body. A thoroughly representative busi- ss in this trade is that of Mr. W. Fearnley, which was originally esta- ished in 1825 by Mr. Hughes. The present proprietor has been in ssession nearly twenty years. The premises occupied are of ample mensions, and comprise shop and hair-dressing saloons for ladies and ntlemen, the shop being well fitted up and containing a fine stock of ilet requisites, perfumery, &c. of the best quality. The hair-dressing loons are elegantly furnished with every possible appliance and appa- tus for the business carried on, and for the comfort and convenience of e customers. Mr. W. Fearnley is a most practical and experienced hair- esser, and he has a very lucrative connection of a high-class nature. e is well known in the trade as one of the most highly respected and fluential members, and he enjoys the esteem and confidence of the local mmunity.

A. Watson & R. Pilling, British Sports Outfitters, , Oxford Street.—Among the sporting industries of Manchester the well-known firm of Messrs. A. Watson & R. Pilling. This firm, cently established in Manchester, is now well known as the great use for supplying the lovers of cricket, lawn tennis, lacrosse, hockey, :., with all the necessary implements for the various games. They ve an immense assortment of bats, wickets, footballs, rackets, lacrosses, :., all of the very best construction, yet at most reasonable prices, and th every possible improvement, and being favourites with the best and ost renowned players, the firm have the exclusive right to supply the cessary goods to many of the leading clubs and colleges in and around anchester. In addition to which large consignments of their well- iown goods are dispatched to all parts of the globe. The principals are ill known, and enjoy a high reputation as professional cricketers, aying in all the leading matches in England. Mr. R. Pilling is known the most celebrated wicket keeper of his day, while Mr. A. Watson is ually well esteemed and remarked for his splendid bowling. The firm cupy fairly sized premises, and employ an adequate staff, while the siness operations are on a large and increasing scale. Both gentlemen e well known and highly respected.

M. Jackson, Hosier, 12, St. Ann's Passage.—The hosiery, ove, lace, &c., establishment of Margaret Jackson has been established der the same name for sixteen years, and has, during the whole time, en carried on in the same premises. These consist of a shop on ground or, and workrooms above, where an efficient staff is employed in the ecial class of manufacture of fancy work for which this firm is noted. well-selected stock is kept, and comprises all the latest novelties at fashion has made popular in this direction. The trade is not only ge so far as the immediate locality is concerned, but extends all er Lancashire and the district. It is also of the very highest class, ery thing dealt in being of the finest make obtainable. No similar siness in the city is held in greater repute, and the renown of the firm widespread.

John Sankey, Manufacturer of Matches, Washing ystal, &c., 10, Dale Street.—This business has been in active and ccessful operation for more than twenty years, and is now extremely ll known all over the northern half of the kingdom. The premises in le Street consist of a capital and spacious warehouse, thoroughly well uipped with all the latest and most approved appliances for the rapid spatch of business. The works, which are very extensive and cover a ge area, are located at Blackley, some three miles from the city. The iding specialities are "Sankey's Celebrated Matches," which are as ll known and appreciated in this city and district, as are Bryant and ay's in London. They are known under the names "Manchester," Successful," "Strike," "Brilliant Star," "Match Me" and "Absolute fety." Mr. Sankey also manufactures sparklers, match-flamers, and Derby fuses. Other departments are devoted to the production of Pickstone's, Rayson's, British, and Sankey's washing crystals, and the Quintessence dry soap. The trade connection, though for the most part local, includes almost every buyer in the city and surrounding districts. Mr. Sankey has no partners; but is himself entirely responsible for the successful carrying on of this important business.

Edmund Salmon, Shirt Manufacturer, Jersey Street Mill, Ancoats.—Mr. Edmund Salmon (who for some years was manager of a large manufacturing company) established a first-class business in Jersey Street Mill, Ancoats, for the manufacture of shirts, jackets, &c. Having had so many years' experience as the manager of a very extensive factory, this gentleman brought a great amount of ability to bear upon his own establishment, and now has a very important connection and a large trade. The premises occupied consist of a large room containing a number of machines, most of which are specially constructed for the purpose of shirt making. All these machines are worked by steam, and as there is a large and very efficient staff, a vast number of these articles are made. Mr. Edmund Salmon is sole proprietor of the firm, and personally manages the whole business. His long practical experience has been very valuable, and by his commercial ability he has made a very successful and thriving affair of this factory. Several travellers are engaged, and the trade is still rapidly increasing. A very large business is done in the manufacture of shirts, and in this branch of industry Mr. Salmon has acquired considerable fame both for quality of material and high class work.

J. H. Rosenberg & Co., Importers of Havanna Cigars, 16, Royal Exchange.—This business was established over forty years ago, under the same title. The shop is an extremely handsome one, and is fitted up in the very best possible manner. The principal speciality is the far-famed "Syrian Mixture," made up of a selection of fine tobaccos, blended with great skill and the nicest discrimination. The "Syrian Mixture" is perhaps the best-known mixture sold in this city, and its consumption is proportionately great. The stock of cigars is practically unrivalled, and there is no choice or reputed kind in existence which is not fully represented amongst the thousands upon thousands of boxes in the stock of this enterprising firm. The family of the Rosenbergs have been connected with the cigar trade in Manchester for over forty years, and no name is more highly esteemed or respected in the business. Messrs. J. H. Rosenberg & Co. employ several commercial travellers. The wholesale trade connection extends over the whole empire, and the turnover is very large indeed. The sole partner is Mr. Joseph Hertz Rosenberg, a gentleman who is justly held to be one of the very best judges of cigars to be found in the trade, and a thoroughly capable *homme d'affaires*.

James Hibbert, Hat Manufacturer, 55, Market Street.—This, the best known hatter's in the city, was established forty-five years ago, and has been located in the present premises some seventeen years. The business of the firm is purely retail, yet Hibbert's hats are sent all over the world. Mr. Hibbert early set himself to master the difficulties of hat manufacture—lightness, coolness, and perfect fit. His hats speedily became known and their merits fully appreciated. Until now there is no civilized country on the face of the globe from which Mr. Hibbert does not receive commissions during the course of the year. The premises were enlarged two years ago, and they are now the handsomest shop and sale-room of their class in the city.

E. Tranter, Cane and Wood Chair Manufacturer, 8 Mayes Street, and 10, North Street, Shudehill.—A very important branch of the furniture industry is the manufacture of chairs, and among the Manchester establishments engaged, a notable position is held by that of Mr. E. Tranter, which was originally established by Messrs. Tranter and Bennell in 1878. Mr. Edward Tranter is considered one of the most practical and experienced chair manufacturers in the city, and his efforts to improve the trade are worthy of imitation. The premises consist of a large commodious three-storied building utilised as works and warehouse, and fitted up with every possible appliance for carrying on the business. A large force of skilled hands are employed in manufacturing wood and cane chairs of every description, the specialties being smoking, bannister, rocking, and lath back chairs, fancy cane, ladies' rockers; also in ply veneer and patent velvet seating and ladder, Quaker and Cambridge backs in birch, mahogany, &c., and cherry arms and rockers, cherry Romans, and the Austrian bent wood chairs, &c. These goods are of the soundest workmanship, and every plank and spar of timber is tested and well seasoned before being used. A very extensive trade is done in the city and its vicinity, which by his efforts to meet the requirements of the trade is rapidly increasing. The premises at 10, North Street, are of ample extent, and comprise work-rooms and show-rooms, the latter well stocked with a selection of all sorts of chairs made by the firm. Mr. Edward Tranter is thoroughly proficient in all branches of the manufacture, and manages with enterprise and energy. He is well known by the many trade members, highly respected for his honour and integrity, and his house holds an honourable place in the furniture industry.

Henry Eaton, Wheelwright, &c., 102, Fairfield Street. —This business was established over fifty years ago in Dale Street, and received an immense impetus with the development of the railway goods traffic, as the firm managed to secure a large amount of work connected with the building and repairing of trollies, vans, and trucks. The premises in Dale Street were found too small for the large and increasing trade done by the firm, and twenty years ago the business was removed to larger and more commodious premises in Fairfield Street. These are very large, covering over an acre of land, and an enormous quantity of timber and other material is constantly in store. The principal work is the building of light and heavy vans, trollies, and floats, and vehicles especially adapted for the Manchester trade. The working staff numbers a very large contingent of skilled wheelwrights, coach-builders, &c., and the reputation of the firm for high-class work of its kind is not surpassed by any house in the kingdom. The sole proprietor is Mr. Henry Eaton, a gentleman most thoroughly and practically acquainted with every detail of the trade, a capital designer, and an experienced man of business. Mr. Eaton is well known in trade circles, and is much esteemed and respected.

Kenneth's High Class Fancy Goods, Jewellery, &c., 85, Market Street.—The fancy goods and jewellery trade of Manchester is one of the important and valuable business interests of the city, and many establishments are engaged therein. A very fine house, one of the most representative in the city, is that carried on by Mr. A. M. Barnicott, under the name of the original founder, T. R. Kenneth, which was originated fourteen years ago, falling two years later into the possession of the present proprietor. The shop is large, of handsome appearance, elegantly fitted up, and there is an extensive and splendid display of fancy goods and jewellery of every description, including ornaments, toilette sets, leather goods, dressing-cases, work-baskets, ivory goods, inkstands and desks, writing-table sets, fans, and other fashionable requisites and specialities. In art manufactures the specialities of the business are fans, albums, and French jewellery, the former articles being in great variety and of exquisite beauty and elegance; and the entire stock is an admirable summary of the one thousand nic-nacks of the fashionable world. The house is the depot for the celebrated Jumeau's Parisian dolls, and throughout the city a finer stock of fancy goods and jewellery cannot be seen. The presentation calendar, known as "Kenneth's," is a daintily got-up little book, and contains much valuable local information. Mr. Barnicott carries on a very fine trade of an influential character, and employs an ample staff of assistants who are most polite and attentive. He thoroughly understands the business, and is a gentleman of talent, strict integrity, and courtesy.

W. H. Prophet, Gentleman's Outfitter, 246, Deansgate.—This admirable business—one of the most compact, profitable, and best of its kind in the locality—was established in 1857, by the present proprietor, Mr. W. H. Prophet. The trade transacted is very valuable, the connection being very large. The different departments are conducted on the most approved lines, and the entire business carried on with the greatest ability. As a gentleman's outfitter, Mr. Prophet has achieved a wide and certainly well-deserved reputation for general and especial excellence. He affords his patrons the most careful attention, and the stock always in hand at his well-appointed establishment is an admirable and comprehensive one, invariably up to date. Orders are fulfilled without delay with all solicitude, and the charges made are based upon a scale that has the pre-eminent advantage of being particularly moderate.

Bamber & Rowe, Cheese Factors, 30, Withy Grove.—This firm, although established but five years ago, has already acquired a large and valuable connection. As cheese factors they keep a large and well-selected stock from all the best known Cheshire dairies, and are noted for several choice kinds from the United States and Canada, the principal trade being confined to Cheshire cheese. Besides this important branch of business, Messrs. Bamber & Rowe have latterly added departments for general provisions, and they have usually on offer an excellent selection of all these goods. The premises are well situated for the provision trade. The warehouse and stores have ample accommodation for a large trade, and the offices are convenient, well arranged, and handsomely furnished. The firm has a branch business in the thriving town of Preston. The sole partners are Mr. Bamber and Mr. Rowe, both experienced gentlemen in the provision trade, each having a special knowledge of a department and an excellent reputation as buyer. Both Messrs. Bamber and Rowe are well known at the various cheese fairs, and are as highly esteemed for their many good qualities as for their keen business abilities.

Edmondsons & Co., General Hardware Merchants, 144, Princess Street, Old Garrett.—This business has been established about fifty years, having been founded by the late Mr. Edmondson. The premises in Princess Street have been in the occupation of the firm some four years only, the business having been previously carried on for fifteen years or more in Sackville Street, and before that at the factory in Charles Street, Old Garratt. At Princess Street Messrs. Edmondson & Co. confine their attention to a general hardware factoring trade, and their connecti lies chiefly amongst railway companies, mine owners, engineers, a machinists. They employ several commercial travellers and an effici staff of clerks and assistants. The trade connection of this department extremely extensive and wide-spread, and the reputation of the fi stands very high. The present partners are Mr. Thomas Edmondson a Mr. F. E. Bracewell. Each of these gentlemen is well skilled in all t details of screw manufacture, and has had a long experience in the tra The firm are looked upon as liberal employers, and are most high respected and esteemed.

The Spread Eagle Hotel, Corporation Street.—T Spread Eagle Hotel is one of the principal and most interesting featu of the locality. It has a history that extends back to the time of t great civil war that agitated the country some two hundred and fo odd years ago. At the present time it is in a position to compete wi the best of the modern hotels from every point of view. The pres proprietor has held possession of the Spread Eagle for a period of abo twelve years, and the enterprise he has shown in catering for the publ and the pains he has taken in order to render his place deserving of wide and generous patronage, are deserving of the highest prai He supplies travellers and visitors with every possible convenience, a eaters alike, and in the same satisfactory manner, for the middle and t upper classes of the community. He supplies the best attendance a excellent general accommodation at a remarkably moderate figure. I premises, which, it is almost unnecessary to add, are fitted up with eve modern improvement, will well repay a visit. The reputation of t hotel is a sound one, and the proprietor is careful to deserve and prese the same.

E. Wilson, Milliner, 22, St. Ann's Square.—This we known and extensive millinery business, with its handsome shop and sho rooms, has been conducted by Miss E. Wilson for upwards of six ye at its present address. During this time Miss E. Wilson has succeed by great taste and skill in adjusting materials and colours, by alwa having intelligence of the newest fashions, and by indefatigable applic tion to business, in obtaining an enviable degree of reputation and suppo All the newest designs and the latest fashions are to be seen displayed the greatest advantage in Miss E. Wilson's capacious and well-light show-rooms, which are daily frequented by not a few of the *élite* of the Ci Miss E. Wilson numbering amongst her patronesses the ladies of some the best families in Lancashire. Miss E. Wilson, in addition to devoti that amount of personal attention and skill to business which is at all tin the surest guarantee of its proper execution, employs a large staff of t most experienced modistes that are to be procured, and is, therefore, every way in a position to execute orders in such a style as is calculated r merely to give present satisfaction, but a continuance of support and extension of that reputation which her establishment now so deserved enjoys.

Wm. Willis, Wholesale Dealer in Smallwares, 4 Shudehill.—Among the many merchants in the city devoted to the tra in smallwares, not one holds a more prominent place than that occupi by Mr. William Willis, whose well-known depôt is one of the features Shudehill. The firm was established in 1812 by a person of the na of Downes, at 6, Shudehill, where, until recently, it was conducted Mr. Willis. The shop at present occupied is of very spacious dime sions and affords ample room for storage, which in such a business a consideration of the first importance. Mr. Willis's place is stocked the very ceiling with all sorts of haberdashery, smallware, wools, hosie stationery, toys, Carr's ladder tape, electro-plate, brushes, boot-lac pins, needles, and hundreds of other useful items for domestic and otl purposes. In all these a trade of very great extent is done all over t country, but particularly in all parts of the city. A very brisk busin is transacted throughout the entire day, many customers being in the dep at once. The goods are of the best quality, remarkably cheap, and being sold are promptly dispatched. Mr. Willis, who is a member of t Board of Guardians, possesses all the qualifications of a first-class bu ness man, and is much respected locally.

E. & S. Warburton, Tea Merchants, 24, Withy Grov —The firm of Messrs. Warburton (trading as E. & S. Warburto tea merchants, is one of very old and reputable standing. It w established some thirty-nine years ago, and now occupies a premi position in the tea trade. The business carried on is to a great exte confined to the locality, and in this particular alone the firm enjo a first-class connection, but orders are received from all parts of t country. The quality of the merchandise offered by Messrs. Warburt has always been of a first-class character, and still retains its reputatio The most careful supervision is exercised, and every care is taken that customer shall have the slightest excuse for complaint. On the premis every courtesy is shown to customers, while all outside orders a promptly attended to. There is a uniform moderation in prices throug out this establishment, and value for money is always given.

Costume Manufacturer,
chester, as in every large com-
costumes, in fact, every article
lustry, and the trade therein is
large number of recently estab-
is that of Mr. Robert Lomas,
has attracted and secured a very
e basis of a trade which promises
he premises are large and com-
al building, with a handsome
with every requisite for the dis-
on of the business. The stock
antles, costumes, millinery, and
ls and in the latest and most
dly employs the best hands, and
prices, polite assistants, skilful
naterials and trimmings to select
usiness, and the convenience of
manner. A very good trade is
s extending to very considerable
t 16, Boar Lane, Leeds, and is
al towns as opportunities arise.
nd enterprise, and is well known
fair to become one of the most

r of the Highest Class
Positions and Temperatures
Mr. McFerran makes four classes
, viz.:—

. . . . .	£2 10
lever, at . . .	£5 0
at.	£7 0
carat, at . . .	£10 0

one of W. McFerran, Manches-
ock largely consists of the finest
in silver ranging up to £12, and
cFerran, who was established in
nd turret clocks. He is railway
, Great Northern, South York,
lines, and supplies the leading
for all kinds of public clocks.

l Die-Sinker, 78, Faulkner
ntinues to occupy the important
ago, and its history is one of
ises consist of a capital shop of
ighted, and commodious work-
ufacture are rubber stamps used
oor and window plates in brass,
branding-irons, seals, dies, and
n addition, Mr. Clarke keeps in
other inks in various colours;
s; a variety of the new rubber-
in which they are used. Mr.
otion of indiarubber stamps to
ving an impression. The trade
s most of the large firms of the
y of the country manufacturers
ness houses that do not occasion-
anufactured or sold by the firm.
he export houses. The working
experienced working engravers
tional talent as a designer is of
rke has no partner; he is consid-
l business man. It may be added
er stamps for the "Manchester
eral satisfaction to all concerned.

Blinds, 4, Long Millgate.
ularity which has attended the
ral use in this country has made
ortant branch of industry, and
l in it in this city is Mr. James
ent is admirably located. Here,
, is to be found an assortment
able for all business or domestic
e and finish, and in the case of
and favourite designs are dis-
l sizes, from the best quality of
he most approved and reliable
ighteen years with Mr. James
ss, in the same locality, brings
cal experience. All contracts are
sion, and upon terms which are
y of the article and workmanship

is taken into consideration. Thanks to the popularity which the concern has acquired in these respects, Mr. Coates has a very large and widespread connection in all parts of the town and country, and the success and prosperity of his undertaking are being daily increased

Frederick J. Merryweather, Men's, Boys', and Youths' Clothier, 126 and 128, Chapel Street, Salford.—The clothing trade of Manchester, as might be imagined from the huge population, is of immense value, and provides employment, directly and indirectly, for thousands of hands. A thoroughly representative house in this line is that of Mr. Frederick J. Merryweather, which for thirty-six years has enjoyed the esteem and favour of the public. The premises occupied are large and commodious, of very attractive appearance, and are fitted up in a most suitable and superior manner, to meet the requirements of the trade. The stock, which is admirably arranged, is very extensive, and consists of clothes in the latest and most fashionable styles, for men, youths, and boys, and these goods are of splendid quality, newest pattern and material, and are of unexcellable workmanship. Mr. Fred. J. Merryweather's knowledge of the trade enables him to secure the most perfect clothing as regards style and quality, and his sound judgment prevents him from overstocking. Thus his goods are always new from the factory. The trade carried on by this energetic clothier is very heavy, of a local and good-class character, and its manufacture provides employment for seventy hands. Mr. Fred. J. Merryweather is a gentleman of undoubted business aptitude and experience, honourable and genial to the highest degree, and he enjoys the confidence of the public.

Thomas Hallam, Saw Manufacturer and Tool Maker, 40, Thomas Street, Shudehill.—This business has been in successful operation since the year 1855, and is at the present time one of the best known in its own line in the city or neighbourhood. The premises include a capital shop, with warehouse and workshop in the rear. The premises are neatly fitted up and substantially furnished. The trade is both wholesale and retail. The speciality is best quality band and circular saws. Of the former the French make are perhaps the most esteemed, as the temper of these goods is as nearly perfect as possible, and is generally considered superior to any of English make. Mr. Hallam, with the view of accommodating all requirements, keeps a large stock of the best quality French band saws, which he supplies at prices varying from tenpence to thirty-three pence per yard, according to width. All classes of saws are re-toothed, set, sharpened, hammered, and trued up. Mr. Hallam has also a capital stock of joiners' and cabinet-makers' tools, augers, braces, bits, files, planes, rules, &c., table and pocket cutlery. The connection is very extensive, and includes customers in both town and country. The sole proprietor is Mr. Hallam, the founder of the firm, assisted by his son, a gentleman of great experience in the tool trade, and a thoroughly clever business man.

Matthew Jackson & Co., Hosiers, Haberdashers, and Trimming Merchants, 218 and 220, Stretford Road.—In the ranks of the retail establishments of Manchester a leading position is held by the concern belonging to Matthew Jackson & Co., where they have been established for the last twenty years, and do a trade of very great value and widespread extent. The premises are extensive, arranged and fitted with taste and skill, and stocked with every class of goods of all qualities in the lines to which the house is devoted. Fringes, gimps, ornaments, buttons, haberdashery, smallwares, knitting yarns, silks, satins, velvets, ribbons, and fur trimmings; laces, lace collarettes, embroideries, collars, handkerchiefs, silk squares and scarves, mob caps, ladies' aprons, frillings, hosiery, and gloves; fur capes, boys' suits and jersey jackets, with hosts of other kinds of articles in constant demand among the residents and frequenters of the important locality in which the business is situated. A staff of competent hands is employed, and the concern is managed with that ability, energy, and regularity for which Manchester houses bear such eminent repute. Mr. Jackson and his partner are both personally very able and persevering in all enterprises demanding tact and judgment, and are very much esteemed by their employés, *clientèle*, and the public generally.

W. H. Bridge, Wholesale Druggist and Drysalter, 50, Oldham Road.—An important place among the many businesses of Manchester is held by the drug and drysaltery trade by reason of its magnitude and value. A fine business in this line is that of Mr. W. H. Bridge, which was founded eight years ago. The shop is of ample dimensions, of attractive appearance, and is heavily stocked with drugs and drysaltery of every description and of the utmost purity and reliability. Mr. W. H. Bridge also deals in white lead, oils, paints, colours, and varnishes of every description, wood naphtha, methylated spirit, finish, shellacs, gums, glues, &c., and these goods are of superior quality. He carries on a very considerable wholesale and retail trade, employs an efficient staff, and he manages with unusual ability and untiring energy. In every sense Mr. W. H. Bridge is a genuine business man, enjoying universal esteem and confidence, and of very high status in the drug and drysaltery trade of Manchester.

Vegetarian Restaurants Co., 5, Fountain Street.—This Vegetarian Restaurant is by far the most superior thing of its kind we have seen. The billiard, smoke, and reading-rooms, plentifully supplied with newspapers, periodicals, chess, draughts, &c., help to make the restaurant a pleasant resort. It is highly thought of by some of Manchester's best citizens, as a counter attraction to places where young men are tempted to spend in a manner beyond their means, and sometimes acquire habits which are undoubtedly bad, and end in ruin. The directorate have made special efforts to meet the wants of young men of the commercial and professional classes. Whether vegeterianism is popular or not, there can be little doubt about the success of the well-known Vegetarian Restaurants Co., Limited, established in 1884. The fact that about twenty-one hands are employed proves that whether the public believe in the principle or not, they like the fare that is provided. There could hardly be a better recommendation for the system than the success this Company has achieved. One great reason for this may be the handsome manner in which the premises are fitted up, containing as they do, in addition to the ordinary dining-rooms, handsomely furnished billiard, reading, and smoke-rooms, lavatories, &c. Another reason is the great ability shown in the management by Mr. Frederick Harrison, who is responsible for the control of everything. This gentleman has succeeded in making an immense business of this establishment, and in studying the wishes of the public and catering for them in the first-class manner shown in this company's premises, has done much for the cause of vegetarianism. In addition to the chief restaurant, with its dining-rooms, lecture-hall, reading-room, billiard-room, &c., there is a small place, the Fountain Restaurant, No. 1, Meal Street, under the same management, where a dinner of three courses is supplied for sixpence, with every advantage of cleanliness and pleasant service. All kinds of methods seem to be adopted to dispense with flesh meat. Breakfasts, luncheons, dinners, made of almost everything in the vegetable world, and in every variety of manner are to be found, and, after all, it must accord with the taste of a great many people, or the Vegetarian Restaurants Co. would not be doing such an enormous trade, have gained such a business, and have such an excellent reputation.

Warbrick & Co., Manufacturers of Improved Fast Pile Velveteens, Dress Satins, &c., 34, Charlotte Street.—As a source of supply for pile velveteens, dress satins, &c., Manchester has been long noted, and in the trade and manufacture many firms are engaged. A well-known firm engaged in this way is that of Messrs. Warbrick & Co., which was originated by the present members in 1877. Messrs. Warbrick & Co. bear an excellent name as manufacturers of improved fast pile velveteens, and they have brought all their productions to the highest state of perfection. The premises occupied consist of a floor of a commodious building, admirably fitted up for the business carried on, and heavily stocked with improved fast pile velveteens, dress satins, &c. These goods are manufactured by skilful hands, and by modern machinery on the most approved methods; and their distinguishing features are beauty and gloss of texture, quality of material, and durability. Excellent in every detail are these goods, and Messrs. Warbrick & Co. carry on a very valuable local and shipping trade, which, owing to their able management, is increasing in a most gratifying manner. An ample staff is employed, and the organization of the business results in the heaviest orders being dispatched with promptitude. The members of the firm, Messrs. G. H. Warbrick and W. H. Hallworth, are gentlemen who have devoted great talent to, and displayed much inventive power in, their manufacture, and their efforts have been eminently successful. They are well known in the industrial and commercial world, and are deeply esteemed for their sterling qualities, whilst their house, in the velveteen manufacture, holds an important place.

Mr. Harry Clegg, Photographic Artist, 12, Stretford Road.—This well-known home of photographic art is one of the most popular and successful which the city of Manchester can boast. Established so recently as 1884, it has made such rapid progress in public estimation that it takes rank with the oldest and best of its class. Its handsome and well-appointed premises, suitably situated, form a most attractive feature in a busy and well-known thoroughfare. Half a dozen large and commodious saloons are devoted to the business, and in these the principal, Mr. Harry Clegg, has arranged a remarkable collection of specimens of his art. Life-size portraits, cabinet photographs, and cartes-de-visite are ranged round the saloons in wonderful profusion. All the necessary appliances are of the newest and most approved character. The adoption, too, of the latest discoveries in the science of photography, renders it possible for portraits to be taken in any weather or at any hour of the day or night. Infants and children are made an especial study, and the numerous splendid examples of juvenile portraiture which are on view show how well Mr. Clegg succeeds in this somewhat difficult department. A very large staff of travellers are engaged in various parts of the country, and the success of their labours is shown in the vast amount of other than local business which the firm transacts. Mr. Clegg, the proprietor, is a gentleman who has made an earnest study of every branch of the photographic art. He has himself served under the best of masters, and the experience he has thus acquired is solely devoted to a studio which is second to none in the whole city.

Geo. Henderson, Dra
the most extensive, importan
that of drapery, and the c
numerous. A fine business in
which was originally founded
carried it on for sixteen year
proprietor. The shop occupi
superior and substantial man
goods, fancy and staple. The
and the selection reflects great
to his trade knowledge and j
business of a high-class natu
admirable manner. Mr. Geo.
is highly respected, and his
popular with the local commun

J. A. Littlewood, Fasl
Salford, and 29, Regent Roa
naturally causes the clothing a
siderable magnitude, and the
have wrought it to its high sta
business in this trade is afford
has been established for severa
the trade, elegantly and compl
stock of ready-made clothing
latest and most fashionable s
The order department is in exc
of cloths, &c. from the best ma
selection of the customers, and
and experienced, and under the
wood. Mourning orders are
effort is made to meet the con
Littlewood carries on a very l
connection of good class charac
respected, Mr. J. A. Littlewoo
the community.

Peace & Norquoy, Joi
—This firm was established c
by its founders. The premis
store-rooms, large workshops,
numbers between forty and
quently doubled or trebled acc
In addition to the ordinary w
Norquoy have a very importa
house, office, and shop-fitter
including all branches of the l
trade in erecting hoardings fo
The works are fitted with mode
and grooving mills, and a lar
available. The two partners
fully experienced builders, and
accounted liberal employers, a
the latest schemes of technical

Thomas Slater, Brus
Place.—This concern has been
one of the oldest of the kind
menced by Mr. Joseph Slater,
the present well-appointed and
by Mr. Thomas Slater for the
industry is a very interesting
his own make, and, besides t
baskets and articles of a sim
Mr. Slater are remarkably mod

J. U. Hallam, Stamp
Gardens.—Stamp-making and
industry, and of a useful and
trade is of considerable extent,
of Mr. J. U. Hallam. It was
1880, and in 1884 came into th
occupied the present premises
modious, fitted throughout wit
trade, and the hands employe
turned out are of excellent wor
and healthy in design, and in e
U. Hallam has a fine connecti
leading companies, public bodi
of Manchester having been de
every branch of the trade Mr.
he is looked upon as a gentlem
honour. He is well known an
trade, and his house is a most i
and industrial world.

Tea Merchants, &c., 17,
industries of Manchester and
rtant branch which relates to
presentative centre is the well-
rooke, Bond & Co., Wholesale
eful housewives buy their tea
know that neither merchant,
ber gain a living off the teas
uence about their article that
. sell an uncorrupted *leaf* tea
ale in this tea, but they do not
the finest and rarest tea in the
, and good. Their 2/- tea is a
money by sending to Brooke,

Brooke, Bond & Co.'s doesn't
low: it means best for least
. Brooke, Bond & Co.'s most
spring leaves of the choicest
choicest beverages, lies in their
sumptuous tea sold by Messrs.
nd most exquisite fragrance,
the wild violet. This it is—
ut of the sunny Orient—which
to this superb tea. Through
ylon tea is now highly popu-
and the North of England.
s, of unequalled strength, free
it may be truly said that the
tea of that incomparable land.
Ceylon tea at 2/- and 2/8 per
same prices by their agents.
pplications for their tea agency
tioners, bakers, and others; a
agents are making substantial
. Prospectus and samples are
d leaf tea is sold at 1/4 per lb.,
most sumptuous tea at 2/8 per
and may be had of accredited

Contractor, Jersey Street,
with increasing trade and popu-
and new buildings, the masonry
nch of industry, and in Man-
a heavy business, is in a high
. to much skilled and unskilled
tion is that of Mr. Isaac Kirk-
bout twenty-five years. The
us, comprising two yards (with
, and offices, the yards contain-
e business. The workshops are
pliances and convenience, and a
employed. Mr. Isaac Kirk-
acts in the city and vicinity.
the business, and Mr. Isaac
xcellence of his work, and the
Mr. Isaac Kirkham's resources
ions at the shortest notice, and
skilled workmen in the city.
ets and builders, &c. Mr. I.
he high standard of his work.
terling qualities

A. Steel, Dealer in Curiosities, "Old Curiosity Shop," 111, Deansgate.—The subject of this notice, Mr. A. Steel, has been in business in Manchester for over thirty years, so that he is a gentleman thoroughly well known in the city. The establishment has not been founded for any lengthened period, nevertheless it has acquired great notoriety, and is familiar to the residents and others as the "Old Curiosity Shop." It would be impossible for us to give a full list of the articles which comprise Mr. Steel's miscellaneous stock. First on the list come diamonds and precious stones of all kinds, some of them being of great value. Next, gold and silver articles, of almost every description, both ancient and modern, watches both complicated and ordinary, old and rare coins in gold, silver, and other metals. Ancient guns and fire-arms of all sorts. Watches and clocks of home and foreign manufacture, both ancient and modern. Optical goods of every kind. Opera glasses, field glasses, telescopes, &c. Musical instruments of every conceivable make, both English and foreign. Bronzes of all descriptions. Pictures in great variety. Magic lanterns and other kindred articles. All the foregoing may very properly be classified as specialities, since Mr. Steel does more in these various wares than perhaps any other house in the north of England and he buys to an almost unlimited extent. He does an extensive trade, too, in pebble spectacles, and we believe he is able to supply the real genuine article of his own manufacture, at the remarkably low figure of 3s. 6d., which is under one-quarter the usual market price. Mr. Steel purchases curiosities of all kinds, and much of his stock at Deansgate is made up of second-hand wares of a rare and valuable description. He is a buyer of old gold and silver, jewellery, diamonds, coins, guns, pianos, medals, and in fact of all second-hand goods which are kindred to his business. He is an *importer* of diamonds, and other precious stones and *gems*, as well as a dealer, and is one of the best connoisseurs of such articles in the kingdom. His business at Deansgate is for the most part local, but we may observe that he has a wholesale emporium at 8, Thomas Street, where he carries on a large and important trade with clients in all parts of the country. At this establishment, (which has been opened about seven years), he keeps—in addition to other goods and merchandise—all kinds of tools and materials used by watchmakers, jewellers, &c., and they are of the best possible quality and make. As will naturally be supposed, Mr. Steel's business, taken altogether, is a most extensive one, and it is only bare justice to that gentleman to say that it is conducted with tact and ability, and upon the most straightforward and honourable lines, and his commercial reputation is of the first order. He is universally esteemed in Manchester and the district, where he has been engaged in business for a great many years, and he occupies a position in the city of which any citizen might well feel proud.

Madame Lillie, Corsetière and Ladies' and Children's Outfitter, St. Ann's Place, St. Anne's Square.—A special department of clothing that has of late years assumed very considerable dimensions is that of ladies' and children's underclothing. No longer carried on so generally in connection with other branches of trade, this particular class of business now occupies a separate existence in the world of commerce. One of the oldest businesses in this line is now in the hands of Madame Lillie, and is located in a good-sized shop and large show-rooms, with fitting, stock, and workroom above. Madame Lillie trades generally as ladies' and children's outfitter in this special department of dress, embracing as it does babies' clothing and millinery for children. The chief feature of the business, and that for which it has been noted for fifty years, is the sale of French and English made corsets, of which there is a first-class stock. Madame Lillie has only taken over the business during the last three years, but in that time has achieved a first-class reputation. Both the articles of French and English manufacture are characterized by the best skill in the make and the quality of the material, and many artistic designs and improvements have been introduced.

Heaton Bros., Tailors, 15, Old Millgate.—Messrs. Heaton Bros. have established an excellent business as tailors and outfitters. Though it has been in existence only about twelve months, still it has already made a very good name in the neighbourhood and does an extensive trade. At the premises in Old Millgate there are several hands engaged, all of whom are specially selected for the work of bespoke tailoring, to which branch this firm is almost entirely devoted. Messrs. Heaton Bros. have gained considerable praise for their special workmanship, and not only in this, but in every branch of the trade, are giving great satisfaction and thriving well

W. Dunkerley, jun., & Co., Butter and Egg Merchants, 76, Corporation Street, Manchester. The well-known firm of W. Dunkerley, jun., & Co., have a widespread reputation. It was established in 1877. The career of this concern is a record of enterprise, good and consistent management, and success. The trade carried on in connection with the importation of Danish, Kiel, and French butter, MARGARINE, and Continental EGGS is large. Their consignments of eggs are of the best quality and specially selected, the particular brands of these commodities dealt in being very popular. They also hold agencies for Dutch mixtures and Margarines, which are rapidly coming into great demand. The premises occupied are fitted up suitably for the business requirements, being really more a sale-room than for storage, most of the goods being forwarded direct from port of arrival to customers. They have been occupied over ten years, and are well stocked with samples of the various commodities dealt in. The admirable manner in which W. Dunkerley, jun., and Co., conduct their concern ensures satisfaction to their customers. Their punctuality and carefulness in attending to orders are deserving of high commendation, and the business is worthy of the most generous patronage and support. The registered trade-mark is D U X, each letter in a star, and the telegraphic address is "DUXENS," Manchester.

Mrs. Cangney, Practical Shirt Maker, Hosier, and Glover, 94, Deansgate.—In all great centres of population, the trade in shirt making, hosiery, and glove manufacture is one of considerable extent and value. It is so in Manchester, where the demand for articles in these lines is very great. It is in this class of trade that Mrs. Cangney is engaged. She has her head-quarters in one of the leading positions in the city, 94, Deansgate. The premises are attractive in appearance, large and commodious, and afford every facility for the transaction of an extensive business. Mrs. Cangney began operations about six years ago, and, though this is not a very long period in which to push one's business on the broad way to success, she has succeeded in doing so. A fine show is made of all kinds of shirts, which are made under the direct supervision of Mrs. Cangney; Oxford, dress, and fancy wools, &c., for night use; gloves and hosiery are also stocked in great variety and abundance, and altogether the establishment is neatly arranged, smartly managed, and enables Mrs. Cangney to do a growing and profitable trade on the ready cash principle.

Sherwood & Co., Accountants and Mercantile Agents, Bow Chambers, 55, Cross Street.—The utility and importance of the mercantile agency and accountancy business in a large industrial and commercial city like Manchester cannot be overrated, and it is of considerable magnitude and in able and energetic hands. A young and promising business in this line is that known as Messrs. Sherwood & Co. (Mr. Thomas Sherwood being the only member), the "Lancashire, Cheshire, and South Yorkshire Mercantile Offices," which were founded between one and two years ago. Mr. Thomas Sherwood, however, has in this short time built up a very good business, which is rapidly extending, and he is winning golden opinions from all. The offices are large and commodious, furnished in a complete and superior manner, and bear every evidence of prosperity. Mr. Thomas Sherwood undertakes all kinds of mercantile commissions, accountancy work, debt collecting, and he has a thorough knowledge of the industries of the country and the leading markets. He carries out all transactions in an admirable manner, promptly and efficiently, and these qualities and his honourable methods and courtesy are rapidly increasing his connections. Mr. Sherwood is well known in business circles, and is highly respected, and the general opinion is that his house is a "coming" concern.

S. Burman, Watchmaker, 41, Oldham Street.—This well-known and important business has been established upwards of fourteen years. The premises are of splendid appearance, and the enterprise and public spirit of the proprietor are seen in the magnificent clock erected on the outside of the shop. This admirable specimen of the work turned out of Mr. Burman's manufactory is a conspicuous object in the neighbourhood. It is in direct communication with Greenwich, and a time-ball mounted upon a pole falls exactly at one o'clock. The stock is an unrivalled display of gold and silver jewellery and plate, presentation and other valuable watches, chains, pins, rings, &c. There are some fine marble and gilt time-pieces, and English, French, and the best descriptions of American clocks. Amongst this portion of the stock are many specimens of the ingenious combination time-pieces that have of late become so fashionable. Mr. Burman is a gentleman of great practical skill and experience. His connection is of the highest class, and his capable judgment and perfect knowledge of his business make his advice and opinion exceptionally valuable.

Mr. Cox's Antique Art Repository, 26, Cathedral Yard.—All lovers of art, and especially collectors of the antique, should pay a visit to the handsomely stocked and attractive repository of Mr. Cox. Those who have not before seen the place and interested themselves in the contents of this fine and large collection will find a new and most pleasant experience. Mr. Cox, the courteous and enterprising proprietor, has been established no less than twenty years. He has during this period achieved a widespread reputation among collectors as an authority whose judgment may safely be relied upon. The stock he has always on hand is of the very best description; he thoroughly understands all multifarious niceties of his business, and is in a position to afford patrons many exceptional advantages; and Mr. Cox is to be congratulated upon the result of his painstaking efforts to deserve well of public, who cannot do better than pay him a visit and inspect the numerous and varied works of art always on view.

J. Child & Sons, Perfumers, 5, King Street, & 166, Brunswick Street.—The trade in perfumery in this country is of consider importance and extent, and as a branch of commerce is a sourc national revenue. The manufacture during recent years has gre improved, the cost of production lessened, and the demand increa Manchester does a very good business in this direction, and among establishments engaged in this trade a prominent place is occupied those of Messrs. J. Child & Sons, which were founded seven years The shop at 5, King Street, is spacious and of elegant appearance, ha the advantage of a splendid corner situation, and is fitted and furni in a superior manner, with every appliance for the display of the s and the convenience of patrons. The stock is very large and comp comprising the choicest and costliest perfumes and every requisite of toilet, the articles being too numerous to particularise. It will suffic say that everything is of the best quality and from the leading ma facturers and importers. Messrs. J. Child & Sons enjoy a most influe connection among the gentry and upper classes of Manchester an vicinity, and they also own another establishment at 166, Brunswick St also in the most perfect order, besides one at West Street, Black Messrs. J. Child & Sons are thoroughly proficient in this most impor business, and manage with enterprise and ability. They are in e respect able and influential citizens, and their business is justly sidered one of the most superior in the city.

J. R. Taylor, Expert and Picture Restorer, 15, Bra nose Street.—In a wealthy city like Manchester, famous as it is fo liberal patronage of art, and numbering amongst its citizens many a known collector of pictures, the presence of an expert and really cl picture restorer is nothing less than an absolute necessity. S wonder then that Mr. J. R. Taylor is held in such high est and his opinion so eagerly sought in cases of doubtful authenticit works of art. Succeeding his father, Mr. John Taylor, who establi the business fifty years ago, the present proprietor has so far gained confidence of picture buyers that his *dictum* is accepted unquestione buyers and dealers alike; while the skill he has acquired in pi lining and restoring renders his assistance invaluable to possesso private galleries. Mr. Taylor is thoroughly acquainted with the s and manner of the different masters, their analogists and imita and through his hands have passed some of the most important ex ples in this part of the country—matchless paintings, some ever almost priceless worth, in the Italian, Spanish, Flemish, Dutch, Fre and English schools. All the public institutions here that pictures have engaged Mr. Taylor's services. Picture lining and re ing, and transferring ancient pictures from panel to canvas, which requ great judgment, are carried out as follows: The surface of the pic has a paper, or paper and gauze, pasted over it, so as to perfectly se the paint itself. The picture is then turned face downwards. The w marked like a chessboard, is sawn carefully until it arrives at the gro on which the picture itself has been painted, and is then rubbed d with pumice-stone, &c., until there at last remains nothing but the shell of paint which constitutes the picture, and which must the secured by composition and heated irons—which are made for the p pose—to a strong canvas. Sometimes it is found necessary to fasten additional canvas, which is known as double lining. Mr. Taylor ha extremely valuable collection of choice pictures, which intending p chasers would do well to inspect.

A. P. Towle & Son, Manufacturers of Chlorodyne, 75, Back Piccadilly.—The manufacture of chlorodyne is one of the important branches of the pharmaceutical trade of Manchester, a well-known firm engaged therein is that of Messrs. A. P. Towle & S originally founded by Mr. Alexander Pearson Towle forty years ago, now carried on by himself and son. The Messrs. Towle & Son are as the proprietors and manufacturers of the well-known "TOWL CHLORODYNE," which they have made for the last twenty-seven ye chlorodyne jujubes, chlorodyne lozenges, liquor chlorodyni, and "Thornton's preparations for the hair." The great demand for t remedies testifies to their merits. Messrs. Towle & Son carry on a extensive trade, produced mainly through a large and wisely arran system of advertising. Their goods are sent to North and South Ame Australia, and India, the chlorodyne being peculiarly efficacious cholera, diarrhœa, dysentery, ague, and spasms, also for throat, ch and lung affections in cold or damp climates. Messrs. Towle & manage their business with ability and enterprise, and they are thoro masters of their calling. Their preparations are universally popular their sterling qualities, and are so uniform in strength and excellen quality that they have gained the confidence of both doctors and public, to such a degree that a large number of imitations have arise every town. Hence it is necessary to ask for and see that you TOWLE'S CHLORODYNE. This firm showed their preparation the Manchester Royal Jubilee Exhibition, 1887.

Thos. Coles, Tourist and Excursion Agent [illegible]

B. J. Robinson, [illegible]

R. & J. Partington, Manufacturers of Cotton Dress Goods, Coloured Shirtings, Jeans, [illegible]

William Greenhough, Wholesale Grindery and Shoe Thread Warehouse, 98, Shudehill.—Among the branches of trade that suffer from excessive competition must be placed the grindery and shoe thread businesses. In this important line Mr. William Greenhough is engaged, and has been for the past fifty-five years. The firm is nearly a century old. His premises are admirably located in a central and commanding district, and are of ample dimensions to meet the demand of storage and a rather numerous *clientèle*. The stock is one of great variety, as is of necessity the case in all first-class businesses of this kind. Indeed the trade is very much like a comprehensive ironmonger's, in that the goods are much of the same kind, but more various. All sorts of tools for all trades, and buttons and other hardware sundries, are embraced in Mr. Greenhough's stock, which is one of the most exhaustive to be found anywhere in the city. Twelve hands are constantly employed in manufacturing; and though the business is local, it is very valuable, and rapidly increasing in importance. Mr. Greenhough is a capital and energetic manager, and his success and popularity are the merited reward of conscientiousness and industry.

Coulborn & Hulme, Military Tailors and Habit Makers, 26, St. Ann's Square.—This firm is one of the oldest of its kind, not only in Manchester but the whole of the North of England. It was originally established about the year 1717, so that it has had an existence of considerably over a century. For many years it was carried on under the style of Scarr & Co., under which title a trade and connection of the very highest class were built up, and still continues to flourish to this day. The establishment has been conducted in the present firm's name for twenty-two years, and will probably be so continued, although the original members of the old firm have passed away. The principal of the firm, as it is at present constituted, is Mr. Edward Robinson Hulme, upon whom has devolved the responsibility of conducting and sustaining a reputation which but few houses of the kind have the pleasure to enjoy. The speciality of the firm is the very highest class of civil and military tailoring.

Cottrill and Jones, Pattern Card Makers and Printers, Finishers, and General Letterpress Printers, 15, George Street, Telephone No. 486.—This business was established in the year 1862, and is now considered one of the leading firms in its line. Messrs. Cottrill and Jones were upwards of fourteen years with Messrs. Bland and Messenger. The premises include several large and convenient machine and workrooms. The speciality of the trade is the manufacture of pattern cards and pattern books, and in this important branch of business Messrs. Cottrill and Jones display great artistic taste and no little ingenuity and inventive talent. Many of the pattern books and pattern cards manufactured by the firm are veritable works of art. In addition, Messrs. Cottrill and Jones have a department for ordinary letterpress printing. The type is extremely well selected, most of it being of modern design and quite new. The machinery is rapid, perfect, and very powerful. A numerous staff of skilled hands is employed. The connection includes a large proportion of the leading houses. The members of the firm are both well known in Manchester.

Aaron Howard, Fishmonger, Wholesale Fish Market, and 9, 10, and 11, Market Place.—Fish is one of the most important articles of food; our fisheries are simply inexhaustible, and the finest in the world, and of late years strenuous and successful efforts have been made to popularise this nourishing food, and bring it within the reach of our dense population. In a large industrial city like Manchester it would be of untold value, and as it is, the trade is very considerable and in a flourishing condition. A very good house engaged in the business of fishmongering is that of Mr. Aaron Howard, which has been in existence for some years, and enjoys the confidence of the local community for the reliability and freshness of its goods. The shop is large and specially arranged, great attention being paid to the ventilation and coolness of the place, and everything is in the most perfect order, satisfying the most fastidious. The stock comprises every variety of the choicest fish, and is procured direct daily from the principal fishing stations. The extent of the trade can be judged from the fact that twelve hands are engaged in waiting upon the connection, which is of a most influential and high-class order. Mr. Aaron Howard is thoroughly versed in all details of the trade, and is looked upon as an honourable and upright citizen, owning a business which is acknowledged by all to be "one of the best fishmongers' establishments in the city and its vicinity."

W. H. Murphy, Professor of the Guitar and Banjo, Dealer in Musical Instruments, 48, Barton Arcade.—This gentleman is a refined vocalist, and has been established in Manchester for more than ten years, and has occupied his present premises since the beginning of the year 1887. His offices are a pair of beautiful rooms, handsomely furnished, and a staff of clerks is employed to conduct an extensive correspondence which is kept up between Mr. Murphy and a numerous body of clients, pupils, and customers in every part of the United Kingdom. Mr. William Henry Murphy is acknowledged to be the very best
guitar and banjo player in the n
pupils come to him from places
instructor of the well-known Man
a very considerable trade as dealer
and he keeps a good stock of the
He is also agent for Mr. S. S. Ste
& Co., New York, the great guit
best-known gentlemen in this city
concerts is proverbial.

Richard H. Sutton, &
Booksellers, 25, Princes Street, a
old and new books is one that is
portance, and increases with the s
city a noted house, one of the olde
Thomas Sutton & Son. This firm
Sutton in 1845, and always duri
done. His son, Mr. Richard He
account about 1874, and now, at
has the largest and most varied st
Mr. Albert Sutton, was partner w
his father's demise has conducted
the old lines at 130, Portland Str
old success. The stocks of books
comprehensive and of a singularly
not only to the diverse requirem
but to bibliophiles generally, who
piled and always welcome catalog
these houses. Both the brothers
their ability and urbanity are mar

The Prince's Restaura
establishment was opened by Mr.
into the hands of the present p
The establishment is on a grand s
There is a handsome dining-saloo
rooms, three billiard-rooms, and n
furnished in the most sumptuou
perfect style. The kitchen is a m
venience, and is supplied with an
ratus. A noted *chef* is in charg
celebrated all over the city. Th
plished corps, as many as eight
are at least thirty household ser
the comfort and convenience of g
ladies' dining-room has lately be
tion of ladies and leading memb
connection is necessarily of a hi
Mr. Wood, the proprietor, is also
famous Prince's Theatre, just opp

E. W. Wollaston, Oil M
business was founded thirty year
premises consist of a commodi
capital office well furnished an
lubricating oil, and in its preparat
the selection being invariably co
vision. As a consequence, Woll
oils are in great request by engine
facturers and mine owners, and a
does a very large trade also in m
and widespread, and requires the
proprietor is Mr. Edwin Washin
great technical knowledge of his
and tact, fertility of resource, an

Hooper & Co., Tailors a
—Among the leading firms of tai
of Messrs. Hooper & Co. They
by strict attention, artistic work,
able dealing, they have already
among the best classes of the city
in Exchange Street are of spacio
fitted up in a neat and attractive
stock is kept. It includes the fi
the leading British and Continen
Co. have won an excellent reputa
costumes, and Ulsters, the garm
beauty and originality of design,
fashionable elegance. The firm
William Hooper, the proprieto
capable business man, liberal a
respects worthy of his substantial

Mrs. M. A. Lee, Corset Maker, 8, St. Ann's Place.—A ry old-established business in anatomical corset and belt making and porting of French goods is carried on by Mrs. M. A. Lee. This siness was established under the same title over forty years ago; the esent premises have been occupied about twenty-five years: the op and showrooms are very large, and contain a great amount of luable stock. Several comfortable fitting rooms may be found in le establishment, and an efficient staff is always kept. The busi-ss of this firm is entirely of the best class, and extends all over e three kingdoms. The term "corset" seems to be of comparatively odern use in its present sense, and although really derived from the tin, was no doubt suggested by the peculiar kind of armour known as rselet. Great ingenuity has been displayed by Mrs. Lee in cutting her rsets to suit the anatomy of the human frame, and in fitting and proving defective figures. Much comfort and support are given to valid ladies, therefore Mrs. Lee is highly recommended and patronised the most eminent members of the medical profession. Mrs. Lee is ecially noted in this branch, not only for excellence of workmanship, d the first-class quality of the materials used, but for the way the ever-rying fashions are dealt with in adapting these corsets to the prevailing le of dress. Great pains are taken to secure an absolutely perfect fit, and very best hands are employed in the manufacture. Mrs. Lee also ports first-class French hand-sewn and woven corsets, and keeps the gest stock of all sizes for ladies and children to be found out of Paris or ndon. This business has acquired great celebrity in the city and rounding counties, and is one of the most prosperous and flourishing uses in the city.

H. Wolstenholme, General Draper, &c., 442 and 444, lham Road.—There are few trades in Manchester of greater import-ce than that of drapery and hosiery. A thoroughly representative use in this direction is that of Mr. H. Wolstenholme, which was nded by this gentleman seventeen years ago. Since that date he has cked up a fine local trade and established a very good business reputa-n. The shop occupied is large and roomy, suitably fitted and nished for the display and accommodation of stock and for the con-nience of customers, and the general appearance is most attractive and asing. It is very fully stocked with drapery goods of all kinds, fancy l staple, smallwares, trimmings, worsteds, wools, hosiery, gloves, rts, underclothing, &c., the made-up garments being in the latest and st fashionable styles. Mr. H. Wolstenholme only purchases superior ds, and he shows a keen knowledge of public taste. A very fine trade carried on in the locality, and Mr. H. Wolstenholme manages with erprise and ability. He is well known in the trade, is highly respected its members for his strict rectitude, and he likewise enjoys the esteem l confidence of the local community.

Mr. John Silvester, Furnishing Saddler and Saddlers' amonger, 39 and 41, Turner Street, High Street.—Prominent among trade industries of Manchester and districts is that of the furnishing dler and saddlers' ironmonger, ably represented by the well-known use of Mr. John Silvester, whose business premises are eligibly uate. Established over thirty years since in Manchester, the business always been known under the same title, and maintains a very high utation for the exceedingly good quality and workmanship of its pro-tions. The name of Mr. John Silvester in connection with saddle king and harness making generally, is most favourably known and roved by every keeper of horses throughout Manchester and the ad-ning counties. The business of this house is very large and widespread, ry description of harness being manufactured on the premises. The mises occupied are very large, and employ a large staff of highly skilled ineymen and harness makers, and highly skilled hands for the saddlers' nmongery department. The stocks held are immense, and comprise ry article in the saddlery trade, with harness in single and double sets, l, silver, nickel, or brass plated, of the highest possible finish, and all prices. Collars, bridles, reins, traces, saddles, in every variety. principal, Mr. John Silvester, is a gentleman well known far and e as a thoroughly practical tradesman of great integrity, and very lely respected.

City Pianoforte Show Rooms (John Steele Higgins, pro-etor), 7, Green Street, Tib Street, Market Street. This firm has been ablished for over twenty years for the manufacture and sale of piano-tes and other musical instruments. In addition to the pianos manu-tured by the firm, the show-rooms contain a choice selection of instru-nts, ranging from the productions of Messrs. Collard, Broadwood, Erard, hmann and others equally eminent, to those of the cheapest reliable kers. In the repairing department, since the introduction of improved chinery, driven by power, and the employment only of skilled work-n, this branch has become the most extensive and successful in the vinces. The visitors to the workshop cannot fail to be impressed by number of instruments of all descriptions, either awaiting repairs or sing through some of its various stages. Owing to the facilities orded by the above department Mr. J. Steele Higgins is never without rge stock of second-hand instruments by all makers, which after being roughly renovated or reconstructed, are offered on such terms as to enable the humblest home to become possessed of a good sound piano. A speciality also appears to be the manufacture of covered strings, which, with the large stock kept of felts, wire, panels, and all materials for the embellishments or restoration of worn pianos, gives the tuner or repairer an opportunity of being supplied, without anxiety or delay. A remark-able feature is noticeable in connection with this house, and one almost unique in an age when it has become an axiom of commerce that no business can be successful unless extensively advertised, is that for years a large and increasing trade has been carried on without the aid of a single advertisement—a fact which can only be attributed to the sterling qualities of the instruments sold, and the thorough integrity of all business transactions, thus enabling the proprietor to rest his reputation solely on the satisfaction given to those whom business has brought into contact with his firm.

T. Bell, Umbrella Maker, 9, Fountain Street.—Something like one hundred years have passed away since the well-known and benevolent Jonas Hanway first astonished the residents of the metropolis by carrying an umbrella through its streets. Like all innovations, it had to endure a great deal of ridicule and abuse; but it soon forced itself into public favour, and Hanway's solitary gingham has been the precursor of millions. Prominent among those who have taken an active part in the umbrella trade is the well-known Manchester firm of Thomas Bell, which commenced business in Nicholas Croft, more than twenty years ago, and removed in 1885 to its present commodious pre-mises. The workrooms, showroom and warehouse are large and well-fitted up. Ladies' and gentlemen's umbrellas, sunshades and parasols are here in every kind of material, and fitted for all classes, from the family umbrella to the dainty little articles which ladies mostly affect. All are of the very best make and workmanship. The materials are well selected and of the best quality, whilst the fashioning of the handles, &c., is elegant. Mr. Bell's establishment is one of the leading centres in the home trade, so far as this particular line is concerned, and he has the satisfaction of knowing that his goods give unqualified satisfaction in every part of the kingdom.

A. B. Brett, Drapers' Valuer and Commission Agent, The North of England General Business Offices, 80, Deansgate.—The retail drapers, and others engaged in kindred trades in the city and sur-rounding districts, have long felt the want of such a business as that conducted by Mr. Brett at the above address. This gentleman began operations in 1887, and the success that has since attended his efforts is ample testimony to his ability, integrity, and enterprise. The offices occupied are well-fitted and efficiently manned by a competent staff. Mr. Brett acts as drapers' valuer and general commission agent, and as such his services are in constant demand, not only in Manchester but in various other parts of the North. He purchases and matches goods for wholesale houses, retailers, and others who confide their commissions to him; acts as a practical valuer of drapery stock and fixtures; negotiates partner-ships and the transfers of business; assesses losses by fire or other causes, and acts as general insurance and guarantee agent. It is well known that many firms now prefer a society to a personal guarantee, and Mr. Brett represents the leading guarantee societies who, for a small annual premium, offer security guarantees of from £100 to £1,000. A very im-portant branch of Mr. Brett's business is the keeping of an employment register wherein are entered the wants of employers who may require travellers, salesmen, or assistants, and by means of which the latter, when out of employment, are brought into communication with those in quest of their services. This, to the parties concerned, has been a most valuable medium and very extensively utilised. Mr. Brett carries on his business in this department in the most capable manner, and on the same lines as are followed by metropolitan houses. His many years' experience in Manchester, Liverpool and London render him thoroughly au fait in the details of his business, and has proved of immense advantage to him, and through him to his numerous patrons.

James Booth, Wholesale Clog Sole and Patten Manufacturer, and Wholesale Dealer in Clogging Material of every description, 14, Rochdale Road. Manchester is the head-quarters of the clog sole and patten industry, and the establishments engaged are numerous and in excellent order. A well-known house so engaged is that of Mr. James Booth, which has been established for sixty years, and enjoys a sound reputation. The premises are large and commodious, and fitted throughout with every appliance for the proper carrying on of the business. The hands employed are able and experienced, and the clog soles and pattens, and every description of clogging material turned out, are durable, of excellent workmanship, and first class material. The trade done is entirely wholesale and very considerable. Mr. Booth is agent for Henry Carter's knives and hollowers, Watt's (late Hale) clasps and silver toed lasts, prize-medal sewing-machines, and for the finest quality machine needles and thread. Mr. James Booth, the proprietor of this extensive business, is thoroughly proficient in all branches of the trade, and manages with enterprise and ability. He is well known among the trade members, and highly respected, and his house is an able representative of the clog sole and patten trade, and clogging materials of every description.

Thomas Entwisle & Co., Calico Printers, 72, St. James's Street.—The firm of Thomas Entwisle & Co. is one of the best known of those engaged in the trade of calico printing in Manchester. The business is very old-established. Messrs. Entwisle & Co. have taken full advantage of all improvements in carrying on their business. The premises occupied consist of a building three stories high, wherein a large and efficient staff is engaged. The trade done is for the most part shipping orders, but a fairly large amount is done locally. The offices of the firm are handsomely fitted up and well lighted. Messrs. Entwisle are noted for the excellence of their work, and the long-standing reputation of this firm is worthily maintained.

E. Liebert & Co., Shippers and Merchants, 10, Dolefield Street, Bridge Street.—A house of high repute in the Manchester export trade is that of Messrs. E. Liebert & Co., which was established in 1860. The firm occupy a prominent edifice of three floors, and a commodious suite of offices is situate on the first floor, the remainder of the building being utilised for warehouse purposes, &c. This house occupies a very conspicuous position in the market, the principal goods handled being yarn and all kinds of machinery. The trade is exclusively of an export nature and particularly well-established among the best houses in all parts of the continent of Europe and the principal Eastern ports. The only partner, Mr. E. Liebert, holds the distinguished office of Consul to the German Empire, his practical knowledge of mercantile affairs rendering him particularly qualified to discharge the functions of such an appointment, while his genial amiability to the numerous patrons of the house has secured for him their unqualified esteem and personal regard.

J. Holden & Son, Architects, Surveyors, and Valuers, 64, Cross Street.—The architectural and surveying professions in Manchester are of considerable importance, and the members are a well-known body. This firm was founded in 1838, under the title of Isaac & James P. Holden, who separated. The senior branch, afterwards J. Holden & Son, is now represented by Mr. John Holden, Fellow of the Royal Institute of British Architects, Fellow of the Surveyors' Institution (London), and Past President of the Manchester Society of Architects. In addition to his architectural practice Mr. Holden has considerable experience as an arbitrator and valuer, and as an expert in connection with disputes as to easements and rights of light. A small book on this subject written by him has been published by the Manchester Society of Architects, and has been well received by the public.

T. S. Alderson, Laces, Gloves, Hosiery and Haberdashery, &c., 391, Oxford Street.—Among the trades of Manchester an important position is taken by the retailers of ornamental dress items. A representative type of this business is the well-known establishment of Mr. T. S. Alderson, noted for laces, flowers, frillings, ribbons, gloves, hosiery, muslins, antimacassars, umbrellas, haberdashery, &c., lace curtains, lace lappetts, &c. Established now several years this depot has long maintained a high-class reputation. The specialities of this house are laces, ribbons, and gloves. A first-rate trade is done in lace curtains. The haberdashery department is always busy. The premises held comprise a compact and well-fitted shop and house, admirably arranged and adapted to the business.

T. H. Bennett, Tea and Coffee Salesman, &c., "Canister Tea Mart," 518, Oldham Road.—The tea, coffee, grocery and provision trade of Manchester is, on account of the immense population, of vast value and importance. A typical business in this line is that known as the "Canister Tea Mart," which was founded three years ago by the present proprietor, Mr. T. H. Bennett. The shop is commodious, well fitted up with the necessary fixtures, and the windows present an attractive appearance owing to the fine display of choice goods. The stock is heavy, and consists of tea and coffee of unsurpassable purity and fragrance, staple and fancy groceries and provisions of all kinds. In three years he has built up a very fine local trade of a good class character. The management is able and energetic. In all details of the trade Mr. T. H. Bennett is thoroughly experienced, and popular with the members of the trade.

Gillespie & Brumbill, Glass, China, &c., 30, Cavendish Street, Stretford Road.—There are probably no members of the great trading community who serve a more useful purpose than do the purveyors of china, glass, and earthenware. Prominent among those who cater in this direction for the city of Manchester must be mentioned Messrs. Gillespie & Brumbill. Established in 1878, Mr. James Gillespie and Miss Mary Brumbill have succeeded in meeting the requirements of the public. Their shop and show-rooms in Cavendish Street are well known for miles around, and at all times display a wealth of stock which it would be difficult to equal. Articles in glass, in china, and in more costly ware, are here to be found in attractive variety. The price list is suited to the purses of all classes, and taking it altogether the concern is one of the most flourishing, popular, and successful of its kind.

Riley's Printing Office
Street, Ardwick.—This business
established (1884) has already n
gives great promise for the futu
several occasions to remove and
amount of patronage bestowed u
capital shops, having considerab
and a roomy printing-office and s
consists of Payne's Wharfedale
machine, with automatic cylind
Minerva printing machine, with
poster press by Figgins, of Londo
numerous labour-saving machine
very choice selection of modern ar
and American foundries. The
descriptions—address, business, m
ing patterns and styles Mr. Riley
inventive faculty. Plain and pic
both as regards cost and producti
circular, catalogue, cut-work, woo
Mr. Riley's specimen and pattern
excellent and first-rate work. T
leading tradesmen resident in th
A competent staff is employed.
manager. He is also the origi
Ardwick Advertiser and Monthly
of publication. Advertisers freq
valuable advertising medium in t
it can receive. It is the original
the largest circulation (which is
in the district. The *Advertiser*
jottings, &c., and is delivered fr
knowledge of his business, combi
and is thoroughly deserving of th

Haron Varbetian & Co.,
Street.—The Levant trade in M
one, and engages the attention of
merchants and shippers in this
Varbetian & Co. is one of these,
ago by Mr. Haron Varbetian. T
wholly confined to the shipmen
Levant. Having a thorough kn
ket to which their consignment
betian & Co. possess an advantag
The firm's name stands exceeding
for business acumen and the stric
ments are always kept.

Wm. Barnes Russell,
and Briar Pipes, 93, Market St
important internal branch of ind
nearly all great cities, is the man
An admirable type of house eng
Barnes Russell, which was foun
Russell has several branches. T
sions, of attractive appearance,
with meerschaum and briar pipes
designs. An ample staff of ha
goods. Mr. W. B. Russell carr
on a very extensive local trad
management, is steadily increasi

J. T. Sawyer, Fancy
Street, Shudehill.—The manufac
of industry extensively carried o
house engaged therein is that of
1849. The premises consist
admirably fitted and arranged wit
A numerous force of skilled ha
The processes are most advance
the boxes produced are durable a
are in great demand among perf

S. O. Prior, Tailor an
A typical tailoring house in this
which was founded in 1859. T
a very elegant manner. The stoc
goods, including cloths of super
the tailoring department. In
on a very fine trade, having a
Mr. Prior is one of the most pop

William Williams, Shirt and Jacket Manufacturer, 1, Dale Street.—Prominent amongst the industries of Manchester and strict are the many manufacturing interests, aptly illustrated by the oll-known and highly patronised establishment of Mr. William Wil-ams, shirt and jacket manufacturer. Established now twenty years, the oprietor is a gentleman well known as a thoroughly practical man of siness, and is highly respected.

Joseph Levy, Tailor, 2, Bull's Head Yard, Market Place. -Although the Manchester population are busily engaged in com-ercial and industrial pursuits, they do not neglect in the least their ersonal adornment, as is plainly apparent by the prosperous condition of e tailoring trade in the city. An excellent example of a local tailoring siness is that of Mr. Joseph Levy, which has a reputation of eight ars' standing. Mr. J. Levy is one of the most expert and practical ilors in the district, and a very good class patronage is accorded to his siness, which is entirely "to measure." The premises occupied are every way admirably adapted for the trade, and consist of shop and orkrooms. The shop is elegantly fitted up for the convenience of stomers, and the workrooms are large and fitted completely with ery necessary appliance. There is a fine stock of the best material for e choice of the patrons, and the clothes are made by able and perienced tailors in the latest and most fashionable styles at very oderate prices. Mr. Joseph Levy superintends all work, and is well sted in the latest fashions. He is well known and very popular in the ighbourhood, and his business fully deserves the patronage accorded it.

The Central Laundry, 72, Quay Street, Deansgate **Mrs. M. E. Southern, Proprietress**).—Prominent among the occupations at promote the welfare of all classes of the community is the vocation of e laundress, exceedingly well exemplified in the well-known establish-ent conducted by Mrs. M. E. Southern, to which she succeeded in 79. The business has been carried on at the present address for the st seven years. The premises are very large, and divided into almost mberless apartments for washing, drying, wringing, mangling, &c.; in ct, every description of laundry work is executed on the premises with nctuality and dispatch. A staff of over thirty experienced hands is nstantly employed. Several carmen and well-appointed vans are con-antly plying to all parts of the city, receiving and delivering goods. e connection is very extensive, and conducted almost entirely among e leading houses of business and private families in and around Man-ester. The proprietress is a thoroughly practical laundress, and she s gained the respect and esteem of her customers.

W. F. Jopling, Hosier, Glover and Outfitter, 127, ford Street.—This business was established in the year 1850, and has en steadily and uniformly successful. The shop is of good size, of cellent appearance and imposing frontage. The business is entirely nfined to a superior class of goods, and it is well understood among . Jopling's numerous customers that the quality of all articles sup-ed may be fully relied upon. The entire stock shows clearly that all ods have been selected with great care, sound judgment, and refined te; and in gloves, ties, and handkerchiefs, Mr. Jopling's stock will ir comparison with any exhibited in Bond Street or the Burlington cade. A large business is done in gentlemen's outfitting. The assort-nt of fancy articles for ladies' wear is extremely attractive. The nnection includes most of the residents in Rusholme, Chorlton, Whalley nge and Old Trafford. Mr. Jopling is the sole proprietor of the siness, which was founded by his father. He is much esteemed and pected, and is considered one of the most successful business men in locality.

William Wardle, Cheese Factor and Provision Mer-ant, 33, Withy Grove.—The most important department of trade in s city is the purveying of provisions of various kinds, such as cheese, on, hams, salted pork, tinned meats, &c., of all of which the weekly sumption is enormous, affording for its supply a fine opening for the rcise of business tact and ability. The establishment of Mr. William rdle has now enjoyed a prosperous business existence since the year 0, from which time Mr. Wardle has succeeded in rendering it one of at magnitude and extent. The merit of this is entirely due to him-, he having been the sole founder, and being now the sole principal in establishment. His business has already become a very extensive , especially in Cheshire and American cheese and Irish roll bacon. . Wardle's trade now extends well over the city and the surrounding ns, the splendid quality of his provisions of all kinds, and their formity of excellence, combined with the thoroughly business manner which all Mr. Wardle's transactions are conducted, always securing him a continuity of support wherever he has once succeeded in ning a footing, which is everywhere throughout the district. Mr. rdle's unswerving integrity, and the perfect straightforwardness with ich he acts, have gained for him a great degree of respect and esteem only in general commercial circles but throughout the city.

Alfred Darbyshire, Architect, Brazennose Street.—Mr. Alfred Darbyshire, F.R.I.B.A., established himself professionally in St. James's Square in the year 1862, and has latterly had associated with him Mr. F. Bennett Smith. The offices are a handsome suite of large airy rooms, admirably lighted, substantially furnished, and capitally situated for business. Mr. Darbyshire is a gentleman of very high-class reputation, of great attainments, and possessed of most extensive professional knowledge. He has great inventive faculty, constructive skill, and genuine artistic feeling. His original designs are invariably characterised by purity of style, novelty of treatment, genuine adaptability to the purposes intended, ingenious contrivance, and economical detail. In all his work there is a freshness of treatment that is as welcome as it is unusual, and it is not surprising therefore that Mr. Darbyshire has already erected most important public buildings, theatres, chapels, schools, warehouses, country residences, hospitals, mills, and foundries. Mr. Darbyshire finds an excellent lieutenant in Mr. F. Bennet Smith. Both gentlemen are well known in the city, and are most highly respected and esteemed in both professional and social circles.

Joseph Bowers, Wholesale Cigar Merchant, 66, Portland Street.—Judging by its extent, the cigar and tobacco trade of this country is one of the first importance. The wholesale cigar warehouse of Mr. Joseph Bowers was established in January, 1882, by its present energetic and enterprising proprietor. Mr. Bowers's trade is a first-class one, especially in the choicest brands of foreign cigars. His extensive and lengthened experience and excellent judgment enable him to offer a magnificent choice and selection of these, of a description to meet the unqualified approbation of the most fastidious and discriminating taste. Mr. Bowers enjoys a very high reputation for dealing in this choice class of goods. There is no description of really choice foreign cigars which he is not prepared to supply. Mr. Bowers has a splendid connection amongst the best classes, and is exceedingly popular with his customers.

J. Pendlebury, Wholesale Smallware, Hosiery, and Haberdashery Dealer, 27 and 29, Thomas Street, and 96, High Street—This business has been established upwards of thirty years, and is well known both in the city and country generally. The premises, which are extensive and well adapted for all the requirements of the business, include the buildings 27 and 29, Thomas Street, and 96, High Street, and are in close proximity to Smithfield Market. The business is wholesale, and the stock, which is of a large and varied character, includes every description of smallwares, haberdashery, and hosiery, noted amongst which are sewing cottons, linen and silk reels; braces, needles, pins, buttons, and tapes of every description; in addition to which there is a large and comprehensive assortment of hosiery, underclothing, baby linen, handkerchiefs, collars, collarettes, frillings, laces and edgings; upholsterers' trimmings, fringes, and bindings; Berlin, German, and fingering wools, and worsteds in great variety. The trade connection consists principally of shopkeepers in town and country, whose wants are attended to by an efficient body of assistants.

G. Adcroft & Co., Waste Paper Dealers, Paper and Twine Manufacturers, 61, Spear Street.—A business in Manchester of great magnitude and importance is formed by the waste paper trade and the manufacture of paper and twine, and among the firms engaged therein a principal place is held by Messrs. G. Adcroft & Co., who were established ten years ago. The premises occupied are spacious, admirably fitted up, and contain a very extensive stock of paper and twine of all kinds. These commodities are noted for high quality and excellent manufacture. Mr. G. Adcroft deals extensively in waste paper, and carries on a very heavy local trade in paper and twines, having a fine connection of long standing. He thoroughly understands the business, and is an honourable and talented man of business.

James Moore, Cheese and Corn Factor, 20A, Hanging Ditch.—The trade in corn and cheese in this country is almost of incredible proportions, and contributes in no small degree to our commercial prosperity. Manchester has a fine reputation for the extent of her business in this direction, and among the firms engaged a leading place is occupied by that of Mr. James Moore, which has been in existence for eleven years. The premises are especially adapted for the business, and comprise offices and cellars which afford excellent accommodation. The stock of cheese and corn always held is very extensive. Mr. James Moore has a house at Antrobus, Cheshire, in the centre of the cheese-making district, hence his English cheese is of the finest quality. The corn is of the best growth. Mr. J. Moore is an excellent judge of both corn and cheese. An efficient staff of clerks, travellers, and others is employed. The trade is very considerable, and extends to all parts of the country. It is an acknowledged fact that Mr. Moore by his business capacity has raised his house to a position of importance in the trade. He is highly respected by all who know him, and manages his business with enterprise and ability.

Richard Ashworth & Sons, Manufacturers, 36, Bloom Street.—This firm was established in the year 1850, when all the work was done by hand looms, and formerly occupied premises at 51, Cannon Street, till 1878. In 1856 power looms were introduced. The mills, which are large, are situated at Middleton and Alkrington, the former being known as Tonge mill and the latter as Bradshaw Mill. The premises in Bloom Street consist of a handsome warehouse with a first-rate suite of roomy offices, well and substantially furnished and fitted up with all the most approved modern appliances for the rapid transaction of business. Mr. R. Ashworth was a hand-loom weaver and began in a very small way. He first kept a draper's shop, and travelled occasionally. In 1866 he commenced finishing his goods, and purchased the Tonge mill, which has since been almost entirely rebuilt. The offices in Bloom Street are under the management of Mr. R. Ashworth, senior, and his son, Joseph; while both mills are controlled by Phillip, the junior member of the firm, and his younger brother Richard. The principal goods manufactured are ginghams and checks, and for these fabrics Messrs. Richard Ashworth and Sons are well known. Doubling is an important branch of the operation conducted. The firm sells none but their own productions. Since 1868 the firm have bleached, dyed, and sized their own manufactures. The trade connection includes many of the leading shipping houses of the city, as well as the principal warehousemen and wholesale dealers. The firm employs nearly five hundred hands at the mills, and in Bloom Street there is an efficient staff of clerks. The members of the firm are Mr. Richard Ashworth and his sons Joseph and Phillip, who are well known in the city, and in general commercial circles. They take an active interest in all that concerns the welfare of the trade of the city and district; and are highly esteemed and respected.

John Reece, Manufacturers' Agent, 65, Dale Street.—The importance of this city as a commercial centre is best pointed out by showing the perfection to which all mercantile arrangements are here carried on. That perfection is clearly manifested in the subdivision of labour in wholesale mercantile pursuits, which is here everywhere apparent. Here the manufacturers' agents are a distinct class, and are again to be classified according to the nature of the merchandise they handle. The manufacturers' agency business of Mr. John Reece was established by its present energetic and enterprising principal, and has been conducted with a remarkable degree of success. His father belonged to the sturdy class of farmers bred and born among the bracing hills of Derbyshire, and his son John coming to Manchester in very early life, at once began to distinguish himself at school by carrying off the highest honours and the silver medal. He was put to business in a manufacturer's counting-house, but very soon entered into business on his own account, and by his undaunted energy and real English pluck quickly made his mark as master of the business which he had made specially his own. He is the duly accredited agent of a very large first-class house (which alone in its line he represents) in what is known as the cut or hat leather department, and owing to his great experience in handling this important class of merchandise, his well-established connection and his first-class business capacity have contributed to make him rank as one of the foremost in the trade. Amongst the great mercantile houses who have become aware of this, and have accordingly confided their business and interests in this city unreservedly to him, may be mentioned the well known name of Thomas Bayley & Company, Limited, of Lenton, near Nottingham, leather dressers, tanners, glue and parchment makers, &c., for whom Mr. Reece does a very large amount of business. This great firm, so ably represented here by Mr. Reece, does a magnificent business throughout the whole of the United Kingdom and abroad, having agents and representatives in all great commercial centres. The testimony of Messrs. Bayley, however, is not an isolated one. Mr. Reece is also sole representative in Manchester of the very old-established house of H. Passadant, furrier, Paris, whose name is well known on the Continent and in America. His unswerving loyalty and integrity to those whose business he transacts, his invariably upright and honourable bearing under all circumstances, and his promptitude and readiness to oblige, have gained for Mr. Reece the universal good opinion and respect of that large section of the mercantile community with whom he is daily brought into contact.

J. Preston & Co., Victoria Chemical Works, Bradford.—In chemical manufacture, as in most other industries, there are many special lines. One of these is the distillation of tar and ammonia, which, in the neighbourhood of Manchester and Bradford, is carried on pretty extensively. A house well and widely known in connection with this branch of industry is the reputable establishment of Messrs. Preston & Co., Limited. Their works are located at Bradford, and are of considerable extent, well kept, and equipped with the newest and most effective kind of labour-saving machinery. They were started about four years ago by Mr. James B. Dunkerley, who alone is responsible for their management at the present time. A staff of between twenty and thirty men is engaged in the operations conducted. These embrace the distilling of all sorts of tar and ammonia, which are both extensively used in the many processes connected with the staple trades of the north, and in many other branches of business. Another important manufacture is white and grey sugar of lead, the firm being about the largest makers of this article in the kingdom, turning out about twenty tons per week. This commodity largely used by the calico printers and paper manufacturers of Lancashi The trade of the house is widespread, and Messrs. Bagnall & Bramwo 4, St. Ann's Square, who represent the firm, are daily making it more Its reputation for the excellence of its special productions is very hig and the supervision and ability of Mr. Dunkerley are likely to st further enhance it in this respect.

John H. Keeble, Accountant, Estate Agent, an Licensed Valuer; also Assessor and Collector of Government Tax for the Wards of New Cross and St. Clement's, Agent to t Northern Assurance Co., 33, Hopwood Avenue, Market Place.—T accountant and estate agency business has now become one of great val and importance in Manchester. A capital business in this line is th of Mr. John Howarth Keeble, which was established in the year 187 Mr. Keeble is a thoroughly capable accountant. His connection is ve extensive. He holds the responsible office of assessor and collector government taxes for two of the most important and wealthy districts the city. Mr. Keeble is, moreover, the secretary to the Failswor Permanent Building Society, one of the most prosperous and substant in the Manchester district. His offices are centrally and convenient situated, within a minute's walk of the Royal Exchange, and he emplo an adequate clerical staff. Mr. Keeble's private address is Canadi Villa, Failsworth.

John M. Sumner & Co., 2, Brazennose Street.—After successful business career of from thirty to forty years, this firm sta out most prominently among the export houses of the city of Manchest The offices on the second and third floors are well and conveniently fit up, and are occupied by a numerous staff of clerks and engineers. T warehouse and packing-rooms occupy the rest of the building, and spacious in extent, well lighted, and admirably arranged for the requi ments of the business. Messrs. Sumner & Co., whose speciality is t export of textile machinery in all its branches, are well and deserve known in all countries where machinery is used, and their thoron acquaintance with the requirements of producers, as well as the care a attention devoted to the details of their business, have secured for th the confidence and respect of all the leading houses, and have enabl them to bring their firm to the position which it now occupies.

John Adamson, Son, & Co., Chartered Accountant 5, Norfolk Street.—This very high-class firm was established in the ye 1865, by the late Mr. John Adamson, who had just retired from the fi of Chadwick, Adamson, Collier, & Co., accountants, of Manchester a London. Mr. Adamson was an active public man as early as 1862, wh he became secretary to the Cotton Famine Relief Fund, and at the cl a presentation was made to him as an acknowledgment of the hi appreciation in which he was held by the committee. To the valua services which his energy and ability (for which he was conspicuo enabled him to render in that capacity was due, in a measure, the succ he afterwards attained as an accountant. For the latter he was specia fitted, and his advice was much sought after and valued highly. T business rapidly increased, and he took into partnership his son, a afterwards several of the old and experienced clerks, when the title of t firm was altered from John Adamson to that of John Adamson, Son, & C The business of the firm is chiefly among the great public compan and large private firms. Besides executorial business, it has also a co siderable share of practice connected with the Bankruptcy and Chance Courts as receivers, official liquidators, trustees, &c. The present pa ners, Messrs. Hill, Carse, & Walkden, have been connected with the fi for nearly sixteen years, and have acquired a thorough grasp of t business and of accountancy practice in general. The commodious offi of the firm have been occupied by them for the past twelve years, a are handsome and well furnished.

G. H. Akhurst & Co., Manufacturing Chemists, Ale andra Works, Bradford, Manchester.—This business was established its present proprietor some few years ago. The works are of a modera size, and are furnished with the most modern machinery. The princip specialities are pitch, creosote oil, naphtha, black varnish, vegetable a lamp black, moulders' charcoal, and mineral blacking and coal dust. moulders' blacking and coal dust for foundry purposes very special atte tion has been paid, and a great deal of money has been spent, so to enable the firm to turn out any quality of blacking or coal dust be suitable for the different classes of work done. Coal dust from 18s. the finest possible. They do the largest business in the city with t foundries. The working staff is large; commercial travellers are em ployed. The sole partner is G. H. Akhurst, a gentleman of experienc He has introduced great improvements in certain processes of manufa turing blacking and coal dust for foundry purposes, which enables hi to supply quickly and reasonably, and is regarded justly as a rising ma The vegetable black ovens are of the best construction, and are consider about the largest in the trade.

Henry Wallwork & Co., Engineers and Malleable and **oft Iron Founders,** harter Street. — To is large and important firm belongs e credit of introducing into this city the anufacture of malleable and soft iron stings. Prior to the undation of this business Manchester was pendent upon Sheffeld and the district round Birmingham r soft iron castings; d it was a great oon to the sewing achine makers when r. Wallwork commenced operations. His usiness grew most pidly, being exemely well conducted: hile as far as the anchester district was ncerned he held a rtual monopoly. The orks were rapidly extnded: new departents were added, until early four hundred ands are constantly nployed. Still the incipal business conaues to be the protection of malleable d soft iron castings r the trade; but a od deal of finished achinery and gas ennes are turned out. ey are the principal anufacturers of machinery for the proaction of every class far and wool hats, d they have fitted complete manufacories in France, Germany, Austria, Italy, d Australia, to proce from 2,500 dozen r week of finished lt hats. They are so makers of Sturson's patent gas engine, which is now coming very popular account of its many cellent advantages, e balancing of all orking parts, regular ing even at highest eed, low pressure of s required, small ace taken up, one apulse in every reolution of shaft, all arts can be readily t at, there being no linder cover to take f, and the balancing the expansive force the charge. There e also produced here e well-known "Wells atent Unbreakable amps," of which the firm have made up to the present date January 1888, 680,000, which have been sent to every part of the globe. They are also making a large number of very powerful lamps that are entirely portable, and can be carried about by two men or boys. These lamps, known as the "Wells Light," are the joint patents of Messrs. Wallwork and Mr. Wells. The light is produced by converting crude oils into gas, the flame when burning producing or making its own gas and giving a light equal to 3000 candle power at a cost of one penny per 1000 candles. These lamps are extensively used by Railway Cos., and also in the construction of the ship canal. Amongst other specialities may be named the manufacture of sewing machines, of which the firm now make a large number, both of hand and treadle machines, being the sole makers of the well-known "Warwick" sewing machines, every part of which is manufactured by the firm. The sewing machine works are situated in Hilton Street. They have also a branch works for the production of malleable castings at Oakengates, in Shropshire, producing there from fifty to one hundred tons per week, of every class of malleable castings. The present proprietors are Mr. Henry Wallwork, Mr. R. Wallwork, and Mr. Charles Henry Wallwork, all well-known in the city, and regarded as highly successful and thriving manufacturers.

John Bardsley & Sons, Flour and Rice Millers, and Dealers in Farina and Sago Flour for Sizing and Dressing Purposes, Mason Street Mills.—This business, which has been established over forty years, is now carried on by Mr. John G. Bardsley, under the style of John Bardsley & Sons. The mills at Mason Street are large and well appointed, and the plant and machinery of every description is of the most modern and improved character.

John Parker, Wholesale and Family Grocer and Tea **ealer,** 113, Long Millgate.—The grocery and tea trade of Manchester one of the most important. A typical house in this trade is that of Ir. John Parker, which was established in 1837 by Horsfall & Arnold, whom the present proprietor became an apprentice in 1843. In 1854 Ir. Parker purchased the business from his original employers, and like e true Manchester man, has stood by the spot where he first commenced usiness, which has steadily increased year by year. In 1863 another business was opened at 114, Great Clowes Street, in 187 one at No. 1, Great Clowes Street, and two years later still another was opened at 63, Bury New Road. The shop at 63, Bury New Road, like the others, is large, commodious, attractive and substantial. It is heavily stocked with staple and fancy groceries, teas, and coffees, cocoas, chocolates, spices, pickles, sauces, and other goods appertaining to the trade. Mr. John Parker carries on a very fine wholesale and retail local trade. Mr. Parker is an energetic, honourable man of business.

Charles Bostock, Dispensing Chemist and Surgeon-Dentist, 277 and 279, Rochdale Road.—The pharmacy business of Manchester is as fine as that of any other city, and the members engaged are an important and well-qualified body. A good type of house in this direction is that of Mr. Charles Bostock, which was established some years ago by the present proprietor. The premises are large, fitted up in an elegant and superior manner, and present a very prosperous appearance. The stock of drugs, &c., is very complete, and every precaution is taken to ensure the quality and strength, the stock being frequently renewed from the leading manufacturing chemists. Mr. C. Bostock dispenses with great care and judgment, and has earned the confidence and patronage of the local members of the medical profession. He also carries on practice as surgeon-dentist, and for his skill and ability enjoys a fine local reputation. His lengthened experience in his profession has made him familiar with all kinds of dental complaints, and the operations are performed with delicacy and dispatch. The consulting-room is fitted up in the most complete manner with all the appliances for the comfort and convenience of the patients, and the instruments used are by the best makers. Altogether, Mr. Charles Bostock carries on a very lucrative business (its value being enhanced by the excellently managed post-office attached) is highly popular with the local community, and his courteous bearing is reflected by his qualified assistance, whilst he is looked upon by the medical profession as an able dispenser and skilful dental practitioner.

Middleton & Co., Manufacturers of Victoria and Bishop's Lawn, &c., 50, Fountain Street.—Among the many branches of the cotton industry of Manchester, a prominent position must be assigned to the manufacture of Victoria and Bishop's lawns, muslin, cambrics, and such like goods. A well-known house engaged in this departure is that of Messrs. Middloton, which was established by the sole member and proprietor, Mr. W. A. Middleton, in 1881. The premises are extensive, and comprise offices and warehouse. The spacious warehouse is densely packed with a large and valuable stock of lawns, plain and fancy muslins, cambrics, jacconets, nainsooks, white and dyed costume fabrics, batistes, brilliantes, brocades, linings, &c. These goods are of splendid quality, and are manufactured with the greatest care from the best materials. The trade done is heavy, spreading all over the country, and large quantities of these goods are exported to all parts of the world. Mr. W. A. Middleton shows much ability and energy in his management, and the house has gradually assumed a position of eminence in the mercantile world.

Alexander Reid, Fashionable Tailor, &c., 290, Stretford Road.—This well-known and important business has been located at the present address upwards of four years, having for the previous sixteen years occupied premises at 6, Upper Moss Lane. The shop is unusually spacious, of handsome frontage, and imposing appearance. It is elegantly fitted and furnished, and is decorated in the very best taste. On the upper floors and in the rear are capital stock, cutting, and work-rooms. All are well ventilated, admirably lighted, and scrupulously clean. Mr. Reid is famous for his choice patterns in best Scotch tweeds, West of England and Leeds coatings, Huddersfield trouserings, and the finest productions of the French houses. He is in direct communication with the leading Parisian and London tailors, and his customers get the full benefit of the connection. Mr. Reid employs a permanent staff of some fifteen to eighteen hands, and the number is increased during busy seasons. He is looked upon as a deservedly successful business man.

Thomas Guest & Co., Confectioners, 92, Carruthers Street, Ancoats.—Among the many branches of industry carried on in Manchester a prominent place is held by the manufacture of confectionery. A well-known, old-established, thoroughly-representative firm so engaged is that of Messrs. Thomas Guest & Co., which is noted for the variety and excellence of its productions. The works occupied consist of two extensive seven-storied buildings, which are completely equipped, regardless of cost, with machinery of the most improved construction. Over one hundred trained hands are employed in manufacturing confectionery of all kinds; the process being on the most advanced principles. All obnoxious colouring matters are strictly avoided, and the confectionery turned out, for wholesomeness, variety, and delicacy of flavour, is absolutely unsurpassable. Messrs. Thomas Guest & Co. spare no trouble or expense, and they expend much talent and patience in maintaining this high standard of excellence. They carry on a very heavy trade in all parts of the globe and United Kingdom, and employ several travellers and colonial agents. Thomas Guest & Co. are gentlemen of great influence and eminence in the industrial and commercial world.

Edward Britnor, Stay and Corset Manufacturer, Hosier, Glover, Shirt Maker, &c., 117 and 119, Oldham Street.—This business was established twenty-five years ago, and is still carried on by its founder. The shop is very large and well fitted up, and there are several commodious stock and workrooms on the upper floors of the building. Mr. Britnor possesses also a branch establishment at 24, Great
Ancoats Street, where he does a
specialities are stays and corsets
and best assorted stock in the U
and other articles, which are mor
trade is also done in gentlemen's
though to a very large extent l
numerous customers in many of
Mr. Britnor is exceedingly wel
highly respected as a liberal and

John Hickling & Co
Quilts, &c., 1, Minshull Street.-
cern was formerly carried on at
however, its growing importance
necessitated) a removal to the
remarkably brisk trade is being c
sheets, quilts, pocketings, jeans,
manufacture, from the large wo
Hickling & Co. were established i
by no means an old one, yet in t
running, advantage has been tal
sented itself. Keen business tal
praiseworthy determination to s
reasonable rate, have been the ch
concern has achieved in so short
has in every way been thoroughl

J. Hyslop, Gentlemen's
111, Oxford Road.—This rapidly
1873 at 72, Oxford Road. In t
years afterwards extended the p
111, while a further enlargement
called for. Mr. Hyslop has al
character at 24, Market Stree
amongst the handsomest and be
admirably situated and adapted
in gentlemen's outfitting is the
fect-fitting, well made, and most
ment is replete with all the o
toilette. The stock of linen an
in the best possible taste. A ve
and the pressure of business kee
Mr. Hyslop is well known in the

Timothy Hibbert, W
facturer, 8, Water Street.—A p
turing trade is the production of
industry is the old-established
Hibbert, which was founded b
quently removed to the present
arranged and well-fixtured the
being very attractive. The wor
very extensive. The industrial
the production of horse-collars.
harness used in vehicular wor
and the high-class quality of
throughout the trade in Manche
tact, push, and energy employ
insuring punctuality and dispat
trade is exclusively of a wholesa
the best houses. The proprietor
in the trade, and highly respecte

Alfred Grant, Carriag
This business was commenced i
was subsequently removed to its
very much larger and more con
The show-rooms are spacious,
factory is capitally situated an
machinery. The offices are a
and well fitted up. In the show
number of extremely elegant,
barouches, landaus, gigs, phaete
especially successful in designin
upon the conventional styles, an
than twelve gold and silver priz
The firm's *clientèle* is extensive
over the United Kingdom, the c
of the world. Mr. Grant's is o
are entirely built, finished, and
hands is employed.

J. F. Mellor, Princess Bakery, 323, Chester Road, d 282, Stretford Road. Also branch establishments at 45, Alexander ad, 91, Preston Street, 72, Radnor Street, Hulme, and 101, Upper ook Street.—Bakers, like most other tradesmen who deal in the cessities of life, generally do a constant and on the whole a paying de. An example of the truth of this assertion is the well-known siness of Mr. James Mellor, popularly known as the "Princess kery." This concern is carried on in a handsome block of buildings, d was started over five years ago. The premises are admirably fitted d equipped, and are models of order and cleanliness, two of the eatest and most important considerations where human food and its eparation are in question. The rapid development of the business and e valuable connections secured in the most legitimate manner in such comparatively short time, speak volumes for the ability and business imen of Mr. Mellor, who is one of the most popular tradesmen in the ighbourhood of his principal shop and branch establishments at 45, exander Road, 91, Preston Street, and 72, Radnor Street, Hulme.

The Alliance Commercial (Temperance) Hotel, Cathe-il Gates.—This handsomely-furnished and wonderfully well managed tel presents many irresistible and exceptional attractions to the abstain-g commercial traveller. It has been established for about twenty years d is superior to any similar contemporary house within a wide radius. is a particularly pleasing feature of the locality, and the present ener-tic and enterprising proprietor, with Mr. J. Utley, and his wife, are cer-nly to be complimented upon the ability they have displayed, and the le manner in which they have followed up the excellent example of their edecessor, Mr. T. H. Hall, and even improved upon that gentleman's anagement. The hotel is situated in a central and convenient position ar the Royal Exchange and the railway station. Every convenience l comfort are afforded visitors and travellers, and the terms are strictly nay, remarkably—moderate. It is conducted on strictly temperance nciples. The hotel is so well patronised that on many occasions they d it not large enough to accommodate their patrons.

Duncan & Spratt, Provision Merchants, 26, Withy ove.—Messrs. Duncan & Spratt are well known throughout the ited Kingdom as shippers of butter and provision merchants; they joy a reputation of the most enviable kind. Besides their establishment Withy Grove, Manchester, they have large export depôts at Nelson reet, Limerick, and Henry Street, Tipperary. They are shippers of st quantities of Irish, Danish, and Hamburg butters, and have en established for about forty years, a period which has been one of ady but rapid and substantial progress, the management deserving high mmendation for the exemplary manner in which the concern has been rked. From their Manchester warehouse a most extensive business is rried on by this firm, who are able to place special value before their ents. The utmost promptness is displayed in attending to all orders, d satisfaction may be safely relied upon by all the patrons of Duncan & ratt.

John Dawson, Chartered Accountant, 80, Cross Street. The industrial and commercial greatness of Manchester makes the artered accountancy business of value and importance. A successful siness in this direction is that of Mr. John Dawson, which was inded in the city by this gentleman over eighteen years ago. The lices are of goodly dimensions, are furnished in a very suitable manner, d ample clerical assistance is employed. Mr. John Dawson is thoroughly oficient in all branches of the chartered accountant business, and he rries out all commissions in a very prompt manner. He has a very ie connection among manufacturers, merchants, and the industrial and mmercial world generally. Mr. John Dawson is well known in busi-ss circles, and his services are in great demand; his honourable business ethods and energy, and his eminent standing in the profession meets ith due appreciation.

Edward Cowper, Hairdresser, Wig Maker, and Per-imer, 34, Bury New Road.—Mr. Edward Cowper has dressed the hair f the ladies and gentlemen of Broughton and district for the past twelve ars. His shop is a very handsome one, and the hair-dressing saloons o elegantly appointed, making, in the skilful hands of E. Cowper and s assistants, hair-dressing and shaving a positive pleasure. As a ladies' air-dresser E. Cowper has been extremely successful; and his method f cutting, singeing and shampooing is exclusively his own. He is equently called upon to dress ladies' hair in all styles—historical, owdered, and otherwise. A beautiful stock of ornamental hair-work rms a department of itself; and in addition E. C. makes and supplies igs, scalps, and fronts; he has also a large stock of theatrical wigs, hich he supplies to dramatic societies. In the sale-shop there is a capital nd well-selected stock of brushes, dressing-combs, soaps, perfumery, and roprietary articles. He has many specialities for the hair which have een recommended by medical men. Mr. Cowper employs many experi-nced assistants, but is himself the prime favourite with his lady and gen-lemen patrons, having for many years been with one of the first London ouses, where he acquired great experience and skill in his trade.

Hudson's Bay House, Furriers, 140, Oxford Street.—This business was established in 1850, and has been remarkably success-ful. The premises consist of a very attractive shop of handsome and im-posing frontage, several capital show-rooms, and a range of extensive and convenient workshops in the rear. The stock displayed in the windows and in the show-rooms includes many costly sealskins, sables, beavers, martens, and racoons; and besides the products of the North American continent, there is a fine stock of expensive Russian furs. The Hudson's Bay House proprietors do a very large business as manufacturing furriers, receiving consignments of skins, and dressing, preparing, and making them up. Thus they have generally on offer seal jackets, vests, and hats, sealskin coats and gentlemen's vests, ladies' muffs in great variety, fur sets for trimmings, capes, boas, and carriage and hearth rugs. The company also undertake the dyeing, cleaning, and repairing and altera-tion of furs. A large staff of hands is employed, and great personal attention is bestowed by the manager upon all work, new or old, under-taken by the company.

Henry R. Price, M.S.A., Architect and Surveyor, 25, Cross Street.—One of the most useful and advanced professions in Manchester is that of architecture and surveying. An old-established house in this line is that of Mr. Henry Price, which was originally founded as Price and Linklater twenty years ago. Mr. H. R. Price, who is a member of the Society of Architects, has been in sole possession for about fifteen years. The offices are of ample dimensions and admirably fitted up. A good staff of clerks is employed. Mr. Henry Robert Price is a thoroughly experienced architect, and he has executed many important commissions. He was architect to St. Paul's Church, Sale, St. Edmund's Church, Alexandra Park, Moss-Side, and St. Clement's Church, Green-heys. Mr. Henry R. Price's work is of great beauty, characterised by originality and freedom. He pays special attention to church work and to villas, and in all parts his services are frequently in demand. His qualifications are of the highest order, and he is universally respected.

Bailey & Williamson, Designers and Engravers on Wood, 24, Exchange Buildings, St. Mary's Gate (corner of Deansgate and St. Mary's Gate).—The art of designing and wood engraving is ex-tensively carried on in Manchester. A typical business in this line is that of Messrs. Bailey & Williamson, which was founded in September, 1880. Messrs. Bailey & Williamson, being men of talent and energy, have succeeded in attracting a connection which is extending in a most gratifying manner. The premises occupied, which are most centrally situated, are roomy, and fitted up in a first-class manner. Messrs. Bailey & Williamson undertake wood engraving in every branch, from the finest style on boxwood to the coarsest pine poster. They make a speciality of the engraving of mechanical subjects. Messrs. James Pollard Bailey and William Williamson are well known and enjoy the esteem and confidence of the members of the trade.

Nathaniel Dodd, General Finisher and Maker-up, &c., Pryme Street Works, Chester Road.—Among the many branches of the cotton industry of Manchester that of finishing holds no unimportant place. A well-known firm thus engaged is that of Mr. Nathaniel Dodd, which has a reputation of nearly forty years' standing. The works are very extensive, and are admirably fitted with the most modern machinery and appliances. Over one hundred skilled hands are employed in cloth-working, waterproofing, general finishing, and making up of all descrip-tions of fancy cotton goods, zephyrs, and Oxford cloths, &c. Mr. Nathaniel Dodd does a trade which for magnitude and extent has no superior in the city, and the energetic travellers employed are rapidly extending it, whilst the rise and progress of his house are important features in the industrial chronicles of Manchester.

Raby & Son, Sanitary Engineers, &c., 78, Cross Street.—Prominent among those firms which devote special attention to sani-tary engineering, land agency, surveying, and valuing, stands that of Messrs. William Raby & Son. It was established more than thirty-three years since, under the name of Corbett & Raby, and after twenty years of most successful work assumed its present designation. The members of the firm are Messrs. William Raby and Joseph Walker Raby. Their well arranged offices are devoted to the work of the firm, which is of a varied and highly responsible character, both of the principals being well qualified, by education, by experience, and special knowledge, to deal with the most difficult and delicate questions. In the important matter of public health as affected by sanitary engineering, Messrs. Raby enjoy a widespread repute. Their speciality, however, is the valuation of railway, gas and waterworks, manufactories, and other premises, &c., for the purposes of assessment. All who have to impose or pay local rates know that this is a task which requires very great care and attention. Both parties have, if possible, to be satisfied, and this is not always an easy task. In all the work of this class undertaken by Messrs. Raby & Son they have achieved a most thorough success, and no firm in the city of Manchester enjoys a more honoured or more respected position.

Richard Twemlow, Chemist, Dentist, &c., 91, Upper Brook Street.—Mr. Richard Twemlow's business is an important one. Soundly established, it is conducted on the most approved lines. As a chemist and dentist the enterprising and skilful proprietor has achieved a well-merited reputation, and he enjoys the custom and confidence of a large and ever-increasing number of customers. He is an A.Ph.S., Lond., by exam., and has had a quarter of a century's experience in the business. It is unnecessary, therefore, to say that he is a gentleman thoroughly conversant with the many details of his interesting and important profession. The premises occupied are admirably appointed. He is a capable and prompt business man, has a most excellent staff of assistants, and his customers are afforded every courtesy, care, and attention. His premises are admirably appointed for the efficient carrying on of his business in its various departments. Mr. Twemlow is also the Registrar of Births and Deaths for Chorlton-upon-Medlock, a district containing some 57,000 inhabitants.

Benjamin Burton, Family Draper, &c., 145, Strangeways.—The drapery trade of Manchester is not behind that of any other city for extent and excellence. A typical house in this business is that of Mr. Benjamin Burton, which was founded by the present proprietor thirteen years ago. The shop is large and elegantly fitted. The stock is extensive, comprising drapery, hosiery, gloves, collars, cuffs, scarves, ties, and other fancy and staple haberdashery and drapery goods. Mr. Burton manages in an enterprising manner, and his house stands well in the favour of local residents.

Joseph Saunders, Tobacco and Cigar Merchant, 2, Palatine Buildings, Victoria Street.—The manufacturing industry of Manchester does not monopolise all the commercial activity of the city, as the tobacco and cigar business is a most representative trade. A prominent house in this business is the establishment of Mr. Joseph Saunders, whose premises are conveniently situated. This house was established forty-three years ago, and came into the hands of the present proprietor some two years ago, and Mr. Saunders has spared neither time nor money in making it one of the most attractive and commodious concerns in Manchester. The establishment contains a most valuable stock of tobacco and cigars of English and foreign manufacture. Mr. Saunders claims some distinction in being an importer of Havana and Mexican cigars, having gained experience in the tobacco-growing countries, a superb assortment of whose productions is constantly kept on the premises, which are elegantly fitted with all the appliances incidental to the business. Mr. Saunders's taste and unqualified judgment are to be perceived in the regularity that is maintained in the progress of the establishment. He, with suitable assistance, personally conducts the business. This establishment bears conclusive evidence of the matured experience of Mr. Saunders. His able judgment and judicious purchases enable him to control a business which is profitable to himself and popular with the public at large.

H. Ranck, Importer of Stamps, Pictures, Stationery, &c., 11, Sugar Lane.—This firm has been established since the year 1872. The business is for the most part local, but many country buyers in search of novelties find their way to Mr. Ranck's warehouse. The stock consists mainly of German oleographs and chromo pictures, cheap engravings, and the thousand and one sundry articles of stationery goods that Continental manufacturers are able to produce at such wonderfully low prices as to utterly defy competition. Mr. Ranck is also a noted importer of foreign postage-stamps, and in connection with this part of his business has correspondents in almost every part of the globe. Mr. Ranck does not employ travellers, but does business direct with many wholesale houses. His advice is much esteemed, owing to his familiarity with all the productions of the Continental fine-art publishers.

Robert Robertson, Plumber, Glazier, and Gas and Hot-water Fitting, 4A, Marsden Square, Market Street.—Plumbing, glazing, and gas and hot-water fitting is a branch of industry of great importance and untold utility in a large city like Manchester. A good type of business in this line is that of Mr. R. Robertson, which was founded four years ago. Since that date Mr. Robert Robertson has worked up a fine connection, and has done much important work in the city. His premises are commodious, with spacious cellarage, and he has a very fine stock of appliances and materials for plumbing, glazing, and gas and hot-water fitting. He carries out all orders in an efficient, prompt, and economical manner, using the best materials and employing only the most skilful workmen. He carries on a good business, and makes a speciality of sanitary work and ventilation. Mr. Robert Robertson is a perfect master of his trade, and in four years he has won the esteem and confidence of the entire community.

Mrs. Samuel Bramall, Furniture Broker, 202, Stretford Road.—This business has been located at the present address since the year 1883, but was previously carried on for twelve years at 109, Great Jackson Street. The shop is spacious and well adapted for the business. Mrs. Bramall's business is that of a first-class furniture broker, and her transactions include the buying as well as the selling of the best second-hand household furniture, which includes drawing, dining, and bedroom furniture, cabinets, sideboards, &c. in great variety. The connection is extensive, and for the most part local. Nevertheless there are many customers in distant parts of the city. Mrs. Bramall is well known in the trade, and is much respected and esteemed.

Mr. John Bowden, Surveyor, Architect, and Valuer, 14, Ridgefield.—The business of architect and surveyor which is being carried on by Mr. John Bowden, is one of the best managed and most successful of local concerns. It has been established for a period of over fifteen years, and at present enjoys a wide and influential patronage. The offices are large and well-appointed, and a staff of clerks is kept in regular employment. An important part of the work done is in connection with the De Trafford estates, for which Mr. Bowden is the specially appointed surveyor. But architecture in all its branches, valuations, surveys, and arbitrations form a very material and important part of the business transacted by Mr. Bowden.

Frank Pearn & Co., Steam Pump Makers, West Gorton.—For seventeen years the names "Pearn" and "Pumps" have been indissolubly connected, and it is safe to say that no firm existing has a reputation at all approaching that of Messrs. Frank Pearn & Co. in the particular line. Pearn's pumps have carried off innumerable honours and distinctions, and they are known and appreciated the world over. The works are at West Gorton, and about one hundred men are kept constantly employed. The partners are Mr. Frank Pearn, Mr. Sinclair Pearn, and Thomas Addyman, all experienced engineers and inventors. The patents held by the firm, though mostly in reference to pumps, yet cover a number of ingenious appliances for steam-engines and tools.

Jno. Maybury, Law Stationer, 5, Clarence Street.—Mr. Maybury occupies an excellent suite of offices at the foregoing address, where, with a very efficient staff of assistants, he carries on a most successful business as law stationer, engrosser, lithographic and public writer. He is widely known amongst the legal profession generally in Manchester, and highly appreciated for the very careful and superior manner in which he executes the various orders with which his numerous patrons entrust him. It is an old-established business, dating as far back as 1864. Mr. Maybury is exceedingly clever in his method of copying, reducing, and also enlarging plans, &c., and is justly noted for his skill as an ornamental writer and engrosser. His staff are chosen from the most skilful and experienced men to be found, and all his work is executed in the very best style. A great feature in Mr. John Maybury's business is the despatch with which he executes orders, and his invariable punctuality down to matters of even the most trifling detail. He has therefore a most deservedly thriving business, and an extensive and distinguished connection, and furthermore, he is a gentleman universally respected, both as a man of business and a citizen.

Jacob Abdela & Co., General Commission Agents and Merchants, 13, Greenwood Street.—An enterprising and highly successful Manchester firm is that of Messrs. Jacob Abdela & Co., general commission agents and merchants. They have been established about twenty years, and they have built up a large and permanent trade. The firm deals in all kinds of Manchester and Yorkshire manufactured goods, earthenware, metals, colonial produce, and general merchandise, of which they carry a large and valuable stock. They both import and export considerably. The firm occupy a prominent position in commercial circles. The individual members of the firm are popular and respected.

G. B. Kershaw, Manufacturers' Agent, 38, Church Street.—Lace and trimmings of all kinds form an important item in the industries of the present day, and a very large number of firms are engaged in their production. Some of the best among these find an efficient and active Manchester representative in Mr. Geo. B. Kershaw, who for more than eighteen years has carried on a successful business at the above address. Mr. Kershaw has well-arranged and commodious offices, and the stock of lace, trimmings, and fancy goods which he has at command is very extensive. A large and widespread demand exists for the goods which are supplied through the agency of Mr. Kershaw. Mr. Kershaw studies the interests of both producer and consumer, and by energy and enterprise has won for himself a high and honourable position.

George C. Melville, Photographer and Dealer in Vorks of Art, 105A, Market Street.—Photography in Manchester is in e most advanced condition. A typical house in this line is that of Mr. eorge C. Melville, which was founded seven years ago. The premises cupied, which were specially built for Mr. Melville, are easy of access, the second floor of a commodious building. Mr. Melville is a most ilful photographer, and his work is of great beauty. He makes a eciality of oil painting on opal, size unframed fifteen by twelve inches, gilt frame and rosewood case, for thirty shillings, including twelve rtes. He has also made a speciality of a smaller-sized picture, eight d a half by six and a half inches, most exquisitely framed. This he pplies, together with twelve cartes-de-visite, for 12s. 6d. This gentle-an also deals in works of art, and he has a very fine collection. He rries on business partly on the club system, and employs eight or nine ualified assistants. Mr. Melville is thoroughly acquainted with his lling and is a gentleman of the strictest integrity.

E. Tucker, Baker and Flour Dealer, 121, Oldham Road. The bread and flour trade is the most important branch of the food supply Manchester, and it is, owing to the enormous population, of great lue, employing many establishments. A steady business in this line is at of Mr. E. Tucker, which was founded nine years ago. The shop is ample dimensions, well fitted up, the appearance is attractive, and it is avily stocked with bread and flour. The bread is absolutely pure and holesome, being manufactured by approved apparatus. Mr. E. Tucker rries on a very extensive wholesale and retail trade, supplying shops, d having a fine family connection. His own vans deliver with punc-ality, and the business is admirably organised.

Lamb & Evans, Makers of Glass and Wood Signs, ire Blinds, &c., opposite Cathedral, Manchester, and 1, Chapel Street, lford.—The manufacture of glass and wood signs, opal letters, wire nds, &c., is an important branch of industry in Manchester, and is of a ogressive and useful character. A well-known firm engaged therein, ving a fine city connection, is that of Messrs. Lamb & Evans, which was ginally established in 1858 by Mr. A. Tucker, who was succeeded in 1879 the present proprietors, who have greatly extended the business. ese gentlemen are looked upon as very expert and practical glass and od sign manufacturers, and they have raised the manufacture to the ghest state of perfection. The premises are large and commodious, nprising office and workrooms, the former substantially furnished, and workrooms completely fitted with every possible appliance for the siness. An adequate staff is constantly employed in making signs, opal ters, and wire blinds, under the careful overlooking of Messrs. Lamb & ans, and the productions are characterised by originality, tastefulness, l elegance of design and general artistic merit. A very lucrative trade carried on, the books containing a connection of long standing. ssrs. Lamb and Evans manage their business with enterprise and ll, and they are well known in the city and honoured as gentlemen unswerving honour and strict rectitude.

Stephen Moseley, Dealer in Toys, Brushes, Cooper-e, Combs, Hardware, &c., 31, Bury New Road, Strangeways.—The ernal Manchester trade in toys, cooperage, combs, hardware and other ods for personal and household use is very considerable. A thoroughly resentative business in this line is that of Mr. Stephen Moseley, ich was founded by the present proprietor thirty-nine years ago. e attractive-looking shop has the advantage of a fine situation at the ner of Cheetwood Street, and it is admirably fitted up with the requi-fixtures. The stock is extensive, well arranged, making a fine play, and consists of toys and brushes of all kinds, cooperage in at variety, combs, hardware of every description, and other like ods for domestic and personal use. They are of the best quality and nufacture, and in stock buying Mr. Stephen Moseley shows a thorough owledge of the trade. He carries on a very lucrative business in locality, employs an ample staff, and his management is able and rgetic. Mr. Stephen Moseley is one of the best known tradesmen in district; he is deeply esteemed for his strict integrity, and he holds an inent place in the trade.

J. R. Lancashire, Cabinet Maker and House Fur-her, 515 and 517, Rochdale Road.—This business has been in active ration for several years, and has apparently entered upon a successful eer. The premises include two very handsome and commodious shops with nerous show-rooms and capital warehouse accommodation. The stock been most carefully selected and is extremely comprehensive and ied in character. Mr. Lancashire was for seventeen years engaged h the noted firm of Messrs. Heaps and Harrison, of Oldham Street, l in commencing on his own account determined to follow out as far as cticable their system of business. Accordingly, great attention is paid quality, material, and workmanship of all goods manufactured or sold the premises. Every portion of the stock is the best of its kind, while selling price is kept as low as possible. Mr. Lancashire undertakes to furnish houses with everything that may be required from drawing-room, to kitchen, and best bedroom to scullery. There is also a department of his workshops devoted to the re-making of bedding and to upholstery remakes and repairs, while very special attention is paid to the absolute purity of the materials used in new work. A staff of some half-dozen experienced workmen are employed in the shops and work-rooms and warehouse, a very large trade being done. Mr. Lancashire is the sole proprietor, and is looked upon by the trade as a most deservedly prosperous gentleman.

R. Davenport, Plain and Decorative Painter, Paper Hanger, and Sign Writer, 58, Chapel Street, Salford.—The painting, paper hanging, and sign writing trade of Manchester is very considerable, and in a flourishing condition. A typical business in this direction is that carried on by Mr. R. Davenport. Although he only started last year, 1886, the ability of the management has attracted and secured a very good connection, which has every promise of a rapid extension. The shop occupied is large and admirably fitted with the trade appliances, the stock of paper hangings being large and of choice and original patterns. The decorative paintings and sign writing of this establishment is marked by tastefulness, and originality of design, and this department enjoys special patronage of a good class character. Mr. Robert Davenport, the proprietor of the business, is a man of enterprise and ability, thoroughly understanding every detail of his trade. He is well known and highly respected by the trade, and his house stands well in the favour of the local community.

Henry Otley, Saw, Tool, and File Manufacturer, 82, Oxford Street.—This business was established in the year 1855. The principal speciality is the manufacture of saws of all descriptions. Mr. Otley's band-saws are most highly esteemed by cabinet makers and carpenters for their excellent temper and durability. In addition to saws, Mr. Otley does a very large trade in machine, plane, and moulding irons, and in general joiners' tools, wood-carving tools, rules and measuring instruments, gauges and rods, and in special tools for engineers, tinmen, coach-makers, &c. Mr. Otley also stocks a good assortment of tool steel and files. The business premises consists of a sale shop of fair size, well fitted up and arranged, and workshops, and stock and store rooms. The trade, though extensive, is for the most part local. Experienced and skilful workmen are employed on the premises, though much of the work of the firm is executed elsewhere. The present proprietor took over the concern in 1877. He has been very successful, and is well known in the trade.

Hugh Stevenson, 71, 73, and 75, Silver Street.—Mr. Hugh Stevenson, the well-known manufacturer of cardboard boxes, &c., has a most thriving business at the above address, in addition to a new branch at 31, Bridge Street, Ardwick. Originally established in 1860, it is still in the hands of its founder, who employs between 100 and 120 hands in making all sorts and sizes of plain and fancy boxes, pattern cards, &c. A speciality of this firm is the sample cases made for the use of travellers, and these have met with a large sale. Many very pretty and artistic specimens of fancy boxes are produced here, and great talent has been displayed in the employment of new and novel cases. Mr. Stevenson is the sole licensee of the United Kingdom Patent Metal-edged Box Company for the Manchester district. The productions of the company are marvels of simple construction, strength, neatness, and general utility. The metal-edge boxes are as cheap as, and often cheaper than, those made in the old style, while their many advantages are such as should win for them universal adoption in trade circles. Mr. Stevenson also deals very largely in all kinds of enamelled and coloured papers, and does a considerable amount of business in card and pasteboards. A judicious and skilful management has done a great deal to give this house the success it has hitherto enjoyed.

The Stock Exchange Restaurant (F. D. Ballard, Proprietor), off Cross Street. That we should find a restaurant of the first class established in the immediate vicinity of the Exchange affords no ground for surprise. Situate off Cross Street, hard by the Royal Exchange, in New-Market and Black Pool Fold, and in the Stock Exchange Building, is a restaurant well-known as the Stock Exchange Restaurant, kept by Mr. F. D. Ballard, who—from his years of connection with the well-known Stork Hotel, of Queen's Square, Liverpool, and the Queen's Hotel, Southport—has qualified himself as few caterers for the public have done. The bar is long and handsomely fitted, and is frequently full of customers. There are also comfortable smoke-rooms, a private and compact apartment for the transaction of any business affairs; dining-room, and all the usual and necessary offices, including kitchens, &c.; the whole making, in fact, about as complete a place of rest or call as can possibly be found in Manchester or elsewhere. The attention bestowed upon Mr. Ballard's guests is marked by promptness and courtesy, and the proprietor himself is a genial and obliging host. The Stock Exchange Restaurant is indeed a pleasant place to visit, and a place that once visited is likely to become a favourite house to the lover of comfort and good cheer.

T. E. Hallewell, Mount-Cutter, Gilder, and Picture-Frame Manufacturer, 50, Hanover Street, Dantzic Street.—The fondness of the Lancashire people of all classes for the adornment of their walls with pictures is well known, and the gratification of this fancy not only gives pleasure to themselves but affords occupation and employment to a numerous class of artists, business men, and artistic workers in various departments of industry. The establishment of Mr. T. E. Hallewell, mount-cutter, gilder, and picture-frame manufacturer, affords an illustration of the above remark. It was established in the year 1877 by Mr. Hallewell, and has been an unequivocal success. The rate at which Mr. Hallewell turns out picture frames may truly be characterised as wholesale, as they leave his establishment by hundreds, and go to adorn alike the walls of the public building, the art gallery, the stately mansion, the snug villa, the house of business, and the parlour or house wall of the artisan and cottager. There is no description of picture frame that is not turned out from his establishment in large numbers in the course of the year. Mr. Hallewell's establishment turns out a large quantity of plain and polished oak and other mouldings of the handsomest kinds. He also undertakes the resilvering of plate and looking-glasses, and regilding in all its branches. He likewise makes a large quantity of show-card and photograph frames, and uses the latest and most improved machinery in their manufacture. The motive power is supplied by a gas engine. Mr. Hallewell furnishes estimates where necessary, per post or otherwise, for any contract embracing work under any of the branches of trade which he conducts. He employs a very considerable number of hands in the various branches of his extensive business, sending men occasionally far and wide for the execution of work. Mr. Hallewell is most assiduous in his business and most upright and honourable in his method of transacting it—facts which are borne universal witness to in the general respect and esteem in which he is held by all classes.

Wm. Garner, Boiler Maker, Perseverance Boiler Works, Blackburn Street, Adelphi, Salford. The manufacture of steam boilers is extensively carried on in Manchester. This branch of industry in the City is indeed in a most perfect condition and the business done represents an enormous sum. About five hundred hands are employed in the manufacture of boilers of all kinds. A well-known house in this way is that of William Garner, known as the Perseverance Boiler Works, which was founded in 1873. The works, sheds, and offices which form the premises are extensive and commodious, and the machinery is of modern and powerful construction. The offices are convenient, and the clerical staff employed is ample. Mr. Garner carries on a steady trade in all parts of the United Kingdom and abroad, and under his able and energetic management the business has rapidly increased. He is well known in the industrial and commercial world, and is highly respected for his business qualifications and courtesy, and is generally acknowledged to be one of the leading boiler manufacturers in the district, and is maker of several specialities in this line.

J. & P. Higson, Civil and Mining Engineers and Surveyors, 18, Booth Street.—Messrs. J. & P. Higson established themselves professionally in this city in the year 1853. Until 1878 they occupied premises in Albert Square, when they removed to the present address. The offices in Booth Street are a fine suite of spacious and handsome rooms, exceptionally well-furnished, and thoroughly and completely fitted up with all the latest and most approved appliances for the rapid dispatch of business. The Messrs. Higson being possessed of an influential personal connection, speedily found themselves entrusted with important business, and as their skill, knowledge, and training were perfect in their way, confidence was inspired, and a steady and remunerative professional business found its way into their offices. As mining engineers they were very successful, and their experience, ingenuity, and resource have been of the very utmost service to not a few mine owners and lessees in this neighbourhood. As surveyors, the Messrs. Higson are frequently commissioned in the interest of the banks and financial associations, and in cases of arbitration their decisions are seldom or never questioned. Mr. Peter Higson died in the year 1880, and the firm now includes Mr. Jacob Higson and Mr. John Higson, gentlemen most highly esteemed in their profession, and greatly respected by their clients and in general commercial circles.

Henry Coffey & Sons, Manufacturers of Shirts, Pinafores, Frocks, and Underclothing, 50 and 52, High Street.—This business, which was established over forty years ago in the present premises, by Mr. Henry Coffey, the senior partner in the present firm, was originally concerned with the Bradford dress goods trade, but in the process of time other departments were added. About sixteen years ago the sewing machine making great progress, and doing much to alter the course of many classes o[f] by which new trades were to be bui[lt] the whole complexion of much of [the] make of the garments worn by the [...] tative efforts were made, first in t[he] wards in the manufacture of u[...] developed until the whole range [...] included. The number of styles [...] ing to hundreds of new designs [...] being continually engaged in the [...] comprise a considerable warehous[e] diately behind it. The latter is a [...] frontage, and five stories in heigh[t] most complete machinery for cuttin[g] employment to over 300 male and [...] ping business with our colonies in [...] here, and in the pinafore depart[ment] week can be turned out, the m[...] stitches per minute not so high [...] the best for the well-made goods [...] duce.

Samuel Smith & Sons [...] **Drapers,** 46 to 54, Deansgate.—T[...] turing interests has had a benefic[ial] every branch of mercantile indus[try] the old-established and thorough[ly] and general drapers is that of Sa[muel] founded in 1824 on the site of its [...] and handsome building at the cor[ner] It is admirably arranged for the t[...] is given to a large staff of experie[nced] valuable, including silks, velvet[s] goods of every description; gl[...] usually found in a first-class est[ablishment] always maintained an excellent r[...] its stock, being specially noted fo[r] by American visitors to the cit[y] McDowall Smith, is one of Man[chester's] respected merchants, and has gi[ven] charities, is a member of the [...] other charities. The present bui[lding] on its improvement, and thus he [...] of the marvellous advancement w[...] thoroughfare in regard to the cha[racter] lishments. To the volunteers of [...] Smith, late of the 3rd M.R.V[...] an active part from its formatio[n] fourteen years.

William Teacher & S[ons] [...] whiskies supplied by this eminent [...] The house was established in Gl[asgow] Teacher & Sons, in the trade i[...] position, has become a synonym [...] chester branch was opened about [...] in importance the other offices [...] prominent blends of the firm is [...] protected by the Trades Mark [...] Cream Whisky is a leading art[icle] sampled at the London office, 26, [...] are moderate, seeing the great [...] stock kept in bond and in duty-p[aid] land—enables Messrs. Teacher [...] a uniform quality, an all-impo[rtant] trade. And this they are enable[d] by them, which is no other [...] stocks of the best of each year [...] matured, and not purchasing ol[d] Samples will be submitted wit[h] careful consideration and justi[ce] claimed for the liquors of this in[...]

I. Levinstein & Co. (I[...] **and Aniline Dye Manufactu[rers]** of dyeing is at once most instru[...] of this country is particularly go[...] class firms engaged in the manuf[acture] is the old-established and reputa[ble] for the superiority of their man[...] best managed, and in this lies the [...] works are situated at Crumpsall [...] fitted with all the latest improv[ements] hands are kept in regular empl[oyment] proprietor, will be remembered [...] of the Manchester Jubilee Exhib[ition]

John Parsons & Co., Glass Bottle Manufacturers, , Water Street, Bridge Street.—The manufacture of glass bottles nstitutes a staple branch of British industrial enterprise, which is orthily represented by the old-established house conducted by Messrs. ohn Parsons & Co., founded in 1760 under the title of Bluun Bros., the present firm having conducted the business for the past thirty years. The depot occupied is very extensive, and divided into spacious offices and ample warehouse accommodation, &c., the entire building presenting a fine street frontage. The working plant and appliances are all of the most improved construction, and kept in excellent working order. Vast stocks of all kinds of glass bottles are held, and the

rgest order can be executed forthwith. A full staff of clerks, working eratives, and warehousemen are permanently employed, excellent organtion being observable in every department, and the whole establishent bearing a thorough business-like aspect. The trade is entirely of a holesale character, and conducted exclusively among the best houses in the city and its environs. The gentlemen constituting the firm are practical bottle manufacturers, and of the highest business integrity and standing in the trade, their courtesy and expeditious completion of all orders confided to the house securing to them the personal regard and esteem of their numerous patrons.

Grimshaw Brothers, Chemical Manufacturers, Canal hemical Works, Clayton.—The firm of Grimshaw Brothers has now een established over twelve years, and not only have they achieved arked success in business, but they have obtained a high reputation in o sphere of chemistry. The list of articles manufactured by the firm is ry numerous, and include chloride of zinc, sulphate and sulphide of nc; also the ferrocyanide, silicate, phosphate, carbonate, acetate, nitrate, ide, chromate, bromide, iodide, &c. The chloride of zinc is made nerally in two forms, the solid and liquid. The former is espeally suited for export, as it insures a saving of at least half the freight, d we believe Messrs. Grimshaw Brothers were the *first* to prepare chlode of zinc in this convenient form. The liquid chloride is used for the eservation of railway sleepers and timber generally; it is also employed r the prevention of mildew in cotton sizing, as a flux in the tinplate anufacture, and for many similar purposes. Besides the foregoing emicals, which are used in manufacture, pharmacy, and medicine, essrs. Grimshaw Brothers are large dealers and makers of sizing mateals for cotton warps and piece goods. The firm also manufacture an ticle known by the name "Universal," used for scaling and cleaning eam boilers. This preparation contains materials which attack and move the scale formed by all classes of water, and also prevents the forution of scale without injuring the boiler plates in any way. Messrs rimshaw have also a wide reputation among indiarubber manufacturers, eir principal articles being recovered indiarubber and indiarubber subitutes of every variety. Nor must we omit to mention that what is own as "Paton's Soap Economiser" (of which Messrs. J. C. Paton & on, Limited, of 5, Chatham Street, Manchester, are the proprietors), is anufactured by Messrs. Grimshaw, and a silver medal was awarded it the Liverpool Exhibition of 1886. The foregoing list merely enumeos the leading commodities of their manufacture. The works are of nsiderable magnitude, and were erected for the special purpose to hich they are devoted, and they are most conveniently arranged and oroughly equipped for meeting all the firm's requirements. The coartnership consists of Messrs. Harry Grimshaw and Ernest Grimshaw, ho are sons of James Grimshaw, Esq., of Broughton Park. Both entlemen received their chemical education at Owens College, under the rection of Sir Henry Roscoe, F.R.S. Mr. H. Grimshaw acted for some me as a Demonstrator in Chemistry. He is an Associate of Owens ollege, Fellow of chemical and other societies, to which he has contriuted many original papers on chemical subjects. The firm employ good staff of hands, some of which are highly trained in science nd technology. We are glad to state that their trade is steadily increasing, their connection extending in all directions, and the future is ot only hopeful but full of promise. It may be noted that the firm had splendid exhibit at the Royal Jubilee Exhibition, Manchester, and they ill also have the same at the Glasgow International Exhibition which pens in May next.

William Holland, Great Ancoats Machinery Depot, 8, Store Street, Manchester.—In reviewing the industries of Manchester and district, the engineering interest calls for special notice. A representative establishment in this line is the well-known business of Mr. William Holland, whose immense warehouse is well situated and is known as "Great Ancoats Machinery Depot." Established now some twenty years, and under the same title, this house of business may well be considered one of the commercial institutions of Manchester. A glance at the circular published by Mr. Holland shows he is prepared to supply a very great selection of new and second-hand steam engines, boilers, and general machinery suitable for packers, bleachers, dyers, calenderers, finishers, engineers, boiler makers, &c. The stock comprises steam engines in pairs, and single, horizontal, vertical, and diagonal steam engines and boilers combined; steam engine attachments, boilers, Cornish, Lancashire, vertical, &c.; tools, &c., in every variety; wood-working machines, &c., weighing machines (various), steam and power pumps, hydraulic hydraulic presses, lifts, and pumps, for hand and power; calenderers' finishing machinery, &c., shafting pulleys, and miscellaneous cisterns, various copper work, &c. To manufacturers and users of steam power and machinery this establishment offers opportunities for the acquisition of sound second-hand engines and boilers of every denomination, and offers a selection not to be surpassed at any other similar establishment in England. The business transactions of the firm are necessarily very large and widespread, the house being well known and much patronised. The principal is well known as a thorough practical man of business of the strictest integrity and widely respected.

S. Megarity & Co., Shop Fitters, &c., Harris Street.—A great deal of business success depends upon the style in which the shop is fitted up and the manner in which the goods are displayed. In the "good old times" but little attention was paid to this important point. Window and shop dressing has grown to be an important factor in all branches of business. Prominent among those who are noted in this respect in Manchester is the well-known firm of Megarity & Co. Established ten years since by Mr. Samuel Megarity, this firm has large offices and suitable warerooms, and in these well-arranged and spacious premises a goodly stock of timber and other requisites for shop-fitting and the manufacture of showcases is kept. The business lies chiefly in Manchester and its environs, and some of the most handsome and elegantly-appointed shops in that district have been fitted up under its auspices, satisfaction of the most pronounced character being in every instance the immediate result. In showcases of every kind the firm has also a well-established reputation, and at all sorts of exhibitions its services are in constant demand. Nor is it to this branch of business that Mr. Megarity confines his attention, for he carries out all contracts for building, joinery, and the general business of a contractor. Perhaps a speciality of his may be mentioned in passing, such speciality being the fitting up of public bars, in which peculiar line he does a large and increasing business. Elegance in design, care and thoroughness in workmanship, and sterling quality in every material made use of, are the great qualifications of the firm; and they have been abundantly recognised by tradesmen and manufacturers in all parts of the city, who bear the highest testimony to the efficiency of Mr. Megarity and his workmen, and to the reasonable character of the charges which are made.

G. A. Chanot, Violin, Viola, Violoncello, and Bow-maker, Dealer in Old Italian Violins, &c., 18, Great Ducie Street.—An important branch of the musical instrument trade of Manchester is the manufacture, fitting, and restoration of stringed instruments, as carried on by Mr. G. A. Chanot, who was a pupil of the celebrated Georges Chanot, of Paris, is eldest son of George Chanot, of London, and is said to be a great adept at his art, that of making exact copies of the celebrated Italian violin makers' instruments, viz., Nicholas Amati, Stradivarius, Guarnerius, Maggini, Ruggerius, &c. Established in this city in 1879, he gained the highest award—a gold medal—at the International Inventions Exhibition, London, 1885, and a silver medal at the International Exhibition, Liverpool, 1886. He has gained a great reputation for restoring old violins, no matter how much damaged or neglected, to their original beauty and tone. He is also the inventor of a combination bag-case for violins, &c., patented; a quartett string gauge, by using which strings can be selected to insure perfect fifths; a preparation called the "G. A. C. Reviver," for cleaning violins, removing atmospheric dirt and resin without damaging the most delicate Cremona varnish. His most recent invention is a composition for preventing violins pegs, etc., from slipping, called the "G. A. C. Peg Slip no More," for which he has received testimonials from the leading violinists in Manchester, and which when it is generally known will be greatly appreciated and prove a great boon to all violinists. Mr. G. A. Chanot has a large stock of old violins and bows by celebrated makers. Special value in cheap violins, bows, cases, etc., for beginners, and imports direct the finest Italian, Russian, German, and French strings and every kind of fittings. He is also special agent or depôt for the "Edition Chanot" violin music published by his brother, Mr. F. W. Chanot, of London. Mr. G. A. Chanot carries on an extensive trade, and has large workshops fitted with gas engine and other tools for the special manufacture of violins, and manages his business personally with enterprise and ability, and is much esteemed in musical Manchester.

Joseph Siepen & Son, Tailors, 5, Police Street.—Established in 1846, this firm continues to be one of the best among the high-class tailors of this city. Originally known as Joseph Siepen, the admission into the partnership of Mr. Siepen, jun., in the year 1868, led to the style of the firm being altered to Joseph Siepen & Son. The firm have occupied the present premises some twelve years. The business is entirely the very best class of bespoke tailoring, and the stock includes ranges of pure West of England, Scotch, and Continental manufactures. Messrs. Siepen & Son's business connection extends far beyond Manchester and Salford. They are distinguished for good taste, style, fit, and irreproachable workmanship. The sole partner is Mr. Joseph Siepen, who is well known in the trade and highly esteemed.

Joseph Rigby, Furnishing Ironmonger, 56, Deansgate.—This well-known firm was established in handsome premises in Piccadilly in the year 1835 by Mr. John Rigby. Subsequently the business was known as John Rigby & Son, and five years ago the firm became known as Joseph Rigby. The trade connection is scattered over the whole of the North of England. For ordinary jobbing purposes a staff of experienced workmen is constantly maintained, but for contract and special work other men are employed. Mr. Rigby himself has had a life-long experience in the manufacture of all kinds of gas and water fittings, and this makes his advice and opinion extremely valuable. His stock includes gas and oil cooking stoves, the most approved lamps and fittings, and brass and ormolu mountings. Mr. Rigby has been entrusted with the lighting of many of the most important public buildings in Manchester, such as the Royal Exchange, the Reform Club, and the Athenæum. He is well known in commercial circles.

John Smith, Auctioneer and Valuer, 27, Dickinson Street.—The auctioneering and valuation business of Manchester is of vast value, and of great utility. A typical business in this line is that of Mr. John Smith, which was founded by the present proprietor thirteen years ago. Mr. S. carries out auctions of houses, lands, furniture, plate, jewellery, and every description of property, and is well-known for his energy and tact. He carefully prepares valuations. In business circles he is well known and highly respected.

Wm. Bourke & Co., Wholesale and Family Wine and Spirit Merchants, 58, Oldham Road.—One of the most valuable branches of businesses in Manchester is the wine and spirit trade. A young but typical house in this line is that of Messrs. Wm. Bourke & Co. It was established over four years ago, and the honourable business methods of the firm have already secured a good connection. The premises occupied consist of compact wholesale and family stores, containing spacious cellar, and also adjacent stores, in which are kept Guiness's stouts, Bass's and Allsopp's ales. The stocks come exclusively from the leading distillers and brewers. This firm have always in bond, at the distillery stores, John Jamieson's whisky from one to ten years old, Geo. R & Co.'s whisky from one to seven years old, and the Bushmills O Distillery Co.'s whisky from one to seven years old, in quarter cask hogsheads, and puncheons. Bonding orders for any of the above cel brated makes are executed at the lowest prices. Messrs. Wm. Bourke & C make a rule of only purchasing produce of the highest standard, and b adhering hereto they have established a sound name for purity ar reliability. Their ports and sherries are worthy of special attentio Messrs. Wm. Bourke & Co. are fully conversant with the trade, ar are excellent judges in buying. These sterling qualities have wo esteem and confidence, and their house enjoys a good reputation.

W. Peace, Hosier, Glover, &c., 294, Stretford Road.- This business has been established about twelve years, and its history one of steady and uniform prosperity. The premises consist of a handson roomy shop elegantly fitted up. In his general business Mr. Peace kee an exceptionally well-selected stock of goods, and having studied careful the precise requirements of the neighbourhood is very largely patronise In ladies' hosiery, gloves and fancy articles, and gentlemen's outfittin and a variety of elegant presents for ladies, Mr. Peace's stock h scarcely a rival in the whole length of Stretford Road. There are r travellers attached to the business, but several experienced assistants a employed. The sole proprietor is still Mr. William Peace, the found of the business, to whose ability the success of the concern is due.

Hulme Booking Office, 121, Stretford Road, **Josep Wray, Tobacconist,** proprietor.—This establishment was opened by M Wray about ten years since, for the purpose of supplying the public wi tobacco, cigars, &c., of reliable quality, for which his long experience wi the late Mr. R. J. Lee, of Market Street, and the late Mr. Charles Rose berg, of Oxford Street, has made him thoroughly fitted. With the bu ness of cigar merchant and tobacconist Mr. Wray combines that of railwa and steamship agent. As railway agent Mr. Wray issues ordinary ar excursion tickets to London, Liverpool, Blackpool, Southport, Dougla and many other places; and as parcel agent receives and forwards parce per Manchester, Sheffield and Lincolnshire, Great Northern, Cheshi lines, Lancashire and Yorkshire, and other railways, to all parts of th kingdom. Mr. Wray also holds the agency for the Atlantic liners of th Guion and Beaver Companies; and through Messrs. Davis, Turner, & Co foreign shippers, forwards parcels to any part of the globe.

C. W. Simpson, Ladies' and Children's Outfitter, 1 and 20, Cavendish Street.—This well-known and flourishing concern enjo a widespread popularity. It was established in 1880 by Mr. Charles Woo cock Simpson, and so much has the business grown that two shops ha been found necessary for its development. The windows of the premis are dressed in an extremely attractive manner, and bear ample testimo to the wealth of stock which may be found within. Every article whi can be included in the most comprehensive list of hosiery and outfitti for ladies and children is to be found in stock, and as Mr. Simpson de only with the very best and most reliable wholesale houses, there is no roo for doubt as to quality. A speciality is ladies' corsets and underclothing, a into this very important line of business so much care and energy ha been thrown that success has been achieved. The result of the honest a fair-dealing policy pursued is seen in the good name and large busine which Mr. Simpson enjoys.

Joseph Pollard, Chemist, Exchange Arcade.—Mr. Josep Pollard is the proprietor of a small but well-fitted homœopathic and d pensing chemist's business in Exchange Arcade. The business was est blished in 1878, and by due attention to the requirements of his custome a very good connection has been got together, and the business is no very thriving. Mr. Pollard exercises great care in making up prescri tions, and this is very important, as any carelessness or accident on t part of a chemist might lead to effects much more sensational than ple sant. The proprietor of this establishment employs an efficient staff, a has, moreover, an excellent reputation in the locality, and during the t years he has been established has had a constantly increasing trade, a now owns a very good connection in the neighbourhood.

James H. Royle, Manufacturer of Dress Good Ginghams, Zephyrs, &c., 41, Faulkner Street.—This business has be in active operation since the year 1880, and now occupies an importa position in the trade. The specialities of manufacture are various kin of dress goods, ginghams, zephyrs, Oxfords, Harvards, ticks, denim regattas, fodens, listados, cotton and union drills, and similar good The connection is large and important, and the trade is both home a foreign. Mr. Royle possesses a most thorough and complete knowled of every detail of the cotton manufacture.

Hayes & Whittle, Grocers and Tea Dealers, 710, ochdale Road.—This business was originally established by the late benezer Turnbull, who built the premises. It subsequently passed into o hands of the present proprietors, Messrs. Hayes & Whittle. The remises consist of a three-storey building, the handsome and roomy shop cupying the ground-floor, while there are warehouse and stock-rooms in e rear and basement. The shop is fitted up in a most expensive style, ost of the furnishing being best-class London made. Messrs. Hayes & Whittle have made a capital blend of Indian tea their leading line, and r this excellent article they are justly celebrated all over the district. hey also bear a celebrated name for Kiel butter, for which they have ecial facilities in obtaining from the finest dairies in the Kiel district. n addition, however, they keep a capitally selected stock of general rocery goods and all the best brands of tinned comestibles, such as corned oef, lobster, salmon, &c., with dried and preserved fruits, and similar oods. Latterly they have added to their grocery business the flour and ovision trade next door, 718, Rochdale Road. They have already established a name for the quality of their English and Austrian flours. Their ead, also, is baked on the most approved principle. They also keep a oice selection of plain and smoked Wiltshire hams and bacon, also finest alities of Cheshire and American cheese. The trade connection includes very large proportion of the best families in the district. Messrs. ayes & Whittle have another establishment at 341, Rochdale Road, ich was established by Mr. Bright; also one at 116, Miles Platting, dham Road, Newton Heath. The joint businesses show a very handme turnover, and each of the two gentlemen named has had a long perience therein.

Shelton & Hallett, Manufacturers of and Agents for nglish and Foreign Hosiery, Laces, Frillings, &c., 3, York Street.—is business was established more than a quarter of a century ago by e late Mr. George Shelton, and in 1881, some alterations in the firm having been made, the present style, Shelton & Hallett, was assumed. Their sale-rooms are centrally situated, have been in their possession for a great number of years, and are therefore well known to every buyer of hosiery and lace goods visiting Manchester. Their trade being so general in these classes, including frillings, curtains, nets, and kindred articles of both British and Continental production, they are always in a position to show the latest novelties and to advise on the special needs of any particular market, this latter being a feature to which they have given the most careful attention. Their large *clientèle* is e result of their experience, not only as practical men and manufacturers, t as agents for several leading makers. Both partners are actively gaged in the concern; they are thriving and prosperous and enjoy the st reputation.

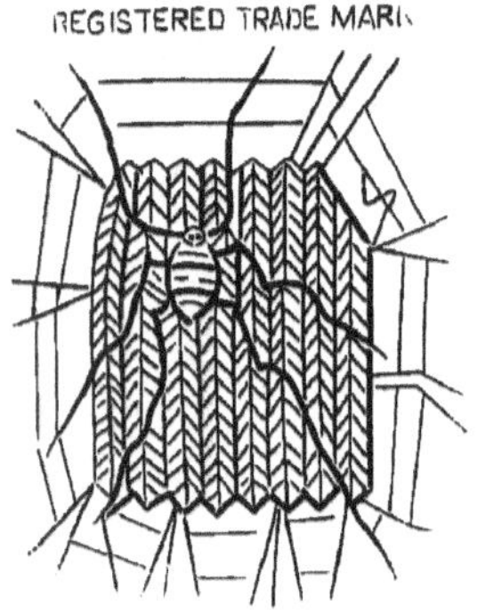

George Whittle, Mat and Matting Manufacturer. 'arehouse, 9, Dale Street.—This branch warehouse was opened about o years ago by Mr. Whittle, in order to meet the expressed wants of veral of his customers and to suit their convenience. It consists of a rge room, filled with a well-assorted stock of cocoa mats, mattings, &c., om which pressing orders can be executed with dispatch. Mr. Whittle's ods have been known in this city and district for several years, and ve the reputation of being best possible value at lowest remunerative otations. The factories for mat making and matting weaving are uated at Long Melford, in Suffolk, and the fibre mills at Janet Street, illwall, London, E., and the London warehouse at 31, Jewin Street, .C.

John Wynne, F.R.I.BA., Architect and Surveyor, Cooper Street.—Mr. John Wynne occupies offices in large and handme premises which were designed by himself. Established in 1881, he as elected a Fellow of the Royal Institute of British Architects in 1878. is intimate practical knowledge of measurements and values has enabled him to erect many difficult and costly works altogether without "extras." This, together with the artistic character of his designs, and his careful attention to the requirements and wishes of his clients, have obtained for him a reputation for architectural ability beyond his own city, and deservedly secured a varied and extensive practice not only in Manchester and its suburbs, but in different parts of the country.

Freud & Co., Manufacturers of Beads, Ornaments, Pearls, Bead Alberts, Collarets, Bracelets, Necklets, Crystal and Black Garnet Jewellery, &c., 71, Lever Street.—Manchester is an important centre of the bead and glass trade, and a manufacturing firm in this industry is that of Messrs. Freud & Co., which has been established for many years. Besides the house in this city, the firm has houses at Paris, Gablonz, and Vienna, and carries on a home and foreign trade. Many bead hands find constant employment. The Manchester premises contain stock of the raw material, and a good selection of samples from the three houses: beads of every colour and shape, ornaments, glass jewellery of the newest designs, pearls of very faithful appearance, and other novelties and leading articles of the seasons. Mr. Freud, the representative of the Manchester branch, thoroughly understands his business, is indefatigable in bringing out new designs, and enjoys the confidence and respect of his customers.

William Lomax, Manufacturer of Useful and Decorative Furniture, Carver and Gilder, and Dealer in Works of Art. Works and Show-rooms, 79, Oxford Street.—This business was established in 1845, by John and William Lomax, in the Old Exchange Arcade, where now stands the Manchester Royal Exchange. After the demolition of the old property the firm removed to 61, Cross Street, and 1, Princess Street, where the business was successfully carried on for a number of years; it is now solely in the hands of Mr. William Lomax at the above address. This gentleman added the manufacture of useful and decorative furniture of every description to the business. Here will be found, in the large show-rooms and picture galleries, some of the finest engravings and etchings from the best publishers, English and continental; also paintings and drawings of many rising and eminent artists. A very important branch of this establishment is that of carving and gilding, also the framing of paintings, drawings, and etchings. The restoring of paintings, drawings, engravings, bronzes, and pottery, &c., is manipulated by competent men of long experience.

The Globe Cotton Spinning and Manufacturing Co., Ltd., 1, Marsden Street.—Among the many Manchester establishments engaged in cotton spinning, &c., a prominent place is held by The Globe Cotton Spinning and Manufacturing Company, Limited. It was founded in 1864 at Cross Street, and in 1878 was removed to the present address. The premises are large and commodious, and comprise offices and warehouse. An efficient clerical staff is employed. The works at each of these places are large and extensive, admirably equipped with the most powerful and modern machinery used in the operations of spinning and manufacturing, and the hands employed are experienced and under efficient supervision. The Company's great speciality is the manufacture of cloth for India, China, and the home trade. Their operations are carried on on a very extensive scale, as may be judged from the fact that they have 200,000 spindles and 3,000 looms continually at work. Their large and well equipped works are located at Macclesfield, Crawshawbooth, Church, and Billington. The goods turned out by this Company have a widespread reputation for their general excellence, and the trade done is very heavy and rapidly increasing. The management throughout is able and experienced.

Sabbato Levy & Co., Levant Merchants and Shippers, 11, Bloom Street.—This compact establishment, founded so long since as 1866, by Messrs. Sabbato Levy & Co., and recently removed to the above address, bears abundant evidence of the sound nature of its transactions. Careful selections of general Manchester goods are periodically made by this house and shipped to the Levant, and other eastern ports and markets, where, as the result of this care, they generally arrive in time to command a ready sale. Almost all Messrs. Sabbato Levy & Co's. transactions are personally conducted, which no doubt accounts to a considerable extent for the solid reputation and the sound business the firm has succeeded in building up. They employ no travellers and keep no extensive staff of clerks and warehousemen, preferring to rely on their own experience and personal care and attention, which have been the essential cause of their success in all commercial transactions.

Worsley Brothers, General Joiners and Repairers of Property.—Good workmanship guaranteed. 67, Hardman Street, Deansgate; 17, Cobden Street, Gartside Street. Funerals completely furnished. Established over forty years.

Henry Hilton & Son, Smallware Manufacturers, 39, York Street.—This important business has been in active operation since 1789, the present head being the fifth generation in the same business. Though established nearly a hundred years, the operatives employed have never struck for an advance of wages, such differences having been amicably settled by mutual agreement. All the operations of a self-contained concern are conducted at the mills, where, in addition to manufacturing, there are also machine-making, bleaching, dyeing, and finishing. The specialities of manufacture are galloons, china ribbons, pink and china tapes, hatters' trimmings, silk and worsted floss, webbs, girdles, &c. The mills are at Parkside, Prestwich, and Hardman's Green, Pilkington. The connection extends over the United Kingdom, and a large export trade is also carried on. A strong body of clerks and warehousemen are actively employed, and the mills find occupation for very many experienced hands. The present members of the firm are Mr. Matthew Hilton, Mr William Henry Hilton, and Mr. Edwin Hilton. Each of these gentlemen has been carefully trained to the business, and is thoroughly conversant with every detail of the trade. They are all well known in the commercial world and no firm is more highly respected.

—

Babcock & Wilcox Company, Boiler Makers, Victoria Buildings, Deansgate.—One of the most notable names in the annals of modern British and American steam engineering is that of the eminent firm so widely known on both sides of the Atlantic as the Babcock & Wilcox Company of New York and Glasgow, manufacturers of the famous patent high-pressure water-tube steam boilers, which have secured the highest reputation. Three years ago this representative company founded their establishment in Manchester. Here spacious premises are occupied, and a large and increasing business is now being carried on in the sale of the boilers above mentioned, which is their leading speciality. The type of boiler now produced by this firm is the outcome of many years of careful and exhaustive research in every phase and aspect of the great question of steam generation, and the success they have achieved speaks for the company's attainment of an unsurpassed level of perfection. The Babcock & Wilcox Patent Water-tube Steam Boilers embody a decided and radical improvement in the disposition and application of the water tubes which constitute an indispensable part in steam generation intended for working at very high pressure with the least possible cost in fuel to the users. The Babcock & Wilcox boiler comprises three constructive parts, all of which are connected together, making up a complete steam boiler. (1) Over the furnace is placed a group of inclined solid-welded water tubes, by which the water is divided into small volumes and quickly raised to a high temperature, transforming it into steam as it passes over the furnace on its upward course through the said tubes and front headers into (2) a horizontal steam and water drum, where the steam separates from the water while it is passing through the drum to the rear end, where it descends through the back circulating tubes into the lower headers, from which it again ascends the inclined tubes and is again subjected to the action of the fire, and again passed into the steam and water drum. Thus a continuous and rapid circulation of water is kept up, consequently a uniform temperature is maintained throughout the boiler and unequal strain prevented. (3) A mud collector (a drum or cylinder) is situate at the rear and lowest point of the boiler, where it is connected to the bottom part of back headers, and as the water descends the heavier impurities fall by their greater specific gravity into this receiver, from which they are blown out through the blow-off pipe attached for that purpose. The water tubes, steam and water drum, and mud collector constitute the three prime features of distinction in the Babcock & Wilcox boiler. They are of the most careful manufacture, and it is sufficient here to state that the materials of which they are severally composed are of the best quality and most suitable character that careful selection can suggest or long experience and general usage sanction. The swift and complete circulation of the water through the boiler scours the tubes by frictional action, and prevents to a very large extent incrustation, even with the worst of waters, except of course in the mud collector provided for that purpose, as before stated. The whole structure of the boiler, when erected for use is suspended on wrought-iron girders and columns, allowing the boiler to expand and contract without undue strain. This is important, and worthy the notice of steam users, as it is well known that many explosions have occurred with cylindrical boilers owing to their having been set upon brick seatings. We understand that the Babcock & Wilcox boiler is erected and tested by hydraulic pressure before being enclosed. The brickwork is then constructed round the boiler, and arrangements made by means of iron doors for easy access to every part of the heating surfaces for examination and cleaning. The entire machine, therefore, can be readily kept in the most perfect order and repair at the least possible cost. On inquiry we learn that these boilers are unsurpassed for their capacity in supplying heavy and steady demands of steam, and yet while large in quantity we are assured that it is of the dryest quality. These boilers, being built in sections of moderate weight, are specially suitable for shipment, and are easily erected. In the matter of freight for transportation they can be conveyed for some 30 to 50 per cent. less than is charged for cylindrical boilers of similar power or capacity. The behaviour of these boilers when working under varied and most severe treatment proves them to be constructed upon principles which endure rougher usage than any other boilers in the market: and the fact that repeat orders have many times been given by large steam users, after having made sufficient trials, is ample proof that these boilers possess the superior merits claimed for them by the maker, viz. simplicity, safety, economy, efficiency, and durability. As regards economy, we may say that we have examined tables of some thirty tests which have been made by twenty different engineers of repute on boilers while doing their ordinary daily duty, and those results give an average evaporation of 11·4 lbs. of water per lb. of combustible. As to durability, many of them have been at work doing ordinary duty for upwards of fifteen years, whilst a large number have been at work almost night and day during that time, without any outlay on them for repairs. In addition to their Glasgow and New York establishments, the Babcock & Wilcox Company control other branches at Boston, Mass.; Philadelphia, Pa.; San Francisco, Cal.; Chicago, Ill.; New Orleans, La.; London, Paris, Havana, and Sydney. They have also selling agencies in Mexico, Holland, Germany, Russia, Austria, Switzerland, France, Belgium, Italy, Spain, and Portugal. The Manchester establishment is situated in a most convenient and central locality, being close to the Royal Exchange, Victoria, and Exchange Stations. Keeping in view the higher attainments and higher requirements of modern boiler making, the Babcock & Wilcox Company have carefully considered and followed those conditions most essential for the construction of such a boiler as will give the highest pressures with perfect safety, whilst at the same time having all the other claimed advantages. The advantages of high-pressure steam are being daily more recognised by the more intelligent steam users and manufacturers, as its use secures results, both in efficiency and economy, far exceeding what can be obtained from low pressures. Now that triple and quadruple expansion engines are coming more and more to the front, for the working of which it is necessary that steam be of very high pressure, consequently requiring a substantial steam generator, the Babcock & Wilcox boilers are being extensively adopted for the purpose, and they are also being put down for numerous other manufacturing purposes requiring high-pressure steam.

Life Association of Scotland, Royal Exchange, St. Ann's Square.—The Life Association of Scotland was founded in the year 1838. The feature distinguishing the Association from other Scottish Offices established previous to, and about, this date was the annual distribution of its *surplus funds* in the form of *cash bonuses;* policies being entitled to participate after being in force for six years. With assurers who wished to make a fixed provision for their families, or a business security at the lowest cost to themselves, the system of the Association soon became popular; so that early in its career the office took front rank in the assurance world. It was originally constituted, and its affairs have been invariably administered, on strictly scientific principles, the aim of the executive having been to secure stability and permanence, as the first requisite. Like some other leading offices it was able to announce at its first annual meeting, after the passing of the Life Assurance Act of 1870, that from the year of its foundation it had always valued its liabilities and assets upon a more stringent basis than the new act imposed. In the year 1860, the Association introduced a new and unique plan of assurance (Class B), designed to secure to that class of assurers who are the most remunerative to life offices, viz., those who live to extreme old age, the largest possible benefits. The plan is that only those assured who reach their "Expectation of Life," the average term of life of persons of their age at entry, realise the profits in the class. By the careful selection of lives for which the Association is noted, more than half the whole number of assurers live to the specified ages. When the assured has thus lived to his "Expectation," the bonuses are at his disposal, six options being given him. First, he may add the bonus as a reversion to the sum assured (the reversionary bonus additions have been at the last five quinquennial divisions at the rate of £4 per £100 per annum); second, he may cease paying premiums and receive a paid-up policy with considerable bonus additions; or third, a cash payment, at most ages carrying an important addition to the original sum assured; or fourth, a life annuity; or fifth, he may receive the bonuses in cash, and leave the amount of the policy intact for his heirs at his death; or sixth, may transform the bonuses into an annuity on his life. Of late years the Association has granted policies in the ordinary way, carrying bonus additions payable with the policy whenever death occurs after the first five years. The Association has taken a leading part in freeing policies from restrictions as to travel, residence, &c. The financial position at the end of the last quinquennium was as follows:—Amount of policies in force, £11,067,400; income in the last year, £474,300; death claims paid in five years, £1,032,215; valuation surplus, £471,175, of which divided, £400,182; accumulated funds, £3,140,679. The home of the Life Association of Scotland is at Edinburgh. Its head office buildings, which form one of the finest architectural features in the city, are located in the centre of the famous Princes Street, affording a very fine view of old Edinburgh and the castle. The local office in Manchester was established thirty years ago, and is at present located in the Royal Exchange Buildings, at the corner of St. Ann's Square. From its earliest years the Association has enjoyed the patronage of the manufacturing and merchant classes, and has obtained from Manchester and district a very large quota of its business. In amount, its risks in Lancashire are larger than perhaps in any part of the kingdom, London only excepted. The Association has offices in London, 5, Lombard Street, and 123, Pall Mall; Birmingham, Leeds, Liverpool, Newcastle-on-Tyne, Glasgow, Dundee, Dublin and Belfast.

Thomas Jones, Hot-Water Engineer and Heating [A]pparatus Manufacturer (High and Low Pressure). Works, 68, [Te]mple Street, London Road.—There is, perhaps, no business which com-[pr]ises so many branches as that of engineer. In each of these depart-[me]nts there has been witnessed a constant display of inventive genius [no]t only marvellous in itself, but in its consequences. This branch of [en]gineering is devoted to the designing and manufacturing of boilers, [pip]es, coils, valves, and other materials for hot-water heating, as adapted [to] the warming of buildings of all descriptions. Mr. Jones's establish-[me]nt is thoroughly representative of this branch of the engineering [bu]siness, including both the high and the low pressure system of heating by [me]ans of hot water. Mr. Jones has been in business since 1866. He has [no]t only acquired a splendid reputation all over the country, but he has [se]cured a large and widespread connection for his manufactures both at [ho]me and abroad. Perhaps no one invention of his has attained greater [fa]me than his noted "Terminal Saddle Boiler," which was the first [sa]ddle boiler made with a complete water-way end. This boiler is worked

[o]n the low-pressure principle, and was designed for warming green-[ho]uses, conservatories, churches, schools, and public buildings. It is [no]ted for its great power, with small consumption of fuel. Speaking of [th]is invention the *Journal of Horticulture* says, "The Terminal Saddle [B]oiler is, in our opinion, the greatest stride made for a long time in heat-[in]g by hot water." The *Gardeners' Chronicle* says, "Taking all the [ad]vantages this boiler possesses into consideration, we have no hesitation [in] pronouncing it the safest and most economical boiler in present use." [T]he *Gardeners' Magazine* remarks with regard to it, "This boiler possesses [th]e rare merit of sucking all the heat from the fire, so that it furnishes [a] maximum of power for a minimum of outlay in respect of fuel." At [th]e Manchester and Liverpool Agricultural Society's Show, held at Staley-[b]ridge, in September, 1874, the silver medal was awarded to Mr. Jones [fo]r this invention; and at the Great National Horticultural Exhibition, [he]ld in Manchester in 1867, it was awarded a first-class certificate, with [th]e following words written upon it: "The judges consider this one of [th]e most powerful and useful boilers for general purposes." The accom-[p]anying plate will show the formation of this boiler, and also a section of

[i]t when set in brickwork. It will be observed that the terminal end and [t]he side wings are valuable extensions of the heating surface. Mr. Jones [m]anufactures other descriptions of boilers, including the independent [c]ylinder, Trentham, tubular, and box boilers, and, in fact, every requisite [c]onnected with hot-water heating apparatus, and he keeps in stock a large [q]uantity of boilers, hot-water pipes, valves, connections, &c., &c. Mr. [J]ones also manufactures heating apparatus on the high-pressure principle, [o]r what is known as the improved "small bore" system, which con-[s]ists of continuous lengths of wrought-iron tube, 1¼ inch in diameter, a [s]mall portion of which is formed into a coil and placed in a furnace (either [b]rick or iron) around the burning fuel. This system has special recom-[m]endations for warming residences, churches, schools, railway stations, [o]ffices or warehouses, as the tubes can be bent round the fixtures, corners, [a]nd recesses of a room, or office, or other building, and it takes up very little space, and its advantages may be summed up as follows: rapidity in heating, economy in fuel, neatness in appearance, simplicity in ma-[n]agement, and smallness of space occupied. Mr. Jones's heating apparatus has been fixed in churches and chapels all over the kingdom, a large number of schools, more particularly in Lancashire and Cheshire, also warehouses and offices, and private residences in the same districts, public gardens all over England, and private gardens belonging to the nobility and gentry. His testimonials are sufficient to make a small volume in themselves. From a perusal of these testimonials, a few of which can be had on application, it is perfectly clear that Mr. Jones has fully established his reputation amongst all classes of his clients as a gentleman of uprightness and integrity as well as of very superior quali-fications in the profession to which he belongs. His works are commo-dious and well arranged; he employs an excellent staff of skilled work-men in all branches of his business, and furnishes estimates for all kinds of heating apparatus free of charge. Mr. Jones is much respected in Manchester and the district, and his business is extending in every direction.

Smithson Brothers, Cotton Spinners and Manufac-turers of T Cloths, Long Cloths, Drills, Twills, and Domestics, 9, York Street. (Telegraphic address, Smithson, Manchester).—This busi-ness was established more than thirty years ago, and is justly considered an important one in the city. The firm has been located at the present premises nearly twenty years. The mills are the Spodden Vale and Lower Mills at Facit, near Rochdale; the Bank Heath Mill at Golborne, near Newton-le-Willows; and the Daisy Hill Mill at Rishton, near Blackburn. A large number of operatives is thus employed, in addition to those employed by the various manufacturers and spinners for whom Messrs. Smithson Brothers are the agents. The main items of production are yarns and grey cloths. The trade connection is extensive, and in-cludes the principal shipping houses of Manchester, the general ware-housemen, and the leading wholesale houses of the city. The working staff at York Street is numerous, and includes many gentlemen of experi-ence and skill in the cotton trade.

Talbot & Co., Chromo-Lithographers and Printers, Pattern-Card and Book Makers, 5, Pool Street.—This newly esta-blished firm makes a strong bid for public favour. The premises occupied are very commodious, and admirably adapted for the purposes of a large business such as Messrs. Talbot and Company propose to establish. A very fine plant, consisting of the very newest patterns and best type of modern machinery has been laid down for the execution of all classes of chromo-lithography, and tons upon tons of litho stones are conveniently arranged in substantial packs. There is a department for pattern-card making and for account book making and binding. Necessarily a large staff is employed; and as excellence is the motto of the firm, the enter-prise of Messrs. Talbot & Co. is pretty sure to meet its usual reward. Being but newly established, the pattern-books of the firm are not as yet very bulky volumes, but already some very cleverly-executed printing has been turned out, notably some beautiful chromo cards for the decora-tion of finished piece goods—velveteens, white calicoes, prints, and the like. There are also some choicely designed and engraved invoice headings and tickets.

Chadwick, Boardman & Co., Chartered Accountants and Financial Agents, 64, Cross Street, Manchester, and 36, Coleman Street, E.C.—This firm was established in 1845, by the present senior partner, Mr. David Chadwick, M.P. for Macclesfield 1868 to 1874, author of various essays on parliamentary representation, working men's colleges, poor rate and principles of rating, and the equitable adjustment of the income tax, and joint stock companies. He is prize essayist and associate of the Institute of Civil Engineers. The partnership consists of Mr. David Chadwick, F.C.A., F.S.S., and Mr. James Boardman, F.C.A. The firm have also a large insurance business, Mr. Chadwick having been the principal agent and superintendent of the Globe Insurance Company, now incorporated with the Liverpool and London and Globe Insurance Com-pany. The firm's connection, as chartered accountants and financial agents, is very extensive. The companies formed and reconstructed by them since 1862 are represented by nominal capital amounting in the aggregate to upwards of £30,000,000, of which over £18,000,000 is represented by iron, coal, and steel industries, the rest being shipping, cotton, chemical, rail-way carriage and waggon, agricultural implements, dyeing and bleaching, india-rubber, copper smelting, &c., and marine insurance companies. Manchester is the headquarters of the firm, the London office having been established upwards of twenty years ago.

Sutton's Parcel Delivery.—In a busy commercial centre like the city of Manchester, the prompt and certain delivery of parcels of all kinds is one of the greatest necessities of the times. Occupying a proud and prominent position among those engaged in this work is the well-known firm of Sutton & Co., whose name is a household word, not only in Manchester but throughout the kingdom. Little more than a quarter of a century has passed since Sutton & Co. commenced in a comparatively small way, and during that period it has grown to gigantic proportions. The head office in Manchester is situate at 32A, Fountain Street, but the sorting and despatching is conducted in a large and splendidly arranged building in German Street, Oldham Road, the busy aspect of which, at all hours of the day, proves the widespread character of the business transacted. In addition to this well-known centre, there are branches in all parts of Manchester and districts. Parcels and packages are received and forwarded from and to all parts of the city and district by means of a finely equipped service of horses and vans. The Company is also in con-nection with all the railways which serve the district, and receives and despatches an enormous number of parcels by their means. Everything is carried out with the one object of serving the public in the best possible manner, and a great and unexampled success has been the result.

Olive & Partington, Paper Manufacturers, 9, New Market Lane.—This business was founded more than twenty years ago, and is recognised as one of the most important in the city. The firm have occupied the present premises some seventeen or eighteen years, and in spite of their great capacity and convenience find them almost too small for the requirements of their very extensive business. The offices are commodious and fitted with all modern appliances for the rapid transaction of business. The working staff includes manager, salesmen, book-keepers, clerks, and warehousemen. The trade connection is both home and foreign, an enormous quantity of paper being shipped to the order of Manchester and London merchants, as well as all that is sent forward by the firm direct. The paper mills belonging to the firm are as follow: in this city the Broughton Bridge Mills; in Glossop, the Turn Lee and the Dover Mills. As Mr. Olive died about twelve years ago, Mr. Edward Partington is now sole proprietor.

Wm. Jackson & Son, Cotton Manufacturers, 13, Mount Street.—This business was established about the year 1870, and is looked upon as a very important one of its kind. The premises in Mount Street are, in point of fact, little more than a town address, the mills and manufactory, at which a large number of hands is employed, being elsewhere. The principal items of manufacture are grey printers' twills, fancy cloths and coloured goods, Oxfords, Harvards, zephyrs, ticks, regattas, linens, lustres, &c. The trade connection is amongst the wholesale houses and the merchant shippers of Manchester and Bradford, and a very large business is done. The members of the firm are all very well known on 'Change, and are considered most skilful buyers and experienced men of business. Liberal employers, the firm generously support all movements likely to improve the trade of the city, or add to the comforts of the less fortunate residents. The firm occupies a leading position in the estimation of the trade.

John Ashmore, Joiner, Builder, and General Contractor, Shop and Office Fitter, and Show-case Maker, Decorative Painter and Paperhanger, 5, Minshull Street and 23, Silver Street.—This old-established business continues its career of steady progress and success. Mr. Ashmore has convenient workshops and offices, which are centrally situated, and from long experience in business can undertake any class of work and carry it through successfully. His speciality is the alteration and fitting up, furnishing, and decorating of shops, offices, warehouses, and show-rooms, and he has always on hand a very large and select stock of thoroughly seasoned and first-class materials. None but competent workmen are employed, and all work is carried out under personal superintendence.

Higgin, Lloyd & Co., Manufacturing Chemists and Drysalters, 22, Little Peter Street.—An important branch of the Manchester industry is the manufacture of gum, starch, drysaltery, &c., and, among the firms engaged, a prominent position is held by that of Messrs. Higgin, Lloyd & Co., which was established thirty years ago. The premises are large and commodious, comprising works and warehouse, the former fitted with all the most modern machinery and appliances used. The manufactures of the firm comprise stannate, arseniate, bin-arseniate, and chlorate of soda; arsenic, oleic and tannic acids, aniline solutions, salt, cake, and oil oxydizing pastes; steam black, Indian blue, soluble oil, oleine, resin, size, finishing gums and starches; farina, sago, rice, sizing, and printers' flour; all classes of British gums, crystal and corn starches, pigments, and artificial alizarines, &c. Messrs. Higgin, Lloyd & Co. also carry on business at Crooke, near Wigan, and at Nutsford Vale, West Gorton; and altogether a widespread business is done, travellers being employed in its extension. The members of the firm are Abraham E. and James Bradshaw Lloyd, and their house exercises a salutary influence in the trade.

Joseph Jones, Merchant, 16, Dale Street.—Among the many grades of Manchester no unimportant place is held by that of general dress goods, &c., and this trade is very valuable, and in many hands. A prosperous house in this line is that of Mr. Joseph Jones, which was founded three years ago. Since that date Mr. Jones has placed the house on a sound basis. The premises are commodious, affording extensive storing capacity, which is completely filled with general dress goods, and other fabrics. These goods bear the stamp of the most noted manufacturers. Mr. Jones carries on a very large trade in the city and suburbs. He has made himself well known in the mercantile and trading world and has earned respect and confidence in commercial circles.

Charles Wood, Waterproof Garment Manufacturer, 71, Chapel Street, Ancoats.—Although this business has been established but a comparatively short time, yet so great has been the satisfaction given, owing to the care and energy displayed by Mr. Wood, that it has assumed a prominent position in the trade, and is yearly improving. This house manufactures and supplies all goods in its line required
by retail establishments, among
fishing goods, shooting goods, an
the way of waterproofs. Mr. W
turned out by him, and in fact h
each and every article. The wo
Manchester Infirmary, and the p
fitted with the latest and most
Wood is held in esteem by the tr
and socially he is respected as an

Henry Lees & Bros.,
10, Corporation Street.—The gr
facturing centre of the country h
years. Among the commercial h
identified with Manchester's dev
& Bros. This business was found
on enterprising, energetic, and l
most gratifying manner, occupyin
trade. They do an extensive b
agents. The superior facilities
enable it to offer special advanta
are gentlemen whose integrity a
the esteem and respect of the com

Messrs. Sutton Brothe
Manufacturers, and Millers,
of the great manufacturing inte
would be complete without due
Messrs. Sutton Brothers. This
years ago, and have developed a
Their operations are exceptionall
prise three distinct departments
the manufacture of chemicals, a
gum and starch Messrs. Sutton
Their productions in this high
every quarter of the globe, and
starches have acquired, for purity
port to public favour. In the che
Messrs. Sutton Brothers are very
of a chemical nature required b
staining, and dyeing trades. M
nently forward among the repre
vicinity, and carry on flour-mi
mises occupied by the house, in
and admirably suited. All wo
with mechanical plant of the hi
house is very great and far-reach
British and shipping branches.
Sutton and Mr. T. A. Sutton, wl
business. To Messrs. Sutton's p
the success in Salford of an indus
developed, that busy suburb of M
and thriving manufacturing and

John Needham, Patter
—This business has been establi
of the most important in its l
George Street in the year 1830,
city improvements, a removal w
year 1886. The premises incl
venience for carrying on a first-c
ness is the manufacture of patt
in each of these departments g
addition a large number of travel
also a stock-room where a brisk
card makers, bookbinders and
fasteners, borders, fancy papers,
&c. The connection is extensive
old-established and well-known s

S. Fletcher & Son, Ta
Upper Brook Street.—The well-k
history that extends back some eig
of the first class, this firm has se
branch of industry it is essential t
to offer the public goods of the la
The stock kept at this establishm
these particulars. The premises
goods, and the visitor may rely
satisfactory reception. Mr. Georg
successful and artistic cutter, with
branch of the trade.

ral, Agricultural, and
atenton Street, Manchester, and
of the oldest concerns in Man-
e been in existence in 1769. A
n eighty-three years of age who
rentice in the wire works by his
many years. These two gene-
ntury, and it is with fascinating
interest that the present
proprietors and hands lis-
ten to the recitals of the
octogenarian touching the
past. Of course the name
of the firm has changed
more than once. Much
fresh energy was thrown
into the concern some six
years ago by a new pro-
prietor, though he main-
tained the old name of
Brookes & Co., and the
ie recent Royal Jubilee Exhibi-
ace to face with the name of the
rh fencing work in the gardens
nough to acquire, through the
nd at the head of affairs in this
ng and flower-bed bordering in
quired by the exhibition. The
t-iron fence along the terrace
easure of tens of thousands of
ved reputation. Besides all the
trade, we observe some clever
firm's catalogue, and we have
tifully ingenious machine, for
e. It is for use in the cotton
ward to its two ingenious in-
her in the proprietorship of the
ent into their own hands. A
of its productions, from wire
n tennis apparatus, ranges of
ard, to window-guards, riddles,
stock; and, we believe, in the
ery.

Manufacturer, 62, Hard-
ad.—Few athletic exercises call
ter share of mechanical industry
of cricket. The time-honoured
manufacture of which is appro-
tablishment conducted by Mr.
City Road, Hulme, in 1859, and
ess. The premises occupied are
cellent front shop and spacious
shment being well fixtured and
he speciality of the house is the
l stock is carried, including all
however, are renowned all over
its of excellence, and the other
er of merit. Another speciality
celebrated game of "Lacrosse."
of these goods, they are now
n fact, they send them all over
anised, a permanent staff of
ad the establishment kept in
is very heavy and particularly
he leading cricket clubs and the
proprietor is a gentleman well
n of no mean order, his genial
ng him their entire personal

r and Stationer, 31,
ationer's branch of commercial
ance, Mrs. Spencer's establish-
ne. It was established about
old the reputation of being one
chester. The specialities con-
somely bound Church services,
ses of every description and in
binding, and artistic printing,
g library stocked with all the
roductions of the best modern
choice of articles, both useful
mentioned "fans," of English
l artistic designs; ladies' and
ases of best material, with the

necessary accompaniments in silver, electro plate, &c.; toilet trays, in china, by best known makers; vases in glass, china, barbotina, satsuma, and imari ware; bronzes, plaques; hand paintings on porcelain, china, &c. This house also bears a long and deserved reputation for the choice and varied selection of articles suitable for presentation on occasions such as birthdays, christenings, weddings, farewells, &c. Another branch is that of address cards, menus, ball programmes, at home, condolence, wedding, and invitation cards, which are got up in every conceivable style and finish; Christmas, New Year, Easter, and birthday cards to suit all comers; and not to be blamed for having forgotten them, gentlemen may see here a capital assortment of tobacco pouches, beautifully embroidered in all colours, designs, and names; boxes for vestas, cigar and cigarette cases, hand-painted and crewel-worked letter-cases and pocket-books in every size; also ladies' and gents' card cases, &c., &c. Carved wood goods are also kept, which comprise brackets, pipe racks, match cases for the wall, work-boxes, writing desks, gipsy tables, smokers' tables; a splendid display of French steel jewellery; also the new silver fine art jewellery, &c.; photographic frames in every size and shape. In fact, the most fastidious could hardly fail to be pleased with the goods kept at this establishment. The stock held is very large and valuable, and comprises every known article in daily requisition at a first-class bookseller's and stationer's. The principal is a lady of the highest integrity, well known and widely respected by the inhabitants of the surrounding district.

Ellinger & Co., Merchants, 8, Minshull Street.—This business has been established upwards of thirty years, and is one of the most important in its line. The premises consist of a large modern-built stone warehouse, with most commodious, well-lighted offices. The trade connections are scattered all over India, and the British and Dutch settlements in the Straits, the Eastern Archipelago, China, Japan, and Persia. The shipments include every description of Manchester goods, from the heaviest twills to the lightest muslins and zephyrs, also velvets. Large parcels of Leeds and Bradford goods, and Batley and Dewsbury cloths; seals and rugs are also sent out. In addition Messrs. Ellinger & Co. ship considerable quantities of hardware, cutlery, tools, bar iron, guns, ammunition, and other Sheffield and Birmingham goods, machinery, and occasionally pottery and glass. Mr. Ellinger and Mr. James Ellinger are the sole partners.

Robert Charlton & Sons, Finishers, Makers-up, Calenderers, and Packers, Irwell Buildings, 42, Blackfriars Street.—Finishing, making-up, calendering, and packing form a branch of industry for the extent and excellence of which Manchester has a splendid reputation; and among the establishments engaged a principal place is held by that of Messrs. Robert Charlton & Sons, which was founded in 1816. The premises occupied are large and commodious, and consist of offices, warehouses, and a mill situated at the back of these. The mill is spacious and commodious, and is admirably equipped with the best machinery and appliances. About two hundred and thirty hands are engaged in finishing, making-up, calendering, and packing, which operations are conducted on the most advanced principles. The warehouse is heavily stocked; and the firm have a mill at Strangeways. Messrs. Robert Charlton & Sons carry on a very extensive trade in all parts, and they manage with enterprise and ability. The members of the firm are Messrs. John and Henry Charlton, who are both well known in the industrial and commercial world.

W. Downing & Co., Tea and Coffee Merchants, 2, Half Street, Hanging Ditch.—This highly-reputed firm is a very old-established concern, and its connection extends throughout the whole of the north of England. The offices, situate in Half Street, are sufficiently commodious, and adjoining are tea-tasting and store rooms. Mr. William Downing, who is now sole partner, is accounted one of the very best tea-tasters in the trade. There is always on offer by the firm a choice selection of the finest and most favourite teas. For fine coffees the Messrs. Downing & Co. stand in the front ranks of the trade, being coffee roasters, and having one of the oldest shares in the Manchester Coffee Roasters Company. Mr. William Downing is one of the best-known men in "the Ditch," and highly esteemed for his great business abilities.

Garside & Andrews, Manufacturers' Agents, 3, Half Moon Street.—This firm, originally known as Hodgson and Andrews, was established about 8 years ago. Three years afterwards, on the admission of Mr. James Garside into the partnership, it became known as Hodgson, Andrews and Garside; and subsequently as Garside and Andrews. The business of the firm is purely that which is known as the Manchester trade, that is to say, they offer shirtings, jaconets, mulls, cambrics, printing cloths, madapollams, taujibs, twills, stripes, Spanish cloths, checks, sateens and similar fabrics. In addition to their own merchant business, Messrs. Garside and Andrews are the absolute agents for several mills and manufacturing companies. The premises in Half Moon Street consist of convenient and well-appointed offices and warehouse. The partners are Mr. James Garside and Mr. Richard Henry Andrews.

Philip Whyman, Tea Merchant, &c., 690, Rochdale Road.—This business was established in the year 1878, and has advanced most rapidly, so that it has now become the largest food-providing establishment in this city. The warehouse and offices are situated at 690, Rochdale Road, and known as the "Electric." In addition to the headquarters, the firm possess thirty-seven other retail establishments within a radius of seven miles of the Royal Exchange. The warehouse is 100 feet long, and consists of three storeys, exclusive of the basement, the whole containing 20 000 feet of flooring space. The front part of the first floor is a large retail shop, quadrangular in shape, fronting the main road, which is brilliantly lit up by the "electric" light. Eight thousand candle-light power is produced at the exterior, as well as the interior—in all, sixteen thousand candle-power, and very attractive is the luminous effect. Two of Gramme's machines have been adopted, which are driven by a powerful horizontal high-pressure engine, which is fed by a twenty-horse power Lancashire boiler, 24 feet by 5 feet. The engine is fitted with the patent electric governors, making it always run accurate and steady. The boiler-house is fire-proof and ventilated, all heat being passed outside. It is enclosed on the warehouse side by an eighteen-inch wall, thereby preventing the heat from getting into the warehouse, thus keeping the other portion of the premises cool. Joining the engine-house are large cement tanks, fitted with hot and cold water pipes, for washing and dressing hams and bacon. Adjoining this is an ice or cooling-house, for the preservation of perishable provisions during the hot weather. On tl other side of this basement are stored large quantities of dried fruits, pr serves, lard, butter, &c. The floor being composed of cement is a pr ventative against moisture coming through. Here are hundreds of packag from different countries—Denmark, in which country the proprietor h secured dairies direct from the farms for his own business requirement These being shipped fresh direct to him each week are of the choice quality. Margarine from Holland, and the enormous stock of Irish bu ter, proves that Mr. Whyman is an immense dealer in this article, ha ing his own buyers in Ireland to export direct from the farmers fres made butter. On this floor also are the fruit-cleaning machines. On tl next, or first floor, are tinned goods, biscuits, flour, sugar, &c., in very lar quantities. The ceiling is scarcely visible, on account of the numero hams and bacon hung thereon. The second floor consists of spice, ric tapioca, sago, cocoa, &c. Great attention seems to be paid to all these in t manner they are stored. The third floor, however, brings us to the artic for which the proprietor has chiefly made his nar and fame, viz., tea. Piles of this English invigorat stand like immense walls, representing fully Chir India, and Ceylon teas. On the same floor is t drying and smoking department: the former admirably arranged, thoroughly closed in, air-tig on the warehouse side. A ventilation shaft is co structed from the bakehouse to the drying-roon to convey the heat from the bakehouse to the s rooms. Here the hams and bacon, after being w washed and dressed, are hung up for the purpose drying, and being thus exposed to a dry heat t process is most effectual. The fire-proof smol room, which provides for the lovers of smoked ha and bacon, so much valued by some for the brea fast table, is arranged with the same care as oth parts of the establishment. The tea-blender is driv by the engine which drives the dynamos for t "electric light." Half a ton can, by this excelle contrivance, be blended in seven minutes, and far more regularly combined than can possibly accomplished by any hand power. The mixer is fed means of a hopper from the room above. On tl floor also is the "coffee-roaster," converting t green berry, as gathered from the tree, to a bro berry, similar to that offered by dealers ready f grinding. A powerful steam hoist traverses from t basement to the top of the building. Arrangemen for loading and unloading are admirable in the e treme, the lurries being drawn into the building on level with the ground floor. The entrance to t breadroom and bakehouse is in Needwood Street, the back of the premises. To the right of the breadroom is the entrar to the bakery; here the mixing, kneading, and general preparations baking are carried on. The stoke-holes of the ovens are to the left, th keeping all fuel and dirt from the bakehouse. The firm is extremely w known in the wholesale markets; and the name is as familiar in Minci Lane and the Commercial Sale Rooms as in Hanging Ditch, Ma chester.

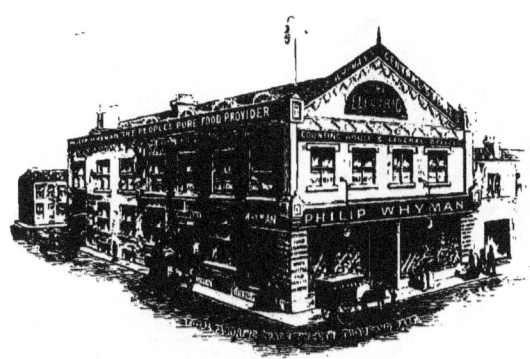

A. Kendal & Co., the "Alert" Automatic Fire Extinguisher, Byron Chambers, 8, Exchange Street.—The danger of fire in large cities is a hundredfold greater than in small and sparsely peopled places. For this reason anyone bringing out a fire extinguisher that can be safely, simply, expeditiously, and effectively brought to bear on the destructive element is almost certain to meet with success. This is just what Messrs. Alfred Kendal and Co. have done in introducing the "Alert" fire extinguisher. The invention is aptly designated the "Alert," for in cases of emergency the patent Self-closing Automatic Sprinkler, as the contrivance is also called, is so constructed that it works automatically, opening and closing itself. In this, quite a novel principle of action is adopted. No fusible metal is used as a sensitive agent. In its place we have an ingenious application of one of the properties of glycerine. A small quantity of this material is placed in a globular brass chamber about two inches in diameter. This is affixed to water pipes by means of a T-piece. As the heat acts upon the glycerine, causing it to expand, the pressure thus created forces open a small valve, from which the water falls in a spray, covering about one hundred square feet of superficial area. Immediately the fire is extinguished and the glycerine cools, its contraction allows the valve to fall and to cut off any further supply of water. The sprinkler will begin to act at a minimum temperature of 100°, but it can be regulated to work at any degree between 100° and 300°. The practical result is that the water is sprinkled when the temperature reaches an excessive point, say 150°, and that the sprinkling ceases automatically immediately the normal condition of temperature is again created by the extinction of the fire. Thus all unnecessary damage to goods and buildings is avoided without the intervention of any person. The apparatus is compact and strongly made, and not liable to damage by ladders, white-washing, or cleaning. The experiments which we witnessed at the works of Alfred Kendal & Co proved its value very conclusively. Two water-pipes were arranged under the roof of a wooden shed 24 feet long by 18 feet wide and 9½ feet high. Heaps of wood and shavings, satura with paraffin, were lighted within the building. The flames rose rapic to the roof, but within one minute and twenty-five seconds from the ti of ignition the "Alert" sprinklers, of which there were six, began play. In another minute they had extinguished the flames, and a f seconds afterwards the water had ceased to flow, having been cut automatically by the fall of the valve. The large number of gentlem present, interested in woollen and cotton mills, and other extensive wor expressed themselves highly satisfied with the efficiency of the inventic and especially with its sensitive and reliable action. The "Alert sprinkler is the first with an automatically closing arrangement—a f which alone promises to ensure its complete success.

W. Marsden, Chemist and Druggist, 251, Ashl New Road, Beswick.—Besides his well-appointed and particularly w stocked premises at Beswick, Mr. Marsden has another establishment 89, Every Street, in the city. At both places the business carried on satisfactory in the extreme, and as a chemist and druggist of no ordin position, the persevering and talented proprietor enjoys a wide reputat and considerable popularity. He does all in his power to give to customers genuine satisfaction, and is rewarded by a connection of wh anyone in his position might well be proud. The business was establisl some ten years ago, and during the ensuing period has been stead working its way to the front. At the present time the most promis signs of vitality are manifest, and a still more useful and profitable car is before this admirable concern.

J. B. Johnston & Co., Shippers of all Classes Merchandise to the East, 1, Parsonage.

William Tristram, Spinner and Manufacturer, 33, ...orlton Street.—The commercial greatness of Manchester constitutes ...e of the most magnificent illustrations of the outcome of trade progress, influenced by the well-directed employment of capital and enterprise, at the present mercantile condition of Great Britain affords. The ...reer of this city has been one of the most brilliant recorded in the whole ...nals of British manufacturing advancement during the latter part of ...e eighteenth and the whole of the nineteenth centuries, and the present ...osperity at which that career has culminated has unquestionably had ...r its chief well-spring and source the textile industries, in the develop...ent of which lies the solid foundation of Manchester's world-wide fame. ...connection with those industries the entire district, of which Man...ester stands as the great central point, has acquired a proportionate ...are in the city's renown. Lancashire as a county is no less celebrated ...r its practical operations in a branch of industrial activity of which ...anchester as a city acts as the commercial headquarters than is the ...ter great community for the part it has played in the same connection;

...d thus it is that we find the warehouse and business offices of Mr. ...illiam Tristram, situate at 33, Chorlton Street, well worthy of note by ...ason of their association with the same firm's extensive spinning and ...aving factories at Halliwell, Bolton, a locality whose fame as a centre ...textile industry needs no accentuation in these pages. The well-...own house of Mr. William Tristram was founded over forty years ...o, and was at first chiefly engaged in the production of plain Man...ester muslins. This original branch of industry has since been much ...veloped and expanded in scope; and now, after several notable exten...ns in the firm's operations, and in keeping with the progress made in ...e art of producing figured and other fancy cotton goods, the house ...nds unexcelled and practically unrivalled in the variety and excellency ...its designs and manufactures in this class of textile fabrics. The mills ...Halliwell, Bolton, constitute one of the greatest industrial features of ...at vicinity, covering a very large area of ground, and affording employ...nt to a most numerous force of operatives. The manufacturing opera...ns there carried on are of the first order of magnitude and importance, ...d a suggestion of the volume of industry accomplished and of the ...mensity of productive facility and capacity possessed by these notable ...rks may be derived from the accompanying cut of the establishment. ...ere is hardly a market in the world that does not absorb some portion ...the annual output of Mr. Tristram's Halliwell Mills; but within the ...ited space and scope of a work of this kind it is not practicable to ...ter into details of a more extended nature than those embodied in the ...regoing necessarily brief, concise, and superficial outline.

Sharp & Scott (by special appointment Purveyors to ...r Most Gracious Majesty the Queen), **Grocers, Tea and Coffee ...erchants, Italian Warehousemen and Importers of Wines, ...irits, and Liquors,** 56, Market Street.—The business of grocer, tea-...aler, and Italian warehouseman, combined with that of wine and spirit ...erchant, is an important branch of trade. Foremost in the ranks of ...uses engaged in this business in the city stands the well-known and ...pular establishment of Messrs. Sharp & Scott. Established in 1830 ...der its present title, this house has maintained for over half a century a ...putation of the highest order for quality of goods, reasonable prices, and ...ict attention to business. In the year 1840 Mr. Sharp was honoured ...the appointment of purveyor to her Majesty the Queen. Its specialities ...e chiefly high-class teas and coffees. Their sugars, refined only from ...re cane sugar at their own extensive manufactories, are well known ...rough the kingdom, as are also their wines, spirits, and liquors which ...e supplied direct from the principal vineyards and distilleries. The ...emises comprise a double-fronted shop, handsomely fitted, bold, large, ...d attractive, with warehouse for stores. The stock held here is very large, varied, and of the very highest character. The principals are Mr. William Sharp, who is an alderman and a Justice of the Peace, and Mr. Frederick Hodgkinson Beswick, both widely respected, of great integrity and business abilities.

Thomas Dyson & Co., Smallware Merchants, Trimmings, Lace, and General Warehousemen, 23A, High Street.—This business has been established since the year 1850, and the firm occupies large premises at the above address, consisting of a six-storeyed building divided for the convenience of trade into departments, whereof the basement is devoted to fents, piece goods, and knitting wools of all descriptions, including Hayfield, German yarns and fingering; knitting worsteds, Berlin, Shetland, Andalusian, and petticoat wools. The first floor is set apart for linen, cotton reels, &c., and the remainder of the building is laid out for and devoted to other departments, among which we may mention smallwares, buttons of all descriptions, trimmings, ribbons, velvets in the piece and in fents; silk plush in all the known shades, silk and cotton lace in great variety; linen, cotton, and silk pocket-handkerchiefs. A large department contains an assortment of babies', children's, and ladies' underclothing; in fact, all that comprises the usual stock of a general warehouseman. The house of Thomas Dyson & Co. is one of good repute, and does a substantial and growing trade; thus wholesale smallware dealers and drapers from the country will find it to their interest to call and inspect the stock at 23A, High Street, when they will be able to convince themselves as to its extent, and of the lowness of the quotations for the same.

S. A. Van Dam & Co., Margarine Importers and Commission Merchants, 22A, Hanging Ditch.—Margarine during the past few years has become very popular in this country and elsewhere, and the trade done is considerable and is steadily increasing. Manchester does the largest amount of business in this article of food, and among the firms engaged one of the most prominent places is occupied by Messrs. S. A. Van Dam & Co., which has been in existence for some years. This firm has the reputation of being the sole importers of the finest margarine, known as the "Blue Circle Brand." The premises occupied are extensive, comprising offices and store-rooms, and employment is provided for an ample staff of clerks and travellers. The blue circle brand of margarine is known favourably everywhere, and the trade is very widespread, extending all over the country, and a heavy export trade to foreign countries in tinned margarine is also done. The margarine is procured from the largest manufactory in Holland, and for purity and wholesomeness could not be excelled. Mr. Christopher Van Dam is now the sole proprietor of the firm. He is well known in mercantile circles, thoroughly conversant with all details of the trade, whilst his house is of considerable eminence in the margarine trade.

John Conery & Co., Umbrella Manufacturers, Joiner Street, Church Street.—The manufacture of umbrellas is of great importance in this city as a branch of industry, and one of the principal firms engaged in this line is Messrs. John Conery & Co., of which Mr. John Conery is the only member. The house was established in 1868. The premises occupied consist of a very large block of buildings of substantial appearance, and comprising works and warehouse. The works are fitted up with the most modern appliances. The umbrellas made on the premises are noted for their excellent workmanship, the fine quality of material, and elegant appearance. The warehouse contains a very large stock of umbrellas noted for their many excellent and original features. An enormous home and shipping trade is carried on. The organisation of the business is perfect. Mr. Conery has devoted his whole energy and talent to the manufacture of umbrellas, with the happiest results. His services in forwarding the manufacture of umbrellas are universally recognised and appreciated among the wholesale and retail traders throughout the country.

Ralph Waller & Co. (Limited), Cotton Spinners and Manufacturers, 46, Dale Street, Manchester.—The firm of Ralph Waller & Co., spinners and manufacturers, established more than sixty years ago, was converted into a limited liability company a few years since, and has a high reputation for the quality of its productions: candle-wicks, twines, heald yarns, banding, sponge cloths, hot-house shadings, cleaning waste, sewing cottons, knittings, mendings, cotton cords, crochet, and all kinds of single and double yarns.

Hughes & Young, 75, Thomas Street.—Amongst the fancy trades which have been developed in Manchester, the manufacture of umbrellas is a striking example. This trade, in England, is little more than a century old, and for sixty years the business we are now sketching has been steadily working its way. In the early days, when Mr. Dow (to whom Messrs. Hughes & Young have succeeded), commenced making umbrellas, the choice and styles were exceedingly limited. All of them were made up with frames of whalebone or cane, and the different kinds of sticks were by no means numerous. Now the variety is unlimited. The export of umbrellas from Manchester has increased in unusual dimensions during recent years, and it is now the centre for all the foreign markets. In tropical countries the umbrella has become almost a necessity. It is computed that to India alone about 5¾ million umbrellas are exported annually, the bulk of which are made in Manchester. It is very interesting to examine the different kinds of umbrellas being prepared for India, Australia, South America, Canada, Africa, China, West Indies, &c., and also to observe that each country requires an entirely different class of umbrella from any other; indeed, the differences are so marked that if by any chance a shipment got to the wrong port, they would scarcely realise freight. To an ordinary observer it is not a little astonishing that the umbrella is capable of being made in such endless styles. Visiting the show-rooms you will find thousands of sticks, suggesting the idea that every material of sufficiently durable nature that can be worked into umbrella handles has been utilised. A very large trade, of course, is always done in natural sticks, such as vines, pimentos, myrtles, oranges, and olives, and also in canes of many kinds. Natural wood and cane never seem to go out of fashion, though many changes are effected year by year in shaping, or dressing, or mounting. Ivory and buffalo-horn have had a large sale for many years, but recently the demand has been more for handles made of vulcanite or of celluloid. Both these materials lend themselves readily to moulding in a variety of elegant shapes. There are some very beautiful examples of artistic carving and chaste designs in gold and silver mounts. The frames are now almost exclusively made of steel in place of whalebone and cane, those made of Messrs. S. Fox & Co.'s Paragon wire being best adapted to general requirement. Messrs. Hughes & Young have introduced several valuable improvements in the manufacture of umbrellas, all tending to combine greater strength and resistance to wear with smartness of appearance. In the rooms containing materials for covering the range extends from the most expensive silks, through numerous qualities of unions, down to the cheapest cottons. The covers of some umbrellas have occasionally been rather troublesome to distributors, and it is sometimes said that umbrellas do not wear so well as in times gone by, a comparison not unfrequently made of a present cheap umbrella with an old expensive one. But in these days complaints of whatever kind have to be met, so Messrs. Hughes & Young, after considerable expense and many experiments, succeeded in introducing the "Phœnix" umbrella, which appears to be practically outside the ordinary effects of wear. In the factory many labour-saving appliances are used, and it is satisfactory to know that though umbrellas to-day are to be bought at lower prices than at any previous time, Messrs. Hughes & Young continue to make theirs under conditions healthy and even comfortable for their large staff of work-people, who are able to earn better wages than formerly.

C. L. Baker & Co. (Limited), Electric Light Contractors, Electrical Instrument Makers, Cornbrook Telegraph Works.—This well-known firm of electric light engineers and wholesale manufacturing electricians claim to hold the unique position of being the only *bond-fide* manufacturers of electric light plant and telegraphic and electrical apparatus in Lancashire. The works are situated in Worsley Street, Hulme, and were founded some years since by Mr. Charles L. Baker, whose varied experience, coupled with the high class of goods turned out, has caused the firm to take front rank in this particular industry. Without mentioning the works in detail, attention may be given at once to the instrument room, in which all the parts of the various instruments are carefully fitted together. In course of construction was seen a Prowett's patent bell-pull switch. It is made in various sizes, to suit either a single incandescent lamp or a large group of lamps or arc lights, and is intended to be fixed, for side lights, on the wall close to ceiling, or, for centre lights, on a rafter under the floor above. The communication to the switch (as shown in the illustration) is effected by means of the ordinary bell-pull cord and tassel. The one operation of pulling the cord alternately opens and closes the circuit. This switch is especially adapted for bedroom purposes, the cord and tassel being hung conveniently to the bed, so that the light can be extinguished after retiring, and at any moment during the night a light can be promptly produced. Moreover, it obviates the necessity of cutting the walls to receive the wires, or the fixing of the wires on the face of the wall to reach down to the ordina switch, thus saving a considerable amount of wire. Another speciali is the "special" testing apparatus. It consists of a portable astatic g vanometer, wound to a resistance of 600 ohms, and mounted on a mal gany base, and provided with three levelling screws. The galvanome is enclosed with a lacquered brass cover and open glass top. The set resistance coils and Wheatstone bridge are fitted in a mahogany case, a the capacity of the apparatus enables tests being taken ranging from of an ohm up to 1,100 ohms. The whole thing has been designed for t use of electric-light engineers, electric bell and lightning conductor fixe students, and amateurs. For dealing effectually with the fine class work here carried out it has been found necessary to design some spe tools. Amongst them is a lathe known as the "Cornbrook." It l 4-inch centres, a mandril of hardened steel, a four-speed pulley, a an extra-sized six-speed fly-wheel and treadle, &c. It is also fit with a divided head and step, a compound slide-rest, a 4-foot ga bed, loose headstock, hand-rest, and two tees. It can, if necessa be run by power as well as by hand. A drilling-machine capable working either wood or metal is another very neat little machine, a has been designed for high-speed working. It has an adjustable be ing in connection with the driving-wheel, the adjustment being ma by means of a screw and a slot. This adjustment tightens up t band as may be required. The machine has a fixed and a movable tal and makes a 2½-inch stroke. For cutting the teeth of certain whe used in arc lamps and the Morse telegraph instruments, an exceedin fine machine has been designed and constructed on the premises. In t winding-room the work done is chiefly covering the wire with silk a winding the wire into coils. Female labour is employed for these pu poses. The engineering shop contains a variety of special tools, one which may be especially mentioned, viz., a screw-cutting machine small screws. On this machine the screws are made from the rod, finis and cut off to the proper length without necessitating a stoppage, a the work done is equal t gross of screws per ho In this department th was being tested at the ti of the visit a new arc lan the prime features of it l ing simplicity of constru tion and a remarkable fe ness of parts. For the ti it was seen burning it w exceedingly steady, notwi standing that it was bei run off the ordinary engi used for driving the circu saws and the rest of t machinery in the wor and that also it was not highly finished lamp, l one used for experimenti upon. Owing to the gr increase which has lat taken place in lighting electricity, the firm ha been compelled to enla their premises, in order keep pace with the dema made upon their resourc Messrs. Baker & Co. (Lim ed) make a special feature this branch of the business, and being extensive manufacturers of dynam arc lamps, switches, &c., they are enabled to tender at a fair price every contract. They are also in a position to guarantee the qual and workmanship of all instruments and materials used by them any installations they undertake. All installations they have carri out have given the utmost satisfaction, and this fact has materially add to their eminent reputation and widespread and influential connecti The firm's works are lighted both by arc and incandescent lamps, a millowners and gentlemen contemplating the adoption of the electric lig cannot do better than pay a visit to Messrs. Baker and Co.'s headquart at Cornbrook, where they will see their ideas practically exemplified a in effective operations.

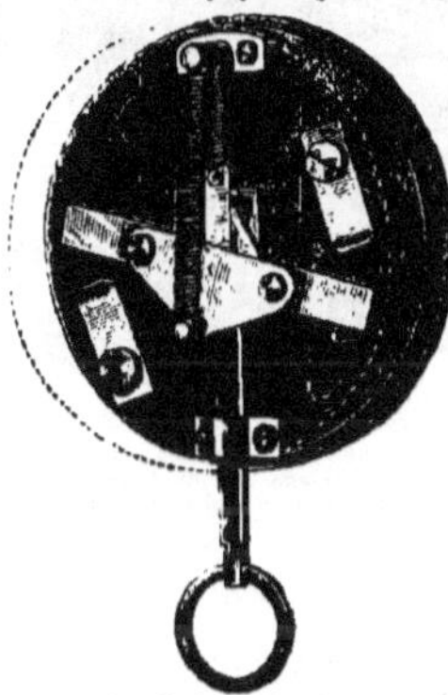

J. V. Farwell & Co. (of Chicago), **Merchants,** 2 Faulkner Street.—This business, which is but comparatively recen established, is making most satisfactory progress. The premises cons of a capital suite of convenient offices. Messrs. John V. Farwell & C are a firm of American merchants, whose headquarters are at Chica Their business in this city is the purchase of goods on account of t American business; and the firm is represented here by Mr. R. T. Edd The purchases include a large assortment of British manufactured goo some of the leading items being special makes of calico, velvets, ve veteens, muslins, cambrics and lawns, pilots and seals, Bradford stu and alpacas, Leicester and Nottingham goods, Scotch and Irish line while their continental trade forms a conspicuous item in their gene business. Mr. Eddy has made himself troops of friends since he settl here, and is extremely popular.

Mr. James Stott, Spinner, &c. Warehouse, 46, Spring ardens.—A leading manufacturing representative centre in the Manches- district is the well-known establishment of Mr. James Stott, Coldhurst all Mill, cotton spinner and doubler, manufacturer of knitting, sewing, d mending cottons, and all kinds of doubled yarns for manufacturing purses. Established in 1860 at Oldham, the Coldhurst Hall Mill has from e very outset been a prominent concern in the industries of the locality, e very magnitude of the undertaking guaranteeing its stability. The mills m an extensive range of premises of modern construction, fitted with comete and highly expensive machinery of the latest patterns and improveents, employing as many as three hundred to four hundred skilled operaves all the year round. The products of this house are well known, and aintain a very high reputation among all classes interested in the cotton dustry. The output is very large, and has a steady sale throughout the ngdom. The various kinds of cottons and doubled yarns are of a rearkably fine quality and finish, the excellent machinery in operation at eir works enabling this firm to successfully compete with any similar tablishment in the trade. The Manchester premises comprise a capaus warehouse well arranged and adapted for the storage of goods pack-g, forwarding, &c. There is a well-fitted office on the ground floor, th an adequate staff of assistants. The principal, Mr. James Stott, is gentleman well known and widely respected, and of great practical siness experience.

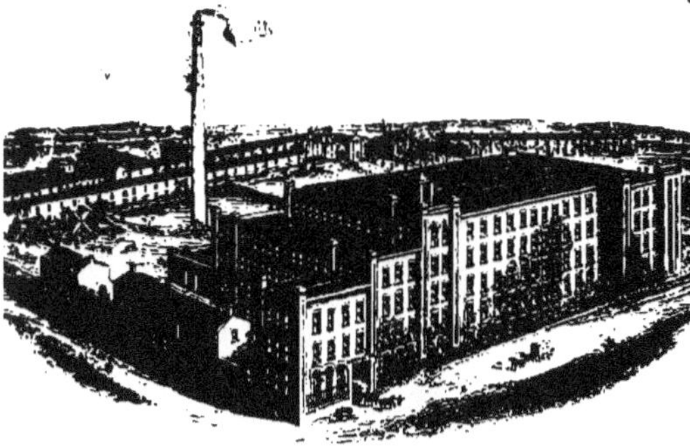

J. P. Westhead & Co., Limited, Manufacturers and erchants, 49, Piccadilly; and at Liverpool, Hull, Leeds, Birmingham, d Newcastle-on-Tyne.—The great representative business now carried under the style of J. P. Westhead & Co., Limited, was founded far back as 1801 by Mr. James Wood and Mr. Edward Westhead, o both commenced operations at the early age of twenty-five, as anufacturers of small wares and fringes. For these lines of goods the use, whose original location was at 6, Marsden Square, speedily acquired asting reputation; and this notoriety, influencing the continuous growth its trade, led to the business being transferred, in 1815, to High Street, ere a much larger warehouse afforded the necessary scope for its greatly tended operations. The year 1824 is marked in the history of Messrs. ood and Westhead by their establishing on the river Medlock the mills own as the "Medlock Smallware Company." The addition of new partments was thenceforward judiciously pursued, year after year, for long period. In 1830 Mr. J. P. Brown-Westhead, son of Mr. Edward estheud, was admitted a partner; and a few years later his younger others, Edward and John, joined the firm. Mr. J. P. Brown-Westhead as born in Faulkner Street, Manchester, on the 18th of April, 1807, and heriting a handsome fortune from his father, he was enabled to devote uch of his time to the public benefit. His natural quickness of perceptn, inventive turn of mind, and close attention to, and aptitude for, usiness, naturally led his fellow-citizens to request Mr. J. P. Brown-Westhead's assistance in almost every public movement. He took an tive part in obtaining a charter of incorporation for Manchester, and in nsequence was elected by the Manchester Town Council as one of their st aldermen. Few men displayed equal tact, more comprehension and ility in railway matters, and no man of his time had a more active or eater experience of them. His connection with the London and North estern and other railway companies led his friends to wish to see him Parliament, and accordingly in 1847 he was returned for Knaresborough. 1857 he was returned for York. Mr. Edward Westhead, senior, died 1833, having lived to see the status and success of the business he had unded practically assured. About the year 1836 the trade of the firm had developed to a degree which encouraged the purchase of the fine site in Piccadilly, upon which their present magnificent premises stand. Here were erected the two superb warehouses which were so familiar to the then residents in, and visitors to, Manchester, and these buildings were so constructed, in juxtaposition, that they could at any time be united and used as one complete warehouse. To this new location Messrs. Wood & Westhead removed in 1847, their firm occupying one of the warehouses, and Messrs. Ralph Hall & Co. the other. In 1839 Mr. John Westhead retired from the firm; and in 1841, partly by reason of advanced age and partly on account of the expiring of the original partnership between Messrs. Wood & Westhead, Mr. James Wood retired from business life. This left the control of the concern entirely in the hands of Messrs. J. P. Brown-Westhead and Edward Westhead. The firm in 1842 engaged as manager Mr. William Butterfield; and this gentleman became in 1847 managing partner in the concern. In the same year the two warehouses were thrown into one. In 1850 (March 21st) the fine warehouses in Piccadilly were visited by a disastrous fire, which destroyed little short of £100,000 worth of stock, and did great damage to the buildings. Owing to the great energy displayed by the firm, and notably by Mr. Butterfield, the business suffered practically no interruption, it being carried on during the rebuilding at two warehouses in close proximity. In 1858 Mr. Marcus Brown-Westhead, second son of Mr. J. P. Brown-Westhead, and Mr. Walter Bousfield Westhead, eldest son of Mr. Edward Westhead, joined the firm. In 1875 the business was formed into a Limited Liability Company, under the title of J. P. Westhead & Co., Limited; and two years later Mr. J. P. Brown-Westhead died, at the age of seventy years. Nine years previously (in 1866) several prominent members of the executive staff of the house had been admitted to partnership, and among these were notably Mr. Royle, now managing director of the Company, and his co-director, Mr. Goodwin. The development and extension of the business since its re-constitution upon a Company basis have been continuous and uninterrupted; so that the present warehouse accommodation has become inadequate to meet the present requirements, notwithstanding the additions—made in 1876—of the new warehouse at the corner of Lever Street, a portion of which is occupied by the export offices, which branch of their business has largely developed. The warehouses constitute unquestionably a complete emporium of the various lines—blankets, carpets, dyed goods, flannels, fustians, grey calicoes, linens, shirtings, prints, sheets and quilts, stuffs and dresses, velveteens, white calicoes and woollen cloths, corsets and buttons, dress trimmings, feathers and flowers, furs, gloves, haberdashery, hats, caps and boots, hosiery and wools, lace and curtains, millinery and straws, men's outfitting, ribbons, shawls and skirts, silks, crapes and plushes, umbrellas, smallwares, and upholstery trimmings. In each department the stock is replete with all the current requirements, both in variety, quality, and price. Messrs. J. P. Westhead & Co., Limited, control a trade entirely wholesale in character and of enormous proportions in its every detail, and have important and flourishing branches in Liverpool, Hull, Leeds, Birmingham, Newcastle-on-Tyne, and New York.

John Ashworth, Land and Mine Surveyor, &c., Hanover Chambers, 8, King Street.—Land and mine surveying is a profession of great importance and utility in this country. Manchester being a great industrial centre is naturally one of the chief headquarters of this profession. A well-known member is Mr. John Ashworth, who has been established in the city for ten years. He is thoroughly experienced in land, mine, and railway surveying, and has varied experience in all branches. He has a very influential and widespread connection among estate and mine owners, and he executes all commissions with fidelity and dispatch. He is well known in the land and mining world, and enjoys the goodwill and esteem of his professional brethren.

James Priest, Furniture Remover, 6, Stephenson Square.—One of the best-known firms in Manchester is that of Mr. James Priest, the extensive furniture remover and general carrier. Established as far back as 1835, this firm has so increased its business that the name of Priest is as well known as any in the North of England. The premises occupied are of very large dimensions. There are over one hundred and fifty hands employed. A firm of this description requires very careful management, great tact and business ability, and it says a great deal for the manner in which the business of this firm is conducted that such an amount of trade is done. In addition to the business of furniture removing, Mr. Priest has a large business as general carrier, and the promptitude with which this department is conducted has greatly increased the transactions of the firm.

Samuel Heginbottom & Sons, Spinners and Manufacturers, 15, York Street; and Junction Mills, Ashton-under-Lyne.—In reviewing the various branches of industrial activity which have made Manchester one of the greatest manufacturing centres of the kingdom, it is instructive and interesting to note the advances and improvements that have been effected in each of the principal departments of trade concerned. In surveying the wide field of industrial and commercial interests thus brought under notice it is easy to see that the manufacture of textile fabrics has been the great factor in the mercantile and general prosperity of the city, and in this connection it is a pleasure no less than a duty to be able to give prominent mention and remark to a firm of such old establishment and thoroughly representative character as that of Messrs. Samuel Heginbottom & Sons. This distinguished house is one of the great "family firms" of England; its history is enwrapped in that of the family of its proprietary during the last two and a quarter centuries (for the actual origin of the house can in reality be traced to the times of the Commonwealth and Protectorate under Cromwell). That excellent work of biography and history, *Manchester Worthies* (p. 47), sets forth a number of authentic details regarding the early annals of the Heginbottom (or Higginbotham, as the name was first spelled) family. As far back as 1650 Samuel Higginbotham is mentioned as a flax dresser and spinner, of Lower Halt Hill, near Ashton-under-Lyne, an industry carried on by him in the upper or third storey of his house. This may without hesitation be set down as the origin of the present firm. From the parish church registers the family, previous to this time (1650), appear to have been tanners and skinners, and, prior to that again, are described as yeomen. One thing is clear—the family of Heginbottom ranks among the oldest, as it stands to-day among the most highly respected, in the Manchester district of Lancashire. The "purposes of marriage between Samuel Higginbotham of the one part, and Mary Turner, of Alt, of the other part, were published three times, as by statute required, on Wednesdays, in the Market Place, (Ashton), *to witte*, the 13th day of January, the 20th and the 27th of the same, 1657-8." In 1657 it is also recorded that Nicholas Higginbotham presented to the Cheetham Library, No. 6,712, *Flores Historiarum*, by Matthew of Westminster, with a continuation to 1326, which was formerly the property of the monks of Westminster. Records show that members of the Higginbotham family, of Alt and from Alt, were churchwardens and overseers of that parish in the years, 1697, 1698, 1726, 1730, 1775, and again in 1838, 1847, 1857, and 1869. They held office also as mayors of the manor and borough in 1839-40, 1849-50, 1850-51, 1853-4, 1854-5, 1861-2, and 1879-80-81; and were county and borough magistrates in 1845, 1852, 1855, 1861, 1867, and 1882. Coming more particularly to the doings of the family in trade and industry, we find from an old day-book in the possession of Mr. Thomas Heginbottom, the present principal of the house, that Mr. William Heginbottom, on January 1st, 1767, is the seller of linen cloth, at 12d. per yard; flax, at 9d. per lb.; hemp, at 10d. per lb.; blow (blown) flax, at 12d. per lb.; flax thread, at 13d. per lb.; yarn, at 2s. 6d. per lb.; check, at 10d. per yard; hemp spun, at 1s. 6d. per lb.; and fustian at 18d. per yard. This Mr. William Heginbottom altered the spelling of the name in the year 1762 from Higginbotham to its present form. He continued to carry on his flax spinning at Halt Hill, the spinning-mule being then driven by hand, and, dying in 1780, was buried in the north aisle of the Ashton parish church. He was succeeded by his son William, who, adding the industry of cotton spinning to that of flax spinning, removed his business to Ashton. In 1814 he handed over the business to his sons Samuel and John. The first mention of cotton yarn in the records of the house is an entry in an account dated October 9th, 1779: "48 lbs. of white yarn, £2 16s. 0d." Samuel and John Heginbottom continued the business at Kenworthy's Mill, in Stamford Street, and at Croft Mill and Charlestown Mill, and eventually Samuel became sole head of the firm. He continued the undertakings of the concern at Jowett's Mill, built for him by Mr. Jowett, and in 1832 built his own first Junction Mill, so called from its being on the side of the canal at the junction of the Peak Forest with the Huddersfield Canal. In 1834 he built a larger mill, and followed this up with the erection of two others in 1836-37 and 1838 respectively, all in the same locality. This group of mills now constitutes the extensive industrial headquarters of the concern. Later on Samuel Heginbottom took his two sons, William and George, into partnership as spinners and weavers, and retired from business himself in 1850. The present principal, Mr. Thomas Heginbottom, is the only son of this last-mentioned William Heginbottom, and by him the mills have been much extended. His uncle, George, who never married, and lived quietly and carefully, left and gave large sums of money to benevolent and charitable purposes. In these respects he displayed a munificence that has largely characterised the family, especially its present representative, and among many existent monuments to his bounty are Holy Trinity Church, Schools, and Parsonage, at Ashton, costing £23,000, and other Ashton churches, towards the erection and improvement of which he contributed nearly £2,000. In addition to this he devoted to educational purposes £3,200; to religious societies, £2,500; and for Church work in Ashton, for the poor of Ashton, for the beautiful Ashton People's Park, and for the lifeboat, about £3,800. In all these he set a magnificent example to others similarly prosperous, and has left behind him a memory that will live for all time in the recollections of the many who have permanently profited by his well-directed beneficence. And thus the family record is brought down to the present head of the firm of Samuel Heginbottom & Sons, Mr. Thomas Heginbottom, Alderman of Ashton, and Justice of the

Peace of Lancaster county, whos
public man has been one of es
entered the business of which he i
and, upon attaining the estate c
daughter of the late Alfred Norton
Works. After this Mr. Heginbot
attention to public matters, and w
zealous efforts in behalf of the
times of depression, and notably f
practical and substantial assistanc
Famine. Becoming churchwarde
Williams, M.A., afterwards Dean
Heginbottom worked with might
stricken workpeople in Ashton a
the deputation to London, in 186
the Mansion House Committee th
1860 Mr. Heginbottom entered th
for three years, and in the same y
and Saltersbrook Trust. The yea
sion of the Peace for Ashton bo
the same connection for the coun
1874, he was made respectively
valescent Hospital, a life governor
and chairman of the Watch Con
his father for many years before h
one of the representative Church
1873 he was elected again to
governor of the Royal Albert Asy
tion stone of Holy Trinity Churc
Ashton. In 1878 he was elected
eminent office for three years w
community, and enhancement t
neglected no opportunity to serve
townsmen. After this he was ag
remains an alderman to the presen
of eminent usefulness, and few
creditably combined their efforts
time a great and prosperous mo
characteristics of which are such
the community in which his lot i
Ashton-under-Lyne, the firm of S
a very large force of skilled oper
the manufacture of plain cloth, twi
jeanettes, serges, cords, diapers, sp
satteen cords, satteen stripes, ca
fancies in general, from 27 to 60 i
these goods have a standard rep
every class of home and export c
Street a large stock is held, and
cute orders of the greatest magn
satisfaction. It will be impossib
dwell adequately upon the many c
which distinguish the working ro
such a business. The great suc
has had its latest and most prolific
of its present principal, Mr. Th
capacity and untiring energy, nev
the magnitude of his public and m
unquestionably made the business
the resources of capital and experi
its splendid manufacturing faciliti
tains, along with the fact that tw
business, it is not possible to look
the past as any other than the ant
advancement and increased and en

Thos. Muirhead & Sons
Game, and Poultry Merchants,
most thoroughly representative fir
in Manchester is that of Messrs. T
was established in 1846, by the lat
inception has enjoyed a prosper
spacious and commodious, admira
convenience for the transaction of b
wholesale and retail trade in t
supplying the same to the best cl
reputation of this establishment is
praise, and it is sufficient to say th
Muirhead and Sons are in a p
customers, and to execute all ord
individual members of the firm, M
gentlemen whose enterprise and
esteem and respect of the commerc
Muirhead was one of Manchest
citizens. He was an alderman of t
and as councillor for upwards o
advocate of every measure having
ment of Manchester.

Bryce & Rumpff, Alizarines, Anilines, Chemicals, . Booth Street, Mosley Street.—This firm has a widespread and valuable putation that extends itself throughout the country. It was originally ablished about eleven years ago as the sole representatives for this intry of the Farbenfabriken Vormals Bayer & Co., whose celebrated rks are situated in Elberfeld, Germany. Besides this firm's works at berfeld, they have branch establishments in Moscow (Russia), and Clers by Roubaix (France), for the purpose of introducing their world-own makes of alizarines and their highly-reputed anilines among large consumers in England, Scotland, and Ireland. With what suc-s their (Bryce & Rumpff's) endeavours have been crowned, the present gh standing and reputation of the productions of the Farbenfabriken iong the whole textile colouring trade, amply prove; for we can safely say there is not a dye-house in the United Kingdom where their products are not known and appreciated, and closely connected therewith is the name of Bryce & Rumpff. They made a very important addition to their trade by the introduction into the English market of the valuable series of new colours for dyeing cotton without a mordant, manufactured and invented by their friends in Elberfeld. This branch of their business has developed a new epoch in the dyeing trade. Besides this department of trade, they have also devoted their attention to the chemical trade at large, and have by reason of the really admirable manner in which their business has throughout been conducted, and the many exceptional advantages the enterprising proprietors have been enabled to offer their customers, made a most rapid and, at the same time, substantial progress on the road to success, thus establishing for themselves a large and

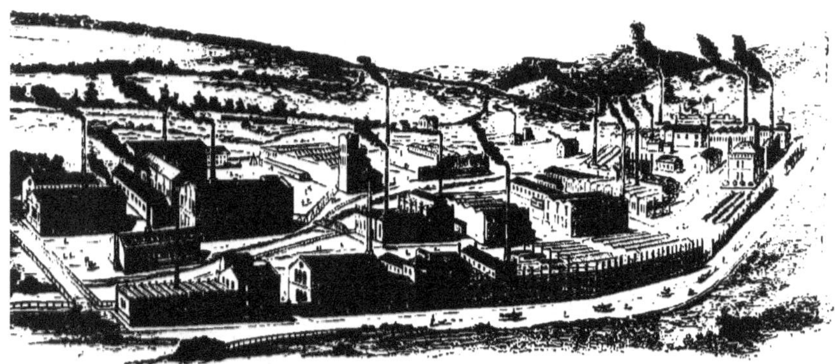

uable *clientele*. The chief office is at Glasgow, in addition to which re are three branches, each of which forms the centre of a brisk l lucrative trade. These branches are situated respectively at Brad-d, Yorkshire, in London, and at 18 and 20, Booth Street, Mosley eet, Manchester. The latter is the medium for the bulk of the Lan-hire connection, which is one of the most important in England, and manner in which it is conducted reflects the very greatest credit upon se who are left in charge. With regard to the goods for which Bryce Rumpff have become so famous—Alizarines, Anilines, and Chemicals—r firms can approach them in general and particular excellence. In lition, moreover, to their well-known quality, the prices charged for them are very moderate indeed. The leading position which Messrs. Bryce & Rumpff now hold in the whole chemical trade, and the reputation they have obtained for themselves enables them to afford every possible care and attention that skill and forethought can secure to their customers. Taken as a whole, the firm commends itself as deserving of widespread and cordial support. The proprietors certainly occupy a prominent position in the front rank of their class. Improvement and thoroughness are their mottoes, and they act up to them in a manner that is hard to equal, but to which is owing the indisputable fact that, through the general excellence of their goods, their business is rapidly increasing, and their popularity is fast becoming more complete and general.

James Hardcastle & Co., Bleachers, Dyers, and lico Printers, 87, Mosley Street.—The well-known and old-estab-ied firm of bleachers, dyers, and calico printers, James Hardcastle & ., of the above address, and Bradshaw Works, near Bolton, has been wards of half a century in existence. It was founded upon principles sound and with resources so considerable that it has withstood all the inges and trials which have since befallen every branch of the cotton de. The extensive operations of the firm are carried on at the Brad-w Works, near Bolton, which are replete with all modern machinery. e firm of James Hardcastle & Co. may truly be said to have gone to fullest possible extent in availing themselves of these resources science, with the result that their productions at all times take highest place on the market. The business of this firm consists receiving cotton goods of almost all kinds from merchants and manu-turers in the grey state in which they leave the loom, and delivering m bleached and finished for the home or foreign trade, or dyed or nted according to the orders they receive with them. Their white ishes are specially suited to the China, Singapore, India, and South aerican markets. They also do a considerable business for Constan-ople, the Levant, Persia, Egypt, and other markets. The dyeing and nting trades of James Hardcastle & Co. consist chiefly in the produc-n of goods suitable for linings for all purposes, many of the designs ng very beautiful and ingeniously adapted to the purpose for which y are intended, and which are largely sold in the London market. e firm employ about six hundred hands, many of them having been th them from childhood, and all holding their employers in the highest pect and esteem. James Hardcastle & Co. are the possessors of several luable and well-known trade marks and tickets, amongst which we y mention their "Tiger Ticket," the crest and arms of the family, isisting of a leopard standing on a shield containing castles and pards' heads; and their "Cock Ticket," the crest of the Lever family, h which Mr. Hardcastle's grandfather was connected. The presence of these tickets upon finished goods is a guarantee that they are as perfect and correct in length and other particulars as possible. Mr. Hardcastle devotes the greater part of his time to personally superintending the business in all its branches, and also employs competent men in Manches-ter and all the works to assist him, and no efforts are spared to meet the requirements of the customers of his firm.

O. Moore, Confectioner and Tobacconist, 14, Victoria Station Approach.—Among the many elegant and attractive establish-ments which are to be found in the Victoria Station Approach, none is more popular or more frequented than the restaurant and confectioner's of which Mr. Oliver Moore is the proprietor. It was only during the present year that the success which had attended Mr. Moore during a twenty-three years' tenure of 57, Long Millgate, induced him to remove to this busy and well-known spot; but he has already won a measure of success that is gratifying in every respect. The premises at the above address in the Station Approach are of ample extent. There is a hand-some and well-fitted shop, replete with every convenience—comfortable seats and well-arranged tables attract those in need of rest or refreshment, and the manner in which their wants are attended to leaves nothing to be desired. The stock, which is arranged in the most effective manner, com-prises all toothsome dainties and triumphs of the confectioner's art. Light wines, or tea and coffee, with other liquid refreshments, such as lemonade, seltzer, &c., are also supplied, and here again the quality is to be relied upon. Mr. Moore also does a considerable trade in cigars, tobacco, and cigarettes; and the brands can always be relied on. This is very convenient for the passengers both coming and going by the various trains in and out of Manchester. First class brands are stocked, and in this connection the house has won a good reputation. Mr. Moore has had a lengthy and successful experience in catering for the public; and the manner in which he has met their requirements has earned for him a most gratifying amount of success.

The Manchester Pure Ice Company, Limited, Minshull Street.—This company, which has been established four years, has in that comparatively short space of time made very considerable progress, and succeeded in making a name for its speciality in Manchester and suburbs. Its extensive works are situated in Minshull Street, and are specially adapted for the manufacture of pure artificial ice; and to those who are interested in the progress of science in this direction, are well worthy of a visit and inspection. They are replete with the newest and most effective machinery, apparatus, and appliances of every description, that the combined efforts of science and mechanism have yet been able to bring to bear for the purpose of artificially producing what has now become an indispensable necessary of life amongst all but the very lowest class of society. Already the Company employs a considerable number of hands, though in consequence of the excellence of the machinery and the perfection to which the process has been brought, not so many as might be expected from the output which the Directors are already able to congratulate themselves upon. The quality of the ice produced by the Manchester Pure Ice Company is of the very highest class, and nothing can exceed its purity and the perfection with which it is manipulated, the surest test of which is the rapidity with which the trade has grown and still continues to expand. The Company have been extremely fortunate in the selection of their staff, and have succeeded in securing a combination of the best scientific knowledge and experience and practical business ability in the management, which to a great extent accounts for the progress already made, and holds out the fairest promise for the success of future operations.

Peter Reid, 39, Dickinson Street, Manchester, and Caledonian Works, Whit Lane, Pendleton.—One of the great and most important industries of the age is that of treating textile fabrics and yarns by the various processes known as bleaching, dyeing, calico printing, and the general finishing of goods; and very wonderful is the change effected by one or more of these processes between the cloth as it leaves the loom and when it leaves the hands of the dyer. The dyer of yarns and warps is also responsible for many of the beautiful effects produced in goods woven with coloured yarns, a very important branch of Lancashire trade. It is, therefore, very evident, that to hold our position among other manufacturing nations, great attention must be paid to the above industries. At the works of Mr. Peter Reid may be seen all the above processes in full operation, and cloth and yarn in all colours and finishes for every market in the world being produced. The works were established in 1853, employ about five hundred workpeople, have fourteen full-sized Lancashire steam boilers, and about fifty steam engines, from 5 to 400 h.p. Their great capacity may be judged of as the weight of finished cloth and yarn that can be turned out ready for the market daily exceeds fifteen tons. We give a brief summary of the principal processes to be seen at these works. *Bleaching* is divided into two departments, one the muslin department, in which are bleached and finished Victoria lawns, mulls, jacconetts, scarfs, and all descriptions of fancy cloths suitable for both home and foreign markets. The beauty of the pure white and excellent finish is much to be admired, and has only been produced by the use of most expensive and excellent machinery. The other and no less important part of the bleaching department is that devoted to the production of white shirtings. A speciality is made of the beetle finish in this department.—*Cloth dyeing and finishing:* This is a very extensive department, and combines every variety of cotton cloth, from the sober colours used for home trade linings, to the brilliant dyes required for the Eastern markets; the dyeing of dress goods is a noticeable feature of this department. Every imaginable finish is put on the various goods when dyed, and a large quantity of calenders and beetling machines are constantly at work.—*Calico printing:* The trade the firm makes a speciality of in this line is the printing of linings for the home and foreign markets, both in fast and loose colours, as required. The stock of copper rollers is a very large one, and the patterns, of which there are an immense variety, are extremely choice and well suited to the trade.—*Indigo blue cloth dyeing.* The dyeing of this colour forms a department of itself. Here are dyed and finished all shades of indigo upon drills, shirtings, twills, and other cloths.—*Yarn dyeing.* In connection with this large department are three dyehouses, one for Turkey red, another for indigo blue, and a third for fancy colours. As in the other departments, both the home and foreign markets are catered for. Great attention is paid to the various colours which are required to stand a bleaching process after being woven in the cloth.—*Warp dyeing:* This department is carried on in a separate works from the main buildings, and forms a complete works in itself. Any colours which can be dyed in the bank the firm will dye also in the warp if required, and with the aid of very improved machinery a good result is obtained. These are the principal features briefly summarised of a works in which perhaps as many varieties of the coloured trade can be seen as any in the United Kingdom, and owing to their large capacity and management offer special advantages to merchants who require prompt and satisfactory execution of their orders. Owing to the great variety of the work undertaken, the merchant is enabled to send his various classes of goods into one hand and thus save a great deal of trouble and expense. The proprietor, Mr. Peter Reid, has been for many years a member of the Royal Exchange, and is a gentleman widely known and respected by a large circle of friends, and to his industry and experience the high position attained by the firm is due.

Thomas & William Southern, Manufacturing Chemists
Wheat Hill Chemical Works, Salford.—Surrounded as this city is b
dyers, bleachers, dressers, and finishers, it follows that enormous quanti
ties of chemicals must be annually consumed, and hence it is nc
surprising that certain chemical works which commenced in a somewh
humble way have in the course of time reached imposing proportion
Over sixty years ago the Wheat Hill Chemical Works, situate close t
Broughton Bridge, Salford, came into the possession of Mr. Thoma
Southern, the grandfather of the present proprietors, Messrs. Thomas an
William Southern, who since that time have gone on increasing the
boundaries in response to the calls of an ever-extending business. Th
requirements of the dyer and the calico printer are to-day infinitely mo
numerous than they were, say, thirty or forty years ago, and as th
manufacturing chemist is called upon to supply most of the dyes, colour
and liquors, in addition to all the acids, alkalis, sulphates, and salts,
follows that in place of the old-fashioned list of one or two specialitie
which formerly sufficed for even large concerns in the chemical trade, th
number of necessary articles has reached a total of one hundred at leas
The Wheat Hill Chemical Works, no way behind the times, is prepare
to supply everything demanded for calico printing, dyeing, bleachin
calendering, and finishing. Its list of productions is an imposing doc
ment. To carry on its multitude of various processes a sufficiency
hands are kept. The general trade of the firm extends over the whole
the United Kingdom, while large shipments are constantly made
foreign ports. The proprietors of the firm are Mr. Thomas Southe
and Mr. William Southern, both gentlemen well known in all publ
matters pertaining to the borough of Salford, and in a somewhat le
degree to the neighbouring city of Manchester.

Alex. Thomson, Coppersmith, Brassfounder, &c., 5
Temple Street.—Working in copper and brass founding form a branch
industry in Manchester of no small importance, and an admirable e
ample of a substantial house in this line is afforded by that of Mr. Ale
Thomson, which was founded twenty-six years ago. The premises a
of adequate dimensions, fitted up in a very complete manner. A staff
about twenty experienced hands is employed in manufacturing all kinds
brass and copper work, baths, boilers, cylinders, brewers', dyers', a
wash pans, beer machines, spirit fountains, soda water apparatuses, a
other industrial appliances. Mr. Thomson carries on a widespread trad
having a fine connection of long standing among brewers, dyers, distille
and mineral water makers.

David Greenwood, Furniture Dealer, 108, Stretfo
Road.—The "City Furnishing Establishment" was founded by M
David Greenwood in the year 1847. Large and well-fitted premises a
here devoted to the work of cabinet making and upholstering; and in t
shop and show-rooms there is a large stock of furniture of a handson
and serviceable description, made in the newest designs and of the be
material. For those who prefer furniture which has been well season
Mr. Greenwood has a very large selection of second-hand articles whi
well repays inspection. This establishment is one of the most prosper
and successful in this particular industry.

James Martin, Bookbinders' Cloth, Materials, Mil
board Merchant, &c., 6, Cross Street, Bradshaw Street.—Bookbindi
being an important branch of industry in the country, the trade in t
cloth, materials, millboards and papers used, is of considerable magnitud
Manchester does a heavy business in these materials, one of the chi
firms engaged being that trading under the name of James Martin, whi
was established twenty years ago, and is now carried on by Mr. Jo
Martin, the son of the founder. The premises occupied are large a
commodious. The offices are well furnished, and the spacious wareho
contains a heavy stock of bookbinders' cloth, material, millboards, pape
&c., from the best manufacturers in the country. Mr. John Martin
agent for the country towns for the sale of Messrs. Dewhurst & Co.
bookbinders' cloths and label cloth, and Sagar's patent tracing cloth, a
he is able to supply those articles on the very best terms. A very good tra
is carried on in the city and its vicinity, and the travellers engaged a
rapidly increasing it. Mr. John Martin is very popular in the city, a
highly respected, and his house holds its own with credit in the trade.

Robert Robson, Yarn Agent, 2, Norfolk Street.—Th
firm was founded about the year 1874, and has been located in the pr
sent premises for the last eight years. Though professedly a yarn agenc
the firm has extensive dealings on its own account. The firm has t
sale of the entire make of yarns of several large spinning concerns, a
their connection includes almost *every* shipping firm in Manchester, mo
particularly in what is known as extra hard yarns, which they have ma
a speciality. Mr. Robson was until his death, caused by an accident, o
of the best-known men on 'Change. The premises at 2, Norfolk Stree
include a very large warehouse and capital suite of handsomely furnish
offices. The business is now carried on by his executors, with who
are allied Mr. Nicholas Alexander and Mr. W. C. Daggatt.

Tailoring Industry.—William Hay & Co., Art Tailors and Specialists in Dress, 5, Cross Street (opposite Royal Exchange). [illegible] "History of the Industries of Manchester" would be [illegible] were we to overlook one so important as that of tailoring, which, [illegible] magnitude and diversity of production [illegible] every other occupation in the [illegible]. Thomas Carlyle [illegible] given this subject a peculiar interest by the production of his [illegible] Sartor Resartus, and shown [illegible] wonderful part which tailoring has [illegible] in the history of [illegible] world's civilisation, from the [illegible] to the luxurious and [illegible] requirements of the [illegible] drawing-rooms of [illegible]. Our present purpose, however, is not [illegible] philosophy of clothes [illegible] a few plain facts respecting one of our Manchester houses, [illegible] in model and artistic tailoring has gained for itself [illegible]

[illegible] Cashmeres, [illegible], Beavers, [illegible] West of England [illegible] and Bedford cords, [illegible] coatings [illegible] also a variety of other makes too numerous to mention. [illegible] the cutting-room, and although we make no pretence to practical knowledge [illegible] department, after Mr. Hay's lucid explanation of the minutiae of the cutting art, we [illegible] that the tailor's claim to rank among the artists of our country [illegible] higher [illegible] deserving of recognition than we had hitherto believed. [illegible] for instance, [illegible] the man who can [illegible] a figure which nature has but poorly endowed, and [illegible] a perfect model, is [illegible] less an artist than the sculptor who takes [illegible] which he [illegible] and shapes [illegible] a figure which is [illegible] better than [illegible] the painter who with his brush and canvas reproduces a landscape [illegible] of the human form. We may say in this [illegible] that Mr. Hay greatly deplores the evident lack [illegible] of even a rudimentary knowledge of the principles of tailoring. The fitting-room, which is at the extreme end of the premises, is richly carpeted, furnished with [illegible] and [illegible] fitted with large handsome mirrors, placed in such positions that [illegible] when trying on garments may see their back and front simultaneously. This room also contains a full-sized horse model, which is used for trying on ladies' riding habits or [illegible] hunting breeches. We believe the firm [illegible] Mr. Hay being the originator of several new improvements in connection with ladies' [illegible] breeches and [illegible] being adopted for the latter. In order to facilitate communication, we observed the cutting and making-up departments were connected by telephone. The advantages of this arrangement will be well understood by anyone who knows how important it is [illegible] the cutter should be always in constant communication with the workmen. After what we have seen of the establishment of Messrs. Hay & Co., and the method of their business, we cannot understand why any Manchester man should consider it necessary to go to London for his clothes. [illegible] that "anything will do for a [illegible]" [illegible] they may think provincial men do not get the best of the London talent. We have only further to add that the head of the firm (Mr. William Hay) is not only a man of exceptionally good [illegible] but a gentleman of the highest probity and honour, [illegible] and widely known and respected throughout Manchester and the surrounding district.

[illegible] reputation. We [illegible] the firm of Messrs. Walter [illegible] & Co., of the above address, a firm which seems fully to have [illegible] [illegible]

Albert V. Sharratt, Joiner, Builder, and Contractor, 19, Hardman Street, Deansgate. A [illegible] house in the building [illegible] by Mr. Albert V. Sharratt, who [illegible] established by him in 18[illegible]. The Hardman Street premises [illegible] arranged [illegible] well appointed in every respect. The working plant and [illegible] very extensive and well [illegible]. The [illegible] of the business are [illegible] the execution of all kinds of joinery and building work, the fitting up of offices, shops and warehouses, and [illegible] requiring [illegible] the house has a widespread [illegible] [illegible]

Mr. R. Wilson, Clydesdale Restaurant, 77, Piccadilly [illegible]

William J. Hall & Co., Manufacturers of Fire Bricks, Silica Bricks, Tiles, &c., 36, Cooper Street.—The firm of fire brick and tile manufacturers, whose offices are at the above address, was originally established by Mr. Lambert, by whom it was carried on for many years with great success and finally transferred to the present proprietors, Messrs. William J. Hall & Co., who have very considerably extended them. The works are at Pott-Shrigley, near Macclesfield, and are very extensive, turning out annually a very large quantity of fire bricks of a very superior quality, which are in great demand for a variety of purposes in connection with the construction of furnaces of all descriptions. The firm also have a very large trade in plain tiles, and their productions, from their extreme durability and toughness, are also in great demand. The speciality of the firm, however, is "pure ground Bessemer gaunister," a most valuable product for a variety of purposes, from the fact of its being almost a pure silica, having scarcely any admixture of foreign substances. It has been submitted to a searching analysis by Messrs. Wilkinson and Grimshaw, the well-known analysts, with the following satisfactory results:—

Silica { uncombined,	90·70 }	96·74
Silica { combined,	6·04 }	
Alumina with a little peroxide of iron,		2·00
Lime, magnesia, and loss,		66
Water,		60
		100·00

Messrs. William J. Hall & Co. are to be congratulated on being able to offer to the public a product of such purity, and which constitutes so important a factor in so many different branches of manufacture. It will have an immense demand which they will be equal to supplying, as they are going to considerable expense in order to complete their facilities for the purpose. The manufacture of glazed and coloured bricks, a special feature of the firm's operations, is also carried on with considerable success.

Dunnill & Craig, Bleachers, Dyers, and Finishers, 26, Kennedy Street.—Bleaching is a very important process in the preparation of many fabrics for the market, and the firms engaged in it are among the most substantial in the city. A notable house conducting this business in conjunction with the allied branches of dyeing and finishing is that known as Dunnill & Craig. This establishment was founded in 1883, but for the previous forty years had been used as a dyeworks, and is noted for the excellent quality of its water. The spacious premises in the occupation of the firm comprise the works in Springfield Lane, Salford, and an office at the foregoing address in the city. The works are extensive, neatly arranged, and fitted with all necessary machinery and mechanical appliances required in the intricate and somewhat delicate operations to which the fabrics must be subjected before being finished. A numerous body of skilled and experienced hands is constantly engaged in executing the orders entrusted to the house. The work done by Messrs. Dunnill & Craig is of the most perfect kind, and has won for them a high position among the bleachers, dyers, and finishers of the city. Both Messrs. Dunnill and Craig enjoy the esteem and patronage of a rapidly increasing and valuable connection among the leading houses engaged in the textile industries of the district.

John A. Wood, Manufacturer of Coach Lace, Reps, &c., also Poncho Cloths, Pellones, &c., 82, Great Bridgewater Street.—The manufacture of coach lace, rep linings, carriage silks, ponchos, poncho cloths, pellones, serges, girdles, webs, fringes, &c., is in Manchester a branch of industry of great value and importance in a very perfect condition, and among the houses engaged a principal place is held by that of Mr. John A. Wood, which was founded about seventy-five years ago, having been in the present proprietor's possession since about 1856. For carriage laces, &c., it is the largest and oldest firm in the United Kingdom. The premises occupied are very extensive and are admirably fitted up. A large staff of trained hands is employed. Carriage trimmings, silks, coach lace, cloths of every description, woollen, worsted and cotton poncho cloth, pellones, garters, coxonilhos, saddle mats, and a variety of other similar goods, are manufactured. Mr. John A. Wood has a world-wide reputation for the excellence of his productions. The warehouse contains an enormous stock of these goods. Travellers are engaged and Mr. Wood carries on an extensive trade, shipping goods to all parts of the world. The railway carriage rep linings in second and third class carriages have been invented and introduced by Mr. Wood. In the manufacture of carriage trimmings, &c., poncho cloths, pellones, girdles, &c., he has rendered services and produced results which place his house at the head of all others engaged in the same industry.

George Howe & Brother, Manufacturers and Agents, 38, Portland Street.—This business was established in the year 1873, and has been very successful. The premises consist of a capital warehouse and a suite of commodious offices, handsomely furnished and fitted with the latest and most approved appliances for the rapid despatch of business. A branch establishment is located at 2, India Buildings, Dundee,
where the firm carry on the busin
also largely engaged in manufact
have lately put down some of the n
turning out of the same. In the I
are occupied mainly as agents for
flax spinners, linen manufacturers
fast, whose works are at Annvale
productions of this firm are mainl
are also agents for Messrs. Cluau
manufacturers, bleachers, and dyer
and for Messrs. Robert Watson &
cotton handkerchiefs, white and
The trade connection is to a larg
general Manchester wholesale wa
heavy shipping business done thr
this city. The staff at 38, Port
book-keepers, and others. The pa
Jason Howe. Both these gentlen
flax and jute trade, and are fully
manufacture, are extremely well k
city, and are everywhere esteemed

E. Moreton, Manufact
Stereotyping Apparatus, &c., 2
carries on an extensive trade in roll
and printing materials. The man
branch of industry and the firms e
concern in this line is that of Mr. I
typing apparatus, and printing n
1870. The works are extensive a
requisite appliances and apparat
manufacturing roller composition,
kinds of printing materials. The
and material, and the processes o
most advanced principles. Mr. E
tures to the highest state of perfe
Street, London. Mr. E. Moreto
stocked, and he employs an effici
very extensive home trade, having
he ships printers' machinery to C
He is well known in printing a
circles, and his status therein is ve
integrity and other genuine qualiti
reputation and an honourable place

Walter T. Glover & Co.
Makers, and Engineers, Mach
firm engaged as makers of electric
neers, machinists, and tool-makers
Co., Salford, whose London addr
whose telegraphic address is "Wa
This business was established in I
wire is carried on at Salford Ele
Lane Cable Works, both being e
perfect and powerful machinery.
facture of conductors for the el
ductors which this firm supplied
1887, took not less than ten tons
cables. This quantity, if drawn
reach a length equal to the circum
wires are variously insulated, the
wear, while the fine wires to whic
most elegantly finished in silk, and
ticular decorations which surround
turers and patentees of a special A
merit, as by its use those distract
telephone are avoided. They also
wires for electric bells, as well as v
to mention armoured and lead-case
are contractors to her Majesty's Go
telephone, and electric light compa
This firm is also the sole maker of
a really useful instrument to all dea
number, diameter in inch as well a
city in ampères of pure copper wire
ness is carried on at the Bridgewate
admirably equipped with the most
kinds of machinery and tools are
cluding "James" patent doubling
making machines, guillotine pape
and punching machines, machines
silk goods, vices, &c. Messrs. W.
and silver medal at the Inventio
the firm devote all their attention
character of their noted manufact
the most influential and noted men

T. H. White, Ordsal Injector and Steam-jet Pump **'orks,** Crowther Street, Regent Road, Salford.—A work on the "In- etries of Manchester" would by no means be complete which did not ntain some mention of what are known in the engineering trade as jectors. These are a very valuable and ingenious invention, and are dely used in place of pumps for feeding steam boilers with water. ey are especially valuable for marine boilers, locomotives, tram and iction engines, &c. The work of an injector is accomplished in a way at to the unmechanical mind seems quite incredible. A portion of the am generated in the boiler is utilised for forcing water into the boiler ainst the pressure of the steam itself. A pipe from the upper part of boiler conveys steam to the pipe containing the feed water, and the ndensation of the steam on coming in contact with the water forms a which is impelled with great force into the boiler. The feed water is course considerably heated in the process (Mr. White guarantees not s than 190° of heat even with his exhaust injectors), and a great economy fuel is hereby effected. The discovery of the principle of this novel in- ation is generally attributed to an engineer named Giffard, who obtained atent for it in 1859; but there is evidence to show that the idea had viously occurred to an Englishman at the beginning of the present century, though it does not seem to have led to any practical results. Indeed, as confirming the old adage that "there is nothing new under the sun," it is stated that the principle is really older than Christianity itself. As with every other invention of any importance, great improvements have been made in it since the days of Mr. Giffard, and most notably within the last few years. Though containing elements of undoubted value, injectors were for a long time very fitful and unreliable, and frequently caused great inconvenience and danger by ceasing to act at very critical times. The steam had to be admitted to the feed water very gradually every time the boiler required water, and in fact injectors had to be as carefully nursed as a fractious baby. But *nous avons changé tout cela*; at any rate, no one who requires an injector need fail to get one in every respect reliable and trustworthy, for that is assured him if he will only go to the right place. The merit of bringing these instruments to their present high state of perfection undoubtedly belongs in a great measure to Mr. T. H. White, engineer, of Salford, who is the sole proprietor of the Ordsal Injector and Steam-jet Pump Works, Crowther eet, Regent Road. This is all the more noteworthy and singular from fact that Mr. White had not in early life received the advantages of engineering training. It would almost seem to be true of injector kers as of poets, that they are born not made, for Mr. White appears iave achieved, and that in a very short time, almost it may be said by tinct, what men trained in the theory and practice of engineering were years trying to reach in vain. Some years ago he entered as an killed labourer the service of a firm of injector makers in his native n, and having ample opportunity of examining these ingenious con- ances for dispensing with pumps, and of witnessing their action, he s struck, like many others, with the great need that existed for im- ving them if they were to become of universal application. He accord- ly made them the great object of his study and attention. The interest took in them attracted the attention of his employers, and he was ulti- tely placed in the responsible position of having to see that all injectors re fit for work before being sent off. Their unreliability sorely an- 'ed him. At that time all injectors were fitted with a steam spindle l water regulator which required the most skilful manipulation in er to make them work at all. But Mr. White disposed most effectu- r and at once of both these troublesome regulators by contriving an ector which automatically relieved itself of any excess of steam or ter, thus enabling the injector—as we might say—to select for itself quantity and proportion of each necessary to form the current, or jet, the required force to enter the boiler, and then to carry in the full iply of water without any waste; and by these means it also *restarts* *if* if from jolting or any other cause its working is interrupted. Con- ucting an injector on this plan, he was surprised at its success. His ployers and all who saw it were equally astonished, for, for the first e in their experience, the steam might be turned on full at once and injector worked quite satisfactorily. This departure became known "Borland's Injector" from the name of the gentleman who purchased This was in 1883. Finding that his inventiveness was not duly preciated by his employers, Mr. White left their service and commenced siness on his own account. Still experimenting with the view of fur- r simplifying the injector, in 1884 he was enabled to take out another ent, to which he gave the name of the "Influx." In the same year he brought out also an exhaust injector. Both these he sold to a well-known firm of injector manufacturers, though he retained the right to make. In 1885 he followed with another improvement, which he named the "Simplex," and since that date he has patented an improvement in his exhaust injector, which is doubtless of great value, as it includes a method of extracting the grease from the feed water on its passage into the boiler, the admission of grease being the greatest drawback to the use of the exhaust injector. It may here be interpolated that, wonderful as is the action of the ordinary or live steam injector, that of the exhaust injector is still more marvellous, and it has baffled the most experienced engineers to account for it. For with a pressure less than that of steam from a tea kettle, White's exhaust injectors feed boilers against a pressure of 90 lbs. per square inch. They are also so constructed that they can be worked by live steam direct from the boiler when the engine is standing; and by a further improvement, very recently patent, he is able to guarantee them to return the whole of the exhaust steam to the boiler; the advantages of which cannot easily be overrated, and especially where the water supply is impure. This latest improvement, to which is attached also a patented arrangement for reviving the steam where it is worked against a very high pressure, is to be known as the "Acme Exhaust Injector;" the word acme, however much abused elsewhere, being obviously appropriate here, for, all the exhaust being returned to the boiler, it is difficult to see how anything more can be accomplished. The inventions of Mr. White have revolutionised the manufacture of injectors. Previous to his experiments all injectors lifted water according to their size, the smaller ones lifting not more than two feet, whereas now White's injectors of any size will lift not less than fifteen feet, and we understand that these are the only injectors that have been approved by the Board of Trade for use on tram and traction engines. Such is the preference for these injectors, not only on account of their marked superiority as lifters, and more especially still as restarters, but for all points claimed for injectors, being in every respect entitled to the best and most unqualified commendations. Mr. White is also the inventor and maker of a unique patent valve with a seating which is removable without disturbing the connections and renewable whilst pressure is in the valve; whilst his steam-jet pumps are unequalled in the trade, as they can be made to lift and force water a distance of 250 feet, whilst those of other makers are not capable of lifting and forcing more than 80 feet. We conclude our notice of Mr. White's specialities by mentioning his patent ejector condenser, one of the chief merits of which consists in the fact that the water condensed by the apparatus is not allowed to go to waste, as with those of other makers, but is sent back to its source of supply to be used over and over again. And after calling attention, even so far as we have done so, to the many advantages possessed by Mr. White as his own inventor, &c., it will not be surprising to learn that he has also a comparable advantage as to prices, &c. We are able to add, however, that in his line he is making still further improvements by sundry contrivances for the further reduction of the cost of production.

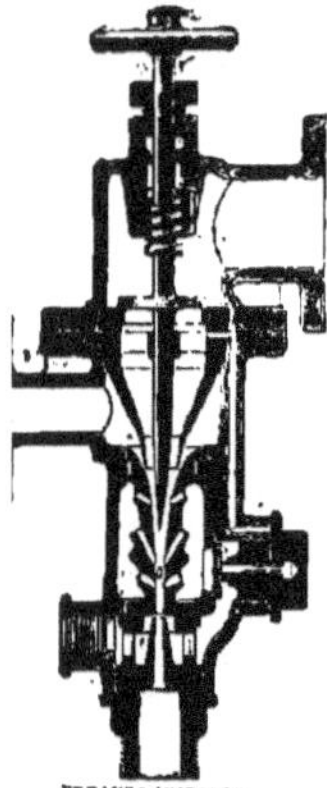

EXHAUST INJECTOR.

A. Bland & Co., Wholesale Tea and Coffee Merchants, 24, Fennel Street.—The now well known firm of Arthur Bland & Co., was established in 1878. During the ten years that have elapsed since that date the progress made has been very satisfactory. The proprietors have certainly been most active in their endeavours to make the business one of the best of its class, and their efforts have been productive of a very gratifying result. As wholesale tea and coffee merchants of the first grade, they now cater for the wants of a widespread connection. They supply goods of the first quality; their charges are based upon a reasonably moderate scale, and their overtures to the public have been well appreciated. Their premises are admirably appointed, and the stock always on hand is a carefully selected and extensive one. Orders receive prompt and careful attention, and the management is all that could be desired.

S. Butterworth, Pattern-Card Maker, 7, York Street.—Pattern-card making is of vast importance to a textile manufacturing city like Manchester. There are upwards of fifty firms in this branch of industry located in the city, over the premises of several of which we have had the pleasure of being shown, amongst them the shop of Mr. S. Butterworth, of York Street, which is specially worthy of note. The premises are very spacious, and arranged in all respects to suit the requirements of the business. All manual appliances and machinery of the most modern type are to be found in abundance. A pretty numerous working staff are continually employed in making pattern cards of every description and for every class of goods. On our visit at one bench they were turning out some very pretty shade cards of satteens; at another part of the "shop" the men were busy on a pile of Oxford and zephyr shirtings; others were hard at work on what appeared to us as very intricate brace cards. We also noted a lot of very neat shade cards for sewing cottons, in fact, the place presented quite a busy hive of industry, and to detail everything we saw would require more space than we can afford. We must not omit to mention the unique pattern-cards intended for the wholesale woollen and clothing trade, of which Mr. Butterworth makes a speciality, and the registered cards of which he is the sole maker. It is certainly the best and handiest way of making patterns up we ever saw, and reflects great credit on Mr. Butterworth, who evidently makes a study of his business. It was exceedingly pleasant to note the cheerful and clean aspect of the place and workpeople.

The Grand Hotel, Aytoun Street, Portland Street.—The Grand Hotel was opened to visitors in the month of October, 1883. It is situated in Aytoun Street, which is a street running off Portland Street, and is within one minute's walk from Piccadilly, and about four minutes' walk from the London Road Station. It is a splendid pile of buildings, and was originally built for a warehouse by the noted firm of Alexander Collie & Co., but was subsequently converted into an hotel. The architects for this work of internal transformation were the well-known firm of Messrs. Mills & Murgatroyd (who were also the original architects), and they certainly effected wonders in converting the structure to its present use, and making it a beautifully arranged, large, and commodious hotel. Externally the hotel has a noble appearance, being six storeys high and having three frontages. Its architectural merits are very great. The internal appearance is singularly imposing, and the most captious critic could not find fault with the structural arrangements. Below the ground-floor are the kitchens, store-rooms, larders, still-room, strong-room, &c., and light and ventilation have been secured to the utmost extent. On the ground-floor is a dining-room of noble dimensions, admirably furnished, which is probably the finest room of the kind in the North of England. It is eighty-two feet long by thirty wide, and twenty-five feet high, and it is lighted by nine windows; adjoining it is a reading and writing room. There is likewise a smoke-room on this floor (perhaps the most commodious and most comfortable smoke-room in Manchester), also a second large dining-room and several private sitting-rooms, besides the manager's private room. The reception office is directly facing the main entrance from Aytoun Street. The entrance hall is splendid, having a tesselated pavement of rich design, and its walls adorned with a dado of tiles of beautiful and artistic fashion. The main staircase is magnificent, having a beautiful dome light and easy ascent. From this floor rises a hydraulic lift for passengers, who by its means can make the ascent or descent to or from any floor of the house. There is a second hydraulic lift which is used for luggage. On the first floor is situated the drawing-room, a magnificent apartment, superbly furnished and upholstered. The tiled mantelpiece in this room is a delightful bit of decoration, and altogether the effect is charming. It contains an excellent grand piano. There are a number of sitting-rooms on this floor, some of which have bedrooms attached. Above this floor are three other successive storeys, and altogether there are a hundred and twenty large and well ventilated bedrooms. The hotel also contains the finest billiard-room in Manchester; and there are spacious lavatories and other conveniences on all the floors. The Grand is well provided against any outbreak of fire, and is in telegraphic communication with Liverpool and other towns in Lancashire and Yorkshire. In winter the corridors are warmed. One great advantage possessed by this hotel is, that although standing in the very heart of the city, being within five or six minutes' walk of all the railway stations, the General Post and Telegraphic Offices, the Town Hall, and the Cathedral, it is so situated as to avoid the noise of the street traffic, which, it must be admitted, is a very great drawback in the case of many hotels in large cities. The hotel is admirably conducted under able management, which has in no small degree contributed to the repute it has acquired both at home and abroad. Whilst the comforts and conveniences of the Grand are unsurpassed, the catering and attendance excellent, and the wines, &c., first-class, the tariff is moderate, and the establishment is fully entitled to rank amongst the very best hotels outside the metropolis. It is patronised by the very *élite* of visitors to Manchester from all parts of the world, and does a most superior class of business.

The Belmont Manufacturing Company (G. T. Peate and R. N. Parkinson, proprietors), Cotton Spinners and Manufacturers, 63, Faulkner Street.—This old-established business continues to occupy the very important position to which it attained some years ago. The premises in Faulkner Street include a suite of convenient offices, salerooms, &c., for the rapid despatch of business. The Belmont Co.'s mills and weaving sheds are situated at a distance from the city. They are of large size, splendidly engined and appointed, and contain none but the very best modern machinery, renewals having been made from time to time when found necessary to keep abreast of the requirements of the day. They are makers of all kinds of clothing drills, shoe linings, stay cloths, &c. The trade connection is mainly with the leading shipping firms of this city and the metropolis, and they also do a large business with the wholesale houses in the home trade and the Manchester general warehousemen. At the mills a very large staff is employed, but as the Faulkner Street offices are little more than a town address, a few salesmen and clerks only are engaged there.

John Horsley, Agent, Pool Fold.—The Lancashire agencies for some of the larger iron-works of the North are posts of great value. One of the most noted agents in the iron trade of the North is Mr. J. Horsley, whose offices are suitably situated in Manchester, a central position for securing a share of the country and city trade. Mr. Horsley represents MacFarlane, Strang, & Co., Limited, of Glasgow, whose productions are known and used in all parts of the universe. Their cast-iron gas and water pipes have long since secured for the firm a foremost place in the estimation of those requiring goods of this description. Iron hurdles, fencing, gates, roofs, bridges, and girders are made by Messrs.

Keay, of the Cyclops Works, W
many of the firm's best orders. T
nection with the celebrated firm o
iron girders, bridge and roof wor
all kinds Mr. Horsley has introd
in this country. Nuts, bolts, spi
machine and hand-made nuts a
Mayer & Co., of the Crown Bolt
these concerns proves the varied
transactions, and when it is adde
on his part is the result, a corre
ability, integrity, and status.

H. Bury, Electrical E
St. Mary's Gate.—This business
by its present proprietor, and fro
engaged in the practical installati
one of the most important and be
not only thoroughly identified hi
inant, but he has devoted his taler
apparatus and machinery and th
the electric light as readily availa
Many ingenious devices are asso
admirable contrivances connected
to him. From the very first he
the cost of the electric light, and l
marked. Saying nothing of the nu
light carried out by this firm, Mr
in business, erected plant and carr
for lighting the premises of upwa
the Swinton Mills of the world-
Rylands & Sons, Mr. Bury has fi
and the whole is working admira
formerly twelve hundred gas je
account, he has established an
superior in illuminating power, a
annum. Indeed the success attai
of the electric light has been
extant; while the sterling chara
is incontestably proved by the fa
up the works of such eminent en
of Openshaw, and Messrs. W.
chester. Theatres, public garde
mills, dye works, bleach works,
private houses are all included in
by this enterprising firm, and ref
them. Though up to the present
in the North of England, the busi
any particular district, but extend
large quantities of apparatus, ma
shipped to the colonies, India a
other electric light businesses. Mr
and limited by the unsatisfactory
At present the ordinary perma
numbers something over thirty
increased when heavy contracts a
the firm has been located during
occupies a suite of offices with co
the general works and stores bei
well-known firm, Davey Paxma
engines were selected to drive th
Healtheries, Inventions, and In
engines carried off the only pa
portable engines at the Royal A
It is needless to add that he has
in the very first rank of practical
doubt that as the vexatious restri
imposes upon the trade are remo
and enter upon the brilliant care
proprietor entitle it.

Hotson, Houston & Co
Packing-case Makers, and S
Crown Street.—This business has
ably more than thirty years, and
concerns in the same trade in t
timber-yard, situated in Bridgew
mill and packing-case manufact
gether, a considerable number c
very large stock of well-seasone
sawing is done for the trade. Th
the shipping and general wareh
specialities. The partners are
Houston, both gentlemen of ex
known in and around Manch
being liberal employers and g
movements.

lia & Co.—It is always a very pleasing duty to nour due to men who occupy a conspicuous position in vorld, and who by dint of well directed energy and sound y, joined to a cultivated training, have originated and lourishing condition a business of the first magnitude. At present, when the keenest competition is rife in every a business can scarcely be successful if it relies on nothing st reputation; on the contrary, the presence of a master- ith the times, and capable of appreciating the perpetually ions under which the operations of commerce must be ispensably necessary in business undertakings, and a man a post satisfactorily must be possessed of merit of a high at the career of Mr. Daniel Melia will suffice to show, n justice lay claim to the distinction of being the origi- n of Daniel Melia & Co., and that the uniform success hich it has enjoyed points to his personal character and ing contributed thereto in a great degree. He was for- receive a thorough education, and his first business ex- ained in a merchant's office, but circumstance came about d no control, and so within a twelvemonth afterwards he ess of a firm at Stalybridge. It will thus be seen that enced at the lowest round of the ladder, and all the more nsequence of the extraordinary success which has followed reat that many of those who knew him while in Staly- w bring themselves to believe that the man who, so few ied a comparatively humble position among them can ole partner and director of the large business which bears so it is, and the result goes to show what can be won by perseverance, and the exact management of business in

cant details. To return, Mr. Melia did not make a long lge, for he soon obtained a position of importance with a nchester, where he had every opportunity of obtaining a ledge of his business, and it was not long before he was man of exceptional capacity and energy. Throughout social and economic changes which it will be the duty of the history of the nineteenth century to record, the work- g principle is everywhere apparent. We allude to the tend- ntralization, which, under varying forms, may be recognised n in almost every sphere of human activity. So wide and nfluence, that centralization may be said, without exag- e watchword of the period through which we are now pass- be no doubt that a very distinct attribute of Mr. Melia's power of organization. The last quarter of a century eat change and development in the retail trade of this modern tendency is to economize in the distribution of ng the producer and consumer closer together, and the th this object in view, which Mr. Melia has proved to be so wonderfully successful, is to open a large number of branches with one buying centre, so that the retailer virtually becomes his own whole- saler. This requires great organization, but it can be readily understood that the proprietor of a number of branches selling for cash, and amalga- mating the requirements of each, can not only place large orders and buy cheaply, but he can pay promptly and to the greatest advantage to him- self and his customers. The great difficulty in conducting retail business on this large scale is in the management and organizing ability required. An uneducated man or a weak man would very soon find himself face to face with the official receiver in the bankruptcy court. Mr. Melia, however, was a very successful manager before he started in business for himself. He was accustomed to travel throughout the country ad- vising where branches should be opened, and organizing down to the minutest details the arrangements of the various establishments. He was, indeed, the pioneer of a system of business which, as in use under his direction at the present day, is a complete success, and as a model of excellence and perfect organization will serve to be studied and copied for many years to come, marking, as it does, a considerable revolution in the retail trade of the nineteenth century. It was in 1881, just seven years ago, that the nucleus of the present business was formed. The first shop was opened in Manchester, but the enterprising spirit who watched over and directed the early growth of the present flourishing concern speedily launched out into wider spheres. Encouraged by suc- cess, and confident in the faith of his system of conducting business, Mr. Melia has gone on adding to the number of his establishments, which are now to be found in London and all the principal towns throughout Lancashire, Yorkshire, and the Midlands. The chief warehouses are at London and Manchester, and contain a most extensive and varied stock. They are fitted up with power and all the latest and most approved machinery for tea blending, coffee roasting, packing, and fruit cleaning, thus dispensing with unnecessary labour, and lessening the cost of distribution to the public. They contain all kinds of general grocery, tinned meats, patent medicines, proprietary articles, and almost every conceivable article of household consumption and do- mestic use. All these goods are bought direct, in very large quantities, from English and Continental manufacturers, so that Mr. Melia is able to retail his goods at the cheapest possible prices. In the conduct of the business proper, Mr. Melia has shown himself a shrewd though scrupu- lously upright business man, neglecting no legitimate opportunity of advancing his business, though always keeping in view the extension of the concern on a thoroughly sound basis. In our interview with him he pronounced the secret of his success to be mainly due to his power of reading character, and the faculty of being thus able to fit the right man to the right place. Possessed of that confidence in himself which is the outcome of conscious power, he has confidence in his fellow-men; and while avoiding that superficial cleverness which merely consists in trying to over-reach others, he strives ably to arrange that the interests of his customers, of his employés, and of himself, shall roll along in happy unison to the benefit of all. But any account of the life of Mr. Daniel Melia would be indeed incomplete, unless it con- tained a more than passing reference to the well-known magazine that bears his name. Throughout his life he has been associated in a more or less direct way with literary men, and has always taken a great interest in the movement for supplying high-class, interesting literature for the homes of the people. This interest ultimately culmi- nated in the production of *Melia's Magazine*. It was an entirely original conception on the part of Mr. Melia, and the high-class manner in which it has been carried out throws a strong light on the enterprise and ability that animates the man. It has been criticised very favourably, as the following extracts serve to show:—The *Manchester Examiner and Times*, writing of the Christmas number, says: "The quality of the work is creditable throughout, and some of the contributions are really good." The *Manchester City News*, noticing the November number, says: "The *Magazine* is a large and excellent miscellany, and, whilst planned on the lines of the celebrated 'journalistic fluke' (*Tit-Bits*), is a much better production. This issue contains memoirs and striking portraits of Miss Ellen Terry and Bismarck." The *Glossop Dale Chronicle*, reviewing the December number, notes "That it is quite a bulky work, there being sixty-four quarto pages of most excellently varied literary matter, with the exception of a few pages of advertisements. The number contains some capital stories, and all the selections are interesting. There are also articles on Adelina Patti and Mark Twain, with portraits of the famous songstress and popular humourist. We advise all our readers not to neglect to obtain a copy of this number." The *Halifax Courier* says: "The prize competitions are alluring, and will set to work the wits of smart people; there are good stories, some of them of local interest; none of them long; bits of humours and bits of poetry." The *Grocers' Gazette* notices that "*Melia's Magazine* for the present month (December) abounds in reading of a light and entertaining character. The chief feature of interest would appear to be the prize competitions, which occupy consider- able space, with specimens of patch-work verse, Christmas stories, personal incidents, enigmas, charades, parlour games, prize receipts, jokes, &c. Biographies of Madam Patti and Mark Twain are included in the number, together with a paper on tea-drinking, the latter being ingen- iously utilized at the close as an advertisement for one of the firm's *specialities*. It is certainly a very readable publication, and is, no doubt, duly appreciated by the firm's customers, more particularly because of its free distribution." The *St. Helen's Lantern*, reviewing the January number, says: "The literary contents of the number before us are of more than ordinary excellence. They comprise stories and anecdotes received in the prize competitions which the journal promotes for its readers; prize recipes and rules of etiquette similarly obtained; two of a series of articles on Men and Women of the Times, with portraits of the Empress Eugenie and Mr. John Morley,—selected, we presume, on the principle that extremes not only do but ought to meet; a description (also illustrated) of Buffalo Bill and his Manchester Show; letters on Fashions and the Household; and, not to put too fine a point on it, odd paragraphs about 'everything else under the sun!' It is not the contents of the *Magazine*, however, that most favourably impress us; it is the omissions! We may, indeed, confess that we were most agreeably surprised to find that none of the contents are mere 'puffs' of the proprietors. Here and there, of course, there is an advertisement; but there is no degradation of literary talent into a mere trick of trade, none of that practical joking with readers which usually earns for these gifts of enterprising commerce a shoulder-shrugging *Timeo Danaos!* We shall look forward with interest to the future numbers of this literary venture. Although Messrs. Melia have opened a shop in St. Helens, and will, no doubt, attract many of our readers as customers, we welcome rather than deprecate the diffusion of their magazine. It deals only, of course, with the general: our mission lies (and that, more and more) with the local; and so, for us, and *Melia's Magazine*, and for all our other contemporaries, there is, in our opinion, an ample field."

Louis W. Waechter & Co., Oil and Asbestos Manufacturers and Importers, 34, City Road.—The firm of Louis W. Waechter & Co. has now been established close upon a quarter of a century—namely, since the year 1866. They are manufacturers and importers of lubricating oils, also of asbestos. This firm are manufacturers of the following:—

SPINDLE OIL.	CYLINDER OIL.
LOOM OIL.	VALVE OIL.
MACHINE OIL.	NATURAL TEN OIL.
ENGINE OIL.	REFINED COLZA, TORCH, OR OPEN LAMP OIL.
SHAFTING OIL.	ASBESTOS ENGINE OIL.
DARK NATURAL MACHINE, ENGINE, AND SHAFTING OIL.	ASBESTOS CYLINDER OIL.
LUBRICATING MINERAL OIL.	CASTOR OIL, finest quality (in original cases).
DOUBLE REFINED GALLIPOLI OIL.	PARAFFIN WAX, PURE OLEINE, OR WOOL OIL.
REFINED LARD OIL.	
REFINED NEATSFOOT OIL.	

Brown, Yellow, or White Refined Tallow, Machinery Wheel Grease, and Water-wheel Grease. We may remark that what is known as the "Spindle Oil" is one of the firm's specialities. By its use the very highest rate of speed can be secured, with a minimum of friction, thus reducing considerably the cost of wear and tear, independent of the other advantages. This oil is consumed in great quantities by cotton-spinners, doublers, woollen manufacturers, &c. Another speciality is their "Cylinder Oil," of which they manufacture several qualities in order to suit the various temperatures to which they are exposed. For instance, Messrs. Louis Waechter & Co. maintain that the same oil cannot be used advantageously for cylinders where the boiler pressure is, say 40 lbs., and in cylinders where it is 90 lbs. In the first-named the temperature in the cylinders is perhaps 360° Fahrenheit, while in the latter the temperature is about 500° or 600° Fahrenheit. As every one knows, all fluids attenuate under heat. The question then arises, to what extent is the body of the oil reduced at this heightened temperature. Messrs. Waechter & Co. have given the matter long attention, and their theory has been proved in practice to be correct. They guarantee to supply the best cylinder oil for each special case on the consumer stating the boiler pressure. Their efforts have been thoroughly appreciated by the consumers of this class of oil, as is evidenced by the important connection which has been formed. The firm manufacture the following articles in asbestos:—

ASBESTOS MILLBOARD AND MILLBOARD RINGS OR WASHERS.	ASBESTOS AND INDIA-RUBBER WOVEN SHEETING RINGS OR WASHERS.
ASBESTOS PLAITED ROPE PACKING AND BLOCK PACKING, with or without Rubber Core.	ASBESTOS AND INDIA-RUBBER WOVEN TAPE.
ASBESTOS WICK OR YARN PACKING AND INDIA-RUBBER WOVEN SHEETING.	ASBESTOS FIBRE, CLOTH, PUTTY, CEMENT, AND PAINT.
PATENT ASBESTOS COMPOUND SHEETING.	ASBESTOS BOILER COVERING COMPOSITION.

Besides having introduced some Specialities for calico printers and others. Our limited space prevents us from entering into any descriptive statement showing the acknowledged superiority of asbestos over any other known article for the purposes to which it is applied, but the firm under notice have issued a printed catalogue which gives the fullest information on the subject, and the same may be obtained free of cost on application; and the catalogue also contains a descriptive list of their oils, greases, &c. The firm carry on an extensive business and employ an efficient staff, and the reputation of the concern is second to none in the kingdom. Mr. L. W. Waechter takes the entire management of the business, and it is conducted with skill and ability and upon the highest lines of commercial honour and probity. We may observe, in passing, that what are termed "lubricating oils," or "fatty oils," even in spite of careful prepa-

ration, are liable to oxidize in th
a kind of gummy matter that p
in the manufacture and method
has been surmounted, and Mess
for their oils of this description,
trade. In conclusion, we will n
gentleman well known in Manch
popular and respected in the city

Richard Knowles & S
and Porter Merchants, 23, Str
are articles of daily consumptio
got absolutely pure and genuin
find that the trade of Manchest
of excellence and of considerab
in this way is that of Messrs.
originally established in this
for a considerable time as Mess
een years ago altered to pres
large and commodious, compris
furnished and presenting a very
very extensive and contain a l
choicest vintages, and spirits,
Messrs. Knowles & Son also ca
their premises contain a vast nu
dealing importers and manufact
tion for the reliability and purit
connection in all parts of the co
M. Joseph Hamilton Knowles,
acknowledged judge of wines,
world, and is highly respected
looked upon as the proprietor of

Andrew Fullerton &
chants, 20, Fountain Street.—T
ginally established in the neighb
ago. The business was carried
made to their present commodi
As manufacturers of and mercha
goods, Andrew Fullerton & Co
reputation. The material suppl
quality, and their charges are
of the concern does credit to t
workmen is kept in regular empl
treated in every way by this firm
and their orders attended to wit

McDonnell & Webste
chants, Bridgewater Buildings,
lished some six or seven years
business being now one of the l
ness was formerly carried on by
joined the firm, the title of whic
Since Mr. Webster became a pa
present commodious location.
Skilful buying ensures an attr
Albert Square stores, convenientl
by buyers from all the country
present a crowded and busy sce
of grey, bleached, and printed c
and ticks, checks and stripes;
ends, and remnants of velvets,
frequently in best colourings.
experienced buyers well known

Groves & Whitnall,
Salford.—Brewing is a very imp
and the trade is of vast proportio
the leading brewing firms a prom
Groves & Whitnall, which has e
years. The brewery is very lar
the district, is admirably eq
machinery and appliances, and
the place a thorough model.
men are constantly employed
delivering ales, beers, stouts, a
esteemed for their strength, qu
demand. Every care is taken i
operation is carefully superinten
steadily increasing. The memb
Groves, Arthur William Whi
gentlemen thoroughly versed i
sedulously employed in maintain
of eminent status, commercially
ance with the motto of their cre

P. Galea Ciantar & Co., Cigar Importers and Bonders, 59, Corporation Street.—This enterprising company started business in September, 1885. In the comparatively short period that has elapsed since their establishment no time has been lost, and their concern is already appreciated as one of the best of its kind. The custom enjoyed is very large and valuable, whilst it is increasing in proportions in a manner that is satisfactory in the extreme. The brands imported by P. Galea Ciantar & Co. are of the first quality. These are placed before the public at a price unprecedentedly low, and it is not to be marvelled at that they command such a ready sale all over the country. The premises at Corporation Street always contain a handsome stock of goods, and are admirably appointed for the requirements of the business. Looked at from every standpoint, this firm thoroughly deserves support, and the future before it is a most promising one. The management is very able and energetic. A competent staff is engaged, and the customer is afforded the most perfect satisfaction.

W. Griffiths & Son, Accountants and Estate Agents, 16, Kennedy Street, Clarence Street.—Among the many important professions extensively followed in Manchester is that of the accountant and estate agent. Among the members of this useful body we find Messrs. William Griffiths & Son, who are also agents to the Manchester, Royal, Lancashire, and County Insurance Companies. Established in 1848, these offices are well known. The estate agency department comprises a list of a very considerable number of high and medium class estates, houses, lands, and business concerns. Mr. Alfred Griffiths, now the sole representative of the firm, is the well-known and much respected secretary to the "Manchester Field Naturalists' and Archæologists' Society," also secretary to the "Chorlton-upon-Medlock Building Society," positions held to the entire satisfaction of the numerous members of both societies.

Joseph Pollard, Chemist, Exchange Arcade.—Mr. Joseph Pollard is the proprietor of a small but well-fitted homœopathic and dispensing chemist's business in Exchange Arcade. The business was established in 1878, and by due attention to the requirements of his customers a very good connection has been got together, and the business is now very thriving. Mr. Pollard exercises great care in making up prescriptions, and this is very important, as any carelessness or accident on the part of a chemist might lead to effects much more sensational than pleasant. The proprietor of this establishment employs an efficient staff, and has an excellent reputation, and enjoys a constantly increasing trade, and owns a very good connection in the neighbourhood.

Joseph Barton, Cabinet Manufacturer and Upholsterer, No. 2, Hewitt Street, Knott Mill.—This is a representative house in the cabinet making trade. Mr. Joseph Barton, the oldest cabinet maker in Manchester, having a reputation of thirty-two years' standing. The business, prior to its removal to the present address, was carried on for nearly thirty years at 55, Oxford Street, Manchester. The works are of ample dimensions, and fitted with every requisite appliance. Twenty able and experienced hands are employed, and the furniture turned out is of elegant and original design. The stock on view is extensive, comprising dining, drawing, and bedroom suites, in all kinds of woods and coverings. A local trade is done of a good-class nature and is rapidly increasing. Mr. Joseph Barton is an able and enterprising man, and fully understands every branch of the trade.

J. Affleck, jun., Medical Agent and Accountant, 22, Tib Lane, Cross Street.—The medical agency and accountancy practice lately established by Mr. J. Affleck, jun., at Tib Lane, is something unique of its kind. Mr. Affleck is to be congratulated on having struck upon and given effect to an idea which in his hands is certain to develop into an undertaking lucrative to himself and exceedingly useful to the medical profession, and indirectly to the community at large. The need of some recognised and thoroughly respectable medium through which medical practices could be disposed of or acquired has long been felt. This has now been ministered to by Mr. Affleck, a gentleman whose antecedents, connections, and business capacity eminently qualify him for the position, in which he has already found opportunities of showing his ability owing to his widespread experience, several important transfers having been successfully negotiated and many others coming into his hands, whilst he is, at the same time, gaining golden opinions on all sides for his honourable integrity and devotion to the interests of his clients.

Jno. M. Thompson, (of London), Court and Military Tailor, 70, Market Street.—This business, which bids fair to become one of the very best in its line in this city, was established by its present proprietor in the year 1883. Mr. Thompson, who is a London gentleman, has similar establishments at 55, Lord Street, Liverpool; 21 & 23, Darley Street, Bradford; and 21, High Street, Sheffield. The speciality is high-class tailoring and habit-making, for which Mr. Thompson's West-end experience is of the greatest importance. The connection is very select, and includes many of the most fashionably dressed gentlemen of this district. Mr. Thompson's system of cutting being designed to artistically drape the figure, the excellent taste displayed in the selection of materials ensures the very perfection of clothing. The business premises at 70, Market Street, consist of a large handsome shop, and a suite of reception, measuring, and work rooms; and a very large staff of skilled cutters and operatives is engaged. The stock of materials is very extensive and well selected, and the business is conducted on the most liberal principles. Although but recently established in this city, Mr. Thompson takes an active interest in all that concerns its welfare and improvement. The Bradford establishment is very large, and embraces hats, ladies' costumes, and jackets, ulsters, &c. In the Manchester establishment a speciality is also ladies' costumes, &c.

Thos. Taylor & Sons, Manufacturers of Linen and Union Drills, Damasks, Worsted Coatings, &c., 46, Faulkner Street.—This business has been established and in active operation for more than a hundred years, and the splendid reputation made during its earlier years has been fully retained until the present day. The premises in Faulkner Street include a warehouse of several capacious floors. The offices are fitted up with all requirements to facilitate business. The mills, which are substantially erected and of very large size, are located at Barnsley, the seat of the Yorkshire linen manufacture. The principal items produced by Messrs. Taylor & Sons are linen and union drills, damasks, worsted coatings, trouserings, and similar goods. The trade connection is very extensive and widespread. There is a very considerable business done with the London shippers as well as those of this city, while important customers are found amongst the wholesale houses and the general Manchester warehousemen. At the Faulkner Street establishment there is an efficient staff of salesmen, clerks, and warehousemen. The Messrs. Taylor are well known and have great experience in the linen trade.

George Beneke, Manufacturer of India-rubber, Gutta-Percha Goods, and Insulated Electrical Wires and Cables, "The Hanover Caoutchouc, Gutta-Percha, and Telegraph Works," 12, King Street.—The manufacture of india-rubber and gutta percha goods and appliances for telegraphy is a branch of industry of no small importance in Manchester. A good example of a firm in this line is that of the Hanover Caoutchouc, Gutta-Percha, and Telegraph Works Co., whose factory is located at Hanover, of which Mr. George Beneke is the agent and export manager, and which has been in existence a considerable time. The works are large and commodious, employing several hundred hands, and are completely fitted up with the requisite plant and apparatus of modern construction for the business carried on. A good staff of skilled hands, under talented supervision, is employed in manufacturing india-rubber and gutta-percha articles and electrical wires and cables. The productions of the house are of the best materials and of excellent workmanship. Mr. George Beneke carries on a very extensive trade, and he manages with enterprise and ability. He is well known in the industrial and commercial world, and his house holds an important and influential place in this branch of industry.

Mr. James Cumberbirch, Wholesale Warehouseman, 27, Rochdale Road.—In reviewing the great industries of the age, a special feature is introduced to notice in the prominent position taken up by the great warehousemen of the city, whose business operations form an extensive and unlimited source of activity and ever-prevailing industry, and who may with every truth be denominated merchant princes, so great are their transactions, so numerous the variety of mercantile requisites dealt in. A thoroughly representative house of this kind is the well-known establishment of Mr. James Cumberbirch, wholesale London, Birmingham, and Sheffield warehouseman. Established in 1852, this business shows unmistakable signs of rapidly growing into a concern of considerable proportions. The premises consist of a large and imposing-looking warehouse of four storeys and basement, and contains on each floor a large and high-class assortment of miscellaneous goods of a quality and character in demand by the leading shopkeepers, dealers, exporters, and others. The trade is very large, and finds ample employment for a staff of some sixteen hands. It is exclusively wholesale, and of a select and first-class character. The stock is very large and high-class. The principal is a gentleman well known and widely respected, whose business abilities command for him universal esteem.

Floyd & McNaught, Chartered Accountants, 5, Norfolk Street.

Geo. Peak & Co., Ltd., Fancy Goods Warehousemen, 9, Portland Street.—The extensive and well-known firm of lace and fancy goods warehousemen, carrying on business under the style of George Peak & Co., Limited, was originally established by Messrs. Kelly, Peak & Barry, forty years ago, and conducted by them with credit and success for a considerable length of time. On the retirement of Messrs. Kelly and Barry some quarter of a century ago, the business remained in the hands of Mr. Geo. Peak, who at once associated with himself as partner Mr. John Kendall (the present managing director), who had already been connected with the firm for many years. After the disastrous fire which entirely destroyed their stock and warehouse, 31, Portland Street, the business was formed into a Limited Liability Company, and temporary accommodation secured until their present premises were ready. Their warehouse stands on undoubtedly the finest business site in Manchester, at the corner of Aytoun Street, and in full view of Piccadilly, and is a very large and handsome erection of six storeys, the appearance of which is an ornament to the street and the city itself. The interior of the building is strictly in keeping with the exterior, the appointments being all modern, convenient, and of first-rate character, and the arrangements for the conduct and classification of business are excellent. The basement contains, besides most ample provision for the entering and despatch of goods, a large department devoted to the sale of lace curtains, lace blinds, antimacassars, Lanrashire, Scotch, and fancy muslins. On the ground-floor are displayed ruchings, bonnet fronts, mob caps, and fancy wool hosiery, &c. The first floor is devoted t velvets, velveteens, crapes, silk handkerchiefs, scarfs, ribbons, &c. second floor to silk and cotton laces, underclothing, trimming, and Edelweiss laces, real laces, made-up lace goods, and ribbon velvets. third floor, which covers an area twice as large as the lower ones, cc four important departments: the first embraces Swiss trimmings, and children's underclothing, infants' bibs, gowns, robes, frocks, fores and aprons, cambric handkerchiefs, infants' millinery, peliss dresses, ladies' and gents' linen and fancy collars and cuffs; the contains corsets, umbrellas, sunshades, mackintoshes, &c.; the third trimming and haberdashery, and comprises dress and mantle trim gimps, ornaments, fringes, buttons, tapes, needles, pins, braids, silks and cottons, boot and stay laces, Berlin and fingering wools, & A fourth, and what is intended to be a very important branch, gloves. This department is entirely new, and will meet a want lo by the customers of the firm. The top floor in the warehouse, whic tains nearly one thousand square yards, is used exclusively for bonnets and hats, feathers and flowers, ladies' millinery bonnets. winter season an extensive business is done in furs, in a department is probably the largest given to these goods by any house in th Everything connected with this business is on a scale commensurat the requirements and enterprising spirit of this great and successful A branch warehouse at 12, Williamson Street, Liverpool, is fc convenience to their customers in that city and the neighbourhood.

www.ingramcontent.com/pod-product-compliance
Lightning Source LLC
Chambersburg PA
CBHW020920230426
43666CB00008B/1511

* 9 7 8 3 7 4 3 3 3 4 9 5 3 *